ALFRED STIEGLITZ

ALFRED STIEGLITZ

A Biography

RICHARD WHELAN

LITTLE, BROWN AND COMPANY
Boston New York Toronto London

FIRST EDITION

Permissions to quote from copyrighted and/or unpublished material appear
on pages 643-644.

Library of Congress Cataloging-in-Publication Data
Whelan, Richard.
     Alfred Stieglitz: a biography / Richard Whelan. — 1st ed.
          p.   cm.
     ISBN 0-316-93404-6
     1. Stieglitz, Alfred, 1864–1946.   2. Photographers — United States —
Biography.   I. Title
TR140. S7W49   1995
770' 92 — dc20
[B]   94-39372

10 9 8 7 6 5 4 3 2 1

MV-NY

Published simultaneously in Canada by
Little, Brown & Company (Canada) Limited

Printed in the United States of America

CONTENTS

∾

Preface • vii

Acknowledgments • ix

Illustrations follow page 310.

PREFACE

⁀

ALFRED STIEGLITZ (1864–1946) is perhaps the most important figure in the history of the visual arts in America. Who can even begin to rival his multiple credentials? He was, of course, a great photographer, but also a great discoverer and promoter of photographers and of artists in other media, as well as a great publisher, patron, and collector. After his death, it would take his widow, Georgia O'Keeffe, three years to distribute among several American museums his own work and his large collection, which altogether would probably be worth today more than $20 million.

It is amazing that there has hitherto been no full-scale biography of Stieglitz. Sue Davidson Lowe, one of his grandnieces, published in 1983 a fascinating "memoir-biography." Ten years before that, Dorothy Norman — with whom the photographer had been romantically involved — edited a richly illustrated volume with a relatively brief, though important, text based largely on her notes of Stieglitz's recollections. Other books have tended to deal in a scholarly manner with some aspect of Stieglitz's career or else to consider him mainly in relation to O'Keeffe. Indeed, outside the photographic community, Stieglitz is known to the public primarily as O'Keeffe's husband. Morever, even many people who should know better confuse Stieglitz (pronounced "STEEG-litz") with his friend Edward Steichen ("STY-ken"), a superb photographer who became head of the Museum of Modern Art's photography department.

Both through the excellence of his own work and through his militant advocacy, Stieglitz won widespread acceptance of photography as a fine art. He was the publisher and editor in chief of *Camera Work* (1903–17), a magnificently produced magazine devoted not only to photography but also to modernist art. It was in 1908 that Stieglitz began his passionate campaign to introduce the most advanced European art to America. At his gallery 291, he presented the first American one-man exhibitions of work by Henri de Toulouse-Lautrec, Paul Cézanne, Henri Matisse, Francis Picabia, and Elie Nadelman; and the first one-man showings anywhere of Pablo Picasso, Constantin Brancusi, and Le Douanier Rousseau. He also pioneered displays of African sculpture and of children's drawings. Stieglitz was the first to print Gertrude Stein's innovative prose, and among his close literary friends were Theodore Dreiser, William Carlos Williams, Sherwood Anderson, Hart Crane, and Henry Miller.

Beginning about 1910, Stieglitz concentrated on nurturing a group of American painters and photographers that eventually included O'Keeffe, John Marin, Arthur Dove, Marsden Hartley, Charles Demuth, Max Weber, Abraham Walkowitz, Paul Strand, Ansel Adams, and Eliot Porter. All are now esteemed among the outstanding American artists of the twentieth century.

But even without any of his other accomplishments, Stieglitz would be remembered for his spiritually rich and technically unsurpassed photographs: sensuous nudes of O'Keeffe, emotion-laden studies of clouds, psychologically penetrating portraits of his friends, chilling indictments of New York's rising skyscraper temples of commerce, and such genre scenes as his famous picture "The Steerage," which shows working-class passengers on a transatlantic steamer. Some scholars, curators, and collectors revere Stieglitz as the greatest photographer ever, and his prints have established world-record prices at auction.

Virtually all of Stieglitz's photographs are autobiographical. He photographed his surroundings, his family, his friends, and the many women he loved. The story of his life and work is one of the great artistic epics of modern times.

ACKNOWLEDGMENTS

∽

I THANK ALL of the many people who aided, in one way or another, my work on this book. I am especially grateful to the Rockefeller Foundation for a residency at its Study and Conference Center, the Villa Serbelloni, in Bellagio, Italy; and to the Gladys Krieble Delmas Foundation for a grant that enabled me to travel to Venice to do research on Stieglitz's photographs of that city.

I would also like to give special thanks to everyone at Little, Brown who worked on this book, in particular to Ray Roberts, who first suggested the topic to me; to Jennifer Josephy, the editor who inherited the project and guided it to completion with enthusiasm and insight; to Abigail Wilentz, Ms. Josephy's assistant, who very ably and graciously coordinated all the details; to Deborah Jacobs, who performed her usual miracles in copyediting the manuscript; to Mark Lipsman, for doing a splendid job of guiding the book through the final stages of production; to Steve Snider and Caroline Hagen, who beautifully designed the jacket and pages, respectively; and to Phillip King, who did an exceptionally fine job of preparing the index.

PART I

"I WAS BORN IN HOBOKEN"

CHAPTER ONE

ALFRED STIEGLITZ'S FATHER, Edward, clearly fancied himself an aristocrat manqué; he had the air of a man who would have liked to call himself the Baron von Stieglitz — and may possibly even have had a distant relative with such a title. Of modest birth in Germany in 1833, Edward immigrated to America in 1849, enjoyed considerable success in business, and dedicated as much of his time as possible to the refined pleasures of the arts, the table, and the track. He was a vain man who well into middle age kept his dark, intense, and wiry Central European good looks and was handsome even in his old age. He prided himself on his honor, his munificence, and his worldliness, and he was as highly strung as the Thoroughbred horses he so loved.

A formal photographic portrait, made by his son about 1894, shows Edward with a large white handlebar mustache and a fine head of white hair brushed back from his high forehead. He sports an impeccably bow-tied and flowing black silk cravat that introduces a bohemian note in contrast to his stodgy black frock coat, his elegant black waistcoat edged with silk, and his primly high and starched wing collar. Disturbingly, however, his expression is cold, arrogant, disapproving, even hostile. True, by the time the photograph was made Edward had endured the death of his eldest daughter and had suffered serious financial losses, but such tribulations do not create character traits; they only exacerbate them.

An unsigned eulogy of Edward Stieglitz, written on stationery of the Lotos Club, in New York, stated that people to whom he "took a fancy were greatly charmed and impressed with his generosity, enthusiasm, praise and appreciation of the conditions and surroundings at the time. Those, however, . . . who perchance were unsympathetic to him, found him as a rule a man given to somewhat free expressions of frankness." For which read bluntness that could be not merely tactless but inexcusably rude.

Edward was at his best when he had an opportunity to lend or give money to his friends and relatives, and even to deserving strangers. His magnanimity confirmed his nobility, established him in a relation of power and patronage, and thus enabled him to relax the tensions that generated his harsh words. "The keynote of his nature was charity," concluded the eulogy. "He could overlook the faults of his friends and others with equal impartiality, and no one, friend or stranger, in search of advice and aid would appeal to him in vain. It was then that the dreamer, the enthusiast, the extremist, became the philosopher, friend and guide."[1]

Although the anonymous eulogist attributed the extremism of his character to "an artistic temperament," Edward Stieglitz seems to have viewed the arts primarily as social graces. To be an amateur, in his highly romantic view, was one of the obligations and delights of being an aristocrat. He loved to dabble as a Sunday painter, and he certainly enjoyed the role of patron. Self-consciously cultivated and urbane, he apparently found socializing with artists more satisfying than the contemplation of works of art, which occasioned pleasure but not passion. Paintings and sculptures were to be collected as mementos of artistic friendships, as decoration, and as trophies of wealth and taste. However, art was not really to be taken any more seriously than were the flirtatious dalliances he affected.

Edward was a poseur, and that aspect of his character was never more candidly displayed than in a letter he wrote, from Saratoga, New York, in July 1873, to his wife's sister Ida. After a rambling acknowledgment of a note from her, he launched into courtly badinage about how a Saratoga gentleman must learn "to keep up a conversation of considerable duration. Particularly when, as in this case, an interesting lady is addressed —and at the end of it —, it must show so little weight & must be so airy, not to molest any in these hot days —."

After that prologue, Edward addressed the serious matter at hand, a promenade he and Ida had recently taken in Central Park, during which her

talents to entertain one showed themselves in all their grand bril-
liancy. . . . It had such a deep & lasting impression on my mind [con-
tinued Edward] that it controlled my whole soul and body and I
thought best to find my way to the mountains and lakes, etc., in order to form new impressions & to drown that one. . . . I think [it]
best . . . to subdue these dangerous flames, which, if not conquered
in time, will perhaps put all Saratoga on fire. . . . In my mind's eye I
see the great damages it would do and I would paint them for you but
dinner hour has come and I relieve you for a little while to take
breath.

> Your affectionate brother,
> Edward[2]

Although one might well assume that this extraordinary letter concerned the possibility of a scandalous liaison, Edward sent it to his wife,
unsealed, and asked her to give it to her sister. Evidently, it was nothing but
a game; the passion was mock, and the eloquence a harmless display of
male plumage. One wonders whether Ida, upon receipt of this letter, was
amused, furious, or crushed.

Edward was born Ephraim Stieglitz in 1833, near the picturesque and
thriving Hanoverian town of Münden, at the confluence of rivers forming
the Weser. He was the youngest of the six surviving children — three sons
and three daughters — of Levi (later Loeb) Stieglitz and Joanna Rosen-
thal. Levi was an educated man whose ancestors, according to Alfred, included a doctor and a banker; Levi himself was a prosperous farmer whose
education earned him a leading place in the local Jewish community.

During the first half of the nineteenth century, German anti-Semitism
mainly took the form of strong pressures on Jews to convert to Christianity or at least to assimilate by abandoning the modes of dress, dietary laws,
and other customs that outwardly distinguished them from Christians. Reform Judaism, which originated in Germany during Napoleonic times in
response to such pressures, was formally established as an organized religion during the 1840s and quickly gained a wide following among German
Jews. Although Loeb Stieglitz retained his orthodoxy, his son Edward
would go to the opposite extreme, rejecting religious belief altogether.

Through the vicissitudes of royal succession, the house of Hanover
had inherited the English crown in 1714; hence, when Edward was born,
the king of Hanover was King William IV of England. His brother Adol-

phus Frederick, the duke of Cambridge, ruled in Hanover as his viceroy. In 1833 William and his brother gave Hanover a new and quite liberal constitution based on that of Britain. The year 1837, however, brought great change. William died and his niece Victoria became queen of England; because an ancient law barred any woman from ascending the throne of Hanover, her uncle Ernest Augustus, the duke of Cumberland, became the Hanoverian king. In his biography of Victoria, Lytton Strachey noted that the duke had been "probably the most unpopular man in England" and that he was "hideously ugly, with a distorted eye, . . . bad-tempered and vindictive in private, [and] a violent reactionary in politics." In 1840 Ernest rescinded the constitution, after having banished Jacob Grimm, one of the fairy-tale-collecting brothers, for having tried to thwart him.

Essentially the same pattern held in the electorate of Hesse-Kassel, where Edward Stieglitz's family lived, during an unspecified period, in a village named Gehau.* In Hesse-Kassel the elector — who was addressed as Your Royal Highness — reluctantly granted a liberal constitution in 1831, then sulkily withdrew from politics and appointed as regent his son, who dedicated himself to subverting the constitution.

In the tumultuous year of 1848 Ephraim's two older brothers, twenty-six-year-old Siegmund and twenty-three-year-old Marcus, left home to immigrate to America. The great wave of German emigration had begun in 1845, the year of the first of the disastrous crop failures that were to spread hunger and unrest throughout much of Europe. The famine triggered the great depression of 1847, in which mass unemployment reached crisis proportions in all the advanced European nations, temporarily halting industrial growth and aggravating the political situation. Between 1845 and 1849, an average of ninety thousand people left Germany annually, nearly triple the statistic of any previous year. By the end of that period about a third of the emigrés were Jews.

In Germany the threat of revolution was in the air, as thick as coal smoke. It wafted westward to London, where Karl Marx and Friedrich Engels could smell it distinctly; to them it had a wonderful fragrance. They wrote their *Manifest der Kommunistischen Partei* at the beginning of 1848 to encourage and guide the German revolutionaries. Marx and Engels were quite correct in predicting the approach of a great storm, but they were as

---

*There are two such villages, a fairly short distance apart. The Stieglitzes probably lived in Waldkappel-Gehau, about twenty miles southeast of Kassel, which is itself only ten miles southwest of Münden.

wrong about its nature as if they had forecast a blizzard in July. Through-out Europe — and especially in Germany — the most effective revolu-tionaries wanted more capitalism, not less. The immediate effect of the revolutions of 1848 was little more than to terrify the European emperors and princelings, who had long outlived their usefulness. In their despera-tion, they attempted to eradicate liberalism. They might as well have tried to stop the winter from yielding to the spring. Because the Jews were widely associated with the liberal movement, official anti-Semitism in-creased. As a result, Jewish emigration from Germany rose dramatically af-ter 1848.

In Hanover, King Ernest survived the storms of 1848 by cynically restoring the constitution of 1833. Two years later, once an uneasy quiet again prevailed, he tried to revert to autocracy. A bitter struggle ensued, but Ernest died in 1851 without having achieved victory. His blind son, however, maintained the fight for feudalism until 1866, when Prussian troops seized Hanover and Bismarck annexed it. A nearly identical sce-nario played itself out in Hesse-Kassel. The Stieglitz family had done well to leave.

Soon after they reached New York, in 1848, Siegmund and Marcus Stieglitz found both work and love; Siegmund married in 1849, Marcus the following year. Ephraim arrived in 1849, changing his name to Edward in the process. He and Siegmund, in whose house he lived, set up shop at the corner of Cliff and John streets, in lower Manhattan, to sell surveying and mechanical-drawing instruments "made to order at very moderate prices." Their business established, the brothers sent for the rest of the family in 1850.

Perhaps their prices were too moderate, for Siegmund and Edward seem to have put up little resistance when, in 1851, Loeb Stieglitz bankrolled a partnership with his three sons and his friend Moritz Isidor to import woolen cloth and manufacture shirts. The field was crowded, but the market was tremendous and growing rapidly. New York was the center of the world's cloth and clothing trades, and within two years dry-goods businesses would constitute fully half of the city's commerce.

Edward remained in the partnership for five years, withdrawing because of Isidor's incompetence, which would eventually take the firm — twice — into bankruptcy. His secession from the family business provides the ear-liest precedent for the many secessions that punctuated Alfred Stieglitz's life. It was a happy example, for the wool business that Edward then estab-lished with Hermann Hahlo would make his comfortable fortune. Hahlo must have contributed a wealth of experience and contacts, since by the terms of the copartnership agreement they signed on December 29, 1856, Edward was to put up 80 percent of the firm's $3,000 capital, and yet the partners were to split the profits fifty-fifty.

Edward's story provides a striking parallel with that of another German-Jewish immigrant to America. In 1841, together with his family, eight-year-old Daniel Stein — Edward's exact contemporary — emigrated from Germany to Baltimore. Soon thereafter the eldest of his four brothers started a retail clothing store that specialized in imported fabrics, and each of the brothers joined the firm as soon as he was old enough to do so. In 1862 the twenty-nine-year-old Daniel felt the need to secede from the family's discordant inner circle and enlisted his younger brother to join with him in opening a branch of the family store in Pittsburgh. Daniel's daughter Gertrude was born in that city's suburb of Allegheny in February 1874. Like Edward Stieglitz, Daniel Stein took his young family to live in Europe for several years. But then the stories diverge. Upon their return to America, the Steins settled in San Francisco. When Gertrude and her siblings eventually expatriated themselves to Paris and bought their Cézannes, Picassos, and Matisses, they paid for them with money made not from fabrics but from their father's investments in streetcars and real estate.

Edward Stieglitz had joined the predominantly German 6th Regiment of the New York State Militia during the 1850s. Commanded by the ardently Republican (which is to say pro-Lincoln and anti-slavery) Colonel Joseph C. Pinckney, the regiment had ten companies, the great majority of whose officers were German. The German immigrants were very patriotic, and the largely ceremonial and social regiment, with its fancy uniforms — confections of red, white, blue, and gold — must have evoked for many of its members the German university dueling societies to which they had belonged as students, or wished they had. All that these holiday soldiers needed was a nice little war to show off their valor.

At the outbreak of the Civil War, there were fewer than seventeen thousand troops in the regular Union Army, the majority of them stationed at forts in the West. On April 15, 1861, the *New York Herald* carried the full text of President Lincoln's proclamation calling seventy-five thousand members of the state militias into national service for ninety days, by the end of which — so almost everyone believed — the insurrection would surely have been quashed.

On April 19 the 6th Regiment enrolled to serve three months, and Edward Stieglitz was commissioned as the first lieutenant of Company F, second in command under Captain Alexander Ebelspacher.[3] Two days later Edward and the more than five hundred men of his regiment sailed for Annapolis, Maryland. The *Herald* hailed the departure as "an event memorable in the annals of New York." During the regiment's march from its headquarters in Centre Market to the fast steamboat waiting at the end of Canal Street, the crowd was so vast and so enthusiastic that "hats and handkerchiefs waved everywhere over the sea of humanity in such profusion that they resembled the migration of an immense flock of pigeons across one of our great western lakes."[4]

With Alexandria, Virginia, a Confederate city, Annapolis was to become Washington's chief port — the principal landing point for troops bound for the capital and a major depot for supplies. Edward's regiment was among those stationed in and around Annapolis to guard the city and intimidate the local secessionists. As soon as the regiment arrived, it was deployed along the railroad line leading from Annapolis to the junction at which the branch line connected with the main line from Baltimore to Washington.

Edward Stieglitz never saw a Southern swamp or had a Confederate rifle aimed at him. During the 6th Regiment's period of service in 1861, not a single one of its men was killed, even by disease. Edward wrote that Annapolis was among the quietest towns he had ever seen. For one thing, there were no naval cadets to enliven the place, since the academy had been moved to Newport, Rhode Island, for the duration, and its buildings were now being used as a military hospital. The quiet suited Edward, for he was a *Feinschmecker*, a connoisseur of good food and of civilized living.

Although Edward's letters did not burden his family with complaints, Siegmund heard through the family of another officer early in May that the regiment was suffering "severe deprivations."[5] His response was to send off at once packages containing a ham, sausages, tongue, mustard, sardines, bread, nuts, chocolate, macaroons, caraway liqueur, rum, and a dozen bottles of wine. We can only wonder whether it was his supply of such luxuries that occasioned a hostile mention of Edward in the daily German-language *New Yorker Demokrat* in mid-May; Siegmund's wife assured him in a letter that "one can read between the lines that they are dictated by jealousy and anger."[6]

Edward's letters, while perhaps presenting an exaggeratedly gilded account of his army life in order to reassure his family, nevertheless reflect a reality that could hardly contrast more dramatically with the horrific tales of hardship usually associated with the Civil War. On June 3 Edward wrote from Fort Morgan, "Here one day is like the next one and if the landscape were not so beautiful, I would be bored. The daily duties, the correspondence with home, bathing and going for walks fill the days."[7] In a letter dated July 14 there is a distinct tone of regret in Edward's statement that "the pleasures of this idyllic life . . . will soon come to an end and we shall soon be coming home."[8]

Because Edward's regiment had not been officially mustered in until May 14, nearly a month after its arrival in Annapolis, the date of that homecoming had been delayed to August 19. Adding insult to injury, the socially elite and battle-seasoned 7th Regiment of the New York State Militia had been mustered in promptly on April 26, as soon as it had reached Washington, and its term of service was set at a mere thirty days.[9] By June 3 the 7th Regiment was back in New York, where, as many feared, it might be needed to suppress riots or worse, for the heavily Democratic city was a hotbed of Southern sympathy. Many New York merchants had strong economic ties to the South, and many of the city's Irish and German immigrants hated Lincoln's Republican party as the party of big business, nativism, Protestantism, and temperance. Indeed, in January 1861 New York's pro-Southern mayor, Fernando Wood, had proposed that the city secede from the Union.

It is ironic that Edward's main accomplishment during his military tenure was to get his regiment released from service at the end of July. The First Battle of Bull Run — which took place near the railroad hub of Manassas Junction, twenty-five miles southwest of Washington, on July 21, 1861 — convinced him that it was time to return to New York. His regiment had remained safely at Annapolis during the battle, but several other New York State Militia regiments did fight, including the 69th (133 of whose men were killed that day), the 2nd, the 8th, and the 14th, as well as the 71st, which had been shipped south at the same time as the 6th. In the war's first engagement, to which gentlemen and ladies rode out from Washington in carriages to witness the expected romp, nearly 500 Union soldiers were killed, more than 1,000 wounded, and 1,200 captured or listed as missing. By the end of that shocking day, the Union retreat to Washington had deteriorated into a rout.

On July 24, after secessionists had marched triumphantly through the streets of Annapolis, the commanding general in Maryland wrote, "The late reverse at Manassas has brought out manifestations of a most hostile and vindictive feeling." He wanted all the troops he could get in order to guarantee the security of the area, but he acknowledged that the 6th Regiment was a problem, for its men were "dissatisfied, and to some extent de-moralized."[10]

Having previously succeeded on a mission to Washington to secure the pay due the officers, Edward was chosen to accompany two captains of companies in his regiment to the capital. There they called on Secretary of War Simon Cameron himself, who issued an order to demobilize the regiment at once. Edward was again fêted by his fellow officers as a hero.

He was mustered out with his regiment in New York City on July 31, 1861. Almost two years later, on June 18, 1863, the 6th Regiment was called up for another thirty days and sent to Baltimore. Edward, by that time a married man, bought his exemption. That common practice would bring about the draft riots that convulsed New York City for four days during July, after Lincoln had called for another round of conscription in the wake of the terrible casualties at Gettysburg. The rioters were mostly Irishmen who resented the fact that for $300 — a year's income for an unskilled laborer who was lucky enough to have steady work — a better-off man could hire a substitute who might well get killed in his stead.

CHAPTER TWO

EARLY IN AUGUST 1862, twenty-nine-year-old Edward Stieglitz proposed to seventeen-year-old Fräulein Hedwig Ann Werner and was accepted. It was to be a brief engagement. Less than six months later, on Sunday, December 21, they were married in a New York hotel. Edward, whose business was flourishing, returned to work on Monday, and soon the newlyweds were settled in the comfortable house that he had rented in Hoboken, New Jersey.

Hedwig Werner had been born in Offenbach, Germany, near Frankfurt, in October 1844. She was the eldest child of Abraham Werner, the proprietor of a clothing business, and Flora Collin, who died about 1850. They were cultivated people who loved music and literature and whose family trees boasted three rabbis. Abraham remarried soon after Flora's death, and in 1852 or 1853, when Hedwig was eight, he moved his family to New York.

As Edward's wife, Hedwig became an exemplary matriarch — nurturing, understanding, and hospitable. She loved music, the visual arts, and the works of Shakespeare, Goethe, Heine, and Schiller. Despite her cultural sophistication, however, she retained a rather childlike quality of innocence and relished a domestic life with traditional middle-class values. Even with the drama of a huge extended family to preoccupy her, she devoured as many as a hundred novels every year and became so absorbed in them that years later she could remember the names of the principal characters and recount their plots. But all her reading didn't do much for her English. Hedwig was notorious for her malapropisms and for her literal, and unintentionally hilarious, translations of German idioms.

Edward and Hedwig Stieglitz's first child, Alfred, was born in Hoboken on January 1, 1864, during a lull in the war. General Ulysses S. Grant's decisive defeat of the Confederate forces at Lookout Mountain and Missionary Ridge late in November 1863, together with the lifting of the Confederate siege of Knoxville early in December, had given the Union control of Tennessee. From then on a Union victory was inevitable, although many in the North still did not recognize that fact. In March 1864 Lincoln would make Grant the first man since George Washington to command the army with the full powers of a lieutenant general, and Grant would use those powers brilliantly. Nevertheless, until General William Sherman's capture of Atlanta at the end of August 1864 buoyed Northern spirits and vindicated Lincoln's military policies, the North was so pessimistic that the Democratic candidate, General George B. McClellan, felt assured of victory in that fall's presidential election.

A lithographic view of Hoboken published in 1860 shows a pleasant and obviously prosperous town, which, except for its busy riverfront, was almost exclusively middle-class and residential, with a population of about 10,000. (It grew to nearly 13,000 by 1865 and to more than 20,000 by 1870.) In the lithograph Hoboken looks much like a planned utopian community, with a rational grid of wide, tree-lined streets and many green squares. There are neither mansions nor slums, only block after block of three- and four-story row houses overshadowed by numerous church steeples. The shipping that was the town's main industry is much in evidence in the foreground, where the sailing ships, steamers, docks, and warehouses of the Bremen line are prominent. The docks became even busier in 1863, when the Hamburg steamship line established its New York terminal in Hoboken. Two lines of side-wheel ferries, with separate cabins for men and women, made frequent trips across the narrow stretch of the Hudson known as the North River to Christopher and Barclay streets in Manhattan. Like Brooklyn, which would not become a borough until 1898, Hoboken was widely considered a de facto part of New York City.

Hoboken's healthful river breezes were among the town's prime attractions, as the yellow fever, cholera, typhoid fever, and malaria originating in Manhattan's crowded and squalid slums gave New York the highest rate of disease mortality in the western world, twice that of London. The river insulated Hoboken not only from the epidemics (ships departing from Hoboken were exempt from quarantine) but also from overcrowding, crime, noise, and filth.

Furthermore, commuting by ferry was far safer, quicker, and more pleasant than riding the jammed horse-drawn omnibuses that clattered along the cobblestone-paved and potholed streets of Manhattan. Poor transportation kept nearly all of the city's businesses concentrated below Fourteenth Street and most of the comfortable housing below Thirtieth Street. In downtown Manhattan, where Edward Stieglitz had his business, pandemonium reigned in the streets. Horses, carriages, horse-drawn trams, and other conveyances attempted to race every which way but often became paralyzed by hopeless snarls. The trams and omnibuses frequently became so packed that the horses were overstrained; it was partly to prevent such abuses that in 1866 Henry Bergh, the son of a wealthy New York shipbuilder, founded the American Society for the Prevention of Cruelty to Animals. Bergh himself was known to dart out into the street to force drivers to discharge some of their passengers.

By 1870 the population of New York was just short of one million, of which 200,000 were Irish and 150,000 German — the third-largest German population of any city in the world, after Berlin and Munich. About 40,000 of the Germans in New York were Jewish, the remainder mostly Lutheran. The predominantly middle-class Germans were a powerful force in New York politics and culture. By the 1870s one of the city's several German-language newspapers, the *New Yorker Staats-Zeitung* (founded in 1834 as a weekly, becoming a daily in 1843), was published in a grand five-story arcaded and mansarded confection that was considerably more impressive than the nearby building of the *New York Times* on Printing House Square, near City Hall. Many middle-class Germans, both Jewish and Lutheran, chose to colonize Hoboken, which became a gemütlich enclave known as Little Germany, complete with Germanic-style architecture, German churches, clubs, publishers, schools, and theaters. Hoboken was, however, by no means exclusively German. An 1873 property map of the town shows that on the block where the Stieglitzes lived for seven years, the names of the house owners included Donally, Brown, Robinson, and Lawton as well as Leipziger, Stein, Bauer, and Engelbrecht.

Alfred Stieglitz was born in the house at One Sea View Place, on the corner of Hudson Street and Fifth Street.[1] The block of row houses was punctuated in the middle by the four-square, Victorian-Gothic brownstone

Dutch Reformed Church. Across Hudson Street was a grassy square on which the first building of the Stevens Institute of Technology would be built in 1870–71. The Stieglitzes enjoyed an unimpeded view of the river and a sweeping prospect of Manhattan.

In 1864, Sea View Place was the last built-up block of Hudson Street before one reached the Elysian Fields, to which Manhattanites flocked on Sundays, though not in such great numbers as they had before 1858, when the public began to use some areas of Central Park, the landscaping of which was just getting under way. They came to the Elysian Fields to enjoy the river breezes in summer, to stroll along the tree-lined walks, to sit in the rustic pergolas, or to play baseball. Indeed, modern baseball had been developed in the park early in the 1840s by the New York Knickerbockers, and many championship games were still played there throughout the 1860s. It was as a child in Hoboken that Alfred Stieglitz would develop his lifelong love of baseball.

In August 1864 Edward Stieglitz bought a three-story house, only two windows wide, at 109 Garden Street, in Hoboken, just a few houses away from the one his brother Siegmund was renting. Set back from the street, it had a front garden, a high stoop, and a so-called English basement arrangement to admit daylight into the dining room, which was on the front of the ground floor, several feet below street level.[2] On Sunday afternoons, Alfred would ride his hobby horse there for hours and listen to the conversation, while his father's friends drank and smoked in the darkened room, its curtains drawn so that no one would notice the passage of time.

The second of Edward and Hedwig's children, Flora, was born on July 1, 1865, a year and half after Alfred. She was a sweet-tempered girl whose intellectual curiosity and musical talent Edward encouraged. She would become Alfred's friend and his ally against their younger siblings.

What was perhaps the decisive trauma of Alfred's childhood occurred in May 1867, when he was three and a half. The arrival of identical twin boys, Julius and Leopold, gravely threatened the firstborn's predominance. (The twins always insisted that Edward favored Alfred, who in turn maintained that the reverse was true. In fact, Alfred appears to have been the clear favorite.) As if it weren't bad enough that he suddenly had two male rivals for his parents' affections and attentions, the twins were also brilliant and mischievous. Intensely jealous, Alfred would spend much of his life searching for a twin of his own to be his reinforcement, soul mate, and companion. In at least partial fulfillment of his wish, he was given to discerning "reflections" of himself — narcissistic projections — often in rather unlikely people and phenomena. Surely, one factor that drew him to photography was that the medium would allow him to capture and collect those reflections.

During the late 1870s an old Italian organ-grinder, accompanied by his monkey, used to play outside the Stieglitz house every Saturday evening, at dinnertime, in all kinds of weather. The old man would always play the Miserere from *Il Trovatore*, as well as other melodies, all of them out of tune. Alfred saved ten cents out of his one-dollar allowance every week to give to him, along with a sandwich and a cup of coffee that the cook obligingly provided. Except during summer vacations, Alfred performed his services faithfully until the family left for Europe in 1881. Many years later he avowed to his mother, "I was the organ-grinder," and went on to explain that he had never given anything to anyone with whom he did not identify.[3] Similarly, he often affirmed that whenever he took a photograph, regardless of the ostensible subject, he was photographing himself — that all his photographs were, in effect, self-portraits and symbolic representations of his feelings.

Late in 1865 Hedwig's sister Rosa Werner had moved in with the Stieglitzes. She would remain a much-loved member of the household until her death, in 1899. Rosa — a kind and sensible woman who knew when to be strict and when to be lenient — enthusiastically took charge of the nursery, to which were added the slighted Agnes, born in January 1869, and spoiled, petulant Selma, born in May 1871. Rosa seemed to be a stabilizing force within the family, but Alfred would later wonder whether there hadn't existed between his father and Aunt Rosa somewhat stronger feelings of love than society deemed proper between in-laws.

Associated with Alfred's third year are two stories that he would repeat endlessly throughout his life to suggest that his love affairs with Georgia O'Keeffe and with photography were predestined. One of these incidents took place in Berlin, where the Stieglitz family spent several months in the spring of 1866, during a six-month trip to Europe on which Edward negotiated deals with his firm's suppliers. Two-year-old Alfred became so attached to a photograph of a young male cousin that he carried it with him everywhere, sometimes securing it under his belt. He later recalled that he had felt no particular attachment to the cousin but was simply fascinated by the sheer wonder of the photograph as a magical object, a talisman.

During the same year, in New York, Alfred developed a crush on one of his father's cousins, a tall woman with smoothly coiffed dark hair and white skin. "While she was in the room I had a lovely but sad feeling about her," he recollected. He would sit and stare at her unremittingly, as if he were mesmerized, prompting the woman to ask whether he was ill. After she left, he would desperately count the days until her next weekly visit.[4]

This captivating woman, who was probably a war widow, always wore black. (Less than a year earlier, at the time of Lincoln's assassination, in April 1865, the American poet Edmund Clarence Stedman had written, "You know that a *vulgar* woman appears a lady *in mourning;* and that a lady is never so elegant as when in black."[5]) For the rest of his life, Stieglitz would say that black was his favorite color (at age twelve, he specified "cardinalian black"), and he remained extraordinarily susceptible to any woman he saw dressed in black or in black and white, a combination that O'Keeffe often wore. Indeed, he claimed that every time he encountered a beautiful nun, he had to control his impulse to speak to her and shake her hand.

CHAPTER THREE

IN 1921 STIEGLITZ wrote for the catalog of a retrospective of his photographs, "I was born in Hoboken. I am an American. Photography is my passion. The search for Truth my obsession."[1] He had devoted his life to inculcating the idea that passion is the sine qua non of art — both for the artist and for the viewer. Just how radical his endeavor was may be gauged if we consider a statement made by the extraordinary American art collector and commentator James Jackson Jarves in his book *The Art-Idea*, published in New York in the spring of 1864, a few months after Stieglitz's birth. Jarves lamented that neither in America nor in England "does aesthetic feeling assume the dignity of a passion. . . . A few minds only receive it as a conviction or sentiment; perhaps none as a portion of the true bread of life." Indeed, continued Jarves, Americans had "scarcely begun to sow the fields of art."[2]

In 1862 Jarves had opened a magazine article with the question "Talk of art during a civil war?" to which he replied, "Why not? War is fleeting, Art permanent."[3] Many New Yorkers were, in fact, quite preoccupied with art throughout the Civil War. Perhaps the grandest public manifestation was the Picture Gallery of the Metropolitan Fair, which was housed in temporary buildings set up in Union Square, in April 1864. The purpose of the fair was to raise money to enable the U.S. Sanitary Commission to purchase medical supplies for the Union Army and to staff field hospitals. For such a noble cause wealthy collectors lent their most impressive canvases, which the public paid admission to see. Among the popular favorites were Emanuel Leutze's *Washington Crossing the Delaware*, Frederic Church's *Heart of the Andes* (which had sold in 1859 for $10,000, then a record price for an American painting), Albert Bierstadt's *Rocky Mountains*, and Daniel Huntington's *Mercy's Dream*, a pretentious illustration of an episode in John Bunyan's *Pilgrim's Progress*, prints of which hung in countless American homes. Landscapes were especially plentiful, since, with the coming of the Civil War, which seemed to represent an expulsion from paradise, the grandiose paintings of such second-generation Hudson River school painters as Church and Bierstadt had assumed new significance. The wilderness was the covenant of the ark; artistic affirmation of the American landscape as a manifestation of God's special love for America became more urgent than ever.

Harper's Weekly boasted that the value of the hundreds of oils, which covered nearly every square inch of wall space from floor to ceiling in the immense gallery, exceeded $400,000 and provided "an eloquent witness of the wealth, magnificence, and progress in art and refinement of the greatest city of the Western continent." Innocently revealing the descending order of priorities of most Americans who claimed an interest in art, the magazine noted that "these paintings are all carefully labeled with the subject of the work, the party to whom each at present belongs, and the artist whose brush produced it."[4]

The Metropolitan Fair, which displayed not only art but also goods of every description, raised more than $1 million. The picture gallery was such a success that many prominent New Yorkers began to feel it was high time for the city to have a permanent art museum. In 1866 several men of that persuasion were present at a gala Fourth of July party in Paris; inspired no doubt by France's glorious example, they then and there resolved to establish a national art museum in New York. That resolution led, four years later, to the founding of the Metropolitan Museum of Art.

In 1864 the splendid new building of the powerful and prestigious National Academy of Design was going up on the northwest corner of Fourth Avenue and Twenty-third Street. Opening the following year, it was a three-story structure, in the style of a thirteenth-century Venetian-Gothic palazzo, with alternating bands of gray and white marble; at the third-story level, red and buff bricks were worked into an elaborate diamond pattern. On the top floor were the skylighted galleries in which were held the academy's great spring exhibitions, limited to works by living American artists. This policy was one manifestation of the wave of American cultural chauvinism that culminated in 1867, when more than seventy members of the academy petitioned Congress to levy a protectionist tariff on imported art. The outrage of collectors and dealers quickly killed the legislation.

The academy was opposed to the importation of European art, but it had no such bias against foreign aesthetic theories. Both the Venetian style of its building's exterior and the accurate stone carvings of native plants that ornamented its interior bore ostentatious witness to the American reverence for the writings of the British art critic John Ruskin (1819–1900). John Durand, the son of Hudson River school painter Asher B. Durand, commented that during the 1850s Ruskin had "developed more interest in art in the United States than all other agencies put together." Durand went on to say that Ruskin's "remarkable word-painting, the theological bent of his mind, his ascetic temperament, his eccentricities, his moral injunctions, furnishing both pulpit and press with material for sermons, news, and gossip about art . . . spread a knowledge of art among people who would not otherwise have given it a thought."[5]

Although Stieglitz liked to think of his obsessive "search for Truth" as unique, it actually had a long and honorable genealogy in the history of American art. It so happened that in January 1863, a year before Stieglitz's birth, a group of New York artists, critics, architects, geologists, and others with a strong interest in painting had founded an organization variously called the Association, or the Society, for the Advancement of Truth in Art.[6] By "Truth," these artists meant the sedulous rendering of nature that was so persuasively advocated by Ruskin. One of their number wrote in an issue of the association's journal, *The New Path*, "By the mercy of God, Ruskin has been sent to open our eyes and loose the seals of darkness. He has shown us the truth and we thank him and give God the glory."[7]

Ruskin — whose five-volume magnum opus, *Modern Painters*, had been published between 1843 and 1860 — really had only one fundamental idea, but that idea was so great and so compelling that it generated a tidal wave of impassioned prose. He believed that God is revealed in nature, by which he meant primarily plants, trees, rocks, mountains, water, and clouds, but certainly not the nude human body, which to earlier periods had represented the divinity's finest creation. In his view, the reverent observation and portrayal of nature by an artist who shared that belief constituted one of the supreme forms of worship, and every work so produced was an epiphany, a new gospel to edify the world.

"The greatest thing a human soul ever does in this world is to *see* something, and tell what it *saw* in a plain way," wrote Ruskin.[8] One might think

that that is precisely what a photographer does. But Ruskin would have disagreed, vehemently. He was himself a highly talented and accomplished
draftsman who made exquisite drawings of nature and architecture. He was
also a photographer, though he would have spurned that label. He deigned
to employ a camera merely to obtain a precise depiction of certain architectural details without taking the time to execute a drawing. Ruskin —
who detested Catholicism and preached that true art could be made only
by the human hand rendering what the eye saw, filtered through the
spirit — believed, in effect, that drawing is to photography as spontaneously uttering a heartfelt prayer is to paying for a mass to be said.

Ruskin deplored the ravages of the Industrial Revolution upon nature,
as well as upon the morals, the faith, and the structure of British society.
Longing for a golden age, he idealized the Middle Ages as a time of belief,
social harmony, craftsmanship, and closeness to nature. He felt that the
machine had been given excessive power and that only a return to artisanal
hand production, in which individual craftsmen would see a project
through from beginning to end, could restore sanity and happiness. The
artist should be a workman, and the workman an artist.

Ruskin's work gave rise to the Arts and Crafts movement, which flour-
ished in England and America from the 1880s until the teens and spawned
both Art Nouveau and the Bauhaus. The Arts and Crafts catchphrase "Art-
Work" — which signified the union of the artist and the craftsman — was
the direct ancestor of the name of Stieglitz's magazine *Camera Work*.
Whether directly or indirectly, Ruskin's writings had a decisive influence
not only on Stieglitz's philosophy but also on his photography.

CHAPTER FOUR

ALFRED STIEGLITZ WAS born six days before the twenty-fifth anniversary of the meeting of the French Academy of Sciences at which it was announced that the painter Louis Jacques Mandé Daguerre had succeeded in inventing a photographic process. In the United States, for most of those twenty-five years, photography had been almost entirely limited to the business of making daguerreotype portraits. Because the process was difficult to master, required cumbersome and expensive equipment, and involved dangerous fumes, there were very few amateurs. On the other hand, by the early 1850s some two thousand professional American daguerreotypists, of whom nearly one hundred had their studios in Manhattan, were exposing three million plates a year. What they offered their public was a breathtakingly detailed, often hand-tinted portrait, usually measuring about 2¾ by 3¼ inches, nestled in a fancily tooled leather case lined with embossed velvet. The portraits have a grim and intense quality, partly due to the strain involved in remaining perfectly still, without even blinking, for the five-minute exposure necessary to secure an image.

In 1851 the English sculptor Frederick Scott Archer developed the technique of coating glass plates with collodion, a clear, sticky liquid in which photosensitive silver salts were suspended. The process combined the detail of daguerreotypes with the reproducibility of William Henry Fox Talbot's negative-positive process. Moreover, the chemistry provided greater photosensitivity, which meant briefer exposures — though still very long by today's standards. But the process had several serious disadvantages. For one thing, the emulsion lost its photosensitivity as it dried, requiring the photographer to coat his own plate, evenly and without any bubbles or streaks, just before he was ready to make his exposure. Once the wet plate had been exposed, it had to be developed immediately, for it would be ruined if allowed to dry. Nevertheless, all the trouble was worthwhile, since the negatives could produce an unlimited supply of extremely detailed prints, usually on paper that had been coated with an emulsion of albumen (egg white) and silver salts. Because all printing had to be done by sunlight, only contact prints were possible, not enlargements. The desire for large prints that could be hung on the wall led some photographers to use enormous cameras that could handle the aptly named "mammoth" glass plates. By 1861, for instance, Carleton Watkins was photographing in Yosemite with plates measuring 16 by 21 inches.

If you had sat for a photographic portrait in New York City in 1855, you would almost certainly have taken home a daguerreotype. By 1864, you would have had trouble finding a single diehard daguerreotypist. You would probably have gone home with an albumen print, the poles of your choice being the miniature and the imposing. The former was a set of *carte de visite* portraits, each mounted on a piece of cardboard measuring about 2½ inches by 4, the size of a calling card. At the other extreme were Mathew Brady's Imperial portraits, on paper measuring 17 inches by 21 and often heavily retouched with India ink, gouache, and even oil paint. The full treatment could cost up to $500, as opposed to a few dollars for a set of cartes de visite.

The carte de visite craze, started in Paris in 1854 by the photographer André-Adolphe-Eugène Disdéri, had spread to America in 1860, just in time for the Civil War. Soldiers going off to fight would get a supply of these little portraits to leave with family and friends. In 1864 the editor of a photography magazine wrote, "Everybody keeps a photographic album, and it is a source of pride and emulation among some people to see how many cartes de visite they can accumulate from their friends and acquaintances."[1]

The real commercial bonanza, however, lay in the sale of cartes de visite of such celebrities as Harriet Beecher Stowe and the Prince of Wales, who visited New York in 1860. Untold millions of these photographs — mass-produced albumen prints, not reproductions printed with ink — were sold for about twenty-five cents apiece. People of all ages and social classes collected such cards and organized them in albums.

The phenomenon was closely related to the rise of American illustrated magazines during the 1850s. *Frank Leslie's Illustrated Newspaper* began publication in 1856, *Harper's Weekly* in 1857, to cater to the increasingly educated public with its insatiable appetite for the edifying lectures of the lyceum movement (Chautauqua's predecessor) and for the acquisition of facts, visual or otherwise. The magazines had been made possible by such technological developments as steam presses, machine-made paper, and wood engravings (which could be printed simultaneously with type). Improvements in transportation and communication enabled the magazines to publish illustrated articles about relatively current events, a great attraction at a time when newspapers carried no illustrations at all. However, even magazines were not yet able to publish facsimiles of photographs. The best that *Harper's* and *Frank Leslie's* could offer their readers were wood engravings of drawings based on photographs.

To satisfy their craving for an illusion of reality, Americans turned to the stereograph, which might be called the mid-nineteenth-century equivalent of television. The introduction of stereographs to the United States in 1858 began what was nothing short of a revolution. The public bought thousands of stereoscopes and millions of stereographic prints, ranging from pictures of the wonders of the world to series of coy or moralistic scenes, the forerunners of movies and soap operas.

A stereograph consisted of two nearly identical images mounted side by side on a card. Taken with a camera whose twin lenses were spaced as wide apart as a pair of human eyes, stereographs reproduced the effect of binocular vision. In 1859, Oliver Wendell Holmes, the Boston physician, essayist, and amateur photographer who invented a lightweight viewer for stereos, wrote that looking at a stereograph produced "an appearance of reality which cheats the senses with its seeming truth."[2] Indeed, the three-dimensional effect, which makes the personalities and milieus of the nineteenth century seem to spring to life, can startle and enchant even today.

Stereographs picked up where Currier and Ives left off. By 1860 the firm was offering hand-colored lithographs of nearly a thousand different subjects, many of them spectacular events or sights that could not yet be recorded effectively by photography: great fires, disasters at sea, whaling scenes, clipper ships under full sail, speeding trains, midnight steamboat races, and such sports as boxing, baseball, and horse racing. Currier and Ives prints of Civil War scenes showed battles raging, while photographs could show only the dead sprawled on the ground after the smoke had cleared.

In 1864 two of the greatest attractions in New York were P. T. Barnum's American Museum and Mathew Brady's photographic gallery. Like Barnum, Brady was a showman, an impresario, a producer. It is ironic that he took very few of the pictures credited to him, despite being probably the most famous name in American photography. He carefully oversaw the work of his operators, but by the 1850s failing eyesight prevented him from operating a camera himself and forced him to wear glasses with thick blue lenses.

What Brady offered the public was snob appeal. Something of a dandy, dressed in finely tailored clothes and scented with English lavender cologne, he hired the best photographers and retouchers to produce tasteful portraits that would appeal to an elite clientele. He knew how to treat the wealthy in the style to which they were accustomed, and the middle class in the style to which it aspired.

Soon after setting up his first New York gallery, in 1844, Brady undertook to photograph every American of importance or prominence — presidents, senators, military men, robber barons, kings of commerce, clergymen, artists and writers, financiers, scientists, explorers, actors and actresses. In 1864 his Gallery of National Portraiture occupied an entire floor of his establishment at the northwest corner of Broadway and Tenth Street, diagonally across Broadway from A. T. Stewart's immense department store, which had opened two years earlier. In the sumptuous exhibition room, furnished as if it were the parlor of a millionaire's house, the walls were almost completely covered with large gilt-framed photographic portraits of notable men and women. New Yorkers and visitors to the city flocked to Brady's gallery to look and to enjoy the fashionable ambiance. While there, those who could afford to do so might perhaps even make an appointment to be photographed. A portrait stamped "Photograph by Brady" offered greatness by association.

The location of Brady's gallery must have afforded him a measure of personal satisfaction, for soon after his arrival in New York, about 1840, he had worked as a clerk in Stewart's first store. The facade of his former employer's new establishment, the largest retail store and the largest cast-iron building in the world, extended along the entire block of Broadway between Ninth and Tenth streets, just below Grace Church.* A. T. Stewart was one of Edward Stieglitz's leading customers. The great department store not only sold fabric by the yard but also employed several hundred women — who sat at long tables in a top-floor loft — to sew the clothes ordered downstairs.

Although opening his gallery in 1860 had overtaxed Brady's already strained finances, the following year he plunged into his great documentation of the Civil War, which would bankrupt him. Despite his partial blindness and poor health, Brady himself photographed at the First Battle of Bull Run, but most of his war pictures were made by men working for him.

In 1859, the twentieth anniversary of the announcement of Daguerre's invention, photographs were admitted for the first time into the official salon in Paris, though they were still relegated to a separate section in the Palais de l'Industrie. But many Frenchmen were not at all willing to concede the status of art to photography. Most notably, the great poet and critic Charles Baudelaire deplored not only the admission of photographs but also the influence of photography upon French painting. In his review of the 1859 salon he sneered that "the photographic industry is the refuge for every failed painter, too little talented or too lazy to complete his studies." Baudelaire hoped that the French would soon reduce photography "to its proper rôle of servant, like printing and stenography, which have neither created nor supplanted literature."[3]

Two years later the controversy over photography's status as an art found its way into the French courts. During and after the crisis that ended with the unification of Italy in 1861, the Paris photographic firm of Mayer and Pierson had had great success selling its cartes de visite of two major actors in the drama, British prime minister Lord Palmerston and Count Cavour, premier of the kingdom of Sardinia. The demand for these portraits was so great that the firm of Betbeder and Schwabbe had found it profitable to publish pirated prints of them. Mayer and Pierson then appealed for protection under the French copyright laws. However, those

---

*James Bogardus had constructed the first building made of prefabricated cast-iron elements in 1849. By the middle 1860s the classical columns and arches of cast-iron architecture had transformed the appearance of New York, and by the end of the decade the elegant cast-iron facades of such stores as Tiffany's, Arnold Constable, and Lord and Taylor would grace the Ladies' Mile, as the shopping district along Broadway and Sixth Avenue between Fourteenth and Twenty-third streets came to be called.

laws protected only works of art. If photographs were to be covered, the court would first have to grant them that exalted status.

To this day, facts per se are not protected by copyright. Only their literary or artistic expression is safeguarded. Therefore, the central question was: Is a photograph simply a bald statement of the fact of the sitter's appearance, or does it reflect the personality of the photographer as well as that of the subject? The corollary was: Are photographs made by photographers or by cameras?

These were tricky questions. Photographers did not want to lose their status as providers of objective truth, but they also wanted to be given credit for their artistry — for their mastery of the very complicated artistic and psychological techniques of making a great portrait.

Of course, every photograph reflects the photographer's taste, intelligence, sensitivity, and imagination. Beyond mere technical ability, the photographer's artistic judgment determines such factors as the angle of vision, the composition, the closeness of the camera to the sitter, the inclusion or exclusion of props, the highlighting of details, and the darkness or lightness of the subject and the print. Furthermore, the success of a portrait depends upon the photographer's ability to elicit and capture a characteristic or revealing expression — or what in his judgment is such an expression.

Nevertheless, on January 9, 1862, the court handed down a decision denying Mayer and Pierson the protection they had sought. Undaunted, the pair appealed in April, and this time their lawyer's arguments were more persuasive. On July 4 the court declared that a photograph was a work of art, entitled to protection under the French copyright laws. Adamant in the face of a petition, signed by many leading French painters, insisting that photography was merely a mechanical trade, the court in November reaffirmed its position: Photography is Art.[4]

CHAPTER FIVE

IN JUNE 1871, one month after the last of Edward and Hedwig's six children was born, the Stieglitz family moved to Manhattan. Their spacious, five-floor brownstone row house, at 14 East Sixtieth Street, not only boasted such advanced luxuries as gas chandeliers, steam heat, and special pipes for refrigerated water but also provided separate bedrooms for Edward and Hedwig.

The house had a large bay window at the rear of the parlor floor, offering an extensive but unlovely view of expanses of mud punctuated by great outcroppings of rock, squatters' shacks, and rather comically stranded houses waiting for the rest of their rows to be built.[1] Fifth Avenue had been paved, with cobblestones, only as far north as Fifty-ninth Street, and Madison Avenue was just packed earth for some distance to the south. In the summer residents had to contend with problems such as malaria and the appalling stench of dead horses decaying in vacant lots. In effect, the area in which the Stieglitz house was located looked more like a western mining town than like part of the greatest city in America.

The block directly north of the house was owned by a speculator who evicted the squatters and their goats, blasted away the rocks, planted grass, and fenced in the entire area. (The eastern portion of the block would be built up during the early 1880s, but the park frontage remained virgin until the construction of McKim, Mead and White's Metropolitan Club in the early 1890s.) Because there were so few houses along Fifth Avenue to the north, the Stieglitzes had a fairly unobstructed view of the park.

Most of the land surrounding Central Park — then generally called "the" Central Park — had been bought by investors who kept the real estate off the market, biding their time until fashionable New Yorkers were ready to move north. But the rich were in no hurry, for they viewed the area surrounding the park as a depressing and unhealthy Siberia. They preferred to live around Gramercy and Madison squares and on Fifth Avenue between Washington Square and Thirty-fourth Street, though a few who were sufficiently daring and socially secure were beginning to move uptown. One such was Mary Mason Jones, an aunt of Edith Jones (later Wharton). In the late 1860s Mrs. Jones, who would serve as a model for Mrs. Manson Mingott, the excessively grande dame in her niece's novel *The Age of Innocence*, had built a group of mansarded mansions, known as Marble Row, on Fifth Avenue between Fifty-seventh and Fifty-eighth streets, reserving the largest for herself. Not until the 1890s would Fifth Avenue above Fifty-ninth Street become Millionaires' Row.

During the 1870s, upper Fifth Avenue could boast only a few scattered houses and, between Seventieth and Seventy-first streets, architect Richard Morris Hunt's Lenox Library. The library's foundation was laid in May 1871, but the noble white marble building, in the classical style of eighteenth-century France, would not open to the public until January 1877. One block to the north, in startling contrast, stood the bright blue clapboard Lenox farmhouse. As for the newly founded Metropolitan Museum of Art, beginning in February 1872 its collections were on view in temporary quarters in a brownstone house at 681 Fifth Avenue, just above Fifty-third Street. Its first building at its permanent location, in Central Park at Eighty-second Street — a small, polychromatic brick-and-stone Ruskinian Gothic structure designed by Calvert Vaux — would not open until 1880.

In 1871, Fifth Avenue was still almost exclusively residential along its entire length. (When the first shop opened on the lower part of the avenue, in 1870, snobs wailed that the decline and fall of New York had clearly begun.) The monotony of row houses was broken only by the many churches, by a few palazzi, public buildings, and clubs, and, looming up at Forty-second Street, by the massive, fortresslike Croton Distributing Reservoir, in the Egyptian Revival style that had been popular in the early 1840s. St. Patrick's Cathedral (begun in 1858) was still under construction. Although the building itself would be completed and dedicated in 1879, its spires would not be finished until 1888.

The tallest structures in the New York skyline were hundreds of church steeples. Most residential and commercial buildings were no more than four or five stories high, though Otis's elevator (perfected in the late 1850s and called a vertical railway) would, by 1875, make possible the first two proto-skyscrapers: the headquarters of Horace Greeley's *New York Tribune*, on Printing House Square, and the Western Union Telegraph Company building, on Broadway at Dey Street. However, neither building was taller than the spire of Trinity Church, and both were soon to be overshadowed by the Brooklyn Bridge, construction of which had begun in 1870 and would be completed in 1883.

Improvements in transportation were drawing the city's upper middle class ineluctably northward. In the late 1860s the Third Avenue horse railway had been extended to Sixty-fifth Street and offered relatively fast service to lower Manhattan, with cars leaving the depot every forty-five seconds during rush hours. By 1871 plans were afoot to construct an elevated steam railway along Third Avenue. The Greenwich Street line had already been opened in 1869, and by 1870 it snaked along Ninth Avenue to near West Thirtieth Street. The Third Avenue line would not open until 1878; it would then cut in half Edward Stieglitz's daily commute downtown. Consistent with the rule that for every gain there is some loss, the horrendous clatter of the locomotive-pulled trains shaking the iron structures on which they traveled made life miserable for the low-income tenants who lived along the routes. Anyone who could afford to do so made a point of living well out of earshot.

But the Stieglitzes themselves were not entirely immune to related problems. Just a block and a half to the east of their house, Fourth Avenue (which was known as Park Avenue only for a short stretch below Fortieth Street) was rendered semivolcanic by the sunken tracks of the railroad lines leading to Commodore Vanderbilt's Grand Central Terminal, which would open in October 1871. From the uncovered gash running up the middle of the avenue, bridged only by the cross streets, every passing train belched forth coal smoke, sparks, and steam.

In September 1870 Walt Whitman found himself forced to admit that everywhere he looked in New York City, "in shop, street, church, barroom, official chair, are pervading flippancy and vulgarity, low cunning, infidelity, . . . everywhere an abnormal libidinousness . . . with a range of manners, or rather lack of manners, (considering the advantages enjoy'd,) probably the meanest to be seen in the world." In short, he summed up, "we live in an atmosphere of hypocrisy throughout."[2]

Another writer, in *Harper's Weekly*, spoke of the "public frenzy" that followed the end of the Civil War and lamented that "enormous speculations, losses, and consequent frauds; an increase of crime, a curious and tragical recklessness in the management of railroads and steamers; a fury of extravagance in public watering places are all observable."[3] This was the period that Mark Twain, in the title of his "tale of today," published in 1873, called the Gilded Age. Ulysses Grant was inaugurated as president in March 1869, and corruption would plague his administration in the middle 1870s. John D. Rockefeller founded the Standard Oil Company in 1870, while men like Andrew Carnegie and Henry Clay Frick were making their vast fortunes in steel. In the late 1860s Jim Fisk and Jay Gould successfully battled Commodore Vanderbilt for control of the Erie Railroad. After one especially dastardly and daring manipulation Fisk quipped, "Nothing is lost save honor!" That could well serve as a motto for the post–Civil War period, which saw the triumph of the voracious vulgarians who swallowed up rivals and resources as greedily as they gulped down gargantuan dinners of terrapin and tournedos.

A fitting symbol of the times was Boss William Marcy Tweed, the three-hundred-pound bookkeeper who rose to absolute control of Tammany Hall, the New York City Democratic organization that based its power on its services to immigrants — aiding them in distress, obtaining jobs for them, expediting their naturalization, and rescuing them from the clutches of the law. Finally coming to completion in 1871 was the county courthouse that Tweed built directly behind City Hall for his corrupt judges. When construction began, the total cost had been projected at $250,000. In the end, the city had spent $12 million (more than the cost of building the U.S. Capitol), a good three quarters of it siphoned off into the pockets of Tweed and his Tammany cronies. Tweed's downfall began that same year, when the *New York Times* published new evidence revealing the magnitude of his wrongdoings, and he would finally be convicted and imprisoned in November 1873.

By 1871 Edward Stieglitz's business, which supplied woolen cloth to stores all over the eastern half of the nation, was thriving. What really made his fortune, however, was the terrible fire that ravaged Chicago from October 8 to 11 that year. When Edward heard the news, he realized that the city's stores would need to buy a tremendous amount of cloth to replace clothes that had been destroyed. His reputation as a businessman was so solid that in very short order he was able to obtain a large bank loan to increase his inventory greatly before prices shot up. His profits were highly gratifying.

For Edward Stieglitz the business world was a means, not an end. He wasn't so much a businessman as a man who found it necessary to engage in trade, and to succeed, in order to subsidize his comfortable and pleasurable life. Not caring to associate with businessmen, he preferred the company of artists, musicians, writers, actors, journalists, editors, sportsmen, and academics. There was nothing he relished more than entertaining his artistic and literary friends — people of high cultural and ethical standards who knew how to enjoy themselves.

The highlight of Edward's week was the large Sunday afternoon gathering of his friends for a generous dinner and animated, opinionated conversation that would stretch long into the evening, accompanied by port and cigars, cards and billiards. At age seven, when the family moved into its Manhattan house, Alfred assumed the duties of sommelier, fetching vintage bottles from his father's fine cellar. The attentive boy took it all in, watching the billiard games so carefully that he was able to imitate all the moves. Practicing on his own, in secret, the nine-year-old prodigy was able to beat his surprised and delighted father.

The company at the Sunday gatherings was diverse and constantly changing. Any artistic soul visiting from Germany was welcome, and Edward might well extend an invitation for a prolonged stay or make a contribution to defray the costs of a national performing tour. But most of Edward's friends were, naturally, New Yorkers. One was Joseph Keppler, the bohemian and marvelously amusing raconteur and caricaturist who founded the overwhelmingly successful satirical magazine *Puck* in New York in the 1870s. Another was Scottish-born John Foord, a genial man with a taste for the arts, who was an editor of the *New York Times*. Having distinguished himself as fearless, persistent, and accurate during the *Times*'s campaign against Boss Tweed in the early 1870s, Foord was made managing editor in 1876, and in the 1880s he would take up the same position at *Harper's Weekly*.[4] Foord and his wife had three daughters; they and the Stieglitzes became close, visiting each other in New York and at the New Jersey shore.

It was presumably through Foord that Edward met Howard Carroll. The son of a general who was killed leading a charge at Antietam, Carroll (who was only ten years older than Alfred) had studied in Germany and Switzerland before returning to New York in 1873. At the age of nineteen he was hired as a junior reporter for the *Times*. Within three years his coverage of events in the South had won him a national reputation, and in 1877, when he was only twenty-three, he was appointed the *Times's* Washington correspondent. A man of many interests and talents, Carroll would write a number of plays — one of which, *The American Countess*, was a hit in cities throughout the country — and he later had a successful career in business.[5] In 1878, however, his finances were shaky. Among Edward's papers is an effusive letter of thanks from Carroll for a loan that got the young man out of a tight spot.

Perhaps the most crucial member of Edward's circle was his wife's cousin Adolph Werner, professor of the German language and literature at the College of the City of New York. Born in Frankfurt in 1839, Werner arrived in America in 1850. Seven years later he graduated, as valedictorian, from New York's Free Academy. In 1861, having worked as a tutor at the academy, which in 1866 would become CCNY, he was appointed a full professor and would hold that position until his retirement, in 1915.

By all accounts the unmarried Werner, who lived with his three sisters, was a paragon. One of his most distinguished students — the publisher and reformer Richard Rogers Bowker — recollected that he "was a great teacher because he was a great man, most beloved of all our instructors, popular in the best and highest sense, a friend of every class and every man coming under his influence." Bowker said that "golden-hearted" Werner possessed "a positive genius for friendship" and stated that "his dignity and charm won him the respect of every boy and man, and in his room discipline was never necessary."[6] Another testimonial spoke of "the superb manner of man" that Werner was and referred to "the dignity and distinction of his presence, his wit, his humor, his poise, his winning charm, his thoughtful and delicate generosity, his affection."[7] As an exemplar, as a mentor, as a recommender of books, and as an adviser on matters regarding education and the choice of career, he was to have a great influence on young Alfred Stieglitz.

In September 1871 Alfred began to attend the best private school in New York. The Charlier Institute — "French and English Institution for Young Gentlemen, under the Direction of Prof. Elie Charlier" — was located at 126–130 East Twenty-fourth Street, in the heart of Manhattan's elite residential district. Founded in 1855 by Charlier, a French Huguenot, the school had become very fashionable and enjoyed a reputation for academic excellence. Among its graduates — who tended to become "Clergymen, Lawyers, Doctors, Merchants, Officers" — were many who bore such distinguished New York names as Astor, Fish, Gallatin, Schuyler, and Van Rensselaer.

The school, which took both boarders and day students, accepted no boys younger than seven and expected them to "know at least how to spell and read a little." After three years in the Primary Department, students entered the five-year General School, at the end of which (at about the age of fifteen) they went directly to college. Charlier assured parents of prospective students that the curriculum of the General School embraced "all the branches of a good, solid English education" of the sort one would receive in an elite British public school.

The school's prospectus particularly emphasized that "FRENCH IS THE LANGUAGE OF THE SCHOOL for ALL YOUNG AMERICANS . . . Pupils are required to SPEAK it, to WRITE it, and USE it, in all the details of every-day life," though much of the instruction was in English. Classes were generally held six days a week, with one Saturday off every month. During the lunch break the boys could exercise indoors or in nearby Madison Square Park, where, in 1876, the torch-bearing arm of the Statue of Liberty was displayed in an effort to raise money to complete the statue and to erect it in New York harbor.

Charlier considered it his "most important duty" to provide his pupils with such religious instruction as he would give his own children. Every school day began at 8:55 with "public worship," and all pupils were expected to be present. "Anything denominational is omitted. . . . I have among my pupils many Catholic and Jewish boys." With no sense of contradiction Charlier demanded that all of his pupils "must be WELL-BRED, HIGH-MINDED, CHRISTIAN boys and young men." He didn't care what specific beliefs they held as long as they manifested what he called "the liberal spirit of living, active Christianity." None of this prevented Edward Stieglitz, an atheistic Jew, from sending his sons to Charlier's school.

In September 1874, when they were seven, Alfred's brothers, Julius and Leopold (whom his family and friends always called Lee) began to attend the Charlier Institute, and Alfred entered its General School. It was fortunate for him that the school was progressive in its pedagogical principles, for he was stubbornly contrary and refused to commit to memory the passages of poetry and prose assigned for practice in elocution and declamation. "Since I was first in my class in every other subject as well as in conduct," he recalled, the teacher "must have felt he could not give me a zero, so he marked me a hundred."[8]

CHAPTER SIX

IN AUGUST 1872, Alfred and his parents, accompanied part of the way by Aunt Rosa, toured several of the outstanding scenic resorts of New York State: Sharon Springs, Niagara Falls, Saratoga Springs, and Lake George. The following summer he and his father would revisit Saratoga and Lake George, as well as traveling to Newport, the White Mountains of New Hampshire, and the Catskills. These trips were partly artistic pilgrimages to see the landscapes favored by the painters of the Hudson River school and partly searches for the perfect spot in which the family could spend its summers, now that Edward's prosperity made such a luxury possible.

Ever since their courtship, Edward and Hedwig had enjoyed occasionally taking the Day Line boat to West Point. During the late 1860s, after Siegmund Stieglitz had acquired a vacation house for his family at Highland Falls, next to West Point, Hedwig and the children would spend a few weeks there most summers. But now Edward wanted something more permanent. His quest would eventually end at Lake George, to which the family would return every year when it was not in Europe. Until his death, Alfred Stieglitz's personal and creative life would have two geographical centers, two opposite poles: New York City and Lake George.

In his 1870s guidebook entitled *Popular Resorts and How to Reach Them*, author John Bachelder noted, "The custom of setting apart a few weeks or months of the year as a respite from labor is fast gaining popularity."[1] The rise of resorts was related to many social, economic, artistic, and technological developments in post–Civil War America. Most important was certainly the tremendous increase in railroad mileage, which made it possible to go almost anywhere in the country with relative speed and comfort. There were approximately fifty thousand miles of track in the early 1870s — and more than ninety thousand by 1880. With the spread of railroads, vast numbers of Americans crisscrossed the nation to see for themselves the picturesque wonders of which paintings by the Hudson River school, as well as the avalanche of stereographs and magazine illustrations, had made them aware.

The trend was summed up in *Picturesque America; or, The Land We Live In: A Delineation by Pen and Pencil of the Mountains, Rivers, Lakes, Forests, Water-falls, Shores, Cañons, Valleys, Cities, and Other Picturesque Features of Our Country*, a splendid work whose two imposing volumes appeared successively in 1872 and 1874. Edited by William Cullen Bryant, the nature poet who was editor in chief of the literate and liberal *New York Evening Post*, the work was a patriotic celebration of the nation's beauties. In the year during which the first volume of *Picturesque America* was published, the U.S. Congress — convinced by William Henry Jackson's photographs that painters had not grossly exaggerated the splendors of Yellowstone — designated that region the first national park.

In scenic areas all over the country, new resorts sprang up and old ones grew. People visited them to see the sights, to meet people from other parts of the nation, to mingle with those who might snub them at home, to forget the horrible ordeal of the Civil War, to relax, to indulge, and to play such newly imported sports as croquet, lawn tennis, and archery. Before the war, sports had been unfashionable, but the games imported from England in the late 1860s became popular because they made possible an unprecedented sociability between the sexes. In 1868 the *Nation* referred to the craze for croquet as "the swiftest and most infectious epidemic" that had ever swept the country.[2]

Archery and lawn tennis would soon follow. Young Alfred took up archery, and late in life he reminisced about the lesson he had learned from the sport. "I wanted to hit what you might call the center of the center of the target. . . . That has been my concern when making my photographs, in my contact with the public and in personal relationships."[3]

Toward the end of August 1872 the Stieglitzes arrived in Saratoga Springs, an impressive place overcrowded with glamorous people enjoying its healthful waters (which the family doctor, concerned about Alfred's pallor, had recommended), band concerts in the park, elegant balls in the evening, games of all sorts, the finest food, and an ambience of luxury and sophistication. In his guidebook Bachelder deplored the "sickly sentimentality of that health-restoring and -destroying spot," but he conceded that Saratoga rivaled Newport for the title of queen of American watering places.[4] The Stieglitzes stayed in the Union Hotel, the most fashionable in town. A. T. Stewart would buy it later that year and spend half a million dollars and nearly two years to transform it into the opulent Grand Union Hotel. In 1877, when Stewart instituted a policy of excluding Jews from the hotel, a Jewish boycott of his department store was organized — presumably costing Edward Stieglitz one of his best customers.

Since 1863 Saratoga had offered the attraction that ultimately came to surpass all others: a track for Thoroughbred racing. It was the track that drew Edward Stieglitz to Saratoga in 1872, and it was the prospect of finally being able to see a real horse race that had excited his son more than anything else on the entire trip. Alfred was already an aficionado. The previous year he had begun to read avidly the British racing magazine to which his father subscribed. Edward owned a Thoroughbred horse, and Alfred would later claim that his father had been the only Jewish member of the New York Jockey Club. That claim is absurd, for August Belmont (né Schoenberg), a key figure in New York racing, was Jewish.[5] Most likely, Edward became a member of the Gentlemen's Riding Club (founded in 1883), which was located on East Fifty-eighth Street between Fifth and Madison avenues, a short distance from his house. His friend Howard Carroll would eventually become president of the club, whose members included August Belmont, as well as Cornelius Vanderbilt, J. P. Morgan, and Stanford White.

Alfred collected lead models of horses ridden by jockeys whipping them on to full gallop. He stabled his models, named them after his favorites, played with them, and used them as springboards for fantasy. He and his friends placed the horses on a Parcheesi board and threw dice to advance them, or they would reenact the great races of the past. In his room at home Alfred hung Currier and Ives prints of famous horses and races, many of them based on paintings by his father's friend Louis Maurer, whose equestrian depictions, ranging from trotters to firehorses, enjoyed enormous popularity.

Given Edward's determination to visit the principal scenic areas associated with the Hudson River school, it was inevitable that he would want to make the short trip from Saratoga to pay homage to Lake George. As early as 1835 the group's founder, Thomas Cole, had hymned the lake "begemmed with isles of emerald, and curtained by green receding hills" in his "Essay on American Scenery." "These scenes are classic," he wrote. "History and Genius have hallowed them."[6] In *The Last of the Mohicans,* James Fenimore Cooper had fixed the lake in the imaginations of countless readers. Among painters it was John F. Kensett — whom James Jackson Jarves called "the [William Cullen] Bryant of our painters" — who had long been associated most closely with the "American Como." It is unclear whether his own reputation or the lake's profited more from the scores of paintings of it that he executed between 1852 and his death in 1872.

Capitalizing on the lake's artistic appeal, an enterprising hotelier had, in 1868, reconstructed and enlarged the old Fort William Henry Hotel in the village of Caldwell, today known as the town of Lake George, at the southern tip of the lake.[7] By 1873 the hotel was so successful in attracting tourists that a writer named Seneca Ray Stoddard (who was also a professional photographer) deemed it worth his while to publish a Lake George guidebook, which would go through thirty editions by 1900. Bachelder included Lake George in his *Popular Resorts,* and in 1874 Lake George and Lake Champlain were given a long chapter in the second volume of *Picturesque America.* The writer of that chapter related that one traveled the eighteen miles from Saratoga to Glens Falls by train, and then the remaining nine miles by stage, on which there was always a free-for-all scramble for the choice outside seats. He then went on to describe the scene that the Stieglitzes would have seen on their first visit, late in August 1872.

> The spacious Fort William Henry Hotel, situated upon the site of the old fort of the same name, stands directly at the head of the lake, with a noble expanse of its waters spread out before it. The coach is driven with a sweep and a swirl through the grounds of the hotel, and, suddenly turning a corner, dashes up before the wide and corridored piazza, crowded with groups of people — all superb life and animation on one side of him, and a marvellous stretch of lake and mountain and island and wooded shore on the other — such a picture, in its charm and brightness and completeness, as the New-World traveller rarely encounters.[8]

On their first trip, the Stieglitzes had time for only an overnight visit — hardly long enough to begin to savor the many pleasures offered by the region. One could, for instance, tour the shores and islands of the lake on one of the four daily excursion steamers, whose arrivals and departures from the dock of the Fort William Henry Hotel were accompanied by the oompah-pah of a German brass band. Or one could pay a dollar for the rough wagon ride from Caldwell to the observatory on the summit of Prospect Mountain, where "a glorious picture of the whole region is spread out before the spectator."[9] Visitors who had more time could rent a canoe to explore the lake's islands, said to number 365, one for every day of the year, with a 366th appearing each leap year.[10]

In the summer of 1873, nine-year-old Alfred and his father paid a visit to the great Catskill Mountain House, long associated with Thomas Cole, who had lived nearby for many years and whose influence had made the surrounding area the most painted region in eastern America. From the village of Catskill, across the river from the town of Hudson, one took a stage to the hotel, dramatically situated high on a jutting rock ledge at an elevation of three thousand feet, between North and South mountains. An advertisement preserved in the Stieglitz archive at Yale University boasts hyperbolically of the view from the hotel's veranda, with its thirteen Corinthian columns (one for each of the original states): "Extending over about ten thousand square miles, [it] is unsurpassed for beauty by any in the world." On the back of the broadside Alfred recorded his accounts:

10	getting blanket
10	carrying book for 1 hour
12	get my and your coat
5	letter
2	buying newspaper
39	cts

Alfred Stieglitz

$3.87 cents of old bill
  39 today
that makes
$4.26 cents[11]

Although Edward, a punctilious stickler, was perhaps trying to inculcate a habit of record keeping that would be useful to his son in his professional life, the nature of the accounts suggests that Alfred, an exceptionally independent and willful child, had to be bribed to perform the simplest chore. He appears to have embraced the practice with a certain vindictive enthusiasm, though perhaps his later contempt for money had something to do with his father's purchase of obedience.

After their stay at the Catskill Mountain House, Edward and Alfred returned to the Fort William Henry Hotel in August 1873 for a longer visit. This time Edward decided that Lake George was the place he had been seeking. For the next seven summers the Stieglitz family traveled the 214 miles from New York to the lake and stayed a month or two, or even three, as guests at one or another of the fashionable hotels there. From 1874 to 1876 they stayed at the Fort William Henry, the last year renting one of the cottages on its grounds. For the following three years they moved into one of the three picturesque cottages at Lake House, the largest hotel in Caldwell. Alfred was evidently content there, for in 1877 he wrote in an album that Lake George was the place where he would most like to live.

In 1880 the family spent the entire summer in one of the cottages at the hotel called Crosbyside, across the lake from Caldwell. Seneca Ray Stoddard noted that as one approached the hotel,

> an air of intense respectability is wafted toward us from the shore, for you must know that Crosbyside is immense in that direction, numbering among its guests Supreme Court judges, D.D.'s [Doctors of Divinity], Japanese princes, and escaped editors, which would be rather strong society for the average touring mortal if the balance of power was not retained on the world's side by the bevy of (*jolly* is the word, I think) young ladies who are annually banished from city homes by confiding mothers, satisfied that they will be safe with Mrs. Crosby. . . . [I]t gets but few "transients," assuming more the appearance of a great home, to which familiar faces come year after year.[12]

For Alfred, Lake George offered not only the beauties of nature but also important contact with photography. In the summer of 1873, accompanied by several friends, he took his collection of lead horses to be photographed by Mr. Irish, the tintyper in Caldwell. Alfred carefully arranged his models on a cloth and, after the exposure was made, was granted permission to follow Mr. Irish into his darkroom. It was not the first time Alfred had entered such a sanctum, for the previous year he had been allowed into the darkroom when his mother had taken him and his brothers and sisters to be photographed by the fashionable Abraham Bogardus, in New York. "I was far less interested in the pictures than in going into darkrooms," recalled Stieglitz. "I wanted to know what went on in those mysterious places."[13]

Now Mr. Irish's shop became a place for Alfred to visit frequently. It was the friendship, not photography, that kept him coming back. He did not make any special effort to learn techniques, nor did he then think of photography as a profession he would like to follow himself. (When he told his father that he would like a camera and darkroom of his own, Edward put his foot down, saying that photography was too messy.) Alfred would simply drop in to chat with the friendly photographer and watch him work. He was fascinated by the skill with which Mr. Irish directed his portrait subjects, and he was opinionated about at least one of his friend's practices, that of touching up the cheeks of his portraits with carmine. Mr. Irish said it made the pictures look "more natural," but Alfred disagreed. In a late version of the story, he claimed already to have an intuition that the integrity of the photographic image should be respected. More likely, he simply thought that the incongruously rouged cheeks looked silly.

CHAPTER SEVEN

IN THE MIDDLE 1870s the most successful photographer in New York was Napoleon Sarony, a tiny man, just over five feet tall. In the late afternoon he might be seen promenading along the "Boulevard de Broadway" (as he called it), wearing an astrakhan cap, a jacket trimmed with Persian lamb, a brocade vest, and checked trousers tucked into knee-high riding boots. With his beard and unruly hair, he looked the part of a miniature Gustave Courbet. Dwarfed by his towering wife, who dressed as flamboyantly as he did, the immensely popular and charming Sarony seemed to know everyone of note in New York and spent much of his walk waving and bowing effusively.

His studio on Union Square, in the heart of the city's theatrical and musical district, was a veritable *cabinet de curiosités*. Crammed together in a self-consciously eccentric jumble were paintings, sculptures, busts, statuettes, Egyptian relics, Japanese and medieval armor, bric-a-brac, carpets, tapestries, feathers, furniture — even a Russian sleigh and a stuffed crocodile. There Sarony photographed actors and actresses, producing not the stiffly posed pictures offered by his competitors but dramatic images of stars in costume, holding climactic poses from their most popular current rôles. He published something like forty thousand theatrical portraits, and so intense was the craze for collecting his pictures that a newly issued one might sell out in hours.

Sarony gained a reputation as the father of artistic photography in America. He was, in fact, the first commercial photographer to become fully accepted as a friend and kindred spirit by the New York community of artists. He was a founder of the Salmagundi Club and a member of the Tile Club — the city's two elite artists' societies. At his death in 1896, the same year in which Mathew Brady died in poverty and obscurity, Sarony's obituary was published on the front page of the *New York Times*.

Had the Stieglitz family traveled to Philadelphia in 1876 to see the great Centennial Exposition, whose organizers honored photography with a pavilion of its own, Alfred would have seen work very different from Sarony's: the large and magnificent views of the American West — counterparts of paintings by Church and Bierstadt — then being produced by men such as William Henry Jackson and Carleton Watkins, both of whom won medals. From sixteen countries the works of 144 photographers, predominantly portraits and documentary photographs, were gathered in what was one of the earliest international photographic exhibitions. Among the visitors from abroad was Professor Hermann Wilhelm Vogel, head of the committee that had selected the German entries, who called the exhibition in Photographic Hall "the grandest display of photographs the world ever saw."[1] Within less than a decade Vogel would be Alfred's first instructor in photography.

The Centennial Exposition was the apotheosis of the wet plate, which was on the verge of being outmoded. The very next year George Eastman, a twenty-three-year-old bookkeeper in Rochester, New York, would take up the hobby of photography. He quickly grew disgusted with the inconveniences of the process, and in 1878 he assiduously studied the reports that appeared, first in British and then in American photographic journals, concerning attempts to substitute gelatin for collodion. In this new process, glass plates were coated with a mixture of gelatin and silver nitrate, then allowed to dry; they could be exposed days or weeks later and developed comfortably at home after a photographic expedition. In 1879 Eastman went to England to learn more, and in July of that year he was awarded his first patent, for a mechanical device to spread gelatin onto glass plates. By the fall of 1881, Eastman's dry plates were widely available in the United States. Because they were cheaper, more photosensitive, and incomparably more convenient to use than wet plates, they were almost solely responsible for the sudden and widespread appearance of a new species: the amateur photographer.

*   *   *

At the Centennial Exposition, young Alfred could also have seen what was the most extensive retrospective survey of American art ever assembled up to that time. Semiphotographic landscape paintings still had pride of place, but the more advanced critics commented favorably on works by such radical young artists as James A. McNeill Whistler, George Inness, and Thomas Wilmer Dewing. The exposition marked a turning point in American taste, away from the dry rendering and the grandiosity of Düsseldorf and the Pre-Raphaelites to the emotionally evocative spirit and freer brushwork of Barbizon and Munich.

The display of Japanese art at the exposition triggered a mass enthusiasm for *japonisme* that would remain an important factor in the American fine and decorative arts well into the first decade of the twentieth century; it would have a tremendous influence on Stieglitz and many of the photographers and painters associated with him. Japan seemed to be a living example of a civilization imbued with the spirit of Ruskin's medievalism, though the writer himself scorned Japanese art as heathen. Many of his American disciples hoped to emulate Japan, where (so it seemed) all levels of society were endowed with exquisite taste and where individual artisans, rejecting technology and commercialism, were creating objects of great beauty based on meticulous observation of — and harmony with — nature. In fact, much of Japanese society was then turning away from its own traditions and avidly embracing Westernism.

Among the sculptures at the exposition was a marble group symbolizing religious liberty that Moses Ezekiel had executed on a joint commission from the Independent Order of the Sons of the Covenant and the Israelites of America.[2] Between January and August 1878, Ezekiel, who was Edward's favorite artist, would live in the Stieglitzes' New York house and share the family's rented cottage at Lake George. During that period he was working on the preliminary sketches for his series of sculptures of the great artists of history — including Phidias, Michelangelo, Raphael, and Dürer — to adorn the facade of William Corcoran's house, forerunner of the present Corcoran Gallery, in Washington. Edward advanced him money to purchase marble.

Ezekiel, whose grandparents were Dutch Jews, was born in Richmond in 1844. A student at the Virginia Military Institute from 1861 until the school was burned by Union troops early in 1864, he and his fellow cadets, some of them only fifteen, then joined the Confederate Army and won themselves a niche in Southern legend by fighting in the Battle of New Market, in May of that year.

In 1869 Ezekiel went to Berlin to study at the Royal Academy of Art. Four years later he won a fellowship from a German foundation for a year in Rome, where he would spend much time throughout the rest of his life. Having thoroughly mastered the techniques of academic realism, he received many commissions for portrait busts, portrait reliefs, and memorials, such as *Virginia Mourning Her Dead* (1872–73), his monument in Lexington, Virginia, honoring his fellow cadets. He evidently had a penchant for traumatic biblical stories, for among his other works were an Eve with the serpent, a David with Goliath's head, and a marble bust of Judith, a copy of which was in Edward's collection.

Edward had met Ezekiel through Fedor Encke, a portraitist and genre painter born in Berlin in 1851. Encke had entered the academy there at the same time as Ezekiel, but in 1872 he left for Weimar to continue his studies. An example of his work from this period, exhibited at the Dresden Academy in 1875, was a piece of historical genre entitled *In the Roman Ghetto*. He lived with the Stieglitzes for nearly all of 1877, during which time he painted the first of his numerous portraits of members of the family. Edward, who judged Encke's work not quite first-rate, underwrote many of his expenses for a year in Paris and often subsidized his summer travels to scenic locations.

Inspired, no doubt, by the resident talent, Edward converted one room of the New York house to a studio and, during 1879 and 1880, engaged the services of a painter named Erxleben to give him weekly lessons in oils. Edward demonstrated passable talent and would long enjoy his hobby, turning out a succession of rather crudely painted romantic landscapes. His son's most affectionate, and most amusing, photograph of him shows the old man standing beside his easel at Lake George. Smoking a cigar and attired in a black frock-coated business suit, he is holding his palette in one hand and his hat in the other. On the easel is a small painting of the trees that would be such an important motif in Alfred's photographs.

In the 1870s Alfred's tastes were still very conventional. When he was thirteen he listed Fedor Encke as one of his two favorite painters. (The other was cryptically identified as "H.L.") Among his favorite works was a trompe l'oeil watercolor by Julius Gerson, another of Edward's artistic friends. Made for Alfred's thirteenth birthday, it depicted, in the style developed by William Harnett in the middle 1870s, a pile of correspondence that included a Western Union telegram, the envelope of a letter, and two postcards, the top one addressed to "Mr. Alfred Stieglitz, 14 East 60th St., New York." The picture struck Alfred as nothing less than "miraculous," for he felt as though he could "lift the postcards and stamps from the very paper on which they were painted."[3]

CHAPTER EIGHT

UNDERNEATH HIS GRACIOUSNESS and love of life, Edward Stieglitz was a tense and brittle man with a hair-trigger temper. His family lived in a minefield, never knowing what ordinarily negligible sound might set him off — the creak of a floorboard, the rustle of a starched petticoat, the rasp of a knife on a plate. As he read in his library one evening after a trying day, for example, he was so tormented by the sound of the maid's footsteps overhead that he furiously ordered her thenceforth to remove her shoes whenever she worked upstairs while he was at home.

The dinner table was all too often the arena in which unpleasant scenes occurred. Edward's hypersensitivity to disturbing sounds could even lead this paragon of hospitality to be rude to visitors. One frequent and esteemed dinner guest was a German named Herman Linde, a vigorous, powerfully built, and splendidly bearded man who toured America giving one-man performances of Shakespeare's plays, reciting all of the rôles himself in his rich voice.

"Linde liked soup," Alfred later related, "and whenever he would take a mouthful of soup you could hear him . . . across the room." One evening Edward was so irritated by this uncouthness that he exploded, "Do you think you could eat your soup without all of New York hearing you eat it?" and then stormed away from the table, announcing that he would go out into the hall and read his paper until Linde had finished. Fortunately,

Linde was a man who could respond to such peevish behavior with good humor. He enjoyed — or at least made a show of enjoying — the rest of his soup and then called out to Edward that it was safe to return.[1]

The family, however, was both embarrassed and terrorized by the bullying of this martinet of the dinner table. Alfred, discovering that he too was overly sensitive to harsh sounds, resolved to harden himself so that he would never succumb to such self-indulgence. He determined to strengthen himself for whatever life might bring.

One hot day when he was about ten or eleven, he passed a knife and scissors grinder on a neighboring street; the noise of metal on grindstone set his teeth on edge and sent chills down his spine. Then and there he decided to mortify this weakness. He paced back and forth beside the grinder until the man had finished and moved on. As if in training for sainthood, Alfred repeated this exercise in self-control and inurement for about a year, whenever he encountered the man on his weekly round. He never did overcome his aversion to the sound. But when the grinder stopped coming around, he regretted the loss of this opportunity for self-improvement.

Edward seems to have weathered the financial panic of September 1873 quite well, though its reverberations would depress the American economy until 1877. But it may have been as the result of a need for thrift imposed by hard times that, when Alfred was about ten years old, his parents began to argue frequently, and heatedly, about money. Unlike her son, Hedwig was simply incapable of maintaining the meticulous accounting that Edward demanded, and she was unable to curb her impulse to give small sums to those she considered deserving. Furthermore, she was expansive and careless about household expenses. "I could not always discern the reasons for either my father's intermittent strictness or my mother's harrowing inability to keep within a reasonable budget," reminisced Alfred. "Her failure to do so never ceased to exasperate my father. . . . I must admit, though, had my father not insisted on a strict budget, I do not know what would have happened to our family."[2] Four decades later, Hedwig's cousin Adolph Werner would describe Edward as "hospitable and generous and lavish to relatives, friends, strangers and meanly quarrelsome about household expenditures."[3]

Alfred observed that wealth could make possible a degree of freedom but that money could also be "a deadly poison."[4] Although he conceded that his father's anger was not without basis, he nevertheless blamed him for introducing discord into the family circle and inflicting pain, not only upon Hedwig but also upon the children. The boy who in his thirteenth year wrote in an album that his "favorite non-religious book" was "a pocket-book filled with money" resolved that he would never allow himself to behave like his father.[5] "The endless family altercations about financial matters made me recoil from all references to the subject of money," he later remarked.[6] Throughout his life Alfred would resort to excessive denial of the importance of money in everyone's life, including his own. He could not, of course, be as indifferent to money as he tried and pretended to be, since the life he wished to live, for all its ostensible simplicity, was an expensive one. There is, after all, no costlier luxury in this world than not having to worry about money.

The arguments over finances were certainly aggravated by sexual tensions between Edward and Hedwig. By 1877 Alfred had become aware that Edward would often climb the back stairs to pay a late-night visit to the chambermaid. After the birth of Hedwig's sixth child, Edward had probably been banished from his wife's bed. But Alfred would not have known that, and would not have understood it if he had known.

For help in comprehending such undiscussable matters, he turned to Goethe's *Faust*, which then became his favorite book, eclipsing even *Uncle Tom's Cabin*, the Horatio Alger stories, *David Copperfield* (whose hero he identified in 1876 as his favorite character in fiction), and Charles Carleton Coffin's popular novel of the American Revolution, *The Boys of '76*. When his mother found him reading *Faust* one day, Alfred told her, "There are two things that attract me in it, Marguerite and the Devil."[7] One need not be a psychoanalyst to state with considerable assurance that in the pure and virtuous Marguerite he saw his mother — and in the clever, cavalier, powerful, and wicked Mephistopheles, his father. Alfred told his mother that the character of Faust didn't interest him. Despite the nobility of his tragic longings, Faust does seem rather a clod — and that, of course, is precisely what makes his tragedy so poignant and universal. Undoubtedly, Alfred's denial of interest in Faust himself was directly proportionate to the discomfort caused by his true feelings: he identified with Faust and envied Mephistopheles.

One day, in the midst of this pubescent confusion, Alfred was reading on a bench in Central Park when along came a French governess and her charges — two sisters, slightly younger than he, wearing black mourning dresses with white collars, the combination that he found so irresistible. He developed an instantaneous crush on the younger girl, whom he thought "very beautiful." As they sat on the opposite bench, they were clearly delighted to be joined by a friend, a blond boy with a hoop. Watching their animated conversation, Alfred became so overwhelmed by his "heartache" over the unbridgeable, indeed existential, gulf separating him from the girl's beauty and happiness that he went home and cried.

The next day the scene repeated itself, and Alfred decided that he must sit on his bench until he had mastered his feelings, even if he had to "sit there forever." He stayed until the group had left, then went home and ran around the block three times. In his old age he would write, "I still see the little girl, I still see the little boy, and I am still the same, — I still have the same heartache. I have not grown up one bit."[8] He went on to state that a related sense of heartache underlay his dedication to his galleries, where he promulgated the doctrine that art can never really be owned or even fully understood. One must be content to contemplate the ideal; the more vigorously one attempts to grasp it, the more removed it becomes.

Alfred wrote of his father that he was a highly strung autocrat. "Yet, even while rebelling against my father and finding him vain, impatient and impossible to speak to, I admired him. Both he and my mother were extremely kind and sentimental at heart."[9] This is the classic formulation of someone who as a child could not understand why an "extremely kind" parent would withhold his love unless the child suppressed his true feelings and impulses and acted like a perfect little adult. The young Alfred had evidently so greatly feared his father that he had not dared to articulate, even to himself, the extent of his fear. Even the mature Alfred did not fully face the dynamics of his childhood. To say that one "admired" a father who was "vain, impatient and impossible to speak to" is both to indict him explicitly and to damn him with faint praise.

In December 1877 Alfred wrote a letter to his father confessing that in July he had presented a story by someone else as his own. He had suffered agonies of guilt. "For the past two months," he told Edward, "I could not think of anything but the lie I told you." The truth of the matter was, he wrote, "I read a book in which this story appeared. I then wrote it from memory, [*inserted, in pencil, with a caret:* 'I would swear to it that I did not copy it.'] & then gave it to you, & tried to make you believe that I wrote out of my own head. . . . I would rather bear the severest punishment from you, than to tell another lie, in my future life. This year is coming to a close, & I have made up my mind, that this was the first & last lie, that my lips shall ever utter."[10]

Capitalized "Truth" was the bogeyman of Alfred's childhood. In 1874 Edward wrote in his ten-year-old son's autograph album:

Be the servant of Truth
Master of Passion.
To his son Alfred
E^d Stieglitz[11]

Two years later Alfred noted that the quality he most respected in men was "honesty," and in women "truth," though he didn't explain the distinction he evidently made between them. The traits he despised above all others, he added, were "dishonesty and deceitfulness."[12] Such attitudes were strongly reinforced at school, for in his prospectus Charlier warned that he insisted upon "TRUTH in every thing. Yes must be yes. No must be no." It is no wonder Alfred would later claim that he was obsessed with his search for Truth. He had to find it in order to feel worthy, even if only retroactively, of the affection that his father had withheld.

Alfred played billiards, bowled, practiced archery, followed horse racing, collected autographs, and read widely. He had begun studying the piano when he was nine; by thirteen he would be accomplished enough to play with gusto, if not with finesse, and even to imagine a career as a concert pianist. Nevertheless, he soon conceded that his talent was not sufficient. Despite all these activities, he lacked an intense form of exercise that would allow him to push himself to his physical limits and to sublimate his rapidly growing sexual energy and frustration.

In May 1874 such a form of recreation presented itself a few blocks away from the Stieglitz house. At the Rink, on the corner of Third Avenue and Sixty-fourth Street, where the American Institute of the City of New York mounted its huge commercial fair every autumn, a famous walker attempted to set a new record by covering five hundred miles in six days. By pure — and ultimately insignificant — coincidence, the name of the walker was Edward Weston; another Edward Weston would become one of the greatest photographers of the twentieth century, and Alfred would be one of the decisive influences on his career.

Edward Payson Weston had first come to national notice in 1861, when the twenty-two-year-old walked the 478 miles between Boston and Washington, D.C., in ten consecutive days in order to attend the inauguration of President Lincoln. He missed the ceremony by a few days, but his feat was widely celebrated in the press. In 1867 he decided to transform his hobby of long-distance walking into his profession and proceeded to walk from Portland, Maine, to Chicago — a distance of 1,326 miles — in thirty days, scrupulously resting on the four Sabbaths within that time. Reports of his progress sparked a national mania for what was then called pedestrianism.

On Monday, May 11, 1874, Weston began his five-hundred-mile attempt, his greatest test to that date. All New York was excited. Some two thousand spectators, including many ladies, cheered Weston on at the Rink that evening as he made his indefatigable circuits of the one-seventh-mile track to the accompaniment of a band. On page 1 the *New York Times* for May 12 reported that, despite heavy betting against him, Weston had exceeded all previous efforts by walking 115 miles in twenty-three hours and fifty-one minutes. A *Times* editorial the following day intoned that his first day's accomplishment "must be placed among the marvels of physical prowess," declaring that "any horse that could be guaranteed to get over the same amount of ground in the same time would bring an almost fabulous price." The *Times* continued, "It is quite certain that his performance will result in a public benefit. There is no more healthful exercise than walking, and there is none which is more neglected in our great cities. The example of WESTON will induce our young men to use their legs rather than the [still dangerously overcrowded] street-cars."

That evening large crowds turned out, including many prominent citizens with their entire families in tow. In the end, Weston failed to reach his goal by the deadline, which had been set to avoid the Sabbath. (In Newark, New Jersey, in December of that year, Weston would finally succeed in walking five hundred miles in six days.)

The most direct result of his attempt was the rise of the six-day "go-as-you-please" races at Gilmore's Garden, the former New York and Harlem Railroad passenger depot at Fourth Avenue between Twenty-sixth and Twenty-seventh streets, which had been vacated by the opening of Grand Central Terminal in 1871. The name sprang from the format: the contestants walked and rested as they pleased; timers kept track of each man's distance, and he who had covered the most ground by the end of the contest won. In 1879 William H. Vanderbilt reclaimed the building and renamed it Madison Square Garden. He forbade pedestrian races, allegedly because the professionals inspired so many amateurs to cover long distances on foot that the railroad business was suffering.

Walking was evidently too sedate for Alfred, who loved the speed of horse races. Thus Weston's example prompted him to take up running. "Racing was in my blood," he later said. "I was a natural runner." He began running every day around the fenced-in vacant block across the street from the family's house, sometimes covering many circuits. After trying the hundred-yard dash and the broad jump, he set up courses for himself punctuated with chairs and ran the hurdles. "I was proud of my running," he recalled. "I loved . . . to do everything as fast and well as possible."[13]

Edward was pleased to see Alfred getting exercise that would improve his health, which had always been worrisome. A rather delicate boy with a shock of dark hair, deeply set eyes, a pale complexion, and an intense, brooding temperament, Alfred inspired his mother's friends to nickname him Hamlet. Later in the decade he grew so tall and thin that, as a friend later reported, he took on a "cadaverous look which periodically frightened his mother into supposing him tubercular."[14]

Throughout the rest of his life, Alfred would suffer terribly from incurable hypochondria, the first cousin of depression, which is itself so often caused by the inability to express one's rage. Some of Alfred's rage was certainly due to his envy of his twin brothers. "I am sick," insists the hypochondriac. "Therefore you must give me extra love." Alfred would employ that strategy to manipulate his parents, his first wife, and his second — Georgia O'Keeffe. His hypochondria may also have been related to his sense of unworthiness and weakness, perhaps the result of guilt and fear concerning masturbation. When he was about seventeen, he told his mother that he would never get married, for no woman he would want to marry could possibly find him worthy.

As an adult, Alfred clearly had strong manic-depressive tendencies. Afraid he could not be loved for who he was, he resolved to ensure that he would at least be loved for what he did. To that end he would expend a tremendous amount of energy in pursuit of perfection and the highest ideals. But periodically, and with increasing frequency as he aged, his obsessive pursuit would utterly exhaust him, and he would find himself unable to sustain the performance that made him feel worthy of love. He would then fall into a depression, usually accompanied by hypochondriacal symptoms, until he regained the strength to resume his perfectionistic labors.[15]

When Alfred was about thirteen, he decided to stage a one-man, twenty-five-mile race against time. On a winter afternoon his brothers and friends watched him as he ran endlessly around a track he had laid out in the sweltering basement of the family house. The whole thing was very professional. One of the assembled boys timed Alfred with the fine chronometer Edward had given him; others manned pails, holding drinking ladles and sponges for mopping the runner's sweating forehead. Alfred crossed the finish line after about three and a half hours.

At other times, he would run races against his friends. "I wanted to beat everybody on earth," he admitted.[16] He insisted that winning meant absolutely nothing to him. Although he conceded that there may have been an element of vanity in his competitiveness, he maintained that it was the quality of his effort that really mattered to him.

Truth, running, photography: the common denominators for Alfred were the intensity of striving, the testing of oneself, and the honor of the gentleman-sportsman. Throughout his life he strove to uphold the basically aristocratic principle of British sportsmanship and amateurism: "It's not whether you win or lose; it's how you play the game." In his old age he would sum up, "I always have had a feeling of sport in relationship to everything I have done."[17] Indeed, he often used to quote Nietzsche's statement that achievers fall into three categories: the artist, the scientist, and the sportsman. He would always go on to emphasize that he considered himself far more the last two than the first.

Alfred would give up his self-described "passion for running" only when he finally found another activity about which he could be even more passionate and obsessive — photography.

CHAPTER NINE

BY 1877 EDWARD and Hedwig Stieglitz were considering Alfred's college education, which he would begin in September 1879. On the advice of Adolph Werner, and because of Werner's affiliation, they decided that Alfred would attend the College of the City of New York.

CCNY was then dominated by three great teachers: Werner, Alfred George Compton, and Robert Ogden Doremus. Compton, the professor of applied mathematics, was a rather quiet and gentle young man who was well liked by his students and highly respected as a teacher. In 1873 he had instituted a postgraduate course in civil engineering at CCNY. Doremus, the professor of chemistry and physics, was a very different kind of man. Dynamic and charismatic, he was widely celebrated for his specialty of forensic toxicology. His electrifying lectures and scientific demonstrations made him extremely popular not only at CCNY but also on the national lyceum circuit, where he attempted to convince the pious and provincial American public that science should play a role in education equal to that of the humanities.

Undoubtedly influenced by his friends Compton and Doremus, Werner advised Edward that Alfred, who had shown an aptitude for mathematics, should become either an engineer or a chemist. The present, and certainly the future, seemed to belong to the scientists and the inventors. Indeed, the technology that would transform the world was rapidly being developed. The 1876 Centennial Exposition had been dominated by the Hoe press and the Corliss engine, and the hand of the engineer was increasingly evident everywhere — in railroads, bridges, and tall buildings. Alexander Graham Bell invented the telephone in 1876, and that same year a German named Nikolaus Otto perfected a four-stroke internal-combustion engine. In 1878 Thomas Edison would patent his phonograph, and the following year he would produce an incandescent electric lightbulb. It was quite obvious to any intelligent observer that the world was in the midst of one of the most profound and far-reaching technological revolutions in history.

Werner, Compton, and Doremus led the progressive faction at CCNY, but their influence was unfortunately counteracted by the reactionary thinking of the college's president. In September 1869, thirty-three-year-old General Alexander Stewart Webb, a graduate of West Point and a recipient of the Congressional Medal of Honor for his bravery at Gettysburg, had become CCNY's second president. Webb, alas, was no scholar. He was an administrator and disciplinarian, whose pedagogical philosophy and methods were rapidly becoming obsolete. In 1874 CCNY strengthened its old-fashioned, classical curriculum. Three years later Compton was forced to teach his civil engineering course outside college hours and without pay. A new scientific laboratory was proposed in 1879, but it would not be built until 1883.[1]

If the only consideration had been to provide Alfred with the best possible preparation for a career as a mechanical engineer, his parents would certainly not have sent him to CCNY. They might instead have chosen the Stevens Institute of Technology, in Hoboken, which had opened in September 1871 and which in 1875 had established a fine mechanical laboratory. Or they could have chosen the Massachusetts Institute of Technology, chartered in 1861, though the Civil War delayed the beginning of classes for four years. Best of all would have been the Rensselaer Polytechnic Institute, in Troy, New York. In 1835 it had become the first American school to grant an engineering degree. During the 1870s the school's most effective advertisement was the fact that Washington Roebling, the chief engineer of the rising Brooklyn Bridge, was a graduate.

Edward and Hedwig undoubtedly felt that at the age of fifteen their precious Alfred would be too young to go away to school. Even more important was the matter of family loyalty. Adolph Werner was devoted to CCNY, and he wanted to recruit as many good students as possible to reinforce the school during a critical period in its existence. (Alfred was not his only catch within the family; Siegmund Stieglitz's son Edward entered in 1878.)

The college had received much criticism during the late 1860s and the 1870s in several New York newspapers, especially the *Sun*. The wealthy, wanting to maintain a monopoly in the professions, resented having their taxes subsidize a free education for hustling boys from the slums who would then provide stiff competition. The argument ran that CCNY served only to educate the poor beyond their station, fostering discontent and making them dissatisfied with their proper work. Moreover, contended the college's opponents, free admission discouraged individual initiative and hard work.

In 1876 efforts to cripple or destroy CCNY were renewed. They were blocked in the state legislature, but the attack resumed in January 1878. It was, however, swiftly and decisively defeated by a petition with sixty thousand signatures in support of the college.

Because Edward and Hedwig had decided to send Alfred to CCNY, he did not return to the Charlier Institute in September 1877, for the college had a rule that excluded graduates of private or parochial schools.[2] Instead, he would attend Grammar School Number 55, on Twentieth Street between Sixth and Seventh avenues. (The term "high school" had not yet come into its current usage; one went from primary school to grammar school and then to college.) Grammar School Number 55 was reputed to be the best public school in the city, and it sent an exceptional number of its graduates to CCNY.

In old age, looking back on his life, Alfred felt that in his youth he had been repeatedly "uprooted," one traumatic instance of which was being taken out of Charlier. He thought that as a result of those constant uprootings he had always been "unprepared." "I find that the keynote to whatever I have done has been unpreparedness," he wrote. "In reality the only thing in which I have been actually thorough has been in being thoroughly unprepared."[3] But he concluded that his unpreparedness had contributed greatly to his ultimate success by developing his sense of adventure and enabling him to approach situations with a fresh perspective, unhindered by rules and expectations.

By his own account, Alfred's career at Grammar School Number 55 was highly unorthodox. Sailing through his classes with little effort, he was bored there. No wonder he wrote in an album in 1877 that his favorite season was "whenever there is no school." His most satisfying accomplishment was demonstrating an extraordinary ability to work out complex arithmetical problems completely in his head. After several minutes of silence, he would usually amaze his teachers and fellow students by delivering the correct answer. A few years later, in Germany, Alfred's professor was shocked to learn that he couldn't explain the intermediate steps. Regarding him as little more than an idiot savant, he told the boy that "he had never encountered such an unmathematical mind." Alfred shot back, "'In America we only care for the answers.'"[4]

The Charlier Institute had placed great emphasis on penmanship, and Alfred — who for the rest of his life would be vain about the strong, flowing script he wrote with a broad-nibbed pen — had been at the top of his class in that skill. Because of Alfred's superb hand and his excellent spelling, Mr. Conklin, the principal of Grammar School Number 55, enlisted him to write out the school's payroll one day each week. "Sometimes I would even get through by noon," he recollected, "and then Conklin would say, 'You have done a beautiful job. I will excuse you from lessons for the rest of the day.' And then I would go to play baseball or something else equally important to me."[5]

Late in May 1879, Alfred spent three days taking the battery of CCNY admission exams, covering everything from English grammar and American history to quadratic equations. A couple of weeks later he must have been pleased and proud to see his name appear in print for the first time, as the *New York Herald* published the list of successful candidates.

After an enjoyable summer at one of the Lake House cottages, Alfred left his family at Lake George in September and returned to New York, where he would live for a month with his mother's parents while beginning classes at CCNY.

The College of the City of New York was located on the corner of Lexington Avenue and Twenty-third Street, in an ugly Victorian-Gothic structure of brown stucco, brick, and red sandstone that looked like a cross between a church and a utopian-socialist factory. Because the course of studies at CCNY was a five-year program, Alfred entered the college as a member of the class of 1884. The first year, called the subfreshman year or Introductory Class, was largely remedial, since so many students were not adequately prepared by the public high schools. (The often-repeated claim that Stieglitz attended Townsend Harris High School before entering CCNY is not true. The first school of that name was not established until 1906, when the subfreshman course at CCNY was expanded into a three-year high school program.) Adolph Werner later recalled that the subfreshmen, confined to a small annex, "did not disturb the scholastic calm of the main building; they never entered it except when they came, under supervision, to the first floor to listen to Professor Doremus and behold his magnificent experiments."[6]

Alfred later wrote that he had continued to feel uprooted when he entered college, for his father was already "always talking about getting out of business and taking the family to Europe." The boy assumed that he probably wouldn't complete more than two years at CCNY, and so he saw no point in trying to be a superlative student. Nevertheless, he managed to rank tenth in his class during his first year — graduating classes usually numbered thirty to fifty students — and sixth the following year.

Since he was not working very hard, Alfred had plenty of time for extracurricular activities and for his own interests. In the CCNY *Microcosm* for 1880–81 he was listed as a member of the Freshman Winter Sports Society and as the vice president of La Société Française Littéraire ("fondée Octobre 1880"). The inclusion of Alfred's name may, however, be misleading, for one graduate in the class of 1883 later recalled that "perhaps a third of these organizations never existed except in these pages, but such spurious clubs gave opportunities for students to see their names in print with official titles attached."[7]

CHAPTER TEN

ALTHOUGH IT WAS because of Adolph Werner that Alfred went to CCNY, the teacher was equally responsible for the decision that Alfred should withdraw and continue his schooling in Germany. One factor may have been the first stirrings of anti-Semitism at CCNY, around 1880, as evidenced in some of the school publications that were born during a wave of student journalism at that time. In addition, Werner was greatly disappointed by the college's failure to adopt the broad and flexible curriculum of the German universities, at which students were free to choose electives in keeping with their interests and career plans. Johns Hopkins University, founded in 1867, had been directly inspired by the German example, and two years later the elective system was instituted at Harvard by its new president, Charles William Eliot. But most American students were far less advanced, scholastically and culturally, than Germans of the same age. President Webb of CCNY dismissed the elective system as "nonsense" and believed that college boys were too young to choose a career until they came of legal age. "Our great trouble is with Webb," wrote Werner in September 1880. "He is good-natured, affable, disposed to do right; but he has no ideas, no plans for the future, and there is nothing Emersonian in his sermons to the students."[1] Werner felt that in order to receive a first-rate education, the Stieglitz children would have to go to school in Germany.

Alfred left CCNY in 1881, at the end of his freshman year, but the school has long considered him one of its most distinguished alumni, eventually even naming a building devoted to cinematic studies Stieglitz Hall.

In January 1881, forty-eight-year-old Edward Stieglitz decided to retire and take his family to live in Europe for at least five years. He himself wanted to be free to travel and to pursue his increasingly consuming hobby of painting. While he did so, his children would attend progressive schools and imbibe the values and the culture of the Old World. Upon their return to America, they would not only lead in their chosen fields but also, he hoped, serve as moral and cultural exemplars.

During the following six months Edward sold most of his share of Hahlo and Stieglitz for the then princely sum of more than $400,000 and invested his capital in the stock market. On June 18 the family sailed from Hoboken on a ship of the Bremen line. They escaped just in time, for that summer the streets of New York were "filthy beyond precedent," and "disease and death stalked through the metropolis."[2]

The ten-day crossing turned out to be far more eventful than it seemed at the time, for on board the Stieglitzes met two boys who would have a tremendous impact on the family. Joseph Obermeyer and Louis Schubart were traveling to Europe to rendezvous with their parents, who had embarked before the end of the school year. Joe and Lou were about two years older than Alfred, but the difference in their ages appeared even greater, since they were tall and solidly built. Responding to Alfred's witty remarks and his funny stories, they initially adopted him as their mascot. Alfred, no doubt, half envied and half resented their self-possession and confidence, which he tended to dismiss as smugness. They were clearly not as sensitive and artistic as he was, but they were probably not so philistine as he later chose to portray them. For one thing, when the elderly Alfred recounted the history of his involvement with these two friends, he never bothered to mention that Obermeyer proved to be quite a good photographer.

By 1881, ten years after the establishment of the German Empire, Chancellor Otto von Bismarck's conservative system was well in place. Terrified by the Paris Commune of 1871, Bismarck had become obsessed by the threat of the international socialist movement. To form alliances against socialism within Germany, he manipulated the various classes and interests as skillfully and ruthlessly as he did the governments of Europe. Beginning in 1881, not out of any humanitarian impulse, but as a sop, Bismarck instituted a great program of health insurance, workers' compensation, and old-age pensions. He even convinced the liberal middle class that its beloved parliament would not be able to maneuver quickly and decisively enough to withstand the attacks of socialism and that a de facto military dictatorship was thus essential. The spirit of militarism permeated every aspect of life, and uniforms proliferated, from the government bureaucracy to the university.

Germany was then in the throes of the second Industrial Revolution. The first had been a revolution of coal and iron; the second was one of electricity and steel, and Germany was a world leader in both. The great firm of Siemens, located in Berlin, was in the vanguard of a huge industry that would produce everything from dynamos to electric streetcars. Germany was also unchallenged in the chemical industry, developing and producing synthetic dyes, explosives, and drugs. Expanding at phenomenal rates were such fields as shipbuilding and maritime trade, the manufacture of optical and precision instruments, banking, and insurance.

During his years in Germany, Alfred would come to think of its people as industrious, socially responsible, deeply spiritual, and devoted to music and the other arts as well as to the ideals of freedom. That was all true enough, but there was also another side. There was the nouveau riche Germany, extremely competitive, extravagant, vulgar, materialistic, and expansive, whose rampage of colonization would begin in 1884. That Germany Stieglitz would either ignore or choose to forget.

At first the plan was for Alfred to attend the Zurich Polytechnik, which was then considered the best engineering school in the world. But Edward was soon told that it was notorious for its cigarette-smoking Russian female students with loose morals and radical politics. His information was out of date, since, in 1873, Czar Alexander II had attempted to cut off the influx of sedition by decreeing that all students must return home from Switzerland immediately or be barred from practicing their future professions in the Russian Empire. Relatively few remained in Zurich.

Edward then decided that Alfred would study in Berlin at the all-male Königliche Technische Hochschule (Royal Technical High School), which had been formed in 1879 by the union of the Königliche Gewerbeakademie (Royal Vocational Academy, known informally as the Polytechnik) and the architectural academy. From the viewpoint of New Yorkers in the early 1880s, the most prominent graduate of the vocational academy, founded in 1821, was John A. Roebling, the designer of the Brooklyn Bridge and father of its chief engineer. One of the Technische Hochschule's most famous twentieth-century students would be Ludwig Wittgenstein, who attended from 1906 to 1908 and soon gave up mechanical engineering for philosophy. Stieglitz and Wittgenstein would share an obsession with absolute truth that would lead many of their colleagues and followers to regard them as spiritual masters. One might argue that mechanical engineering's concern for basic structure and logic served them both well, providing them not only with an experience of materialism against which to react but also a methodology for their reaction.

In 1881 neither Alfred's German nor his scientific education was adequate to qualify him for the Technische Hochschule. He would therefore spend his first year at the Realgymnasium in Karlsruhe, which his twin brothers would also attend. (It offered a curriculum more modern than that of a classical gymnasium, with courses in physics and chemistry.) Agnes and Selma would attend a school in Weimar, while Flora would study piano at the conservatory there. Edward, Hedwig, and Aunt Rosa would alight in cities from Paris to Vienna for the concert, opera, and theater seasons, and then migrate to the various fashionable spas in warmer weather.

During the summer of their arrival in Europe, the entire Stieglitz family spent the month of August in the Black Forest resort of Baden-Baden, of which Mark Twain had written in *A Tramp Abroad*, published in 1880, "It is an inane town, filled with sham, and petty fraud, and snobbery, but the baths are good."[3] Then the three boys were sent off to nearby Karlsruhe. The avenues of this beautiful city radiated like spokes from the duke of Baden's palace, which lay at the center of an immense circle, half of which was occupied by the city and half by the ducal gardens. Edward and Hedwig had chosen Karlsruhe for their sons because one of Fedor Encke's closest friends, a painter named Wilhelm Gustav Friedrich Hasemann, lived there and could not only help to make arrangements but also keep an eye on the boys. Alfred would board with the family of Professor Doktor Karl L. Bauer, a kindly man who taught mathematics at the Realgymnasium, while the twins would live with the congenial and intellectual family of Professor Träutlein, director of the town's classical gymnasium. In addition to their regular classwork, Julius diligently studied the cello, and Lee the violin. Eventually the Träutleins arranged for the twins to play piano quartets with the Stieffel sisters, daughters of a local government official. In 1891 Julius would marry violinist Anny Stieffel, and three years later Lee would marry her sister Elizabeth. The latter was so talented that she had been summoned to Baden-Baden to serve as pianist-in-residence at the summer court of Queen Elizabeth of Rumania, who, under the pseudonym Carmen Sylva, wrote poems, *pensées*, and a collection of folktales.

Although Alfred immediately found that his schooling in New York had not prepared him sufficiently even for his preparatory courses, and despite a difficult period of adjustment when he felt that the Germans could do nothing right, he spent a reasonably happy year in Karlsruhe. During the Easter vacation he enjoyed a stay with Wilhelm Hasemann in the picturesque Black Forest farming village of Gutach, which was completely unspoiled by factories or railroads.

Born in 1850, Hasemann had met Fedor Encke in the early 1870s, when they were both students in Weimar. At that time Hasemann began to specialize in sentimental portraits of peasants. In 1880, while studying in Munich, he first visited Gutach, where he soon established an artists' colony. His genre scenes, landscapes, and idealized character studies of farmers became very popular, even in America, and his work was widely known through reproductions.

Over the next twelve years Alfred would return to Gutach several times with his camera. In 1895 he would write that "the inhabitants have taken something of the sunshine and the odor of the pines into their souls, making them cheerful simple natures, ever willing to assist, entering into the spirit of the artist, and the smallest gratuity prompts the willing spirits to long hours of posing . . . in their quaint caps and mediaeval costumes."[4]

The Stieglitz family spent the first half of the summer of 1882 visiting such lovely German villages as Badenweiler, Schlangenbad, and Mittenwald. They then toured Austria — Innsbruck, the Engadine Valley, and Vienna. Toward the middle of September, Alfred went to Berlin, the Biedermeier charm of which was rapidly being overwhelmed by the grandiose excesses of Second Empire architecture. At first he stayed with Fedor Encke's older brother, Erdmann, a highly successful academic sculptor who was making a second career as a portrait photographer.

In October, Alfred entered the Technische Hochschule, which had five departments: architecture, civil engineering, mechanical engineering (by far the largest department, with more than 250 students enrolled in its main course and an additional forty specializing in shipbuilding), chemistry and metallurgy, and general science. The head of the mechanical engineering department, in which Alfred was to enroll, was Franz Reuleaux (1829–1905), whose specialties were machine design and kinematics, the physics of motion. Reuleaux, an engaging and persuasive man with a flair for public relations, greatly enhanced the prestige of the engineering profession in Germany. A polymath who translated Longfellow's *Hiawatha* into German and wrote several travel books, he was seduced by the German reverence for philosophy and logic; he loved to formulate ambitious theoretical systems, some of the grandest and most influential of which soon proved to have been built on sand. Nevertheless, his writings about the analysis and classification of machinery provided a secure foundation for modern kinematics.

Because of Alfred's talents in mathematical calculation, Edward and Adolph Werner assumed that he would make a good mechanical engineer. But Alfred had never been one of those children with a compelling need to take things apart, see how they work, and then put them back together again with precocious skill. As he entered the Technische Hochschule, he was neither enthusiastic nor optimistic about his course of study.

Alfred's annual allowance of $1,200 or $1,300 enabled him to live very comfortably in Berlin, since his tuition and basic living expenses didn't amount to much more than $600.[5] After a month or so he found pleasant lodgings and moved out of Encke's apartment to live on his own.

Late at night the archromantic Alfred — completely naked — would often sit at his upright piano and play an intense, if hardly note-perfect, rendition of Chopin's *Funeral March*, a Tyrolese song, or one of his other favorites. Above the piano hung a portrait of his mother by Fedor Encke, a birthday present from the artist. Over the portrait was draped a twelve-foot-long American flag that a fellow student, a German, impressed by Alfred's love of America, had sewn by hand for his friend. Against another wall he kept his gleaming Columbia bicycle, whose front wheel measured nearly five feet in diameter.

Alfred spent many hours in his room reading. In 1884 he listed his favorite authors as Shakespeare, Byron, and Edward Bulwer-Lytton, author of extravagant historical novels, among them *The Last Days of Pompeii*. Soon Alfred discovered the Russians. He was especially delighted by Lermontov's *A Hero of Our Time* and came to love Turgenev, Pushkin, Gogol, and finally Tolstoy. For comic relief Alfred adored the works of Mark Twain, which he would read aloud to his friends among the American students in Berlin. Later in the decade he would be profoundly moved by Zola's naturalistic novel *Madeleine Férat*, after which he became engrossed in the Rougon-Macquart series, with its scientific approach to the bitter realities of life. Zola's naturalism would strongly influence Alfred's early work in photography.

Many evenings Alfred would buy standing-room tickets to hear *Carmen* or *Tristan und Isolde* at the Royal Opera, or he might attend the theater to see a play by Shakespeare or Ibsen. Thoroughly content with such simple fare as bread, cheese, and sausages, washed down by *vin ordinaire* (he didn't care for beer), Alfred would often meet friends at the Café Bauer, where he could always find someone with whom to talk or play chess or billiards; he later claimed that he had become the German amateur billiards champion. Still passionate about running, he also enjoyed skating or rowing with his friends on the Wannsee. At the racetrack, to which students were admitted for a reduced fee, he was thrilled by the riot of colors and speed, by the "comedy and tragedy" of the spectacle, and by the relationship between the jockeys and their horses, which symbolized for Alfred man's mastery of nature.

None of these activities, he recalled, either complicated his life or interfered with his work. Nor, he insisted, was he distracted by the pursuit of romance. "I was interested in Woman," he remarked, "but not in women."[6] Nevertheless, in a question album he filled out in 1884, he said that the place where he would most like to live was the mythical Venusberg, of Wagner's opera *Tannhäuser*. As for his sexual fantasies, we know that he was deeply aroused by Peter Paul Rubens's great portrait of his voluptuous wife Hélène Fourment, nude except for a fur wrap, which he saw in the Kunsthistorisches Museum in Vienna in 1882.

All in all, it is no wonder that Alfred asked rhetorically, "What more could life offer anywhere?"[7] He felt completely at home in Berlin, where his life was, he later said, "congenial, free — the freest I have ever experienced."[8] He remembered the Technische Hochschule and the University of Berlin as "havens of perfect freedom."[9] "There were no set times when I had to do anything," he reminisced. "If tired, I slept; if hungry, I ate. When I wanted to read, I read."[10] A few years later a study of German universities would state that the student's life was, "in very truth, the time of greatest and fullest freedom which comes during one's whole life."[11]

During his first term at the Technische Hochschule, Alfred discovered that he could attend lectures at the University of Berlin, on Unter den Linden, across from the opera house. At the Hochschule he was obligated to follow a fixed course of study, for which he paid a fixed tuition. Matters stood quite differently at the university; students were entirely free to choose their courses, and they paid lecture fees directly to each of their professors.

At the leading German universities the teachers of science were the greatest German scientists, while in France and Britain the outstanding scientists were rarely involved in teaching. Thus it was that Alfred had the opportunity to attend a course of lectures given by the physicist and physiologist Hermann von Helmholtz, the most famous German scientist of the nineteenth century. Alas, Helmholtz — who was then preoccupied with the thermodynamics of chemical processes — spoke of questions far over Alfred's head in complex terms and in a voice that could barely be heard. Finally, in utter frustration, Alfred overcame his timidity and went up to Helmholtz after a lecture to ask whether he could perhaps express himself a bit more simply. Very quietly, and with a note of sadness, Helmholtz told him that he was setting forth "the ABC of physics" and couldn't possibly make the course any simpler.[12] Alfred did not return. (He would have done far better to stay in his room and read Helmholtz's book *Popular Lectures*, published in English in 1880.) It must have been galling to him when, toward the end of the decade, his brother Julius achieved considerable distinction in his work at the University of Berlin under Helmholtz, among others.

Alfred wasn't doing much better at the Technische Hochschule than at the university. He found it torture to sit through Professor Reuleaux's lectures on mechanical analysis, and he began to fear that he had no aptitude whatsoever for engineering. In any case, the field held very little interest for him. Although he dreaded appearing a failure in his father's eyes, he thought about leaving school. He felt trapped, lost, and frightened. He had no idea what he wanted to do with his life. It was then that he stumbled upon photography.

PART II

THE PROGRESSIVE PHOTOGRAPHER

CHAPTER ELEVEN

A PERSON WHOSE natural impulse is always to tell the simple truth, as he sincerely understands it, is unlikely to feel any need to announce that he is obsessed with Truth. Stieglitz was indeed obsessed with a search for uppercase Truth, but, in the process, lowercase truth sometimes suffered. When it came to telling the story of his life, he was not one to allow the specifics of mere circumstance to interfere with his vision of how things should have been. By the time he began dictating his reminiscences to various friends, when he was over sixty, they had undergone not only the inevitable unconscious distortions due to the passage of time but also many minor conscious and self-serving revisions. Stieglitz was constantly telling and retelling his stories, changing them and elaborating on them both to gratify himself and to illustrate moral lessons. His anecdotes became parables. Adherence to fact was far less important than making a point. Perhaps he told them in altered forms so many times that he came to believe the new versions as literal truth. It behooves us to approach them with circumspection.

Stieglitz's late-in-life account of how he first became interested in photography relates that quite by chance in January 1883, when he was returning to his room after a boring lecture, he happened to see a camera in a shop window on Berlin's Klosterstrasse and bought it purely on impulse. However, in the spring of 1882, while he was still in school at Karlsruhe, Alfred was already taking photographs. In a letter dated May 17 of that year, his mother suggested that the family found the snapshots he had sent them overly melodramatic and sentimental. We haven't a clue about either the nature or the ownership of the camera with which he made these first, and long-vanished, pictures.

Perhaps it was to the period of these proto-photographs that Stieglitz was referring when he stated in a 1944 interview that photography had fascinated him "first as a toy."[1] Regarding the events that soon followed, he seems to have told two contradictory versions — though the confusion was possibly introduced by the recorders and editors of his reminiscences. In one version, it was only after he had bought his camera on the Klosterstrasse that he began taking a photography course with Dr. Hermann Vogel at the Technische Hochschule.[2] But the earlier, and thus probably more reliable, version suggests that Vogel preceded the camera.[3] This makes more sense, especially since the photograph that Alfred identified as the first he made with his new camera is one that strongly implies he was already studying with Vogel.

Alfred would have gravitated to Vogel for two main reasons: the professor liked Americans, and he was a teacher from the same admirable mold as Adolph Werner. Alfred could not have had a mentor better suited to his needs than was Herr Professor Doktor Hermann Wilhelm Vogel of the Technische Hochschule's department of chemistry and metallurgy. Despite his portentous title, Vogel, who turned fifty in 1884, was not a pompous and punctilious Prussian. He was said to have "an extremely likable personality" and to be "a kindly critic."[4] In a photograph taken about 1872, his expression is one of sympathetic bemusement. Sporting a full beard and disheveled hair that foster a resemblance to Karl Marx, and wearing light-colored striped trousers and a windowpane waistcoat, he looks quite dapper and rather bohemian — not at all like a formal German professor.[5] In a dramatic and expressive portrait shot by Alfred about 1886, the goateed Vogel, turning toward the camera, looks like an operatic bass quite capable of singing Falstaff. Stieglitz would later say of him, "I looked upon that man as a perfect god."[6]

Vogel had close ties to the professional photographic community in the United States. In 1865 editor Edward L. Wilson recruited him to write regularly for *The Philadelphia Photographer*, which had begun publication the preceding year. Through Wilson, Vogel was invited to the third annual convention of the National Photographic Association, in Cleveland, in 1870. As we have already seen, he returned in 1876 as the German commissioner for the photographic section of the Centennial Exposition, and in the summer of 1883 he attended another convention of the NPA, this time in Milwaukee. In his address to that conference, he told his audience that in America photography was "much more esteemed by the scientific men, by the men of industry, and the people in general, than in Europe."[7] Photographic historian Robert Taft records that although Vogel "did not understand or speak English well, he was able to fit into the programs of the Americans with ease" and that at one convention he even provided the piano accompaniment for the opening rendition of "The Star-Spangled Banner."[8]

Because retouching was anathema to Stieglitz, it is ironic that Vogel first achieved celebrity in American photographic circles through his role in introducing the technique of retouching collodion negatives, thereby revolutionizing portrait photography in America. Now an unlimited number of finished prints could be made without having to retouch each one individually.

In 1899 Stieglitz's friend Theodore Dreiser wrote,

> It was in Berlin that Mr. Stieglitz first studied photography. There, in 1885, he was studying mechanical engineering at the Polytechnic School, when Dr. Vogel, of the photo-chemical laboratory, persuaded the young man that a course of theoretical photography would be of great value in his profession. Mr. Stieglitz took up the work and followed it closely, only to become convinced that it was a worthy field in itself, and suitable to his ambition.[9]

The date of Stieglitz's first course with Vogel got successively earlier as he told his story over the years. In his *Who's Who* entry in the 1910s, he stated that he studied "photo-chemistry and photography" at the Berlin Polytechnic from 1884 to 1888. And in 1938 he wrote, "My career in photography might be said to date from 1883 when I took up photography as a course in the Berlin Polytechnic with Professor Vogel."[10] Stieglitz appears to have been embarrassed by having been a late bloomer and consequently exaggerated his precocity. As a result of his inconsistencies, all we can say with certainty is that during the period 1882–85 he was drawn to photography — which, by the end of that time, had become his passion and obsession.

We know something of the arguments that Professor Vogel would have used to induce young Alfred to take his course. In the introduction to his *Handbook of the Practice and Art of Photography* he wrote that the camera "makes for the engineer in a few moments faithful copies of the most complicated machinery, and reproductions of his drawings and plans, which would occupy the time of the most skillful draughtsman for weeks" and that "it supplies him with an authentic foundation for the construction of plans and maps."[11]

One aspect of photography's usefulness that especially interested Vogel was its power to create what André Malraux would later refer to as "the museum without walls" — that is, an endlessly reproducible and reasonably affordable gallery of photographs of works of art. In Vogel's view, the photographer who could make an undistorted copy of a work of art was contributing significantly to the civilizing process. The professor clearly considered photography the servant of art, not its rival.

Alfred, who had probably not yet bought a camera of his own, was evidently given special permission to enroll in Vogel's course after the semester's classes had already begun. This put him at an immediate disadvantage; at first he understood little, and he feared a repetition of the Helmholtz fiasco. But if the lectures on theory were over his head, he caught on quickly in the sessions devoted to practical demonstrations and training.

In his book, and presumably in his course as well, Vogel began with a thorough explanation of the camera and a discussion of the pros, cons, and special uses of lenses of various sorts. Then followed the preparation of chemicals for coating, sensitizing, developing, and fixing the glass plates of the wet-collodion process, which even in the middle 1880s was still widely used by professional photographers.

Only after all that did Vogel move on to "Photographic Operations" — the actual taking of a picture. (For their own practice, the students used wet-plate cameras owned by the school.) Here he began with stern warnings, exhortations, and injunctions concerning the cleanliness of the plates. Alfred, frightened into thinking that if his plates were not perfectly clean they would deteriorate hopelessly in short order, washed, wiped, and polished them obsessively. He later claimed that after he had worked at this task for weeks, without proceeding any further, Vogel finally told him that it would be impossible to get a plate *perfectly* clean unless one lived in "a hermetically sealed room which would have to be chemically clean."[12]

In his course at the Technische Hochschule, Vogel emphasized the photographic reproduction of charts, drawings, paintings, and sculptures. Preoccupied by the scientific challenge of making the most accurate possible record of the work in question, translating its true range of colors into black-and-white, he concentrated primarily on the chemistry of photography. In 1873 he had invented the first successful orthochromatic plates. Until then, the silver bromide emulsion of the wet-collodion process had been overly sensitive to blue (which recorded as white in prints) and had tended to darken green, yellow, orange, and red. Vogel, taking advantage of progress in the booming German dye industry, discovered that adding certain dyes to the emulsion extended its sensitivity to color values, though not until panchromatic film became available in 1906 could a red object be photographed clearly against a black background.

Early in the 1880s Vogel was able to apply his method to dry plates, and the manufacture of orthochromatic dry plates began in 1884. Thereafter, Vogel continued his search for the formula that would allow silver bromide to render the entire visible spectrum in an accurate balance of light and dark. For two years Alfred, who called Vogel "the father of scientific photography,"[13] spent much of his time assisting the professor in testing new batches of chemicals.

Improper lighting of a subject to be copied could obscure as much detail as could the color insensitivity of the photographic plates. And so Vogel worked assiduously with his students to initiate them into the art of controlling and adjusting the fall of light. In those infant days of electricity, that usually meant painstaking adjustments of curtains over large studio windows. One of the first assignments that Vogel gave his class was to photograph a bust of the Apollo Belvedere partially draped with black velvet. The challenge was to make a negative that would simultaneously capture all the modeling of the white cast and all the details in the folds and texture of the black velvet. "Generally speaking," wrote Vogel, "*the lights are too white and the shadows are too black* in photographic representations."[14]

Alfred spent weeks obsessively photographing what he came to call "that damned plaster cast." Finally Vogel told him that he was trying to do the impossible and that the best anyone could hope for was a print that achieved an acceptable compromise between the lights and the darks. Alfred was shocked. "I do not think I had heard the word compromise before in my whole life. I really didn't understand."[15]

Vogel had written that it was nearly impossible to make a photograph of an outdoor sculpture in which the work of art and the trees in the background would be equally sharp. Telling Alfred that something was impossible was like waving a red cape before a bull, and it is thus no surprise that among his early works are preserved several of his successful images of outdoor sculptures, such as an 1886 photograph of Erdmann Encke's memorial to Queen Louise, in Berlin, in which both the intricately carved white marble relief and the background of dark foliage are clear. This is precisely the kind of technical tour de force in which the young Stieglitz delighted. At first his interest in photography was strictly technical, not artistic. In

1901 critic Charles Caffin would write of his friend that he united "the scientific and the artistic temperament" and that "if one is to assign their relative positions, I am inclined to believe that the foundation threads of his purposes are scientific, and that into these he has woven the artistic woof."[16] Confirming this insight, Alfred told Dreiser, "The camera always fascinated me; so did chemistry; I began to make mechanical drawings with it, and gradually switched over to the art side."[17]

It was the challenge of breaking down barriers through intensive striving that held Alfred. Photography was for him at first essentially a sport — a substitute for running. Some of his early photographic exploits are even oddly reminiscent of his athletic endeavors. Once, for instance, he set up his camera on a tripod in the basement of the Technische Hochschule, which was illuminated only by a dim electric lightbulb. Vogel had said that it would be impossible to photograph in such light, but Alfred left the shutter of his camera wide open for more than twenty-four hours and produced a perfect negative of a dynamo. We can only wonder whether he was reminded of the earlier triumph of his basement marathon.

Nor was Alfred able to resist introducing the element of speed into his work in photography. He once conducted a race against time to see how quickly he could take, develop, and print a picture. It took him thirty-four minutes. When his fellow students asked him why he bothered with such an exercise (which he repeated at the photographic exposition in Berlin in 1889), he replied that the question of speed would soon be important for photographers rushing to meet newspaper deadlines.

If Alfred at first favored the technical and the scientific over the artistic, it was partly because his artistic tastes were relatively undeveloped and conventional. Judging from the works of which he chose to make copy photographs, he tended to prefer the sentimental confections of such fashionable academicians and society painters as Franz von Lenbach, Pierre Cot, and Jules Bastien-Lepage. Soon after he arrived in Berlin, Alfred told Erdmann Encke that "Rembrandt was rot." Rather than argue with him, Encke, whom Alfred considered "a very wise person," sent him out to the museums. "Gradually things began to happen to me," Stieglitz remembered. "That's the best you can do for a person — keep putting things in front of him."[18] Nonetheless, he thought that most of the paintings in Berlin's Royal Museum looked like old leather and preferred the collection of Egyptian antiquities. In 1884 he said that his favorite artists were Rubens, Van Dyck, and Michelangelo. He also listed Raphael but then crossed him out. On a visit to Venice later in the decade, he encountered Tintoretto and, perhaps under the influence of Ruskin, decided that he loved his paintings "more than Titian and Giorgione and all the rest put together."[19]

Having mastered the wet-collodion process, Alfred asked a fellow student about dry plates and learned where he could buy a camera for them. It was presumably then that he went to the store on the Klosterstrasse (where some of the Technische Hochschule's buildings were located until the fall of 1884, when the school moved). Stieglitz later said of his simple first camera that "a more beautiful one never has been made."[20] What he bought was probably something like the Rochester Optical Company's "New Model" view camera, which first appeared on the market in 1883. It came in two sizes, the smaller of which used dry plates measuring 5 by 8 inches, the approximate size of Alfred's. The camera had a collapsible bellows, but since it had no shutter, exposures were made by removing the lens cap for something between a few seconds and a minute or more. The list price of $16 included a lens, a tripod, a wooden carrying case, and a plate holder.[21] For a few dollars more one obtained a supply of dry plates, the necessary chemicals and developing trays, a candle lamp with a ruby canvas hood for use in the darkroom, and an instruction booklet.

Alfred's reasons for buying a dry-plate camera were technical rather than aesthetic. The first image he made with it was not a picture of his friends or his surroundings but a copy photograph that showed, pinned kaleidoscopically to a drawing board, a group of carte de visite photographic portraits of Alfred that Erdmann Encke had taken over a period of time. The student simply wanted to apply a new technique to the problems that Vogel had been assigning him.

In four of the Encke portraits in that first image, Alfred is wearing a North African burnoose. The others show him clean shaven or with a mustache or even a full beard and wearing various outfits. (Except for a brief period during the middle 1880s, when Alfred again ran the gamut of experimentation, he would sport a mustache for the rest of his life.) There is an oddly cubistic feel to the result, which is also reminiscent of the Julius Gerson trompe l'oeil watercolor that Alfred had loved. The picture presents an unformed personality searching for a self-image and questioning his identity, as if asking, "Which of these images shows the real Alfred Stieglitz?"

Unwilling to wait until the next day to develop his negatives at school, Alfred improvised a darkroom at home using the tiny triangular space that was formed behind an interior door when he swung it open so that, like a screen, it blocked off a corner. That night he closed the curtains and draped all his blankets over the door to make a ceiling for his "darkroom" and to cover the cracks through which light might enter. The cubbyhole was so cramped that he could fit nothing more than a chair inside; under it he placed a pitcher of water and a slop pail, while on the chair he precariously balanced his ruby lamp and his developing tray, which, when the time came, he awkwardly replaced with another tray containing fixer. Even under these primitive conditions he was able to produce what he considered a perfect negative on his first attempt.

When Alfred took his new camera out-of-doors, it was to make what were essentially copy photographs of advertising kiosks (*Litfaβsäule*) and of the facade of the Technische Hochschule. These were five-finger exercises. Since there were as yet no exposure meters, every photographer had to develop his ability to assess the available light and choose the appropriate length of exposure. To practice, Alfred shot — hundreds of times — the plain plaster wall of the house opposite his own. He photographed at every hour of the day, from dawn to dusk, and in conditions ranging from bright sunlight to heavy overcast. Then he would vary, in turn, the strength of the developing solution, the proportions of the chemicals, the duration of the development bath, and the number of rinses. "I started with the real A.B.C. — at the rudiments — and evolved my own methods and my own ideas virtually from the word go," he recalled, "even to the method of learning the A.B.C."[22] His aim was to develop a reflexive sense of technique, so that he could count on it absolutely as the secure foundation of his art.

Once Alfred had transferred out of the mechanical engineering program and into Vogel's chemistry department, his attitude toward the Technische Hochschule changed completely. Revealing his infatuated bias, he wrote in 1887 of the new building, in the Berlin suburb of Charlottenburg, to which the school had moved: "Thanks to the munificence of the city, which devoted upwards of £1,000,000 to the purpose . . . the building is a grand work of architectural art, unsurpassed by any educational institution on the face of the globe, both in exterior and interior beauty, and practicality." As for the photochemical laboratory — "a model one in every respect, no expense having been saved in its appointment" — there he was in very heaven. Within the complex, which was equipped with electric lighting, there were

> an elaborate studio, five dark rooms (one for the "wet," and three for the "dry" processes, and one for the preparing of gelatine plates); a

"finishing" room for the negative process; a room to store away finished plates; three rooms for the printing; glass shed to print under, in case of storm; . . . all supplied with not only the necessities, but also all the luxuries that an inventive mind could suggest.[23]

The only problem was that the laboratory closed at the end of regular school hours. The administration finally agreed that if Alfred would assume responsibility he could keep the lab open as late as he wanted. There, in the best-equipped darkroom he would ever use, he was free to conduct his experiments far into the night.

Stieglitz never had hobbies, only passions. "The camera was waiting for me by predestination," he wrote, "and I took to it as a musician takes to the piano or a painter to the canvas."[24] He recalled in his old age, "I went to photography really a free soul — and loved it at first sight with a great passion."[25] On another occasion he reminisced, "The other students [in Vogel's course] had no inkling about the driving force within me."[26] In short order, "photography had become a matter of life and death. I worked like one possessed."[27]

Alfred soon decided that, one way or another, he wanted to pursue a career in photography. In the summer of 1885, when Edward announced that he and Hedwig, together with their three daughters and Aunt Rosa, would be returning to America the following spring, Alfred told him that he was in a quandary. On the one hand, he wanted to remain in Berlin to continue his photographic studies at the Technische Hochschule and at the university — though he believed it would be a waste of time to work toward a Ph.D., as his brother Julius and his friends Joe Obermeyer and Lou Schubart were doing. On the other hand, Alfred felt a responsibility to return home with the family and to begin earning a living. Edward, pleased to see his son so enthusiastic about photography — the technical side of which, after all, united engineering and chemistry — assured him that he need not worry about money or feel any pressure to get a job. Indeed, Edward promised both to continue giving him a generous allowance and to leave him a large sum of money in his will. Alfred told photo-historian Nancy Newhall that when he received that news, he "cheered up . . . and began to enjoy himself."[28] His close friend Paul Rosenfeld put it more forcefully: "Since he has set earnestly to work with the camera, he has come to feel for the first time that he has a right to life, and a right to be living there in Berlin."[29]

CHAPTER TWELVE

IN AN ALBUM now in the National Gallery of Art, in Washington, D.C., Alfred wrote beside one print, "Mittenwald, 1886. One of my earliest attempts at picture making." The self-consciously posed photograph shows, standing in a field in an alpine region, a young woman who has stopped raking to look off into the distance, shading her eyes with her right hand. Although Stieglitz later claimed, "I never felt like photographing anything I ever saw painted," the image is closely related to many German canvases of the time.[1]

   That picture, together with another album (also in the National Gallery), gives us a fascinating glimpse of Alfred's progress as he "switched over to the art side" of photography. Stamped in gold letters on the leather cover of the second album are the words "A Souvenir of the Summer of 1886 to the Family. Mittenwald." Alfred sent it to his parents, who had returned to New York in the spring of that year, both to demonstrate his improving skill and to remind them of the family's happy visits during three of the previous summers to Mittenwald, a village in the Bavarian Alps that, as the photographer noted, was "famous for its violin and 'cello builders."[2] The images in the album include landscapes of mountainous terrain, views of a rustic hotel against a dramatic Alpine background, scenes of peasants in fields, and a picture of a sleeping hobo propped up against a cross in the village cemetery. The lack of technical and aesthetic distinction suggests that these were among Alfred's first efforts of this sort. Until then his photographs probably tended to be of the variety that he collected in yet another album, recording the antics of seven of his schoolfriends (most of them Americans) celebrating the Fourth of July, 1886, in the countryside. ("Eight Little Boys from School are we / Happy that our Country's free," wrote one, parodying Gilbert and Sullivan's *Mikado*, first performed the previous year.) Among his friends and traveling companions in this period were his two brothers, as well as Joe Obermeyer, Lou Schubart, and Frank Simon ("Sime") Herrmann, a CCNY classmate who was studying painting in Munich, where Alfred visited him frequently.

Although clearly imitating German painting in his first attempts to make artistic photographs, Alfred was also influenced by work published in special numbers of *The Amateur Photographer*, a British magazine that had begun publication in 1884. Its first issue had referred to "the best pictures taken this year by amateurs — which is almost tantamount to saying the best photographs which have yet been produced." Since then the magazine had taken the lead in propagating the radical assertion that photography was the one art form in which amateurs consistently surpassed the professionals.

Of course, many amateurs did not aspire to such heights. By the summer of 1884 so many visitors to the fashionable American resorts were snapping away at their fellow vacationers (especially pretty ones at the beaches) that the *New York Times* complained of the "camera epidemic," which seemed nearly as pestilential as the cholera epidemic then ravaging Europe.[3] Throughout the 1880s and 1890s the ranks of photographic amateurs, both serious and frivolous, would burgeon as the Eastman Company outdid itself in developing roll film to replace dry plates and as advances in glassmaking and lens design eliminated distortion, improved focus, and reduced exposure times.

"In England amateur photography was flourishing," wrote Stieglitz in a statement published in 1938. "There was virtually no such thing in Germany. I might say that I was the first amateur photographer in Germany."[4] That claim is certainly at variance with his observation, in a letter published in the German magazine *Der Amateur-Photograph* in March 1887, that "Germany is teeming with amateur photographers." The previous month, in his first published article, "A Word or Two about Amateur Photography in Germany" (which appeared in *The Amateur Photographer* in February 1887), Alfred had written that the Technische Hochschule was responsible for the appearance of German amateurs, since prohibitive "expense is attached to the acquiring of a practical knowledge of photography through unaided experiment."[5] Professor Vogel strongly encouraged the spirit of amateurism. "Why is Germany the most musical land of the world?" he asked. "Why do you find music there more appreciated than in any other part of the world? Because we have so many musical amateurs."[6]

In his letter to *Der Amateur-Photograph*, Alfred went on to reveal for the first time what would be one of his principal obsessions for many years to come: the importance of societies within which amateur photographers could "learn from one another and strive together for the goal of artistic and technical perfection."[7] He sanguinely stated in his article in *The Amateur Photographer*, "I hope soon to be able to report the organisation of a [German] society for the promotion of amateur photography, the sure sign of its firm hold and rapid advancement."[8] In fact, the Deutsche Gesellschaft von Freunden der Photographie (German Society of Friends of Photography) would be founded that year under Vogel's leadership.

Proud of the photographs he had made during the summer of 1886, Alfred selected seven to send to *The Amateur Photographer*'s Holiday Work competition that fall. A few months later he learned that he had won an honorable mention. Too, the Stieglitz photographs that Professor Vogel showed to a group of Berlin artists of his acquaintance one evening were probably from that summer's work. The next day Vogel reported that the prints had "created quite a sensation" and that the artists "could not believe that these pictures were photographs." The painters were all so impressed that they asked to meet the photographer, and when this meeting took place, one of them said, "Why, young man, if those photographs of yours had been made by hand they would be art, but not having been made by hand, wonderful as they are, they are not." This remark incensed Alfred and prompted him to question the very nature of art. He found himself drawn to the modern and romantic conclusion that the essence of the work of art is in the artist's vision, without which technical virtuosity is empty show. Academic painters might have superb techniques at their command, but that did not necessarily mean that they were *artists*. Vogel's friends excluded Stieglitz's photographs from the status of art because they had been "made by machine," but the photographer realized that his control of the camera, and his mastery in the darkroom, enabled him to use his medium as a very direct means of recording his vision. The camera became an extension of himself, even part of himself, "the machine and myself being one," as he wrote.[9] It was on account of such dawning realizations that he began his "fight for photography," which, according to a statement he made in 1910, dated from 1886.[10]

Early in August 1887, Alfred — accompanied by Joe Obermeyer and Lou Schubart, both of whom he had interested in photography, and possibly also his brothers and Sime Herrmann — set out from Munich, on foot and carrying thirty pounds of camera, tripod, and plates, for a photographic journey through northern Italy. When they arrived at Bellagio, spectacularly situated on a promontory in the middle of Lake Como, surrounded by mountains, Alfred was enchanted. Mark Twain, in his book *The Innocents Abroad* (1869), had described at length the pleasures and beauties of Bellagio, which he called "a paradise of tranquil repose." Of the prospect across the lake to the mountainous shore Twain enthused, "Beyond all question, this is the most voluptuous scene we have yet looked upon."[11]

Alfred was undoubtedly well primed to fall in love with Lake Como, even more beautiful than the similarly set Lake George. His friends were determined to push on, but he decided to remain in Bellagio for a few days and catch up with them later. He installed himself in the Pensione du Lac, on the waterfront, and set out to explore this magical old town, in which long stairways served as pedestrian streets.[12] Early one morning, on the Salita Mella, just around the corner from the entrance to his pensione, he came upon a sixteen-year-old fruit seller named Maria and her mother.[13] Moved by Maria's simple beauty, Alfred bought five pounds of grapes from her and began to take photographs. Struggling with his poor Italian, extrapolating from French, and relying much on gestures and empathy, he struck up a friendship with the girl, her brother Leone, and their mother.

At an alfresco fountain and laundry place in front of his pensione, Alfred took his best-known photograph from this period, *A Good Joke*.[14] It is obvious that an instant before he exposed his plate, someone had made a funny remark — quite possibly at Alfred's expense. In the picture a young boy in a sailor suit is squealing with delight and hilarity as he turns toward the photographer, either to invite him to join in the laughter or to laugh at him directly. The image — a piece of rather sentimental genre rescued by spontaneity and genuine high spirits — has a certain modest charm, though it is by no means a masterpiece.

Perhaps the strongest of Stieglitz's Bellagio photographs is his forthright and sympathetic portrait of a mason, an aging man with a kindly, deeply lined face adorned with a white walrus mustache and chin whiskers.

The picture is extraordinary because it makes obvious, without any sentimentality, that this man — whose hat, clothes, and hands were heavily spattered with mortar — is a genuinely noble person.

During this period Alfred's portraits were his strongest photographs, though his landscapes tended to be technical tours de force. One of the latter, entitled *The Approaching Storm*, he shot from the veranda of his pensione, looking toward the Punta Balbianello, a small peninsular promontory on which a famous villa was situated. Having hoped for some time "to capture by photography a gathering storm — a sight at once overpowering and of great potential beauty," he was able to take full advantage of his opportunity in Bellagio because he was well supplied with Vogel-Obernetter orthochromatic plates. Using them with a yellow filter, through which it was difficult to see for focusing, he managed to capture the magnificent play of light and clouds over the lake.

Alfred's perceptions of life in Bellagio were highly romanticized, as he was forced to acknowledge when his friendship with Maria and her family suddenly became complicated. Until reality intruded, he had been interested in them because he assumed they were stoically content with their lives. Eventually, Maria's mother, who saw a savior in Alfred, told him that she had a relative living in America; she hoped that he could take Maria to him. At that point Alfred beat a hasty retreat, insisting that he couldn't keep his friends waiting any longer.

In the issue of *The Amateur Photographer* dated August 26, 1887, Alfred saw, on the first page, an announcement headed "HOLIDAY WORK," in which the editor invited "*bona fide* amateurs" to submit, by September 30, photographs made during the summer. Three prizes would be awarded, and the winners' work would be reproduced in a special issue of the magazine. Alfred mailed off to London twelve prints of his best images from his Italian journey, including one of *A Good Joke*.

The magazine's November 25 issue listed "Mr. Alfred Stieglitz, 54 Kronenstrasse, Berlin" as the winner of the first prize, two guineas and a silver medal.[15] The distinguished British photographer Peter Henry Emerson had judged the submissions "from an art point of view," though he had "not lost sight of the merit due through careful photographic manipulation." None of the winning photographs was reproduced (the magazine never included photographs in its regular issues), but the editors would publish an illustrated supplement in January.

Some months later, Emerson remarked in a letter to Alfred that his had been "the only *spontaneous* work in the whole collection," then qualified his praise by saying, "I was delighted with most of it."[16] Stieglitz would later insist that the prize had not meant much to him and that at the time he had told his friends, with saintly modesty, "I'm very glad for my father; it's a tangible proof for him that I am not wasting my time — but for myself, I can only think how bad my competitors must be." Just how much the prize really meant to him may be reflected in his later exaggeration of the size of the award to a gold medal and $300.[17]

CHAPTER THIRTEEN

DURING THE LATE 1880s, the British photographic community was deeply divided by a fundamental conflict concerning the very nature of photography and its potential as an art form. The chief protagonists of this struggle were Peter Henry Emerson and Henry Peach Robinson.

Robinson — a cheerful, optimistic, self-made man with a profitable business as a portraitist in the fashionable spas of Leamington and Tunbridge Wells — specialized in ambitious images that blatantly imitated the work of the Pre-Raphaelites and French academic painters, in which every detail throughout the entire picture was in equally sharp focus. Since it was impossible to achieve the desired effect with a single camera exposure, Robinson practiced "combination printing," which meant that he assembled his pictures as if they were jigsaw puzzles, using separate negatives for the background and for each figure or group of figures.

He began by conceptualizing his picture, next drew a sketch, and only then set about realizing the image photographically. In effect, Robinson was as much a director as a photographer, since he posed his figures as if they were actors and actresses, sometimes working in an indoor studio complete with painted backdrops. Although he made some images of genuine charm, his pictures — with such titles as *The Lady of Shalott, Bringing Home the May, When the Day's Work Is Done,* and *Wayside Gossip* — tend to be mawkish.

Emerson, the advocate of naturalism in photography, detested the artificiality of Robinson's work. Pedro Enrique Emerson was born in 1856 on the seven-square-mile Cuban sugar plantation owned by his American father, a fourth cousin of Ralph Waldo Emerson's. In 1869, two years after his father's death, Pedro Enrique's British mother took him and his brothers to live in England, where he anglicized his name to Peter Henry.

Emerson was a natural athlete, a brilliant scholar, and one of the greatest photographers of the nineteenth century. Possessing an insatiable appetite for scientific knowledge, as well as an independent fortune, he had studied physics, chemistry, and botany at Cambridge and gone on to earn several medical degrees. Since his love of nature and adventure led him to plan a career as an explorer, he eschewed Harley Street and dreamt of the Himalayas.

It was nature that had drawn Emerson to photography, and in a sense he always remained a naturalist first and a photographer second. An amateur ornithologist, he had, in 1882, bought his first camera to make stop-action photographs of birds. He was so captivated by the "truth and beauty" of what he saw on the ground glass that all his photographic efforts were directed toward capturing, as faithfully as possible, that natural image — which, as he admitted, he always greatly preferred to his finished photographs.

Although Emerson condemned Robinson for his slavish imitation of paintings, Emerson himself was not, for all his professed naturalism and spontaneity, immune to such criticism. The difference was that while Robinson emulated sentimental genre paintings, Emerson was influenced by the work of such artists as John Constable and Jean-François Millet. Ironically, in his insistence upon the high status of photography, Emerson had the unintentional effect of encouraging amateurs to become self-consciously "artistic." Like the Robinsonians, they carefully distanced themselves as much as possible from what we now tend to view as the strongest — and most modern — tendency in nineteenth-century photography: the absolutely straightforward, sharp-focused documentary style that the Emersonian "pictorialists" dismissed as scientific and, Heaven forbid!, professional.

This last distinction points to an important and unfortunate aspect of the Emerson-Robinson conflict — namely, that it was as much a class war as it was an artistic one. The wealthy Emerson represented the tradition of the aristocratic amateur of means and leisure — the gentleman who would never deign to engage in trade — while the professional Robinson was very much a man of the bourgeoisie. The antagonism that their rivalry ex-

acerbated had been an undercurrent ever since photography had been invented more or less simultaneously by the wealthy amateur Fox Talbot and
the bourgeois professional Daguerre, but from the late 1880s onward
snobbery became a powerful, if unacknowledged, force within the photographic world. Stieglitz naturally embraced the cause of amateurism and,
although he professed idealism and disinterestedness, did much to perpet-
uate the class war.

Emerson felt that matte platinum (platinotype) printing* and photogravure (both of which were greatly refined during the early 1880s) were
the only two processes suitable for making positives. On this point, especially, Emerson's influence was so great that within a few years no self-
respecting amateur would dream of using semiglossy albumen or glossy
gelatin-silver papers, which were stigmatized as the materials of professionals and mere hobbyists.

Although Alfred still favored silver chloride gelatin aristotype paper as
late as October 1889, he did so because he had developed a method of toning it with platinum, so that even such an expert as Dr. Vogel would mistake the results for platinum prints.[1] Early in 1892 Alfred would write that
prints made by the platinotype process, "that prince of all processes," were
"indispensable" for exhibition and that every serious amateur "will have to
discard all albumen-paper, glazed aristotype (that *bête noire* for every fine-
feeling eye), etc."[2] He would become a master of making luminous and
subtle platinum prints, which he toned with various chemicals to yield anything from a cool blue to a warm brown, depending on the emotional tem-
perature of the image. Praising its "range of yielding the strongest blacks
with pure lights and a long scale of intermediate half-tones of grays," he
concluded that "the platinum print has an indescribable charm, suggesting
atmosphere, though the negative printed on another medium may be entirely devoid of this valuable pictorial quality."[3]

Once he began to use platinum paper, Alfred — who until then had
been more concerned with his negatives than with his prints — developed
an enhanced respect for the photographic print as a work of art. In an 1887
letter to *The Amateur Photographer* he stated the still rather radical argument that "an amateur who has the printing done by a professional ought
not to be eligible to [enter] prize competitions for *amateur* work, as there

---

*Photosensitive platinum salts — somewhat more expensive than silver salts, which
yielded harsher contrast — impregnated the paper instead of being held in an
emulsion on its surface.

is no question that it is as difficult to turn out a good positive as a good negative."[4] In 1903 he would write, "The fact that it is impossible to produce two totally identical prints is generally, albeit gradually, being recognized. . . . Each individual print may have its own merits, but there will always be one print that more than any other from the same negative reflects the purpose and conception of the artist."[5]

Emerson staunchly believed that if a photographer of intelligence, sensitivity, and character made very direct, spontaneous, and intuitive photographs of nature and of people living and working in nature, the result would be art. He argued that "any Art is a fine Art which can, by pictures, express these beauties of Nature." He conceded that until photography could reproduce the colors of nature, it could not challenge the supremacy of painting, "but all other branches of Pictorial Art we are able to surpass."[6]

Wanting to make photographs that would be true to the way the human eye actually saw, Emerson believed that "the principal object in the picture must be fairly sharp, *just as sharp as the eye sees it and no sharper*, but everything else, and all other planes of the picture, must be subdued . . . slightly out of focus."[7] He called his guiding principle "differential focusing" and sought to achieve it photographically by means of a special lens. Some photographers came to believe, however, that Emerson favored pictures that were simply out of focus, leading critics to speak disparagingly of "fuzzygraphs."

Because of his fascination with technical challenges, Alfred's natural impulse was to strive to achieve Robinsonian sharp focus with a single exposure. In any case, many of his early pictures (such as *A Good Joke*) are more Robinsonian than Emersonian in appearance, though he apparently never set up scenes. He claimed, for instance, that his photograph entitled *The Card Players* (1887), in which three young men dressed as Renaissance guardsmen gamble in front of a tapestry, was an impromptu shot made at a costume party. Nor was the affinity between Stieglitz and Robinson merely superficial. The young Stieglitz was quite a sentimentalist. We must wonder how much his later austerity of photographic style and personal manner arose in overcompensation — or even a sort of penance — for his youthful excesses.

Despite his close alliance with Emerson for a few years, Alfred never attacked Robinson in print. Emerson, by contrast, was an arrogant and self-important man who had no patience with the politics of the photographic world and gave free rein to his most offensive opinions. He enjoyed lambasting the famous and would not hesitate to say that the work of some universally respected photographer or clique was "vapid, bigger and more inane than ever." Since he believed that his scientific approach provided him with definitive answers to all questions regarding art and photography, he felt that anyone who had the temerity to challenge him must be an "ignorant fool," insane, or given to telling "envenomed and malicious" lies. Unfortunately, as Stieglitz aged he would increasingly take after Emerson.

Miraculously, Emerson's photographs transcend all his bluster. His pictures of the people and the landscapes of East Anglia's wetlands are sensitive and highly sympathetic, gentle, intelligent, and ethnographically informative. Like Eugène Atget's photographs of Paris, they occupy that most potent of artistic territories — where all distinctions break down between the documentary and the poetic, between the specific and the universal, between science and art.

On June 20, 1888, Emerson wrote to Alfred (whose name he always misspelled "Steiglitz"), "Although we are unknown to each other in the flesh we are I trust friends in the spirit." He went on to say that he had nearly finished writing a book to be entitled *Naturalistic Photography for Students of the Art* and hoped that it would be published in England before Christmas. He asked the younger man whether he would "care to undertake the translation of it into German, a task for which you are undoubtedly highly qualified?"[8] Alfred replied that he was interested. Revisions, however, delayed publication of the British edition until the following March, at which time Emerson renewed his offer. Alfred still endorsed the plan and evidently even began his translation, but by September 1889 he had become discouraged at the prospect of finding a publisher, since the Germans were alarmed by all the controversy over the book in the British press. "It is very noble and magnanimous of you to go on with translation in spite of such opposition and I do hope you will get a publisher," wrote Emerson.[9]

The beleaguered Emerson clearly felt that in Stieglitz he had found an ally. To cement the bond, he emphasized that they were compatriots, asking in a postscript, "Aren't you an American?" and when Alfred replied in the affirmative, the thoroughly anglicized Emerson responded rather disingenuously, "Shake — I am an American too."[10] Emerson's principal connection with the nation in which he had lived only five years was that he was the British correspondent of *The American Amateur Photographer*, which had begun publication in July 1889. (Photographs by Stieglitz had appeared in the first issue.) Now Emerson asked his young friend whether he would "write me a short resume of the Berlin Jubilee Exhibition to forward in my letter? I will of course attach your name to it."[11] Emerson suggested that Alfred offer to become the Berlin correspondent for the magazine. The German translation project quietly fell by the wayside.

The appearance of Emerson's book began what amounted to a civil war. Stieglitz later commented that to say that its publication had "created a whirlpool of comment is putting it mildly. In truth, the book was the talk of the photographic world for months and was the cause of many bitter controversies. Dr. Emerson had struck a blow which shattered idols without mercy; the lucid and forcible style could not be mistaken."[12]

In one of the first skirmishes, Robinson's supporters were able to arrange for the ouster of *The Amateur Photographer*'s pro-Emerson editor, thereby ensuring that the magazine would publish Robinson's hostile review of *Naturalistic Photography*. The unsigned review concluded, "While giving Dr. Emerson all credit for sincerity, we cannot help feeling that his system is pernicious, and tending to lead the amateur into slovenly ways, and into a habit of excusing bad photography by calling it good art."[13]

Reviewing the 1889 exhibition of the Photographic Society of Great Britain, Emerson proclaimed rather smugly that "nearly all the best workers have discarded silver printing, sharp focusing, artificial compositions, made-up interiors, combination printing." From that observation he deduced "the *complete triumph of naturalism*."[14] His satisfaction was short-lived, for the following year he had a crisis of faith that devastated the very foundations of his belief in photography as an art. For one thing, he was disgusted by the way an English photographer named George Davison had appropriated and distorted his theories of naturalistic photography and differential focusing to justify a style that imitated the allover blur of Impressionist paintings. (Davison used a pinhole camera, with no lens, to get that effect.) Then, after conversations with "a great artist" — probably Whistler, who admired his photographs — Emerson began to change his mind about the relationship between nature and art.

An exhibition of prints by Hokusai, whose quick, abbreviated sketches captured the spirit of a scene better than a detailed picture possibly could, further convinced Emerson that photography was not an art. Still more fuel was added to the fire by William James's book *The Principles of Psychology*, which created a sensation when it was published, in 1890. Emerson became convinced that the literalness of photography was not true to the way human beings perceived things, since so much was adjusted and interpreted by the mind. A painter could make the necessary adjustments, but a photographer could not.

The last straw was provided by the findings of two chemists working together in England, Vero Charles Driffield and Swiss-born Ferdinand Hurter. Their shared hobby of photography, and their dissatisfaction with the hit-or-miss unpredictability of results, led them to years of painstaking experiments to establish precise relationships among such variables as the chemical composition of the photographic emulsion, the intensity of light reflected by the subject, and the proper length of exposure. The findings of Hurter and Driffield (H & D, as they became universally known), published in a British scientific journal in May 1890, forced Emerson to conclude that photography was a science, not an art. His intellectual vision was like his photographs: only the central subject was in sharp focus, everything beyond it somewhat blurred.

Emerson lived up to the advice of his illustrious relative, who had written in the first edition of his *Essays*, "If you would be a man, speak what you think today in words as hard as cannon-balls, and tomorrow speak what tomorrow thinks in hard words again, though it contradict everything you said today." In January 1891 he sent to the editors of all the major British and American photographic magazines a letter asking them to publish a statement in which he apologized both to his former adversaries and to all whom he had misled with his claim that photography was an art. Soon thereafter he published a small black-bordered pamphlet on whose cover he printed the epitaph of naturalistic photography, "which ran a short but active life, upset many conventions, helped to further monochrome photography to the utmost of its limited art boundaries, stirred men to think and act for themselves, produced many prigs and bubble reputations, exposed the ignorance of the multitude, [and] brought out the low morality of certain persons in the photographic world." In the pamphlet, which was entitled *The Death of Naturalistic Photography*, he stated, "The limitations of photography are so great that, though the results may, and sometimes do give a certain esthetic pleasure, the medium must rank the lowest of all arts, *lower than* any graphic art, for the individuality of the artist is cramped." Many years later Stieglitz recalled that he had been "furious" when Emerson published *The Death of Naturalistic Photography*, which he condemned as "a betrayal, for ignorance, of his pure aesthetic."[15]

It was difficult to remain friends with this bitter and obnoxious man, a crank whose fulminations bordered on insanity. Paradoxically, Emerson made some of his finest images after his apostasy. The sixteen magnificent photogravures in his book *Marsh Leaves*, published in 1895, certainly bear out his contention that photographs "are sometimes more beautiful than art . . . just as Nature is often more beautiful than art."[16]

In the end, despite his retraction, Emerson had transformed photography. He had created a superb body of work unlike anything anyone had done before. He had expressed ideas too powerful and too appealing to suppress. And even if he disavowed his many disciples, among whom we must number Alfred Stieglitz, he had started a movement with irreversible momentum. Photographic historian Nancy Newhall rightly asked, "Who else, before, had proclaimed that photography was an independent and potentially great art form capable of expressing thoughts and emotions beyond the scope of the other and older art forms?"[17]

In 1893, Stieglitz inquired of the readers of *The American Amateur Photographer*, "How many appreciate the enormous benefit that P.H. Emerson has bestowed upon photographic art? Call him by whatever name you may, criticise him from any point of view, and still the fact remains: his teachings formed the basis of what we saw in this exhibition."[18] And in his review of a revised and enlarged American edition of *Naturalistic Photography*, published in 1899, he wrote that the book, which he called "part of the education of the pictorial photographer," had gradually come to exert "such an influence that now it is regarded as a 'classic' in photographic literature. To it pictorial photography owes the stability which it now enjoys."[19] More forcefully, in 1899 Alfred described Emerson as the person to whom pictorial photography "owes more than to any other man."[20]

CHAPTER FOURTEEN

DURING THE LATE 1880s, Stieglitz devoted far more of his time to
chemistry — photographic and otherwise — than to photography. The focus of his work continued to be Vogel's experiments to develop a dye that
would extend the color sensitivity of his orthochromatic plates. In pursuit
of that goal, Alfred studied and worked extensively with Dr. Karl Liebermann, Vogel's colleague on the chemistry and metallurgy faculty of the
Technische Hochschule, who was engaged in research on aniline dyes,
made from derivatives of coal tar.

By 1887 or 1888, when Alfred was ready for more advanced work than
the Technische Hochschule could offer, he began to attend the lectures
given at the University of Berlin by the great organic chemist August Wilhelm von Hofmann (who added the noble "von" to his name when he was
made a baron on his seventieth birthday, in 1888). Hofmann, who had
taught in England for twenty years before returning to Berlin in 1865, was
a genial man given to flights of grandiloquence. A practical chemist rather
than a theoretician, he had developed several commercially important dyes
during the 1860s, but many of his working concepts were out of date by the
1880s.

In the latter part of that decade, Alfred was not only working on aniline
dyes but also constantly experimenting with photographic processes. In
numerous brief letters to *The Amateur Photographer* and in dozens of articles

published in Vogel's *Photographische Mittheilungen* (Berlin), *Der Amateur-Photograph* (Düsseldorf), and *Die Photographische Rundschau* (Halle), he expounded on such highly technical subjects as new developments in platinum printing, how to tone aristotype prints with platinum, how to save an overexposed plate by bathing it in potassium bromide before immersing it in a weak developing solution, how to increase the photosensitivity of gelatin negatives with mercuric chloride and ammonia, and how to tone gelatin chloride printing-out paper with solutions of potassium oxalate, potassium phosphate, and sodium chloroplatinate. During this period one might have predicted that Alfred would become a scientist with a dilettante's passion for artistic photography.

Early in 1888 he received the happy news that in August his sister Flora would marry Alfred Stern, manager of the Los Angeles office of Charles Stern, California Wines and Brandies, proprietor of a "Model Winery and Distillery." The firm's business was booming at that time, for devastation by the phylloxera aphid reduced French vintages by nearly 50 percent during the 1880s, and California wines rushed in to make up the domestic and foreign deficit.

Before going to New York in July for the wedding, Alfred spent more than two weeks in Venice with Lou Schubart. "Tired of landscape and architecture" and "hunting around for genre pictures and studies from life," they were advised by an English artist whom they met in the city to explore Chioggia, a fishing village on the Venetian lagoon. They went with Sime Herrmann, who had surprised them by turning up at their hotel. In Chioggia, which was "inhabited only by fishermen and their families — a picturesque but rough and unsociable set of people," they took pictures of such scenes as "a little fellow sitting outside a shoemaker's shop, mending a shoe quite as big as himself."[1] At that rate, it is a wonder that Alfred's photographs garnered even the third prize in *The Amateur Photographer*'s annual holiday-tour competition. Perhaps he won it for his fine picture of a woman on the harborside Ponte Vigo or for his study of fishing boats moored beside the Ponte della Cuccagna, an image whose proto-cubistic composition strikingly anticipates that of one of his most famous photographs, *The Steerage*, which he would shoot nineteen years later.

Late in July 1888 the three Stieglitz brothers returned to the United States for their first visit since 1881. Seeing the new Statue of Liberty as they steamed into New York harbor, Alfred must have mused that a permanent return to New York would mean, for him, the loss of the liberty that he enjoyed in Europe.

The brothers immediately joined the family at Oaklawn, the grandly gabled, turreted, and verandahed Queen Anne mansion on Lake George that Edward Stieglitz had bought in the fall of 1886. The house, named for an ancient oak on the five-acre property, about a mile northeast of the village of Lake George, had been built very recently, but evidently the revelation of an illicit romantic liaison had forced the owner to sell. Edward — having just returned to New York with his wife, his daughters, and Aunt Rosa — rented the capacious and beautifully situated house for the summer of 1886; at the end of the season he exercised his option to buy.[2] The principal drawback was that the hypersensitive Edward was nauseated by the aromas that occasionally wafted down from the pigsty of the farm on the hill across the road. In 1891 he would finally succeed in buying the sixty-three-acre farm. At first he used its house, which had a splendid view of the lake, as his hermitage and painting studio. But soon, since Oaklawn could not accommodate all of the relatives and friends who came to visit for weeks at a stretch, the Spartan farmhouse was commandeered to serve as an annex for children and hardy guests.

Among the visitors to Oaklawn in the summer of 1888 were John Foord and his family. Edward and Hedwig had ulterior motives for the invitation, since they felt that Alfred should soon be finding himself both a wife and a job. Hedwig, who was hoping that romance might blossom between her son and the pertly attractive Maggie Foord, was encouraged as Alfred played love songs for Maggie on the piano and the two wandered the picturesquely landscaped grounds of Oaklawn hand in hand. Nothing came of it all, but Hedwig — perhaps under the influence of her romantic novels — continued to hope.

In the matter of a job, Edward first suggested that Alfred sell his photographs to publishers and collectors. Alfred exclaimed that he could never bring himself to sell his beautiful prints. Then Edward proposed a gallery to sell photographs by others. Again the idea was dismissed as out of the question. That seemed to leave no possibility except the printing of fine reproductions of photographs. Alfred was not at all enthusiastic about going into that or any other business, but he said he would at least *consider* photoengraving — though preferably not until he had completed several more years of study in Germany. Edward hoped that John Foord, then managing editor of *Harper's Weekly*, might have some useful contacts in the printing industry.

On the editorial page of the *New York Daily Graphic* for March 4, 1880, had appeared a picture of a West Side shantytown, the first halftone illustration ever printed simultaneously with the text of a newspaper. Then the race was on to improve the quality and reduce the cost of black-and-white halftones, as well as to develop a method of printing halftones in color. It was into this arena that Alfred's father wanted him to enter.

Having spent much of September in New York exasperatedly submitting to job interviews with the owners of several photoengraving firms, Alfred, accompanied by his brothers, returned to Germany early in October.

Alfred apparently remained in Berlin during the entire summer of 1889, for he was extremely busy with his work and with preparations for the great exhibition that was being sponsored by the Deutsche Gesellschaft von Freunden der Photographie to celebrate the fifty-year jubilee of the announcement of photography's invention. When the exhibition opened in August, Alfred deemed it "a perfect success in every way."[3] Among its four sections was one devoted to artistic photographs — portraits, landscape, genre, and so forth — by amateurs from all over Europe and America, judged by a jury headed by Erdmann Encke and consisting mostly of painters. The other sections were for scientific photography, photomechanical reproduction, and apparatus and chemicals, in the last of which Alfred himself was a judge. His own photographs won a silver medal, and he was awarded the prize for technical excellence offered by the Steinheil camera and lens manufacturing company. Among the many other amateurs exhibiting photographs was Joe Obermeyer, of whom Alfred commented that he showed several expressive genre studies from Italy and a very beautiful portrait of a young Italian woman with a guitar. Obermeyer's two published photographs of Italian women are both warm, natural, and sincere.[4]

Another reason for Alfred's remaining in Berlin that summer may have been his involvement with a young woman — an apparently charming prostitute named Paula — who became his Eliza Doolittle. Alfred was so taken with her that he invited her to live with him in his apartment at 44 Kaiser Wilhelmstrasse. She became the first woman to whom he made love with his camera, though no nudes of her survive. Indeed, we have only one of Alfred's photographs from this time, entitled *Sun Rays — Paula* (1889), but in it appear two other photographs of his lover.

The existing picture is essentially an example of Robinsonian sentimental genre, a set piece, a *tableau vivant* strongly reminiscent of Vermeer, in whom popular interest was increasing during the 1880s, after two centuries of neglect. Paula models in her Sunday best — a voluminous, multilayered dark dress trimmed with lace at the collar and cuffs. She wears a large, dark, extravagantly feathered hat, and her hair is done up in a bun at the back. Seated with her back partly to the camera, she is writing at a table placed beside a window; sunlight is streaming into the room through the slats of a venetian blind. On the wall are pinned up six of Alfred's photographic prints, a studio portrait of him, and three valentine hearts. A seventh print has been inserted into a frame placed on the table. Three of the prints, one of them reversed, were made from the same negative of Paula in a white dress and white hat. Another, a close-up of Paula's head as she lies in bed, is a kind of trophy or boast, for it clearly implies that the photographer was intimate with the subject.

Alfred's photographs of Paula in white idealize her into a perfectly respectable, and even virginal, lady of the bourgeoisie. Decades later, Stieglitz told Nancy Newhall that he had felt that Paula was "as clean as his mother." In practically the next breath he added that he had never seen "how or why any woman could love him."[5] Still plagued with guilt, Alfred probably felt comfortable only with a prostitute.

This would all still have been somewhat shocking in 1889, though that was the year in which the French government bought Edouard Manet's *Olympia* for the Louvre. Stieglitz always loved to *épater les bourgeois*, and his photograph is one of his first mature attempts to do so. Indeed, in addition to being an homage to Zola's naturalism, the photograph is a declaration of Alfred's independence and a testimony to his coming-of-age. Although he later claimed that he had had his sexual initiation when he was "nearly twenty," it seems quite likely that his first experience was with Paula, when he was twenty-five.

Alfred's photograph hints that there was already trouble in paradise. Most heart-wrenchingly, the pattern of stripes cast on the wall by the light entering through the blind suggests that Paula, as a prostitute, is a caged songbird. To emphasize that point, an actual birdcage hovers at the right side of the photograph. Furthermore, it is surely not without significance that the two landscape photographs on the wall are both prints of Alfred's Bellagio image *The Approaching Storm*. It was probably intended to allude to the storm that would be brought on by his impending return to America. After their parting, in 1890, Alfred would send Paula $150 out of his allowance every year "so that he could feel she was not on the streets."[6] Sometimes he implied, or even stated, that he had had a son by her and that the money was to support this child. Eventually Alfred heard that another admirer had established Paula as the hostess or proprietress of a café.

It is rather disturbing to realize that, for all the layers of personal meaning in his photograph, Alfred may well have been more concerned with its technical than with its artistic aspects. To capture equal detail in sun and shadow was the kind of tour de force in which he still delighted, and in those terms the picture was an astonishing triumph over the usual limitations of emulsions and processing.

In December 1889 Hedwig Stieglitz went out to Los Angeles to be with her daughter Flora, who was in the final weeks of her pregnancy. The baby was due early in January, but it was not until about February 10, five weeks late, that Flora at last went into labor. On February 14, 1890, after four agonizing days and nights, she was delivered of a stillborn child. Three days later the exhausted mother died of blood poisoning. Alfred was heartbroken by the news, for he had been far closer emotionally to Flora than to any of his other siblings.

To drown his grief, Alfred threw himself into his work. He went to Vienna that spring to undertake "a severe and long term of experimental laboratory work" at the recently founded state printing and photography school, the Graphische Lehr- und Versuchsanstalt, headed by Josef Maria Eder.[7] While in Vienna, Alfred became a member of the Wiener Club der Amateur-Photographen, which was then very busy with preparations for the photographic salon it would hold the following year.

During August, having nearly once again worked himself into a state of prostration, with his experiments in Vienna, Alfred took "a few days of vacation in order to take a run down to that picturesque, and at the same time grandly-situated village, Cortina, the headquarters of mountain tourists in the Ampezzo Valley." On the way back to Vienna he stopped off for a few hours in the Tyrolean town of Sterzing, famous for its narrow, precipitous, and winding streets lined with houses that he described as the "queerest bits of architecture my eye ever struck."[8] Having won £25 in *The Amateur Photographer*'s competition for a "Traveling Studentship," Alfred then spent a couple of weeks on the Ile de Ré and in Arcachon, Biarritz, and St. Jean-de-Luz, all on the west coast of France, to photograph "Cathedrals, Castles, Ruins, . . . beaches, promenades."[9]

Although he would have liked to remain in Europe indefinitely, the forces pulling him back to New York now grew irresistible. His mother, still devastated by grief, wanted all her children close to her. Julius, who had received his Ph.D. from the University of Berlin in December 1889, was already home. Only Lee would remain in Germany, since he was in his last year of medical training at Heidelberg. (He would graduate summa cum laude in May 1891.) Joe Obermeyer and Lou Schubart had both been awarded their doctorates in chemistry by the University of Berlin and were ready to return to New York. Finally, new tariff regulations were cutting into Hahlo and Stieglitz's profits, leading Edward to inform Alfred that he would not be able to continue to give him so generous an allowance. Toward the end of September 1890 a sad and apprehensive Alfred said goodbye to Berlin and sailed home.

CHAPTER FIFTEEN

ALFRED, AN INDEPENDENT twenty-six-year-old who had been thriving for the previous nine years in an exhilarating atmosphere of culture and science, suddenly found himself ignominiously living in his parents' house, in a vulgar and provincial city. He felt completely alienated. He was anguished by the barrenness and filth of New York, disgusted by its rampant materialism, and depressed by its seeming lack of any real spiritual values. He later claimed that he had been so lonely after his return that he cried himself to sleep every night.

The city to which Alfred had returned was certainly very different from that which he had left in 1881. By 1890 much of Manhattan was lighted by electricity, indoors and out, making possible more nightlife. Perhaps the city's most impressive bid for sophistication was Stanford White's new Madison Square Garden, nearing completion at Madison Avenue and Twenty-sixth Street, with its vast arena, a concert hall, a restaurant, an elegant roof garden, and, topped by Augustus Saint-Gaudens's nude *Diana*, its soaring tower modeled after Seville's Giralda. The only taller structure in New York was Trinity Church's steeple, which was finally surpassed by the Manhattan Life Insurance Building in 1893.

A hotel–apartment house, the most enormous and luxurious in the city, was under construction on the site of the present Plaza Hotel, at Grand Army Plaza, just a block from the Stieglitz residence. Increased appreciation of Central Park and the cachet of the Metropolitan Museum were acting as powerful forces to overcome the initial reluctance of the wealthy to live uptown. Fifth Avenue from Fifty-ninth to Eighty-sixth Streets, and even beyond, was well on its way to becoming Millionaires' Row. By the end of the decade that stretch would be one of the most garishly ostentatious boulevards on earth, with an appalling jumble of mansions parading as Loire Valley châteaux, Venetian palazzi, and classical Parisian *hôtels particuliers*, with pastiches and travesties of practically every other style in the history of architecture thrown in. In 1893 the extravagant Renaissance palazzo designed by McKim, Mead and White for the Metropolitan Club would open on the northeast corner of Fifth Avenue and Sixtieth Street, across from the Stieglitz house. In 1890, however, the Fifth Avenue side of the Stieglitzes' block still represented the opposite extreme, with a row of flimsy, single-story wooden buildings that housed a saloon, a stable office, and a dairy kitchen.

The picture galleries of the rich were filled with John Singer Sargent portraits, Barbizon landscapes, and nudes and genre scenes by the favored French salon painters — Bastien-Lepage, Cot, Ernest Meissonier, Alexandre Cabanel, and William-Adolphe Bouguereau. Many of the canvases were purchased at the gallery of M. Knoedler and Company (a branch of Goupil et Compagnie, in whose galleries in Paris, London, and The Hague Vincent van Gogh had worked between 1869 and 1876) or at Durand-Ruel's, the New York outpost of the Parisian firm that championed the Impressionists.

Among the most sophisticated of New York's millionaires were the Henry O. Havemeyers, who had made their money in sugar and who in 1891 would move into their vast Tuscan Romanesque mansion, on the northeast corner of Fifth Avenue and Sixty-sixth Street, with sumptuous interiors by the Tiffany Studios. Already possessing an extraordinary collection of Oriental ceramics and textiles, the Havemeyers had only very recently begun to supplement their paintings by Rembrandt, Corot, and Degas with works by Courbet and Manet, all of which are now among the glories of the Metropolitan Museum of Art.

In 1890, a great controversy was raging over whether that museum should adopt the policy of opening on Sundays. Clergymen and other guardians of public morality insisted that visiting an art museum was an amusement in violation of the Sabbath. More enlightened New Yorkers, including settlement-house workers and many prominent journalists, retorted that one of the most important functions of the Met should be to edify the humble, who worked six days a week and found the museum closed on the seventh. In May 1891 the issue was finally settled in favor of opening.

George Eastman had patented his Kodak camera in September 1888 (he had given much thought to devising a name beginning and ending with the letter *k*, which he considered the punchiest letter), and it appeared on the market early in 1889. That year the Eastman Company sold an astonishing fifteen thousand Kodaks. The small, lightweight box camera came loaded with a roll of nitrocellulose film that could yield up to one hundred pictures. After the film had been exposed, the photographer would send the entire camera to Rochester, where the film would be processed and the camera reloaded. The resulting pictures were round rather than rectangular, since the camera's image frame was circular.

In America, photography tended to mean the rampages of the snapshooters who were more interested in titillation than in art, as parodied in the beach scene entitled "The Peeping Toms of the Camera" that appeared on the cover of *Puck* magazine in July 1891. Alfred, for whom photography was a noble calling, was sickened by the Kodak slogan "You press the button, and we do the rest." Everyone, he later wrote, was "shooting away at random, taking the chance of getting something. To me it seemed rotten sportsmanship. I had been brought up with the idea of the tripod and awaiting one's moment to do what one willed to do."[1]

One day in September 1890, over lunch in the popular rotunda dining room of the Astor House hotel (near City Hall and Printing House Square, where *Harper's Weekly* had its offices), John Foord persuaded Alfred to accept a job with the Heliochrome Company, a firm developing a process for printing photographic reproductions in color. Foord, who had invested heavily in the company, told him that Edward Stieglitz had already bought $1,000 worth of stock. Foord went on to insist that Alfred, with his chemical and photographic expertise, could surely develop a three-color process that would make a lucrative proposition out of the company, which was on the verge of collapse. On October 17, 1890, unconvinced but no longer able to refuse, Alfred began reporting daily to Heliochrome's ramshackle brownstone on Fulton Street, where his position was that of de facto director. Over the course of the following months, he would induce his friends Joe Obermeyer and Lou Schubart to join him in the enterprise.

Alfred had absurdly idealistic theories about how Heliochrome should be run. He assumed that if he was completely honest and fair with the firm's six employees, if he treated them with respect and paid them well, they would respond with total devotion, performing their jobs with Germanic application and excellence. The owners and workers would be like one happy family, cooperating for their mutual benefit.

During the first year, the business did not receive a single order but nevertheless spent heavily on experiments, under Alfred's direction, to develop both black-and-white and color printing processes. Much of the time the workmen had nothing better to do than oil the machinery, while the partners sat in the office reading newspapers. Alfred was dreadfully bored, but he was not entirely distressed about the lack of business, for he hoped the firm would soon go bankrupt so that he could be finished with the whole fiasco. By the end of the first year, he was no longer willing to put up with the futile tedium. Despite the disapproval of his doggedly dutiful partners, he began to spend less time at the office and more time wandering the streets of New York, with his new 8 x 10-inch tripod-mounted view camera, looking for subjects.

Heliochrome finally did go bankrupt. Alas, Edward insisted on giving Alfred and his friends $5,000 with which to buy the firm's equipment. In September 1891 the partners started the Photochrome Engraving Company and moved to a new loft building at 162–166 Leonard Street, between Baxter and Centre streets, around the corner from the Egyptian Revival prison known (like its successor) as the Tombs. They hired all the workmen from Heliochrome as well as a few newcomers, and their salesman redoubled his efforts.

Eventually orders began to trickle in from *Cassirer's* magazine, devoted to mechanical engineering, and from *The National Police Gazette*, which billed itself as "The Leading Illustrated Sporting Journal in the World." Alfred — who, with his head for figures, had been given responsibility for making estimates — was shocked that customers objected to the high prices he quoted. He had assumed that everyone would want the best possible work, no matter what it cost. In any case, he felt that customers should recognize that Photochrome's prices were very low for such fine work, since he and his partners drew no salary. (Alfred continued to receive a generous allowance from his father, though living at home meant that he had few basic expenses.) He calculated his estimates simply to cover operating costs — but because the firm paid its men generously, deducting neither for holidays nor sick days, as other firms did, they were high. "The greatest misfortune," wrote Alfred, "is that the majority of customers believe that reproductions by photographic methods are entirely mechanical, and therefore refuse to pay a fair price to the better class engraver."[2] He was appalled when he realized that the customers didn't give a damn about craftsmanship. They simply wanted acceptable work done as quickly and cheaply as possible.

Photochrome lost the race to perfect the process to print color reproductions by means of three photoengraved halftone plates (a yellow, a magenta, and a blue), the impressions of which would be superimposed by three successive runs through the printing press. The victor was William Kurtz, also of New York, who early in 1892 enlisted the aid of Ernst Vogel, Professor Vogel's son. By the end of that year Kurtz and Vogel had worked out a procedure for making three-color separations and printing the plates. The honor of announcing and demonstrating the breakthrough was given to Professor Vogel's magazine, *Photographische Mittheilungen.* Bound into every copy of its January 1, 1893, issue was a full-color photographic reproduction, printed by Kurtz, of fruit on a table.

Kurtz patented his process, but Photochrome apparently developed another sufficiently different to guarantee independence. Eagerness to show off his firm's new capability led Alfred to what was perhaps the worst artistic lapse of his entire career. Inserted as a frontispiece into every copy of *The American Amateur Photographer* for January 1894 was a color reproduction of a hand-colored platinum print of his photograph *The Last Load*, an alpine haying scene. The quality of the reproduction is fine, but the coloring of the print, though delicately toned, is painfully inappropriate. In an editorial comment Alfred conceded that colored photographs "are generally crude and inartistic," but he went on to state, with unjustified optimism, that this example was an exception.[3]

Photochrome's first large orders for color printing were from the Murphy Comedy Company, a traveling theatrical troupe, which would need a thousand cartes de visite of its actors and actresses whenever it moved on to a new town, as it did every couple of weeks. The Photochrome salesman assured the partners that Murphy would eventually distribute more than one hundred thousand of the cards. The problem was that, as the months passed, although the orders kept arriving as promised, there was no sign of payment. Desperate for business, Obermeyer and Schubart insisted nonetheless upon continuing to fill the orders. Finally, Alfred decided to consult the editor of *The National Police Gazette*, who told him, "You mustn't trust theatrical people. You'll never see a cent of this money owed to you." Outraged by the troupe's bad faith and disgusted by his partners' foolishness, Alfred threatened to resign from Photochrome at once.

But he was not to win his freedom so easily or so soon, for his friends cajoled him into remaining.

Not long after this brouhaha, Photochrome received a very large order from the Wagner Palace Car Company (a railroad-car manufacturer whose president, J. Watson Webb, was the Havemeyers' son-in-law) for small advertising cards printed in color. Obermeyer and Schubart were overjoyed — even if perhaps Alfred was not — for this was the kind of business that could finally put Photochrome on its feet. However, sensing a bonanza at last, the firm's employees announced that they would not proceed with their work unless they received an immediate 10 percent increase in their wages. The partners had no choice but to give in, though Alfred shrewdly insisted that the firm no longer pay the men for holidays or sick days. He was furious at the workmen, who had obtained their raise by virtual blackmail and thereby betrayed the firm's paternalistic benevolence. Worse, the men's greed and stupidity filled him with contempt, since the net result of the new arrangement was that their wages were 6 percent lower than before.

CHAPTER SIXTEEN

SOON AFTER RETURNING to New York in 1890, Alfred renewed his connection with Frederick C. Beach, the editor in chief and one of the founders of *The American Amateur Photographer*. One motive for this approach may have been the young man's hope that Beach would commission Heliochrome to engrave and print illustrations for the magazine.

Beach, whose family had formerly owned the *New York Sun* and who had himself been an editor of another family publication, *Scientific American*, had served four years as the first president of the Society of Amateur Photographers of New York, founded in 1884; in 1890–91 he was its secretary. Early in 1891, Alfred — who, as we have seen, was an ardent believer in the usefulness of photographic societies — joined the SAP. Joe Obermeyer also joined, at that time or soon thereafter. The club occupied an entire floor of the new Telephone Building at 113 West Thirty-eighth Street, where it held frequent meetings, at which members presented technical papers, told of photographic adventures at home and abroad, showed lantern slides of their work, described experiments, announced discoveries, and gave demonstrations of new equipment, techniques, and processes. The society also organized social evenings — "smokers," dances, and musicales — as well as photographic field trips.

From Alfred's point of view, however, the SAP's most important function was to sponsor exhibitions. Since 1887 it had collaborated with the

Photographic Society of Philadelphia and the Boston Camera Club to hold a Joint Exhibition every year (except 1890), rotating among the three cities. The aim of these shows, the only ones in the United States of more than local interest, was to promote the "artistic, scientific, and technical excellence of Photography." All of the hundreds of entries submitted by American and European photographers were hung, and a jury awarded silver medals to outstanding work.

At the fourth Joint Exhibition, held in New York during the spring of 1891, Alfred was one of only three members of the SAP to receive a medal. The show spurred him to write a fiery article for the 1892 edition of the annual *Photographic Mosaics*. He poured out, in "A Plea for Art Photography in America," all his anger, frustration, and shame in regard to the state of photography in his native country. In his view the British, who were developing P. H. Emerson's principles despite the latter's repudiation, were the greatest photographers in the world. "Granting that we are, in our technique, fully equal to the English, what we lack is that taste and sense for composition and for tone, which is essential in producing a photograph of artistic value — in other words, a *picture*."[1]

This last point was essential. At that time an artistically successful painting was generally called a "picture." Sophisticated photographers now began to argue that their works were also "pictures." (It was this usage that would give rise to the term "pictorial photography.") Many of the English were determined "to make their pictures look as little like photographs as possible," observed Alfred. They were increasingly turning to soft-focus, romantic images that resembled "reproductions from paintings or etchings."[2]

This was the tendency of the so-called new school, whose members claimed to be disciples of Emerson but who were about as Emersonian as the Renaissance popes were Christian. Ironically, even Emerson's long-time antagonist, Henry Peach Robinson, couldn't resist this trend. Alfred said he was glad to see that Robinson "had met the new school half way at least" and that his new work wasn't as "posey" as the old had been.[3]

Sounding the keynote of his own vision, Alfred wrote, "Artistic sense . . . loves simplicity and hates all superficial make-up. Simplicity, I might say, is the key to all art — a conviction that anybody who has studied the masters must arrive at."[4] That conviction underlay all of his future photographic work. The clarion statement of that principle, here in his first important article that was aesthetic rather than technical, marks the real beginning of the metamorphosis of Stieglitz the scientist into Stieglitz the artist.

*   *   *

To give weight to his words, Alfred needed the prestige of European triumphs. He scored a major one in May 1891 when he was among the very few Americans whose work was accepted at the Exhibition of Artistic Photography, in Vienna, a show that he had helped to plan before he left Europe. In previous European and American exhibitions, all submissions had been hung — resulting in a frightful chaos composed of the good, the bad, and the ugly. Under such circumstances, even the most devoted connoisseur of photography would find it difficult to contemplate the good with any serenity. But the organizers of the Viennese exhibition, the first anywhere devoted entirely to pictorial photography, had resolved to imitate the Parisian salons of painting and sculpture, to which only works accepted by the jury were admitted. Since they would exclude all but the good, they would not award any medals; it would be sufficient honor to have one's work hung.

Amateurs from around the world had sent some 4,000 photographs to Vienna. The jury, made up of painters and sculptors, was so highly selective that it hung only 600 prints, by a total of 176 photographers. More than forty Americans had entered, but only ten — eight men and two women — had their work accepted, a mere 25 pictures in all. Stieglitz, one of the two Americans to have five prints hung, was outshone only by the now-forgotten John Dumont, of Rochester, with six.

Alfred did everything he could to improve the quality of work being done by members of the SAP. He encouraged and exhorted, he wrote perceptive and candid reviews, he offered special medals as incentive, and he got himself appointed chairman of the exhibition committee. Although he was consistently among the members winning the most medals in every show, he was regarded no more highly than three or four other photographers in the society.

His popularity was perhaps limited by his self-appointed role of gadfly and critic. He wrote in his review of the 1893 Joint Exhibition that, taken as a whole, the work on view by members of the SAP was "photographically very good, artistically very poor."[5] And in his review of the following year's show he commented that the New York club seemed "to insist upon being the most 'conservative' of the leading societies, in other words, the least progressive."[6] During this period, "progressive" was one of Alfred's favorite terms; for a competition to which all work was to be submitted under pseudonyms, he chose the name Progressive.

"I would rather be a first-class photographer in a community of first-class photographers, than the greatest photographer in a community of nonentities," he remarked.[7] And so it was that, beginning in the early 1890s, Alfred threw himself into the herculean task of building up "a community of first-class photographers" in America. To that end he became a crusader, an evangelist, and a Jeremiah. He worked tirelessly to organize and to judge exhibitions. He wrote dozens of articles, some of them still about technique but now more often about the aesthetics and politics of photography. And he strove to set a standard of excellence in his own work. He was relentless and uncompromising, for he was on a spiritual quest. He believed, then and later, that the more he succeeded in preventing the American public from seeing anything but first-rate art, the more he would have contributed to the moral health of the nation.

Alfred was somewhat encouraged by the sixth Joint Exhibition, held in the galleries of the Pennsylvania Academy of the Fine Arts during April 1893. He called it "without doubt, the finest exhibition of photographs ever held in the United States" and claimed that it surpassed all previous shows except for that in Vienna two years earlier.[8] In all his writings, Alfred was highly appreciative of the work being done by women — as he would remain throughout his life. Among the medalists in the 1893 Joint Exhibition, he singled out for special praise Emma Justine Farnsworth, of Albany, New York: "Every one of her pictures is full of life and artistic quality, bold in conception and execution. . . . Her work is unaffected and full of individuality."[9]

The photographic community was remarkably egalitarian for the time. Although there was undeniably some condescension toward "lady amateurs," women played a leading role in photographic societies and exhibitions, both in America and abroad. There were several reasons. One was that photography was still widely viewed as something of a social sport, on a par with croquet or tennis. It was a very genteel — and relatively easily mastered — art form for those whose artistic longings perhaps exceeded their talents. (Queen Victoria, an accomplished watercolorist, was such an enthusiastic amateur photographer that she had a darkroom installed at Windsor Castle.) Excursions and soirees, which provided valuable opportunities for socializing and courting, drew many men and women into the photographic clubs. ("The field day has become an institution with the amateur societies, and woe to the sensitive who get in the path of one of these armed bodies," warned an article in *The Century Illustrated Monthly Magazine* in 1887.[10]) More important, women were gaining recognition in the decorative arts through the Arts and Crafts movement. Some of the outstanding American ceramicists, graphic designers, and silver-smiths were women, and the often-victorious struggle of all Arts and Crafts workers to have their work bought by art museums had a very direct bearing on the status of photography.

Too, a multitude of economic and social factors was drawing educated and talented women into the workforce. The profession of photography was attractive to many of these women, to whom law, medicine, and the other professions were still largely closed. In 1897 Frances Benjamin John-ston — a very successful Washington portrait photographer and photo-journalist who covered such topics as Pennsylvania miners, Massachusetts working women, and life on board a battleship — published the article "What a Woman Can Do with a Camera" in *The Ladies' Home Journal.* "Photography as a profession should appeal particularly to women," she stated in this virtual manifesto, "and in it there are great opportunities for a good-paying business." She listed the prerequisites for entering the pro-fession as "good common sense, unlimited patience to carry [one] through endless failures, equally unlimited tact, good taste, a quick eye, a talent for detail and a genius for hard work."[11] She might have added that for a woman to succeed as a photographer in those days she also needed to be exceptionally independent, to be defiant of convention, and to have a sense of humor. That Johnston herself was well endowed with these qualities is clearly demonstrated in her 1896 self-portrait, in which she sits before the fireplace of her Arts and Crafts–style studio brazenly smoking a cigarette and holding a stein of beer, with her skirt pulled up comfortably but scan-dalously to reveal an expanse of petticoat.

To foster the development of "a community of first-class photographers" in America, Alfred clearly needed a forum larger than that provided by the SAP. He was writing fairly regularly for *The American Amateur Photog-rapher,* but he longed to have editorial control so that he could publish im-ages by the most progressive photographers and enlist them to write articles. When circumstances led to his being offered a position as an edi-tor of the magazine in the spring of 1893, he accepted with alacrity. He would not be editor in chief, but, significantly, his name would precede Frederick Beach's on the revised masthead. Furthermore, to protect him-self from being forced to compromise, he would work without salary. The job would be only part-time, and Alfred would continue to work for Pho-tochrome, which was already producing gravures for the magazine.

The July 1893 issue announced,

We are happy to say that we have induced Mr. Alfred Stieglitz, so well-known both here and abroad for his artistic work, to become an active editor on our staff; with his co-operation we have no doubt but what important improvements in the magazine will be undertaken, which will include, perhaps, a greater number and variety of illustrations. His judgment of the value of photographic work is always good, while his technical knowledge . . . is unsurpassed.[12]

Although *The American Amateur Photographer* suffered from a preponderance of pieces about travel photography, it also regularly contained aesthetic and technical articles. Most of Alfred's contributions had been of the latter variety, with titles like "Points on Developing Cold-Bath Platinotypes" and "Uranium Toning of Platinotypes," both of which had appeared in the May 1893 issue. The back section of the magazine was filled with news from photographic societies all over America, with short book reviews, notices of new photographic patents, and announcements of upcoming exhibitions and competitions. The text was illustrated with halftones and an occasional photogravure printed on rag paper, though, until Stieglitz's advent, few of the images were memorable.

One of Alfred's first triumphs as editor was to sign up George Davison (of the pinhole camera) to contribute regularly to the magazine. Davison would fill the gap left by Emerson's resignation as British correspondent in the spring of 1890. An editorial note in the November 1893 issue called Davison "probably the foremost of living photographers," and in the May issue Stieglitz had written of his work that it "stands in a class by itself. Here we are dealing with a genuine artist. Every one of his pictures is a delight to the eye, a gem in its way. His work is full of individuality, full of power and effect."[13] Moreover, Davison was a warm and generous man who loved to entertain his many friends from the photographic world aboard his houseboat on the Thames.

Ten years older than Stieglitz, the shrewd Davison had invested heavily in Eastman stock and, in 1889, became one of the founding directors of the Eastman Photographic Materials Company of Great Britain. By the end of the 1890s his investments in Eastman had made him a wealthy man, and in 1900 he was appointed managing director of the British company.

Davison was no ordinary millionaire. A Christian Socialist, he believed that he had been blessed with a fortune in order to help others, and to that end he immersed himself in left-wing politics. This so embarrassed

the Eastman management that, in 1912, they asked him to resign. Thereafter he left his family and retired to his mansion in Wales, which he
opened to such activities as weekend seminars on the principles of Christian Socialism.

Davison was little less radical in his photography. The evocatively
blurred, pseudo-Impressionistic pictures that he began to show in 1890 appealed greatly to the fin de siècle mood of Symbolism and, in equal measure, outraged both Emerson and the traditionalists. "The new school, for
Mr. Davison's work is called so, goes in for suggestiveness," wrote Stieglitz
in 1893. He went on to explain that the Englishman's pictures were so revolutionary that they could not be judged "upon the principles hitherto
used in criticising photographs."[14]

Alfred was especially interested in Davison because of the latter's involvement with the British photographic society that called itself the
Brotherhood of the Linked Ring. The conservative members of the Photographic Society of Great Britain, who were primarily interested in
technique and equipment rather than aesthetics, had been horrified by
Davison's soft-focus images. Late in 1891, when the reactionaries seized
upon a technicality to exclude his pictures from the annual exhibition,
Davison and his rather surprising ally, Henry Peach Robinson, resigned
from the society. Others soon followed. In May 1892 fifteen of these men
decided to form the Linked Ring, a "small Society, an inner circle, a kind
of little Bohemian Club" devoted to "bringing together those who are interested in the development of the highest form of Art of which Photography is capable."[15]

The members, who called themselves Links, would meet periodically
for an evening of simple food, music played by members, conversation, and
business. In the style of the artistic clubs of the day, there was not only
much show of good-fellowship, often in the form of sophomoric puns and
verse, but also a certain amount of vaguely Masonic, secret-society ritual.
Most members, for instance, adopted such nicknames as Hangman (in
charge of installing exhibitions), High Executioner, and Philosopher.

The most important function of the Linked Ring was to sponsor an annual exhibition in London, the Photographic Salon, which not only embraced work that was anathema to the Photographic Society of Great
Britain but also influenced the organization, selection, and hanging of
photographic shows all over the world. The annual exhibitions of the Photographic Society, at the New Gallery on Pall Mall, looked like the display
in an auctioneer's salesroom, thousands of frames being hung without
rhyme or reason (pell-mell, so to speak) from the chair rail practically to

the ceiling. All submissions were hung, and the jury then awarded prizes. The Linked Ring decided to follow the example of Vienna's 1891 exhibition, hanging only what the jury selected and eschewing prizes and medals. Weeding out all the inferior work meant that what remained could be hung more tastefully, in two or three rows at eye level. "The idea is to have a very select exhibit of art photographs or those which are to be pictures," stated the announcement in the August 1893 issue of *The American Amateur Photographer* inviting entries from the United States for the first Photographic Salon, to be held that fall.

Alfred sent several of his prints, but when the salon opened in November, at the Dudley Gallery, not far from the more or less concurrent exhibition of the Photographic Society, none of his work was to be seen among the three hundred photographs hung. That was a painful blow, but Alfred recovered. So passionately did he believe in the work of the Linked Ring that he forgave, even if he never forgot, his initial snub. In 1902 he wrote of the Photographic Salons that their advent in 1893 had "mark[ed] the beginning of modern pictorial photography."[16]

P. H. Emerson would certainly not have been pleased to read that statement. Because the Linked Ring was dominated by his enemies Robinson and Davison, Emerson would never have consented to join. But he was never invited. In the view of the new leaders of the movement to develop "the highest form of Art of which Photography is capable," Emerson's apostasy merited his total excommunication. In revenge, Emerson threw his lot in with his old bugaboo, the Photographic Society of Great Britain, and in 1894 was instrumental in winning permission for it to add the prefix "Royal" to its name.

Alfred became virtually obsessed by his wish for a grand American version of the Photographic Salon to be held annually in New York. "The Exhibition should be purely pictorial," he insisted; "only work to be hung which shows individuality and is of artistic value."[17] Such a policy would, he assumed, force American photographers to do more progressive pictorial work. Since all those with any talent would want to be included in the show, they would have no choice but to rise to its standards.

If Alfred felt an exhibition would advance the cause of artistic photography, he would do everything possible to promote it. Since, however, he disapproved of the judges who had been appointed for the seventh Joint Exhibition, to be held in New York during April 1894, he decided to boycott it and encouraged his friends and others to do likewise. "First class men are rather chary in submitting their pictures to judgment to unknown quantities," he explained.[18] Later that year he went so far as to exhort his compatriots, "Abolish the joint exhibitions, which have done their work and served their purpose, and let us start afresh with an *Annual Photographic Salon*, to be run upon the *strictest* lines." He himself, so he assured his readers, would, "with much pleasure, sacrifice time and money in order to bring about a revolution in photographic exhibitions in the United States."[19]

For the moment, Alfred was granted only half of his wish. The 1895 Joint Exhibition was to be held in Boston, but the Bostonians withdrew from the series. "No one was willing to shoulder the responsibilities, and face the inevitable criticisms of every move to be made," recounted Alfred. He thought that "the natural death of these joint exhibitions has its decided advantage," for he hoped it would lead to the establishment of "an exhibition run on the Salon basis, and it is probably only a question of a short time [before] we shall have one."[20]

CHAPTER SEVENTEEN

ON THE EVENING of January 23, 1893, Alfred happened to walk past the Fifth Avenue Theater, on West Twenty-fourth Street, behind the great old Fifth Avenue Hotel. As he did so, he noticed a large poster announcing that in a few minutes the curtain was to go up for Eleonora Duse's New York debut, in Alexandre Dumas fils's masterpiece, *La Dame aux camélias*. Although he disliked the play and had never heard of Duse, he impulsively bought a ticket for his favorite seat, on the aisle in the first row of the orchestra.

When Duse walked onstage without saying a word, Alfred was enraptured. With his opera glasses he scrutinized her every expression and gesture. In Europe he had been impressed but not moved by Sarah Bernhardt's performance in the role of Marguerite Gauthier. Duse could not have been more different. Bernhardt, the mistress of histrionic emotionalism and stage effect, subsumed all of her rôles into her own personality and always relied upon her repertoire of highly developed mannerisms. In contrast, the younger Duse (she was thirty-four when Alfred saw her) was a consummate actress who penetrated the specific psychology of each of her characters and represented them all with unprecedented naturalism, subtlety, and grace. Her costumes were unspectacular, and on her face — not pretty but radiant with intelligence and inner strength — she wore no makeup. Alfred, convinced that he had never seen a more brilliant performance or a more beautiful woman, was moved to tears. He was in love. During the last intermission he went to the box office and reserved the same seat for three more evenings. He would, however, make no attempt to meet Duse, who the following year would fall deeply in love with the poet, novelist, and dramatist Gabriele D'Annunzio. Because Duse, onstage, had instantly become Alfred's ideal woman, as she would long remain, he did not want to jeopardize his memory of perfection by meeting her offstage.

On Washington's Birthday, one month after seeing Duse, Alfred encountered his friend William B. Post at the Society of Amateur Photographers. Later that year he would write of Post that he was "without doubt one of the most talented men in the society. He is an ardent and serious worker, knowing exactly what he wants and bent upon 'getting there.'"[1]

Post — a jaunty, trimly bearded, and sociable fellow seven years older than Alfred — was a wealthy man who would become a member of the New York Stock Exchange in 1898. Before then, traveling seems to have been his principal occupation. During 1893 he photographed in Maine, the White Mountains of New Hampshire, Nassau in the Bahamas, Texas, California (where he focused on Yosemite and old Spanish missions), and Japan. Because he found it too awkward to carry a large camera, a tripod, and all the other necessary equipment on such extensive journeys, Post had bought a medium-size handheld camera that used 4 x 5-inch plates. The camera, a leather-covered box whose front folded down to provide support for the sliding bellows that connected the lens panel and the plate holder, was probably a Kodak Number 4 Folding Camera. A version of that model, adapted for plates instead of the standard roll film, had been introduced in 1892.[2]

Alfred was amazed by the photographs that Post had made with his hand camera during the sojourn in Nassau from which he had just returned. In fact, he was so impressed that he would soon write that Post's "hand-camera work is of high artistic merit, some of the little bits are real gems . . . extremely delicate and atmospheric."[3] Stieglitz had previously regarded the hand camera "as a mere toy, good for the purposes of the globetrotter who wished to jot down photographic notes as he passed along his journey, but in no way adapted to the wants of him whose aim it is to do serious work."[4] Part of his prejudice against the small cameras was due to the misleading advice, universally given, that they could be used successfully only in bright sunlight.

When Post offered to let him borrow his camera, Alfred jumped at the chance. It had been snowing prodigiously for several days, and the depressed and lonely young man found his mood reflected in the bad weather. He had conceived an idea for a picture that would have been almost impossible to make in the raging blizzard with his cumbersome view camera. Having been assured that Post's camera was waterproof, he set out from the SAP. With snow falling heavily and the wind blowing fiercely, he stood for three hours (or so he claimed) at the corner of Fifth Avenue and Thirty-fifth Street, waiting for an opportunity to get the shot he wanted. Looking down the avenue, past the houses of A. T. Stewart and Mrs. William Astor and the brand-new, thirteen-story Waldorf Hotel, at Thirty-third Street, he was stalking a heroic shot of a horse-drawn omnibus, its driver up on the box, exposed to the elements, urging his horses steadily forward against the howling wind.

Coincidentally, the young writer Stephen Crane, also out during that storm, would write: "The drivers of vehicles hurried their horses furiously on their way. They were made more cruel by the exposure of their positions, aloft on high seats. The street-cars, bound uptown, went slowly, the horses slipping and straining in the spongy brown mass that lay between the rails. The drivers, muffled to the eyes, stood erect and facing the wind, models of grim philosophy."[5] He could have been describing Stieglitz's photograph. It is probable that both men were influenced by Walt Whitman in their choice of subject. Whitman, who had loved to ride up top with the drivers, called them "a strange, natural, quick-eyed and wondrous race" in whom not only Rabelais and Cervantes but also Homer and Shakespeare would have delighted.[6]

Once he finally had his shot, Alfred rushed back to the SAP to develop the negative. It turned out exactly as he had hoped, though one of his fellow members thought it was so badly blurred that he should throw it away. Alfred's primary concern, however, was not with a "microscopic sharpness . . . of no pictorial value."[7] His aim was to capture the feeling — the inward experience rather than merely the outward appearance — of the scene that resonated so powerfully in his own emotions. He considered his picture a symbolic self-portrait, for he felt that the driver struggling up Fifth Avenue against the blasts of a great storm represented his own plight as an artist in a philistine city.

Alfred believed that his photograph, which he entitled *Winter — Fifth Avenue*, marked the beginning of a "new era." Indisputably, it marked the beginning of his mature work. The picture was still a technical tour de force, since flakes of falling snow were notoriously difficult to record, but it had an emotional urgency and authority previously lacking. In 1898 critic Sadakichi Hartmann would write perceptively that the photograph "reminds one of nothing else, while most of [his] others suggest in some way or another the faint reminiscences of some school of art."[8]

Within twenty-four hours of developing his negative, Alfred had produced a vertical lantern slide in which he reduced the overall contrast and cropped off much distracting detail from the left and right sides of the original horizontal negative. "My hand camera negatives are all made with the express purpose of enlargement," he would write, "and it is but rarely that I use more than part of the original shot. . . . Prints from the direct negatives have but little value."[9]

Excited though his colleagues were by the slide, that was only the beginning of Alfred's work on this image. Our source is no less than his friend Theodore Dreiser, who was so impressed by the photograph that in his novel *The "Genius"* (1915), he describes a painting by the protagonist that is obviously based on it. Dreiser wrote in an 1899 article about Stieglitz, "Often months of work are devoted to such a picture: not constant, of course, but six or eight hours a week. In this case, the photograph was taken four or five years ago, and only completed a few months since. It had grown to an eleven-by-fourteen print, a gem of art."[10]

By the morning of the day after Washington's Birthday, 1893, the blizzard had ended. With several feet of snow on the ground, the city seemed hushed and deserted. Still enjoying the loan of Post's hand camera, Alfred made his way downtown to the huge, ugly Second Empire–style Post Office that occupied the lower part of City Hall Park. Across Broadway was the Doric-columned, Greek Revival–porticoed Astor House hotel; here, on the complex pattern of tracks crisscrossing Broadway and Park Row, the Third Avenue and Madison Avenue railway cars turned around to head back uptown to Harlem. Alfred's eye was drawn to one of the drivers, wearing a rubber coat and hat, giving water to his horses while clouds of steam rose from their bodies. Alfred, whose love of Thoroughbreds extended to their poor cousins, admired the nobility of this man doing his job with love and tenderness, and he envied the horses for having such a person to care for them. He also regretted that the horse-drawn omnibuses were already being rendered obsolete, for the first cable cars would appear on the Broadway line later that year. Alfred crystallized his emotions in his great photograph *The Terminal*, also known as *The Car Horses*, an extraordinary juxtaposition of the eternal and the ephemeral.

He soon bought a camera like Post's and began to wander with it all over the city. That winter he photographed ragpickers, more omnibuses, and men paving the streets. He went down to Coenties Slip, on the East River, to photograph the moored sailing ships, their bowsprits jutting far over the street. And early in April an evening at the SAP was devoted to his lantern slides of "scenes on the Battery, the squalid localities of New York, as well as some interesting souvenirs of life on Fifth Avenue between Murray Hill and the Central Park."[11] He hoped to complete a series of one hundred photographs that would sum up his feelings about New York in all its complexity, to capture the feeling of life in the city.[12] He wanted to document "the New York of transition. — The Old gradually passing into the New. . . . the Spirit of that something that endears New York to one who really loves it — not for its outer attractions — but for its deepest worth — & significance. — The universal thing in it."[13]

In Stieglitz's New York photographs of 1893 there is a power new to his work. Immediate, spontaneous, direct, and sincere, they are pervaded by a tragic sense of life. He had at last gone beyond the picturesque and the merely technical to create images that resonate with intensely personal feelings. These were by far the most Emersonian photographs that Stieglitz had yet made.

Most days Alfred would spend only a few hours at the Photochrome office. Then he would take his camera and explore the streets nearby, in one of the poorest sections of the city, the notorious Five Points neighborhood, named for the intersection of Baxter, Worth, and Park streets, just two blocks east of the Photochrome office.

Alfred's motives, approach, and results were very different from those of Jacob Riis, the reformer-photographer whose book *How the Other Half Lives*, published in 1890, also focused on the area around the Five Points. Stieglitz was not interested in documenting the appalling conditions in which the slumdwellers were forced to live and work; he was drawn instead to individuals who seemed to transcend the misery that surrounded them. He claimed to envy them, since their struggle for life was elemental, in what he considered a refreshing contrast to the artificiality and superficiality of the business and social worlds in which he found himself trapped.[14] By photographing these people he was engaging not only in an act of rebellion and protest against bourgeois values but also in an act of love, though sadly without the warmth of actual human contact. He wandered the streets searching for kindred spirits in the hope that he was not completely alone, not a total anomaly.

One afternoon in June 1893 Alfred found himself walking by Tony Pastor's Theater, on the ground floor of Tammany Hall, on East Fourteenth Street, where the Consolidated Edison building now stands.[15] During the 1880s, Pastor had cleaned up vaudeville — banning obscenity and blasphemy from his stage and forbidding his audience to smoke or drink — thereby making it suitable entertainment for families.

Since the day was warm, the doors of the theater were open to the street, and Alfred heard hearty laughter coming from inside. Peering in, he saw that two men — the poster outside proclaimed them to be Weber and Fields, of whom Alfred had never heard — were performing a routine involving billiards. Having been "a fiend at billiards," he was intrigued and decided to buy a ticket, but he was told that he could go in for free, since the show was nearly over.

Very shortly after Weber and Fields' Own Company was organized in 1890, it had become one of the most popular traveling vaudeville acts in America. Every year during the early 1890s the two-man company played in New York for a few weeks late in the spring and then hit the road, covering the entire nation from coast to coast.

The characters, Mike and Myer, were German immigrants who massacred the English language with their outrageously thick accents, malapropisms, mispronunciations, literal renderings of German syntax, and just plain nonsense so uninhibited that it spun off into a sort of proto-surrealism. Joe Weber played Mike, short and fat, his belly grotesquely padded with pillows and his derby reinforced with iron to protect him from the blows that Lew Fields — as Myer, the tall, wily bully — gave him with his cane or any other available weapon. The tenor of their physically abusive yet oddly affectionate slapstick was summed up by Field's best-known lines, "Ven I'm away from you, I cannot keep mein mind from off of you. Ven I'm mit you, I cannot keep mein hands from off of you. Oh, I luff you, Mike."

What Alfred saw was their sketch "The Senators in a Pool-Room," which was to become one of their most famous. Amid jokes based on Weber's shortness and on money having been placed on a high shelf, with all sorts of slapstick involving billiard cues and balls, Weber and Fields launched into a hilarious sequence of misunderstandings, illogic, and non sequiturs. Alfred was so convulsed with laughter that other spectators began to turn around to look at him. He went back every day during the rest of the run.

"The first human thing I saw in New York," Stieglitz recalled many years later, was the man tending his horses. According to a friend, that sight together with Duse and the comedians Weber and Fields "constituted the trinity which gave him hope, made New York bearable."[16]

CHAPTER EIGHTEEN

⟡

SEX WAS VERY much on Alfred's mind, judging from his photograph entitled *A Study*, reproduced in the February 1893 issue of *The American Amateur Photographer*. It shows a young woman with long wavy hair, tilting her head and looking provocatively toward the camera — which is to say at the photographer. She is wearing what could be either a loose, peasant-style white blouse or a nightgown. It is obvious that if Alfred did not in fact go to bed with her, he would have liked to. The picture leads the viewer to believe that, unless the model was simply a talented actress assuming a pose as directed, she would probably have been quite willing.

The pressure that Edward and Hedwig had been putting on Alfred to find a wife surely increased after Julius married Anny Stieffel in 1891 and Selma married Lou Schubart in 1892. Joe Obermeyer, who would have liked to marry Selma himself, thought that his younger sister Emmy would make an ideal match for Alfred.

Ever since the deaths of their parents during the preceding several years, Joe had been Emmy's guardian and had shared a house with her in Manhattan. It must have been late in 1892 or early in 1893 that the lonely and impressionable Emmy, who seems to have wanted desperately a re-placement father figure, had developed a crush on her riding instructor. Joe, fearing an elopement, whisked Emmy away to St. Augustine to cool her passion. The episode made him feel that it was urgent to get her happily married and off his hands before she got herself into trouble.

Alfred was not interested. He had known Emmy since 1889, when the sixteen-year-old girl, attending a boarding school in Stuttgart, visited her brother in Berlin. Alfred found her hopelessly spoiled and selfish, frivolous and materialistic, obnoxiously pushy, and far from beautiful. In photographs dating from the 1890s, she occasionally displays a certain fresh charm, but more often she looks as though she belongs in one of Francisco Goya's unflattering portraits of the stupid and coarse-featured Spanish royal family. Although she dressed the part of a Gibson girl, she tended to look like a scullery maid to whom the master has taken an unaccountable fancy, snatching her from the kitchen to the tennis court.

For her part, Emmy was terribly impressed by Alfred, who in 1893 was twenty-nine to her twenty. He was becoming a famous photographer — a flattering article about him had appeared in *Cosmopolitan* magazine the previous year. He was handsome, amusing, and sophisticated. Emmy soon fell in love with him. She didn't care anything about photography, about which he was somewhat frighteningly vehement (one writer noted that the tone of Alfred's voice changed whenever he began to discuss the subject), but she didn't see that as an obstacle to their happiness. She undoubtedly assumed that the marriage ceremony would miraculously transform Alfred into a conventional husband.

One day in the spring of 1893, Alfred, Joe, and Emmy, together with a party of friends, sailed up the Hudson to have a picnic in Nyack, New York. On the way home that evening, Emmy dozed off, and her head came to rest on Alfred's shoulder. Always disdainful and defiant of social conventions, he chose to view this innocently enough. Everyone else, however, took it as a sign that they would soon announce their engagement. As they were saying good-bye, Emmy invited Alfred to pay a formal call on her two evenings later. He dutifully went and spent about three hours with her in the parlor, unchaperoned, though Joe was upstairs. Alfred found the evening boring, but he felt that it would be rude to leave too early. It was all very proper, an empty formality, a favor to a friend whose younger sister was lonely. He was, therefore, appalled when Joe informed him that he considered them as good as engaged.

Alfred had come to like Emmy somewhat better than he had at first, but he certainly didn't love her. In any case, despite his wish for someone to take care of him as faithfully and tenderly as the driver of the horsecar watered his horses, he neither intended nor wanted to marry anyone. Still suffering from low self-esteem, he felt completely unable and unwilling to assume responsibility — financial or otherwise — for a wife and family.

Furthermore, he wanted to dedicate his life to photography, and that meant being free to go wherever he wanted, whenever he wanted.

Joe, who considered it his solemn duty to protect both the feelings and the reputation of his younger sister, was furious. Warning his friend that if he refused to marry Emmy she would be seriously compromised, he sternly informed Alfred that he expected him to do his duty.

In an attempt to appease Joe, and at the same time escape from his predicament, Alfred proposed a five-year engagement. During that time he would consider himself obligated to Emmy, though she would have no obligation to him. He was obviously hoping that she would fall in love with someone else. But he was trapped. Both Edward and Joe insisted upon a brief engagement, which was announced in June 1893.

Edward's financial situation certainly contributed to his eagerness to see Alfred married. He was badly hurt by the panic that began on May 5, 1893, when the prices of shares on the New York Stock Exchange plunged in response to European fears about the soundness of American monetary policy. Agricultural failures and the unavailability of European credit led to panic in Chicago a month later. By the end of June the nation had entered one of the worst depressions in its history. Hahlo and Stieglitz would soon be in such bad shape that Edward felt himself obliged to return to work lest the firm go bankrupt. Indeed, the year 1893 alone saw the failure of six hundred American banks and fifteen thousand businesses, after which the nation would take several years to get back on its feet. Edward was clearly worried about his ability to provide for his family's future. A rich wife for his son would alleviate some of his fears — and those of Alfred himself, who was undoubtedly horrified at the thought that he might have to depend upon a Photochrome that his father would no longer be able to subsidize.

In discussing the engagement, Edward told Alfred that breweries prosper even in hard times, and Obermeyer and Liebmann, Brewers, Maltsters and Bottlers, was a very profitable business. Founded by Emmy's father, David Obermeyer, and his brother-in-law Joseph Liebmann (not to be confused with the latter's cousin of the same name, who was president of S. Liebmann's Sons Brewing Company, later to market its beer under the name Rheingold), the brewery was located on Bremen Street in Brooklyn. Obermeyer had lived at 495 Bushwick Avenue, Liebmann next door at number 493. Since David Obermeyer's death, about 1890, the firm had continued to thrive. Emmy's shares probably yielded her an income of about $3,000 a year, enough to live in modest luxury. Edward told his son that he would give him an equal sum each year. It was agreed that Alfred and Emmy would split their basic living expenses, after which he would have plenty left over for his photographic pursuits. Emmy would pay out of her own pocket not only for her extravagances but also for the support of any children they might have.

Marriage certainly promised advantages, both practical and sexual. Despite his later denials, Alfred seems to have grown fond of his fiancée, as suggested by photographs he took during the several weeks she spent with the Stieglitz family at Lake George in the summer of 1893. One day the engaged couple took a small boat out to Tea Island, where they found a sylvan glen for a picnic. Having arranged on the ground the striped cushions from their boat, Alfred photographed Emmy — looking very happy and very much in love — stretched out on them. As a symbol of the wedded bliss he was hoping for, he placed her bonnet and his own boater together, leaning against his box of camera equipment. He was looking forward to photographing her in the nude once they were married, and he claimed that she had given him reason to expect that she would cooperate.

Alfred later conceded that Emmy had been "quite dulcet and charming" in the months before their marriage. But at the wedding things began to go seriously wrong.[1] They were married at Sherry's ultrafashionable restaurant, on Fifth Avenue, on the evening of November 16, 1893. Inauspiciously, the officiating judge was obviously drunk when he arrived, and someone later pointed out that Alfred had stood on the wrong side of Emmy during the ceremony. In an act that seems half a gesture of self-immolation and half a sign of profound distrust of his bride, Alfred took his mother's advice and, just before the wedding, burned the diary he had kept since he was nine years old.[2]

Since the couple had decided to postpone their honeymoon until the following summer, when they would tour Europe for several months, they spent their nuptial night in their apartment in the Savoy Hotel, located at Fifth Avenue and Fifty-ninth Street, just a block and a half from Alfred's parents' house. One of the most luxurious hotels in New York, the Savoy had opened in 1892.

The marriage was not consummated that night, nor would it be for at least a year — in one version, Stieglitz claimed four years. He said that Emmy, terrified of sex, "became a stern prude" after the wedding and would not let him touch her or even allow him to photograph her in the nude. She excused herself by saying (probably quite rightly) that he would show the pictures to all his friends.[3]

Alfred, who later insisted that he had never found Emmy alluring, was perhaps somewhat relieved at not having to make love to her, though he also confessed to feeling great frustration. In any case, he sublimated his sexual energies into his work and such other activities as playing the piano. Emmy, finding his passionate renditions of Beethoven and Wagner upsettingly intense, exasperated him by requesting an occasional waltz. He had the movers come and take the piano away. He didn't utter a word of reproach to Emmy, instead coldly regarding her with contempt. There was a terrible cruelty in his refusal even to argue with her. Alfred's colossal self-righteousness was his most destructive — and self-destructive — failing. He was a man incapable of compromise, and what is a happy marriage but an extended and loving exercise in gentle compromise?

Alfred had mistakenly believed, or at least hoped, that Emmy would play Galatea to his Pygmalion — that he would be able to shape the sensibilities of this impressionable-seeming young woman. His happiness would depend upon his success in transforming her into a helpmate and companion who would adopt his simple tastes and accompany him on his photography expeditions. Instead, she would play Xanthippe to his Socrates. Alfred would soon discover, to his chagrin, that his wife was resolutely uninterested in all that he cared about most passionately. He then found himself trapped in an unbearable marriage to a woman who was (according to him) obsessed with social climbing, clothes, and luxury.

For her part, Emmy certainly hoped that Alfred would settle down to what she had been brought up to regard as a normal life. She was a conventional girl of the upper middle class who should have married a man who would relish swank parties, posh travel, a lavish dinner at home every night, the paternal rôle, and all the comforts and trimmings of domestic life. Instead, she found herself with a fanatic who abhorred the very idea of the kind of life she wanted.

Each stubbornly and successfully resisted all efforts to change his or her outlook, interests, and values. One is reminded of John Ruskin's even more dismally unsuccessful — but mercifully briefer — marriage, about which he understated, "When we married, I expected to change *her* — she expected to change *me*. Neither have succeeded, and both are displeased."[4]

Although Emmy tried to show an interest in her husband's work, her efforts were clumsy, and Alfred dismissed them. His friend Paul Rosenfeld, writing in the 1930s, tells us that in the early 1890s Alfred had "almost regularly spent his evenings developing and printing his negatives at the Camera Club [the SAP]. Marriage has only brought about this change, that his evening trips to and from the clubhouse have been made in the company of his young wife."[5] That wasn't enough for Alfred. Emmy seems to have been a decent enough woman, but he resented her bitterly for not becoming his twin.

Just as he boycotted and propagandized to wreck photographic exhibitions that did not meet his standards, so he in effect boycotted his marriage and described his wife, to anyone who would listen, as uninterested in his work, uncomprehending, and unsupportive.

Alfred punished Emmy by flirting with every attractive woman who came along. There was, for instance, the very pretty Miss Issacs, whom he photographed, apparently in Central Park, in 1894. Her raised eyes and the slight smile on her full lips give her a dreamy and amused expression. How Alfred must have wished that he could be married to such a woman. And how well Emmy, when she saw the photographs, must have understood.

CHAPTER NINETEEN

ON MAY 5, 1894, six days after Lee Stieglitz married Elizabeth Stief-fel, Alfred and Emmy sailed for Europe on the French liner *Bourgogne*. As far as Alfred was concerned, the main purposes of the trip were to photograph, visit photographic exhibitions, and meet European photographers. He wanted and expected the kind of travels he would have had alone — except that Emmy should now be his devoted companion, admirer, and assistant.

Having been away from his beloved Europe for four years, Alfred felt he had much time to make up. Some days he would get up at 4:00 A.M. so that he could be out on location when the sun rose. He might then devote the entire day to photographing. (He had taken both his 4 x 5 and 8 x 10 cameras.) At night he would either develop his plates or stay up late talking shop with his friends. As he saw it, he was fulfilling his obligations to Emmy by inviting her to accompany him.

Emmy — who had been looking forward to a round of fashionable sightseeing excursions, shops, parties, and restaurants — was miserable. Often she chose to remain alone at their hotel. She cried and complained, but Alfred thought she was just being foolish. Even when she made an effort to please him, she was out of her element. For instance, one day in Switzerland when she agreed to go with him on a photographic outing, he insisted, although she was terrified of heights, that they take the recently opened electric railway up to the village of Mürren (at an elevation of over one mile) to photograph the splendid view of the Jungfrau. Emmy became hysterical and, to Alfred's embarrassment, screamed that he was trying to murder her. To spite her, he hired a guide and (so he claimed) practically ran up the mountain, carrying his heavy photographic equipment, without her.

Among their first stops was Milan, to see the huge international photographic exhibition in which Alfred was one of only four American exhibitors, the others being Emma Farnsworth, Emilie V. Clarkson, and William Post. From there they went up to Bellagio and on to Venice, where Alfred photographed the people and buildings of the city extensively. Some of his architectural studies could easily pass for the work of the Fratelli Alinari, the great Italian firm of topographical documentarians, while his genre scenes reflect the sympathetic naturalism of his New York photographs. Remembering the success of his picture *A Good Joke*, Alfred was especially drawn to scenes around the wells in the center of piazze. He felt that these wells were the true foci of Venetian life and that by photographing the people gathered around them he could capture the essence of the city.

In Paris, where the Eiffel Tower was only five years old, Emmy was a bit happier, for here at last she and Alfred enjoyed together some of the pleasures to which she had been looking forward. They promenaded in the Bois de Boulogne, made an excursion to the forest of Fontainebleau to visit the eponymous village of the Barbizon school, attended plays and concerts, and went to the races at Longchamps. We can only wonder whether they went to the café-concert Les Ambassadeurs to hear the chanteuse Yvette Guilbert, of whom Alfred told Sadakichi Hartmann in 1898 that he was "a great admirer."[1] Hartmann characterized the red-haired singer, wearing her trademark elbow-length black gloves, which heightened the effect of her gestures, as "Ugliness singing the misery and frivolity of modern society."[2] Perhaps a short, homely man — Henri de Toulouse-Lautrec — was in the audience, sketching her, as he often did in that period. In 1909 Alfred would exhibit the Frenchman's work in New York.

Alfred's interest in the Parisian photographic community had been piqued by reports of the first Paris salon, which had been hung in the art gallery of Durand-Ruel during January 1894, under the sponsorship of the Photo-Club de Paris. His photograph *The Card Players* was included in the sumptuous book published as a record of the exhibition.

The chief organizer of the salon was Robert Demachy, son of a wealthy

Parisian banker. Rebellious and bohemian, Demachy was a gregarious, generous, and humorous man of leisure who had avoided going into the family firm. A passionate amateur photographer, as well as a violinist and painter, he set up his darkroom on the top floor of his palatial house on the rue François 1er and established his Spartan personal quarters next to it, scandalously adjacent to the servants' rooms. Whether or not Stieglitz met Demachy in 1894, the two men would soon become close friends and carry on a warm and lengthy correspondence. They would have had much to discuss — not least their unhappy marriages.

Demachy's photographic work is of very uneven quality. Worst are his leering studies of women and girls. Somewhat better are his studies of ballerinas in the wings — though they are sadly prosaic in comparison with the works of Degas, by which they were obviously inspired. Best are his gorgeous portraits, landscapes with horses, and studies of Breton peasants and villages, which ensure him a lasting place as one of the leading Pictorialists.

In addition to making photographs, Demachy wrote five books and hundreds of articles about photography. An outspoken, acerbic, and perceptive critic, he is perhaps best remembered as one of the foremost practioners of, and propagandists for, the gum-bichromate process of printing, which had recently been revived after long neglect. It had been invented in 1855 by Alphonse Louis Poitevin, who added pigment — which could be of any color — to the emulsion. The Pictorialists came to favor the process because gum-bichromate prints looked somewhat like monochromatic watercolors, especially since the photographer could manipulate the surface of the print with a paintbrush while it was wet, eliminating details, changing tonal values, and making painterly brush marks.

Stieglitz was not impressed by what he saw of the work by Parisian photographers, dismissing it as "rather mediocre, nothing worth speaking of."* He thought this was odd, for he found Paris "full of fascination and beauty."[3] Alfred's own best-known photograph from this sojourn shows people crossing the street in front of the Old England Shop, at the corner of the boulevard des Capucines, on a rainy day. (He complained in August that "since leaving New York there have actually been not more than 18 fine days."[4]) *Rainy Day, Paris* — also known as *A Wet Day* — is a charming picture suggestive of Impressionist paintings by Gustave Caillebotte and

---

*Eugène Atget, whose penetrating studies of Parisian architecture and life Stieglitz would admire when he first encountered them in the 1920s, did not begin photographing until 1898.

Camille Pissarro. If the photograph were hung next to Alfred's *Winter —
Fifth Avenue* of the previous year, the two images might be taken to represent the contrast between the harshness of New York and the cultivated
gentleness of Europe.

Alfred took some of his most beautiful photographs of the trip when he revisited Wilhelm Hasemann in Gutach. He made a number of character
studies, such as *Village Philosopher*, an old man lost in thought as he sits at a
table on which rests an open book. More memorable are his outdoor shots
of people working, though it might be argued that the pictures are really
about the magnificent qualities of the light: the early morning sun turning
hay into spun gold while clouds billow above; the gently dappled light in a
scene at a rustic pump; and the diffuse glow of old wood in a shot of a girl
standing in the doorway of a barn, her head highlighted against the rich
and velvety black of the interior space behind her.

In an article on which he collaborated with Lou Schubart — who, together with his wife, was evidently with the honeymooners in Germany
and the Netherlands — Alfred wrote, "In Gutach, nature smiles; in Katwyk, she is forbidding and pessimistic."[5] The place that Stieglitz always
called Katwyk is actually Katwijk aan Zee, a fishing village about fifteen
miles north of The Hague that was favored by painters. Alfred's old friend
Sime Herrmann, then still living in Munich and painting in an Impressionistic style, was in Katwijk while Alfred and Emmy were there; he may
even have been responsible for their visit. Max Liebermann, one of the
foremost Munich painters, spent many summers during the 1880s and
early 1890s in Katwijk and its neighboring villages.

Katwijk was, however, most closely associated with the so-called Hague
school of painters. Influenced by the stalwart Millet and his saccharine im-
itator Bastien-Lepage, as well as by the long tradition of Dutch genre
painting, the Hague school included Jozef Israëls (who was known as the
Dutch Millet), the three Maris brothers, and Anton Mauve, with whom his
wife's cousin Vincent van Gogh had worked during the early 1880s. The
sentimental realism of their paintings of women mending nets, waiting for
the return of the fishing boats, and gathering the day's catch into baskets
was very popular by the 1870s, in New York as well as all over Europe. A
strong affinity with the Hague school is obvious, for example, in the oils
and watercolors that Winslow Homer painted in the northern English
fishing village of Cullercoats in 1881–82, works to which Alfred's photographs of Katwijk bear a striking resemblance.

The residents, according to Alfred, were "immense in stature, hardy, brave beyond belief, stoical from long habit." His pictures of them are among his most Emersonian, which is to say straightforwardly naturalistic, though they are still tinged with a vestige of Robinsonian sentimentality.[6] Perhaps the strongest depicts a solitary woman, seen from the side as she sits on a flat, grassy expanse of sand mending a fishing net. (The solitude of the figure makes the photograph much more powerful than the canvas showing dozens of such women that Liebermann had painted at Katwijk between 1887 and 1889. Alfred told Sadakichi Hartmann that "Liebermann's representation of Dutch fishing folk had never entered his mind."[7]) The photographer would write of *The Net Mender*, which, in 1899, he called his "favorite picture," that it

> expresses the life of a young Dutch woman: every stitch in the mending of the fishing net, the very rudiment of her existence, brings forth a torrent of poetic thoughts in those who watch her sit there on the vast and seemingly endless dunes, toiling with that seriousness and peacefulness which is so characteristic of these sturdy people. All her hopes are concentrated in this occupation — it is her life.[8]

There is a timeless, mythic quality to this photograph of a woman who is like Penelope waiting for Odysseus, or like the figure of one of the Fates from a Greek pediment. It becomes all the more poignant — disturbingly so — when we realize that Alfred intended it partly as a rebuke to Emmy. The photograph was his favorite because it represented his ideal wife.

London was the last stop on the honeymoon. Here Alfred was at last to meet some of the leading lights of the Linked Ring, among them George Davison and Alfred Horsley Hinton, laying the foundations for what would become important friendships. He may also have met the Glasgow photographer J. Craig Annan, who specialized in portraiture and genre and who was to be represented in that fall's Linked Ring salon by fourteen photographs, more than anyone else. Alfred would certainly have been eager to meet Annan, of whom he had written earlier that year, "Here we deal with a true artist, and a decidedly poetical one at that. We have seen but few pictures to equal that called 'Labor — Evening.' . . . The picture breathes of atmosphere, it is a piece of nature itself. We can give it no higher praise."[9]

The parallels between Stieglitz and Annan are astonishing. They were almost exact coevals, for Annan was born two months after, and died one month before, his colleague. Moreover, their photographic styles and interests were closely related during the 1890s. In 1892 Annan had made a number of photographs in the Dutch fishing village of Zandvoort very similar to Alfred's Katwijk pictures, and both men worked in Venice during the summer of 1894. Stieglitz would eventually acquire some sixty prints by Annan, more than he owned by anyone else except Edward Steichen, and he would reproduce photographs by Annan in five issues of *Camera Work*.

Furthermore, Annan was professionally involved with photogravure. In 1883 he had accompanied his father, Thomas Annan (himself a superlative photographer, the Atget of Glasgow), to Vienna to purchase the British rights to the newly developed process from its inventor, Karl Klíč. The firm of T. and R. Annan and Sons soon became known for its magnificent printing.

During his weeks in London, Alfred was able to ensure that he would be elected to the Linked Ring. On October 26, he and Rudolf Eickemeyer became the first two Americans to be offered membership. The status of being a Link not only satisfied Alfred's vanity, though he would never have admitted that fact, but also gave him the prestige he needed to have a real impact on the course of photography in America.

He would have liked to remain in London for the October 1 opening of the Linked Ring's Photographic Salon, but many responsibilities were calling him back to New York. His photograph *Rainy Day, Paris*, would, however, represent him in that show, winning the praise of George Davison, who called it "a very effective subject, . . . well selected and very uncommon."[10] Alfred would also show work in the annual exhibition of the newly Royal Photographic Society that fall, for the animosity between the RPS and the Linked Ring was already beginning to abate.

In mid-September Alfred and Emmy returned to New York, their honeymoon — which was to have brought them closer together — having driven them further apart. It would be ten years before they revisited Europe. By that time Alfred would have played a leading rôle in bringing about a revolution in American photography.

PART III

CAMERA NOTES AND CAMERA WORK

CHAPTER TWENTY

EIGHTEEN NINETY-FIVE and 1896 saw great changes in Stieglitz's professional life. During those two years he finally extricated himself from his job at Photochrome and firmly established himself on the course that would lead to *Camera Work* and his first gallery.

The January 1895 issue of *The American Amateur Photographer* announced that "beginning with this issue, Mr. Alfred Stieglitz assumes sole charge of the general management" and will also be "the responsible editor."[1] His promotion came about largely because Frederick Beach had embroiled the magazine in a legal battle. In 1893, when he published a photograph of a yacht by E. C. Bolles, a member of the SAP, Beach paid the photographer for the use of his picture and printed a copyright line with it. The following year, however, Beach reprinted part of Bolles's photograph as a decorative vignette. (Incredibly, Stieglitz allowed many of his own photographs to be used similarly, as background for initial letters.) Since Bolles was neither paid nor credited, he sued. In December 1894 the management of the Outing Company, which owned *The American Amateur Photographer*, demoted Beach to editor of the magazine's "scientific and society news departments."

The existing copyright law stipulated that if a plaintiff won his suit, he was to be awarded one dollar for each of the magazine's paid subscriptions. In order to charge high advertising rates, Beach had always claimed that

The American Amateur Photographer had fifty thousand subscribers. When the case finally came to trial in the spring of 1895, he hastened to expose his own lie and showed that, in fact, the magazine had only nineteen thousand. Bolles would still have received the then very substantial sum of $19,000. But Stieglitz saved the day on a technicality. He pointed out that Bolles himself had not been in strict compliance, for he had stamped on his print "Copyright, '93. By Bolles, Brooklyn." The law specified that the year had to be given in full and that the photographer's last name alone was not sufficient. The court therefore denied Bolles's suit.[2] Stieglitz was disgusted by the whole episode, but he would remain at the magazine for almost another year.

Within a few weeks of the announcement of his appointment to the editorship of *The American Amateur Photographer*, that new responsibility, together with a serious bout of illness, brought about his liberation from Photochrome. In January 1895, Alfred developed abdominal pains that were diagnosed as a "kidney colic," and he subsequently came down with pneumonia. He had been weakened by depression caused both by his discouragement with Photochrome and his despair over his marriage, which Emmy still had not consented to consummate. When it looked as though Alfred's life was in danger, a frightened and guilt-stricken Emmy pleaded with him to muster the resolve to live, and she promised that she would have intercourse with him as soon as he regained his health. Dr. Leopold Stieglitz brought his brother back to health and then prescribed a recuperative vacation. Alfred and Emmy went to Rockledge, halfway down the eastern coast of Florida. Unfortunately, the state was in the midst of a cold snap. Although Emmy made good on her promise, the fact that "there was ice on the orange blossoms" struck Alfred as appropriately symbolic.[3]

Family and friends advised Alfred to retire from business — from *The American Amateur Photographer* as well as Photochrome — and travel in Europe for a few years with Emmy. Instead, he simply seized the opportunity to abandon the sinking Photochrome, which was losing its few accounts despite the fact that by the beginning of 1895, halftones had almost completely displaced wood engravings in newspapers and magazines thanks to fine screens, coated paper stock, improved inks, and precision-made cylinder presses.

Photochrome was suffering not only from the aftershocks of the panic of 1893 but also from Stieglitz's uncompromisingly high standards. An article in the October 1895 issue of *Anthony's Photographic Bulletin* stated that he was "too modest" about Photochrome's achievements in color printing and reported that "a bit of still life which they show is equal to anything that has been done, and yet Mr. Alfred Stieglitz, the artist of the firm, is seeking effects still higher before permitting them to bear the imprint of his company."[4]

Because of his heavy financial losses in 1893–94, Edward was unable to bail out Photochrome. Having Alfred hold down a job was a luxury he could no longer afford. And so, in March 1895, the thirty-one-year-old partner retired. He would not participate actively in the firm's day-to-day business, but he would retain a voice in shaping its policies and continue to use the firm's address for his professional correspondence.

The announcement of Stieglitz's promotion had assured, or warned, the readers of *The American Amateur Photographer* that "the same independent and fearless course" the magazine had taken since he had begun to work for it would be continued. Eventually, that course proved to be just a bit too independent and fearless.

The September 1894 issue had informed subscribers that they could send in their photographs to have them "candidly and impartially criticised" by Stieglitz.[5] Trouble soon began. In its January 1895 issue the magazine published a letter from a subscriber complaining that the prints he had sent in for constructive criticism and advice were returned to him with a curt note calling them "pictorially valueless." Stieglitz defended himself by stating that at least he had been sincere, whereas most artists would have offered a hypocritical and conciliatory judgment of "very good."

Soon Stieglitz had settled on the formula "Technically perfect, pictorially rotten" to describe the overwhelming majority of the photographs that readers sent him.[6] The president of the Outing Company was not amused when the offended recipients began canceling their subscriptions. With his perennial idealism, Stieglitz argued that such untalented subscribers were best lost anyway and that if the magazine adhered unswervingly to the highest standards in its text and illustrations, circulation would inevitably increase.[7]

Stieglitz made himself unpopular during 1895 not only through his criticism but also through his rôle in ending the joint exhibitions. Furthermore, he hated the petty compromises he was constantly forced to make as editor. Because of all these factors, he was presumably asked to resign. In February 1896 he announced that he had "severed his connection" with *The American Amateur Photographer* and declared, "I shall henceforth devote all my spare time to pictorial photography."[8]

*   *   *

In fact, he would be devoting far more of his time to the politics of pictorial photography than to the actual making of photographs. Specifically, in the spring of 1896, he would be one of the principals who negotiated the merger of the Society of Amateur Photographers and the New York Camera Club, a project that he referred to as "an amalgamation of the dying and the dead."[9]

The SAP was, as Theodore Dreiser reported, "a rather exclusive body" composed chiefly of men and women "who had done interesting things with the camera." He claimed that although it "had artistic talent to compel recognition and position," the SAP "lacked numbers and revenue to give it corporate greatness and importance." That was only partly true. The SAP had many more members than did the Camera Club, but even the former's numbers had declined drastically from a high of about 270 in 1891 to fewer than 200 by 1896. On the other hand, the Camera Club, founded in 1888 by a group of secessionists from the SAP, was primarily for hobbyists, "photographers and would-be photographers, who could lay no claim to achievement but were ambitious to learn." According to Dreiser, who had received his information from Stieglitz, it "had numbers and revenue, but no talent to compel recognition and public esteem."[10] In fact, the Camera Club had only about 90 members in 1896, down from a high of just over 100 in 1893. However, its members tended to be wealthier than those of the SAP.

As far as the Camera Club was concerned, the bloom was off the rose. The hobbyists, as opposed to the serious artistic photographers, were embarrassed by the tremendous popularity of the Kodak, since the snapshooter had become a comic figure. For the club's leisured members, photography had been largely a pretext for outings, smokers, and gentlemanly competitions. Their desire for camaraderie could be satisfied just as well by a cycling organization.

"Photography as a fad is well-nigh on its last legs," wrote Stieglitz late in 1896, "thanks principally to the bicycle craze. Those seriously interested in its advancement do not look upon this state of affairs as a misfortune, but as a disguised blessing, inasmuch as photography had been classed as a sport by nearly all of those who deserted its ranks and fled to the present idol, the bicycle."[11]

Photography and cycling were linked in many minds, not least because the bicycle enabled less than affluent photographers to explore the countryside in search of subjects. (The cornerstone of the Outing Company was its cycling magazine, *Outing.*) As early as 1891 steel mounts were available for attaching a camera to the handlebars of a bicycle in lieu of a tripod; with the advent of faster films, one could even snap while riding along.

Cycling mania was at its peak in 1896. Although the $100 price tag on a good bicycle was high, a horse cost considerably more to buy and far more to maintain. Several million Americans had already purchased bicycles, and some four hundred U.S. manufacturers were turning out more as fast as they could — about two million in 1897 for a population of sixty-five million. Three inventions had sparked this revolution: the development of the modern bicycle, with a diamond-shaped frame and equally sized wheels (1885); the pneumatic tire (1889); and the drop frame for women (mid-1890s).

In 1896 cycling was having a dramatic impact on the American economy and way of life. The sale of books, pianos, and theater tickets plummeted because so many people chose to spend their hours of leisure on a bicycle. Outings on Sunday led to a decline in churchgoing and an increased disregard for injunctions against pleasure on the Sabbath. Prudes warned that cycling would lead women astray, literally and figuratively, but the bicycle became an important symbol, as well as a practical means, of women's liberation. The Gibson girl's bloomers and leg-of-mutton sleeves (Charles Dana Gibson first drew her in 1895) were designed specifically for comfort on a bicycle.

An 1896 editorial in *Scribner's* magazine observed that the bicycle had had a greater impact on the human race than any other invention since the railroad. But a far more momentous invention was already making its appearance. That same year Henry Ford built his first experimental automobile, which he called the Quadricycle because it rode on four bicycle wheels. Three years later he would found the Detroit Automobile Company.

Stieglitz was one of the leaders of the group of dedicated photographers from both clubs who succeeded in merging the Society of Amateur Photographers of New York and the New York Camera Club on May 7, 1896, to form the Camera Club of New York. "Immediately, the combination of talent and numbers prospered," wrote Dreiser. "The membership increased to over three hundred, and the entrance fee and annual dues were doubled. . . . In little more than a year, the club had become one of the wealthiest organizations of the sort in the country."[12] In 1900 the membership of the club reached an all-time high of 344.

Stieglitz was not initially an officer of the reconsolidated club. The first president was Dexter H. Walker, of whom nothing is known; the vice president was the wealthy William D. Murphy, a former president of the old Camera Club and a leading member of the Republican Club. Early in 1897 Stieglitz was considered for the presidency, but he declined in favor of Murphy because the duties were mostly social and diplomatic. He wasn't interested in making after-dinner speeches. He had more important business in mind and felt he could achieve his goals more effectively as vice president. Holding that office, he became the club's virtual dictator. In 1900 Sadakichi Hartmann would write, "Not only during my first visit to the Camera Club but often since, it has seemed to me that artistic photography, the Camera Club, and Alfred Stieglitz were only three names for one and the same thing."[13]

At first the new club occupied the SAP's quarters on West Thirty-eighth Street, but in January 1898 a five-year lease was signed for the top floor of the handsome new eight-story Bancroft Building, at 3–7 West Twenty-ninth Street. On the committee in charge of the move were Stieglitz, Murphy, and Charles I. Berg, the club architect. Stieglitz, Joe Obermeyer, Emilie Clarkson, and William Post were among the members who contributed most to the drive to raise several thousand dollars to convert the empty five-thousand-square-foot space into one of the finest photographic facilities in the world. (Beginning in April 1898, Obermeyer would serve for two years on the club's Publication Committee, headed by Stieglitz, but thereafter he disappeared from the record.) When it was completed, in May, the new headquarters had a loftlike floor plan, divided principally into a large exhibition and lecture room and a huge workroom, off which were numerous darkrooms. Cameras of various sizes, for the members' use, were placed around both rooms. The club's well-stocked library subscribed to all the major international photographic periodicals.

Members on all levels of proficiency benefited from the merger. Dreiser wrote that the "veriest tyro" was "taught concerning the practical and awakened to the artistic," since he found himself "shoulder to shoulder with the leaders of the art, who, after the boasted spirit of the club, are ready to advise and correct; to give of their full and often costly experience to those who stand in need of it."[14]

One of those "leaders of the art" was Stieglitz, who spent most of every day, and many evenings, at the club. The photographer, whom his friends called Al, was a cheerful and helpful presence, though he would occasionally lash out with the sort of criticism that had cost him his job at *The American Amateur Photographer*. In portraits of him dating from this period, one sees a sensitive face with deeply set, piercing dark eyes. A large brush mustache sprouted above what Dreiser described as his "firm mouth, and sharp, forceful chin."[15] Long but carefully combed wavy black hair covered the tips of his ears. In his expressions one could read fire, sadness, disappointment, fatigue, but also a twinkle of mischievousness.

Dreiser evidently first met Stieglitz when he interviewed him for an article published in *Success* magazine's June 1899 issue, where he hyperbolized, "There is one man among the master photographers who so towers above his followers that there is no longer any dispute as to his leadership."[16] A few months later Dreiser expanded his *Success* one-pager into a twelve-page article for *Ainslee's Magazine* about the Camera Club of New York. His interview with Stieglitz marked the beginning of a friendship between the two men, who, however, do not seem to have seen each other very frequently.

Dreiser wrote that Stieglitz had three projects that he hoped to realize through the club. "The first of these is to elevate the standard of pictorial photography in America. The second, to establish an annual exhibition, of a much higher order than anything yet known, giving no awards, but only a certificate of acceptance, which shall be, in itself, a treasure."[17] This exhibition, obviously modeled on the Linked Ring's Photographic Salon, was, of course, to be held annually in New York. Late in 1896 Stieglitz had reported that the club had appointed him "a Committee of One to draw up the general lines for the undertaking."[18]

The third of Stieglitz's goals was by far the most ambitious. He wanted the Camera Club to establish a National Academy of Photography, "endowed as colleges are," and to "open a large and commodious building, where an accepted course of study, with thoroughly competent men as instructors, may be followed." In addition to courses in every scientific and technical aspect of photography, "there should be classes in drawing, composition, design, clay modeling, and even painting, supplemented by a thorough study of the works of the masters old and new."[19] Stieglitz believed that in photography the study of composition "is even more essential, if possible, than in painting, for the photographer, usually working in monochrome, has not the resource of color upon which the painter can draw."[20]

Nor were Stieglitz's goals limited to the three he had enumerated, since he also dreamt that the Camera Club would eventually found a great museum of pictorial photography. All in all, he hoped the club would develop into an institution that would be recognized as "the world center of photography."[21]

CHAPTER TWENTY·ONE

AS FAR AS Stieglitz was concerned, the most important immediate purpose of the Camera Club of New York was to sponsor the world's greatest annual exhibition of artistic photography. He told Dreiser that he wanted to make "the club so large, its labors so distinguished and its authority so final, that [it] may satisfactorily use its great prestige to compel recognition for the individual artists without and within its walls."[1] For the club to become such an artistic beacon and arbiter, to whose exhibitions the world's foremost photographers would hasten to submit their finest work, it would have to publish a magazine setting a new standard of excellence in pictorial photography.

With the experience he had gained as editor of *The American Amateur Photographer*, Stieglitz felt he was the man to produce such a magazine. He therefore made a proposal at a meeting of the Camera Club's trustees in March 1897. After pointing out that the budget allotted $250 each year to publish a "semi-occasional leaflet," an unillustrated newsletter of club proceedings, he said that for no additional cost to the club he could publish a splendid illustrated quarterly, beautifully designed and printed. He would print one thousand copies of each issue and sell subscriptions to outsiders for one dollar a year. (Copies for members would be covered by their dues, without any increase.) He was certain that he could raise another $1,000 every year through the sale of advertising space in the influential magazine, which was to be called *Camera Notes*.

Stieglitz's plan, as he later wrote (referring to himself in the third person),

> readily received the unqualified approbation of all the Trustees. . . .
> As a condition precedent to undertaking this labor of love and en-
> thusiasm, it was stipulated by our Editor that he was to have the un-
> hampered and absolute control of all matters, direct or remote,
> relating to the conduct of the proposed publication; in short, *Camera
> Notes*, while published for the club, was nevertheless an independent
> institution.[2]

Stieglitz was appointed chairman of the Publication Committee and editor of the magazine.

The first issue of *Camera Notes* appeared in July 1897, its green cover embellished with an Art Nouveau sunflower — which, because of its constant turning toward the sun, was the floral symbol of photography. In an average issue about half the articles dealt with individual photographers and aesthetic questions, the rest with scientific and technical matters. Reviews of books and of local, national, and international exhibitions were followed by a sizable section devoted to Camera Club news and, as Stieglitz had hoped, a substantial number of advertisements.

Every issue was illustrated not only with numerous halftones but also with at least two, and usually three or four, meticulously hand-pulled photogravures "representing some important achievement in pictorial photography." In the first issue Stieglitz stated, "The utmost care will be exercised to publish nothing but what is the development of an organic idea, the evolution of an inward principle; a picture rather than a photograph, though photography must be the method of graphic representation."[3] The quality of the gravures — many of which were made by the Photochrome Engraving Company — was to be the finest possible, for they were to constitute, in effect, a monthly exhibition that would reach more than a thousand photographers throughout the world.

Never one to hide his light under a bushel, Stieglitz published eight gravures of his own photographs during his editorship of *Camera Notes* — more than by any other photographer. Among his cronies from the SAP, Rudolf Eickemeyer and William Post were well represented, as were such foreign friends, and fellow Links, as J. Craig Annan, Robert Demachy, and Alfred Horsley Hinton. A wide range of styles was included, from straightforward, purist landscapes to a study of the back of a woman's head by Demachy that could almost pass for a red chalk drawing.

Stieglitz, who was not paid for his work and who made up for the magazine's frequent deficits out of his own pocket, spent long hours in the Camera Club's boardroom, which doubled as the *Camera Notes* office. For the first year and a half, his right-hand man was William M. Murray, a fearlessly outspoken man who supported the editor in his artistic views and his ambitions for the club. Indeed, in the articles he wrote for *Camera Notes*, Murray zealously attacked second-rate photography, thereby offending so many members that after about a year Stieglitz felt compelled to speak out in his defense. "Just criticism," he argued, "is exceedingly healthy for the welfare of the Club. There is much, too much, back-patting in the ranks of photography."[4]

Murray copyedited most of the articles and gave so much "able and unselfish assistance" that when "urgent business obligations" forced him "to sever his connection" with the magazine late in 1898, Stieglitz wondered whether he would be able to continue the publication. "Within the Club," reported one of his colleagues, "he knew of no one in sympathy with the seriousness and purpose of his policy, nor with the ability to help him as he would require."[5]

Stieglitz had, however, recently met a young man named Joseph T. Keiley, whose nine exhibited photographs had impressed him at the Philadelphia salon that fall. Keiley called on him at the Camera Club for advice about some photographic matter and, while there, showed him the manuscript of his very long review of that salon, prepared with all the thoroughness and eloquence of a legal brief. Although Stieglitz was mildly criticized as well as highly praised in the review, he decided to publish it in the January 1899 issue of *Camera Notes* and soon induced Keiley both to join the Camera Club and to help him edit the magazine. At first he did not take over the copyediting. For that Keiley recruited his friend Dallett Fuguet, a tall, bearded poet of French descent who was a desultory photographer. But Fuguet was so exasperated by the state of many of the submitted manuscripts that Stieglitz finally had to switch him to proofreading the galleys, where he proved to be indispensable.

The charming and pixieishly handsome Keiley, a Wall Street lawyer who never married and who lived with his mother and sister in Brooklyn, soon became Stieglitz's closest friend and most valuable ally. By the summer of 1899 Keiley was already so indispensable that he was invited to Lake

George for a working vacation of several weeks' duration. The editor of the British magazine *Photography* wrote that "Keiley was a man of very high ideals, quiet, tactful, unselfish to a most uncommon degree, a loyal friend, a doughty and honourable opponent."[6] And the flamboyant Sadakichi Hartmann wrote to Stieglitz after Keiley's death in 1914: "Brave, narrow minded soul that he was, so impossible from the Bohemian point of view and yet so subtle, pure, and appreciative."[7]

Although Keiley was certainly not a great photographer, or even a very interesting one, Stieglitz called him "an artist of marked individuality," enthusiastically featured his landscapes and portraits in exhibitions and on the printed page, and, in December 1899, saw to it that he was elected a member of the Linked Ring.[8]

In the April 1898 issue of *Camera Notes*, the Publication Committee — which is to say Stieglitz — boasted that

> part of the recent large accession to our club membership may be traced directly to the influence of *Camera Notes*. . . . It is not too much to say that the Camera Club, of New York, stands higher today in the estimation of the photographic world than either of the old organizations prior to consolidation, and this mainly by reason of the general appreciation of the character of its official organ.

But not everyone was enthusiastic. In the issue dated October of that year appeared a letter from Daniel K. Young, an outraged Camera Club member, who wrote,

> A growing and very dangerous Tarantism has inoculated the club, and it appears that nothing is artistic which is not *outré*, nothing beautiful which is not *bizarre*, nothing worthy of attention which is not preposterous, nothing serious unless untranslatable. . . . This fad for muddy, fogged, bombastic, indistinguishable, unguessable monstrosities will soon pass away and we will recognize that a photograph to be artistic need not be hideous. But in the meantime cannot the editors of *Camera Notes* preserve us from them? Their production may be glossed over as mere senile inebriety, but their reproduction is a heinous crime.[9]

Controversy along such lines had become so intense by the middle of the following year that the Publication Committee felt compelled (or perhaps actually was compelled) to publish a disclaimer entitled "Free

Speech," in which it stated that the articles in the magazine did not represent the official opinions of the Camera Club. The committee went on to assure readers, "*Camera Notes* is not only freely open to all topics relating to photography, but . . . it invites and will heartily welcome both original articles and discussion of matters which may appear in its pages."[10] Of such discussion, much of it heated, there would be no shortage from then on.

CHAPTER TWENTY·TWO

∞

THE YEAR 1898 saw the partial realization of one of Stieglitz's most cherished dreams. That fall, in Philadelphia, was held a photographic salon modeled closely on the Linked Ring's and sponsored jointly by the Photographic Society of Philadelphia and the Pennsylvania Academy of the Fine Arts. Stieglitz would, of course, have preferred for the exhibition to be held in New York, but the active participation of the academy, acclaimed as the oldest and most prestigious art institution in the United States, was a powerful argument in favor of Philadelphia.

From the very beginning, he was involved in planning the salon. Robert S. Redfield, a bookseller and talented amateur photographer who had recently been elected president of the Photographic Society of Philadelphia, had long known and admired Stieglitz, who reciprocated the admiration. In their first correspondence about the salon, Redfield assured him that he hoped to meet all the criteria for which the latter had been arguing so forcefully. The salon would be a truly international exhibition devoted entirely to "only such pictures produced by photography as may give distinct evidence of individual artistic feeling and execution."[1] A jury composed entirely of eminent photographers would determine which prints were to be hung, and no medals would be awarded.

However, as Stieglitz later explained, "it was absolutely essential to imbue this first exhibition with an artistic tone so convincing that the public mind could be left in no doubt as to the artistic character of the photographic Salon." That necessity, and probably the insistence of the academy as well, forced the committee to invite two painters who were not themselves photographers to serve on the jury. The five jurors finally chosen were Redfield, Stieglitz, painters William Merritt Chase and Robert William Vonnoh, and illustrator and amateur photographer Alice Barber Stephens. But, Stieglitz would report, "as was anticipated, at the day appointed, Messrs. Chase and Vonnoh failed to put in an appearance, having 'more important duties to perform elsewhere.'"[2]

Fifteen hundred photographs were submitted from all over the world, though both the number and the quality of the entries from abroad were disappointing, and much of the American work was not impressive. The standards of the jury were so high that they "accepted unconditionally only 190 [photographs], placed about 70 in a doubtful class, and rejected the balance, which was about 80 per cent. of the whole," wrote Stieglitz. "After the Jury had finished their labors the Hanging Committee, a separate body altogether — in fact a local committee . . . decided, after some deliberation, not only to exhibit these doubtful works on the walls of the Academy of the Fine Arts, but also to reproduce some of them in the catalogue as illustrations."[3] Stieglitz was furious.

The First Philadelphia Photographic Salon opened on October 24, 1898, in the galleries of the academy's Ruskinian Gothic building. Two hundred fifty-nine pictures by a total of one hundred photographers — seventy-six of them Americans, and seventeen of them women — were hung. One rule stipulated that no more than ten pictures by any one photographer could be exhibited. The only four to achieve that paramount distinction were Stieglitz himself, the seasoned and respected Mathilde Weil, and two brilliant newcomers: Clarence H. White and Gertrude Käsebier. In his review of the salon, Joseph Keiley had high praise for Stieglitz but commented that he had perhaps been so busy politicking that he had neglected the "proper interpretation of his negatives."

The Philadelphia salon of 1898 catapulted several photographers from obscurity to celebrity. One of the most important for Stieglitz was twenty-seven-year-old White, a bookkeeper for a Newark, Ohio, wholesale grocery firm. An autodidact whose knowledge of works of art came mostly from books and magazines at his local public library, White was a sweet and gentle man who adored, and was adored by, his family and neighbors. He and Stieglitz quickly became friends and would long carry on a warm and frequent correspondence. In 1900 Stieglitz successfully sponsored White for membership in the Linked Ring.

A Pre-Raphaelite in small-town Ohio, White photographed his wife, Jane Felix, and her doubly happily named sister Letitia Felix, wearing flowing gowns in sun-dappled apple orchards or posed melancholically, and vaguely erotically, in Arts and Crafts interiors. At first he made very few pictures, since he could afford to buy only two large photographic plates a week. By the end of the 1890s, when he could afford more plates, he would work with his models from sunrise until he had to go to work at 7:00 A.M., and then he would try to get another shot or two in during his lunch hour.

From these unpromising circumstances came many lovely pictures. Influenced by Japanese prints and by Whistler, Chase, and Thomas Dewing, White managed with remarkable success to translate not only their compositional principles but also something of their spirit into photography. His photograph *The Ring Toss* (1899) is certainly a more successful work of art than is the painting Chase had done of the same subject a few years earlier. And yet, if White's photographs affect us today as almost unbearably poignant, it is as much because of the failure of their artistic aspirations as because of their success. As Stieglitz's friend Jerome Mellquist later wrote, White "longed to sing, but he did not always know the notes."[4] Nevertheless, even the most mawkish of his pictures command a respect that is rarely due to similar efforts by his contemporaries.

Gertrude Käsebier was the third newcomer, along with Keiley and White, to emerge from the Philadelphia salon of 1898 as one of Stieglitz's closest friends and colleagues. A sparkling conversationalist with a quick wit, she was also a person of great natural dignity, self-reliant and unconventional. After Käsebier — who was twelve years older than Stieglitz — became a grandmother in July 1900, her friends began calling her Granny. Although she was only forty-eight, the nickname fitted and stuck.

She had been born Gertrude Stanton in 1852 in Fort Des Moines, Iowa, and had spent her childhood in the Colorado Territory. When she was twelve, the Stantons moved to Brooklyn. To make ends meet, Mrs. Stanton took in boarders, one of whom was Eduard Käsebier, a prosperous German shellac importer. On her twenty-second birthday Gertrude married him. They were not happy together, and Gertrude would entitle one of her photographs, of two oxen, *Yoked and Muzzled — Marriage*.

In 1889, by which time her three children were grown, Käsebier enrolled in Brooklyn's Pratt Institute, which had been founded only two years earlier. Specializing in portrait painting, she completed the four-year regular art course and then stayed on for an additional year to study with Arthur Wesley Dow, at that time working closely with Ernest Fenollosa, the great American scholar of Japanese art. Dow would indoctrinate many American artists, including Georgia O'Keeffe, with Japanese principles of composition.

Käsebier, who had made snapshots of her children, became serious about photography as a medium for portraiture, and in 1896 she opened a professional studio close to the headquarters of the Camera Club of New York.[5] Stieglitz's virtual mouthpiece, Charles Caffin, wrote in 1901, "Mrs. Käsebier will tell you that she is a commercial photographer; unquestionably she is an artist."[6] But her artistic claims rested less on her portraits than on her "amateur" allegorical photographs of women and children. In the fall of 1899 *The Manger* was the sensation of the second Philadelphia salon. Shot in a whitewashed stable in Newport, Rhode Island, where she maintained a portrait studio during the summer, it showed a woman dressed luminously in white, with a white veil flowing from her head to the floor, holding what is ostensibly an infant swaddled in white. (There was, in fact, no child inside the swaddling clothes.) That year a print of *The Manger* was sold for $100, more than had previously ever been paid for a pictorial photograph.

Stieglitz was so impressed by Käsebier's work that in 1899 he called her "beyond dispute the leading portrait photographer in this country."[7] In April of that year he published five of her images in *Camera Notes*. He was also instrumental in getting her elected, in October 1900, to the Linked Ring, in which she and the British photographer Carine Cadby, admitted at the same time, were the first women.

That was all very well, but Käsebier's feelings for Stieglitz were considerably stronger than his for her. She wrote to a friend in December 1899, "I think [Stieglitz] is one of the fairest, broadest, finest men I ever knew."[8] More explicitly, she later told her daughter that she had been "perfectly devoted" to Stieglitz and that she had once written on the back of her personal print of a portrait she had made of him, "The only man I ever loved."[9] Alas, Stieglitz probably had no inkling. In any case, he was invariably drawn to women younger than himself.

CHAPTER TWENTY·THREE

AROUND CHRISTMASTIME IN 1897, Alfred and Emmy conceived their first and only child. Alfred probably thought that a baby would provide a focus for Emmy's life, and thus liberate him somewhat from the brunt of her frustrations, while she undoubtedly hoped that having a child would bring her and Alfred closer together.

The misery of his marriage had led him to throw himself totally into his work. In order to spend as little time as possible at home with Emmy, he put in long hours every day at the SAP or, after the spring of 1896, the Camera Club. If he returned home for dinner, it was usually with a group of colleagues who obviated any need for him to talk to his wife. Afterward, the men would shut themselves in Alfred's study to work for the duration of the evening.

One piece of evidence suggests that Emmy's pregnancy did perhaps effect a détente. In his book *Photography as a Fine Art* (1901), Charles Caffin reproduced a photograph by Alfred, dated 1898, which is a profile shot of a handsome, if not beautiful, young woman of evident poise and charm. Looking at this photograph, one's first assumption is likely to be that Alfred was at it again. Surely (while his poor wife was pregnant, no less!) he had gone and fallen in love with this upper-class paragon, his attraction to whom is easily understood. But then one realizes, with a shock, that the woman in the photograph is Emmy. Her huge brown eyes, heavy eyebrows, slightly bulbous-tipped nose, and pronounced chin are unmistakable, though she is wearing her hair in a style that uncharacteristically conceals much of her forehead and her large ears. The profile angle certainly flatters her, but it appears that the happiness of pregnancy may also have brought out her latent beauty.

Alfred printed the image so that Emmy's bust emerges from a cloud of white that covers the bottom third of the picture, making it look like an unfinished painted portrait. He had apparently posed his wife in profile to record her bulging abdomen, and although he might perhaps have been prepared to exhibit or publish a photograph of her in "a delicate condition," she would certainly never have allowed any such transgression of middle-class gentility.

After a few weeks at Oaklawn during August 1898, Alfred and Emmy returned to New York to move into their new apartment at 1111 Madison Avenue, between Eighty-third and Eighty-fourth streets. The full-time staff in this rather grand establishment, the couple's first real home, would include a cook, a chambermaid, and a governess. (In the near future Edward Stieglitz's financial reverses would force him and Hedwig to sell their house on East Sixtieth Street and move to an apartment in the Majestic Hotel, on Central Park West.)

Alfred and Emmy's daughter, Katherine (nicknamed Kitty), was born on September 27. Almost at once, Alfred began to photograph her. First he snapped while she was held by her mother. Later he chronicled her excursions outdoors, focusing especially, as he told Nancy Newhall, on "her moments of delight and discovery."[1] Although that sort of documentation has become irksomely universal, Charles Caffin praised "both the originality of the idea and the methodic completeness" of Stieglitz's series, which was entitled *The Photographic Journal of a Baby*. Stieglitz exhibited and published many of these photographs, both singly and as a series, but he did not regard them as *pictures*. "They are simply studies of baby life," related Caffin, "artless, lovable incidents that had been watched and noted many a time before they were permanently recorded."[2] They also demonstrate that Alfred, in spite of himself, was a doting and adoring father — though perhaps one who felt most comfortable when there was a camera between him and his child.

He later said that he was fascinated by the idea of a photographic record of an entire life, which would constitute the richest possible cumulative portrait — the only really adequate portrait of a human being. (We can only wonder how the New York debut of motion pictures in 1896 may have influenced his thinking about sequences of images.) He blamed Emmy for putting an end to his hope of making such a document of his daughter's life. When he became obsessive about photographing Kitty, insisting that she remain still until he could record a cute gesture or incident, Emmy justifiably complained that "he was spoiling the child's fun and making her self-conscious."[3] He nonetheless continued intermittently until about the time he founded *Camera Work*, late in 1902. Kitty remained an occasional subject for his camera for a few more years, after which she disappeared from his work.

In his memoirs Edward Steichen recounted that after he returned from Paris in 1902 he often dined at the Stieglitz apartment. On those occasions, he wrote, Emmy "was all cordiality and always urged me to come back soon."[4] That directly contradicts Stieglitz's own insistence that Emmy scorned his photographer friends as riffraff and was inhospitable to them.

But in his description of the pictures hanging on the wall of the Stieglitz apartment, Steichen unintentionally provided a clue to how bad Alfred and Emmy's marriage was by 1902 — the bond of childbearing having clearly frayed by then. Among the pictures in the living room were large reproductions of two recent paintings by Franz von Stuck, a founder of the Munich Secession. One, entitled *Sin*, depicts Eve as a temptress, her seductive face in dark shadow and her nude torso highlighted, as an enormous snake slithers up her body.[5] In the second Stuck painting, *The Kiss of the Sphinx*, the full-breasted creature of the title is sinking a bloody claw into the back of the kneeling, naked man whom she is embracing.[6] A third reproduction hanging in that room was one of the five versions of Swiss painter Arnold Böcklin's extremely popular *Island of the Dead*, which shows a coffin being ferried to an island into whose cliffs, surrounding a grove of immense cypresses, vaults have been carved.

Steichen was puzzled by the discrepancy between the heavy-handed fin de siècle eroticism and Symbolism of these works and the naturalistic spareness of his host's own photographs. One of Stieglitz's virtues as a publisher and impresario was that his tastes and interests were by no means limited to work that resembled his own. However, he presumably chose the reproductions to hang in his apartment not because of their style, but because of their subject matter. This becomes clear when we consider the three other pictures that Steichen remembered seeing there. One was a reproduction of a portrait of Eleonora Duse by Franz von Lenbach in which the actress is holding the artist's child. Another, hanging in the bedroom, was "a very handsome photograph of a nude torso by Rubens," most likely the magnificent painting of his wife Hélène Fourment in a fur robe, which had made a powerful impression on eighteen-year-old Alfred in Vienna in 1882. (Though the figure is full-length, it is easy to understand why Steichen would have remembered only the buxom torso.) Finally, the "place of honor" was occupied by a large, "handsomely framed" print of Alfred's photograph *The Net Mender*. These three works represent Alfred's ideal women — in pointed contrast to Emmy. (A self-portrait shows Alfred seated beside a framed print of *The Net Mender*, exactly as many nineteenth-century photographic portraits included a framed portrait of a departed loved one.[7]) To hang those three pictures on the walls of his home — where they would taunt his wife, who must have intuited their significance — was nothing short of sadistic.

In that light, by hanging the two Stuck paintings Alfred was vicariously uttering anguished and defiant cries of sexual frustration. Trapped in what he clearly viewed as a claustrophobic nightmare of a marriage, he must have felt as though he were being strangled and mauled, like the sphinx's victim. Every attractive woman he saw was an Eve, a seductress, tempting him to sin. Even the Böcklin was probably chosen to reflect his feelings of being dead in his marriage. One can easily imagine Alfred, whose humor could be mordantly sarcastic, referring to his apartment as the Island of the Dead.

CHAPTER TWENTY·FOUR

DESPITE THE SUCCESS of the 1898 Philadelphia salon, Stieglitz was very discouraged about the lack of progress in American pictorial photography. The specific cause of his disappointment was the slowness of Americans to experiment with gum-bichromate printing, which was, so he reported in the October 1898 issue of *Camera Notes*, "all the rage in continental Europe," especially in Paris and Vienna.[1] The use of this form of printing had led to the emergence of "a new school of pictorial photography, tearing itself away from the accepted conventionalities and bringing out individualism wherever possible."[2]

On the other hand, complained Stieglitz, in some quarters conventional platinum and carbon prints, regardless of their actual merit, were being "generally decried as weak and ordinary" in comparison with gum prints. He felt compelled to state, therefore, that "while granting that pictures produced by the gum process may be exceedingly beautiful, and oftentimes possess a charm not obtainable by any other photographic printing process, yet a print produced by that interesting and novel printing method is not *necessarily* a picture. . . . We contend that a real picture remains one whether produced in carbon, platinum, or gum."[3]

Gum printing had Stieglitz in a real tizzy. It was not in accord with his personal aesthetic, but he hoped that gum prints would perhaps finally induce the public to recognize photography as a fine art. Once a foot was in the door of the sacred precincts, and as the increasingly sophisticated public came to understand that the manipulations in gum printing were only exaggerations of what purists did in the darkroom, then "straight" photography would also be accepted as art.

Gum printing did have certain undeniable advantages for the photographer who aspired to be seen as an artist. "He can supply, correct, or eliminate," wrote Stieglitz; "he can even introduce color or such combinations of color by means of successive printings — similar to those resorted to in lithography — as to produce almost any effect that his taste, skill, and knowledge may dictate."[4] Picking up that line of argument, Theodore Dreiser gushed that "it is at this point in his progress that the photographer, *per se*, kicked off his chrysalis, and became a real live artist with silken wings and a chance to get glory."[5]

Not everyone was so enthusiastic. One bitter attack was written in 1897 by Joseph Pennell, an expatriate American etcher who was Whistler's disciple and later his biographer. "The art of the photographer, as now explained, is to make his photographs look as much like something they are not as he can," he sneered. "The man who sells margarine for butter, and chalk and water for milk, does much the same, and renders himself liable to legal prosecution by doing it."[6]

However ambivalent Stieglitz may have been about the aesthetics of gum printing, he was, as an inveterate experimenter, very interested in the process from a scientific point of view. His one-man exhibition at the Camera Club, in May 1899, included some gum prints as well as platinum and carbon prints, photogravures, and a number of works in another manipulative process, glycerine-platinum, which was brought to his attention by Joseph Keiley.[7] For nearly two years, Stieglitz and Keiley collaborated on experiments to refine this process. By brushing on solutions of developer and glycerine, in varying proportions, one could intensify or arrest the development of any area of a platinum print. It was by means of glycerine-platinum printing that Alfred had eliminated from his 1898 portrait of Emmy all trace of her pregnancy.

Regarding the glycerine process, Charles Caffin wondered about "the difference between its use by the straight photographer and the other one — I cannot call him 'crooked' — who claims unrestricted liberty of action. The former only *modifies* the result; the latter reserves the right to *alter* it."[8] Although Stieglitz occasionally crossed the line between modification and alteration, Caffin wrote in 1901 that he was by conviction and instinct an exponent of the "straight photograph;" working chiefly in the open air, with rapid exposure; leaving his models to pose themselves, and relying for results upon means strictly photographic. He is to be counted among the Impressionists; fully conceiving his picture before he attempts to take it, seeking for effects of vivid actuality, and reducing the final record to its simplest terms of expression.[9]

When Dreiser once asked Stieglitz, "In a word, what is the secret of serious pictorial photography?" he replied, "Individualism, working out the beauty of a picture as you see it, unhampered by conventionality."[10] Enthusiastically summing up Stieglitz's photographic work during this period, Dreiser wrote, "No man has done subjects more widely apart in conception and feeling, and none has done better. . . . If he has one desire it is to do new things — not in an erratic way, but only new as showing to all the sentiment and tender beauty in subjects previously thought to be devoid of charm."[11]

During the late 1890s and the first years of the new century, Stieglitz concentrated primarily on pictures of New York and on portraiture. In 1901 Caffin wrote, "No picture has secured its author more deserved reputation than the *Portrait of Mr. R.*"[12] The subject of this intense three-quarter-length portrait, dating from 1895, was Anson Davies Fitz Randolph (1820–1896), whose modest cottage was near the Stieglitz house at Lake George. The widely revered Randolph, a New York bookseller who specialized in religious and theological works, was best known for his devotional and patriotic verse. Stieglitz had long admired Randolph's balance of sweetness and dignity, but whenever he persuaded him to step in front of the camera, the old man became hopelessly self-conscious. So Stieglitz decided to try a trick. One day he took Randolph on a stroll around the grounds of Oaklawn until they arrived at the spot where he had set up his camera. He then offhandedly asked Randolph to stand in front of it for a moment while he checked its placement for a figure study he was planning. As soon as the unsuspecting and thus completely relaxed Randolph complied, Stieglitz squeezed the rubber shutter-release bulb he had hidden in his pocket. The result, in which the subject's face and hands are dramatically highlighted against the featureless dark background and against his black frock coat, in the style of the French painter Léon Bonnat, is the equal of any daguerreotype by the great American portraitists Albert Southworth and Josiah Johnson Hawes.

*   *   *

In the fall of 1896 *The Amateur Photographer* published a two-part article by British photographer Paul Martin entitled "Around London by Gaslight." Reading of Martin's experiences and techniques led Stieglitz to become preoccupied with night photography, which posed the sort of technical challenges he loved.[13] His nocturnal photographs of New York reflect his continued interest in city streets under adverse weather conditions. *An Icy Night*, for instance, was made in January 1898, about one o'clock in the morning, after a few inches of snow had fallen. Standing at Fifth Avenue and Sixty-third Street, on the sidewalk beside the wall of Central Park, Stieglitz photographed the bare, overarching trees; the two in the foreground, illuminated by the harsh light of a street lamp, look especially, as he noted, "like specters."[14] It is a haunting, unearthly picture — but also a slightly embarrassing one, for the sharp focus of the trees (despite a three-minute exposure) contradicts Stieglitz's claim that a gale was blowing at the time. Perhaps the fact that he was still recuperating from a recent bout of pneumonia made the night seem wilder to him than it really was.

Just after New Year's Day — his thirty-fourth birthday — Alfred had come down with pneumonia. When it became clear that he needed intensive care, his brother Lee, by then established as one of the foremost physicians in New York, insisted that the patient and Emmy move into the third floor of his new brownstone house at 60 East Sixty-fifth Street. (Although maintaining a general practice, Lee was a qualified neurologist and published a number of papers in medical journals.) Alfred loved to tell — and no doubt to embroider — the story of how he had tiptoed out in the middle of the night to shoot *An Icy Night*, horrifying and outraging his wife and brother when they later learned what he had done. He wanted the world to know that he certainly wasn't one to let a trifle like pneumonia stop him from making a great photograph.

Several of Stieglitz's most beautiful night photographs were shot from Manhattan's Grand Army Plaza, at Fifth Avenue and Fifty-ninth Street, looking across the wet pavement of the avenue to the Savoy Hotel, where he and Emmy had been living. Tinted yellow to approximate the effect of incandescent light, the prints of such pictures are gentle, romantic, and rather melancholy nocturnes. But Stieglitz wrote that night photographs "are best reproduced by means of lantern slides, for by this method only is it possible to preserve the luminosity of the original scene. Prints are always more or less disappointing, and process reproductions still more so."[15]

Stieglitz nevertheless maintained his hope to publish an ambitious collection of fifty or one hundred of his photographs of New York. In 1898 he issued a portfolio of twelve photogravures entitled *Picturesque Bits of New York and Other Studies*, but it contained only three New York views: *Winter — Fifth Avenue* and two nocturnal pictures of the Savoy. The other images had all been made in Europe.

Most of the photographs Stieglitz made during the next several years were intended for his documentation of New York in transition. One, the Dreiserian *Hand of Man* (1902), shows a steam-belching locomotive approaching across the grim expanses of a railroad yard. In this picture, which Stieglitz said was meant to demonstrate the "pictorial possibilities of the commonplace," the tracks seem to outline the fingers of a great hand reaching forward.[16] Another photograph depicts the entrance to one of New York's first subway stations, outside City Hall, about 1904. Yet another — a pale, delicate urban snow scene dominated by a magnificent tree — is the first of hundreds of photographs that Stieglitz would shoot from the windows of his various New York homes and galleries.

Spring Showers (1900) is a very Japanese composition, playing with the kind of scale-distorting juxtaposition used so effectively by Hiroshige. Cropped to a tall, narrow, vertical format, it shows a street sweeper in the middle ground who seems dwarfed by the foreground sapling and its protective iron cage. The photographer was standing in Madison Square Park, looking down Fifth Avenue; one can barely make out, on the right, the tall cupolaed building that still stands at Twenty-second Street and, on the left, the old Erie Railroad office at Twenty-third. The picture was prescient, for the iron cage anticipates the steel structure of the Fuller Building (nicknamed the Flatiron because of its resemblance to that implement), which would, in 1901, begin to rise on the site of the Erie office. Alfred was fascinated by the construction and, as the great building went up, greatly admired "the seeming simplicity of that, to me, amazing structure, the lightness of the structure, combined with solidity."[17] Oddly, he later said that it had never occurred to him to document that steel skeleton.

He didn't photograph the Flatiron Building until the winter of 1902–3, by which time construction had been completed. As he stood in Madison Square Park one day after a snowstorm, the building — whose twenty stories rose far above the trees in the middle distance — looked to him "as if it were moving toward me like the bow of a monster ocean steamer, a picture of the new America which was in the making."[18] Over the course of the next few days he photographed the building in various lights. The most famous of the resulting images he cropped to a narrow vertical to match its companion, *Spring Showers*. The Hiroshige-like forked tree that soars in the foreground of the Flatiron picture not only represents the triangular plan of the building but also echoes the delicate tree in the companion picture. Together, the two photographs compose Stieglitz's most beautiful before-and-after study of New York in transition.

When Edward asked his son why he would photograph such an ugly building, Alfred replied, "It is to America what the Parthenon was to Greece." He even announced that when he died, he would like to have his ashes cast into the wind from the top of the Flatiron. Alfred was pleased with his picture and published it, along with both an article and a poem by Sadakichi Hartmann celebrating the building, in the October 1903 issue of *Camera Work*, which featured Frederick H. Evans's photographs of cathedrals. Stieglitz conceded, however, that when he saw the Flatiron in later years, it "did seem rather ugly and unattractive to me. There was a certain gloom about it."[19]

CHAPTER TWENTY·FIVE

BY THE SPRING OF 1900 grievances against *Camera Notes* had become widespread, and the vociferous condemnation from conservative quarters now extended to all of Stieglitz's activities within the Camera Club. Many members accused Stieglitz of being egotistical, undemocratic, cliquish, and high-handed, if not downright despotic. Every complaint only made him all the more determined to shame the club into renouncing its philistinism. He simply could not comprehend the members' perverse resistance to his efforts to enlighten them and lead them on to artistic glory.

Beyond the membership of the Camera Club, criticism of Stieglitz became pointed in the wake of an article that Joseph Keiley wrote for the 1899 edition of the British annual *Photograms of the Year*. Critic Osborne I. Yellott groused that Keiley "had claimed that *Camera Notes* and the small band referred to as the 'New School' had alone and unaided accomplished the advancement of artistic photography in America."[1] The editors of a number of conservative American photographic magazines — including *The Photo-American*, *The Photo-Era* (which Stieglitz liked to lampoon as the "Photo Error"), and *The Photo-Beacon* — resented Keiley's version because they felt they had played an important role in popularizing pictorial photography. The most embarrassing expression of their pique was "The Keely [*sic*] Cure; or, How It Came to be Written, a Comedy in Two Acts," a spoof on Keiley and Stieglitz signed pseudonymously by A. Smiler (in fact, Yellott) and published in *The Photo-American* in the spring of 1900.[2]

On April 10 Stieglitz had been reelected vice president of the Camera Club, but at the regular club meeting on May 8, "the President announced with regret, on behalf of the Trustees, that, on account of the many demands on his time, and the condition of his health, Mr. Stieglitz had felt it incumbent upon him to tender his resignation" from his office.[3] The claim of illness was not entirely trumped up, for Alfred had worked and worried himself into one of his periodic bouts of nervous prostration.

He was distraught not only about the Camera Club brouhaha but also about the dénouement of his assignment from the U.S. government to select pictorial photographs for the international exposition in Paris in 1900. He had begun by demanding the submission of all photographs to the American fine art jury "to be passed on like the paintings, sculpture, etc., and if any one or more of the photographs be considered of sufficient merit, that the same be hung in the Fine Arts Palace. Those not accepted would be sent to the Liberal Arts Building."[4] Since his demand was rejected, Stieglitz refused to assemble an exhibition. In a state of collapse, he was even forced to relinquish his prized appointment as the American delegate to the international congress of photographers to be held in Paris late that spring.[5]

Many members had expressed outrage over the Stieglitz-sponsored exhibition of Frank Eugene's work at the Camera Club in November 1899. In the eyes of the club's rank and file, Eugene's work was the worst ever, perhaps even the worst possible. His most serious offense was that he often roughly scratched cross-hatching or crude shading directly onto his negatives, thereby causing the printed images to be partly obscured by black lines. Stieglitz was interested in Eugene's work because he hoped that an accomplished painter's highly original use of photography as a medium of personal expression might finally convince the public that photographs could be works of art.

Born in New York in 1865, Frank Eugene Smith (he dropped his inartistic surname) had studied painting in Munich during the 1880s and then returned to New York, where he specialized in oil portraits of actors and actresses and began to experiment with the camera. After their first meeting Stieglitz referred to him as "the sloppy fellow with the black finger nails" and said "I don't want him to come to my house," but once he had seen Eugene's photographs and had shared memories of Munich with him, they quickly became close friends.[6] The tenor of their friendship, which would last for many years, is reflected in the title of a portrait that

Eugene made late in 1899: "Alfred Stieglitz Esquire. Photographer and Truthseeker."

It was in 1900 that the foundation was laid for an even more important friendship, that with Eduard Jean (later simply Edward) Steichen, the greatest of the Pictorialists and one of the most outstanding artists in the entire history of photography. Twenty-one years old in 1900, he was six feet tall and bore a striking resemblance to the young Abraham Lincoln. Sadakichi Hartmann spoke of Steichen's "square shoulders, his pallid, angular face, his dark, disheveled hair, his steady eyes" and observed that he reminded one at times of a Stoic or a visionary and at others of a gallant eighteenth-century artist.[7] Although he often gave the impression of being taciturn and brooding, Steichen was an ambitious man who spoke trenchantly and acted decisively. He was strong and lean, had exceptionally large hands, ate ravenously, needed little sleep, and worked long hours day and night.

In 1881, when he was two, Steichen's parents had emigrated from Luxembourg to the United States. Unable to find work in Chicago, Jean Pierre Steichen had in desperation become a copper miner in Hancock, Michigan, an insalubrious job for this rather frail man, whose own father had been a moderately prosperous landowner. When Jean Pierre's health gave out, he was forced to accept a low-paying position in a local department store. His hardworking wife, Marie, supplemented the family income by making dresses and trimming hats. In 1889 the family moved to Milwaukee, where Marie established a profitable millinery shop.

Having shown talent in drawing, Eduard left school at age fifteen and began a four-year apprenticeship at the American Fine Art Company, a Milwaukee lithography firm that specialized in advertising and commercial design. Since he aspired, however, to become a *real* artist — a painter — he organized a group of his artistic friends and co-workers to form the Milwaukee Art Students League. By pooling their resources, they were able to hire models and engage professional artists to teach them.

Steichen bought his first camera, a second-hand Kodak, when he was sixteen. Discouraged because only one of his first fifty pictures came out, he never shot another roll with it. Instead, he traded it in for a 4 x 5-inch bellows camera that he needed for making photographs on which to base advertisement drawings. Once he had mastered that camera, the relentlessly enterprising Steichen began showing up at all sorts of meetings and functions to photograph the participants, selling the pictures to his subjects for a dollar a dozen.

The romantic young artist, who loved the mysterious and moody qualities of the woods at twilight, on overcast or rainy days, and in the moonlight, soon began to imitate Whistler's work in his watercolors and photographs. To obtain the effects that he sought, he would sometimes shake his tripod during an exposure or sprinkle drops of water onto his lens. Some of these early landscapes are so dark and murky that they were nearly impossible to reproduce.

In the fall of 1899 Steichen submitted to the second Philadelphia salon his two pictures that were most unlike anything he had seen in the photographic magazines. His strategy worked, for both were accepted and hung.

The previous year he had read an article by Robert Demachy explaining the technique of gum-bichromate printing. The process appealed to Steichen because the materials were inexpensive and because it gave him a semi-painterly control over his printing. He sent ten gum prints to the First Chicago Photographic Salon, held in April 1900, for which Stieglitz, Keiley, and Clarence White traveled to Chicago to serve on the jury. White was extremely impressed by Steichen's work, but Keiley — whose position as Stieglitz's right-hand man would soon be threatened by Steichen — was less so.

After the end of his apprenticeship in 1896, Steichen stayed on at the American Fine Art Company, where his talent and dedication were rewarded with a very generous salary of $50 a week. By the spring of 1900 he had saved enough to quit his job and study painting in Paris for a year or two.

When the twenty-one-year-old Steichen arrived at the Camera Club one day early in May 1900, on his way to France, Stieglitz was busy hanging an exhibition of members' work, but he stopped what he was doing and spent more than an hour looking at Steichen's photographs and paintings. Stieglitz, touched by the young man's optimism, was also quite impressed by his work. Here at last, he felt, was someone whose photographic talent was equaled by his ability as a painter. Steichen was to be the messiah for whom the less gifted Frank Eugene had been John the Baptist. By way of encouragement, Stieglitz bought three photographs for five dollars apiece and apologized to the amazed and delighted Steichen, "I am robbing you, at that."

When the young photographer was ready to leave, they walked together to the elevator. Just as Steichen stepped in, Stieglitz asked him whether, now that he was going to Paris to become a great painter, he would abandon photography. Through the closed doors of the already descending elevator Steichen shouted, "Never! I shall use the camera as long as I live; for it can say things that cannot be said in any other medium," or at least words to that effect.[8] Stieglitz told Sadakichi Hartmann that Steichen had "taken up artistic photography as another painter might take up lithography or etching."[9] That evening Stieglitz announced to his wife, "I think I've found my man."[10]

In Paris, Steichen conceived a project that would unite his interests in painting, sculpture, literature, music, and photography: a series of photographic portraits of the figures he most admired in those fields. He set out to be the Mathew Brady of art — to produce a collection of portraits, "present the series of enlargements to a big museum, and publish the same in book form." It would, he said, be his lifework.

Steichen was a brilliant portraitist, and his portraits may well be the greatest of all Pictorialist photographs. Having always dreamt of becoming an actor, he brought to his work an extraordinary sense of drama, character, lighting, expression, and pose. During his two years in Paris, he photographed many artists, including painters George Frederick Watts, Alphonse Mucha, Franz von Lenbach, and Franz von Stuck. In 1898 Stieglitz had told Hartmann that (despite the reproductions hanging in his apartment) his favorite painters were not Stuck but the conservative, decorative *pasticheur* of Impressionism Albert Besnard (whom Steichen also photographed) and Frits Thaulow, a Norwegian Impressionist who had studied in Karlsruhe during the 1880s and whose work Stieglitz may have encountered through Wilhelm Hasemann.

Steichen's most momentous encounter, in 1901, was with Auguste Rodin, to whom he was introduced by Thaulow. Steichen visited Rodin's studio almost every Saturday for an entire year before venturing to photograph the master, who was at that time perhaps the most widely revered artist in the world. The greatest of the resulting portraits — which shows a silhouetted Rodin contemplating his sculpture *The Thinker* while a marble Victor Hugo, glowing in the background of the murky image, seems to contemplate Rodin — was a combination print, à la Robinson, made from two negatives. Hartmann wrote of the portrait, "It can not be improved upon. . . . A medium, so rich and so complete, one in which such a masterpiece can be achieved, the world can no longer ignore. The battle is won!"[11]

Alas, not quite. In March 1902 Steichen successfully submitted to the Salon de la Nationale, also known as the Salon du Champs de Mars, one painting, six charcoal drawings, and ten photographs — gum prints and ozotypes.[12] There was much excitement in New York when the news arrived that for the first time ever a salon jury had admitted photographs. The story even made it into the *New York Herald.*[13] Stieglitz, elated, exulted that "the approval of a body of such known talents . . . must put a stop forever to the sneer of those not willing to give certain photographic pictures rank as works of art."[14] Imagine the disappointment, then, when word followed that "notwithstanding acceptance by the Jury, jealousies and political intrigue within the salon itself proved powerful enough to prevent the hanging of photographs."[15] It turned out that Steichen had called his photographs prints, and they had been accepted as such. When members of the jury subsequently learned the truth, they forbade the hanging of the impostors.

CHAPTER TWENTY·SIX

F. HOLLAND DAY (the *F* stood for Fred, not Frederick) was one of the most colorful characters among the "progressive" photographers around the turn of the century. The same age as Stieglitz, this wealthy Bostonian was dismissed by some critics as a self-indulgent aesthete, a self-styled Decadent with a taste for flowing Turkish robes, Oriental art, incense, and candles. Indeed, Day — a thin man whose foxlike features were accentuated by a scraggly beard and a pince-nez and whose long, thin fingers were habitually adorned with rings — was a dandy who loved exotic costumes and the occult.

But there was a great deal more to him. During the 1890s his publishing house, Copeland and Day, issued an impressive list of titles, many of the volumes inspired by the designs of William Morris's Kelmscott Press. In 1895 the firm issued not only Stephen Crane's first book of poems but also the first American edition of Oscar Wilde's *Salomé*, albeit with Pan's genitals deleted from Aubrey Beardsley's illustration on the title page

Moreover, Day was a serious and highly accomplished photographer — though few of his pictures other than his most straightforward portraits will appeal to the modern viewer who lacks a taste for camp. His woodland studies of naked young boys holding lyres or caressing herms are the homosexual, soft-focus counterparts of the female nudes turned out by bad academic painters and photographers throughout the nineteenth century.

His photographs of his black chauffeur decked out in pseudo-African costumes are embarrassing, but his more direct nude and portrait studies of the man are quite sensitive and beautiful. Day's most egregious photographs, however, are those in which he himself acted the role of Jesus on the cross.

Nevertheless, in January 1896 Day became the third American elected to the Linked Ring. Stieglitz reproduced the work of his fellow Link in *Camera Notes* in 1897 and gave him a one-man show at the Camera Club the following year. It seemed as though Stieglitz had found a valuable ally, since the two men were equally adamant in their determination to create an American equivalent of the Linked Ring.

In 1899 Day retired from his publishing firm to devote himself to photography. Throughout that year he tried to persuade Stieglitz to help him organize an "American Association of Artistic Photography." The problem was that Day wanted its headquarters to be located in his beloved Boston. He wrote to Stieglitz that although he had many friends in New York, he had "never found a place in the world I dislike more."[1] What's more, Boston could offer something that New York could not: affiliation with a great art museum. A close friend of Day's was Sarah Sears — Mrs. J. Montgomery Sears, as in Sears, Roebuck — a talented amateur photographer and watercolorist as well as one of the leading Bostonian collectors of contemporary French art. Mrs. Sears, whose portrait was painted by Sargent that year, had used her very considerable influence to get the Museum of Fine Arts to agree to sponsor the organization and to mount its exhibitions if Stieglitz were in charge. Day even offered to put Stieglitz up whenever the association's business might bring him to Boston. None of that was sufficient incentive for Stieglitz to abandon his hopes for New York as the photographic center of the world.

Day implored, flattered, and cajoled, writing at one point, "I would sooner think of flying than undertake a photographic movement which you would refuse to head in the fullest possible way."[2] But Day was soon thinking of flying. He had told Stieglitz that he wanted to take action to force the condescending Europeans to acknowledge the greatness that American photography had achieved. Since Stieglitz showed no interest in cooperating, Day decided to act on his own. Early in 1900 he wrote to many of the outstanding American photographers and asked them to send him work for an exhibition that he was planning to mount in London and Paris. Stieglitz declined to send any prints and advised his friends to do the same. This time, however, many ignored him, for Day had two very devoted supporters in Gertrude Käsebier and Clarence White. Nothing more eloquently testifies to Day's true sweetness of soul than these friend-ships, which would endure for decades, long after all three had broken with Stieglitz.

On April 14, 1900, Day sailed from New York for Europe, having assembled a collection of about 150 prints. Stieglitz was quite annoyed that Day had canceled their appointment to meet the day before he sailed.[3] There matters rested until July, when Alfred Horsley Hinton wrote Stieglitz to tell him that the Linked Ring was planning to include Day's collection in its salon as a separate, unjuried section. Stieglitz immediately cabled Hinton not to make any commitment before receiving the letter he was sending at once. Stieglitz, who had not seen Day's collection but who had presumably discussed the issue with some of the contributors, mali-ciously claimed in his letter that it consisted mostly of second-rate prints and did not fully represent the diversity of the best American photogra-phy.[4]

Steichen later countered that the prints were first-rate, but the second half of Stieglitz's charge was true — for no exhibition of American pho-tographs from which his own were missing could be said to be truly repre-sentative. Day's collection, in which there was a far greater proportion of portraits and figure studies than would usually be seen in British and Continental exhibitions of the time, strongly emphasized evocative, anti-naturalistic, soft-focus work influenced by Whistler, Japanese prints, the Pre-Raphaelites, and the Symbolists. A critic for the *Amateur Photographer* would write of the photographs, "Most of them are indefinite and elusive in character; the mere suggestion of forms and textures leaves a great deal for the imagination, yet the delicacy of treatment, the selection, the com-position, in most cases denote intense feeling."[5]

Perhaps Stieglitz was worried that in a preponderance of such company his own sharply focused, naturalistic, and straightforwardly composed work might look old-fashioned. There would not even be Stieglitz pho-tographs in the Linked Ring salon or the Royal Photographic Society's an-nual exhibition for the sake of comparison. As a note in the September 21 issue of *The Amateur Photographer* explained, "Mr. Stieglitz, through ill-health and preoccupation, has been unable to do anything this year to keep up the succession of interesting works which his hand has produced."[6] The Day affair had literally made him sick.

Stieglitz's criticisms persuaded the Linked Ring not to show Day's col-lection. But Day was not to be deterred. He headed straight for the rival Royal Photographic Society, which agreed to hang the exhibition.

In September, Steichen went to London in hope of having some of his photographs included in the upcoming Linked Ring salon and RPS annual show. Day was so excited when he saw his work that he decided to include twenty-one Steichen prints in his exhibition. Only White, Käsebier, and Day himself would be represented by more. Steichen, who had a great flair for design, remained in London to help with the hanging.

On October 10, 1900, "an exhibition of prints by the New School of American Photography, supplemented by an additional collection of one hundred examples of the work of F. Holland Day, of Boston, U.S.A.," opened at the RPS galleries on Russell Square. Within the British photographic community it sparked the most impassioned controversy since the publication of Emerson's *Naturalistic Photography* and its retraction. The rage in some quarters was aggravated by the fact that nearly a third of the prints in that year's Linked Ring salon were by Americans. Thomas Bedding, the editor of *The British Journal of Photography*, ranted that Day's exhibition was a collection of "deplorable travesties of photographic work which a handful of American photographers, encouraged by the adulatory writings of neurotic 'appreciators,' were deceived into believing were 'artistic' or 'pictorial.'"[7] Among the chief of these "appreciators" was Sadakichi Hartmann, who had written earlier that year that one of Day's portraits was "a plastic psychological synthesis of the person represented."[8] Day's opponents now seized upon that phrase and adopted "plastic psychological fiddlesticks" as their battle cry.

Stieglitz and Day were struggling not only over the question of who should be the primate of American photography but also over the loyalty of Steichen. As if it weren't bad enough for Day to challenge Stieglitz as a roving ambassador, the Bostonian was also alienating the affections of Stieglitz's prime protégé. Steichen was flattered by Day's attentions, and his fleeting acquaintance with the far-off Stieglitz was soon supplanted by a warm in situ friendship with Day. When Day took an abridged version of his exhibition to Paris early in 1901, Steichen invited him to share his studio on the boulevard du Montparnasse. The younger man, whose representation in the show was increased to thirty-five prints, painted a portrait of Day that was hung prominently in the Salon de la Nationale the following spring.

Throughout his European trip, Day was accompanied by his distant cousin and fellow Bostonian Alvin Langdon Coburn and Alvin's mother, Fannie. Coburn — eighteen years old, three years younger than Steichen — was already such a proficient photographer that Day included nine of his prints in the London and Paris exhibitions.

Auspiciously, one of Coburn's seventeenth-century ancestors, Edward Colburn, had, before immigrating to America, lived in the Wiltshire village of Lacock — where, in the 1830s, William Henry Fox Talbot would invent the negative-positive form of photography. Alvin's father, who had made a modest fortune manufacturing shirts, died when the boy was seven. Receiving a Kodak as a gift on his eighth birthday, Alvin quickly became an enthusiastic amateur. The course of his life was determined when, in 1898, he first met Day, who encouraged and instructed him.

In his autobiography Coburn wrote, "My mother was a remarkable woman of very strong character, who tried to dominate my life. . . . It was a battle royal all the days of our life together."[9] Nor did she battle only her son, for whom she was extremely ambitious. Something of a warhorse ready to take on all comers, Fannie Coburn devoted much energy to trying to convince both Day and Stieglitz that Alvin was a greater photographer than Steichen.[10]

Some notable critics agreed with her. In 1907 Hartmann wrote: "[Steichen's] portraits of celebrities [are] always self-explanatory, even melodramatic. Coburn is subtler, more poetic and elegant. One has only to look at the two men. Steichen [is] proud, eccentric, intolerant. Coburn is genial, cheerful, more temperamental."[11] George Bernard Shaw, Coburn's first famous portrait subject, wrote of his friend and fellow photographer in 1906, "At age twenty-three he is one of the most accomplished and sensitive artists living." Scoring a coup in 1906, Coburn would both parody and upstage Steichen's *Rodin* by photographing Shaw, nude, in the pose of Rodin's *Thinker.*

CHAPTER TWENTY·SEVEN

WITHIN THE CAMERA CLUB the outcry against *Camera Notes* as "synonymous with freak photography" had become so loud that Stieglitz called a special meeting of the club on the evening of October 25, 1900, to air the charges and refute them.[1] He began the meeting dramatically. "Tonight he had a confession to make," reported the magazine's account. "He had been guilty of having lied to the world. *Camera Notes* was a lie; its tone, assumed by the public to represent the tone and standard of the Club, was in reality far in advance of that of the larger body of the Club-members."[2] Despite some passionate condemnation of the publication and its editor, the meeting ended with a surprising vote of confidence for Stieglitz and his management of *Camera Notes*.

Earlier that year, in response to complaints about the "shabby treatment" that the club's annual exhibitions of members' prints had received in the magazine, the board of trustees had passed a resolution ordering the editors to refrain from criticizing the work in these shows. (Hypersensitivity was not limited to those on the receiving end of criticism. The official club critic, conservative photographer and watercolorist J. Wells Champney, eventually resigned because he couldn't bear the thought that his remarks might hurt someone's feelings.) Like the Revolutionary War general Nathanael Greene, whom he had admired since childhood, Stieglitz was capable of making a strategic retreat. In the October 1900 issue he commented that the members' exhibition that year was "an unqualified success from nearly every point of view" and a great improvement over the previous year's show. No sooner did he give this praise than he turned it to his own advantage, writing that the progress "must be of special satisfaction to all those who have been claiming that good example by word and deed must eventually have a beneficial effect on the Club at large." In other words, credit was largely due to the Stieglitz faction and *Camera Notes* — "notwithstanding the seeming dissatisfaction during the year by many, who claim that the exhibitions and magazine of the Club are run in the interests of a select few."[3]

Nonetheless, at the board meeting on February 25, 1901, a new relationship between *Camera Notes* and the Camera Club was adopted. It wasn't quite a divorce, but it was certainly a trial separation. Instead of being the chairman of the Publication Committee, Stieglitz would now be the editor and manager of the magazine, free to appoint his editorial associates. A contract, renewable annually, would replace the old informal arrangement under which the magazine had received an annual subsidy of $250, which was no longer adequate to cover the club's share of the costs. Now the club would pay "a stipulated rate for copies of the publication distributed to the members." Stieglitz would have full control over the section of the magazine devoted to "all general discussion of photographic and artistic topics." A new committee, composed of conservatives, would be responsible for the section "relating to the affairs of the Camera Club, including reports of meetings and criticisms, if any, of exhibitions of prints upon the Club-room walls." Stieglitz would handle the finances of the magazine, subject to quarterly reports to the trustees. The redesigned cover would no longer state that *Camera Notes* was the "Official Organ of The Camera Club, N.Y.," instead now proclaiming it to be "An Illustrated Photographic Quarterly Edited and Managed by Alfred Stieglitz — Published by the Camera Club, NY."

The Philadelphia salon of 1900 did nothing to quiet Stieglitz's opponents. The jury, made up of Stieglitz and four of his friends — Gertrude Käsebier, Clarence White, Frank Eugene, and Eva Watson-Schütze (a gifted photographer who had studied painting with Thomas Eakins at the Pennsylvania Academy) — selected for hanging only 112 prints out of the approximately 1,000 that had been submitted. An additional 86 photographs by the judges and their cronies were hung *hors concours*. "Of course, the photographic world is in a great stew over it all," commented Stieglitz, "but that will end in good instead of harm."[4] He felt that the Philadelphia salon had finally "reached a position in American photography comparable to that held by the 'Linked Ring' Exhibition in London."[5] But many photographers and editors were outraged by such elitism.

In the spring of 1901 the reactionary members of the Philadelphia Photographic Society, calling themselves the Rationalists or the Old School, revolted against the domination of the New School, which they ridiculed as the "Mop and Pail Brigade" or the "Photographic Oscar Wildes." The Rationalists announced their intention of making the salon inclusive rather than exclusive. Running on that platform, one of their number was elected president of the society. The Rationalists also gained control of the salon committee, which promptly resolved to exhibit scientific and documentary photography together with artistic. The committee chose a conservative Philadelphia photographer to serve on the jury along with Charles I. Berg and Frances Johnston, both of whom were sympathetic to the Old School. Stieglitz boycotted the exhibition and persuaded most of his friends at home and abroad to do likewise. F. H. Day was the only major Pictorialist to show. In the wake of this fiasco, the Philadelphia society and the academy decided not to hold a salon in 1902.

In the fall of 1900, J. Craig Annan had asked his fellow Link Stieglitz to select seventy photographs to represent the United States in the photographic section of the Glasgow International Arts and Industrial Exposition, to be held from May through October 1901, to mark the opening of the new Glasgow Art Gallery and Museum. This was to be the first international exposition in which photography would have its proper place in the fine arts section, to be housed in the new museum.

Glasgow gave Stieglitz his opportunity to make a rebuttal to Day's New School exhibition, and he leapt at the chance. Then, briefly but infuriatingly, it looked as though Day's collection would go to Glasgow. Once the crisis was resolved in Stieglitz's favor, he chose photographs by thirty Americans. The selection was dominated — as would be all of Stieglitz's projects for the next several years — by his own work and that of Käsebier, White, Eugene, Edward Steichen, and Joseph Keiley, each of whom was represented by five prints. When Day declined the invitation to participate, Stieglitz sent two Days from his own collection.

During the run of the boycotted Philadelphia salon (November 18 to December 14, 1901), Stieglitz was expecting the imminent return of the photographs that had created a sensation in Glasgow. He had wanted to exhibit them before he sent them off; having failed to do so, he was now determined to rent gallery space in New York for a show. He also resolved that the time had finally come to found an American version of the Linked Ring, which would, in the coming years, mount an annual salon to replace Philadelphia as the premier event in American photography — and perhaps even eclipse the Ring's salon.

Disgusted by the Camera Club, Stieglitz wanted to form not only a new organization but an entirely new kind of organization, which he originally intended to call the Pictorial League. In January 1902 he told John Aspinwall, the president of the Camera Club, that he hoped to start a "group of pictorial photographers and their patrons" with "no president no secretary no dues no club rooms no regular meetings." Aspinwall replied, "I cannot imagine that you seriously believe that an aggregation of pictorial photographers could be held together, to accomplish any distinct work, by such a loose organization as proposed to me the other night." He assumed that the "common centre" of the new organization would be "a new *Camera Notes*" edited by Stieglitz and that its members would resign from the Camera Club. To prevent that, Aspinwall went so far as to suggest the formation of an elect inner circle within the existing club.[6]

Stieglitz took no immediate action on that front, but he did proceed with his plans for an exhibition and asked Charles Caffin to find out how much it would cost to rent the Durand-Ruel Gallery. On November 15, however, Charles de Kay — the art editor and associate editor of the *New York Times* as well as a founder and the managing director of the National Arts Club — wrote Stieglitz that February would "do very well for an exhibition of select artistic photographs" at that club. Founded in 1898 to foster both the fine arts and the decorative crafts, it exhibited not only paintings and sculpture but also ceramics and textiles. Although the show of photographs would draw heavily upon the Glasgow prints, Stieglitz would revise and enlarge that collection. Indeed, when he began to solicit prints, many photographers assumed that he was doing so for a salon under the direction of a new organization.

For a while the exhibition was a sponsorless orphan, but events at the Camera Club would finally resolve the issue. It was an announcement regarding the members' print competition, to be held from May 1 to 15, that brought matters to a head. At a special meeting on December 3, 1901, in reaction to the elitism that had caused so much resentment, one of the anti-Stieglitz members, Ferdinand Stark, proposed that the club should hold regular intramural competitions in which the members would cast votes for their favorite pictures. The three receiving the largest number of votes would be reproduced in *Camera Notes*. For once, Stieglitz agreed on a compromise. He would accept the proposition if he could also publish three prints chosen by a jury of artists — by which he meant painter-photographers drawn from the ranks of the Pictorialists he most admired.[7] It would be an interesting and perhaps even instructive exercise, reminding the members yet again how far their taste fell short of true artistic judgment.

The crisis came on February 17, when Messrs. Stark and C. H. Crosby (who was soon to be elected president of the club) released a circular announcing the rules of the competition. All was pretty much as had been agreed, except that they stipulated that the jury of artists be composed of three nonmembers, and it turned out that Stark and Crosby had already invited a trio of third-rate painters: William A. Coffin, Louis Loeb, and Frederick S. Church (not to be confused with the famous Frederic Edwin Church) to serve.[8] Stieglitz, surely feeling tricked and betrayed, must have been furious over this victory for the philistines. Now he would have to print six dreadful photographs in *Camera Notes* instead of edifyingly juxtaposing three bad and three good. That was the last straw. He immediately resolved to establish a new organization, which he would call the Photo-Secession. He always cited February 17, 1902, as the date on which it had been founded, though historians, failing to understand the significance of the Stark-Crosby circular, have expressed puzzlement about what happened on that day to precipitate his move.

The question of the composition of photographic juries — which had been directly responsible for the crystallization and naming of the Photo-Secession — would figure largely in Stieglitz's public statements over the course of the next year. In the lecture he gave at the opening of the National Arts Club exhibition, just two weeks after the announcement of the Camera Club competition, he made a special point of stressing that a painter was by no means necessarily an artist — a remark that those in the know would have understood to be a criticism of Coffin, Loeb, and Church.

In an editorial published in the second issue of *Camera Work*, Stieglitz would write that he strongly opposed juries composed of "painters and sculptors ignorant of photographic technique." He conceded, however, that "given a jury of painters, etc., familiar with the processes, scope and limitations of photography and themselves imbued with the full spirit of art, untrammeled by convention or prejudice, we stand ready to hail them as *the ideal jury*."[9] In other words, to have one's work admired by an artist such as Whistler would be the ultimate accolade.

*　　*　　*

Even though no actual organization yet existed, Stieglitz called the National Arts Club show American Pictorial Photography, Arranged by "The Photo-Secession." There was an element of snobbery in the name, since most Americans, even most photographers, would not understand what it referred to. "The idea of Secession is hateful to the American," Stieglitz told de Kay; "they'll be thinking of the Civil War. I'm not."[10]

Secessionism — a revolution against the waxwork nudes, maudlin genre scenes, and grandiose history paintings of the academic artists — had been rife in Europe, and even in America, during the 1890s. The Munich Secession was founded in 1892, the Viennese in 1897, Berlin's in 1898. In New York, the painters in the group that became known as the Ten (including Childe Hassam, J. H. Twachtman, and J. Alden Weir) seceded from the Society of American Artists in 1898. Secessionism embraced Realism, Impressionism, Symbolism, Art Nouveau, and the Arts and Crafts movement — all that was modern and adventurous in the arts. Because many European secessionists favored breaking down the traditional boundaries between the fine and decorative arts, their exhibitions often included ceramics, glasswork, silverware, jewelry, furniture, and books. It was, therefore, quite natural for the secessionists to accept photography as an art form.

Secession and photography had been linked in Stieglitz's mind at least since November 1898, when the Munich group mounted an International Elite-Exhibition of Artistic Photographs in conjunction with a show of graphic arts that included work by such artists as Aubrey Beardsley, Edvard Munch, and Toulouse-Lautrec. The following year Stieglitz wrote,

> In Munich, the art-centre of Germany, the "Secessionists," a body of artists comprising the most advanced and gifted men of their times, who (as the name indicates they have broken away from the narrow rules of custom and tradition) have admitted the claims of the pictorial photograph to be judged on its merits as a work of art independently, and without considering the fact that it has been produced through the medium of the camera.[11]

Despite the implication of his new organization's name, Stieglitz seceded only from *Camera Notes*, not from the Camera Club. At the trustees' meeting on February 24, 1902, he gave notice that "he elected not to continue as editor" of the magazine.[12] To justify his resignation, he cited "the official policy of the club, as indicated by the deliberate nominations of a new Board of Officers avowedly out of sympathy with the policy so long maintained by *Camera Notes*." He had decided to let the club make a mess of things, "unhampered by the convictions to which we are so uncompromisingly pledged."[13]

To ensure continuity, however, Stieglitz agreed to edit the July 1902 issue, which would go to press before May 1. Thereafter — as Stieglitz and his editorial associates Keiley, Dallett Fuguet, and John Francis Strauss stated in a letter they sent to various photographic magazines in America and England — they would "be neither directly nor indirectly connected with any branch of this publication, our severance being absolute and complete."[14] Even the conservative *Photo-Era* regretted the news and conceded, "Under the direction of Mr. Alfred Stieglitz, 'Camera Notes' has achieved a notable artistic and pictorial triumph which it can never hope to excel."[15]

Juan C. Abel, who had been the editor of *The Photographic Times* and one of Stieglitz's editorial associates on *Camera Notes*, would be the new editor. Over the course of the next year and a half Abel would manage to bring out only three issues of the magazine, with a completely redesigned format and cover, after which it ceased independent publication, though it ignominiously lingered on for years as a single page in the magazine *American Photography*.

Stieglitz's only other secession in the spring of 1902 occurred on March 31, when the three members of the Camera Club's Print Committee — Keiley (the chairman), Stieglitz, and E. Lee Ferguson — submitted their resignations. This move was occasioned by the committee's disgust at the club's unwillingness to buy prints for a permanent collection of pictorial photographs, "the general lack of interest in and general apathy towards the wall displays on the part of the Club," and the approach of the club elections, in which the stodgy C. H. Crosby seemed certain to become the new president (as he in fact did).[16]

American Pictorial Photography, Arranged by "The Photo-Secession" opened on the evening of Wednesday, March 5, at the National Arts Club, which was then located at 37 West Thirty-fourth Street. Despite a raging blizzard, the audience attending Stieglitz's opening-night lecture, "Pictorial Photography and What It Means," included such celebrities as the duke of Newcastle and the Pre-Raphaelite painter Sir Philip Burne-Jones.

Stieglitz had more than doubled the size of the Glasgow collection, primarily by increasing the representation of his favorites. He also added prints by nine minor photographers — presumably so that he could claim that "all recognized workers of repute who had proven themselves in thorough sympathy with the spirit of the modern movement were invited to contribute, regardless of their photographic affiliations." He went on to boast, "Not only was the exhibition national in the localities represented, but, strangely enough, all printing media from aristo to 'gum-bichromate' on the one hand, and bromide to 'glycerine platinotype' on the other, were embraced, thus showing that the Photo-Secessionist is committed to no other medium than that which best lends itself to his purpose."[17]

Determined to emphasize the diversity of American photography beyond the Symbolist murkiness that Day's exhibition had featured, Stieglitz nevertheless gave pride of place to the ultra-Symbolistic work of painter-photographer Steichen. Keiley designed the decorative scheme and worked with Stieglitz to hang the show. "All the work of each contributor was grouped together, to enable the visitor to make a comparative study of the individual work and scope of the photographer," wrote Stieglitz. "Great care had been taken to so place each picture that its tone, color, and line would harmonise with its surroundings."[18] The photographs meandered along the wall in a rhythmical arrangement from one to three frames high. The effect was rather busy, but, by the standards of the day, very modern. Although there were still many large prints in heavy, dark wooden frames, the shift in taste toward smaller prints mounted artistically on several layers of colored tissue and placed in thin white frames was evident. This so-called American mounting had been originated by Day.

In a letter published in *The British Journal of Photography*, Stieglitz vaunted, "Our bitterest opponents amongst the artists, the greatest nonbelievers amongst the critics, in fact, all who have seen the show, are astounded at the ensemble. . . . The exhibition is a greater success than I dared expect. It is the fairest photographic exhibition which can be shown to the most critical without an excuse. It stands on its own feet, and it stands the test of time."[19] Even de Kay's brother-in-law, Richard Watson Gilder, whom Stieglitz called "that most conservative of conservatives," had been sufficiently impressed to invite the photographer to write an article about Pictorialism for the prestigious *Century* magazine.

CHAPTER TWENTY·EIGHT

THE PHOTO-SECESSION was a very curious organization, not least because its members did not in fact secede from the Camera Club of New York. Indeed, a note in the July 1902 issue of *Camera Notes* stated, "Any person wishing to know further particulars concerning . . . the organization 'Photo-Secession' may address Mr. Alfred Stieglitz, No. 3 West 29th Street, Manhattan."[1] That was, of course, the address of the Camera Club. Stieglitz did not want to hurt the club, and he still hoped to elevate its standards by example. There was also a less idealistic factor. Neither Stieglitz nor most of his friends had darkrooms of their own. They remained members of the Camera Club so that they could use its magnificent facilities — "the like of which I had never seen before," wrote Steichen. The club even continued to mount occasional exhibitions by a Photo-Secessionist; Alvin Langdon Coburn made his debut with a sixty-print solo there in January 1903.

During the first year of his new organization's existence, Stieglitz wrote a number of statements defining the Photo-Secession. It was, he proclaimed, a "secession from the spirit of the doctrinaire, of the compromiser." It was a "protest against the reactionary spirit of the masses." The attitude of its members was, he said, "one of rebellion against the insincere attitude of the unbeliever, of the Philistine, and largely of exhibition authorities."[2]

Stieglitz wrote that the aims of the Photo-Secession were "loosely to hold together those Americans devoted to pictorial photography in their endeavor to compel its recognition, not as the handmaiden of art, but as a distinctive medium of individual expression"[3] and "to hold from time to time, at varying places, exhibitions not necessarily limited to the productions of the Photo-Secession or to American work."[4]

Who were the members of this mysterious organization, and what were the criteria for membership? First of all, Stieglitz had temporarily abandoned his dream of founding an international society; the Photo-Secession was to be strictly American. Its roster would eventually include two Canadians and one Alaskan, but there would be no British members and only two Europeans: Baron Adolf de Meyer (Dresden) and Heinrich Kuehn (Innsbruck). However, American members Frank Eugene and Coburn (who had opportunistically transferred his allegiance from Day to Stieglitz) would live in Munich and London, respectively.

Stieglitz loved to tell the story of how Gertrude Käsebier had demanded at the opening of the National Arts Club show, "What's this Photo-Secession? Am I a Photo-Secessionist?" He replied by asking, "Do you feel you are?" She said she did. "Well, that's all there is to it," he announced.[5]

But it was not always quite that simple, as many would soon learn. Charles Berg, vice president of the Camera Club, had three prints in the exhibition at the National Arts Club, of which he was a member. When, at the opening, he asked whether he was a Photo-Secessionist, Stieglitz coldly informed him that he was not.

As Stieglitz's conception of the Photo-Secession evolved during 1902, it would be dominated by a council of fourteen founding fellows. At the heart of the council he hoped to have, in addition to himself, the seven photographers whose work he then admired most: Day, Eugene, Käsebier, Keiley, Steichen, White, and William B. Dyer, a Chicago professional photographer who specialized in portraiture and book illustration. One of Stieglitz's greatest disappointments was that Day declined his repeated invitations to join.

Also among the founding fellows were *Camera Notes* editorial associates Dallett Fuguet and John Francis Strauss. Two others were John Bullock and Robert Redfield, excellent photographers whom Stieglitz admired as much for having founded the Philadelphia salons as for their own pictures. The last two were Eva Watson-Schütze, elected to the Linked Ring in 1901, and Edmund Stirling, elected in September 1902. As a matter of course, Stieglitz invited all of the American members of the Ring to become fellows of the Photo-Secession.[6]

In 1903 he explained that fellows were "chosen by the Council for meritorious photographic work or labors in behalf of pictorial photography. . . . The photographic work of a possible candidate must be individual and distinctive, and it goes without saying that the applicant must be in thorough sympathy with our aims and principles." With self-satisfaction he noted, "It has been found necessary to deny the application of many whose lukewarm interest in the cause with which we are so thoroughly identified gave no promise of aiding the Secession."[7]

In the fall of 1902 Stieglitz wrote, "For the present, the details of organisation of this body must be denied to the public."[8] That was only partly due to Stieglitz's wanting it to be something of a secret society. More to the point, there were hardly any "details of organisation" to reveal. He hoped to hold to his original vision of "no president no secretary no dues no club rooms no regular meetings," but the eminently practical Steichen had very different ideas. "Restive and a little belligerent about the vagueness of the 'Photo-Secession'," he called for an organizational meeting, which took place on December 22, 1902. Stieglitz refused the title of president as "too ostentatious," but he agreed to be the society's director. To inform out-of-town members about these developments and keep them posted in the future, it was agreed to publish occasionally a one- or two-page newsletter. [9]

At the December meeting, and at another in February 1903, the society granted the secondary status of associate to thirty photographers and patrons. The Photo-Secession would eventually list 120 members, of whom nearly one quarter were women. In the April 1906 issue of *Camera Work* Stieglitz stated that "of the eighty-odd members . . . about sixty are photographers."[10] Emmeline Stieglitz was among the nonphotographers made associates because of their financial contributions. Coburn's mother, some of whose own photographs were exhibited in the Linked Ring's 1906 salon, was also an associate. Joe Obermeyer's name is, however, conspicuous by its absence.

At least one of Stieglitz's oldest friends — William Post, who had been forced by illness in 1901 to retire to his home in Maine — was less than thrilled about being made an associate. He wrote Stieglitz in January 1903,

> Am I to understand it as an invitation to join, or is it a notification of election? As I read over the paper it appears to be a clique, who vote to themselves absolute command for all time, but who wish outsiders (like myself) to come in under the name of "Associates" — This class

will have to pay $5.00 per annum and also bind themselves to pay pro rata for all the mistakes of the first class called "Fellows" and "Council."[11]

Stieglitz responded by making Post a fellow.

It wasn't until January 1904 that the Photo-Secession began to hold regular meetings. An associate named Albert Boursault suggested that all the members who were in town should gather once a month for dinner, conversation, and business. They went to Mouquin's — at Sixth Avenue and Twenty-eighth Street, conveniently close to the Camera Club — a popular and lively French restaurant frequented by the Philadelphia artists who would become the core of the group known as the Eight. (In 1905 William Glackens would immortalize Mouquin's in one of his finest paintings.) The conversations in the restaurant's main dining room — dominated by the nightly arguments between the *New York Sun*'s two Irish art critics, Charles FitzGerald and Frederick James Gregg — were loud. So the Photo-Secessionists gathered upstairs in a private room "decorated with southern smilax vines," as Steichen later recalled.[12]

In its early days, the primary function of the Photo-Secession was to send collections of photographs to museums and expositions throughout the United States and around the world. Early in 1902, shortly before the founding of the new organization, Stieglitz was invited to the Metropolitan Museum of Art, whose East Wing, with its imposing Beaux Arts facade on Fifth Avenue, designed by Richard Morris Hunt, was just being completed. (The wings that stretch along the avenue to the north and south of Hunt's structure were added considerably later.) His appointment was with General Louis Palma di Cesnola, the first director of the Met, who had just been designated the American commissioner for an international arts exposition to be held in Turin. The smug, obese Cesnola (who established a first-class restaurant in the museum) was best known for the huge collection of second-rate Cypriot antiquities he had acquired for the Met while American consul on Cyprus, after having fought with distinction in the Union Army during the Civil War.

The duke of Abruzzi, patron of the Turin exposition and himself an enthusiastic amateur photographer, had asked his friend Cesnola to arrange for Stieglitz to send a collection of prints by the Photo-Secession. Stieglitz told Cesnola that he would provide the collection only if, when it was returned to New York, the Met would exhibit it and accession the photographs into its permanent collection as works of art. Cesnola, who did not dare to disappoint the duke, reluctantly agreed to the terms.

Stieglitz, assisted by Keiley and Charles Berg (head of the Camera Club's Print Committee, who was mustered into service despite Stieglitz's dislike for him), within twenty-four hours assembled sixty prints by thirty photographers, most of them members-to-be of the Photo-Secession. Since Stieglitz was then collecting the very finest prints for the National Arts Club exhibition, he had to include a number of seconds for Turin. Nevertheless, he learned in November 1902 that his entry had won the "special award offered by His Majesty the King of Italy, for the best collection of prints exhibited."[13] However, because Stieglitz had given his address as in care of the Camera Club of New York, the prize was mistakenly awarded to the club. He had the error corrected and deluged the editors of photographic magazines in America and England with the information that "the King's prize has been awarded to Alfred Stieglitz as an individual."[14]

Stieglitz later claimed that Cesnola died before the collection was returned to New York and that since there had been no written agreement, the Met did not acquire the collection. But Cesnola did not die until November 1904, and he remained in office until that time. No photographs would be acquired by the Met as works of art until 1928, when a group of photographs by Stieglitz was accepted.

Stieglitz claimed that by the end of 1903 he had received from 147 American and European organizations "urgent" requests for exhibitions. "It is the policy of the Photo-Secession to exhibit only upon invitation," explained Stieglitz, "and this necessarily implies that its exhibit must be hung as a unit and [in] its entirety, without submission to any jury."[15] Once the new group's council had "satisfied itself of the earnestness of purpose of these bodies and their willingness to accept the terms upon which the Photo-Secession feels it necessary to insist," Stieglitz sent collections of varying size as far away as Russia.[16]

Given the number of prints that had to be framed and packed for shipment, it is no wonder that Stieglitz said the Photo-Secession's first office was in the basement of young George Of's frame shop at 3 East Twenty-eighth Street, just one block from the Camera Club. Of, born in 1876, would himself go to Paris late in 1903 to study painting for a couple of years, but his shop remained open.[17] After he returned to New York, he resumed framing for Stieglitz.

Invitations from the organizers of "salons" in Minneapolis and Denver were all very well, but such triumphs were overshadowed by the Linked Ring's infuriating refusal to accept Stieglitz's suggestion that the 1903 London Photographic Salon include an *hors concours* section of work by the Photo-Secession. The predictable response of Stieglitz and Steichen was to lead a boycott of the salon.

In a statement about the Photo-Secession that Stieglitz wrote in 1903, he blatantly revealed the revolutionary nature of his endeavors and methods. "In all phases of human activity the tendency of the masses has been invariably towards ultra conservatism," he declared.

> Progress has been accomplished only by reason of the fanatical enthusiasm of the revolutionist, whose extreme teaching has saved the mass from utter inertia. . . . In this country photography also has followed this law, and whatever have been the achievements which have won it exceptional distinction, they have been attained by the efforts of the enthusiastic so-called extremists.[18]

The philosophy articulated in this pronouncement is shockingly close to the doctrine that Lenin had set forth the previous year in his revolutionary handbook *What Is to Be Done?* There he called for a disciplined party of full-time professional radicals, intellectuals unswervingly dedicated to the cause, who would write and distribute propaganda, commit acts of terrorism, and otherwise incite the proletariat to revolt. No factionalism or doctrinal dissent was to be tolerated.

In Stieglitz's case, the Photo-Secessionists were his Bolsheviks, his magazine *Camera Work* would be his seditious propaganda, and the exhibitions he organized would be — judging from the reactions of conservative critics — little short of acts of terrorism. Stieglitz even eschewed the term "artist," tainted by Oscar Wilde–style aestheticism, and preferred to call himself and his associates "workers."

Stieglitz was basically an adversarial and dominating personality who was never happy unless he had a battle to fight or a cause to champion. From the photographers whose work he exhibited and published he demanded gratitude and unshakable loyalty. A difference of opinion or an attempt to challenge — or even to question — Stieglitz's leadership would usually cause the offender to be lambasted and then ostracized. "If [anyone] crossed him in any way," recalled Georgia O'Keeffe long after his death, "his power to destroy was as destructive [i.e., as great] as his power to build — the extremes went together."[19] Stieglitz might well have envied Lenin his later power to send his enemies to Siberia.

"There was a constant grinding like the ocean. It was as if something hot, dark, and destructive was hitched to the highest, brightest star," recollected O'Keeffe of her husband. "He was either loved or hated — there wasn't much in between."[20]

CHAPTER TWENTY·NINE

ALTHOUGH STIEGLITZ WAS excited about the Photo-Secession, he was very depressed about the Camera Club and the demise of *Camera Notes*. Following his usual pattern, he was done in by excessive stress and emotion. After a vacation at the New Jersey shore with Emmy and Kitty in June 1902, he collapsed at Lake George early in July and spent much of the summer recuperating.

Concerned about his friend's despair regarding *Camera Notes*, Joseph Keiley wrote to many of Stieglitz's supporters, asking them to encourage him to begin a new magazine. It didn't take much to persuade him. "In response to the importunities of many serious workers in photographic fields that I should undertake the publication of an independent magazine devoted to the furtherance of modern photography," he wrote in a two-page brochure dated August 25, 1902, he was going to publish a quarterly entitled *Camera Work*. The brochure tempted prospective subscribers with the claim that it would be "the best and most sumptuous of photographic publications." Continuity with *Camera Notes* was assured by the fact that Keiley, Fuguet, and Strauss would serve as Stieglitz's editorial associates. They were joined in 1905 by John Barrett Kerfoot, the literary critic for the humor magazine *Life*, of whom one writer observed that "his pleasant, full-cheeked countenance [was] made child-like and inviting by a pair of innocent laughing light blue eyes."[1] As a member of the Camera Club,

Kerfoot had begun contributing to *Camera Notes* about 1900, and beginning with the first issue, he wrote dozens of pieces for *Camera Work*, many of them humorous.

Stieglitz sent his prospectus "to people whom I thought might be interested, and more particularly to the libraries of the country."[2] The size of the magazine and the number of illustrations per issue would be determined by the number of subscriptions sold, at a cost of three and a half dollars per year. The publisher promised that, whatever the format, subscribers would get their money's worth. The first issue, dated January 1903, would be mailed out in the middle of December 1902, by which time there were 647 subscribers. Nevertheless, before the year was out, Stieglitz was forced to announce that the subscription price was being raised to five dollars. "No expense was stinted," he explained, "with the result that the costs of publishing have far exceeded our original estimate."[3] With typically extravagant impracticality, and unwillingness to compromise, Stieglitz printed one thousand copies of every issue regardless of the number of subscribers.

Neither Stieglitz nor his editorial associates received any salary. Nor were photographers paid; the honor of having one's work reproduced was to suffice. Only writers who were not on the editorial staff were paid for their articles. The greatest expenses were for paper, printing, and postage. Stieglitz and his friends wrapped the issues to be mailed, and he himself would take to the post office those to be sent by registered mail, for which he advised all subscribers to pay a premium.

In his 1902 prospectus, Stieglitz made no mention of the Photo-Secession, averring that *Camera Work* would be edited and published by himself, "owing allegiance only to the interests of photography." In the first issue he was more forthcoming, though barely. *Camera Work* "owes allegiance to no organization or clique," he wrote, "and though it is the mouthpiece of the Photo-Secession that fact will not be allowed to hamper its independence in the slightest degree."[4] Advertisements for *Camera Work* called it "The Magazine without an 'If' — fearless — independent — without favor." Stieglitz announced that it was his "intention to reproduce the best examples of all 'schools,' both American and foreign," but "only examples of such work as gives evidence of individuality and artistic worth." Stating the obvious, he conceded that "the pictorial will be the dominating feature of the magazine."[5]

Camera Work was by far the most beautiful of photographic magazines. The editors of *Photography* exclaimed in response to the first issue that "Stieglitz had out-Stieglitzed Stieglitz." On the plain gray front cover, designed by Steichen using an Art Nouveau typeface, the words "CAMERA WORK" appeared, in white, within a white box. In a smaller box was the information: "A PHOTOGRAPHIC QUARTERLY EDITED AND PUBLISHED BY ALFRED STIEGLITZ, NEW YORK." And in the lower right corner, the number and year were given in Roman numerals. Despite Stieglitz's vituperation of Eastman Kodak for the declining quality of its materials, an Eastman ad (also designed by Steichen) appeared on the back cover.

An average issue contained about ten articles, the majority of them written by Stieglitz's cronies. Most dealt with individual photographers or aesthetics, technical articles being very sparse. Almost every issue also contained exhibition reviews; from late in 1904 on, many of them, pro and con, were reprinted from other publications.

While planning *Camera Work*, Stieglitz apparently approached the firm of Charles Scribner's Sons, and perhaps other publishers as well, about a copublication deal. Scribner's proposed that he issue "a de luxe affair with numbered and autographed copies," but he rejected that idea.[6] Nonetheless, the magazine was so sumptuous and so closely associated with the exclusive and mysterious Photo-Secession that Stieglitz had to run, in the July 1904 issue, a full-page "Appeal to Our Subscribers." In it he hastened to correct "the erroneous impression" that had "gone abroad that the edition of *Camera Work* is limited and that only the favored few are admitted to our subscription-list."

When Steichen returned to New York in August 1902, Stieglitz hardly recognized him. Instead of the enthusiastic midwestern boy of two years before, here was a long-haired and conceited Parisian artist, wearing a cloak, constantly gesturing in a rather affected way. Steichen said that the Photo-Secession should exclude everyone but Käsebier, Day, White, Stieglitz, and himself. To include anyone second-rate would only pull the whole thing down to a lower standard. He consented to join only when Stieglitz showed him the dummy of the first issue of *Camera Work*.

He was, in fact, so impressed that he wanted the first issue to be devoted to his work rather than to Käsebier's. He told Stieglitz that because he was planning to get married and open a portrait studio in New York, he urgently needed the publicity. He had assumed that Käsebier, who was present but who was deaf in one ear, would not overhear. She heard everything and, quite understandably, felt betrayed by this young man whom she had befriended. During the summer of 1901 she and her twenty-one-year-old daughter, Hermine, had spent a good deal of time with Steichen in Paris. Steichen reported to Stieglitz that Käsebier "has been goodness itself . . . and pumped much new energy and enthusiasm into me."[7] She in turn felt that she had found a kindred spirit — and perhaps even a son-in-law. But that was not to be. Steichen became engaged to Clara E. Smith, a singer studying in Paris. Stieglitz, who considered Clara "a terror," assumed that because her posing nude for Steichen had led to intimacy, she forced him to propose.[8] On October 3, 1903, they were married in New York's Trinity Church, after which they spent their honeymoon at the Stieglitz farmhouse at Lake George.

Although Steichen had to wait until the second issue for his photographs to be featured, he would do very well by *Camera Work*. His work, and articles about it, appeared in fifteen of the fifty issues, and the reproductions in three issues were entirely his. Altogether, sixty-five Steichens were published in the magazine, more than by anyone else. Stieglitz was next with forty-seven, plus another four that he had made in collaboration with White. Photographs by Stieglitz or Steichen added up to nearly one quarter of the total number reproduced.

During its fifteen-year existence, *Camera Work* published a total of 473 photographs. Of these, 357 were the work of a group of fourteen photographers. In addition to Stieglitz and Steichen, they were, in descending order, Frank Eugene, Clarence White, Alvin Langdon Coburn, J. Craig Annan, David Octavius Hill (in collaboration with the unacknowledged Robert Adamson), Baron Adolf de Meyer, Heinrich Kuehn, George Seeley, Paul Strand, Robert Demachy, Gertrude Käsebier, and Annie W. Brigman. The remaining 116 photographs were by a total of thirty-nine photographers, represented by from one to nine photographs apiece.

The most serious omissions among pictorial photographers known to Stieglitz — F. H. Day and P. H. Emerson — were not voluntary. Day spurned the offer to devote the third issue to his work. And in 1904, when Stieglitz invited Emerson, the cantankerous eccentric replied dismissing Steichen's portraits (in Number 2) as "flat, banal, and terribly crude and amateurish in composition," condemning Clarence White's work (in Number 3) as "commonplace, false in values and childish in composition," and advising that Coburn's photographs would be "best destroyed at once." He concluded, "I cannot accept your very kind offer to appear in that crowd in any capacity, for as far as I can see excepting yourself they are a lot of incompetent poseurs."[9]

Stieglitz did everything to ensure that the photogravures in *Camera Work* would be nearly like prints. Indeed, in 1904, when a Photo-Secession exhibition failed to arrive in Brussels on time, a selection of gravures from the magazine was hung instead. Most viewers of the exhibition assumed they were looking at original photographs. The gravures were printed on very fine, thin Japan tissue paper, which was nearly grainless and which had only recently become available. They had to be hand mounted — by Stieglitz and his associates — either directly onto the pages of the magazine or onto brown or gray mats that were then pasted onto the rich cream-colored pages. Stieglitz himself would check each example of every gravure and carefully ink out any light spots caused by dust.

At first, these beautifully printed gravures were produced by Photochrome, still run by Lou Schubart, whose cooperation had been a vital factor in Stieglitz's decision to launch *Camera Work*. (Initially, Stieglitz used the address of the Photochrome office for all correspondence regarding the magazine.) Soon, however, most of the plates would be printed in Germany, at the Bruckmann Verlag in Munich, where the supervisor and chief technician was Fritz Goetz, a former employee at Photochrome. Stieglitz found that for far superior work, the cost "including shipment, duty, and not having to fight the printers [was] 75 per cent of the price asked in the United States."[10]

To anyone looking through a set of *Camera Work* in chronological order, the fourth issue, dated October 1903, featuring the work of Frederick H. Evans, comes as a bracing astringent after the numbers devoted to Käsebier, Steichen, and White. Evans was the purest of the purists, the antithesis of Steichen. His views of English cathedral interiors are simultaneously the most austere and the most beautiful photographs ever published in *Camera Work*. George Bernard Shaw, as one might expect, cut to the truth of the matter when he wrote, in 1901, "Mr. Evans made himself the most artistic of photographers by being the most simply photographic of artists."[11]

Given Stieglitz's propensity for politicking, it may have been at least partly for extraphotographic reasons that Evans's images were the first by an Englishman published in the magazine. Evans, who had not become a member of the Linked Ring until 1900, had in 1902 been made its honorary secretary and the chairman of the committee in charge of the annual salon.

A dynamic elf of a man with thinning red hair and a beard, Evans had retired from his London bookstore in 1898, at the age of forty-five, to pursue photography full-time. As a passionate bookseller and photographer, he had been befriended by both Shaw and Day and, in 1892, had persuaded the firm of J. M. Dent and Company to commission an unknown young artist named Aubrey Beardsley to illustrate an edition of *Le Morte d'Arthur.*

Evans was a perfectionist who would haunt a cathedral for weeks before photographing it. He badgered the dean of Ely Cathedral until the chairs and gas jets were removed from the nave and aisles so that he could photograph the interior as it had been in the Middle Ages. His luminous platinum prints are so profoundly spiritual — so imbued with divine light and with a noble vision of order, faith, and hope — that it seems as though Evans reconsecrated the cathedrals by photographing them.

In his prospectus, Stieglitz announced that he had already been assured by the critics Charles Caffin and Sadakichi Hartmann that they would write for *Camera Work.* Sadly missing was the name of Theodore Dreiser, who would never write anything for the magazine. Stieglitz had been so enthusiastic about Dreiser's novel *Sister Carrie,* published reluctantly and without publicity by Doubleday in 1900, that he had given copies of it to many of his friends. As late as May 1902 an unsigned article by Dreiser, in which both of the illustrations were by Stieglitz and two of the five pages of text were devoted to him, appeared in the popular magazine the *Great Round World.* But by the summer of 1902 Dreiser's depression over the reviews and sales of *Sister Carrie* had translated itself into a host of physical torments. The writer spent the next several years recovering and scrambling for money. He and Stieglitz fell out of touch during that period and never managed to resurrect their friendship.

The most prolific and important of the *Camera Work* writers was Caffin, who contributed more than thirty pieces for the magazine between 1903 and 1912, during which period he also authored numerous books about art. Between 1913 and 1917, while Caffin was the chief art critic for the *New York American,* Stieglitz regularly reprinted his reviews from the paper. Writing of one sort or another by Caffin appeared in nearly three quarters of *Camera Work*'s issues. His special talent was to engage the general public, without either oversimplification or condescension.

Caffin, ten years older than Stieglitz, was a remarkable Englishman. Educated at Oxford, he spent much of the 1880s as an actor in, and stage manager of, an itinerant company that performed Shakespeare under canvas all over England. Paradoxically, Caffin was to become the least theatrical of the New York art critics. He was a genial and serious man without the airs and affectations endemic in the profession. Not for him was Wildean decadence or art for art's sake. A robust proponent of the Arts and Crafts movement, he believed that the primary function of art was to enhance life both for the artist and for his audience.

Almost immediately upon settling in New York in 1897, Caffin landed jobs as an occasional art critic for both the *New York Evening Post* and *Harper's Weekly*. Beginning in January 1901, he was the editor of the prestigious *New York Sun*'s art page and its principal writer, turning out hundreds of articles and reviews every year. He lost his job with the *Sun* in 1904 because a remark in one of his reviews offended the head of the Stern Brothers' department store, one of the paper's biggest advertisers. For the next eight years Caffin wrote principally for *Camera Work*.

Early in 1901 the editor of *Everybody's Magazine*, the house organ of the Philadelphia emporium Wanamaker's, had proposed to Stieglitz that he write a series of articles about outstanding American photographers. Stieglitz suggested that they ask Caffin instead. The seven resulting essays were collected in his first book, *Photography as a Fine Art*, which appeared at the end of that year. Although Caffin expressed his own judgments, it is clear that much of what he wrote reflects long conversations with Stieglitz, for whom the book was an important triumph. Here at last was an influential art critic stating, "In short, if he has the equipment of an artist and an artistic individuality, the photographer can surmount or evade the limitations of his mechanical tool, the camera, and produce work which, barring colors, may have the characteristics of a beautiful picture."[12]

The second most important contributor of articles to *Camera Work* was Sadakichi Hartmann, born in Japan in 1867, the son of a German merchant and his Japanese servant. When his mother died in 1868, Sadakichi was sent to Hamburg to be raised by his father's wealthy and cultivated relatives. Refusing to attend a German naval academy, the fifteen-year-old went to live with relatives in Philadelphia, where he befriended Walt Whitman, whom he frequently visited at his home in Camden, New Jersey. Between 1885 and 1900 Hartmann wrote about art for a number of American publications and traveled in Europe, enlarging his knowledge of avant-garde art.

In the June 1898 issue of *The Photographic Times* appeared his first article devoted entirely to photography, "An Art Critic's Estimate of Alfred Stieglitz," calling him "indisputably the foremost artistic photographer of America . . . a man whose personality and accomplishments are worthy of being treated by the critic with the same consideration as the life and work of a master artist."[13] Not surprisingly, Hartmann began at once to write regularly for *Camera Notes* and later for *Camera Work*, as well as for many other American photographic magazines. He was so prolific that he employed numerous pseudonyms (his most frequent was Sidney Allan) so that he could publish several pieces in a single issue of a magazine.

Hartmann, who modeled himself on Whistler and Wilde, was a cosmopolitan, a dandy, a bohemian, and a Mephistophelian rake. (Settling in Hollywood in 1923 as the correspondent for a British movie magazine, he was typecast that year when he played the rôle of the court magician in *The Thief of Bagdad*, starring Douglas Fairbanks.) A *raffiné*, Hartmann was exasperated by stupidity and lack of elegance. He prided himself on being outrageously outspoken, and his criticism could be highly enthusiastic or ruthless, though never gratuitously so. Because he was such a mercurial free spirit, one could never be sure what position he would take. As a disciple of the Belgian Symbolist writer Maurice Maeterlinck, Hartmann observed, in a typically aphoristic pronouncement, "Accuracy is the bane of Art." Similarly, his 1903 essay in *Camera Work* entitled "The Value of the Apparently Meaningless and Inaccurate" proclaimed, "The love of exactitude is the lowest form of pictorial gratification." And yet the following year, in "A Plea for Straight Photography," he wrote, "Legitimate photographic methods are the great expressional instrument for a straightforward depiction of the pictorial beauties of life and nature, and to abandon its superiorities in order to aim at the technical qualities of other arts is unwise."[14]

CHAPTER THIRTY

A CRISIS THAT had been brewing for more than a year came to a head in the spring of 1904. The authorities of the Louisiana Purchase Exposition, to be held that summer in St. Louis, had assigned photography to the department of liberal arts — which is to say decorative and industrial arts. Stieglitz made it clear that unless photography was placed under the jurisdiction of the fine arts department, he would like the members of the Photo-Secession to boycott the exposition. There was much grumbling in conservative circles and magazines to the effect that he was trying to gain complete control of the photographic section so that he could exclude everyone but the Secessionists.

When Stieglitz's terms were finally accepted, around March 1, he claimed that "so much time had been lost that it was too late to undertake to do in a few weeks what would require months to accomplish."[1] He had been able to assemble a collection for the Turin exposition overnight, but many prints were now out in traveling shows. Perhaps more to the point, Stieglitz was by then fed up with the whole business. The Photo-Secession and, as he put it, "all other self-respecting photographers" boycotted the exposition, to the disgust of many American amateurs, professionals, and editors.[2]

*   *   *

In the spring of 1904, Stieglitz felt overwhelmed by the problems that seemed to beset him on every side. He was also exhausted from overwork. That year he had already prepared Photo-Secession collections to be sent to Washington, Pittsburgh, Dresden, Paris, Vienna, The Hague, and elsewhere. He was certainly justified in complaining, or boasting, that "the European authorities seem to think that there is no end to the photographs which we are supposed to have up our sleeves."[3]

Offsetting such triumphs was the threat of a challenge to his authority even greater than that posed by F. H. Day in 1900. Early in 1904 Stieglitz heard the first rumblings of the plan of the Metropolitan Camera Club of New York, recently founded by photographers in upper Manhattan, to hold a salon in December. The organizers, who had the temerity to call it the First American Photographic Salon, claimed that no previous exhibition had been "under the control of a committee from all sections of the United States." With tacit reference to the Stieglitz-dominated Philadelphia salons they insisted, "There will be no favors to any and no discrimination against any. All work, whether from the famous or the comparatively unknown artist, will be exhibited equally, and the jury will not know the names of contributors until after the selection has been made."[4]

The mastermind of this project was Curtis Bell, a professional portrait photographer who had opened a studio on Fifth Avenue soon after his recent arrival in New York from the Midwest. (Stieglitz maintained that Bell organized his salon expressly to get publicity for his business.) In a portrait by the St. Louis photographer Julius C. Strauss, Bell looks like a tough young scrapper — a rowdy with the pudgy, immature face, pleading eyes, and crudely cut, slicked-down hair that one associates with western outlaws. His garishly patterned tie accords especially badly with his satin-lapeled frock coat. One of Bell's surviving "pictorial" photographs is an image of calendar-art cuteness, depicting two long-haired cats exploring a food cupboard.

Bell was nevertheless a formidable rival. Not only was he the president of the Metropolitan Camera Club, he also held that same office in the Salon Club of America, composed of about twenty photographers from around the nation who circulated among themselves a monthly portfolio of work for mutual criticism. Moreover, Bell was president of the American Federation of Photographic Societies and cashier of the prestigious Lotos Club, New York's foremost club devoted to the arts, whose members included J. P. Morgan and Henry Havemeyer.

To further his cause, Bell recruited two men — Day and Sadakichi

Hartmann — who would have been glad to see Stieglitz get his comeuppance. It is easy enough to understand Day's resentment, but Hartmann's was and is more surprising. Stieglitz had published articles by him in every issue of *Camera Work*, and in the April 1904 issue alone were five pieces of his writing, including a satire under the pseudonym Klingsor the Magician. But, with a bitterness probably unsuspected by Stieglitz, Hartmann had been accumulating grievances. "I have simply got tired of your dictatorship," he wrote in a letter, going on to accuse Stieglitz of having treated him "shabbily." Hartmann, who believed that Steichen and Käsebier had turned Stieglitz against him, was offended that he was no longer invited to the Photo-Secession's monthly dinners at Mouquin's. Even when Stieglitz did take him out with a group, Hartmann felt ignored in favor of others at the table. He said that Stieglitz had been "abusive" to him and had embarrassed him publicly. On he continued with other petty complaints, which undoubtedly had some basis in fact, though they were obviously blown out of proportion by his oversensitivity.[5]

The critic's first thrust was in the form of an article about the Salon Club and its upcoming show. Written under one of his pseudonyms and published in the July 1904 issue of *The American Amateur Photographer*, it concluded, "All this sounds like open revolt! . . . A duel between Messrs Alfred Stieglitz and Curtis Bell would prove indeed a great attraction. . . . It will stir up the stagnant waters of pictorial photography — they surely need it — and make us all more happy at the end."[6]

Stieglitz worked himself into a state of nervous exhaustion not only over the threat of Bell's salon but also over his own marital predicament. There is little written evidence regarding the state of his relations with his wife and daughter during this period, but we may infer much from photographs of the three. In 1904 Steichen made two series of double portraits, one of Emmy and six-year-old Kitty, the other of Alfred and Kitty. In the first series Emmy — wearing a cape and looking corpulent, homely, and unhappy — suggests a Wagnerian soprano cast as Brünnhilde.

In the photographs with her mother, Kitty looks spoiled and willful. But at least they appear comfortable with each other. The three photographs of Alfred and Kitty, on the other hand, convey a sense of forced affection, discomfort, and alienation. In one, father and daughter are holding hands very awkwardly, though with evident good humor. In another the father stands behind his daughter and gazes down at her rather quizzically and with some concern. In the third, Alfred and Kitty both stand with their hands in their coat pockets. Kitty — despite the halo formed by her light-colored, broad-brimmed hat — seems precociously hardened. If she is a saint, she is Mary Magdalen. It is telling that Steichen did not make a series of Alfred and Emmy together, and there do not seem to be any photographs at all, by anyone, of the three members of the family.

Alfred's relationship with Kitty had become troubled and complicated. Seeing relatively little of her father, she favored her attentive mother in the household schism, and Alfred resented that fact. He was alternately optimistic and pessimistic about her chances of developing into a person whom he could admire. When they were together, his responses were rendered disproportionate to the circumstances. There was little middle ground between his excessive indulgence of her demands and his harsh reprimands. Evidently he would try to win her love, then decide that perhaps she didn't deserve his.

Further evidence of familial dysfunction is provided by one of Alfred's own photographs, dated 1905. It is a deeply disturbing picture of Kitty, who is looking directly at the camera — that is, at her father — with an expression that is coldly appraising and resentful. Suggesting that the hostility may have been mutual, for Alfred was evidently disgusted to see his daughter becoming more and more like her mother, he has photographed her against a wall that bears a stenciled children's book illustration of a Dutch woman who is running and carrying an enormous butcher knife, with which she appears about to attack Kitty's throat.

Alfred certainly abused his daughter psychologically, through his neglect and his destabilizing inconsistency, but it seems unlikely that he abused her physically, as a previous biographer has implied. For one thing, the presence of her hovering mother and a resident governess would have given him few opportunities to do so. As he aged, Alfred became increasingly attracted to adolescent girls, but none of his photographs suggests that he had any erotic interest in prepubescent children.

Badly needing a rest, Alfred sailed for Europe in May 1904 with Emmy, Kitty, and her governess. It was his first visit in ten years, and he had planned an ambitious itinerary of photographic exhibitions, meetings, and excursions. But the ship had hardly docked in Germany before Alfred, as he reported, "collapsed completely" and had to be admitted to a private clinic in Berlin. He was told that he should undergo "a rest-cure which implies absolute quiet all summer." He was, he said, "paying the penalty for ten years of incessant strenuousness."[7] He had spent that decade involved in the struggles of pictorial photography against, in his words, "the hostile environment of ignorance, prejudice, selfishness, vanity, conceit, intrigue, provincialism and a host of other malign influences."[8]

Stieglitz routinely exaggerated the gravity of his physical ailments to obtain sympathy, to secure his privacy from Emmy, and to provide the necessary background for his accounts of his heroic efforts on behalf of photography. Too, his hypochondria was certainly an attempt to translate his psychological pain into physiological terms, to display physical ailments in lieu of the emotional ones that could not be revealed or treated.

After having been in the clinic for about four weeks, Stieglitz made a brief trip to Dresden late in June. "Hardly out of my sick bed, and against the express instructions of my physician," he wrote, "the ruling passion asserted itself." (In fact, his doctor had reluctantly given him permission to go.) He went to see the International Art Exhibition, at that time the foremost such show in Europe, to which the Photo-Secession had sent a "small, but choice, collection."[9]

In July the Stieglitz family went to the lovely Tyrolean village of Igls, near Innsbruck. Still recuperating, Alfred spent many days photographing the beautiful countryside, accompanied for a while by Frank Eugene. Perhaps it was in Igls that Alfred met "Miss S. R.," his photograph of whom shows an attractive, Germanic-looking young woman with seductively half-closed eyes and lasciviously parted lips, wearing her pertly narrow-brimmed hat at a rakish angle. The picture clearly implies mutual infatuation, at the very least.

It is tempting to speculate that an account of a "dream" (actually more like a parable) written by Stieglitz in 1915 might refer to his involvement with "Miss S. R."[10] She had clearly remained on his mind, for he had published his portrait of her in the January 1913 issue of *Camera Work*. The "dream," which was set in the mountains at a time when Stieglitz was very ill, implies that he had wanted a spiritually erotic relationship but was so frightened or repelled by the woman's carnal voracity that he fled.

Another visitor to Igls was Heinrich Kuehn, who enthusiastically accepted Stieglitz's invitation to become the first foreign member of the Photo-Secession. In a portrait by Kuehn dating from this encounter, Stieglitz — nattily dressed in a three-piece suit and a bow tie — looks tired, exasperated, and filled with smoldering anger. He was furious about the latest developments in regard to Curtis Bell's salon. In June, Hartmann had written to the leading European photographers inviting them to send work. As soon as he learned of this, Stieglitz sent letters to the major British and Continental photographic magazines stating that he had nothing to do with the exhibition and that, in fact, it had been organized specif-

ically to counter his influence. He went on to disparage the salon's professed popularization of photography as nothing more than the lowering
of standards. *The Amateur Photographer* soon haughtily commented that the
salon would probably "not be conducted on the lines which would be required by those who insist that exhibitions of this kind must be conducted
disinterestedly and in a dignified manner." The editorial added that "from
private advice we are in a position to say that the leading British workers,
whose practical support has been solicited by the American Salon, do not
see their way to accord it."[11]

There was also a great flap — about which Keiley's letters kept Stieglitz
informed — over an article entitled "The Three Factors in American Photography," published in the August issue of *The American Amateur Photographer*. It had been written by Roland Rood, a painter who taught aesthetics
at Columbia University. (He was the son of the physicist Ogden N. Rood,
whose color wheel had been important in Georges Seurat's development of
pointillism.) Rood had been very friendly with both Stieglitz and Hartmann, and he praised them both in his article, stating that the latter "was
the first art critic who realized the possibility of photography being developed into a fine art." But Hartmann, jealous of the attention that Stieglitz
was paying to Rood, had been shown the manuscript by one of the magazine's editors and had, without Rood's knowledge, revised it extensively,
going so far as to add a paragraph about the upcoming salon. Presented
with this fait accompli upon publication, Rood repudiated the article.[12]
That fall he began contributing regularly to *Camera Work* while continuing
to write for *The American Amateur Photographer*, where he complained of
feeling benumbed by the icy perfection of Frederick Evans's work and
harshly criticized Steichen. When Stieglitz took exception, Rood rebelled
as angrily as Hartmann had done, though far less publicly.

In the hope of ostracizing Bell, Stieglitz revived his dream of establishing
an international society of pictorial photographers. Inspired, no doubt, by
his rival's American Federation of Photographic Societies, Stieglitz was
hoping for an alliance among the Photo-Secession, the Linked Ring, and
the leading French, German, and Austrian societies, which would retain
their individual identities. The new superorganization would be governed
by the combined councils of the member societies, these councils already
being composed mostly of Links. Kuehn, a founder of the new Photo-Club
of Vienna, was all for it. But the key negotiations would take place in London.

Keiley hoped to call the new organization the World's Secession, but the British preferred the International Society of the Linked Ring. Stieglitz, who believed that the chief Links would never agree to the society unless it was headed by a Briton, proposed J. Craig Annan. Unfortunately, Annan had left in mid-August for America, where he was to serve on the photographic jury at the ill-fated St. Louis exposition.

When he arrived in London on August 22, after a stop in Paris, Stieglitz was delighted to find that Alfred Horsley Hinton and George Davison were in favor of the new society — partly because the Linked Ring was then suffering from internal dissension and financial difficulties. (There was also, within the RPS, an abortive movement afoot to win back the Ring; the RPS made Stieglitz a life member in the hope that he might facilitate reunification.) At the next meeting of the Ring, on October 28, Hinton and Davison would set forth their proposal of alliance, at which time they were appointed members of a committee to draft a constitution. In the October 1904 issue of *Camera Work* Stieglitz would optimistically state, in a direct challenge to Bell, that "the squally appearance of the photographic sea is more apparent than real, for the recognized leaders and their friends throughout the world are working in entire harmony toward an end which in our next number we hope to make public."

Preparing the photographic community for Annan's presidency of the new organization, Stieglitz published six gravures by him in that same issue. In an accompanying article, Keiley called Annan "one of the foremost artists in photography, not only in England, but of the whole world" and stated that "the character and influence of his work, his known views, his conservativeness of action and broad catholicity of taste, have all gone to make him what he is today, the real leader of British Pictorial Photography."[13]

Elsewhere in the issue, Stieglitz reviewed the Dresden show and remarked that "in the British exhibit but two deserve mention — Hill, the painter-photographer of fifty years ago, and J. Craig Annan. Their pictures will always hold their own in the very best of company — sane, honest, temperamental." In 1867 Annan's father photographed a huge painting by the Scottish artist David Octavius Hill (whose photographic collaborator Robert Adamson went unmentioned until fairly recently), and when Hill moved out of his house in Edinburgh two years later, the Annan family moved in. Annan, who was only six when Hill died, in 1870, had fond memories of the old man. During the 1890s he began to print and exhibit many of the hundreds of magnificent paper-negative portraits made by Hill and Adamson. Unfamiliar with Hill's work before Dresden, Stieglitz was so impressed that he began to refer to Hill as the founder of pictorial photography and would publish a total of twenty-one of his photographs in three issues of *Camera Work*.

Despite all of Stieglitz's efforts and optimism, the international society never materialized. On January 31, 1905, Hinton and Davison presented their draft constitution, which was printed and sent to all the foreign Links. But the project soon died as a result of apathy — and perhaps also because of the British suspicions that Annan was to be merely a figurehead. The Links surely realized that Stieglitz was determined to be in control and that the new society would eventually shift the center of power to New York.

While he was in London, Stieglitz attended the opening of the Linked Ring's Photographic Salon on September 16. Although for the past eleven years he had been citing the annual salon as the best example of all that he was trying to achieve in America, he had, amazingly, never before actually seen one. The 1904 salon would be of special interest to him because for the first time (as a result of the 1903 boycott) the American photographs had been selected in New York by the American Links and sent over as a collection. Since Stieglitz had been in Europe the entire summer, he had not served on the jury.

Told that this was the best salon ever held, Stieglitz was keenly disappointed when he walked into the Egyptian Hall of the Dudley Gallery in Piccadilly. The room was small and poorly lighted, and the walls seemed overcrowded with frames. Many of the American prints, which constituted about a third of the show, struck him as second-rate. Reversing his recurring criticism throughout the 1890s, he nevertheless concluded that "the artistic average of the American prints was far in advance of that of the English." He went on to observe that "a striking feature in some of the English exhibits was the marked influence of the American school, and notably that of Gertrude Käsebier. In fact, throughout Europe I found her influence dominant."[14] Making up for lost time, Stieglitz would visit the exhibition seven times during the following weeks so that he could study it in detail.

Actually, Stieglitz was making a virtue of necessity, since he had intended to sail for America immediately after the opening of the salon. He wrote, however, that he had been detained in London "on account of the illness of my whole family."[15] He himself was again ill in London, and that led to the disappointment of his hopes to meet two men whom he admired greatly: George Bernard Shaw and Peter Henry Emerson.

According to one story, Stieglitz developed a sore throat during the

Channel crossing and lost his voice. Since it would be absurd to meet Shaw under such circumstances, he canceled their luncheon date and was unable to reschedule. He had no better luck with Emerson. One day when Stieglitz was in bed with a fever so high that he was barely conscious, he became vaguely aware that he had a visitor. Only later was he informed that it had been Emerson. Stieglitz had probably wanted to enlist his support for the new international organization, though Emerson was unlikely to endorse any organization related to the Linked Ring.

When Stieglitz finally returned to New York, in October, he threw himself into preparing the delayed October issue of *Camera Work*, but he was seriously distracted and upset by the approach of Bell's salon. The first direct attack upon Stieglitz was an article by Hartmann, under the pseudonym Juvenal, in the September issue of *The Photo-Beacon*. Entitled "Little Tin Gods on Wheels," this merciless diatribe did not mention Stieglitz by name, referring to his inner circle as the "T.G.O.W." Hartmann raved that "the self-conceit of the Little Tin Gods on Wheels has become abnormal, preposterous, has grown into the very heavens" and then announced that "war has been formally declared on the T.G.O.W." by Bell. The author demanded, "And you pictorialists throughout the land . . . will you any longer stand the undemocratic, un-American policy of these little T.G.O.W.?" Striking a low blow, he listed the many fellows and associates of the Photo-Secession whose work had been ignored or given token representation in *Camera Work* and in exhibitions organized by Stieglitz.[16]

That was only the beginning. The November issue of the same magazine contained more of Hartmann's vitriol — an article entitled "The Inquisitorial System," in which the critic accused the still-unnamed Stieglitz of being a Torquemada.[17] Finally, in the November issue of *The Camera*, Hartmann equated Bell with William Tell, who refused to bow down to the hat belonging to Gessler, the Hapsburgs' evil and marauding governor. The article was illustrated with a caricature of a huge and unmistakable Stieglitz wearing a broad-brimmed slouch hat, while around him a group of tiny people cower with fear and reverence. Hartmann made it clear that he owed allegiance to no one, not even to Bell, of whom he wrote there, "Also he is hunted by envy and ambition, also he would like to become a Gessler, but as his time is still far off, he speaks the broad democratic word."[18] Perhaps Hartmann, writing under the pseudonym Caliban, was covering his bases. In *The Tempest* Caliban revolts against Prospero and supports the usurper Antonio. But Hartmann knew perfectly well that Prospero ultimately triumphs.

*   *   *

Stieglitz, who had assumed that Bell's salon would be hung in one of the city's large and prestigious galleries or perhaps at the Lotos Club, was greatly relieved to learn that it would be held on the top floor of the small brownstone building, at 381 Fifth Avenue, housing the Clausen Galleries. The disturbing news now was that Bell had assembled a jury of twenty-one distinguished painters, headed by John La Farge and including William Merritt Chase, Kenyon Cox, Childe Hassam, Robert Henri, and Dwight W. Tryon. In his article about the salon, Stieglitz would make much of his claim that the judges had looked at ten thousand photographs in sixteen hours to select the 369 mediocre or worse prints "with which the walls were literally plastered."[19]

The salon, which opened on December 5 and ran for almost two weeks, had attracted a considerable amount of foreign work, but most of Stieglitz's friends, at home and abroad, had boycotted it. The only first-rate photographer in the exhibition was Day, whose display was rendered extremely poignant by the fact that his Boston studio had burned on the night of November 11. All of his negatives were destroyed. (Stieglitz, the owner of fifty-four Day prints, sent a laconic telegram of sympathy to his longtime enemy.)

The only other photographers of serious interest were Rudolf Eickemeyer, Arnold Genthe, and a twenty-four-year-old unknown from Stockbridge, Massachusetts, named George Seeley, who was represented by fourteen prints. Bell regarded Seeley as his artistic trump card and had written to him in November, "I have already taken measures to bring your extraordinary work before the public in such a way that I feel *financial* returns will begin to materialize as soon as the December magazines are out and the Salon is underway."[20] Inspired by Day and White, Seeley's gauzy Symbolist fantasies (one shows a toga-wearing but farmer-tanned man holding a lyre in a soft-focus landscape) have not aged well, but they created something of a sensation in 1904. Roland Rood wrote that Seeley had "already acquired a power of expression which places him in the foremost ranks of American photographers."[21]

Stieglitz, badly in need of a first-class "discovery" to diversify *Camera Work*, wasted no time before attempting to steal Bell's protégé, writing to Seeley on December 27 with an offer of fellowship in the Photo-Secession, "an honor not readily conferred, you know."[22] Seeley held out for a year but then became a pillar of the organization.

PART IV

"291"

CHAPTER THIRTY·ONE

WHILE STIEGLITZ WAS in Europe during 1904, Keiley wrote him, "I have quietly and industriously circulated the idea that the Bell Salon is nothing more than an attempt to forestall & over set an international exhibition for 1905 — long contemplated by you."[1] Nor was Keiley bluffing. Stieglitz was particularly eager to found an international federation precisely because it would sponsor an annual salon, to be held in New York, that would render Bell's salon irrelevant and even overshadow the Linked Ring's.

Although his hopes for the international society were dashed early in 1905, Stieglitz persevered in his efforts to organize a great international salon in New York. His plan was to rent one of the big art galleries for a few weeks early in the spring of 1906 and to mount "an exhibition consisting of the very best that has been accomplished in pictorial photography throughout the world, from the time of Hill . . . up to date."[2] He went so far as to assemble many prints, and he intended to show others that were already in his rapidly growing personal collection.

Stieglitz's hopes for the exhibition were strongly supported by Steichen, who was doing quite well financially, not least because, as he put it, "the entire Stieglitz clan" bought canvases from him. Edward Stieglitz was especially fond of Steichen, who found himself more or less adopted into the family. Moreover, his exhibition of paintings at the gallery of Eugene

Glaenzer and Company in February and March 1905 had nearly sold out. He was also thriving as a photographic portraitist. On one extraordinary day in 1903 both J. P. Morgan and Eleonora Duse sat for him. Morgan came because Fedor Encke, who had been commissioned to paint an official portrait, wanted to work from a photograph to supplement his brief and frustrating sittings. In Steichen's dramatic image, the position of Morgan's arm in relation to a reflection on the arm of the wooden chair in which he is sitting makes it look as though he is about to thrust with a dagger.

Steichen felt that he should concentrate either on painting or photography, but he couldn't decide between them. His wavering prompted Sadakichi Hartmann to pen an amusing parody that found its way into the pages of *Camera Work*.

> To paint or photograph — that is the question:
> Whether 'tis more to my advantage to color
> photographic accidents and call them paintings,
> Or to squeeze the bulb against a sea of critics
> And by exposure kill them?
> . . . . To paint — to snap;
> Perchance to tell the truth: aye! there's the rub.
> How may a fact be lost in fuzziness
> When we cast aside the painter's brush . . . [?][3]

In September 1905 Stieglitz found himself forced to accept "the impossibility of securing at any price adequate gallery accommodations [for his salon] during the desirable New York season."[4] One night shortly thereafter, he and Steichen hit upon a brilliant idea during a long conversation at the corner of Fifth Avenue and Thirty-first Street. They decided that even if they could not find a space in which to hang a large exhibition, they surely could at least rent a room or two in which to present the various international sections of the aborted show serially over the course of a few months.

After some deliberation, Steichen exclaimed that he knew of just the place. The success of his Glaenzer show in the spring had enabled him to vacate his top-floor apartment-studio at 291 Fifth Avenue — a few doors from where they were standing — and move across the hall into a larger space with a big skylight. (Hallways had been broken through on every floor to connect the two adjoining brownstones at 291 and 293 so that both could be serviced by a single elevator.) His old studio was still empty, but it would not be big enough for a gallery unless it was combined with the two small rooms behind it, which were occupied by two artists. Steichen, who knew that these two women had only a monthly lease, had been bothered by the odors of their cooking and would therefore be very glad to see them leave. The next day the agent of the landlord, the Chicago department store magnate Marshall Field, said Stieglitz could have the three rooms for $50 a month if he signed a one-year lease. Steichen estimated that renovations, decoration, and the installation of electric lighting would cost about another $300. He told Stieglitz that he would design the interior and oversee the work.

Since Steichen mistakenly assumed that Stieglitz would not want to spend his days at the gallery, he said that whenever people stopped by to see an exhibition, Mrs. Steichen could unlock the door and let them in. The gallery would at first be open mornings from ten to noon and afternoons from two to six every day except Sundays and holidays; eventually Stieglitz would keep it open every day.

He was at first reluctant to sign the lease, for he was worried that he and Steichen would not be able to find enough first-rate photographs to fill the gallery with an uninterrupted series of exhibitions throughout the six-month New York art season. Steichen then countered that since the established art galleries still refused to show photographs, the new place could turn their flank by exhibiting paintings and other works of art, either together with photographs or in alternation. Such exhibitions could confirm the artistic claims of photography and inspire photographers to strive for more sophisticated artistic standards in their own work. Stieglitz naturally approved.

Since Steichen was so enthusiastic, so capable, and so willing to take care of everything, Stieglitz finally agreed to sign the lease. In a letter dated October 14, 1905, he informed the members of the Photo-Secession about the new gallery,

> where will be shown continuous fortnightly exhibitions of from thirty to forty prints each. These small, but very select, shows will consist not only of American pictures never before publicly shown in any city in this country, but also of Austrian, German, British, French, and Belgian photographs, as well as such other art productions, other than photographic, as the Council of the Photo-Secession can from time to time secure.

He went on to say that the new space would be as much a clubroom, the "headquarters for all Secessionists," as it would be a gallery open to the public "generally without charge." The rooms would be made "as attractive as possible to all art lovers, who will find there, besides the exhibitions, art magazines and publications, foreign and American."[5]

Steichen's decoration of the gallery was inspired by the work of the Viennese Secession architect Josef Hoffmann, who had in turn been influenced by Glasgow designers such as Charles Rennie Mackintosh and George Walton. In 1897 J. Craig Annan had asked his friend Walton to redo the room in the Dudley Gallery in which the Linked Ring's salons were held. Walton's design featured a green and buff color scheme, a shelf running around the room, and canvas hangings below the shelf. Steichen saw that room in 1900. In 1902 Frederick Evans modified it with undyed canvas covering the walls, white moldings at top and bottom, and a diffusing scrim suspended under the skylight. Evans described the room in a letter to Steichen, and Stieglitz saw it in 1904. According to the description of the new gallery at 291 Fifth Avenue published in *Camera Work*, the main room, in which photographs were displayed mostly in dark wooden frames, was "kept in dull olive tones, the burlap wall-covering being a warm olive gray; the woodwork and moldings similar in general color, but considerably darker." The pleated canvas hangings that concealed storage below the shelf running all around the room were "of an olive-sepia sateen," and the ceiling and scrim were "of a very deep creamy gray." In the smaller room, where matted photographs were hung unframed or in simple white frames, the walls and doors were "covered with a bleached natural burlap," boldly outlined by rectangles of white, with hangings of grayish yellow. The little hallway, also used as an exhibition space, was "decorated in gray-blue, dull salmon, and olive-gray."[6] A few Japanese vases were placed on the shelf in the main room. On the burlap-covered table in the center of that room, filled with flowers or branches, sat a large, nearly spherical bowl of hammered brass, a three-dimensional version of the golden disk that was the gallery's logo. Outside the building, beside the entrance, was a little vitrine containing a photograph and a small sign on which a golden disk was placed between the words "Photo" and "Secession." The meaning of the golden disk was explained thus by John Kerfoot in *Camera Work:* "In our sun-whirl there is one planet which has a moon which is turning the other way. And if it be strong enough, and last long enough, sooner or later the whole mighty Wheel of Light will return and follow that one little moon."[7]

In his October letter Stieglitz had announced that the inaugural exhibition would be "a collection of work by Secessionists." He urged all members to send work and assured them that at least one picture by each person who responded would be hung. "The Exhibition Committee will undertake to negotiate sales in behalf of the owners of the pictures exhibited," he continued, "charging a commission thereon of 15 per cent for the benefit of the Photo-Secession treasury."[8]

On the evening of November 25, 1905, "without flourish of trumpets, without the stereotyped press-view or similar antiquated functions, the Secessionists and a few friends informally opened the Little Galleries of the Photo-Secession."[9] (The "little" in the name was literally true, but it also had significant connotations. It was an Arts-and-Craftsy catchword implying sophisticated simplicity, informality, camaraderie, and exclusiveness. From the early 1890s until about 1910, Chicago's artists and intellectuals gathered in their Little Room. The years after 1910 would see a proliferation in America of "little theaters" and "little magazines" — notably *The Little Review*.) After a festive dinner at Mouquin's, the assembly made its way to Fifth Avenue to see the new gallery and to view the first exhibition, which had been tastefully hung by Steichen. The prints were in a single row, well separated "so that, as you examined each, it was quietly detached from all its neighbors."[10]

The exhibition amounted to a miniature but superb salon of American photography. Of the approximately sixty photographers in the Photo-Secession at that time, thirty-nine were represented in the selection of one hundred prints. Steichen led with eleven, followed by White, Käsebier, Stieglitz, Keiley, Eugene, and William Dyer. Among those represented by from one to three prints were A. L. Coburn, John Kerfoot, William Post, Sarah Sears, and Eva Watson-Schütze. The names of most of the other exhibitors mean nothing today.

Of the Photo-Secession and its first exhibition the *New York Evening Sun*'s caustic critic Charles FitzGerald wrote, "The vanity of these people is unbelievable. The fopperies displayed in their work, their eccentric frames, the whimsical flourishes in which they habitually indulge, and their incurable gravity — all these are but symptomatic of their essential frivolity. Not that all of the exhibitors come under this condemnation. There are some earnest workers here."[11] He protested that the photographers "are exceedingly jealous of their claims, make a great mystery of their calling, and throw the words Master and Masterpiece at each other with a prodigality that would astonish most painters."[12]

The opening show was followed by one of French photographs selected by Robert Demachy (January 10–24, 1906). The first one-person exhibition (January 26–February 2) was an anomaly: Herbert G. French's series of illustrations of Tennyson's *Idylls of the King*. One may safely assume that it was the $75 contribution made by the wealthy Mr. French, an executive of Procter and Gamble who would later pay for a new wing of the Cincinnati Art Museum, that secured him a one-week slot in the exhibition schedule. Then came a Käsebier and White duet, succeeded by a show of work by Stieglitz's three favorite British photographers, Hill, Annan, and Evans.

Steichen's solo exhibition (March 16–31) was a retrospective of sixty-one photographs, including some experimental color prints made by exposing three separate black-and-white negatives through blue, green, and red filters, then printing them in superimposition with red, green, and blue gum bichromate. In April, shortly after the show closed, the Steichen number of *Camera Work* appeared; it reproduced ten of his images and was accompanied by a special supplement containing another sixteen.

Bringing the first season to a close at the end of April was an Austrian-German show that featured fourteen large multiple-gum prints by the self-styled Viennese Trifolium (Heinrich Kuehn, Hugo Henneberg, and the late Hans Watzek). Stieglitz had thus succeeded in presenting all but the projected Belgian section of his serial salon. He had, however, failed to mount two announced exhibitions: a "Salon des Refusés" to have been made up of "a collection of paintings, by American painters, that have been refused at the Society of American Artists, National Academy, Carnegie Institute, and Pennsylvania Academy of [the] Fine Arts," and a second "general exhibition of work by members of the Photo-Secession."[13] Steichen recalled that the painting show was abandoned because "there was nothing good being refused" and because, in any case, the gallery's rooms were too small to permit the hanging of any large canvases or more than a few medium-size ones.

Stieglitz had assumed that "those who love and understand and have the art-nose" would find their way to 291 Fifth Avenue.[14] They did so in such unexpected numbers — an estimated fifteen thousand visits the first season — that he found it worth his while to spend all day at the gallery. Not only did they come, they also bought. Stieglitz reported that at an average price of $45.86, sixty-one prints were sold for a total of $2,797.46, Steichen's work claiming the lion's share of the sales.[15]

Stieglitz himself, determined to assemble one of the world's greatest collections of pictorial photography, was the principal buyer at 291, as he generally called the gallery. Early in 1902, before General Cesnola reneged on his promise regarding the photographs for Turin, Stieglitz had told Theodore Dreiser that he planned to give his holdings to the Metropolitan Museum someday. Now, in 1905, he was hoping that the Photo-Secession might eventually found the photography museum of which he had dreamt in the early days of the Camera Club.

The new Photo-Secession gallery was certainly well located from a commercial point of view, since by 1905, Fifth Avenue above Thirtieth Street was replacing the old Ladies' Mile as New York's most fashionable district of stores and hotels. (Despite the concentration of wealth, there were still surprisingly few automobiles to be seen. Most of the vehicular traffic passing by Stieglitz's gallery when it opened consisted of hansom cabs. Two years later, with the appearance of the first taxis, people began to complain about the number of automobiles on the avenue.) A couple of blocks north of the gallery, on the southwest corner of Fifth Avenue and Thirty-fourth Street, the splendid, seventeen-story Astoria Hotel, joined to the Waldorf next door, had opened in 1897. Diagonally across Thirty-fourth Street, Benjamin Altman had begun construction of his immense new store in 1905 even though he had not yet succeeded in buying the brownstone on the northeast corner of Thirty-fourth Street occupied by Knoedler's art gallery. Directly across Fifth Avenue the old A. T. Stewart mansion had recently been torn down and replaced by Stanford White's Knickerbocker Trust Company building.

This was the heyday of McKim, Mead and White, whose Italian Renaissance palazzi for the competing jewelers Gorham's and Tiffany's were going up on Fifth Avenue at Thirty-sixth and Thirty-seventh streets, respectively. During February 1906 Stanford White stopped by 291 Fifth Avenue to see the Käsebier–Clarence White exhibition, in which Gertrude's portrait of the architect was displayed in a frame that he had designed himself. He was even listed as a purchaser in Stieglitz's summary of the first season. But in June 1906, before he could become a dependable patron of the Photo-Secession, Stanford White was shot to death in the roof garden of Madison Square Garden by Harry K. Thaw, whose wife, the former Evelyn Nesbit, had been White's mistress before her marriage. Käsebier's suggestive 1902 portrait of Nesbit, commissioned by White, had been exhibited in her two-person show.

Alfred's "round table" at the Holland House, an opulent hotel on the southwest corner of Fifth Avenue and Thirtieth Street, just half a block from the gallery, quickly became an institution.* Opened in 1891, the hotel had a superb restaurant. With the help of a special allowance that

---

*The handsome building still stands. No longer a hotel, it is now filled with offices and Oriental carpet showrooms.

Emmy gave him from her own income, Alfred would take a group of friends there for lunch almost every day. Photographers and writers would drop by 291 during the morning to see the current show, to help Alfred mount photogravures into copies of *Camera Work* (the gallery now doubled as the magazine's editorial office), or to chat for a while, knowing that if they hung around they could get a free lunch that might be their best meal of the week.

By this time, Emmy was probably glad to have Alfred out of the apartment most of the time. The principal evidence regarding the state of their problematic marriage during this period consists of two Käsebier portraits of Emmy that date from late 1905 or 1906. In one, holding a portfolio whose cover is embossed with the golden disk of the Photo-Secession, she actually looks quite happy, as if she still hoped that her efforts (including the lunch allowance) might yet win her Alfred's approval, and even his love. In the other, however, her shoulders are rounded; her big, longing eyes look defeated; and her faint smile suggests reflection upon shattered dreams.

CHAPTER THIRTY·TWO

IN THE SPRING of 1906, Steichen decided that he would give up his "lucrative but stultifying" portrait business and move back to Paris that fall with his wife and their two small children. There he would be able to devote more time to his painting and his personal work in photography. When Stieglitz informed Emmy of his friend's decision, she exclaimed, "Thank God, he's going. Now we two can travel and you can give up all that nonsense, for without Steichen you can't go ahead."[1] Stieglitz, who had been undecided, resolved on the spot to continue with his gallery. He called the real estate agent the next morning and renewed the lease for two more years.

He did so although he found spending all day at 291 a "horrid torment and task." He went every day because he felt it was his duty to be there, since even many of the most intelligent visitors did not understand the works hung on the walls. "You should really hear how A. S. often holds forth not only on photography but on art and social conditions in America," he wrote to Heinrich Kuehn. "It is surely not in vain—that I know and feel."[2]

Stieglitz was already developing serious misgivings about the Photo-Secession, for he was becoming exasperated by the conceit, the competitiveness, and the commercialism that seemed increasingly rampant among the members. He had even expelled one who had been so crass as to print on his business card the words "Member of the Photo-Secession." Looking back on that time, he would write, "They had come to believe that my life was to be dedicated solely to them and did not realize that my battle was for an idea bigger than any individual."[3] He was, in fact, wondering whether perhaps his work on behalf of photography was done. Keiley, still one of Stieglitz's chief spokesmen and once again his closest ally after Steichen's return to Paris, wrote in the October 1906 issue of *Camera Work*, "Today in America the real battle for the recognition of pictorial photography is over. The chief purpose for which the Photo-Secession was established has been accomplished — the serious recognition of photography as an additional medium of pictorial expression."[4]

Nor was it only the Photo-Secession about which Stieglitz was upset. He was equally disgusted by the conservative forces that were gaining control of the Linked Ring. Early in the summer of 1906, he learned that Frederick Evans would be away on assignment for *Country Life* and would thus be unable to serve on the selection committee for that year's salon. Because Evans's absence would give a majority to the conservatives, Stieglitz decided that the Photo-Secession should boycott the salon. Nevertheless, twelve Secessionists — including Coburn, Coburn's mother, and Käsebier — were represented.

All that notwithstanding, Stieglitz began the second season at 291 with another show of members' work, which ran from November 10 through the end of December. Astonishingly, he had been hoping to follow with a Day retrospective. In his reply to Stieglitz's letter of November 26, Day stated that his recent work did not satisfy him. "Regarding an exhibition made up of any possible collection of my prints dating prior to 1900," he continued, "I can but assure you that it would be wholly and seriously without my approval and contrary to my wishes."[5]

One day early in December a young woman named Pamela Colman Smith appeared, unannounced, at 291. Stieglitz was feeling very discouraged, and even rather morbid. When she asked whether Mr. Stieglitz was in, he replied testily, "No. I'm not."[6] But he was intrigued by this eccentric-seeming twenty-eight-year-old American who had been living in London. He relented when she told him that all the dealers were afraid to show her work. Indeed, she had had little success since her two-person show, with Robert Henri, at the Macbeth Gallery in 1897. One reviewer had then praised the "remarkable decorative quality" of her work, though the titles of two of the drawings — *Our Pets* and *Hark! Hark! The Dogs Do Bark* — suggest that he was perhaps being generous.[7]

By 1906 Smith had become more serious. Having mentioned that she counted among her friends William Butler Yeats, the British Symbolist poet and critic Arthur Symons, and the great English actress Ellen Terry, she proceeded to show Stieglitz several portfolios of her drawings and watercolors. Many of them were in the spirit of the French Symbolist painter Odilon Redon, and most had been inspired by the theater (Shakespeare and Maeterlinck) or by music (Robert Schumann's *Carnaval*). Outstanding was a small blue and yellow wash drawing entitled *Death in the House*. Illustrating an Icelandic legend, it was an interior scene with a skeleton standing in profile in the foreground. Cowering, terrified, in the rafters above was a creature of uncertain species. To Stieglitz, the work powerfully represented his own mood and symbolized the unhealthy spirit that had infected the Photo-Secession. He immediately decided to exhibit Smith's work in the slot left open by Day's refusal.

It had, of course, been planned all along to exhibit nonphotographic works, though Steichen's intentions were primarily aesthetic, while Stieglitz's — as was so often the case — were partly moral and didactic. He wanted to rebuke the errant Photo-Secessionists and remind them that his function was not solely to act as their publicist. To ensure that they got the point, he wrote in *Camera Work*, employing a phrase from Ruskin's book *The Seven Lamps of Architecture*, "The Secession Idea is neither the servant nor the product of a medium. It is a spirit. Let us say it is the Spirit of the Lamp; the old and discolored, the too frequently despised, the too often discarded lamp of honesty; honesty of aim, honesty of self-expression, honesty of revolt against the autocracy of convention."[8]

When Steichen received Stieglitz's letter informing him of the upcoming Smith exhibition, he was furious. Upon his return to Paris, he had told Rodin that he and Stieglitz wanted a show of his drawings to be the first nonphotographic exhibition at 291. Rodin had expressed his enthusiasm for the project, but Steichen had not been quick enough to select and send the drawings to New York. Since Stieglitz had signaled that he would leave the selection of nonphotographic work to Steichen, the *peintre-photographe*, the latter was angry at being preempted, and he was embarrassed to have to tell his hero what had happened. Until the end of his life, Steichen would remain annoyed that the sequence of events gave many people the impression that the idea of showing modernist drawings, paintings, and sculpture at 291 had been Stieglitz's.

For the first ten days after the opening of the exhibition of seventy-two drawings and watercolors by Pamela Colman Smith, on January 5, 1907, the gallery was virtually empty. Then there appeared in the *New York Sun* a highly complimentary review, by the distinguished critic James Gibbons Huneker, which began, "Pamela Colman Smith is a young woman with that quality rare in either sex — imagination." Huneker went on to call *Death in the House* "absolutely nerve-shuddering" and to say that not even Munch "could have succeeded better in arousing a profound disquiet." Although he found her technique "naively crude," Huneker concluded that because of the poetic nature of her work, Smith belonged to the "favored choir" of William Blake and his mystics.[9] According to Stieglitz, this review "brought the Whitneys and Havemeyers, Vanderbilts and all classes of people. . . . The place was literally mobbed."[10] The exhibition, which ran until January 24, sold out; and Stieglitz issued, in an edition of only seven, a portfolio of platinum prints of his own photographs of twenty-two of the drawings and watercolors.

Many members of the Photo-Secession resented Smith's show, for they felt there were plenty of other galleries in which nonphotographic artists could exhibit. Stieglitz appeased his colleagues somewhat with the remainder of the season's schedule, which was entirely devoted to photography. (Furthermore, in an attempt to halt cancellations by members who were fed up with *Camera Work*'s elitism, Stieglitz published in the magazine, during the course of 1907, photographs by six not especially gifted Secessionists.) A two-man show of prints by George Seeley, recently made a fellow, and Adolf de Meyer, not yet a member, was followed by an exhibition of work by two fellows who had been neglected, Alice Boughton and William Dyer, together with nonmember C. Yarnall Abbott (February 19–March 5). A small Coburn retrospective (March 11–April 10) brought the second season to an early close.

The most important debut of the gallery's 1906–7 season was that of Baron Adolf de Meyer, about whom secure facts are hard to come by — as is fitting, for de Meyer's life was devoted to fantasy, glamour, outré costumes, and the transformative effects of shimmering light. This Wildean caricature of a Whistlerian dandy, this foppish ultra-aesthete and worshiper of chic who became the first great fashion photographer, was born, perhaps in Paris, in 1868 or 1869. His father was a wealthy French or German Jew who may or may not have been a baron; Adolf's mother, Adele Watson, seems to have been a Scotswoman. Raised by her in Dresden and Paris (his father having died young), Adolf settled in London about 1896 and soon met the exquisite sixteen-year-old Olga, who had been painted or sketched by Whistler, Sargent, and Giovanni Boldini. The illegitimate daughter of Blanche, duchesa (or perhaps only baronessa) de Caracciolo, and the Polish grandee Prince Poniatowski, Olga was the goddaughter of Edward, Prince of Wales (whom many people believed to be her father). Soon — although Adolf was obviously homosexual — she became his wife, muse, model, and entrée into the highest society. They would remain blissfully married, in a sort of brother-and-sister relationship, until her death, in 1931.

Adolf, who had taken up photography in the early 1890s and had exhibited internationally, was made a member of the Linked Ring in 1898. With an exotically decorated apartment in London, a house in Dresden, a rented palazzo in Venice for the late-summer season, and properly timed stays in all the right resort hotels, he became a celebrated portraitist of international high society, as well as an interior decorator and a camp follower of Sergei Diaghilev's Ballets Russes.

De Meyer seems an unlikely candidate for friendship with Stieglitz. But sensible Gertrude Käsebier, in whose portrait the mid-thirtyish Adolf appears positively boyish, was charmed when she met him in Venice. And when Steichen encountered him in 1906, he relayed to Stieglitz high praise for de Meyer's elegant still lifes. These were ravishing platinum studies, in which the arrangements of fruit or flowers — two hydrangeas drooping over the lip of a tumbler or a few water lily blossoms floating in a crystal bowl — were placed on a glass-topped table to create diffused reflections or against a wall to cast shadows. Charles Caffin would write of them, "I had never before seen photographic prints of so deliberate and convincing an exquisiteness of refinement." As photographed by de Meyer, the surfaces of a bunch of grapes offered "a complex system of facets for the reflection of the infinite nuances of light."[11]

For two years after he finally quit his job, in 1904, Clarence White struggled to make a living as a commercial photographer and portraitist. Because there was so little work for him in his small Ohio town, he was forced to travel a great deal within the region, a hardship for White, whose life was centered on his wife and their two sons. In 1906 the Whites moved to New York, for Clarence had concluded that was the only way for him both to make an adequate living and to spend time with his family. Stieglitz later claimed that he had "warned him to stay in business in Ohio — New York would be too much for him. But the Photo-Secession beckoned. Vanity and ambitions."[12]

White was indeed disappointed in New York. Even though he had the imprimatur of the Photo-Secession, clients did not flock to his portrait studio. Nor did he receive many commercial assignments. During the school year 1907–8, at the invitation of Arthur Wesley Dow, White gave a series of lectures on pictorial photography at Teachers College, Columbia University. The lectures proved to be so popular that the following year he was asked to offer the series both in the afternoon and in the evening, and also to give them at the Brooklyn Institute of Arts and Sciences, the parent organization of the Brooklyn Museum. Although he was grateful for the income, he was depressed over his failure to prosper as an artist. In February 1908 he would write to his friend Day, "I hate to look at the future and see myself as a dried up teacher of photography. But I guess that is the only cog I've even started in this year's wheel."[13]

It was largely to cheer up White that, in the spring of 1907, Stieglitz suggested they collaborate on a series of photographic experiments for two weeks, a period that the older man later remembered as "very pleasant days."[14] According to Stieglitz, the idea arose "in consequence of various lively discussions with some painters about portrait painting and the impossibility of the camera to do certain things." Stieglitz and White resolved to "demonstrate the pliability of straight photography as a medium for portraiture and figure work and so disprove the painters' contentions."[15] The experiments would also give them an opportunity to test a new lens and a new brand of plates.

Having engaged a young woman named Mabel Cramer to pose for them, they began with very diffused images of her dressed in white, either holding or standing beside a large glass sphere. The images are much closer to White's typical work than to anything by Stieglitz, whose rôle was principally that of adviser. After making a series of portraits of Cramer, fully or partially clothed, they progressed to nude studies. When the undressed Cramer proved to be rather uncomfortable in front of the camera, White and Stieglitz engaged a less bashful Miss Thompson.

They exposed sixty negatives, but "circumstances made it impossible to produce more than a few finished prints."[16] Eventually they experimented with gelatin-silver, platinum, and gum-bichromate-over-platinum processes, varying papers and developing formulas to yield differing degrees of contrast. Some of the platinum prints were waxed, some were toned with various chemicals, and some had highlights softened with pencil. The prints that satisfied them they signed with a monogram composed of their interlocked initials.

To help White further, Stieglitz would publish sixteen of his photographs in the July 1908 issue of *Camera Work*, four of the collaborations in July 1909, and, that same year, the *hors série White Book*, with twenty-three gravures.

*   *   *

While Stieglitz's friendship with White was growing stronger, that with Gertrude Käsebier was deteriorating, for she was an independent and practical person with little patience for autocratic idealism. Their friendship was showing signs of strain by 1904, but matters didn't pass the point of no return until May 1907, when she joined the Professional Photographers of New York. Stieglitz took her move as a deliberate repudiation of the amateurism for which he and the Photo-Secession stood.

In the October 1907 issue of *Camera Work* he went on the attack. The velvet glove was a reprint of Keiley's 1904 paean to Käsebier. Then came the iron fist: a cruelly mocking parody of an article by Mary Fanton Roberts (who wrote under the pseudonym Giles Edgerton) entitled "Photography as an Emotional Art: A Study of the Work of Gertrude Käsebier." Roberts's article, published in the Arts and Crafts magazine *The Craftsman*, especially praised Käsebier's images on the theme of motherhood. Charles Caffin's satire, "Emotional Art (After Reading the 'Craftsman,' April 1907)," refers only to a character named Theodosius Binny, but all the insiders would have understood that he was attacking Käsebier.

The onslaught came at an especially bad time, for that same month Käsebier lost much of her savings in the failure of the Knickerbocker Trust Company. On top of that, in December she would be evicted from her studio at 273 Fifth Avenue with only three days' notice, since the tenant from whom she was subletting had failed to pay his rent. No sooner was she resettled at 315 Fifth Avenue than appeared the January issue of the *Century*, with an article by Stieglitz's friend J. Nilsen Laurvik that took some swipes at her. It is no wonder that she wrote to Day, her one reliable friend through all this, "Stieglitz has certainly loosed all his dogs of war on me and why I do not know. It is a poor return for my years of loyalty. Neither he nor White have been near me, or showed any sign of feeling in all the great strain I have been passing through."[17]

De Meyer tried to reconcile Stieglitz and "poor old mother Käsebier," attributing her thorniness to "ill health" and "fading energy in creating new work."[18] But his efforts were to no avail. For the next several years, Stieglitz and Käsebier would barely remain on speaking terms.

CHAPTER THIRTY·THREE

AROUND JUNE 1, 1907, Alfred, Emmy, Kitty, and Kitty's governess sailed to Le Havre on the fashionable new flagship of the North German Lloyd line, the *Kaiser Wilhelm II.* Alfred was so repelled by the faces of the nouveaux riches among their fellow passengers in first class that he spent much of the first few days sitting in his steamer chair with his eyes closed. Finally, feeling that he had to escape from their voices as well, he ventured far forward, to take a look at the steerage passengers who occupied several levels in the bow. Standing alone at the railing that separated him from the steerage, he wished that he could change places with any of the people before him.

Neither the situation nor the feelings were new. Stieglitz always identified with the poor, and he had photographed a similar scene (entitled *Nearing Land*) in 1904. This time, however, he was especially struck by the formalistic qualities of what he saw. He felt that his own emotions were perfectly embodied by the specific, complex arrangement of shapes at that moment — as he himself described it, "a round straw hat, the funnel leaning left, the stairway leaning right, the white draw-bridge with its railings made of circular chains, white suspenders crossing on the back of a man . . . below, round shapes of iron machinery, a mast cutting into the sky, making a triangular shape."[1]

Stieglitz ran back to his stateroom, grabbed his 4 x 5-inch Graflex camera (which was loaded with one plate; he didn't dare take the time to un-pack more), and ran forward again. All the way, he prayed that no one would have moved. No one had. As his heart thumped, he carefully com-posed his shot and exposed his plate. Soon after arriving in Paris, he went to the Eastman Kodak office. The firm did not have a darkroom of its own but referred him to a photographer who had a well-equipped one he could use. Insisting on employing his own solutions, Stieglitz nervously devel-oped and fixed the plate. When at last he could turn on the light, he was thrilled to see that the negative was perfect. But to produce a print that sat-isfied him would take days, and so he deferred that labor until he returned to New York. For four months, as he traveled around Europe, he had the precious glass plate, which he had slipped into a protective holder, in his luggage.

It is amusingly ironic that Stieglitz's photograph — which is frequently reproduced to represent hopeful immigrants on their way to America — actually depicts people returning to Europe. Although some of them may have been turned back because of failure to meet the financial or health re-quirements for entrance, most were probably "birds of passage," skilled ar-tisans who worked in the construction trades and more or less commuted between Europe and America in two-year cycles. Moreover, it is often as-sumed that the people on the upper deck were first-class passengers look-ing down at unfortunates; everyone in the photograph was in steerage.

Stieglitz later claimed to have realized immediately that he had made one of the most important photographs of his career, but he neither exhib-ited nor published *The Steerage* until October 1911, despite numerous op-portunities to do so. If he really had known that he had just produced a masterpiece, he would probably not have been so depressed during his Eu-ropean vacation that summer. Late in June he wrote Caffin a whining let-ter in which he complained that he had done all he could for photography, to little avail. In July he told his father that he considered his own life a fail-ure.

Alfred's depression about the Photo-Secession and his loveless marriage was perhaps exacerbated by his worries over money. Edward had suffered financial losses early in the summer, and Alfred feared that Emmy's extrav-agance was getting out of hand, since she always insisted on the most lux-urious hotels, the most expensive restaurants, the most fashionable couturiers, and the best seats at the theater.

Worse was yet to come. On October 21 the currency panic of 1907 be-gan with a run on New York's Knickerbocker Trust Company, which soon led to the closing of other banks throughout the country. The crisis was ended by J. P. Morgan and a group of businessmen, who combined their resources to import $100 million in gold from Europe. But nothing could restore the losses of individuals. About half of Edward's already diminished capital had evaporated. He and Hedwig soon left their apartment in the Majestic Hotel for a more modest one elsewhere.

Perhaps Alfred's depression at least partly explains his boorish reaction when he first saw the work of Paul Cézanne, who had died the preceding year. One morning in June, the Stieglitzes and Steichens went to Bernheim-Jeune et Fils to take in a large exhibition of the artist's watercolors. Stieglitz had never heard of Cézanne and was "flabbergasted" by what he saw. When he inquired about prices and was told that the drawings cost 1,000 francs apiece, he retorted, "You mean a dozen . . . Why there's nothing there but empty paper with a few splashes of color here and there."[2]

The highlight of the summer was the appearance on the market of Autochrome plates for color photography, originated and manufactured by the brothers Auguste and Louis Lumière, of Lyons, who were already pioneers of motion pictures. Stieglitz had heard in mid-1906 that the Lumières had developed a process by which "everyone could make color pictures as readily as he could snap films," but he was skeptical, because he had come "to the conclusion that color, so far as practical purposes were concerned, would ever remain the perpetual motion problem of photography."[3] Frustratingly, he had had to wait a full year to evaluate the new process, for the Lumières were not ready to begin marketing their invention until June 1907.

One morning that month, a demonstration was to be given at the Photo-Club de Paris. Illness prevented Stieglitz from attending, but Steichen went. Although disappointed by what he saw, he purchased a supply of plates that morning and soon produced results that convinced Stieglitz that "the color problem for practical work had been solved, and that even the most fastidious must be satisfied."[4]

Stieglitz felt that the new process would rank in the history of photography with Daguerre's "startling and wonderful" invention. Autochromes actually had several important characteristics in common with daguerreotypes, principally that neither process produced a negative from which positive prints could be made. An exposed and developed Autochrome was a unique positive transparency on a glass plate, best viewed by holding it up to sunlight, though small plates could also be projected onto a screen. Stieglitz speculated that "no print on paper will ever present the colors as brilliantly as those seen on the transparencies." Viewed through the light, an Autochrome resembles a pointillist painting, its mosaic of starch grains dyed blue-violet, green, and red-orange melding to create an effect of surprisingly naturalistic color.

During the summer of 1907 Stieglitz, Steichen, Frank Eugene, A. L. Coburn, and Adolf de Meyer were all seized with "color fever," whose principal symptom was a temporary loss of interest in black-and-white photography. When Steichen returned from a trip to England in July, Stieglitz was so impressed with the Autochromes he had made there that he took three of them, along with a Steichen portrait of Emmy, to Munich at the end of the month to have the Bruckmann Verlag make four-color halftone reproductions of them for *Camera Work*. The three were published — in vibrant color — in the April 1908 issue, but the portrait of Emmy was inexplicably missing.

During August, Stieglitz continued to work with Autochromes in the company of Frank Eugene in the picturesque village of Tutzing, on the shore of the Starnberger See, not far from Munich. "Owing to circumstances over which we had no control," he wrote, their experiments "were only of a comparatively short duration and made under great difficulties."[5] Among the problems were Emmy's boredom and the wrinkling of the emulsion on incorrectly developed plates.

Upon his return to New York in late September, Stieglitz demonstrated the amazing new color process "at an exhibition, reserved exclusively for the Press, in the Photo-Secession Galleries." But his enthusiasm would last only about a year, and Steichen's three images were the only Autochromes ever published in *Camera Work*.

CHAPTER THIRTY·FOUR

AFTER THE OBLIGATORY exhibition of photographs by members of the Photo-Secession — to which the novelty of color transparencies by Stieglitz, Steichen, Eugene, and White brought large numbers of the curious — the real business of the gallery's 1907–8 season began on January 2 with the opening of an exhibition of fifty-eight drawings by Auguste Rodin. Selected by Steichen in collaboration with the artist, these pencil and watercolor studies of the female nude were, as one critic put it, "swift, sure, stenographic notes . . . seldom beautiful, according to accepted standards of beauty."[1] Rodin, who worked from models performing a sinuous and highly erotic dance in his studio, often didn't even look at the paper as he dashed off one sketch after another, not wanting to interrupt the flow of feeling from his eye to his hand. Later he would rework some of the sheets, adding a wash of watercolor to emphasize the figure.

These drawings, close in spirit to Rodin's great works in bronze, naturally shocked those in the public who revered the sculptor for his sugary marble portraits and acceptably romanticized nudes. To shock was precisely Stieglitz's aim. Lest anyone miss the point, he reprinted in the exhibition catalog an extract from an essay in which Arthur Symons had written of the figure in the drawings, "She turns upon herself in a hundred attitudes, turning always upon the central pivot of the sex."[2]

Recent years had seen a revival of activity on the part of Anthony Comstock, who in 1873 had founded the New York Society for the Suppression of Vice and successfully lobbied for a federal statute prohibiting the mailing of obscene material. From then until his death in 1915, Comstock worked (without pay until 1906) as a special agent of the U.S. Post Office Department and oversaw the destruction of some 160 tons of printed matter that he deemed obscene. Stieglitz would later write that the idea underlying the "Comstockian Society" had always given him the creeps, "as it must give the creeps to everyone who has the slightest conception of freedom of expression, of intellectual integrity, of art. Of the reality of life itself."[3] Comstock's rampages prompted J. Nilsen Laurvik to write in the *New York Times* that the Rodin exhibition was "also a challenge to the prurient prudery of our puritanism. As one looks at these amazing records of unabashed observations of an artist, who is also a man, one marvels that this little gallery has not long since been raided by the blind folly that guards our morals. . . . It is a hopeful sign of the changing order of things when work such as this can be shown here in New York."[4]

From this time on, Stieglitz was committed to fighting American prudery. He would greatly admire the first book by the critic Van Wyck Brooks, *The Wine of the Puritans* (1909), which argued that materialistic puritanism had strangled America's artistic life. The following year Stieglitz would publish in *Camera Work* an important article by the reinstated and everprolific Sadakichi Hartmann (broke, he had solicited "a helping hand for old time's sake") entitled "Puritanism — Its Grandeur and Shame."[5] For all these men the standard-bearer was Walt Whitman, who had sung in *Leaves of Grass*, "Without shame the man I like knows and avows the deliciousness of his sex, / Without shame the woman I like knows and avows hers."[6]

The New York press was surprisingly receptive to the Rodin drawings. James Huneker, widely considered the most sophisticated of the city's critics because of his annual pilgrimages to the art centers of Europe, wrote that the exhibition was "artistically the most important that is to be seen in the city at present."[7] But William Merritt Chase, the most famous art teacher in the nation, was outraged. An enthusiastic visitor to 291's photographic exhibitions, Chase was so fascinated by odd camera angles that he offered prizes to students who introduced the "queerest" viewpoints into their paintings. He also respected the camera's honesty, for he always exhorted his students to paint what they actually saw. Greatly admiring Velázquez, Hals, Chardin, Whistler, and Sargent, he advocated rapid execution and virtuosic bravura.

The diminutive Chase — with "quick nervous manners," a neatly pointed gray beard, and an extravagant mustache — played the rôle of

Whistlerian coxcomb to the hilt. At the Saturday morning critiques of his students' weekly output, he habitually showed up wearing a top hat, a cutaway with a carnation in its buttonhole, striped trousers, and spats. The cravat around his bat-wing collar was drawn through a gold ring embellished with a turquoise, and from a black ribbon hung his pince-nez, at hand as he lunged to point out some *maladresse*.

By 1908 Chase, who had been elected a replacement member of the Ten three years earlier, was something of a has-been. He had done his best work during the 1880s and 1890s: shimmering Impressionistic views of Long Island and of Central and Prospect parks, studies of the opulent interior of his studio, and glowing — if not always penetrating — portraits of women. Now he was producing little more than showy still lifes of fish.

Only six weeks before the Rodin show opened, he had angrily resigned from the New York School of Art, which he had founded in 1896. He left because he had become disgusted with the popularity of one of the teachers, Robert Henri, whose earthy, Whitmanesque personality and philosophy represented the antithesis of Chase's studied refinement — though their painting styles were remarkably similar. Immediately after leaving the school, Chase resumed teaching at the Art Students League, where in his first class was a young woman named Georgia O'Keeffe.

One day in January 1908 O'Keeffe and several of her friends from the league made their way through the snowy streets to 291 Fifth Avenue to see the Rodin drawings. Chase, who was so angered by the exhibition that he vowed never to set foot in 291 again, had enticingly denounced them as deliberate hoaxes. Forty years later O'Keeffe recalled, "One instructor told us that he didn't know whether Rodin was fooling Stieglitz and America too by sending over such a ridiculous group of drawings to be shown here, or maybe Stieglitz knew what he was about and had his tongue in his cheek trying to see what nonsense he could put over on the American public."[8]

As far as O'Keeffe could see, the drawings were "just a lot of scribbles," and Stieglitz himself looked something of a fright with his lean face and his "shock of very dark hair standing up straight on the top of his head."[9] He was working in his darkroom when they arrived. Annoyed at being interrupted, he glared at the students "in rather unfriendly fashion" when he emerged, his hands still dripping wet. The men in the group had come not so much to see the drawings as to bait Stieglitz, to "get him going." But O'Keeffe was very put off by the talk, which grew "louder and louder till it became quite violent." She withdrew to another room of the chairless gallery to wait until her friends had finally taken enough verbal drubbing from Stieglitz.[10]

O'Keeffe ventured back to 291 a couple of times over the next few months, but then she left New York, not to return until the fall of 1914.

On January 4, 1908, two days after the opening of the Rodin exhibition, the secretary of the Camera Club of New York, John Hadden, wrote Stieglitz an official letter, the entire text of which consisted of a single sentence: "I have been instructed by the Board of Trustees to request your resignation from the Camera Club."[11] No reasons were given or charges made. Indeed, the letter seemed to come out of the blue, "without warning, without quarrel or words."[12] Thus began a contretemps, aptly characterized by Charles Caffin as a "rumpus in a hen-house," lasting into April.[13]

The Camera Club — under the leadership of Charles Berg, whom Stieglitz had excluded from the Photo-Secession — was in a desperate state. After Stieglitz abandoned *Camera Notes* in 1902, the club's prestige diminished drastically. Membership had fallen from 344 in 1900 to about 160 in 1907. Although the annual dues had been doubled, mismanagement had almost fatally depleted the treasury. In December 1907 the board had proposed that the nearly bankrupt club dissolve itself. The members voted to persevere, and the club would move in the spring to smaller and less convenient headquarters, at Broadway and West Sixty-eighth Street.

Many members blamed Stieglitz for the collapse. In March the trustees would formally state that he had

> continued the practice of building up and increasing the membership in his own Organization from within the Camera Club, creating a body which has no interest in the Club except to use its rooms for business purposes, and its facilities almost exclusively for the benefit of the body alluded to; that this Organization, as originated, enlarged, and continuously directed by him, has been from the start, and is today more than ever, the center of disaffection to the general interests of the Camera Club.[14]

Stieglitz claimed, "The Trustees trumped up charges against me to get me out, expecting that some who could not keep up to the standards I had set and had dropped out would come back, with the 'bars down.'"[15] In fact, in reaction to his expulsion, about forty photographers — many of them members of the Photo-Secession — resigned from the Camera Club and formed an organization called the Camera Workers, "an active working association which in its sphere shall be comparable and complementary to the Photo-Secession." The new club rented space for its headquarters at 122 East Twenty-fifth Street and installed darkroom facilities. The membership, limited to one hundred, included Stieglitz, Steichen, Keiley, White, and former Camera Club secretary Hadden.[16]

Stieglitz ignored the letter of January 4, as his friends advised him to do. "Although the action of the Board of Trustees was illegal and outrageous," wrote John Francis Strauss in *Camera Work*, "the matter was too trivial and ridiculous to be noticed except as a joke."[17]

Stieglitz naturally boycotted the hearing to which the club's trustees had summoned him. The following day, February 4, he was informed that he had been "expelled from membership in the Club and from all rights in or to any of its property," and he was ordered to remove his belongings "from the Club Rooms forthwith."[18]

All was quiet for ten days. Then, on Friday, February 14, the leader of a story centered at the top of the front page of the *New York Times* announced:

CAMERA CLUB OUSTS
ALFRED STIEGLITZ

Trustees Expel Well-Known Amateur
When He Refuses to Resign

SAY THERE ARE CHARGES

He Denies That These Exist, and Says
Row Is Due to "Animus and Jealousy"

Stieglitz, whom the story called "probably the best known amateur photographer in the world," told the reporter who had interviewed him at 291 the previous evening, "There are no charges against me. My friend, L.B. Schram, who is a lawyer, went before the Board of Trustees and demanded that the charges against me be read. They were not forthcoming. . . . Mr. Schram demanded that his resignation be accepted and left."

In fact, Stieglitz had certainly been told by Hadden that the exaggerated charges were that he "made himself obnoxious to Club members; gave the false idea to the world that the Club was dependent on him for financial and technical assistance; made personal use of the Club's custodian; removed Club property without authorization and lured away Club members to join his own organization, the Photo-Secession."[19]

As rumors regarding the nature of the charges proliferated, Stieglitz brought suit against the club, at the same time notifying it, through an intermediary, that "he desires no further connection with an institution of the caliber of the Camera Club and will gladly tender his resignation if the Trustees will specify the charges which prompted the original request for his resignation."[20]

On March 10, the Camera Club informed Stieglitz that he had been reinstated as a life member. And on the twenty-first Berg wrote to the intermediary to state that at a meeting the previous evening the Camera Club's board of trustees had formally resolved "that the charges against Mr. Stieglitz were not based upon any act involving any reflection upon Mr. Stieglitz's morality or personal character, but were based upon the fact that both by deed and action he has for many years worked against the interests of the Camera Club."[21] Although that charge was "contrary to the facts and . . . susceptible of being disproved," Stieglitz was fed up with the whole business. He dropped his legal suit and submitted his resignation, which was accepted.[22]

During this unsettled period, Stieglitz met a young woman named Agnes Ernst. Born in New York in 1887, she came from a long line of Hanoverian Lutheran ministers, but her father was a lawyer who had adopted a bohemian style of life, writing unsalable works and sinking the family into poverty and debt. After graduating from Barnard College, in 1907, the energetic, enterprising, and engaging Agnes persuaded the *New York Morning Sun* to hire her as its first female reporter. When she announced that she was going to take up newspaper work, her mother wept and her father said that he would rather see her dead.

A beautiful twenty-one-year-old with dark blond hair, blue eyes, fine features, and a tall, statuesque figure, Agnes first appeared at 291 about eleven o'clock one morning during the Rodin show. She told Stieglitz that this was her first important assignment, and she insisted that she was deeply interested in his work. He resisted for a few minutes, but the combination of her Germanic good looks, her intelligence, and her youthful spirit prevailed. He overwhelmed her with "a perfect avalanche of words" for the next six hours.

When her unsigned article appeared, several months later, there was no mention of Stieglitz's expulsion from the Camera Club or of the Rodin drawings. The one-and-a-half-column piece simply related what the photographer had told Ernst about his background and provided a forceful statement of his philosophy at that time:

We are searching for the ultimate truth, for the human being who is so simple in every way that he can look at things objectively, with a purely analytical point of view. We are striving for freedom of experience and justice in the fullest sense of the word. . . .

We have no formulated theories, like George Bernard Shaw's, because we believe that a formulated theory is a narrowing thing, lacking in that perfect freedom which we are looking for. . . . We believe that if only people are taught to appreciate the beautiful side of their daily existence, to be aware of all the beauty which constantly surrounds them, they must gradually approach this ideal. . . . And we believe the camera is one of the most effective means of teaching people to distinguish between what is beautiful and what is not. It forces upon them a realization of line and composition and forms in them the habit of looking for the pictorial side of everything.[23]

Stieglitz was so enchanted by the radiant Miss Ernst that he began calling her, intending a double entendre, the Sun Girl. She, in turn, exulted that at 291 her "sails were filled by the free air [she] craved" and began to visit the gallery regularly. Stieglitz encouraged her intention to spend a year or two in Paris, beginning that fall. There she studied French, attended classes at the Sorbonne and the Collège de France, heard lectures by Henri Bergson and others, and went to the Comédie Française and the Ballets Russes. She took in the Salon d'Automne, interviewed Henri Matisse, and visited Steichen at his rose-embowered cottage, the Villa l'Oiseau, in the little village of Voulangis-par-Crécy-en-Brie, outside Paris. She frequented the Saturday evenings at 27, rue de Fleurus, where she was impressed by Leo Stein's opinions about art but disliked the masculine and massive Gertrude. And she became great friends with Rodin, who would have liked to seduce her but settled for guiding her through the Louvre and the Luxembourg museums. To Stieglitz she wrote, "Over here I feel almost like an apostle, and every time a *Camera Work* comes, I wave it like a red flag in the face of my friends."[24]

On a visit to London in the spring of 1909, Agnes went to the British Museum and was captivated when she wandered into a room of Chinese paintings — a *coup de foudre*. For the rest of her life, Chinese art would rival modernism among her passions.

Two months after her return to New York in December 1909, Agnes married financier Eugene Meyer. (It is likely that Stieglitz had already met Meyer, whose sister Aline had married Emmy's cousin Charles J. Liebman in January 1908. Mrs. Liebman would become one of Stieglitz's most important patrons.) Partly because of Agnes's new interest in Asian art, she and Eugene took a trip around the world on their honeymoon, proceeding westward to Hawaii, Japan, Korea, Manchuria, Siberia, and Russia, ending up in Paris, where, with Steichen's guidance, they bought their first canvases by Cézanne and Picasso.

On January 4, the day the Camera Club notified Stieglitz of his expulsion, a Special Exhibition of Contemporary Art, which was "composed almost entirely of work by the leading artistic rebels of America," opened at the National Arts Club. The show had been organized by Stieglitz's friend J. Nilsen Laurvik, a blond-haired, blue-eyed, Norwegian-born critic who had begun writing for *Camera Work* in 1907 and wrote regularly about art for the *New York Times* and various magazines.

Photographs by Stieglitz, Steichen, Käsebier, White, and other Photo-Secessionists were hung alongside paintings and sculptures by a wide cross section of American artists. All the members of the Eight were included, as were Chase, Mary Cassatt, Childe Hassam, and Pamela Colman Smith. A review in the *New York Evening Mail* noted that the exhibition seemed "to be a pretty complete anticipation of the show of the great innovating Eight . . . which is to take place at Macbeth's next month. It takes the wind out of the sails of that exhibition."[25]

The leader of the Eight was Chase's nemesis, Robert Henri (who pronounced his surname "HEN-ryc"), a tall, charismatic man, whose high, prominent cheekbones and almond-shaped eyes gave his broad, pockmarked face a Eurasian cast. Deeply influenced by Ralph Waldo Emerson and Whitman, Henri placed his faith in self-reliance, self-expression, and personal and artistic freedom. He was a fiery, inspiring teacher, stressing individual experience and direct observation.

Born Robert Henry Cozad in Cincinnati in 1865, he spent his early childhood on the Nebraska frontier. After his father fatally shot a man during an argument in 1882, the family fled to Denver and then split up, the parents and children adopting a variety of names. Henri went to Philadelphia in the fall of 1886 and enrolled in the Pennsylvania Academy of the Fine Arts, where he studied under Eakins's disciple Thomas Anshutz.

Elected a full member of the National Academy in 1906, by which time he was living in New York, Henri served as a judge for the spring annual in 1907 but was still unable to prevent the exclusion of many of his friends and students. He was particularly friendly with painters John Sloan, William Glackens, George Luks, and Everett Shinn, who had all worked as artist-reporters for the Philadelphia newspapers before moving to New York. Drawing on their journalistic experience and influenced by Whitman's belief that *everything* was fit subject matter for poetry, they sketched such gritty subjects as life in the streets and tenements of the immigrant neighborhoods, and they painted the riverfront, coal deliveries on snowy streets, the Staten Island ferry, street urchins and old people, sporting events, bar interiors, the theater, and Sunday in Central Park. Henri was outraged when the American collectors and academicians who found Italian poverty picturesque denounced depictions of such New York scenes as being in bad taste.

In May 1907 Henri and seven of his friends — Sloan, Glackens, Shinn, Luks, Symbolist Arthur B. Davies, American Impressionist Ernest Lawson, and the Bostonian Neo-Impressionist Maurice Brazil Prendergast — announced that they would have a show together in February 1908. It would take place at William Macbeth's gallery, in the basement of the brownstone at 450 Fifth Avenue, where Henri, Davies, Lawson, and Prendergast had all had solos. Although the group was promptly dubbed the Eight by their friend James Huneker, in playful reference to the Ten, the number had been limited by the size of the gallery, not by any resolution to form an enduring group. As it turned out, the Macbeth exhibition was the group's only eight-man show.

Stieglitz dismissed paintings by the Eight as illustrations or "colored photographs." Charles Caffin could have been speaking for him when he wrote in *The Story of American Painting* (1907) that the work of Sloan, Henri, Glackens, and Luks, despite being "a natural and wholesome reaction from the vogue of frippery, tameness, and sentimentality . . . reveals a tendency to be overoccupied with the appearances of life, and makes little or no appeal to the imagination or spirit."[26] Stieglitz's only friend among the members of the Eight was Arthur Davies, whose most characteristic paintings (which the photographer judged poetic but irritating) depict dreamy nude women encountering unicorns in landscapes of the Hudson River valley as Pierre Puvis de Chavannes might have painted it.

Davies was a quiet man, rather formal, reserved, and fastidious. Cultivating the persona of an excessively sensitive and spiritual Welsh poet in paint, he could, however, also be extremely charming — and he genuinely loved art, for which he had an astonishingly adventurous eye. That combination of qualities provided the basis for his friendships with the sculptor and patron Gertrude Vanderbilt Whitney and with Miss Lillie P. Bliss. The latter, who would buy any work of art Davies recommended, would become one of the founders of the Museum of Modern Art.

Around the time of the Eight show, Davies was living with his wife and their two sons in the Westchester County village of Congers. When she refused him a divorce, he began spending more and more time in New York, ostensibly in his studio. In fact, under the pseudonym David A. Owen, he moved into an apartment on East Fifty-second Street with one of his former models, a woman named Edna Potter, with whom he had a daughter. Not even Davies's closest friends knew of his double life, and it was not until after his death, in 1928, that his wife learned his secret.

The exhibition of sixty-three paintings by the Eight opened at the Macbeth Gallery on February 3, 1908. By the time it closed, twelve days later, about seven thousand people had seen the show and seven paintings had been sold, four of them to Gertrude Whitney.

Whenever there was a major exhibition elsewhere in the city, Stieglitz would carefully choose a show to balance it. George Seeley was given the challenge of running against the Eight. The Seeley show (February 7–25) and the succeeding trio of Pamela Colman Smith, Willi Geiger, and Donald Shaw MacLaughlan (February 26–March 11) were pointedly Symbolist, in contrast to the harsh materialism of the Eight. Geiger, a friend of Frank Eugene and a disciple of Franz von Stuck, showed bookplates and etchings in which people and animals were bizarrely distorted. MacLaughlan was a Canadian who had settled in New York after studying in Paris, and he specialized in etchings of landscape and architecture. These exhibitions at the Little Galleries were largely ignored, by press and public alike, in the face of all the favorable, and well-deserved, publicity that the Eight received from their many friends among the city's art critics.

CHAPTER THIRTY·FIVE

STEICHEN WROTE TO Stieglitz in January 1908:

> I have another cracker-jack exhibition for you that is going to be as
> fine in its way as the Rodins are. Drawings by Henri Matisse, the
> most modern of the moderns — his drawings are the same to him &
> his painting as Rodin's are to his sculpture. . . . [His paintings] are to
> the figure what the Cézannes are to the landscape. Simply great.
> Some [of Matisse's drawings] are more finished than Rodin's, more of
> a study of form than movement — *abstract* to the limit.[1]

In a subsequent letter he warned Stieglitz, "I would not show any of the
things even to the fellows at the Secession — till we get them up."[2]

Soon after returning to Paris in 1906, Steichen had begun to attend the
weekly Saturday evenings at Gertrude and Leo Stein's. Through them he
met their brother Michael and his wife, Sarah, who were then buying Matisse's finest canvases before they were even dry. Steichen spoke to Sarah
Stein about having a Matisse exhibition at 291, and she gradually convinced the artist, who then enthusiastically selected the works together
with Steichen, launching a warm friendship.

Stieglitz agreed to exhibit Matisse's work almost sight unseen — since
he had done nothing more than glance dismissively at a few of his paintings

when he went to the Cézanne show at Bernheim-Jeune in 1907 — though he probably saw at least one Matisse oil in New York as early as the fall of 1906. In the summer of that year, when Sarah Stein paid a visit to the city, she had with her two Matisse nudes, one a drawing and the other an oil sketch. Among the people to whom she showed them was George Of, Stieglitz's framer. Of asked Stein to select a small Matisse painting for him when she returned to Paris; she sent him *Nude in a Wood*, the first Matisse to be owned by a collector living in America. Of would surely have shown his new acquisition at once to Stieglitz, who would borrow it for the Little Galleries' show as the sole representative of Matisse's oils.

Steichen arrived in New York a week before the March 12 opening of his own one-man exhibition at the gallery. With him he brought a selection of Matisse's watercolors, drawings, etchings, and lithographs for the artist's American debut. In retrospect, Stieglitz would view the exhibition, which followed Steichen's, as "the first blow of 'Modernity' in America."[3]

Stieglitz showed Matisse's work less because he had either a strong belief in or understanding of its aesthetic significance than because he hoped it would serve to shock his fellow photographers — and, beyond them, the American public — out of their complacency. An unsigned editorial in *Camera Work*, written by Stieglitz or at his instigation, boasted of the Matisse exhibition: "Here was the work of a new man, with new ideas — a very anarchist, it seemed, in art. The exhibition led to many heated controversies: it proved stimulating. The New York 'Art-World' was sorely in need of an irritant and Matisse certainly proved a timely one."[4] In 1921 Stieglitz would recall that when one couple (who by that later year were very enthusiastic about modern art) visited the show, the husband "asked his wife to go home with him at once so both could take a bath in a disinfectant!"[5]

Characteristically, Stieglitz emphasized the radicalness of Matisse's work, not its beauty or the pleasures to be derived from looking at it. There was, ironically, a certain puritanism in his anti-puritan stance. Stieglitz was like a doctor prescribing medicine that would be good for the American public. Indeed, he had told Agnes Ernst, "Just as physicians take care of people's bodies, we try to take care of their minds so that they may live in the fullest sense of the word."[6] In 1913 one of Stieglitz's friends would write, with reference to the candy store that occupied the ground floor of 291 Fifth Avenue, "Below, Mary Elizabeth, distributor of melting sweets, above, Alfred Stieglitz, dispenser of bitter pills."[7]

Although the Matisse exhibition suffered from the absence of any major paintings, Steichen had chosen the graphic works to demonstrate, as much as possible, the artist's development, for he knew that Stieglitz was more interested in the work of art as a manifestation of personal evolution than as an independent aesthetic entity. Stieglitz would write in 1910,

> As far as exhibitions are concerned, to me they are only of any meaning whatever if they are a public demonstration of a *positive advance* in or a *summing up* of the really genuine work that has been done in any field of work. Exhibitions, as exhibitions, to me, have always been an abomination, for, as a rule, they are nothing more than a marketplace for the mediocre or the parading-ground for the stupid vanities of the small mind.[8]

Steichen included several of the landscape watercolors Matisse had made in the Mediterranean town of Collioure, where, during the summer of 1905, he had pioneered a style characterized by radically intensified, anti-naturalistic color. Matisse's friend André Derain later said that he and his colleagues had reacted "against anything that resembled a photographic plate taken from life. We treated colors like sticks of dynamite, exploding them to produce light. The idea that everything could be lifted above the real was marvelous in its pristine freshness."[9] When some of their new paintings were hung in the 1905 Salon d'Automne, in a room that also contained a classicizing bust, one critic exclaimed, "*Donatello chez les fauves!* [Donatello in the lair of the wild beasts!]" The new style was promptly christened Fauvism.

The New York critics and public alike were shocked and outraged by Matisse's drawings of the female nude. James Huneker, for instance, wrote in the *New York Sun:* "Compared to these memoranda of the gutter and brothel the sketches of Rodin are academic, are meticulous." And yet, writing of one drawing of the back of a reclining nude, he conceded, "It is difficult not to applaud, so virile and masterly are its strokes. . . . His sketches are those of a brilliant, cruel temperament."[10] J. Edgar Chamberlin snarled in the *New York Evening Mail:* "There are some female figures that are of an ugliness that is most appalling and haunting, and that seems to condemn this man's brain to the limbo of artistic degeneration. On the strength of these things of subterhuman hideousness, I shall try to put Henri Matisse out of my mind for the present."[11]

In February 1908 Stieglitz had been notified that when the two-year lease for the gallery space expired, he would have to commit himself to four more years with a 100 percent rent increase. He had been paying most of 291's expenses out of his own income, since the Photo-Secession dues had fallen off to less than $300 a year as members resigned in protest against the shift to nonphotographic work — or else simply failed to pay. Because he feared that he had neither the money nor the energy to continue, he refused to sign a new lease and decided not to seek another location for his gallery. He had completely used up his own capital by underwriting *Camera Work* and 291, and he felt he couldn't count on his friends — except Steichen — for financial or even moral support.

Camera Work reported that on April 30, five days after the Matisse show closed, "the galleries, stripped of their decorations, passed back into their original condition of an uninviting and dilapidated garret."[12] The "fashionable ladies' tailor" who had taken over Steichen's studio at 293 Fifth Avenue in 1906 now moved across the hall into the former Little Galleries.

A rescuer appeared in the form of a handsome twenty-eight-year-old Frenchman named Paul Burty Haviland, whose half-American father directed the family's famous china-manufacturing firm in Limoges. Paul's mother was the daughter of Philippe Burty, an eminent art critic who had started out as the champion of Delacroix and ended up befriending and defending the Impressionists.

Paul had grown up surrounded by art and music and had developed a special love for the theater. After receiving his bachelor's degree from the University of Paris in 1898, he went on to Harvard for three years to improve his English and to become familiar with his grandmother's native land. Upon graduating, in 1901, he settled in New York as the American representative of the family firm. He did so at his father's insistence and spent as little time as possible in his office.

Accompanied by his younger brother, Frank Burty Haviland, Paul had paid his first visit to 291 early in 1908 to see the Rodin exhibition. Both men bought drawings, and Paul fell in love with the gallery, which he considered a unique oasis of cultivation in New York. In the spring, after Stieglitz had told him that 291 was going to close because of the rent hike, Paul went to the landlord and, without saying a word to Stieglitz, signed a three-year lease for the front and side rooms of 293 Fifth Avenue, to be vacated by the ladies' tailor. The rent would be $500 a year. At first Stieglitz said he could not possibly accept Haviland's generosity. In any case, he was not at all sure that he wanted to continue in a gallery with greatly reduced space. When Haviland promised to take care of having the rooms cleaned, painted, and furnished, Stieglitz relented. He announced his decision in the July issue of *Camera Work*.

By the fall of 1908, an observer might have concluded that Haviland's office was at 293 Fifth Avenue, where he became a leading participant in discussions and one of Stieglitz's most valued co-workers. Beginning in January 1909 he regularly wrote a column for *Camera Work* about the gallery's exhibitions, and in July 1910 he would become an associate editor. His clear and informative contributions show him to have been an eager student of Stieglitz's views. Indeed, it was precisely because Haviland was so receptive and diplomatic that he was indispensable. Stieglitz's friend Jerome Mellquist would write that Haviland, "quiet and cultured, a friend to all, served as the balance-wheel."[13] With his well-tailored tweedy suits, his considerate manners, and his careful observations delivered in French-accented English while he gestured with a cigarette between his fingers, Haviland was the very image of a cosmopolitan gentleman. Stieglitz was delighted that he also proved to be a talented photographer; his pictures — mostly portraits and cityscapes — would be reproduced in three issues of *Camera Work*.

Forced by economy to do without her usual month at the New Jersey shore, Emmy reluctantly accompanied Alfred and Kitty to Lake George in June. Her boredom yielded to hysteria late in July, when Kitty developed acute appendicitis, which necessitated a dramatic operation on the dining room table. Emmy was so shaken by the episode that she made everyone in the house miserable for a month, until finally, early in September, the family gave Alfred an ultimatum: If Emmy didn't leave at once, there would be civil war. Emmy huffed off to New Jersey, but Alfred decided to remain at Oaklawn with Kitty.

Throughout the summer's commotion, Alfred would escape by rowing on the lake. In the quiet he found there, he reflected on his situation and decided that the new gallery should be turned "virtually into a facsimile of the main older room."[14] He would respond to the reduction of wall space simply by maintaining even higher standards of quality than before.

Because he didn't want Haviland to carry the entire burden, and because he was not comfortable approaching potential contributors himself, Stieglitz asked John Kerfoot to see what he could do. Kerfoot arranged an informal tea at the Holland House, to which he invited a group of prospects. Among them was George DuPont Pratt, of Brooklyn, whose father, Charles Pratt, the founder of Pratt Institute, was one of John D. Rockefeller's partners in the Standard Oil Company. George Pratt, who had resigned from the Camera Club in January to become a member of the Camera Workers, was a regular at the Little Galleries and frequently dropped by to ask whether there were any odd jobs that needed doing.

Stieglitz had boasted to Agnes Ernst, "As long as we can do that to the American business man I don't think we are working for nothing."[15]

Also invited were previous contributor Herbert French and his brother-in-law, F. W. Hunter, a wealthy lawyer who collected Chinese and Japanese art and was an authority on early American glass. Pratt agreed to give $100 a year. French, Hunter, and Kerfoot each subscribed $50. Haviland would pay the remainder of the rent, and Stieglitz would somehow or other scrape together enough to cover the other expenses.

"On December 1, 1908, after a house-warming dinner at Mouquin's," reported *Camera Work*, Photo-Secessionists gathered at 293 Fifth Avenue to assist in opening the new gallery.[16] What would prove to be the last members' show opened a week later. Sadly absent was the work of Gertrude Käsebier, whose friendship with Stieglitz continued to disintegrate.

The transformation of the new rooms was astonishing. The tiny rope-operated elevator, which could carry no more than three or four people at a time and was described by one regular as an "inverted toast-rack," deposited visitors in a hallway where Stieglitz would place one beautiful photograph or drawing to be seen immediately.[17] From the hall, one could enter either the tiny side gallery or the main room, fifteen feet square. To create additional space for hanging in the latter, a wall parallel to the facade had been constructed a few feet away from the front windows. The gallery was thus windowless, but a scrim was suspended beneath its skylight to provide what one artist would describe as "a quiet light . . . full of a soothing, mystic feeling."[18]

The rear half of the floor was a large room, twenty-two feet square, occupied by a decorator, Stephen B. Lawrence, who spent much time away from the city, working on the houses of clients up and down the Eastern Seaboard or buying antiques in New England or Europe. Whether he was away or in town, Lawrence let Stieglitz use his telephone. Even more important, since the gallery was unheated, Lawrence's back room had a coal stove, around which Stieglitz and his friends would sit and talk — or work, preparing shows and editing *Camera Work* — during the winter. A bathroom that doubled as Stieglitz's darkroom completed the layout.

Although the new gallery was technically in 293 (the street entrance of which was in its Siamese twin), Stieglitz defiantly ignored the change and, more emphatically than ever, used the old number. "Somehow 291 sounded more euphonious to me than 293," he wrote.[19] At first he employed the number as a convenient code name for what was officially the

Little Gallery (as opposed to the former Little Galleries) of the Photo-Secession; then, after about 1910, as the gallery's universal designation; and, finally, as the mystical, numerological symbol of the conflation of his personality, the gallery, and all that it represented. One could never be quite sure, when Stieglitz uttered the pregnant trinumeric formula, whether he was referring to the gallery or to himself.

CHAPTER THIRTY·SIX

ON JANUARY 4, 1909, a two-man exhibition of caricatures by Marius de Zayas and Autochromes by J. Nilsen Laurvik opened at 291. The combination was appropriate, since it had been on Laurvik's recommendation that Stieglitz first met de Zayas, a rakish, urbane, and sardonic man who regularly caricatured figures in the arts and society for the *New York Evening World*.

His drawings were linear and straightforward, with fairly slight exaggeration, so that the subjects would be easily recognizable to the paper's readers. For his own pleasure, however, without any intention of publication or exhibition, de Zayas drew much more sophisticated caricatures, mostly of famous dancers and actresses and of his friends in the arts. In these Symbolist charcoal drawings — in which the influence of Beardsley, Max Beerbohm, Toulouse-Lautrec, and Redon can be discerned — highly exaggerated figures emerge from dark backgrounds. De Zayas's friend Benjamin de Casseres wrote that in these works the caricaturist showed himself to be a "divinizing psychologist."[1]

By late 1908 Stieglitz had himself begun making portraits of his artistic friends in the Little Gallery. He was perhaps prompted to do so by a desire to surpass Gertrude Käsebier's idiosyncratic photographs of the Eight, recently published in *The Craftsman*. It was probably during that same year that Laurvik, knowing of Stieglitz's concern for capturing each sitter's essence rather than his or her mere appearance, had suggested he take a look at de Zayas's work. He went without an appointment, found the studio door open, walked in, and glanced at the work all around. Without even introducing himself, he offered de Zayas a show, which the latter curtly declined. When Stieglitz persisted, de Zayas nonchalantly acquiesced, telling him to take whatever he wanted and to keep it all.

The caricatures that Stieglitz exhibited some months later were, as Paul Haviland wrote, distinguished by their "daring characterization of well-known people about town as they appeared to [de Zayas] in the street, in the theatre or on the stage. Members of New York's social set had the place of honor on the main wall, flanked on one side by members of the Photo-Secession, and on the other by foot-light stars."[2]

De Casseres reported in *Camera Work* that the exhibition "was treated jocularly by a few reviewers and comparatively neglected by the public." He explained that "the art of the caricaturist is not an amiable art — and in New York amiability is a cardinal principle of success." The caricaturist had violated "the Anglo-Saxon injunction: Thou shalt not commit irony!"[3] Perhaps, but Haviland observed that "the characterizations were without the sting of malice."[4]

It was not the most auspicious debut for a man who would be one of Stieglitz's chief friends, protégés, lieutenants, and spokesmen for the next seven years. Marius de Zayas Enriquez y Calmet, an aristocratic Mexican, was born in Veracruz in 1880. Young Marius had begun by drawing caricatures for the two liberal newspapers owned by his father, Rafael de Zayas — a lawyer who was also a historian, an orator, and the poet laureate of Mexico. Early in 1907 dictator Porfirio Díaz shut down the papers and confiscated the family's property. After a trip to Europe in the spring of 1907, during which he met artist John Marin in Venice, Marius settled in New York, where the rest of his family had fled.

The de Zayas–Laurvik show was followed by one of Coburn's work in color and black-and-white, and then a second exhibition of Baron de Meyer's. While that show was at 291, the National Arts Club housed an International Exhibition of Pictorial Photography, curated by Stieglitz and composed of prints by twenty-four Photo-Secessionists and European members of the Linked Ring.

The 291 season included only one other show of photographs: Steichen's images of Rodin's *Balzac* (April 21–May 7). One night in September 1908 Steichen had photographed, by moonlight, the white plaster cast in the garden of the sculptor's house in Meudon, making many exposures, ranging in length from fifteen minutes to one hour. When Rodin saw Steichen's magnificent pigment prints, he exclaimed with pleasure that in them the sculpture looked "like Christ walking in the desert." As for Stieglitz, recalled Steichen, "He seemed more impressed than with any other prints I had ever shown him."[5]

There would be only four more photographic exhibitions at 291 before it closed in 1917: one devoted to Steichen's color work in 1910; another de Meyer show, in December 1911; a Stieglitz retrospective in February-March 1913; and Paul Strand's debut in March 1916. In the January 1909 issue of *Camera Work*, Haviland had announced that since photography was now recognized as one of the fine arts, the gallery and the magazine would "champion modern tendencies" in all the visual arts and display "new and interesting work" that embodied "personal expression."

Among such shows that season was one of etchings and bookplates "in the spirit of the old German masters" by Allen Lewis. Stieglitz exhibited Lewis's work on the recommendation of Paul Haviland's cousin Hamilton Easter Field (1873–1922), a painter and the art critic for Walt Whitman's old paper, the Brooklyn *Daily Eagle*. Next came Pamela Colman Smith's second one-person show, this one "of drawings in monochrome and color" recording "visions evoked by music, sketched during the concert or opera." At the private opening, on the evening of March 16, Smith's "secessionistic friends" were "delighted by her recital of West Indian nursery rhymes and her chanting of ballads" by William Butler Yeats.[6]

On March 30 Stieglitz opened the gallery's first show of work by young American modernists — Alfred Maurer and John Marin, two painters who were members of an organization that Steichen had started the preceding year. Since the reactionary American Art Association of Paris rejected anything more modernistic than Impressionism, Steichen had invited his friends Maurer, Marin, Max Weber, D. Putnam Brinley, and Arthur Carles to his studio one evening in February 1908 to discuss the formation of a secessionist society.[7] Joined by a few other friends, including Patrick Henry Bruce and the sculptor Jo Davidson, they soon announced the birth of the New Society of American Artists in Paris.

Before sending the Maurers over, Steichen had warned Stieglitz that they were "certainly howlers as *color* and ought to make the people that kicked at Matisse feel ashamed of themselves."[8] But Stieglitz was delighted by the fifteen small Fauvist landscape sketches in gold frames.

As usual, he was especially interested in what the work meant in terms of the artist's personal development. Before going to Paris in 1897, the painter had been a student of William Merritt Chase and had developed a gray-toned Whistlerian style. Maurer, who was described by his close friend Gertrude Stein as "a little dark dapper man . . . with hair, eyes, face, hands and feet all very much alive," had continued painting academically for his first ten years in Paris, but in 1905 he had seen Matisse's work, and within the next two years he had been "reborn" or "gone red," as Stieglitz variously put it.[9] The latter was pleased that Maurer, who had been the "great hope" of the American academics, had become the first American to emulate Matisse. Adding to his pleasure was the fact that Maurer was the son of Edward Stieglitz's friend Louis Maurer, whose Currier and Ives prints of racehorses had hung in Alfred's room when he was a child. Too, Alfred Maurer was a cousin of the Californian amateur photographer Oscar Maurer, a member of the Photo-Secession.

Although Stieglitz liked the work of Winslow Homer, he had not generally been interested in watercolor. But when he unpacked the twenty-four Marins he responded to their gentle poetry and agreed with Steichen, who had written him that they were "about as good as anything in that line that has ever been done."[10] Stieglitz hung them in a single line and concentrated the effect of the Maurers by placing them all on one wall, in three rows of five. "Marin's watercolors sang their quiet song," he recalled, "while the Maurers seemed like instruments of music run riot."[11]

The exhibition attracted what were for 291 large crowds, since the critics outdid themselves in damning Maurer and praising Marin. J. Edgar Chamberlin reported in the *Evening Mail* that in the foreground of one Maurer was "a great gob of color" and asked "What is it? A bursted tomato? A fireman's hat? A red rock? A couple of people under an umbrella?"[12] And Arthur Hoeber wrote in the *Globe*, "Frankly, of all the pure forms of imbecility that have overtaken youth time out of mind, these are the limit."[13]

At the other extreme, James Huneker savored Marin's watercolors as "delicious in tonalities, subtly evocative" and concluded, "There is the poet in this young man; he has a creative touch."[14] Chamberlin was for once on the mark when he wrote, "It is a fair prediction that some time these broad yet delicate things, in which there is the spirit of Whistler and a color that is pure, original, vivacious and subtle, will be famous."[15]

John Marin was born two days before Christmas, 1870, in Rutherford, New Jersey. Nine days later his mother died. His father, a wealthy public accountant, then entrusted him to the care of his puritanical Yankee maternal grandparents and their two unmarried daughters in Weehawken, only a couple of miles from Hoboken, where the Stieglitzes were still living.

Because his family demanded that he practice a "respectable" profession, Marin submitted to a four-year apprenticeship and then set himself up as an architect in Union Hill, New Jersey. But his heart was never in such work. A stubborn fellow, he managed to spend most of his time hiking, fishing, sketching, and, beginning in the late 1880s, painting in watercolor. When John was twenty-nine, his father finally relented and agreed to pay his way through two years at the Pennsylvania Academy of the Fine Arts, where he studied under Thomas Anshutz. For several years after his graduation, he devoted himself to painting. His own wryly terse account of that period read:

> 1 year blank
> 1 year Art Students League, N.Y. . . .
> 2 years blank.

Bankrolled by his reluctant father, Marin finally set off for Paris in September 1905. Between then and 1910 he worked as a professional etcher and made more than one hundred views of cities and villages in France, Italy, Germany, and the Netherlands, for which there was a fairly lively market.

It was probably in the fall of 1908 that Marin's Philadelphia friend Arthur Carles, who had arrived in Paris in June of the previous year, introduced him to Steichen. Soon, Marin's etchings became freer, with rougher and more expressive sketching. He allowed himself the greatest freedom in the watercolors he did for his own pleasure, some of which have a delicate, Oriental quality. Although he denied that he spent much time in the Parisian museums and galleries, he clearly had been looking at Matisse and Cézanne, as well as at the old masters. He had perhaps even learned a thing or two about watercolor from the despised John Singer Sargent.

If the dominant mood of Marin's work was joy, that of another artist who entered Stieglitz's life at this time was brooding. Sometime around April 1, 1909, the effusive and temperamental Irish-American poet Shaemas O'Sheel (né James Shields) asked Stieglitz whether he would be willing to take a look at the work of a young painter, Marsden Hartley, who had just arrived in New York and was in desperate financial straits. Hartley's paintings of his native Maine had an intense, visionary quality that O'Sheel thought would appeal to Stieglitz.

After Stieglitz agreed to a meeting, O'Sheel and Hartley stopped by the gallery early one evening. The thirty-two-year-old Hartley was a tall and gangly English-looking man with big ears, a giant beak of a nose, and awkwardly but expressively gesturing hands. Most striking of all were his large eyes, which he would open wide into an almost insane stare. The features of this romantically poetic soul, who wrote of himself that he had "a tendency toward ecstasy and exaltation," revealed great sadness, torment, and confusion.[16]

O'Sheel at once proposed that Stieglitz give Hartley an exhibition before the end of the season, but the photographer replied that he couldn't possibly do so. The gallery's current schedule was the most crowded ever, with so many shows that none could stay on view for more than ten days or two weeks. Stieglitz had already resolved to have fewer shows during the next season, for a minimum of three weeks each. The Marin-Maurer exhibition on the walls during Hartley's visit was to be followed by Steichen's photographs, and finally Japanese prints from the collection of one of 291's financial backers, F. W. Hunter. (Stieglitz was fascinated by the similarities between de Zayas's caricatures and the work of the nineteenth-century printmaker Sharaku, five of whose portraits of actors were to be featured in the exhibition.) As it was, a number of shows announced for the season had had to be postponed or canceled: photographs of nudes in wild landscapes by Californian Annie Brigman; work by Frank Eugene, Heinrich Kuehn, and Hugo Henneberg, as well as by the now-forgotten William J. Mullins; prints from Stieglitz and White's collaboration; and a group show of the New English school (Malcolm Arbuthnot, Walter Bennington, Dudley Johnston, E. Warner, and others).

Even if 291's schedule had not been crowded, Stieglitz was tempted to resist Hartley both because he was "dead tired" and because he had already turned down an equally urgent plea from Max Weber, a member of Steichen's New Society who had recently returned to New York. Without giving Weber a chance to introduce himself, Stieglitz had told him that even if the artist were "Leonardo da Vinci, Rembrandt, Michelangelo and God himself rolled into one," a show was out of the question. Stieglitz had refused even to look at Weber's portfolio. But he didn't dismiss Hartley so abruptly. Years later, in a letter to Hartley, he recalled,

> When I suggested you should have a show elsewhere you remarked you'd have a show at 291 or nowhere, as you liked the spirit of the place & didn't like the spirit of the other places. I asked you a few questions & then, in spite of myself & my great tiredness & determi-

nation not to have any more shows, I gave you a show to <u>help you</u>. And for no other reason. I believed in you & your work, because I felt a spirit I liked — or rather, thought very worthwhile.[17]

In another letter Stieglitz told Hartley, "You were given your original Show in '291' because of my reading Suffering — Spiritual anguish — in your face. And because I felt a supreme worthwhile struggle of a Soul. No other reason."[18] Stieglitz agreed to show Hartley's work for ten days in May, inserting it between Steichen and the Japanese prints. It would be the first of the painter's five one-man shows at 291.

Deeply moved by the writings of Emerson and Thoreau, Hartley considered art a spiritual discipline and tried to express in his paintings a mystical, pantheistic vision of nature. He said that he wanted to paint with the innocence of a child or with the revelatory insight of a mystic whom ordinary people would dismiss as mad. In the fall of 1908, while living in an abandoned building on a farm in the White Mountains of southwestern Maine, Hartley began using a pointillist style derived from the work of the Italian Giovanni Segantini (1858–99), whose paintings are essentially Pre-Raphaelite images of Alpine meadows executed in a Neo-Impressionist technique of overlapping strokes. Adopting the so-called Segantini stitch, Hartley made a series of bold and dramatic paintings of Maine mountains covered with varicolored autumn foliage or attacked by fierce blizzards. Thirty-three of these small canvases made up his first show at 291.

For Hartley, mountains were symbols of strength, invulnerability, and stoic impassivity in the face of the ravages of natural forces. The artist — a restless and susceptible man who never remained in one place, or worked in one style, for more than a few months — must have envied the unmovable massiveness of mountains. His feelings about them were perhaps not so different from his obsessive attraction to extremely muscular men.

The dealer Newman E. Montross, who was on friendly terms with Stieglitz, went to see Hartley's exhibition and took a paternalistic interest in the artist. For the next two years, asking nothing in return, Montross would give Hartley four dollars a week, the amount on which he had said he could live. Montross invited him to visit his gallery at 372 Fifth Avenue and there introduced him to the work of the great American visionary painter Albert Pinkham Ryder, who was living on West Fifteenth Street, one block from Hartley's boardinghouse. The first painting he saw left the young artist "breathless."[19] Hartley soon made a point of meeting Ryder and later wrote of him that he "saw with an all too pitiless and pitiful eye the element of helplessness in things, the complete succumbing of things in nature to those elements greater than they that wield a fatal power."[20]

During the summer of 1909, living in a bleak and tiny room, painting in a friend's jumbled studio, and suffering from deprivation, Hartley set out to paint, from memory and imagination, a series of "Dark Landscapes," which were, he said, "as close to Ryder as possible." Stieglitz wrote on the back of the one he bought, depicting a tiny farmhouse overwhelmed by huge, sinister mountains, "Hartley undoubtedly was on the verge of suicide during the summer which brought forth this picture."[21]

That fall Hartley returned to Maine, since he needed contact with his muse and could live there more cheaply than in New York. A gregarious man, Hartley was forever torn between his desire for creative solitude and his need for companionship. He sought inspiration and found solace in nature, but he was also hungry for artistic and intellectual friendships that would partly compensate for his lack of sexual and emotional relationships. A devotee of Whitman, whom he called "that great and beautiful man," he would always write poetry as well as essays about art and wonder whether his true vocation was to be a writer or a painter. He was condemned to an endless search for an ideal friendship, for a place where he could be happy, for a style in which he could make great art, and for a social group in which he would be appreciated.

CHAPTER THIRTY·SEVEN

THE MONTH OF May 1909 saw two momentous events in Stieglitz's life: his resignation from the Linked Ring and the death of his father.

For several years the Linked Ring had been torn by a civil war between the Perfectionists (led by George Davison), who insisted upon maintaining the highest standards for work to be shown in the annual salon, and the Latitudinarians (led by F. J. Mortimer, the editor of *The Amateur Photographer*), who demanded more democratic representation. The virtual boycott of the 1906 and 1907 salons by the Photo-Secession had hurt. Davison, temporarily in the ascendant, wanted the Americans back. He saw to it that the Committee of Selection for the 1908 salon would be decidedly Perfectionistic; besides himself, it would include J. Craig Annan, Malcolm Arbuthnot, Walter Bennington, A. L. Coburn, Edward Steichen, Robert Demachy, Frank Eugene, Heinrich Kuehn, Adolf de Meyer, Clarence White, and Stieglitz. The last five were honorary, since they were not able to be in London for the judging.

In their zeal, the jurors lost their sense of proportion and chose 133 photographs by Steichen, Coburn, White, Eugene, de Meyer, Annan, Arbuthnot, and Demachy. Everyone else was represented by a grand total of seventy prints. Some outstanding British Links, such as Frederick Evans, had only one accepted, and many regular exhibitors were excluded altogether. Joseph Keiley reported that "in some quarters it was not merely hinted but openly intimated, that the stronger English work had been re-jected to make the foreign work stand out more prominently by contrast." The embittered Britons generally "accepted as a fact that the Americans had a majority on the Committee of Selection, and that the tyrannical Photo-Secession had ridden rough-shod over English work."[1] In fact, only two of the men who actually served on the jury, Coburn and Steichen, were Americans.

Mortimer proceeded to organize a photographic Salon des Refusés fea-turing the work of the slighted Links, including Evans and himself, in *The Amateur Photographer*'s gallery. Stieglitz was outraged. He later wrote to Davison that when the Ring "practically repudiated its own Committee's work it made it impossible for me at least to continue feeling any sympathy for it."[2]

To make matters far worse, in reaction to the brouhaha of 1908 and as a result of the recent death of Alfred Horsley Hinton, who had been an im-portant stabilizing force, the Latitudinarians gained the upper hand in 1909. Stieglitz was terribly upset when he learned, early in the spring, that letters had been sent to many photographers whom he considered inferior, assuring them that their work would be hung in the coming salon without being submitted to the selection committee. When Davison wrote to enlist his help, Stieglitz replied, "The work begun 26 years ago by me is about to be finished. This is no exaggeration, it is all literally true. For that very rea-son we can't be identified with anything which we ourselves do not believe in."[3]

A letter of resignation bearing the names of seven members — Stieglitz, Coburn, Eugene, Keiley, Kuehn, de Meyer, and White — was read aloud at the Union of the Linked Ring on May 10, 1909. That fall, by which time Eva Watson-Schütze and Gertrude Käsebier had also resigned, Annan wrote Stieglitz that the Ring was in a state of "voluntary liquidation." In February 1910 it met for the last time. With the demise of the Ring, the Photo-Secession became the preeminent photographic organization in the world.

On May 24, 1909, Stieglitz's seventy-six-year-old father died as a result of kidney ailments. Whatever grief Alfred may have felt he kept very private. Indeed, the family seems almost to have been relieved and liberated by the death of the silence-loving tyrant. Hedwig, whose inheritance guaranteed her an adequate but certainly not lavish income, soon rented an apartment in the Hotel Fourteen, at 14 East Sixtieth Street, the site of the demolished

Stieglitz brownstone. She would spend every summer at Lake George, and the rest of the year in New York, visiting friends and family and attending cultural events.

Alfred inherited $10,000, and although he had sworn that if he ever again had any capital he wouldn't touch it, he now decided to draw upon it for the $700 he needed annually to keep 291 going, over and above the $500 subscribed by Pratt, French, Hunter, Kerfoot, and Haviland, which covered only the rent but not the cost of electricity, printing, framing, shipping, and so on. "I could not let the idea of money get in the way of doing work properly," declared Stieglitz.[4]

He had begun his move toward modernist art more than a year earlier, but those first steps were essentially passive, for (with the exception of Pamela Colman Smith's work) he had simply hung on the walls of 291 what Steichen had selected and sent from Paris. Now, with the end of his long involvement with the Linked Ring and the death of his father, Stieglitz seems to have felt free to play a more active rôle in the crusade for modernist art.

A month after Edward's death, Alfred and his family sailed for Europe. When they arrived in Paris late in June, Steichen took Alfred to visit Rodin in Meudon. Unfortunately, it was not possible to arrange a similar meeting with Matisse, who was busy overseeing the construction of his new studio in Issy-les-Moulineaux, a southwestern suburb of Paris. Matisse had been impressed by Steichen's prefabricated wood-framed studio and was having one built for himself so that he could work on large canvases.

Steichen did, however, take Stieglitz to see the extraordinary collection of Matisses owned by Michael and Sarah Stein. The afternoon of the next day they called on Leo and Gertrude at 27, rue de Fleurus, where Stieglitz was overwhelmed by the walls thickly hung with Cézannes, Matisses, and Picassos. Leo, a balding, red-bearded, nervous man wearing rimless glasses, proceeded to lecture on art for the next hour and a half. Stieglitz was, as he later wrote, "spellbound" by this discourse, which ranged from the old masters to the newest of the new. Stein dismissed Whistler and Rodin as second-rate, or even third-, and insisted that although Matisse was certainly not a great painter, he was perhaps the greatest of all modern sculptors. Then Stein pointed to canvases by Picasso, of whom the bewildered Stieglitz had barely heard, and proclaimed the young Spaniard the leading genius of the age.

Stieglitz was so awed, both by the apparent logic of Stein's arguments and by the eloquence with which he expressed them, that he invited him to write down what he had said to be published in *Camera Work*. Stein replied that until he had completely worked out every detail of his philosophy of art, he could not possibly write anything.

Also present was Gertrude, whose name Stieglitz did not catch when Steichen introduced them. Throughout Leo's dissertation she remained off to one side, silent and impassive except for an occasional "knowing smile." Stieglitz perceived her, dressed in her usual brown corduroy, simply as a "dark and bulksome" presence.[5] But it was to be Gertrude, not Leo, whose writing would ultimately be published in *Camera Work*.

Stieglitz was especially eager to meet John Marin, to whose work he had responded so warmly in the spring. He was not disappointed by the man, a boyish leprechaun — quiet and serious, yet also wry and joyous — whose dark, curly bangs nearly hid his eyes. There was an almost instantaneous rapport between the two men. Decades later Stieglitz would boast, "We have never had a word of difference, we have never questioned one another, and each has remained free, true to himself, true to the other."[6]

Immediately upon entering Marin's studio, Stieglitz was struck by a recent watercolor whose drawing was freer, and colors brighter, than of those he had exhibited. Marin said he kept such works to himself, since the dealers had told him that such "wild" paintings would never sell. But Stieglitz counseled him to develop his self-expression and tell the dealers to go to hell. He then informed the artist that during the upcoming season he would like to hang a one-man show of his wildest work at 291.

Stieglitz felt that he had discovered a talent to be nurtured and protected at all costs. Once, when Marin's father visited 291 and suggested that John at least devote his mornings to producing salable work, Stieglitz retorted that to do so would be artistic prostitution. The shrewd photographer perhaps realized that there would be no need for such an abomination, since Marin's work would prove very popular. There wasn't much risk in promising to make up any difference between the artist's sales and what he needed to live on.

Although Stieglitz would have liked to spend all of his time that summer immersing himself in visits to studios and galleries, discussing the new art that had seized his imagination, Emmy insisted that they visit family and friends and take the waters at various fashionable resorts in Germany. Any healthful benefits of the spas were more than negated by Alfred's upset over the news that Lou Schubart had declared bankruptcy; Selma's love of luxury and the decline of his business had used up all his capital and driven him deeply into debt.

With Emmy safely ensconced in the pretentious splendors of Marienbad, Alfred was finally able to get away from her. He went first to Munich
to meet with Frank Eugene, Heinrich Kuehn, and Steichen. After a few days
spent in further experiments with Autochromes, they all went off to Baden-
Baden, where they had arranged to rendezvous with Adolf de Meyer, whom
Stieglitz had never met. He found the "baron" quite delightful.

The five men traveled together to Dresden, where de Meyer had a
house, to see the vast International Photographic Exhibition that had
opened in May. In addition to the professional and amateur sections, a special *hors concours* exhibition, installed in the Hall of Honor, was devoted to
the International Group of Art Photographers, in which all five were included. Stieglitz had asked Käsebier to participate in the Dresden show,
but she replied that in recent years she had been concentrating entirely on
her business and could not very well exhibit the results in a section devoted
to amateur photography. Besides, she didn't want to show her old Pictorialist images yet again. So she submitted five of her portraits to the professional section. Stieglitz, unreasonably incensed, wrote early in March to
Kuehn, "Now she must leave the Secession. Rarely have I heard of anything so low. I'd rather give up the whole thing than have anything further
to do with such rabble."[7] In the April issue of *Camera Work* he published a
revised Photo-Secession members' list, on which Käsebier's name was conspicuously missing from the newly created category of fellows of the di-
rectorate, to which Stieglitz, Steichen, Coburn, Eugene, Keiley, and White
were elevated.

Alfred endured two more weeks at Marienbad and a quick trip to Paris
to get Emmy established for the early September season before taking
Kitty and her governess to Tutzing. There he finally had ten enjoyable days
with Frank Eugene. The family returned to New York early in October.

After Stieglitz had refused to look at Max Weber's paintings in the spring
of 1909, the young artist spent the summer living and working in a barn on
Long Island. That fall Weber — whom Stieglitz described as a "short,
stocky, smooth shaven, pallid young man" — ventured back to 291.[8] The
photographer now volunteered to look at his work, which he found "thoroughly alive" but worryingly imitative of Cézanne and Matisse.

Weber was born to Orthodox Jewish parents in 1881 in the Russian Pale
of Settlement. When he was ten, the family settled in the Williamsburg
section of Brooklyn. After studying at Pratt with Arthur Wesley Dow,
Weber taught in Virginia and Minnesota. In September 1905, having saved
every penny he could, he sailed for France.

Toward the end of 1908, when Weber was running out of money, Steichen, who was as yet unaware that Weber envied his success to the point of hatred, assured him that he could get the best prices for his paintings in New York. So Weber resolved to spend a few months or a year in New York, make a large amount of money very quickly, and return to Paris. In December, his friend Henri Rousseau threw a farewell dinner for him, attended by Picasso, the poet Guillaume Apollinaire, and the painter Marie Laurencin, among others. Le Douanier gave Weber a small painting, which he took with him to New York along with four others he had bought for modest sums. Until Weber's arrival, Rousseau was completely unknown in America.

After his second visit to 291 had failed to produce an offer of a show, Weber did not reappear until one morning early in 1910, telling Stieglitz that he was penniless and had been evicted from his studio. Since Stephen Lawrence would be working on commissions in the South for some time, Stieglitz told Weber he could live in the decorator's workroom, where there was a sofa on which he could sleep. When Lawrence eventually returned, he said Weber could continue to live there as long as he was out by seven o'clock every morning. Stieglitz then let the painter use the gallery as a studio from seven to ten, when it opened to the public. During the day Weber spent most of his time with Stieglitz, and because Emmy liked the artist, he was always welcome at 1111 Madison Avenue for dinner. Stieglitz later wrote of that period, "Weber and I had become so intimate that there was nothing that I did in the name of 291 or pertaining to my own family that I did not share with him." Elsewhere he recalled, "The closeness of Weber and myself and my study of his work — living with it — gave me the opportunity to enlighten myself in a way in which I couldn't have otherwise in America. Weber had a knowledge of art only equalled by that of Arthur B. Davies."[9]

For nine months in 1910, Weber was the leading member of the Stieglitz circle. His most important contribution was to stress the centrality of Cézanne, on the one hand, and of so-called primitive art, on the other, as the vital sources of modernism. In New York, Weber studied the collection of pre-Columbian Mexican objects at the American Museum of Natural History and was one of the first to write about them as art.

Knowledgeable, articulate, and highly opinionated, Weber would argue about aesthetic matters with Stieglitz and the regulars for hours on end in the gallery, in Lawrence's room, or over lunch. Unfortunately, the extremely ambitious Weber — to whom Stieglitz still had not offered a show — generally had kind words only for the dead, since he had trouble regarding a living painter as anything but a competitor. He constantly expressed his contempt for his rivals and attempted to demolish the reputations of the artists whom he was accused of imitating. For instance, he accused Matisse of having "begun to prostitute his genius for gain" and claimed to have stopped going to Matisse's school because the Frenchman was envious of his talent.

At the slightest provocation, Weber would launch into a harangue about the mediocrity of Steichen's paintings and photographs. Steichen, he maintained, "was a better business man than he was an artist. . . . He was shrewd, very clever and facile as a colorist; a hard worker, and an excellent talker; but an artist! . . . He knew how to advertise."[10]

Because Stieglitz was eager to help Weber earn some money, he mentioned his plight to N. E. Montross, whom the artist resented bitterly as the dealer who managed to sell Steichen's paintings for large sums. Montross was interested in Weber's work and commissioned him to paint his portrait. One wonders what exactly Montross expected. In any case, the Cézannesque result so displeased him that he refused to accept the painting or to pay Weber his $100 fee. The understandably furious artist destroyed the painting and inveighed against Montross at every opportunity.

He soon became so notorious for his arrogant and contemptuous pronouncements that Laurvik assembled a collection of Weberisms. Generally sooner rather than later, Weber managed to offend nearly every painter who frequented 291. Only the photographers — at least those who didn't also paint — were safe.

CHAPTER THIRTY·EIGHT

"YOU STEPPED AWAY from the brittle brilliance of Fifth Avenue," wrote man of letters Waldo Frank about what was for many people the sacrament of visiting 291. "The door was always open. Perhaps, Stieglitz was not in. Possibly no one, although this was rare. Only some watercolors of Cézanne or the latest plastic harmonies of Marin. If you were a thief, you could have stolen. No thief did. It was the one open door in burglar-harried Manhattan. Except some churches."[1] One significant difference between a church and 291, however, was that to gain admission to the latter, one was expected to be genteel enough to present a calling card.

Frank went on to make what now strike us as embarrassingly reverential claims about the gallery. "'291' is a religious fact: like all such, a miracle," he affirmed. "It is an altar where talk was often loud, heads never bared, but where no lie and no compromise could live."[2] His words may make us wince, but we must not ignore them if we are to understand what Stieglitz meant to several generations of artists, writers, and intellectuals who optimistically felt an urgent need to uproot the brutal materialism that had pervaded American life and replace it with a spiritual vision.

Steichen recalled that "with only a brief interruption for lunch," Stieglitz "stood on the floor of the Galleries from ten o'clock in the morning until six or seven o'clock at night. He was always there, talking, talking, talking;

talking in parables, arguing, explaining."[3] In 1912 Stieglitz claimed that in seven seasons, during which the gallery had had 160,000 visits (many of them, naturally, by the same few hundred people who saw every show), he had been absent from the gallery only two days. According to Paul Rosenfeld, "Stieglitz was on his shoe leather all day long; and if you did not go into the back room, like as not he would come out into the gallery and begin speaking to you with his fierce and informal, jovial and passionate, address."[4]

The man who would cast his verbal net over visitors was described by Rosenfeld as "a slight slender figure clad in a pepper and salt business suit: gray bristling mustache, gray fighting hair, and shining brown eyes behind glasses."[5] In photographic portraits of Stieglitz one is first drawn to the eyes, large, direct, challenging, and questioning, deeply set beneath exuberant eyebrows. "Eyes too pent with passion and with dream to flash their vision lightly," wrote Frank,[6] while *saloniste* Mabel Dodge Luhan outpoured that his eyes "were like two powerful lenses surrounded by dark shades, and when he turned them upon one they burned through to the core."[7] His face was open and mobile, his most characteristic expression somewhat quizzical, skeptical, but kind, with a hint of a smile. With his pince-nez glasses and a flaring brush-style mustache he looked a bit like a sensitive version of Teddy Roosevelt, whom he despised. (In 1912, when Roosevelt was about to campaign for a third term as president, Stieglitz wrote a letter to the editor of the *New York Sun*, the entire text of which read: "His ideal of the square deal, his idea of every ideal: I deal."[8])

Set somewhat incongruously in the middle of this fine face was a broad nose that a childhood accident had bumped and skewed. Once, when Alfred was about six months old, his mother dozed off while holding him on her lap as she sat in front of the fireplace. He fell onto the floor, landing on his nose. The doctor mispronounced the broken nose intact. Stieglitz always finished telling this story by forcing upon his listener the perhaps unwelcome confidence that ever since the accident he had been able to breathe through only one nostril.

Marius de Zayas based one of his caricatures of Stieglitz on a South Pacific "trap for catching souls" that he had seen in the British Museum. He also depicted him as "a midwife who brings out new ideas to the world."[9] It was not only through his exhibitions but also, and perhaps to an even greater extent, through his conversations with, and endless monologues directed at, 291's regulars and its casual visitors that Stieglitz caught souls and served as a midwife for ideas. In a "slow, solid voice" with more than a trace of a German accent, "Stieglitz spoke almost incessantly — punctu-ated by long and pregnant silences — to all comers, whether in his gallery-demonstration centers, in restaurants, or in his living quarters," wrote his friend and amanuensis Herbert Seligmann.

> Talks continued for hours and days, people came and went during volcanic outpourings to a silent and fascinated audience of from one to twenty or more. Here, in a sustained flow of narration, assimilat-ing into its unbroken course whatever questions, discussions, or self-revelation might come from the participants, Stieglitz developed his main themes. . . . The foe was commercialism . . . its accompanying indifference to quality . . . and its disregard for the spirit.[10]

"It is sometimes a question in our minds whether it is Mr. Stieglitz or the pictures on the wall at the Photo-Secession that constitute the exhibi-tion," wrote critic Henry McBride. "The pictures change from time to time in the little room, different artists emerge from somewhere to puzzle us, and having succeeded go again into the mist, but Mr. Stieglitz is always in the centre of the stage, continually challenging us, continually worrying us, teasing us, frightening and inflaming us according to our various na-tures." On his most recent visit McBride had "spent an hour and a quarter in the gallery, ten minutes of which were devoted to the pictures and one hour and five minutes to delightful conversation."[11]

"Alfred Stieglitz was something of a mesmerist," claimed writer Ed-mund Wilson. "Since the opening in 1905 of [291]. . . , he had been delivering a monologue, a kind of impalpable net in which visitors and dis-ciples were caught from the moment they came within earshot."[12] James Huneker half seriously recommended to the readers of the *New York Sun* that they visit 291 while Stieglitz was out to lunch, as

> a safeguard against the seductiveness of his golden voice. Once open the porches of your ears to his tones and ere long you will begin to believe that photography it was that originated impressionism; that camera and Monet rhyme; that the smeary compound of mush and mezzotint which they have christened the New Photography is one of the fine arts. There's no resisting Stieglitz. He believes what he preaches, a rare virtue nowadays.[13]

More than thirty years later author Henry Miller would write, "Everything that Stieglitz says is based on pure conviction. Behind every word that comes from his lips is his whole life, a life, I must repeat, of absolute devotion to the things he believes in. *He believes!* — that's the essence of it all. He isn't giving his opinions — he is saying what he knows to be true, what he Alfred Stieglitz has found to be true through personal experience."[14] Nevertheless, remembered Georgia O'Keeffe, "he thought aloud and his opinion about anything in the morning might be quite different by afternoon, so that people quoting him might make quite contradictory statements."[15]

Some people simply could not put up with Stieglitz's logorrhea. Not long after 291 first opened, John Sloan dropped in. He later complained to Van Wyck Brooks that the photographer had talked his ear off, and he never went back. Another artist who turned hostile, though only after several years of friendship, was Thomas Hart Benton, who wrote that Stieglitz "never talked directly to the point but wove a web of discourse over, under, and around a subject. One of Stieglitz's actual conversational sentences would, Faulkner-like, run to two or three pages of print."[16] "Without reference directly to modern art," recalled de Zayas, "Stieglitz made soliloquies which his friends, who sensed what he meant and did not listen to what he said, accepted as the outburst of an 'illuminated,' the unbelievers as the outburst of a 'charlatan' and the practical ones as the twaddle of a 'perfect bore.'"[17]

Even when Stieglitz was alone, the outpouring of words rarely stopped during his waking hours, for he maintained a correspondence of staggering volume, writing in his bold, graceful script. He wrote at least three or four letters almost every day, and he would occasionally write twenty or more.

Stieglitz's friend Hutchins Hapgood felt that "it was not because he was an artist in words" that he was able to captivate his listeners. "No, he does not feel the word with the sensitiveness of a gifted writer. He is rather maladroit in speech, too redundant, too emphatic, hardly ever is there a perfectly selected word or a happily chosen phrase; never the poetic phrase — the picture in words that tells the whole of truth." The key to his impact upon his listeners was "the passionate sincerity which moved him."[18]

Hapgood maintained that "conversation with Stieglitz is extremely difficult, as he talks nearly all the time. . . . Although Stieglitz does not converse, and does not seem to listen, yet somehow he often grasps the character of the other by a kind of intuition."[19] But he could never have had such a powerful effect on people if his talk had been entirely monologous and egotistical. Herbert Seligmann was by no means alone when he insisted that "not least of [Stieglitz's] amazing powers was the ability to release people so that sheer and often unconscious impulse on their part took form in words."[20] Paul Rosenfeld rhapsodized that 291 "was a place where people got very hot and explanatory and argumentative about rectangles of color and lumps of bronze and revealed themselves; and a place where quiet unobtrusive people suddenly said luminous things in personal language about paintings and drawings . . . and revealed life." The atmosphere of 291, he recalled, "seemed to demand that you be yourself utterly — for in this place nothing but that final self, that utter, inner design of the soul was revered."[21]

Stieglitz's R. W. Emersonian goal — for himself, for artists, and for all — was the spontaneous and forthright expression of one's deepest feelings. Such expression was the sine qua non of art — and of a life worth living. In 1922 he would counsel Edward Weston, "The struggle is to live and express life untouched by the ideas of neighbors and friends."[22] "The trouble with most photographers," he wrote in 1911, "and for that matter also with painters, and other people, is, that they are always trying to do something which is outside of themselves. In consequence they produce nothing that means anything to those who have the gift of or intuition for truth: all else is really not worth a tinker's damn."[23]

Inexorably, and with what he claimed was a spirit of scientific inquiry and exploration, he delved into his interlocutors' secrets. A devoted reader of Richard von Krafft-Ebing's *Psychopathia Sexualis* (1886) and of Havelock Ellis's seven-volume *Studies in the Psychology of Sex* (1897–1928), Stieglitz asked visitors to his gallery blunt and searching questions about their innermost beliefs and prejudices, their feelings, and even their sex lives — everything that fear usually prevented people from discussing honestly. Some were affronted, but many felt relieved and liberated. Once, in the 1930s, a woman who dropped by Stieglitz's last gallery asked him as she was leaving why the Marins on exhibition didn't arouse any emotion in her. He replied by asking why she didn't give him an erection.

In December 1911, Stieglitz wrote in a letter to Sadakichi Hartmann, "Daily I realize, more and more, that in sacrificing my own photography I have gained something I could have never possessed in any other way — and that is certainly . . . a bigger thing than merely expressing oneself in making photographs, no matter how marvelous they might be."[24] He always considered works of art as means to an end, never as ends in themselves. He liked to tell the critics, "You are interested in the fruit. I am interested in the tree."[25] He considered the artist vital to society as an exemplar of the creative life, developing and expressing all the potential of the individual. The principal function of works of art was to inspire those who saw them, and understood them, to reject the venality, the hypocrisy, and the puritanism that poisoned American culture.

In 1922 Stieglitz would write,

> Photography is not an art. Neither is painting nor sculpture, literature nor music. They are only different media for the individual to express his aesthetic feelings; the tools he uses in his creative work. . . . You do not have to be a painter or sculptor to be an artist. You may be a shoemaker. You may be creative as such. And if so you are a greater artist than the majority of the painters whose work is shown in the art galleries of today."[26]

"It would be a mistake to think that Stieglitz's purpose and objective was to make people understand modern art," wrote de Zayas. "In Stieglitz's hands modern art had transcendental value. He showed it not only for what it was but for what it could be for the individual to find his own real self. . . . Modern art was to most incomprehensible; for that reason it was the best tool to make people understand themselves."[27]

"The 'work of art' was never . . . of much interest to Stieglitz," opined Hutchins Hapgood. "It is what the work of art symbolizes, what is behind it, that counts. . . . Apropos of a picture by Marin, a drawing by Rodin, or a painting by O'Keeffe, Stieglitz would talk by the hour about 'life,' as it manifests, or should manifest, itself in all human relations — marriage, politics, morality."[28] In the photographer's view, however, any attempt to explain a work of art, to analyze it or to fit it into a theory, was antithetical to the spirit of art.

Stieglitz said that at 291 he had "nothing but the thought of liberating the people from superstition, from labels, from bias and the idea that money could buy everything."[29] He strove to keep 291 "devoid of all commercial taint," for he wanted it to be "a place where human beings could meet without all the dirty ugliness which the struggle for existence seems to bring out sooner or later in most artists."[30] One of the surest ways to call down upon oneself the full blast of Stieglitz's wrath was to suggest that he was a dealer, or that 291 was a business. In fact, the gallery was like an adoption agency for works of art. Stieglitz once wrote that "certain pictures should find homes instead of owners," and he could be obnoxiously fussy about prospective parents.[31] "If he thought they wanted to buy just because they had money, he might double the price of the painting," recalled his secretary. "If someone else came in and was just crazy about something, and had nothing else in mind, he would let them have it for half-price!"[32]

"Owning a picture, putting pictures away in the homes of the rich, or in museums," Stieglitz wrote, "is not caring, is not really putting art to its best use or helping the artist to develop to his fullest capacity. Until the feeling that makes one want a picture . . . is mirrored in one's way of life; unless what one does, all the way through, in the name of art mirrors the spirit in which the pictures themselves are painted, there can be no meaning to the having of pictures."[33] He especially deplored the way the American squillionaires (as their favorite art historian, Bernard Berenson, called them) were then buying up old masters by the boxcarload.

Because a great many works of art left the gallery after money had changed hands, some people felt that there was a degree of hypocrisy in Stieglitz's disclaimers. Even the kindly Montross was sufficiently annoyed to remark sarcastically to his formidable competitor, "Surely, some time, Mr. Stieglitz, you are going into the art business."[34]

CHAPTER THIRTY·NINE

THE 1909–10 SEASON at 291 opened on November 24 with an anomalous exhibition of drawings and monotypes by Eugene Higgins, whose sentimental depictions of the urban and rural poor owed much to J. F. Millet and Honoré Daumier. We can only wonder why Stieglitz exhibited such work, unless as a foil for the Toulouse-Lautrec exhibition that followed. (Paul Haviland observed of the latter that "nothing could be more different from the Higgins monotypes."[1]) This first American show of Lautrec's work consisted of thirty lithographs and posters that Stieglitz had bought that summer in Munich. One critic informed his readers, "Mr. Stieglitz exhibits them more as a protest than anything else, against that commercialism which has led so many of our men to waste their undoubted talents."[2] Lautrec, as Stieglitz pointed out, had succeeded in maintaining the highest artistic standards even in his drawings for advertisements.

Steichen arrived in New York in January 1910 to mount concurrent exhibitions of his paintings and photographic portraits at Montross and of his Autochromes at 291 — the gallery's only show of photographs that season. Although the critics tended to agree that Steichen showed more talent with a camera than with a brush, the $8,000 he cleared from his Montross show persuaded him to concentrate on painting — and on hybridizing his beloved delphiniums — for the next four years. He almost totally ne-glected photography, with the exception of a 1911 series of fashion shots commissioned by the magazine *Art et Décoration* for a fat fee.

Since Matisse had become, as one writer then noted, "the object of a cult, the reputed possessor of strange secrets and philosophies," Stieglitz and Steichen felt it was time to have a second show of the Frenchman's work.[3] The purpose was to represent "the power and sanity of the man, his scientific and almost mathematical attitude toward form, his almost Orien-tal sense of decorative spotting [i.e., composition], so irreconcilably op-posed to some of the more emotional tendencies for which critics have tried to make him responsible."[4]

Steichen had brought from Paris a collection of Matisse's figure draw-ings with color wash over pencil, as well as black-and-white photographs of a few paintings done between 1905 and 1908. Of course, the photographs eliminated precisely what was most important and radical in those can-vases — their color — but they at least provided a glimpse of what all the fuss was about. And fuss there was, though in the *New York Sun* a newly en-lightened James Huneker called Matisse "an amazing artist" and declared that he did much "good in stirring the stale swamp of respectability."[5]

The April 1910 issue of *Camera Work* noted that "not only the number, but the quality of the visitors" to the gallery's exhibitions that season had been "gratifying."[6] One of the many visitors to the Matisse show was Eu-gene Meyer's sister Florence, who was married to George Blumenthal, a partner in the investment firm Lazard Frères. When she inquired, Stieglitz told her that the drawings were priced at 100 francs (about $20). But when she said she had selected three, he refused to sell them, assuming that she wanted to buy them as curiosities. Her husband's collection of standard-issue old masters certainly gave Stieglitz no reason to believe that she could possibly have any real appreciation of Matisse. She then informed him of her intention to give the drawings to the Metropolitan Museum, to which he replied that it would never accept them. After all, late in 1908 the mu-seum's director, Sir Caspar Purdon Clarke, had told an interviewer, "There is a state of unrest all over the world in art as in other things. . . . And I dis-like unrest."[7] As it happened, the Met's curator of paintings, the English-man Roger Fry, who spent most of his time in Europe buying old masters for the museum and for J. P. Morgan's personal collection, fully appreci-ated Matisse's work — but Morgan, the Met's president, fired him in February. That fall Fry would organize, at London's Grafton Gallery, an extremely important exhibition of Post-Impressionists (he coined the term for the exhibition's title) from Manet, Cézanne, Van Gogh, and Gauguin to Matisse and Picasso.

In his conversation with Mrs. Blumenthal, Stieglitz failed to take into account that her husband — who in 1934 would become president of the museum — was already a very generous trustee. The grande dame insisted, haughtily and quite correctly, "The Museum will take what I offer it." Not only did the Met accept the three pencil studies of nudes, thereby becoming the first museum in the world to own any nonacademic works by Matisse, it even hung them the following year, to Stieglitz's amazement.[8]

In the fall of 1909 Steichen had proposed that 291 mount an exhibition of work by eight painters who belonged to the New Society of American Artists in Paris: himself, Putnam Brinley, Patrick Henry Bruce, Arthur Carles, Lawrence Fellows, John Marin, Alfred Maurer, and Max Weber. Stieglitz liked the idea for several reasons. For one thing, the show would give New Yorkers their first strong dose of Fauvist oils. That was particularly important to him, because Autochromes had revealed that the colors in most representational paintings "were all wrong and that better results along this line could be secured mechanically. That knocks the pinning out from under the artistic house and the builder must set to work anew to secure more color and a new idea in painting."[9]

Another reason for the show was that Stieglitz had grown tired of hearing all artists who rebelled against the academic tradition indiscriminately accused of being under the influence of Matisse. He wanted to demonstrate how much variety there was among the alleged "Matissites." Haviland stated in *Camera Work* that the only points Steichen's friends had in common were "a departure from realistic representation, the aim toward color composition, the vitality of their work, and the cheerful key in which their canvases are painted."[10]

Stieglitz carefully timed the Younger Americans show to compete against a much-touted Exhibition of Independent Artists (April 1–27) organized by Robert Henri and John Sloan, with the cooperation of Arthur Davies and Walt Kuhn. Renewed trouble at the National Academy had led Henri and Sloan to discuss the possibility of a yearlong exhibition or even a permanent gallery, but they settled for a huge, unjuried, and prizeless show that would coincide with the academy's 1910 spring annual. They rented a three-story warehouse building at 29–31 West Thirty-fifth Street, covered the dirty walls with light gray cloth, and installed 265 paintings, 344 drawings, and 22 sculptures, following the alphabetical order of the names of the 103 artists, more than half of them Henri's present or former students. Despite Henri's misgivings, Davies had asked Stieglitz to encourage his artists to show. But Stieglitz preferred to let his young Fauves upstage the rival enterprise. Most gratifyingly, Huneker wrote of the Independent exhibit: "Something is lacking — art; the chief devil possessing this show is the devil of empty display. . . . As for novelty, at Alfred Stieglitz's Photo-Secession Gallery a week ago there was a grouping of the minor spirits of the Matisse movement that were actually new, not mere offshoots of the now moribund impressionists as are the majority of the Independents."[11]

The exhibition that opened at 291 on March 21 differed somewhat from that originally planned. Bruce was not included, and two men, Hartley and Arthur Dove, had been added. Dove, who had recently appeared at 291 with an introduction from his friend Alfy Maurer, was a natural participant, since he had been friendly with several of the other exhibitors during his stay in Paris, though he had not joined the New Society. Hartley, the only one who had not been to Paris, was the odd man out, but Stieglitz was eager to show a few of his "Dark Landscapes." The effect of the show upon Hartley was that he threw off some of his gloom and, during the summer and fall of that year, painted a series of small, nearly abstract Fauvist landscape sketches. Still desperately poor, he defiantly began to sport a silver-headed cane and to wear a fresh gardenia in the buttonhole of his coat, whose worn spots he attempted to render invisible with black ink.

Arthur Dove, who became one of Stieglitz's closest friends and most loyally championed artists, was born in 1880 and spent his childhood in the town of Geneva, in the Finger Lakes region of New York State. His father, a prominent brick manufacturer and construction contractor, assumed that Arthur would be trained as a lawyer and then take over the family business. Mr. Dove seriously misjudged his son.

After graduation from Cornell University, Dove settled in New York and began working as a freelance illustrator for such magazines as *Harper's* and *The Century*. Critic Arthur Hoeber would later write that his "delightful" drawings depicting "the follies of present day men and women" were distinguished by the artist's "charming notion of the humorous [and] a rational view of humanity."[12]

When Dove met Robert Henri, John Sloan, and William Glackens, they encouraged him to concentrate on painting. In mid-1908, having saved a few thousand dollars from his well-paid work as an illustrator, Dove and his wife, Florence, left for a year in Paris. After his return to New York, Dove resumed illustration but longed to paint full-time and eventually mustered his courage to approach Stieglitz about an exhibition. Although his paintings provided few clues about his potential, they sufficed.

In July 1910 the Doves, who had a newborn son, took over a farm in Westport, Connecticut, a town with a lively artistic and literary community. Since his father refused to give them any financial help, Arthur and his wife had to struggle along on $100 a month. Rising at 4:00 A.M. to tend the chickens whose eggs were his principal source of income and often not finishing his farm chores until midnight, Dove didn't have much time for painting. Nonetheless, during the next two years he would make the most radically abstract works that had yet been painted by an American.

The group of artists and writers who frequented 291 was at its largest and liveliest around the time of the Younger Americans show in March and April 1910. Weber was living at 291. Steichen, Hartley, and Marin were all in New York for several months early in the year, and Dove would occasionally come down from Westport, an hour away by train. In 1910 the writer Temple Scott described a Holland House lunch at which, in addition to himself and Stieglitz, the company included Weber, de Zayas, Laurvik, Marin, Caffin, Hartley, White, Haviland, Kerfoot, and Keiley. Also among the regulars were Benjamin de Casseres, Sadakichi Hartmann, and the poet Alfred Kreymborg, a friend of Hartley's.

They would arrive at 291 late in the morning, when the gallery was still quiet. Sitting around the coal stove in Lawrence's room, they would talk earnestly about art, philosophy, poetry, politics, psychology, and life in general. At the table by the windows that looked out onto a cubistic assemblage of rooftops, chimneys, hanging laundry, and towering rear walls, Stieglitz might be pasting gravures into copies of *Camera Work* or addressing copies to be mailed. Perhaps he would also be keeping careful watch over a batch of freshly exposed sheets of platinum paper in frames on the fire escape as they printed out to the precise degree of darkness he desired.

About noon they would all traipse across the street to the Holland House, or occasionally Stieglitz would lead them down Fifth Avenue and around the corner to the Prince George Hotel, on East Twenty-eighth Street, or to Mouquin's. In the gallery, in Lawrence's room, or over lunch Stieglitz dominated as host, instigator, Socratic gadfly, and referee.

It has been suggested that the men (and, before and after 1910, a few women) who gathered around Stieglitz constituted an extended family, a counterpart to the sprawling clan that reunited every summer at Lake

George. His friend Paul Rosenfeld even suggested that the desire to be surrounded by such a family of artists and kindred spirits was an expression of Stieglitz's Jewish heritage. More to the point, the photographer dreamt of a community of individualists who would encourage one another, offer constructive criticism, and cooperate in a spirit of true friendship.

There was, however, a basic contradiction in Stieglitz's approach to individualism and the group spirit. A month after his death his intimate friend Dorothy Norman wrote in a letter to Steichen, "His great power was in getting people to question themselves." And yet, she continued, "his whole philosophy was based on evasion of questioning himself. He believed in group activities and how decisions must be arrived at by mutual consent. If anyone else was against something he was for, however, he 'blamed' the person disagreeing, saying that the person simply did not 'see.'"[13]

Stieglitz was an extraordinarily self-righteous man who could almost always convince himself that whatever he wanted to do was absolutely right. He claimed that his decisions were so selfless, so objective, and so logical that anyone who disagreed with him must be selfish or blind. This attitude was a fatal flaw — in his relations with those he loved, with artists, with collectors, with the critics, with dealers and curators, and with the public.

After another exhibition of drawings by Rodin, intended to show a wider range of the artist's work than was represented in 1908, a dramatic display of caricatures by de Zayas opened at 291 on April 26, 1910, and ran through the summer. On a low stage that covered nearly two thirds of the main gallery's floor space, de Zayas spent several days setting up dozens of cutout caricatures, nearly life-size, executed with charcoal on thick cardboard. The subjects, reported *Camera Work*, were

> well known New York characters from the theatrical world and the world of art and letters, and prominent people from the social world . . . disporting themselves up and down Fifth Avenue on foot, in hansoms, taxicabs, private carriages, or public busses. The Alfred Vanderbilt coach driven by the young millionaire and occupied by half a dozen theatrical stars was a feature of the show.[14]

Soon after it closed, de Zayas left for Paris, where he would remain for nearly two years, befriending Picasso and becoming an evangelist of the Cubist faith.

Although 291 was usually closed from about May 1 until mid-November, it was open intermittently during the summer of 1910, because Stieglitz was spending a lot of time in New York preparing, with Weber's help, an ambitious photographic group exhibition that would open at the Albright Art Gallery in Buffalo on November 3. Emmy and Kitty were in Deal Beach, New Jersey, for all of July and August, joined several days a week by Alfred and Weber. The latter, eager to repay his benefactor, performed various services, including trying to teach a disinclined and hostile Kitty to draw.

PART V

"THE REAL MEANING
OF ART"

CHAPTER FORTY

DURING THE YEARS 1909 to 1913, Stieglitz was engaged in nothing less than a redefinition of photography and a reevaluation of its relationship to the other visual arts. The essence of his argument was that since the camera naturally surpassed even the most talented painter in the accurate depiction of form, it was pointless for painting and the graphic arts to attempt to do what photography did better — and absurd for photography to imitate second-rate illustration. Stieglitz maintained that photographers should devote themselves to the straightforward and purely photographic representation of form and that painters should attempt to render not outward appearances but their own emotional responses to what they saw. In other words, photographs should not be painterly, and paintings should not be photographic. "The works shown at the Little Galleries in painting, drawing, and other graphic arts have all been non-photographic in their attitude," wrote Haviland, "and the Photo-Secession can be said now to stand for those artists who secede from the photographic attitude toward representation of form."[1]

Stieglitz had begun to exhibit modernist art not because he was repudiating photography, but because he believed that looking at such works would help photographers and others to understand what photography was *not*, and would thus provide valuable insights into what it could and should be. He would write in 1912, "Before the people at large, and for that matter the artists themselves, understand what photography really means, as I understand that term, it is essential for them to be taught the real meaning of art. That is what I am attempting to do . . . in such a conclusive manner that it will have been done for all time."[2]

The majority of Photo-Secessionists simply could not understand why Stieglitz admitted modernist art to their gallery. They felt betrayed by the high priest of photography, whose apparent apostasy seemed as outrageous as Peter Henry Emerson's had when he proclaimed the "death of naturalistic photography."

In the July 1910 issue of *Camera Work*, the first in which Haviland is listed as an associate editor, replacing J. F. Strauss, the new editor acknowledged that the inclusion of only one photographic exhibition in the calendar of the 1909–10 season had "led many of our friends to presume that the Photo-Secession was losing its interest in photography and that 'That Bunch at 291' was steering the association away from its original purpose." He countered that the upcoming Albright exhibition offered "a complete vindication of the fact that the interests of photography have never been lost sight of by the Director of the Photo-Secession."[3]

The pages of *Camera Work* had so far remained inviolable, except for the four de Zayas caricatures in the January 1910 issue. Since October 1908 Stieglitz had even compromised his standards somewhat and published the work of some slighted members in order to appease the Photo-Secession. In October 1910, however, two drawings by Matisse and a stage design by Gordon Craig would appear. From then until the magazine ceased publication, in 1917, sixty reproductions would be devoted to nonphotographic works of art, a fairly modest number compared with the 147 photographs illustrated during the same period. Many subscribers would nevertheless see more red than black-and-white.

In his July editorial Haviland argued, "Those photographers who hope and desire to improve their own work can derive more benefit from following the modern evolution of other media than by watching eternally their own bellies like the fakirs of India."[4] But the ranks of dissenters grew, and early the following year Stieglitz would feel obliged to send out a notice stating, "Those who are not in full sympathy with the present activities of the 'Photo-Secession' are in honor bound to return this bill unpaid and have their names stricken from the list of members."[5] Whether hoping for a purge or a vote of confidence, Stieglitz got only a tepid response.

He had hoped to show, in the spring of 1910, a selection of the drawings by the Polish-born sculptor Elie Nadelman that he had seen in Paris the previous summer. Nadelman sent the drawings to New York, but Stieglitz was unable to exhibit them before they had to be returned. Nonetheless, he printed in *Camera Work* the preface that Nadelman had written for the catalog of the postponed exhibition. The artist stated, "It is form in itself, not resemblance to nature, which gives us pleasure in a work of art. . . . The subject of any work of art is for me nothing but a pretext for creating significant form, relations of forms which create a new life that has nothing to do with life in nature."[6] Stieglitz would later echo that statement when he remarked about his photograph *The Steerage*, "You may call this a crowd of immigrants. . . . To me it is a study in mathematical lines, in balance, in a pattern of light and shade."[7]

Nadelman's preface had an immediate impact on Stieglitz, as did Gelett Burgess's article "The Wild Men of Paris," which appeared in the May 1910 issue of *The Architectural Record*, thanks, no doubt, to its former editor, Herbert Croly. It is odd that the first illustrated article about Cubism to appear in America should be incongruously sandwiched between features on office buildings and opulent Fifth Avenue mansions, but it is perhaps no odder than that such a serious piece was written by a popular humorist.

Wanting a body of new work to show in the Albright exhibition, and eager to apply the lessons of modernist art, Stieglitz photographed more prolifically during 1910 than he had for several years. An important influence on his new images was Max Weber's penetrating perception; as they looked at prints, the painter pointed out strengths and weaknesses that the photographer himself had overlooked.

The great theme of Stieglitz's 1910 work was the juxtaposition of striking contrasts and similarities — of related forms, of light and dark, of the old and the new. One photograph records the uncanny negative-positive resemblance of a ferryboat and a formation of wooden piles along its dock. Another juxtaposes four of those piles with the four smokestacks of the liner *Mauretania* as it steams out of New York harbor. Yet another shows a row of old houses dwarfed by the gigantic steel structure of a building going up on Thirty-fourth Street.

One of the finest of Stieglitz's photographs from 1910 is a view of lower Manhattan shot from the deck of a ferryboat. Entitled *The City of Ambition*, it is a powerful image of ruthless materialism and was probably intended as a statement about why advanced art found such a cold reception in New York, a city in which there was no place for spirituality or freedom.

The Albright exhibition was to be the cornerstone of Stieglitz's inquiry into the essence of photography. In it he would sum up the history of pictorial photography to suggest what the medium might yet become, just as he was exhibiting abstract art at 291 to define what photography was not.

The first seed of the show had apparently been planted when Dr. Charles M. Kurtz, the Albright Gallery's director, had found himself fascinated by the Photo-Secessionist prints that J. Nilsen Laurvik had included in his Special Exhibition of Contemporary Art at the National Arts Club in 1908. Kurtz then approached Stieglitz about organizing, for Buffalo, a strictly invitational show that would be broadly representative of American and European work.

In February 1909, while Stieglitz's International Exhibition of Pictorial Photography was at the club, he and Kurtz had a long meeting at which they reached an agreement. The heart of the Albright show would be a section consisting mostly of twenty- to thirty-print retrospectives of the masters, with some emphasis on their most recent work. A supplemental open section, to be judged by Stieglitz and a group of his allies, would "give all American photographers an opportunity of being represented."[8] Two weeks after the meeting, Kurtz died and the plan was shelved.

Early in the fall of 1909, when A. L. Coburn was passing through Buffalo, he paid a visit to the Albright's acting director, Cornelia B. Sage, who had been Kurtz's assistant, and proposed that she revive the plan. After meeting with Stieglitz at 291, Sage wrote him, "I felt I had found a friend and one who was in tune with my innermost thoughts."[9] She endorsed the agreement that he and Kurtz had reached, and she promised to state, "unequivocally" and "publicly," that the museum "officially recognize[d] photography as a medium of art expression."[10]

In Sage's announcement of the show, printed in the April 1910 issue of *Camera Work*, she invited photographers to submit work to be judged in accordance with the mysterious-sounding "Principles of Independent Vision and of Quality of Rendering" but warned that to "eliminate accidental successes," no photographer would be included in the open section unless at least three of the prints he or she entered were found worthy.

The fact that the show would be organized by the Photo-Secession raised a firestorm of controversy. All "the petty intrigue" that had been "going on continuously for some years in the photographic world," as Stieglitz put it, boiled over. "Self-seeking and jealousy are the root of virtually all intrigue," he wrote in the summer of 1910. "In no field of activity is this truer than in that of photographic ambitions."[11]

Conservative photographers were incensed that although the Albright claimed the exhibition would be representative, they were certain to be excluded. Photographers belonging to the national movement of Photo-

Pictorialists of America, which had developed from Curtis Bell's Salon Club, were especially outraged that the title, International Exhibition of Pictorial Photography — the same as that of Stieglitz's 1909 show — did not acknowledge the Photo-Secession's monopoly.

The most vocal opposition came from *American Photography*, which continued to publish the "Camera Notes" page for the Camera Club of New York. In the August 1910 issue the editor, a Mr. Fraprie, announced that many "prominent workers and groups of workers in the United States have no intention of participating in this show." He lamented

> that Mr. Stieglitz, whose services to photography no man can deny, and whose artistic ability is beyond dispute, should not be broad enough to perceive the value of photographic work of artistic merit which does not conform to the particular style which is so character-istic of all exhibitions under his auspices. Half a generation ago this school [the Photo-Secession] was progressive, and far in advance of its time. Today it is not progressing, but is a reactionary force of the most dangerous type.[12]

Throughout the spring, summer, and fall of 1910, Stieglitz labored mightily to demolish all challenges to his authority and to assemble a de-finitive collection of prints, culling the finest examples from his large col-lection, goading Photo-Secessionists to send their best recent work, and judging the images submitted for the open section. He was also busy preparing the catalog. To emphasize the full acceptance of photography as one of the fine arts, it would provide such curatorial apparatus as notes on the career and distinctions of the leading photographers and would spec-ify the date of each negative (and of the print as well, if it was made in a later year), the type of print, and the name of the lender.[13]

Stieglitz wrote to George Seeley, "The reputation, not only of the Photo-Secession, but of photography is at stake and I intend to muster all the forces available to win out for us." Late in August he went so far as to publish his lengthy replies to Fraprie and others in a privately printed pam-phlet entitled *Photo-Secessionism and Its Opponents: Five Letters.* No effort was too great for him, since, as he assured Coburn in September, "the show at Buffalo will knock spots out of anything yet done, if I remain alive until it is up on the walls. Quality will be the keynote and there will be quality in quantities, too."[14]

When Stieglitz, Max Weber, Clarence White, and Paul Haviland traveled to Buffalo late in October, a week before the scheduled opening, they were horrified to find that the Albright's grandiose galleries, with their arching neoclassical spaces, were not at all suited to photographs; the light from the huge skylights was too harsh; and the burlap covering the walls was dusty. So they hung scrims to lower the ceilings and diffuse the light, and they stretched friezes of blue cloth at the level of the scrims. By covering the burlap with cheesecloth, they gave the walls a light, cheerful tone.

Weber was in charge of the hanging. Standing far back, he treated the frames as windows to be placed rhythmically, and he was careful to create a balance of light and dark prints on each wall. He placed all the prints as low as possible to reduce reflections from the glass of the frames. But since Weber refused to hang Steichen's work, Haviland and Stieglitz (who also took charge of his own prints) had to install it. Even the critic for *American Photography* granted that "no show was ever better hung."[15]

In the six galleries of the invitational section, most of the photographs were grouped by nationality. One exception was Adolf de Meyer, whose work was assigned to the large central room with that of Steichen, Coburn, and Seeley. The other exception was the sanctum sanctorum devoted to the old masters: Hill, Annan, and Stieglitz. Hill (still without any acknowledgment of Adamson) was represented by forty prints, more than anyone else; and he was listed first in the catalog, which called him a "worker" who "at the very threshold of the new art" had "realized its possibilities — restricted though they were technically — for pictorial and individual expression, and for the production of results that have yet to be equalled." Of the two others in the room, Keiley wrote in his review (his last signed piece for *Camera Work*) that both were "marked by a curiously keen sensitiveness, of which Annan's was perhaps the more poetic and gentle, Stieglitz's the more symphonic and aggressive."[16]

Stieglitz showed twenty-nine of his own photographs, ranging from *Winter — Fifth Avenue* and *The Terminal* to prints from eight negatives he had exposed during 1910. Eight images, including *The Net Mender* and three others from Katwijk, dated from 1894. He hung *An Icy Night, Spring Showers, The Flatiron*, and *The Hand of Man*, but neither *The Steerage* nor any portraits.

There were nearly five hundred photographs in the invitational section and few surprises among its thirty-seven names. The most unexpected presence was that of F. H. Day, whose work Stieglitz felt "morally bound" to include, even though the photographer forbade him to do so.[17] Stieglitz exhibited eight early Day prints from his own collection, and he managed to obtain one print dating from 1904, which, so the catalog stated, "marks the beginning of his later work, which is not ready for exhibition." Since the 1904 fire in his studio, Day had mainly concentrated on photographing nude boys outdoors, with such "pagan" props as a marble herm of Pan or a lyre, though he had also done some portraiture in a style influenced by his friends Käsebier and White. He had become especially close to the latter after accepting an invitation to visit the Whites in Ohio during the spring of 1905. They then spent that summer at Day's cottage at Five Islands, Maine, and at his house outside Boston, where their two young sons posed nude for both photographers.

By the terms of a tense compromise reached by Stieglitz and Käsebier, she showed not only fourteen of her classic images but also a group of her professional portraits dating from 1910. The catalog reported that Käsebier's "work has had a strong influence in raising the standard of 'professional' photography, and this influence has been exerted as much in Germany as in America." It also called her "the most distinguished woman photographer living, and possibly the foremost since Mrs. Cameron (England in the sixties)." It is odd that Stieglitz did not include any work by Julia Margaret Cameron (Virginia Woolf's great-aunt), five of whose portraits he would publish in the January 1913 issue of *Camera Work*.

The open section was hung in two galleries, separated from the invitational section by a grand sculpture court. It contained 124 prints by about thirty photographers, including Haviland and F. J. Mullins, who had been scheduled to have a show at 291. Among the "unknowns" whose work was most favored by a jury consisting of Stieglitz, White, Weber, and Charles Caffin were Arnold Genthe, Francis Bruguière, and Karl Struss. To the last of these, a student of White's, Stieglitz wrote, "You and Mr. Haviland, and one or two others, are the only photographers of the younger generation in this country who seem to have anything to say."[18]

Although the catalog claimed that the work selected for the open section had "proved to be of sufficiently high standard to link it with the spirit and quality of the Invitation Section," many viewers inevitably disagreed. In his review for *American Photography*, F. Austin Lidbury gloated that "the Open Section was somewhat of a mistake," for it contained much that did "not imply any higher standard than that of the ordinary camera club show" and thus provided "final and conclusive refutation of the claim that the Photo-Secession is divinely commissioned to uphold a standard of unusual excellence."[19]

Stieglitz himself was extremely pleased with the exhibition. To George Seeley he wrote, "The show seems like a dream to me. Even Mrs. Stieglitz who saw it finally realizes that something *has happened* — it was all a revelation to her!! Yes, it does mean one gigantic sacrifice, but everything lasting probably means that. Life-blood is the price."[20]

The critics were, for the most part, complimentary about the show as a whole, however much fault they found with the work of individual exhibitors. Even Lidbury granted that the show contained "a great deal of the very best pictorial work that has ever been done." All would have been well, he felt, if only the organizers had avowed that the exhibition was essentially a history of the Photo-Secession and a monument to Stieglitz. Such a monument, he conceded, was well deserved by "this Napoleon of pictorial photography," who had "put into the movement for internal progress and external recognition the fanaticism of a Mad Mullah, the wiles of a Machiavelli, the advertising skill of a P. T. Barnum, the literary barbs of a Whistler, and an untiring persistence and confidence all his own, — a confidence that could move mountains, to say nothing of the mere prejudiced conservatism of artistic persons."[21]

CHAPTER FORTY·ONE

⟨∾⟩

EVERY SPRING STIEGLITZ would be so exhausted and discouraged that he would say he could not face another season at 291, and every fall he was ready to plunge in again. He was especially eager in the autumn of 1910, for he was excited about the Albright show and conceived of 291's exhibition schedule as a complement to it — a small but fine survey of Post-Impressionism from Cézanne to Picasso, with Max Weber's one-man exhibition demonstrating the influence of the French modernists on young Americans. Because all of the photographs that Stieglitz admired would be on view in Buffalo, he would not mount any photographic shows in New York that season.

His gallery opened on November 18 with an exhibition of lithographs by Manet, Cézanne, Toulouse-Lautrec, and Renoir, as well as a selection of drawings by Rodin. But it was the work in the smaller room that drew the most attention — Max Weber's collection of five oils and two drawings by Rousseau, who had died early in September as a result of blood poisoning from an untreated leg injury. The little memorial was the first show anywhere devoted solely to him.

The New York critics were blind to Rousseau's charms. Chamberlin wrote in the *New York Mail*, "A little portrait of a woman and child is of unbelievable ugliness," and Huneker sneered in the *Sun* that as an artist Rousseau was "a joke."[1] Stieglitz was so enchanted that he tried (unsuccessfully) to import a group of Le Douanier's paintings for another show, in 1911.

Then followed, as Steichen put it, an "understandable" exhibition of forty-six drawings and etchings of fantastic and actual stage designs by Gordon Craig (1872–1966), the illegitimate son of actress Ellen Terry and the architect E. W. Godwin. Although Craig, a friend of Steichen's, had already created sets for Eleonora Duse in Florence and for Konstantin Stanislavsky in Moscow, many of his cubo-futuristic designs were too fanciful to realize.

In January 1911, 291 itself became the setting for a drama that was to have far-reaching consequences in Stieglitz's life. As early as November 1910, serious tensions arose between Stieglitz and Weber. Because the painter had been paid well for his work on the Albright show, and because he had managed to sell a couple of paintings to Buffalo collectors, he was finally able to afford a studio of his own, on East Fourteenth Street. As soon as he was no longer dependent on Stieglitz for a place to live, all the resentment he had suppressed burst forth. He became outspoken in his criticism of the Albright exhibition, and his denunciations of other painters became so obnoxious that de Zayas and Haviland threatened to secede from 291 if Stieglitz didn't at least rein Weber in.

Matters were surely worsened by the appearance of an *histoire à clef* by Temple Scott in the December 1910 issue of *The Forum*. The central character's name was Michael Weaver (Weber is German for weaver), and most of what he said had obviously been taken directly from the author's conversations with Max. Stieglitz (*goldfinch* in German) was called Finch in the story; he fared quite well, though Weaver/Weber had told the narrator, "Finch was kind, and good, and a fine fellow, but even Finch did not know all that a true artist felt in his innermost heart."[2] Most infuriating was the appearance in print of Weber's malicious comments about Steichen, transparently called Stecker.

All that notwithstanding, Stieglitz went ahead with Weber's show, which was to open on January 11, 1911. Weber spent the entire preceding night hanging his work with the young Australian poet and occasional *Camera Work* contributor William D. MacColl, "a sort of Byronesque figure."[3] When Stieglitz, who usually hung the shows at 291 himself, arrived at the gallery on the morning of the eleventh, he was amazed to see how brilliantly the two men had managed to arrange a very large number of fairly small paintings.

The trouble began when Stieglitz asked Weber to draw up a list of prices. Because the artist had been too poor to afford canvas and oil paints, he had executed most of his work during 1910 with gouache, pastels, charcoal, and/or watercolors on cardboard. Stieglitz was worried about the durability of such works and expected them to be priced accordingly. On the contrary, Weber announced that he was asking fantastic sums, up to $1,000 apiece. Stieglitz, knowing how badly the painter needed money, encouraged him to be more realistic. In a direct reproach to Weber, Haviland would state Stieglitz's arguments in the next issue of *Camera Work*:

> What fair-minded man will claim that the purchaser who acquires a work of art on the assumption that he becomes the possessor of a "thing of beauty" which will be "a joy forever," is treated honorably when . . . he receives an article which in a short period of time will have lost, through deterioration, much of its exchange value, as well as its power to give esthetic pleasure?[4]

Weber would not think of lowering his prices. Stieglitz recalled, "When Mr. MacColl informed me that it was my business to see to it that the people who came into 291 to see the Webers were to lay their gold at the feet of Max Weber, the genius, I was amazed at the tone. And when I asked Weber what sort of cardboard he used and what sort of colors . . . he snapped at me and said, 'Tell them it's Whatman paper and Winsor and Newton colors.'" After MacColl accused Stieglitz of sounding "like a grocery clerk," the photographer said to the two men, "Either you or I will have to get out of here."[5] Weber left stormily and told everyone that Stieglitz had thrown him out. When Stieglitz related to his friends what had happened, they advised him to put Weber's paintings on the street. Instead, during the three-week run of the show, Stieglitz kept up his monologue, which, we can be certain, contained much about how Weber failed to understand the spirit of 291 and how Stieglitz was martyring himself for the good of an ungrateful artist in whose work he continued to believe.

The critics were not kind. One called the show "a brutal, vulgar and unnecessary display of art-license," while Arthur Hoeber condemned it as "the high-water mark of eccentricity" and protested, "Here are travesties of the human form, here are forms that have no justification in nature, but that seem all the world like the emanations of someone not in his right mind."[6] When collectors came in, even those who didn't laugh at the paintings laughed at the prices. Agnes Meyer, who had received $500 for her birthday, offered the entire sum for one work that was priced at $1,000. Stieglitz let her have it, since Weber had said that he could live for a year on the smaller amount. It was the photographer's practice to buy a painting from almost every show or to accept one in lieu of a commission, but he maintained that he could not afford Weber's prices and would not accept a painting in the unlikely event the painter offered him one.

Weber didn't return to 291 until late on the last day of the exhibition, and then only to inquire what had been sold. When he learned of Agnes Meyer's purchase, he complained that if he and Stieglitz hadn't quarreled, Meyer would probably have paid the full price. Still hoping to repair their friendship, Stieglitz invited Weber to dinner. He accepted but then burst out that he blamed Stieglitz for something one of the critics had written. Since the photographer was too tired to argue, Weber left in a rage, never to return.

He went on to a career of uneven achievement and constant struggle. His richly colored, complexly fragmented, and dynamic paintings of New York, dating from 1915 and 1916, are perhaps the most satisfying Cubist works ever produced by an American artist. In 1917, however, Weber shifted to rather mawkish imitations of Picasso's Synthetic Cubism, and soon he would turn to the less modernistic renditions of Jewish themes that would occupy him until his death, in 1961.

Alvin Langdon Coburn arrived from England in January 1911 and quickly developed a close friendship with Weber. Coburn, a year younger than Weber and a fellow student of Arthur Wesley Dow, admired his new friend's paintings and was primed to absorb what he had to say about Cubism. They explored the city together, and each, in his own medium, made a portrait of the other. During the summer of 1912, Coburn and Weber worked together on An Exhibition Illustrating the Progress of the Art of Photography in America, which would open at the Montross Art Galleries on October 10. Coburn got married the next day and sailed for England with his bride. Although he had crossed the Atlantic twenty-three times since 1900, he would never again visit America, and in 1932 he would become a British subject.

Coburn continued to help Weber in every way he could. He successfully lobbied for his inclusion as one of only two foreign artists (Wassily Kandinsky was the other) in a show of British artists organized by Roger Fry in 1913. The next year Coburn offered a substantial subsidy to persuade a London publisher to issue Weber's book *Cubist Poems*.

Stieglitz had been very fond of Coburn and had promoted his work vigorously, but the fickle young photographer — we have already seen how he jilted his cousin F. Holland Day to join the Photo-Secession — now threw his lot in with the anti-Stieglitz faction that was beginning to form around

Weber. He delivered the coup de grâce in 1913 with the publication of his book *Men of Mark*, which included portraits of Weber and Clarence White but, as a deliberate insult, omitted one of Stieglitz.

White's disaffection from Stieglitz had its roots in his increasingly close friendships with Day and Weber. Although White appeared to be on the best of terms with Stieglitz during the period of their collaboration on the Cramer-Thompson series and on the Albright exhibition, some seeds of discontent had already been sown. For one thing, White took umbrage at Stieglitz's ill treatment of Käsebier. For another, he had taken a decisive step in 1909 toward a professional alliance with Day. He had bought an old house in the Maine town of Seguinland, on Georgetown Island, very near Day's cottage, with the intention of starting a summer school of photography. He had some repairs made, and in the April 1910 issue of *Camera Work* appeared an advertisement for his first season. The ad noted that Day would cooperate in criticizing the students' work. Day was already becoming like an uncle to White's sons; he would eventually pay Maynard White's way through Brown University.

If these events tested White's friendship with Stieglitz, it was the Albright exhibition and its aftermath that destroyed it. Only David Octavius Hill was represented by more prints than White's thirty-four, but Stieglitz's high-handed inclusion of Day placed White in an awkward position. Then Stieglitz had his falling-out with White's friend Weber. Finally, White was gravely affronted when the January 1911 issue of *Camera Work* reprinted the entire text of F. Austin Lidbury's Albright review from *American Photography*, in which the critic had written, "The White room is the disappointment of the show." Lidbury went on to say that although the room contained "a few of the prints which brought him reputation, and one or two later gems, it also unfortunately contains a great deal entirely unworthy of the artist, or, indeed, of being hung at all."[7] In April 1912 Stieglitz himself would comment that because White was so busy with his pupils, he had "not developed intellectually so his work cannot develop."[8]

White maintained diplomatic relations until May 1912. For more than a year he had been asking Stieglitz to locate and return two prints loaned for the Albright exhibition: a de Meyer still life belonging to Käsebier and a portrait of Rudyard Kipling by White's friend Sidney Carter, a Toronto photographer. On May 15, White wrote Stieglitz that he could not search for the prints himself, since "it is no longer pleasant for me to visit the gallery of the Photo-Secession."

In Stieglitz's lengthy reply, a week later, he accused White of "aspersions and sneers" and of a "poisoned frame of mind." He made excuses about the misplaced prints and parried that although White blamed Buffalo for their "strained relationship," the Albright show had "simply hastened a sickly condition on your part." In his letter of May 15 White had registered complaints about the Cramer-Thompson collaboration, to which Stieglitz responded, "I am astonished and grieved, more than I can tell you, to see that it is your desire to even soil the pleasant memories of a past friendship and those very pleasant days."[9] Of the eighty-nine prints from the series that Stieglitz had in his possession, he returned all but fourteen to White, as well as all of the negatives, with the demand that his name never again be mentioned in connection with the photographs. The two men would not speak to each other again for many years.

After his break with Stieglitz, White's career as a photographer was largely replaced by his career as a teacher and organizer. The year 1914 saw the opening of the Clarence H. White School of Photography in the lovely old house, with New Orleans-like ironwork on its exterior, that still stands at the southwest corner of Irving Place and East Seventeenth Street. In this so-called Washington Irving House, America's first fashionable professional interior decorator, Elsie de Wolfe, and her friend Elizabeth Marbury had lived and maintained a glittering salon from 1894 until 1911. One of the first teachers White hired was Max Weber, who would lecture — there and at the summer school in Maine — on art history, art appreciation, and design until his resignation in 1918. A book based on Weber's lectures, which emphasized the intensity of personal vision, untrammeled by any rules, was published in New York in 1916.

The Buffalo exhibition also brought about the final rupture between Stieglitz and Gertrude Käsebier. The Albright's trustees were so pleased with the public and critical response to the show that they authorized Cornelia Sage to spend $300 to buy some of the exhibited prints, and Sage assured Stieglitz that the museum would permanently set aside one room for them. Stieglitz, feeling that this would be the supreme vindication of photographs as works of art, encouraged the leading members of the Photo-Secession to reduce their prices, thereby enabling the Albright to acquire as many superb images as possible. He went so far as to ask Käsebier to sell a print of her record-setting $100 picture *The Manger* for the insulting price of $35. Exasperated, she replied, "I am an amiable woman as well as a very busy one. Yes."[10] Because of the concessions by Käsebier and her colleagues, the Albright was able to acquire twelve prints for one-half their catalog value. The museum did not, however, dedicate a gallery to their display.

Käsebier was even more offended by the January 1911 issue of *Camera Work* than was White, for the wounding remarks about his work had at least been made by a writer outside the Photo-Secession. She was attacked by Keiley, who, in his review of the Albright exhibition, contrasted de Meyer's work — "vivacious, finished and delightful, always showing exquisite taste and a masterful knowledge of technique" — and Käsebier's "with its artistic irresponsibility and indifference to mere technique; its curious impulsiveness; its inner blind groping to express the protean self within."[11] Who could blame her for soon thereafter canceling her subscription?

Almost a year passed, during which Stieglitz and Käsebier dealt curtly with each other, before she wrote him a one-sentence note on January 2, 1912: "I present to you my resignation from the Photo-Secession." Although Stieglitz had told Heinrich Kuehn more than two years earlier that he wanted to expel Käsebier, he again drew back from the breach. Instead of the condescending missives that he usually dispatched to her, he wrote a kindly reply:

> Through Mrs. Stieglitz I had heard of your troubles and the load you were carrying. When you cancelled your subscription to *Camera Work* I interpreted it as meaning that you were forced to economize. When now I also receive your resignation from the Photo-Secession without any explanation I assume that it is for the reason you wish your name dropped. Inasmuch as membership to the Secession is not dependent upon payment of dues, — you being one of the very few who paid them regularly, I cannot accept your resignation without knowing that you are no longer in sympathy with the Secession's work, nor believe in its aims and activities.[12]

Käsebier, not to be deterred, wrote back, "I thank you for your generous offer which I cannot accept. I have contemplated the step which I have now taken for a long time. Please let my resignation go through with dignity and without bitterness. It is final." Years later she reminisced, "When I saw that [Stieglitz] was only hot air, I quit."[13]

Käsebier, who would never again have any contact with Stieglitz, now confirmed her membership in the Day-White-Weber faction. They all spent summers together in Maine, where Käsebier occasionally lectured at White's school. Photographs by White and Käsebier appeared frequently in *The Platinum Print*, founded in October 1913 by Edward R. Dickson, a New York photographer, who was both the magazine's publisher and its editor in chief. An article by Weber was featured in the first issue, and Coburn was designated the magazine's "foreign correspondent." Karl Struss, yet another defector from the Photo-Secession, became the associate editor in 1914.

In 1916 White, Käsebier, Coburn, and other Pictorialists associated with *The Platinum Print* established an organization, the Pictorial Photographers of America, to replace the moribund Photo-Secession. White was the new society's first president, Käsebier the honorary vice president. The PPA was launched, as, of course, the Photo-Secession had been, with a large exhibition at the National Arts Club. Unlike its predecessor, the PPA was to be democratic and committed exclusively to photography. It would endorse a great deal of work that was saccharine, imitative, and old-fashioned.

After the ending of his friendships with White, Käsebier, and Coburn, Stieglitz would have little to do with either photography or photographers for several years. Summing up his situation, he would write to a British colleague in January 1913:

> Outside of Baron de Meyer, who is here in New York very busy photographing society and doing it in a masterful fashion, I see none of the photographers. They seem to steer clear of "291" as well as myself. It is very amusing but fortunately I don't miss them. Not because they are not nice fellows but because they have not developed mentally but have stood still during the past six or seven years.[14]

CHAPTER FORTY·TWO

"SINCE YOU LEFT a year ago I have undoubtedly had the most remarkable year in my career," wrote Stieglitz to Sadakichi Hartmann in December 1911. "Beginning with the Albright Art Gallery show it has been
one crescendo culminating with a most remarkable three weeks spent in
Paris."[1]

Stieglitz followed the Weber fiasco with John Marin's second one-man
show, the highlight of which was his series of watercolors executed the previous summer in the Austrian Tyrol. In these lyrical and luminous works,
Marin had spontaneously brushed violet, blue, and yellow onto wet paper
to imbue the magnificent Alpine landscape with his exhilarated response.

The Marins introduced the Cézanne watercolors that were hung next;
the show was the first in America devoted to the Frenchman's work.
Stieglitz's attitude had changed completely since his derisive reaction in
1907. In the interim, Weber had convinced him that Cézanne was the
supreme master whose work was the foundation on which all modernist
painters were building. So when Steichen cabled that Bernheim-Jeune was
willing to lend some twenty watercolors, Stieglitz eagerly accepted the offer. He would have liked a few oils as well, but the watercolors would have
to do.

Stieglitz later recalled that when he opened the box, he was amazed that
the Cézannes looked so beautiful — and so realistic — to him. Most of

them were landscapes, and in such works the artist generally sketched a delicate armature of pencil lines onto which he hung quivering dabs of color like tinted protoplasm. These gossamer documents of the act of perception, in which the data gathered by an extreme of representational honesty become quite abstract, are as pantheistic, or at least as panvitalist, as anything by van Gogh. Stieglitz recounted that the exhibition was "a complete frost" and that no one but Arthur Davies bought anything.[2] Only Stieglitz's artist friends were moved by the show, but most of them, of course, couldn't begin to afford the $200 at which Bernheim-Jeune had priced the Cézannes.

In the summer of 1910 Steichen had written Stieglitz to propose a show of Picasso's drawings for the upcoming season's requisite "red rag." Steichen himself didn't much like the Spaniard's work, but he had no doubt that it would give New Yorkers a real jolt. "I am sure that Picasso would fill the bill if I can get them," he continued, "but he is a crazy galloot, hates exhibiting, etc. — however, we will try him."[3]

Stieglitz, who had been primed by Leo Stein's extravagant praise and by Gelett Burgess's recent article, replied with enthusiasm. Steichen then enlisted Gertrude Stein to recruit Picasso. The eighty-three works chosen for his first exhibition in America included early and recent drawings, watercolors, and etchings, chronicling his evolution from Realism to Cubism. The emphasis was on the latter style, of which these were the first examples publicly exhibited in the United States.

Believing that the Picasso show was "possibly the most interesting yet held" at 291, Stieglitz tried to persuade Bryson Burroughs, the untalented young painter who had replaced Roger Fry as curator of paintings at the Met and who had actually managed to sell the trustees a Renoir, to get the museum to buy all the works in the exhibition for $2,000. But Burroughs dismissed Picasso as a madman. Most of the critics agreed. For example, Arthur Hoeber foamed in the *New York Globe*, "Any sane criticism is entirely out of the question; any serious analysis would be in vain. The results suggest the most violent wards of an asylum for maniacs, the craziest emanations of a disordered mind, the gibberings of a lunatic!"[4]

Stieglitz bought the most advanced work in the exhibition, a 1910 charcoal of a standing nude, a radical and virtually abstract example of Analytical Cubism that prefigures Duchamp's *Nude Descending a Staircase*. He claimed that he had bought it precisely because he didn't understand it.[5] But one writer reported: "Mr. Stieglitz declares in all sincerity that when he has had a tiring day in his gallery or elsewhere he goes home at night, stands before this drawing in black and white, which hangs over his fire-place, and gains from it a genuine stimulus."[6] In 1913 he would say that the drawing, which he would publish three times in *Camera Work*, reminded him of a Bach fugue.[7]

What excited him most, however, was that the drawing reminded him so strongly of his own photograph *Spring Showers* (1900). There was, indeed, an amazing structural and compositional resemblance between the two works, which Stieglitz published in sequence in the October 1911 issue of *Camera Work*. Clearly he felt that the coincidental affinity validated both. The fact that he was able to discern cubistic structure in a photograph he had made long before the evolution of Cubism proved to his satisfaction that modernism was firmly rooted in reality. It also demonstrated that photography was capable of matching the intellectual and emotional pen-etration that distinguished the most powerful abstraction, which he considered "a new medium of expression — the true medium."[8]

In that same issue of *Camera Work* Stieglitz published a total of sixteen of his own photographs, nine of them dating from 1910 and one from 1911. Much of the selection was subtly based on parallels between pairs of photographs: the wing structure of a biplane in one image resembling the skeleton of a building under construction in another, the steam from a lo-comotive in a snowy railroad yard parodying that from the horses in *The Terminal*. A picture of children on and around the diving board and slides at the public swimming pool in Deal Beach obviously echoes the configu-ration of forms in *The Steerage*, which was at last making its debut. For those who were able to discern the connections between the photographs, the similarities and differences could be taken to illustrate Ralph Waldo Emerson's principle of "the unity of cause, the variety of appearance."

In the April-July 1911 issue of *Camera Work* Marius de Zayas wrote that, before he arrived in Paris in 1910, he thought he

> had formed a complete idea of the movement in French Art, princi-pally in so far as painting was concerned, through the exhibitions that the Photo-Secession of New York held of the works of some of the artists who belong to this movement. . . . But I was mistaken. In spite of the efforts of Mr. Steichen, who selects in Paris the works of this kind that are shown in New York, and in spite of the heroism of Mr. Stieglitz, who gives them frank hospitality, . . . the exhibitions of the Photo-Secession give but a faint idea of the intensity of this movement.[9]

Although Stieglitz had seen paintings by Cézanne, Matisse, and Picasso during his visit to Paris in 1909, it was only after his conversations with Max Weber the following year and 291's Cézanne and Picasso exhibitions in the spring of 1911 that he was ready to appreciate their canvases fully. To Sadakichi Hartmann he wrote of that summer's trip, "Paris made me realize what the seven years at '291' had really done for me. All my work, all my many and nasty experiences, had all helped to prepare me for the tremendous experience," which came at the right "psychological moment."[10]

When he sailed for Europe with his wife and daughter in May, Alfred could hardly wait to get to Paris and immerse himself in the new art. But wait he did. The first three months abroad were extremely frustrating, for he was tied to Emmy and thirteen-year-old Kitty in pursuit of fashionable company and rich boys. Late in July he managed an interlude of several days in Munich, where Frank Eugene introduced him to some of the more progressive painters in the city's Secession, but much of the summer was, from Alfred's point of view, wasted on a tour of southern France. The end of August found the family luxuriating (stagnating, as Alfred saw it) in the Palace Hotel in Montreux, Switzerland.

Not until mid-September did the Stieglitzes finally reach Paris, where Alfred devoted three glorious weeks to a feast of modern art — the climax of his annus mirabilis. Steichen and de Zayas gave him the grand tour. They went to see the two great dealers, Bernheim-Jeune and Vollard, and the incomparable collection of more than ninety Cézanne canvases owned by the industrialist Auguste Pellerin.

One morning Steichen took Stieglitz out to Issy-les-Moulineaux to meet Matisse, who pleased the photographer by looking more like a mathematics professor than an artist, let alone a revolutionary one. Stieglitz was, however, disappointed by most of his recent paintings, remarking in a letter that "Matisse is doing some beautiful work, but some how or other it didn't grip me. Possibly he is ahead of me!"[11] Nevertheless, Alfred was sufficiently gripped by a "magnificent flower piece" to offer 5,000 francs for it, but Matisse said that he had already promised the painting to one of his Russian patrons.

De Zayas, of whom Stieglitz wrote that he had "developed remarkably and is a big fellow," conducted him to Picasso's studio. Stieglitz left convinced that the Spaniard was a greater artist than Matisse. Although Picasso "may not as yet fully realize in his work the thing he is after," Stieglitz ventured, "I think his viewpoint is bigger [than Matisse's]."[12]

One day Steichen told Stieglitz that Rodin had invited him to pay a visit. The April–July issue of *Camera Work* had been largely devoted to superb

color reproductions of nine of the sculptor's drawings, along with a Steichen portrait of him and three photographs of his monument to Balzac.
Half of the magazine's six hundred subscriptions were canceled in reaction
to the issue, but Rodin, a wily businessman, was so impressed by the production that he had conceived a grand project. He wanted Stieglitz to publish an edition of one hundred portfolios, each containing fifty gravures of
Steichen's photographs of his sculptures and fifty facsimiles of his drawings
and watercolors. This would be the summation of his career, his artistic
testament. He assured Stieglitz that he could easily get one hundred collectors to pay 1,000 francs apiece for such a production. But Stieglitz eventually declined on the grounds that the undertaking would be too complicated and time-consuming.

Stieglitz also rejected Steichen's suggestion that they attend one of the
Saturday evening soirees at Leo and Gertrude Stein's, for he was certain
that he would not enjoy such a gathering and that it would only cloud his
memory of his extraordinary visit with Leo in 1909. He did, however, accept an invitation to visit the studio in which Steichen's good friend Constantin Brancusi lived and worked, surrounding himself with his sculptures
as if they were his family.

In addition to all that, Stieglitz spent two days at the Louvre, where he
felt he was really seeing the paintings for the first time. He also "saw the
various Salons beginning with the old one, then the Champs de Mars and
the Salon des Indépendants, finally the Salon d'Automne." "Think of it,"
he jubilated to Hartmann in December, "several hundred Cézannes, any
number of Van Goghs and Renoirs — these are the three big modern
painters."[13] A few days before he wrote Hartmann, Stieglitz had declared in
a letter to the editor of the *New York Evening Sun* that the Metropolitan
Museum of Art

> owes it to the Americans to give them a chance to study the work
> of Cézanne. . . , [which] is the strongest influence in modern paint-
> ing. . . . I firmly believe that an exhibition, a well-selected one, of
> Cézanne's paintings is, just at present, of more vital importance than
> would be an exhibition of Rembrandts. . . . The study of van Gogh is
> nearly equally essential, if not quite so.[14]

Stieglitz was hoping to mount an exhibition of work by van Gogh and
Gauguin at 291 in 1912, but the plan fell through.

There was no question about it: Paris couldn't be rivaled for the sheer
wealth, indeed the prodigality, of art on display. But, Stieglitz told Hartmann, "Europe has nothing similar to [291]," which had "certainly shown

the quintessence of some big men's work." There had been "greater, larger exhibitions" in Europe, but never "such a series with such a definite purpose" as that at 291 during the preceding seven years.[15]

After spending three weeks among the Parisians, who seemed so thoroughly alive, so unpuritanical, and so connected to their work, it took Stieglitz, as he told Hartmann, "about three weeks to reconcile myself to New Yorkers — New York itself was as wonderful as ever." Talking to his friends at 291, he "felt the way Tannhäuser must have felt when he returned from the Venusberg and lost his patience listening to his colleagues theorizing about love."[16] Nonetheless, Stieglitz would never return to Europe.

CHAPTER FORTY·THREE

IN JANUARY 1912, Stieglitz wrote Heinrich Kuehn that "America is going through a period of luxury and unrest bordering nearly on madness."[1] So it seemed to many Americans, in a nation where 2 percent of the population owned 60 percent of the wealth. The muckraking movement, which had begun when Lincoln Steffens took over *McClure's* in 1902, reached a climax in 1911. Early the following year Theodore Roosevelt, who had left the White House in 1909, announced, coining a phrase, "My hat is in the ring." Failing to win the Republican nomination, he campaigned as a Progressive and was overwhelmed by Woodrow Wilson. The turkey trot and the bunny hug were in fashion, and *Life* magazine reported in 1912 that the favorite slang phrases included "getting your goat," "It's a cinch!" and "Beat it!" No wonder Stieglitz complained, "There is certainly no art in America today; what is more, there is, as yet, no genuine love for it. Possibly Americans have no genuine love for anything; but I am not hopeless. In fact I am quite the contrary."[2]

Stieglitz prophesied during 1912, "We stand before the door of a new social era."[3] There seemed to be cause for optimism, since radicalism was very much in the air. This was due to many factors, including the rise of monolithic trusts and of firetrap sweatshops (146 employees, most of them women and girls, had died in the Triangle Shirtwaist Company fire in New York in March 1911); the growing power of labor unions, despite vicious attempts to suppress them; the great wave of immigration from Eastern and Southern Europe, which brought many Italian anarchists as well as followers of Mikhail Bakunin; the opening of public libraries and settlement houses; the increase of educational opportunities for women; the impact of the typewriter; the tremendous growth of cheap, popular magazines; advances in science; and the influence of European modernist art.

The young men and women who came of age around 1910 rebelled against prudery, hypocrisy, and injustice. They had left their farms and small towns, gone to college, then settled in the cities, where they became poets, journalists, artists, socialists, feminists, and anarchists. To them, change per se was a virtue. Benjamin de Casseres sounded this note in the January 1912 issue of *Camera Work*, where he wrote, "In poetry, physics, practical life there is nothing . . . that is any longer moored to a certainty, nothing that is forbidden. . . . Nothing which lasts is of value. . . . That which changes perpetually lives perpetually."[4]

The Masses, founded in 1911, was the avowedly socialistic magazine that gave the widest and most powerful expression to such sentiments. Max Eastman, a charismatic twenty-nine-year-old poet and Columbia University graduate student in philosophy, became its editor late in 1912, and in January 1913 he announced that his was "a revolutionary and not a reform magazine; a magazine with a sense of humor and no respect for the respectable; frank, arrogant, impertinent, searching for the true causes; a magazine directed against rigidity and dogma wherever it is found; printing what is too naked or true for a money-making press." John Sloan was its art editor, and among the artists who regularly drew for its pages were George Bellows, Stuart Davis, and Art Young.

During 1911 and 1912 Stieglitz developed several important friendships to replace the rebel angels. One who showed up in December 1911 was an eighteen-year-old voice student named Marie Rapp, whose part-time secretarial services the photographer would share with Stephen Lawrence, a friend of Rapp's brother. Stieglitz was immediately charmed by Rapp, who, in a portrait he made in 1916, appears lovely and pensive, with an expression at once tenderly affectionate, concerned, and ever so slightly amused. He would introduce her to Mrs. Albert K. Boursault, a voice teacher married to a Photo-Secessionist; beyond whatever benefit Rapp may have received from her singing lessons, she would marry the Boursaults' son George in 1918. Several days a week, as Stieglitz paced around Lawrence's room, he would dictate letters for Rapp to type. She became his confidante — with whom he flirted, upon whom he depended for her

good sense and optimism, and with whom he would continue to correspond for years after she stopped working for him, in 1917.

The other woman who now became one of the regulars at 291 was
Agnes Ernst Meyer. Back from their honeymoon in the fall of 1910, the
Meyers had moved into a house on East Fifty-first Street but soon bought
a mansion at Park Avenue and Seventieth, for whose spiral staircase they
commissioned Steichen to paint a series of murals entitled "In Exaltation
of Flowers."

Steichen, who became a close, lifelong friend of the Meyers, wrote in his
memoirs that they had "the healthiest and soundest marriage" he had ever
seen. Perhaps the secret was that Eugene and Agnes saw so little of each
other. He was completely absorbed in his work, day and night; and, after
the birth of their daughter Florence, in 1911, Agnes spent little time at
home. Spurred on by her passion for Asian art, she would study Chinese at
Columbia University for several years and then move on to courses in biology, economics, and history. When she wasn't at Columbia, she was
likely to be at 291. By the time she returned home late each afternoon, the
baby would be howling with hunger. Disdaining her social obligations as
the wife of a prominent financier, she would simply dump into the waste-
basket all the calling cards left during the day.

Agnes, enthralled by 291, where she continued to find the "free air" she
craved, soon persuaded her husband to donate $500 a year to the gallery's
maintenance fund (replacing the disenchanted George Pratt, who withdrew his support in 1913), and she would buy many works that Stieglitz exhibited. Late in 1913 Stieglitz referred to the Meyers as "the only 'rich
people' who have done anything at all for 291."[5] Unfortunately, he seems
not to have asked Eugene Meyer for financial advice. Investment tips from
Meyer would eventually enable Steichen to achieve "a modest degree of financial independence."[6] By 1912 Stieglitz found himself forced to borrow
money from Joe Obermeyer and would soon accumulate a discouraging
pile of debts.

Despite his downcast spirits and his zeal for modernism, Stieglitz opened
the new season, on November 7, 1911, with an exhibition of watercolors by
Gelett Burgess that poked fun at the avant-garde. Inspired by the work of
the painters he had interviewed for his 1910 article, Burgess had made a series of whimsical watercolors in a style that he, with his tongue in his
cheek, called "subjective symbolism." Since he had written and illustrated
a book entitled *Goops and How to Be Them* in 1900, the critics naturally
dubbed his spoofs "goops."

Charles Caffin wrote in *Camera Work* that there was "a streak of malice aforethought" in Stieglitz's timing of the next exhibition, a show of Adolf de Meyer's photographs. According to Caffin, now that the critics were "foaming in impotent bewilderment at the vagaries of modern painting, [Stieglitz] offers as an antidote the sanity of the photographic process."[7] He had additional reasons for the first photographic show at 291 in nearly two years and the only one that season. He considered de Meyer and his wife, who were then in New York, "interesting people" and called the baron's work "distinguished" and "sincere," though leaving room for development.[8] Furthermore, Stieglitz was evidently intrigued that even in the work of a fashionable portraitist who charged $100 for a sitting, there were affinities, albeit unconscious ones, with Picasso. Specifically, two de Meyer images of women wearing exquisite turbans bear a remarkable resemblance to a Picasso sculpture, of a woman's head, that Stieglitz had bought and photographed. Alas, not even de Meyer's flattering camera could endow matronly Emmy, who tried desperately to look at least happy, with anything remotely like glamour.

After a show of paintings by Arthur Carles (January 18–February 3, 1912), Stieglitz hung Marsden Hartley's boldly painted, even primitivistic still lifes, which merged the influences of Cézanne, Matisse, Picasso, and Max Weber, through whose tutelage Hartley had fallen under the spell of the Aix master. It seems rather ironic that Hartley had abandoned his own direct, expressionistic style in favor of eclecticism and formalism. He was, however, at the end of one of the broad swings of his ceaseless pendulum. In the summer of 1911 he had written to Stieglitz, "I want to strike out & get something of outer life into my blood. This inward life is depleting so much of it. . . . It seems as though I've had nothing but denials for most of my life." He was tired of "unpalatable dry crust" and was ready for "a little caviar."[9] What he really wanted was to go to Paris.

Stieglitz and Arthur Davies made it possible for him to go. The former arranged for Agnes Meyer to provide Hartley with a one-year stipend of $15 a week, enough for him to live on, in return for a selection of the paintings he produced. Davies procured a check from Lillie Bliss to cover his travel expenses. In April the thirty-five-year-old Hartley sailed for the promised land.

Arthur Dove's only one-man show at 291 (February 27–March 12) was among the gallery's most important exhibitions. Dove called his series of ten astonishingly original pastels on linen the *Ten Commandments* and explained that they depicted "the form that the idea takes in the imagination rather than the form as it exists outside."[10] These works, ranging from highly idiosyncratic renderings of landscape and animals to purely abstract distillations of movement, were the first modernist paintings by an American artist, at home or abroad, able to hold their own beside the most advanced work being done in Europe. Scholars debate endlessly (since the dating of certain key works is uncertain) whether it was Kandinsky or Dove who first crossed over the boundary into total abstraction, though Kandinsky seems to have the edge.

Stieglitz related that Dove's father was aghast when he saw the show at 291. The photographer told him, "Some day there will be as much a vogue for the things your son is doing as there is now for the things you like, whatever they may be." The businessman replied, "If that is so, I don't want to live."[11] He decided that if his son could afford to give up the $15,000-a-year income he had made from illustrating to perpetrate such horrors, he would not leave him a cent in his will.

Because of the demands of farming and occasional illustration assignments, Dove would not be able to produce enough work for another show before 291 closed in 1917, and he would not have another one-man exhibition anywhere until 1926, when Stieglitz showed his work in his new gallery. Throughout the intervening years, during which Dove struggled simply to survive, he would spend a day in New York every few weeks, and he maintained a warm correspondence with Stieglitz, who would occasionally sell a painting or send a relief check.

On one of Dove's frequent visits to 291, Stieglitz made a highly ironic portrait of the artist that is obviously a collaborative parody of Steichen's 1903 portrait of J. P. Morgan. Wearing a suit, a wing-collared shirt, and a tie with a stickpin, Dove grasps the arm of a wooden chair, just as Morgan does in the Steichen. Although the portrayal of the struggling artist as a millionaire is quite wry, Stieglitz perhaps also intended the photograph to make the point that Dove was as rich spiritually as Morgan was monetarily.

During the last two weeks of March and the first week of April 1912, Stieglitz mounted his third and final Matisse show, this one of sculpture and drawings. Among the bronzes was the tactilely modeled three-foot-tall armless male nude entitled *The Serf* (1900–1904), which Leo Stein had said was greater than any Rodin. On the recommendation of a friend, Gertrude Vanderbilt Whitney went to see it and would have bought it if she hadn't been dissuaded by her mentor, the socially prominent portrait painter Howard Cushing, who, having accompanied her to the gallery, was revolted by the sculpture.[12] The only piece sold was the one bought by

Stieglitz himself, a little bronze torso with pointed breasts, a rounded belly, and jutting buttocks, reminiscent of a Neolithic fertility figure but probably inspired directly by a Baule carving from the Ivory Coast.

Also in the show were *La Serpentine* (an extremely elongated female nude in which Eve and the snake seem to have merged) and the first three of the eventual five progressively more exaggerated — or, as most New Yorkers regarded them, degeneratively more grotesque — heads of a young woman named Jeanette. Arthur Hoeber spoke for all but the most perceptive when he wrote in the *New York Globe* that some of the sculptures, "to put it very mildly, seem like the work of a madman, and it is hard to be patient with these impossible travesties on the human form. There are attenuated figures of women . . . which make one grieve that men should be found who can by any chance regard them with other than feelings of horrible repulsion."[13]

The season's last show — the first in America to present artwork by children as art — owed much to Abraham Walkowitz, whom Hartley had introduced to Stieglitz early in 1912. A journalist reported that the exhibition had come about because one artist "ascribed his success to the fact that he looked at the world through the eyes of a child."

"That is impossible," replied Stieglitz; "you can't do that because you are not a child. To prove it I'll give an exhibition of children's work and show you how far off the track you are."[14]

Walkowitz was instrumental in securing, through a friend who taught art at a Lower East Side settlement house, a group of drawings, pastels, and watercolors by children between the ages of two and thirteen. The exhibition provoked the kind of controversy that Stieglitz relished. The critics naturally had a field day debating the question of whether the drawings — or, for that matter, modernism itself, which struck so many of them as childish — could possibly be taken seriously as art. One called 291 a "Nursery of Genius" and claimed that "one of the young artists saw a painting by Mr. Max Weber and made one just like it — only better."[15] Another astutely observed that some of the drawings had "that evanescent something about them that marks the true work of art."[16]

The exhibition apparently had a strong effect on Walkowitz's own work, for among his drawings and watercolors reproduced in the October 1913 issue of *Camera Work*, several — including one depicting a man conducting an orchestra and another of a nude man and woman embracing — could easily have been made by a modestly talented teenager.

Although Walkowitz's production was of very uneven quality, Stieglitz respected the artist and would give him four one-man shows at 291, a number surpassed only by Marin and Hartley and equaled only by Steichen. Furthermore, Walkowitz would be very important to Stieglitz as a friend, as a helpful assistant around the gallery — and as an anarchist.

Born in western Siberia in 1878, Walkowitz arrived in New York eleven years later with his family. They lived in poverty on the Lower East Side, where his widowed mother sold newspapers. While attending public school, Walkowitz took art classes at Cooper Union and the Educational Alliance. In 1906 he went to Paris, where he met Max Weber at the Académie Julian. Walkowitz was excited and influenced by the work of Rodin, Matisse, Picasso, Rousseau, and Cézanne, but his decisive experience was seeing Isadora Duncan dance. She became his muse, and he later said of her, "Her body was music. It was a body electric, like Walt Whitman."[17] Walkowitz began making, from memory, the first of his thousands of Rodin-like drawings of Duncan in motion, in which he attempted to express the freedom, spontaneity, and dynamism that she represented to him. In 1912 critic Samuel Swift would write in the *New York Sun* that these drawings were "alive with rhythmic beauty and the very essence of joyous grace."[18]

Called home in the summer of 1907 by news that his mother was ill, Walkowitz began the routine he would follow into the early teens. He made his living by lettering signs and office doors, and when he had earned enough money, he would take two or three months off to draw. Inspired by Walt Whitman, whose *Leaves of Grass* was his Bible, he would wander all over Manhattan and Brooklyn, sketching groups of people in the street, picnickers on the grass in Central Park, men digging subway trenches, bathers on the beach at Coney Island, or whatever else caught his eye. Eventually he would work some of these sketches up into paintings that did not differ much from those of the Eight.

Walkowitz's interest in the working-class was political as well as poetic. As Paul Haviland noted in *Camera Work*, the artist was "in close contact with the social movement of the day." And that movement was anarchistic. "The spirit which urges men to free themselves from the bonds of absolute laws and conventions permeates his work," continued Haviland.[19]

Stieglitz had long been a de facto anarchist, and in that spirit he told a reporter in 1912 that the Photo-Secession stood for the "idea of revolt against all authority in art, in fact against all authority in everything, for art is only the expression of life. . . . Some people accuse us of demolishing old theories only to build up new theories of our own. They misunderstand us.

We insist on remaining relaxed and not theorizing."[20] Stieglitz approved neither of the orthodoxy nor of the violence of hard-line anarchists. Unsympathetic to the bomb throwers and those drawn to anarchism as justification for self-indulgence, he surely approved of Haviland's assurance that "the orderly and dignified tone" of Walkowitz's drawings and paintings "prove that anarchy does not mean license."[21]

It was probably in 1911 that Walkowitz's anarchistic leanings first took him to the Modern School of the Ferrer Center, located in a brownstone on East 107th Street. The center had been founded in 1910, largely through the efforts of the anarchist Emma Goldman, with whom Stieglitz would develop a casual but friendly acquaintance. Dedicated to freedom of expression, to Whitmanesque individualism (which many viewed as America's homegrown brand of anarchism), and to pedagogical experimentation, the school offered classes for children during the day and for adults in the evenings and on weekends. Most of the students were working-class Jews from Eastern Europe and their children, but the Modern School also attracted many professional artists, by no means all of them Jewish. What lured them was the life class that Robert Henri taught on Thursday and Friday evenings, assisted by George Bellows. Henri, sympathetic to socialism as a way to increase individual freedom, had accepted Goldman's invitation to teach at the school, without pay, beginning in November 1911. On Wednesday evenings, John Weichsel, whose first contribution to *Camera Work* would appear in the special issue dated June 1913, lectured at the Modern School on art and its rôle as a cultural and educational force.

Walkowitz became Stieglitz's best friend in a complex network of overlapping friendships and collaborations that linked 291 with the Modern School and with the artistic and poetic communities in Greenwich Village and, across the Hudson, in Ridgefield, New Jersey. One of the outstanding figures in this network was Man Ray, né Emmanuel Radnitsky. In January 1908 the seventeen-year-old senior at Boys' High School in Brooklyn — where he was enrolled in a course of engineering, mechanical drawing, and lettering in preparation for architecture school — had gone to 291 to see the Rodin drawings. Upon graduation from high school, when he declared himself an artist and began dreaming of Paris, his parents gave him a room in the family apartment to use as his studio. There he painted an occasional commissioned portrait and experimented with modernism. Although he taught himself camera technique to document his paintings, it would not be until the late teens that Man Ray blossomed as an outstanding photographer.

About the time he adopted his new name, in 1911, he began to visit 291 frequently and to join the regulars at lunch. In the fall of the following year he started going to the Modern School, where he met the Belgian-born sculptor, Whitmanesque poet, and anarchist Adolf Wolff, who taught the children's art class during the day and attended Henri's evening life classes. A few months later, Wolff offered to let Ray move into his studio on West Thirty-fifth Street, not far from the offices of the McGraw Hill Book Company, where the young painter got a job doing calligraphy and layout in the cartographic department. Since 291 was only a few blocks away, he often dropped by the gallery.

In the spring of 1913 Ray moved to the artists' colony in Ridgefield and shared a house with a friend from the Modern School, painter Samuel Halpert, recently returned from a nine-year stay in Paris. Together with Alfred Kreymborg they soon started a poetry magazine called the *Glebe*; its first issue was entirely devoted to the "Songs, Sighs and Curses" of Adolf Wolff, who had also moved to Ridgefield. Before long, Ray was living with Wolff's gorgeous blond former wife, the Belgian-born Adon Lacroix, whom he would marry in May 1914.

Wolff and Halpert joined Ray and Kreymborg as friends of Stieglitz's, along with two other occasional Ridgefield residents, Alanson Hartpence, a poet who was Kreymborg's best friend, and the outrageous character Hippolyte Havel, another Ferrer Center anarchist, identified in *Camera Work* as "dishwasher, editor of *Revolutionary Almanac*, editor of *Don Quixote.*" Havel also worked on Goldman's magazine *Mother Earth* and was the psychopathic companion of the notoriously promiscuous Polly Holladay, in whose popular Greenwich Village restaurant he washed dishes and waited on tables. Havel's moment of glory came when he jumped up at one of the monthly editorial meetings of the *Masses* collective and exploded, "Bourgeois! Voting! Voting on poetry! Poetry is something from the soul. You can't vote on poetry."[22]

Yet another of Stieglitz's anarchistic friends was Emil Zoler, a young artist whom Hartley had brought to 291 in 1909. He would be an invaluable if undependable helper around the gallery until it closed — so much so that Steichen described him as "a sort of shadow to Stieglitz."[23] Zoler never considered himself an employee, but Stieglitz gave him money from time to time. "Though a gifted caricaturist," wrote Jerome Mellquist, "Zoler has never cared to exhibit."[24] In *Camera Work*, Stieglitz listed Zoler's occupation simply as "observer."

But Zoler, whom Stieglitz respected as an example of the idealistic Old World craftsman out of place in America, did a great deal more than observe at 291. Whenever an odd job needed to be done, whether heavy lifting or a bit of fine carpentry, Zoler was called upon. In Stieglitz's 1917 portrait of him, the ruggedly handsome man, with crow's-feet at his eyes and with strongly veined forearms, stands in a doorway looking upward, disappointed and aspiring.

Living in Jersey City and feeling a deep sense of brotherhood with the silk workers who went on strike in March 1913 in nearby Paterson, Zoler would join the Industrial Workers of the World, the syndicate of labor unions led by Big Bill Haywood. The IWW — whose members were known as Wobblies, supposedly because Chinese-American workers pronounced the initials as "Eye Wobble Wobble" — advocated direct and, if necessary, violent action. Having given up on Progressive reform, and believing that the time for revolution had arrived, they saw themselves as the successors to the patriots who had staged the Boston Tea Party and to the abolitionists who had broken the law to destroy the inhuman institution of slavery. During 1913 Stieglitz became so sympathetic to the IWW, and so depressed about the conditions that it was fighting, that Emmy finally asked him to stop bringing "Zoler, Wolff and Co." home to dinner.

Big Bill himself once put in an appearance at 291, doing more to alienate Alfred from the IWW than Emmy's protests could ever have done. Without bothering to look at the works on exhibit, the one-eyed Haywood began (as the photographer contemptuously recalled), "Mr. Stieglitz, a man of your calibre shouldn't waste his time in a dinky little place like this, surrounded by pictures, by artists, by pseudo workers of all classes. . . . You ought to be out amongst the people, amongst the workers in real open spaces. . . . Why don't you leave this place and join the real fight?"[25]

CHAPTER FORTY·FOUR

IN DECEMBER 1911, the frustrated painter Walt Kuhn and a few of his equally disgruntled friends formed the Association of American Painters and Sculptors for the purpose of organizing an annual show along the lines of the big 1910 Exhibition of Independent Artists, though they resolved to add some foreign work. Kuhn felt that if the AAPS could unite all the various circles of progressive art, it would rival, and perhaps even surpass, the National Academy as the leading force in American art.

The painter and critic Guy Pène du Bois wrote that when Arthur Davies was elected president of the AAPS, in January 1912, that quiet and gentle man "underwent an amazing metamorphosis." On behalf of the cause of modern art, he became "a dictator, severe, arrogant, implacable."[1] Specifically, he seized the opportunity to shape the organization's first show, the great International Exhibition of Modern Art, now known universally as the Armory Show, which was to take place in New York during February and March 1913. Davies almost certainly asked Stieglitz to help, but the latter declined to become directly involved — perhaps because of his antipathy toward Walt Kuhn, whose paintings, he would later say, he disliked intensely. He did, however, promise to loan some works and to give his blessing for 291 artists to participate. He also agreed to be listed as an honorary vice president of the exhibition, along with Claude Monet, Odilon Redon, Mrs. Jack Gardner of Boston, and Mabel Dodge.

The Armory Show launched Dodge's New York career. She was a stoutish and rather plain manic-depressive woman with bangs and an insatiable and grasping hunger for physical, intellectual, social, and spiritual fulfillment. At the end of November 1912, after years at her Villa Curonia outside Florence, she moved into the third floor of the rather grand house at 23 Fifth Avenue, on the northeast corner of Ninth Street. Symbolically, Dodge — who would eventually advertise her services as an interior decorator — began by painting all the dark woodwork white, covering the walls with white fabrics, and hanging long white curtains. She was starting a new life.

She had learned about the Armory Show from the sculptor Jo Davidson, whom she had met through her friend Gertrude Stein. Soon, Dodge wrote, "I felt as though the Exhibition were mine. . . . It became, over night, my own little Revolution. *I* would upset America; . . . *I* was going to dynamite New York and nothing would stop me."[2]

Having disencumbered herself of her supernumerary husband, Dodge began, late in January 1913, her weekly "evenings," held on Wednesday or Thursday, and sometimes more than once a week, where the discussion would focus on a single announced topic, such as psychoanalysis, free love, or socialism. She soon could boast that at her salon

> Socialists, Trade-Unionists, Anarchists, Suffragists, Poets, Relations, Lawyers, Murderers, "Old Friends," Psychoanalysts, I.W.W.'s, Single Taxers, Birth Controlists, Newspapermen, Artists, Modern-Artists, Clubwomen, Woman's-place-is-in-the-home Women, Clergymen, and just plain men all met . . . and, stammering in an unaccustomed freedom a kind of speech called Free, exchanged a variousness in vocabulary called, in euphemistic optimism, Opinions![3]

Most of the *Masses* crowd showed up (Dodge gave money to the magazine), along with writers Carl Van Vechten and Lincoln Steffens and (depending on who was in town) artists Andrew Dasburg, Maurice Sterne, Marsden Hartley, Charles Demuth, Francis Picabia, and Adolf de Meyer. Stieglitz dropped in occasionally, but the inner circle at 291 resented Dodge because (according to Agnes Meyer) "she played with life as if it were a game in which the stakes were not very high."[4] Dodge, on the other hand, was a frequent visitor to 291. In her memoirs she generously wrote: "At '291' I met people who became the friends of a lifetime. There we gathered over and over again, drawn and held together by the apparent purity of Stieglitz's intention. He was afraid of nothing, and always trusted his eyes

Alfred Stieglitz, *My Father*, 1894. Platinum print. *(Alfred Stieglitz Collection, © 1995 Board of Trustees, National Gallery of Art, Washington, D.C.)*

Alfred Stieglitz, *Sun Rays — Paula*, Berlin, 1889. Platinum print. *(Alfred Stieglitz Collection, © 1995 Board of Trustees, National Gallery of Art, Washington, D.C.)*

Alfred Stieglitz, *Winter — Fifth Avenue*, 1893. Photogravure from *Camera Work* no. 12, October 1905. *(Permanent Collection, The International Center of Photography, New York.)*

Alfred Stieglitz,
Miss S. R., 1904.
Photogravure from
Camera Work no. 12,
October 1905.
*(Permanent Collection, The
International Center of
Photography, New York.)*

Alfred Stieglitz,
The Terminal, 1893.
Photogravure from
Camera Work no. 36,
October 1911.
*(Permanent Collection, The
International Center of
Photography, New York.)*

Adolf de Meyer,
Mrs. Alfred Stieglitz
[Emmeline], 1912.
Platinum print. *(The*
Metropolitan Museum of
Art, Alfred Stieglitz
Collection, 1933.)

Edward Steichen, *Alfred*
Stieglitz and His Daughter
Katherine. 1905 print
from 1904 negative.
Platinum print. *(The*
Metropolitan Museum of
Art, Alfred Stieglitz
Collection, 1949.)

Frank Eugene, *Alfred Stieglitz*, 1907. Platinum print. *(The Metropolitan Museum of Art, Alfred Stieglitz Collection, 1955.)*

Alfred Stieglitz, *Katherine* [Stieglitz], 1905. Photogravure from *Camera Work* no. 12, October 1905. *(Permanent Collection, The International Center of Photography, New York.)*

Opposite, left: Pablo Picasso, *Drawing,* 1910. Photogravure from *Camera Work* no. 36, October 1911. *(Permanent Collection, The International Center of Photography, New York.)*

Opposite, center: Alfred Stieglitz, *Spring Showers — New York,* 1900. Photogravure from *Camera Work* no. 36, October 1911. *Permanent Collection, The International Center of Photography, New York.*

Opposite, right: Alfred Stieglitz, *The Flatiron,* 1902–3. Photogravure from *Camera Work* no. 4, October 1903. *(Permanent Collection, The International Center of Photography, New York.)*

Above: Alfred Stieglitz, *The Steerage,* 1907. Photogravure from *Camera Work* no. 36, October 1911. *(Permanent Collection, The International Center of Photography, New York.)*

Edward Steichen,
*Portrait of Clarence H.
White*, 1903.
Photogravure from
Camera Work no. 9,
January 1905. *(Permanent
Collection, The International
Center of Photography, New
York.)*

Edward Steichen,
Solitude [portrait of
F. Holland Day], 1901.
Photogravure from
Steichen Supplement to
Camera Work no. 14,
April 1906. *(Permanent
Collection, The International
Center of Photography, New
York.)*

Edward Steichen, *Self-Portrait*, 1902. Photogravure from *Camera Work* no. 2, April 1903. *(Permanent Collection, The International Center of Photography, New York.)*

Clarence H. White, *Alvin Langdon Coburn and His Mother*, 1907. Photogravure from *Camera Work* no. 32, October 1910. *(Permanent Collection, The International Center of Photography, New York.)*

Alfred Stieglitz, *Marsden Hartley*, 1915–16. Gelatin silver print. *(Alfred Stieglitz Collection, © 1995 Board of Trustees, National Gallery of Art, Washington, D.C.)*

Alfred Stieglitz, *The Little Galleries of the Photo-Secession*, 1905. Photogravure from *Camera Work* no. 14, April 1906. *(Permanent Collection, The International Center of Photography, New York.)*

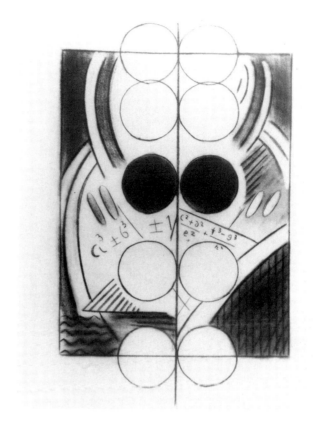

Marius de Zayas, *Alfred Stieglitz*, 1913. Photogravure from *Camera Work* no. 46, April 1914. *(Permanent Collection, The International Center of Photography, New York.)*

Alfred Stieglitz, *Paul Strand*, 1919. Palladium print. *(Alfred Stieglitz Collection, © 1995 Board of Trustees, National Gallery of Art, Washington, D.C.)*

Alfred Stieglitz, *Portrait of Katharine N. Rhoades*, 1915. Platinum print. *(Charles Lang Freer Papers, Freer Gallery of Art Archives, Smithsonian Institution, Washington, D.C.)*

Alfred Stieglitz, *Georgia O'Keeffe: A Portrait — Profile*, 1920. Palladium print. *(Alfred Stieglitz Collection, © 1995 Board of Trustees, National Gallery of Art, Washington, D.C.)*

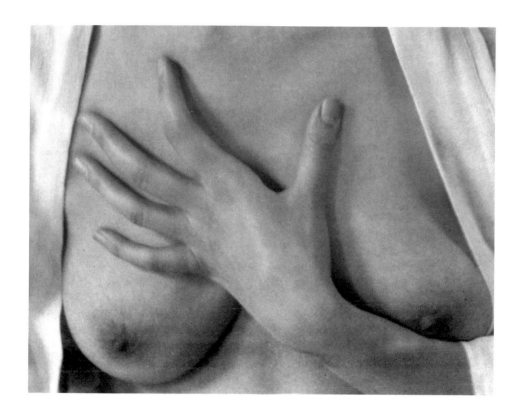

Above: Alfred Stieglitz, *Georgia O'Keeffe: A Portrait — Hand and Breasts*, 1919. Palladium print. *(Alfred Stieglitz Collection, © 1995 Board of Trustees, National Gallery of Art, Washington, D.C.)*

Opposite, top: Alfred Stieglitz and Clarence H. White, *Torso*, 1907. Photogravure from *Camera Work* no. 27, July 1909. *(Permanent Collection, The International Center of Photography, New York.)*

Opposite, bottom: Alfred Stieglitz, *Rebecca Strand*, 1923. Gelatin silver print. *(Alfred Stieglitz Collection, © 1995 Board of Trustees, National Gallery of Art, Washington, D.C.)*

Alfred Stieglitz, *Georgia O'Keeffe: A Portrait — Head*, 1920–22. Gelatin silver developed-out print. (*Alfred Stieglitz Collection, © 1995 Board of Trustees, National Gallery of Art, Washington, D.C.*)

Alfred Stieglitz, *Dorothy Norman XIX, New York*, 1931. Gelatin silver print. (*From the Collection of Dorothy Norman, on loan to the Philadelphia Museum of Art.*)

and heart. . . . He provided an *ambiente* where the frightened artist dared to be himself."[5]

Dodge's salon was a shooting star that had pretty much spent itself by early 1915, when the hostess moved to a house in Croton-on-Hudson, New York, with her lover, the flamboyant journalist John Reed, who had just returned from the Western Front. It would revive intermittently until Dodge and her new, and quite temporary, husband Maurice Sterne moved to Taos, New Mexico, in 1917.

Dodge's best friend was Hutchins Hapgood, "a stocky basso profondo" who in 1912 began writing a column three times a week for the *New York Globe*.[6] The editor let him write about anything he liked — as Hapgood himself put it, "the warm spring day, a French girl, a picture at Stieglitz's, an inspired bum in a saloon, a suffrage meeting, an interview with Bill Haywood, or a strike at Hastings."[7] A good friend of Stieglitz's, Hapgood praised 291 in one of his first columns as a place where "for several years the voice of freedom has been quietly shouting in the wilderness."[8]

In another column, Hapgood set forth his perverse principles. "I merely defend and exalt what is generally condemned," he wrote. "I do this irrespective of the merits of the case, and simply in order to defend the extremely small minority, just because it is the minority . . . I attack the powerful and prevailing thing, in art, industry, in all fields, just because it is prevailing."[9] Moving from the general to the particular, Hapgood wrote during the Armory Show, "Bergson, Post-Impressionism, the I.W.W., anarchism, the radical woman movement, the thrill of the socially and politically new, these things make up the sum and substance of my existence."[10]

Paradoxically, if not downright hypocritically, while Hapgood was championing the anarchistic spirit in print, he and his family were living in the posh Hudson River town of Dobbs Ferry, New York, in a twenty-room brick mansion with "acres of polished oak floors, high ceilings, white marble mantels, and a superb outlook on the great river."[11] (His father, a wealthy Chicago plow manufacturer, had bought the house without bothering to ask them whether they wanted it.) Hapgood would take the train into New York every morning, and after making his rounds of the radical hot spots, he would often retire to the Harvard Club to write his articles.

Stieglitz was pleased by the prospect that the Armory Show might bring to completion his work of introducing modern art to America. Since he also believed he had done just about all that he could for photography, he considered not only closing 291 after the upcoming season but also discontinuing the publication of *Camera Work*. "Isn't my work for the cause about finished?" he asked rhetorically in a letter to Heinrich Kuehn in May 1912. "Useless to sacrifice time and money simply to repeat oneself — I don't believe in that and therefore I feel far too much the need for my own photography."[12]

Stieglitz had hoped to return to Europe in the summer of 1912, but a shortage of money and an excess of work prevented him from going. In response to the announcement of the Armory Show he threw himself into producing a special issue of *Camera Work*, dated August 1912, in which he broadcast his prior claim as the impresario of modernism by publishing black-and-white reproductions of five paintings and two sculptures by Matisse and of four paintings, a drawing, and a sculpture by Picasso. One can all too easily imagine the reaction of the amateur photographers who received the issue and found it completely lacking in the usual photographs (though Stieglitz's two views of the Picasso sculpture are masterpieces of the art of photographing a work of art; Professor Vogel would have been proud of his pupil). As if the pictures were not sufficiently aggravating, the text consisted of Gertrude Stein's word portraits of the two artists, the first publication anywhere of her patience-trying prose. Many subscribers sent in cancellations, some of them presumably infuriated by the first sentences (more than which they cannot have read) of Stein's portrait of Picasso: "One whom some were certainly following was one who was completely charming. One whom some were certainly following was one who was charming. One whom some were following was one who was completely charming. One whom some were following was one who was certainly completely charming."[13]

When Alfred finally joined Emmy and Kitty at Lake George early in August, the family was shaken by the news of the latest development in Lee Stieglitz's already ten-year-long extramarital affair. On a visit home in 1890, Lee had fallen in love with Amanda Liebman, yet another of Emmy's many cousins, but he had honored his engagement to Lizzie Stieffel. He hadn't encountered Amanda again until 1902, by which time she was married to Samuel Hoff. She then became one of Lee's patients — and his mistress. The secret was a fairly open one, even more so once Lee, Lizzie, and their two daughters, during the summers of odd-numbered years, began joining the Hoffs on their annual European sojourns. In the summer of 1912, violating their schedule and all proprieties, the desperate Lee, alone, impetuously followed the Hoffs to the Swiss resort of Sils-Maria. There the cuckolded husband surprised him and Amanda as they, with wildly foolish indiscretion, held hands in public on the terrace of the hotel. Mortified to the point of developing angina pectoris, Lee fled back to New York. Lizzie promptly left Lake George for the city, where she would try to nurse her husband and, with less success, their marriage, back to health. Amid the inevitable recriminations at Oaklawn, Emmy evidently defended her cousin so vehemently that she became persona non grata. In future summers she would not accompany Alfred and Kitty to Lake George. Lee and his family would, however, soon resume their European jaunts with the Hoffs.

Stieglitz decided to open the 1912–13 season on November 20 with a show of theatrical caricatures by Alfred Frueh (pronounced "free"), who had recently left for Paris to dabble in modernism. "While Frueh's work is not to be considered as a contribution to the advancement of modern art," commented *Camera Work*, "it reveals a fresh and independent point of view. His show afforded a refreshing relaxation, in its sympathetic humor, from the tension of New York life."[14] In the 1920s Frueh would become an outstanding caricaturist for *The New Yorker*.

Next came Walkowitz's first one-man show (December 15–January 14, 1913) and then a Marin exhibition that would close two days before the February 17 opening of the Armory Show, in which Marin would have ten watercolors. There would be nothing on the walls of 291 the following week, for no one would pay any attention to any exhibition but the big one. On February 24, Stieglitz would unveil the first and only 291 exhibition of his own photographs.

The Marin show included watercolors of the Berkshires and the Adirondacks, but the highlight was a large selection from his series of more than thirty watercolors of the fifty-five-story Woolworth Building, then the tallest in the world, construction of which was just being completed a block from where Stieglitz had shot his photograph *The Terminal* in 1893.

"The great geniuses," Stieglitz believed, "are those who have kept their childlike spirit and have added to it breadth of vision and experience."[15] Marin was such an artist. Stieglitz, himself trying to preserve a sense of play in all he did, was very excited about how the Woolworth series playfully, with what Benjamin de Casseres called Marin's "luminous humor," progressed from fairly traditional to nearly abstract treatments, culminating in an uninhibitedly joyous depiction of the building as a swelling, Dr.

Seuss–like bubble. When curiosity brought the building's architect, Cass Gilbert, to the gallery, he stared sadly, shook his head, and was heard to mutter something that sounded like a question about the artist's sanity.

"'291' has been seething with life since about the middle of December," wrote Stieglitz to a friend at the end of January. "To give you an idea of the strenuousness of it all I might tell you that during the four days last week I got only sixteen hours of sleep and the other eighty hours were taken up in intellectual discussions, a nerve racking physical test but a most stimulating and invigorating intellectual treat."[16] The fruit of some of those discussions appeared in the *New York American* on Sunday, January 26, three weeks before the Armory Show was to open. The half-page article entitled "The First Great 'Clinic to Revitalize Art,'" claimed to be "By ALFRED STIEGLITZ" but had been, as the first paragraph admitted, "contributed . . . in the form of an interview." It was probably conducted by Charles Caffin, who earlier that month had become the paper's art editor, a position he would hold until his death, in January 1918.

Stieglitz, perhaps not considering how excerpts from one of his usual tirades might look if printed verbatim, spoke candidly. Carried away, he said that despite the revolution in art, "the Chase School and the Henri Academy and the Alexander manufactory will go on doing business at the old stands. Sometimes the dead don't know they're dead." Such remarks led a surprisingly embarrassed Stieglitz to write to a friend the week after publication, "I was staggered to see in print all the things I was supposed to have said," some of which, he complained, were "virtually the reverse" of his actual statements.[17] But most of the article rings very true, including his advice to the public about how to approach the Armory Show: "Don't adopt the enemy's impudent device of plastering these emancipated artists and their work with labels. There's the result — the picture; take it or leave it. If a name is necessary in writing about these live ones, call them 'Revitalizers.'" After some lengthy observations about Brancusi, van Gogh, and Marin, the article concluded with an outburst of Stieglitz's contempt for both illustrational painting and pictorial photography: "If you decide that you would rather that art stay dead, then go out with your kodak and produce some faithful imitations. Good machine work is always preferable to indifferent hand-made products."[18]

Because the AAPS could not afford to rent Madison Square Garden for its International Exhibition, it settled instead on the 69th Infantry Regiment's armory, located on the west side of Lexington Avenue between Twenty-fifth and Twenty-sixth streets. During the week before the formal opening, which began at three o'clock on the afternoon of Monday, February 17, flimsy wooden partitions were hastily erected and covered with burlap to divide the immense drill floor of the armory into a honeycomb of eighteen more or less octagonal rooms. Dozens of pine trees — alluding to the flag of the American revolutionaries, which had been adopted as the emblem of the exhibition — were placed strategically around the hall, and festoons of pine boughs ran all along tops of walls and around doorways. Hundreds of narrow strips of yellow cloth stretched from the center of the soaring barrel-vaulted ceiling to the walls, creating a tentlike effect more appropriate for a political convention or a debutante ball than for a show of modernist art.

The Armory Show not only provided a cross section of contemporary American art but also presented, as genealogy and context, a condensed history of the development of the "independent spirit" in nineteenth- and twentieth-century French painting. It ranged from Ingres and Delacroix, through Impressionism and Post-Impressionism, to Fauvism and Cubism, and included a smattering of work from other European nations. Altogether, about 1,300 works of art — approximately 650 paintings, 150 sculptures, and 470 drawings, watercolors, pastels, etchings, and wood cuts — were exhibited; an additional 300 lithographs, which were not hung, could be viewed upon request. About one third of the works, most of which were for sale, were by foreign artists. Many of the Americans — who had, after all, conceived the exhibition to develop a market for their own work — were enraged when the Europeans stole the limelight in the press and garnered well over two thirds of the sales.

Stieglitz bought only one American work, a drawing by Arthur Davies, in addition to five Aleksandr Archipenko drawings, a Cézanne lithograph, and a bronze by Picasso's friend Manuel Martínez Hugué Manolo. His most important purchase was the one Kandinsky painting in the exhibition, for which he paid $500. Although Royal Cortissoz dismissed the 1912 work *The Garden of Love (Improvisation No. 27)* as "fragments of refuse thrown out of a butcher's shop upon a bit of canvas," the photographer (who conceded that Kandinsky was "not the master like Cézanne or Picasso") regarded the painting as the most important example of lyrical abstraction in the show.[19] He hoped to mount a Kandinsky exhibition at 291, but despite the painter's enthusiasm, it never came about.

Of the American artists to whom Stieglitz had given one-man exhibitions, only Hartley, Marin, and Walkowitz were represented in the Armory Show. Max Weber, who considered himself the most important American

Post-Impressionist, felt so insulted when the selection committee chose only two of his paintings that he refused to participate at all, though he did agree to lend his collection of paintings and drawings by Rousseau. Weber was compensated with a sweet triumph that summer, when the Newark Museum, at the invitation of its director, John Cotton Dana, gave him a solo exhibition of seventeen paintings, the first such show given by any museum to an American modernist.

Having been tantalized at 291, the New York art public now had its first opportunity to see a good selection of Matisse's paintings. Although Picasso was represented by five oils and Georges Braque by three in the Cubist room (the "Chamber of Horrors"), the Cubists who received the most attention were members of the group called La Section d'Or, which was attempting to present an alternative to Picasso. They were taking Cubism in the direction of "pure painting," with an emphasis on mathematical relationships and musical analogies. Among the leaders were Jacques Villon (born Gaston Duchamp), at whose studio in the Parisian suburb Puteaux many of these artists congregated on Sundays; his younger brother Marcel Duchamp; their intermediate brother, the sculptor Raymond Duchamp-Villon; Albert Gleizes; and Francis Picabia.

The succès de scandale of the Cubist room was *Nude Descending a Staircase, No. 2*, painted in 1912 by the twenty-four-year-old Duchamp. Although most people assumed that the nude was a woman, the French title painted directly on the canvas specified *Nu*, not *Nue*. The painting was lampooned as "an explosion in a shingle factory," and one cartoonist cleverly parodied it as "The Rude Descending a Staircase (Rush Hour at the Subway)." In the end, a San Francisco dealer bought the work, sight unseen, as a curiosity, for $324. That was precisely the kind of philistinism that most thoroughly disgusted Stieglitz.

Some writers poured forth enough vituperation to keep things interesting, but the press was generally, as Kuhn put it, "friendly and willing." Even the conservative Cortissoz, who fumed in the *New York Tribune* that the show included "some of the most stupidly ugly pictures in the world and a few pieces of sculpture to match," nevertheless judged it overall "a fine and stirring exhibition."[20] A week later he gallantly wrote,

> The Photo-Secession Gallery is filled with photographs by Mr. Alfred Stieglitz. It is interesting to see them there, but we cannot forbear noting that if any worker with a camera might have claimed admission for his prints at the Salon of the Independents [the Ar-

mory Show] it is Mr. Stieglitz. . . . With his delightful breadth of mind, his enthusiasm for liberty and all those who fight for it, Mr. Stieglitz has been an exemplary pioneer. . . . His liberality is a noble trait, and there is no better occasion than this one for offering it a public tribute.[21]

Stieglitz had written that he would exhibit his own work during the Armory Show to put it "to a diabolical test." If it couldn't stand up to such competition, he mused, then "it contains nothing vital."[22] His show contained about thirty prints — all of them, as *Camera Work* insisted, examples of "the straightest kind of straight photography" — ranging in date from 1893 to 1912 and including *The Terminal, The Flatiron, The Hand of Man, The City of Ambition*, ferryboats and docks, and a recent winter view of the towers of Madison Square Garden and the Metropolitan Life Insurance Company building, seen from Fifth Avenue, as a snow-covered tree dances in the foreground.[23] Most were views of the city, for, as *Camera Work* explained, "a comparison between Marin's rendition of New York and Stieglitz's photographs of the same subject afforded the very best opportunity to the student and public for a clearer understanding of the place and purpose of the two media."[24]

In their reviews of Stieglitz's show, the well-trained critics regurgitated the doctrines with which the photographer had bombarded them at the gallery. J. Edgar Chamberlin, who called Stieglitz's photographs "practically unsurpassable," wrote in the *New York Mail* that the purpose of the exhibition was "to convince the instructed observer that everything that may be rendered at all by photography is already better rendered by photography than it could possibly be by painting, and that the painters had therefore better devote themselves to the subjects and methods which photography cannot touch — to futuristic pictures, in short."[25] And Samuel Swift dutifully noted in the *Sun*, "It is not the subjects of these photographs that alone make this little exhibition one of the significant events of the art season. It is the lesson clearly enforced that photography, even without the aid of any manipulation of plates or special arrangement of composition, can represent actualities with something positive and undeniable in the way of expression."[26] There is no record of anyone's concluding that Stieglitz's photographs had failed the "diabolical test" to which he had put them.

His images of New York illustrated most effectively the objectivity that Marius de Zayas celebrated in his article "Photography," the lead text in the January 1913 issue of *Camera Work*, which served, in effect, as a catalog essay for the show. Echoing P. H. Emerson, de Zayas shocked his readers by opening his article with the declaration "Photography is not Art. It is not even an art." Defining the essential distinction, he explained, "Photography is the plastic verification of a fact. . . . Art presents to us what we may call the emotional or intellectual truth; photography the material truth."

It was far from de Zayas's intention to relegate photography to its old inferior status. In fact, he maintained that the medium was much more in tune with the modern psyche than was traditional art. In de Zayas's view, and in Stieglitz's, a camera in the hands of one who *sees* is a scientific instrument, a sort of metaphysical X-ray machine, capable of revealing the essence of what is photographed. "The photographer — the true photographer," de Zayas wrote, "is he who has become able, through a state of perfect consciousness, to possess such a clear view of things as to enable him to understand and feel the beauty of the reality of Form."[27]

All this owed much to the French philosopher Henri Bergson, who was so popular in America that when he lectured at Columbia University in February 1913, the automobiles of his fashionable audience created a traffic jam on Broadway. In his best-seller *Creative Evolution*, published in 1911, he had argued that analysis distorts experience by breaking it into discrete, static fragments; intuition, on the other hand, perceives the perpetual flux that is the true essence of reality. And in his *Introduction to Metaphysics* (1913) he wrote that intuition is "the *sympathy* by which one is transported into the interior of an object in order to coincide with what there is unique and consequently inexpressible about it." Bergson argued that through intuition human beings are capable of perceiving absolutes, while through the intellect they perceive only the relative. Stieglitz, who published two excerpts from Bergson's writings in *Camera Work*, believed that if he concentrated intensely enough upon his subject, he could force his camera to record his intuitive perceptions.

De Zayas's interpretation of photography was very much in keeping with Stieglitz's sense of himself as a scientist. An egotist dealing with one of the most highly subjective realms of human experience, Stieglitz delighted in claiming that his aesthetic judgments were scientifically impartial. For instance, he wrote in 1912 that the investigation of the "real meaning of art" was for him "not a question of personal likes and dislikes; not a question of theory; I approach the subject in a scientific way, objectively, impersonally."[28] Such a stance certainly reinforced his tendency to dismiss the arguments of his adversaries.

*   *   *

Stieglitz's assessment of the Armory Show was equivocal. In one letter he quipped that it "was a sensational success, possibly primarily a success of sensation" but went on to note gratefully, "One thing is sure, the people at large and for that matter also the artists, etc., have been made to realize the importance of the work that has been going on at '291' and in *Camera Work*. This much the Exhibition accomplished for us."[29]

Although Stieglitz visited the exhibition several times and no doubt gave expostulatory guided tours to a few privileged friends, he was mostly content to observe the proceedings from 291, taking care to distance himself from the sensationalism. He was not, however, so self-righteously aloof that he refused to attend, on March 8, the boisterous stag dinner the AAPS gave for its "friends and enemies," including the leading critics, at Healy's steakhouse, on Columbus Avenue at Sixty-sixth Street. Amid much laughter, singing, and dancing, jocular toasts were given and burlesque messages purporting to be from notable absentees were read.

One of the toasts was given by John Quinn, a driving force behind the show. Quinn, forty-three in 1913, had made a fortune as the legal adviser to corporations and millionaires. An Irish-American who worked actively for Irish home rule, he had a passion for the literature of his ancestral land and collected Irish books and literary manuscripts before he became a serious acquisitor of paintings. He was something of a radical masquerading as a conservative; despite being a member of the Democratic National Committee, he gave money to *The Masses* and was the legal adviser to the AAPS.

Bald, with a skeptical but kindly glint in his penetrating blue eyes, the tall Quinn carried himself like a general or a prince of the church. He was imperious and moody, had a fiery temper, and was a fearsome adversary in court. But in a drawing room or an artist's studio, he could be delightfully engaging and witty.

On a 1912 visit to Paris, Quinn, whose tastes in painting had favored the Eight, bought his first great Post-Impressionist canvases: a Cézanne portrait, a van Gogh self-portrait, and a Tahitian Gauguin. He lent all three to the Armory Show, along with seventy-four other works (twenty of them by his friend Augustus John, the rakish, bohemian painter who had introduced him to Post-Impressionism). That show — at which he spent nearly $6,000 on works by Redon, Derain, Duchamp-Villon, and others — radicalized Quinn's taste in art. He wrote that "after studying the work of the Cubists and Futurists, it makes it hard to stomach the sweetness, the prettiness and the clawing [cloying] sentiment of some of the other work."[30]

From then on he would demand that a painting or sculpture contain "radium." He found more radium in European art than in American, though he had a weakness for American landscapes and for the work of his friend Walt Kuhn. He would soon become an important, though hardly maecenean, buyer at 291.

During the Armory Show, the painter Francis Picabia, the only European modernist in New York at that time, attracted almost as much attention as did Duchamp's notorious painting. With four large and colorful abstractions in the show, Picabia overshadowed Picasso, with whom he was undoubtedly confused by many New Yorkers. He was welcomed as the leading Cubist and treated like a celebrity, but nowhere in the city did he receive a warmer welcome than at 291, which he visited almost daily.

Thirty-four-year-old Picabia — whose grandfather, like P. H. Emerson's father, had made a fortune as a planter in Cuba — was a flamboyant and restless playboy, a true enfant terrible, who drove his Bugatti much too fast, smoked opium, and had genuine artistic talent. With a rich boy's sense of possibility, he was always hatching sweeping plans of revolution and liberation, expressed in sophomorically intellectualizing terms. Gertrude Stein wrote that Picabia annoyed her "with his incessantness and . . . the vulgarity of his delayed adolescence."[31] But Stieglitz found him warm and engaging — and took him on as one of his many sons. He was also very impressed by the artist's wife. Gabrielle Buffet-Picabia, an attractive young woman who had studied to be a singer, would contribute a lucid article to the Armory Show issue of *Camera Work*. Stieglitz wrote that the Picabias "were about the cleanest propositions I ever met in my whole career. They were one hundred percent purity. This fact added to their wonderful intelligence made both of them a constant source of pleasure."[32]

After a show of Picabia's nearly abstract drawings and watercolors — inspired by subjects as diverse as skyscrapers, ships in the harbor, and an African-American singer in a nightclub — 291's season closed with an exhibition of de Zayas's "relative and absolute caricatures." They were abstract drawings in which the artist (playfully, one hopes) claimed to illustrate "(1) The spirit of man by algebraic formulas; (2) his material self by geometrical equivalents; (3) his intellectual force by trajectories within the rectangle that encloses the plastic expression and represents life."[33] In one of them de Zayas had elaborated his drawing of the South Pacific "trap for catching souls" with a vestige of Stieglitz's brush mustache and some fanciful algebraic notations. His "absolute" caricatures of 291ers affected not only Picabia's future work but also Stieglitz's. The photographer had, of course, been making portraits of his friends for the past five years. But now, during 1913 or early in 1914, he rose to the challenge posed in the catalog text for de Zayas's show. There Paul Haviland had reported de Zayas's claim that photography "gives us only the exterior or objective appearance of the subject, and only so much of his character as we would be able to discover by looking at the person himself according to our faculties for judging of character."[34] Stieglitz redoubled his efforts to make photographic portraits that would rival or surpass caricatures as revelations of the subject's psychology. He would, as Paul Rosenfeld wrote, expose "the skyscraper civilization as it lies in the struggling psyche of the male. These are men, full of a marvelous potential life, full of richness . . . but men caught and held and torn in the fearful psychic conflicts of our day."[35] Some of the intensity of Stieglitz's portraits is due to the slowness of the plates he used, requiring exposures of up to four minutes, during which the subject had to remain absolutely immobile. The portraits were impromptu, each subject being taken aside for an hour or so if he happened to arrive at the gallery on a bright day in what struck Stieglitz as a revealing mood and characteristic garb.

Perhaps the most powerful example of Stieglitz's heightened penetration is his 1915 portrait of Marsden Hartley, bundled up against a chill that seems more than merely physical. Wearing a dark, heavy overcoat and a white silk scarf, his hat pulled too far down over his forehead, the artist looks somewhat confused and furtive. His eyes, under which there are dark bags, seem to be looking into his lonely future.

In 1917 Stieglitz would photograph wistful Hodge Kirnon, the young, sensitive West Indian elevator man at 291, his sad face haloed by a bright window. Having written in *Camera Work* that 291 had taught him "that our work is worthy in proportion as it is the honest expression of ourselves," Kirnon appears pessimistic about finding a job that would be an honest expression of himself.

Fittingly, one of the first portraits in Stieglitz's new series was of de Zayas, his mouth almost grimacing beneath his British officer's mustache and his eyes askance beneath his high forehead. A study in black-and-white formality, he looks a bit like a maître d' about to show a wealthy matron to her table. One might have predicted that he would open an art gallery.

Stieglitz declined when his friend Frank Crowninshield, who became editor of *Vanity Fair* in March 1914, offered to publish one of his portraits each month. After Adolf de Meyer and his wife returned to New York in

September 1914, having fled London under suspicion of espionage, Stieglitz persuaded Crowninshield to hire the baron as the magazine's principal portraitist and fashion photographer.

Just before they left New York, on April 10, the Picabias and a group that included Mabel Dodge, Jo Davidson and his wife, the critic Charles FitzGerald, and the Rumanian-born chemist Maurice Aisen (who wrote an article about Picabia for *Camera Work*) made tentative plans for, as Dodge later wrote,

> a really altruistic group life in Paris where we would be devoting all our vitality to an understanding of modern art, for the benefit of artists, giving them a vehicle of expression somewhat along the same lines as Stieglitz's *Camera Work*, and a little place as much like "291" as possible, where their work could be seen, and where our "vie interieure" would have a chance to deepen.[36]

Although the Picabias sailed alone, Gabrielle took the idea quite seriously and actually opened a small gallery in Paris in January 1914. Moreover, Jean Cocteau agreed to edit a magazine based on *Camera Work*. But the gallery closed within a few months, and the magazine was never launched. As for Francis, he told his Parisian friends that he was "enchanted with the land of dollars," where collectors paid well for paintings "brushed in half a day."[37]

CHAPTER FORTY·FIVE

AT ABOUT 1:00 A.M. on June 14, 1913, Stieglitz was awakened by a
telephone call informing him that a fire had broken out in the apartment
below his gallery. Assuming that everything would be destroyed, he saw no
point in rushing to 291 Fifth Avenue. Instead he sat and talked with Emmy,
telling her that although he was sad about losing his negatives and prints as
well as his personal collection of photographs and other works of art, much
worse was the destruction of so much of the output of the young artists in
whom he believed. He told Hutchins Hapgood, who published an account
of this episode in the *New York Globe*, that "he knew that the loss of their
work would to them mean tragedy and might change the course of their
lives.

"For several hours Alfred Stieglitz went through perhaps the most intense experience of his life," continued Hapgood. "When he went to the
gallery and found that nothing had been touched he had no feeling of relief or pleasure. His capacity for emotion had been exhausted." But he told
Hapgood that "if those pictures, plates, photographs, and drawings had
been destroyed, he would have gone to some pseudo art collection, to some
gallery of respectable paintings, to some museum in which academical
compromise in the way of art was stored, and would have burnt it up."
Stieglitz was so pleased with Hapgood's article, entitled "Fire and Revolution," that he had it privately reprinted as a pamphlet.[1]

This episode brought to a climactic close one of the most intense and exhausting periods in Stieglitz's life — from the Armory Show and his retrospective through Kitty's serious bout of diphtheria in May, after which Emmy decided that a trip to Europe would do them all good. But Alfred, who couldn't stand the thought of another European ordeal with Emmy, didn't want to go. For one thing, after the 291 season closed on May 20, he had to work with Haviland and de Zayas on the special Armory Show issue of *Camera Work* to be published in June. Besides, he had seen enough art at the big show, the hoopla surrounding which had, in any case, diminished his enthusiasm for European modernism. Fortunately, Emmy accepted his suggestion that she go instead with a nineteen-year-old niece. They booked passage on a ship leaving New York early in August.

A few days after the fire, Emmy and Kitty settled in for a six-week stay in the New Jersey seaside resort of Elberon, near Long Branch. Six days a week, Alfred would commute to New York, a two-hour train ride in each direction. His only recompense was that he could occasionally go to the races at Monmouth Park. After Emmy finally set off for Europe on August 8, Alfred and Kitty went to Lake George for two months of relaxation and immersion in the delights and horrors of spending time with their huge extended family. At Oaklawn twenty adults might sit down to dinner, the innumerable children eating separately. It was like a self-contained and bustling resort, with a variety of sports during the day and elaborate amateur theatricals and musicales in the evening. Despite so much commotion, Alfred always managed to enjoy such private pleasures as printing his negatives in his improvised darkroom in the carriage house, reading, and catching up on correspondence.

Alfred still had profoundly ambivalent feelings about his daughter, now nearly fifteen. He adored his idealized image of her from a distance, periodically lavishing money and sentiment — if not genuine affection — upon her whenever he briefly and guiltily became conscious of his neglect. An hour later he might vent his fury upon her for some trivial offense.

There was so much distance between father and daughter that Kitty had only a vague idea of the nature of Alfred's work. One day the girls in her class at the Veltin School were asked to state their father's vocation, and Kitty was forced to admit that she didn't know hers. When the teacher said, "Why, he's the greatest photographer in the world," Kitty responded that that couldn't be true, since, although her father did photograph, she had never heard him called a photographer — and, besides, he always called Steichen the greatest. Neither teacher nor pupil seems to have mentioned a gallery.[2]

Kitty's sixteen-year-old cousin Elizabeth, of whom Alfred was very fond, characterized her as a "selfish little rotter." In the summer of 1913, however, Kitty benefited from the absence of her mother and the far more than usually focused attentions of her father. As the two swam, played tennis, hiked, and boated together, Alfred enjoyed one of the happiest times that he had ever had, or would ever have, with his daughter.

That summer he devoted much thought to the question of whether he should bother to reopen 291 in the fall. After the Armory Show, a 291 exhibition of a few small works by Picasso or Matisse would inevitably seem anticlimactic. To regain the old éclat, de Zayas even suggested that they mount an exhibition of overtly erotic art.[3] But Stieglitz reached the conclusion that his work was far from done, for he could not desert Marin, Hartley, Walkowitz, Dove, and the other artists in whom he passionately believed. He would be the champion of the men who were steadfastly attempting to express their inner life. Other dealers might opportunistically take up Cubism, but Stieglitz would (as he saw it) represent the individuals whose work did not fit neatly into any movement and would therefore probably not be exhibited anywhere except at 291.

A shrewd impresario with a good sense of timing and drama, Stieglitz realized that Hartley, recently hailed in Europe by Gertrude Stein and Kandinsky, was his trump card for the new season. Hartley, who had been living in Berlin since May, maintained that he was making the most important paintings of any artist in America or Europe, but only his earlier work had been included in the Armory Show. Therefore, on October 20 Stieglitz wrote him, "I am not opening the little gallery until I know definitely whether you are coming or not. Everything is held in abeyance for you. You are to have the first chance. A certain responsibility toward the others rests on your shoulders."[4]

In July 1912 Hartley had discovered Kandinsky's book *Uber das Geistige in der Kunst* (Concerning the Spiritual in Art), published late the previous year. Although he got his German friends to translate some of it for him, the mere title was enough to spur him to experience "a recurrence of former religious aspirations."[5]

That recurrence, together with his belief that the Native Americans represented the purest expression of spirituality in the New World, resulted in a group of paintings that are inspired jumbles. The recognizable symbols and images in them range from treble clefs, stars, crosses, flowers, and statuettes of Buddha to Indian pictographs. At first his breakthrough paintings — in the style that he called Intuitive Abstraction, Cosmic

Cubism, or Subliminal Cubism — attempted to represent on canvas the effect of music. But even in these free-association, stream-of-consciousness semi-abstractions, in which the ungainly artist seems to shake off his American inhibitions and begin to dance, one can clearly see traces of his Maine mountains in the large, centered arches and triangles that often rise from the bottom of the canvases.

Hartley had settled in Berlin partly because he preferred contemporary German painting to French, and partly because he wanted to be with two Germans he had befriended in Paris, the sculptor Arnold Rönnebeck and Rönnebeck's twenty-three-year-old cousin Karl von Freyburg, by whose beauty and charm the painter was captivated. Hartley responded to the color and brassiness of the ubiquitous military pageantry of Berlin, swarming with handsome men in splendid uniforms, as if he were a child in a toy store. Soon he was painting kaleidoscopic visions of mounted cavalrymen with plumed helmets and gold epaulets.

That fall Hartley was invited to exhibit five paintings in the prestigious Herbstsalon (Salon d'Automne) organized by Herwarth Walden, who was, to some extent, Stieglitz's German counterpart. In his Sturm (Assault) Galerie, the hyperkinetic, chain-smoking, and vociferous Walden had, since 1912, shown the work of the German Expressionists, the Italian Futurists, the Russian Constructivists, and extremists of genius from everywhere. In 1910 he had begun publication of the art magazine that gave the gallery its name. Produced on newsprint to keep costs down, *Der Sturm* was illustrated with striking woodblocks by the likes of Oskar Kokoschka and Kandinsky. World War I put a damper on both the gallery and the magazine, but the former didn't close until 1924, and the latter subsisted until 1932. In the late 1920s, however, the fellow-traveling Walden went to Russia for a visit and disappeared there without a trace.

By September 1913, Hartley had run out of money. In a desperate letter to Stieglitz he said Gertrude Stein had suggested that surely some benefactors — perhaps the Meyers once again — could be found in New York who would give him $100 a month to remain in Europe. But Eugene Meyer had run into financial troubles in the fall of 1912. After their second daughter was born, in February 1913, the Meyers had to give up their splendid house and make do with a large apartment in the St. Regis Hotel. Although Eugene — still a millionaire many times over — was elected to the board of governors of the New York Stock Exchange that same month, he continued to suffer losses throughout the year and consequently was in no mood to give more money to Hartley.

Stieglitz replied with a check of his own for $150 and an almost brutally stern letter in which he chastised, by no means disinterestedly, "I personally don't see any reason why any American should be called upon to give you additional cash without seeing what you have done."[6] Hartley capitulated. He sailed for New York in mid-November, bringing enough paintings for an impressive exhibition at 291.

The night before Thanksgiving, Stieglitz mailed off to France the first copy of the third issue of *Camera Work* to be devoted entirely to Steichen's work. Among the fourteen photogravures were portraits of Yvette Guilbert, Isadora Duncan, Anatole France, Henri Matisse, William Howard Taft, Gordon Craig, and George Bernard Shaw. One of the three paintings reproduced in color halftones was a portrait of Alfred's temperamental and self-indulgently arty sister Selma, who impressed the family by having a dalliance with the great tenor Enrico Caruso.

Stieglitz wrote in his accompanying letter to Steichen, which he signed "291," "Nothing I have ever done has given me quite so much satisfaction as finally sending this number out into the world."[7] Steichen's satisfaction with the issue may well have been diminished somewhat by Marius de Zayas's included article, "Photography and Artistic-Photography." "When man uses the camera without any preconceived idea of final results," wrote de Zayas, "when he uses the camera as a means to penetrate the objective reality of facts, . . . then, man is doing Photography." By contrast, "the artist photographer uses nature to express his individuality. . . . Up to the present, the highest point of these two sides of Photography has been reached by Steichen as an artist and by Stieglitz as an experimentalist."[8] It was perhaps at Stieglitz's request that de Zayas disingenuously concluded, "It would be difficult to say which of these two sides of Photography is the more important."

Walkowitz's second one-man show at 291 opened the 1913–14 season on November 19 and ran for seven weeks, raising enough money to enable the artist to spend five months looking at art in Italy, Greece, and North Africa. The most perceptive review of the exhibition was written by one of his former teachers at the Educational Alliance, Henry McBride, who had recently been made the senior art critic for the *New York Sun*, a position he would hold for thirty-six years. In 1913 the forty-six-year-old McBride already looked, as artist Peggy Bacon would later write, like a "well-bred hunting dog." Although his reviews were amusing, gossipy, even arch, he himself was serious and sympathetic, fearless and sincere, and he had a good eye. Stieglitz considered him by far the ablest of the New York critics — even if he did have high praise for Max Weber's work.

Hartley's spectacular exhibition opened on January 12, 1914, and ran for a month. Mabel Dodge, whose salon the artist began to frequent, contributed a foreword to the catalog, bought two paintings, and arranged for a selection of the paintings to be shown at the homes of friends in Buffalo and Chicago. Unhappy in New York, Hartley left for Berlin about six weeks after his show closed. This second European sojourn was made possible by the dealer Charles Daniel, who bought several of Hartley's paintings for a total of $600.

After another display of children's work (February 18–March 11) came the highlight of the season, Constantin Brancusi's first one-man exhibition anywhere, one of the very few shows at 291 devoted to sculpture. It had been proposed by Steichen, who felt that the gallery was losing its edge because it was showing second-rate work. At the Armory, Brancusi had been represented by five works, four of them in plaster, but 291 would exhibit finished works in marble and bronze. The Meyers would pay for the cost of shipping them to New York and back to Paris.

Brancusi sent eight sculptures to New York, despite the advice of painter and critic Walter Pach, who warned him that Stieglitz "is a rich, or comparatively rich man who fancies himself the protector of art in America. He is a pretty decent sort, but he does not push an artist's work the way a dealer would, nor does he have the self-interest of people like us, whose whole career is at stake. . . . Frankly, I feel you would be doing yourself a disservice if you sent him your marbles."[9]

Steichen installed the exhibition, which opened on March 12 and ran until April 4. He removed the brass bowl from the central platform and replaced it with the large, striding, African-inspired *First Step* (1913), Brancusi's first sculpture in wood.[10] Beside it he laid the egg-shaped marble head called *Sleeping Muse*. Among the sculptures placed on pedestals around the room were a bronze of the eaglelike *Maiastra* and a marble version of his elegantly reductionist, but also rather coy, *Mlle Pogany*.

Of the latter, J. Edgar Chamberlin wrote in the *New York Evening Mail*, "The beauty of this surface, of the mere workmanship, in this head is so great that it almost makes one forget the strange character of the head itself. . . . Brancusi is a splendid artisan at any rate. Is he also a great artist? It doesn't appear so."[11] More sympathetically, Henry McBride commented in the *Sun* that Stieglitz's gallery "has the faculty of showing off modern wares that seem dubious in other places to extreme advantage — like the tailor's mirror in which you can never locate the imperfections that you fancied in the glass at home." He enthused that at 291 *Mlle Pogany*, of which a plaster had appeared somewhat lackluster in the Armory Show, "seems to expand, unfold and to take on a startling lucidity."[12]

On April 14, as if specifically refuting Pach's claim, Stieglitz wrote Brancusi, "We feel that your show has been a complete success, artistically speaking, and we hope that you will also look upon it as a complete success, financially speaking."[13] Stieglitz himself — who had, in vain, asked Emmy to choose between the bronze and marble versions of *Sleeping Muse* when she visited Steichen at Voulangis in the summer of 1913 — decided on the bronze, perhaps because it was less than half the price of the marble. Arthur Davies took the marble *Muse* and Agnes Meyer the bronze *Maiastra*, beginning her collection of Brancusis. John Quinn bought the *Mlle Pogany* as well as a marble *Maiastra* of which the sculptor had sent only a photograph. These were the first Brancusis bought by Quinn, who would eventually acquire more than a dozen. Even after the 15 percent commission that Stieglitz charged for fire and theft insurance and general expenses, Brancusi netted more than 10,000 francs (about $25,000 in 1995).

Rather anticlimactically, Stieglitz ended the season with an exhibition of twenty-five paintings and eleven drawings by Paul Haviland's younger brother, who used the name Frank Burty. It was certainly a favor to one of 291's chief supporters, for the work was not profoundly original. In 1910 the twenty-four-year-old Burty, a music student, had been inspired by Picasso to take up painting — though not Cubism. In response to the 291 show, one critic noted that Burty "seems to be a realist; he paints women, peasants, draped and undraped, with startling fidelity to rather squalid facts."[14] Even Haviland conceded that "the quiet reserve" of his brother's paintings had "disappointed the New York public, ever looking for sensationalism."[15]

CHAPTER FORTY·SIX

∽

STIEGLITZ HAD TURNED fifty on January 1, 1914. Two weeks later he was informed (prematurely, as it turned out) that the brownstones on Fifth Avenue between Thirtieth and Thirty-first streets might soon be torn down to make way for an office building. And, on January 21, Joseph Keiley died of Bright's disease. Stieglitz was grief-stricken by the passing of his most loyal friend, who had persevered despite his lack of enthusiasm for modernist art.

One night late in May, after the Burty show had closed, Stieglitz found himself reflecting about the past and the future. There had been several thousand visitors to the gallery that season. "Not, by far, as many as in former years," he wrote. "Curiosity seekers have fallen away."[1] He wondered what the point of it all was. What had he really accomplished? Should he continue? He then decided to devote an unillustrated issue of *Camera Work* to the question "What Is '291'?" He would solicit answers from "twenty or thirty people, men and women, of different ages, of different temperaments, of different walks of life, from different parts of the country, and some in Europe." Stieglitz explained to Charles Caffin, "I have carefully chosen those who are represented, chosen in the same spirit as I have chosen the exhibits during my whole life."[2] Believing that this stocktaking would dictate his future course, he found his sense of purpose renewed.

*   *   *

Before the Armory Show, 291 had been pretty much alone in New York as a showplace for the most advanced European and American art. During the winter of 1914, however, the situation changed drastically. In February, *American Art News* complained that there were then in New York six simultaneous exhibitions devoted to the "Faddists." That same month Henry McBride suggested in the *New York Sun* that someone should organize a company to give bus tours of the galleries exhibiting modernist art. "At $1 'per' there would be millions in it for some one."[3]

One factor was the success, in October 1913, of John Quinn's campaign to remove the 15 percent tariff that had been levied on works of art less than twenty years old. Contemporary art could now profitably be imported for sale instead of being brought in under bond for exhibition and then returned to Europe. Stieglitz had refused to sign Quinn's petition, for he felt that American artists did, in fact, need to be protected. He argued, not quite convincingly, that both the cost of living and the price of materials were higher in New York than in Paris. More to the point, he was becoming increasingly committed to "the art which grew in the soil of the United States."[4]

After the Armory Show and the change in the tariff regulations, several galleries were established in New York for the explicit purpose of exhibiting and selling modern art, while some hitherto conservative dealers began to mount occasional shows of modernism. The new gallery with which Stieglitz had the closest connection was that opened by Charles Daniel, on the tenth floor of the building at 2 West Forty-seventh Street, in mid-December 1913.

Charlie Daniel, who had for many years been the proprietor of a saloon and hotel on Ninth Avenue, was a rather unlikely art dealer. A scrawny man whose parents, like Stieglitz's, had been born in Germany, Daniel could be rather abrasive, but he was nevertheless a good-hearted and decent fellow with a genuine feeling for art. He had educated his eye by making the rounds of the moderately progressive galleries in the company of young artists he had befriended. In 1908 he had made his first serious purchase, a landscape in oil by Ernest Lawson, for which he paid $22. Two years later he made his first visit to 291, to see the second Matisse exhibition. But it was Marin to whose work he responded. He bought two watercolors and soon returned to buy more. At 291 and elsewhere Daniel acquired paintings by Hartley, Walkowitz, Weber, Maurer, and Samuel Halpert.

In 1913, as Stieglitz put it, Daniel's "passion for pictures moved him to retire in order to become a collector-dealer."[5] During his first year he showed the work of several members of the Eight (Lawson, Glackens, Prendergast), peripheral artists of the Stieglitz circle (Demuth, Halpert, and Maurer), and independents such as Stuart Davis, Preston Dickinson, and William Zorach.

It wasn't until December 1915 that Ferdinand Howald, a quiet, Swiss-born bachelor from Columbus, Ohio, who had made a fortune as the owner of West Virginia coal mines, began buying extensively from Daniel's gallery. Howald would eventually own twenty-eight Marins, an equal number of Demuths, and sixteen Hartleys, as well as hundreds of works by other artists, most of them American and most represented by Daniel. Unwilling to get down on his knees to ask for the privilege of being allowed to buy the works he loved, Howald seems never to have bought a single painting at 291.

Stieglitz, who somewhat contemptuously accused Daniel of having a second-class eye and a commercial spirit, seems to have viewed the new gallery not as competition but as a welcome annex that could benefit his own artists. Two Ninety-one would show their newest work, Daniel their older or less successful productions. He would also provide a useful outlet for artists whom Stieglitz liked personally but was not willing to show. One such was Man Ray, whose exhibition at the Daniel Gallery in October 1915 was his first solo. The Chicago lawyer Arthur J. Eddy, author of *Cubists and Post-Impressionism* (1914), bought six paintings by Ray for $2,000.

Another artist Stieglitz sent to Daniel was Charles Demuth, who had struck up a friendship with Hartley in Paris. Soon after Demuth returned home to Lancaster, Pennsylvania, in the spring of 1914, he went up to New York to introduce himself at 291. Alas, until the end of the decade Stieglitz would tend to regard Demuth's landscapes as too close to Marin's; his watercolors of flowers as too delicate; his illustrations for works by Zola, Henry James, and others as too literal; and his depictions of circus and vaudeville acts and bohemian New York nightspots as too frivolous. Fortunately, Daniel admired his work and, in the fall of 1914, gave him the first of his annual one-man shows.

Demuth — whose family had been prosperous tobacconists for generations and who fancied himself a sophisticated, elegant, and charming man about town — was certainly stung by Stieglitz's rejection. Much of the tension between them is evident in a 1915 portrait made at 291; we see a spoiled dandy who, overcompensating for his insecurities, has assumed an unconvincing expression of defiance and suspicion.

* * *

Among the exhibitions of progressive art in New York in February 1914 was one of paintings and drawings by fourteen contemporary Americans, organized by Arthur Davies and Walt Kuhn for the relocated Montross, at 550 Fifth Avenue. Although the AAPS would never sponsor another exhibition, the leaders of the association (Davies and Kuhn, together with their friends John Quinn and Walter Pach) formed a powerful clique that dominated many of the activities of the galleries that began to feature modernism after the Armory Show. Montross — whose schedule had traditionally included American painters such as Childe Hassam, George Bellows, and the Ten, in addition to old Chinese paintings and ceramics — felt that the Armory Show had created a market in New York and that it would be simply foolish not to take advantage of the situation with a few shows each season devoted to modernism. In January and February of 1915, with the help of Pach as emissary and selector, he would mount a spectacular Matisse show: fourteen paintings, eleven sculptures, and a large selection of drawings and prints. The following year, again with Pach's assistance, Montross exhibited a large group of Cézanne oils and watercolors. Quinn became his most valued customer.

Two other galleries entered the lists of contemporary art in the spring of 1914. The back-from-Paris painter Robert J. Coady, whom Kreymborg called a "pugnacious, red-headed Irishman," opened the Washington Square Gallery at 47 Washington Square South.[6] With the help of his partner, Michael Brenner, an American sculptor living in Paris, Coady was able to show works by Cézanne, Picasso, Juan Gris, and other European modernists.

Early in 1914 an interior decorator named Harriet Bryant decided to upgrade the exhibitions at her firm's showcase, the Carroll Galleries, at 9 East Forty-fourth Street, just around the corner from Delmonico's Fifth Avenue restaurant. Taking advantage of the European art market's collapse, Bryant dispatched Pach to the Continent to buy everything he could get his hands on. In December, when she mounted her first show of his findings — including work by Jacques Villon, André Derain, Raoul Dufy, and Georges Rouault, as well as a group of Picassos consigned by Vollard — the fashionable began to drop by the gallery after lunch to see the latest Paris canvases. Over the course of the next year, Quinn would acquire most of Bryant's inventory.

Stieglitz would certainly have preferred to close 291 rather than be forced to compete with opportunists. In January 1915 one journalist reported that he had threatened "to devote his gallery to exhibitions of academic work in order to escape being obvious." He quoted Stieglitz as having said, "If the worst comes to the worst, and the members of the National Academy of Design can find no other place to exhibit their pictures, I will cheerfully give them the use of No. 291. An exhibition of work by Mr. Edwin Blashfield and Mr. Will Low might help a lot to start the pendulum swinging back the other way."[7] A friend recalled of this period, "A new academy was commencing to form under [Cézanne's] sign; and Stieglitz, who had first shown the essential Cézanne, wished he could place his foot squarely through every one of the beatified canvases of the beatified painter."[8]

Stieglitz always wanted to stand alone. And so it was that his thoughts turned at this time back to photography. The January 1914 issue of *Camera Work*, published in June of that year, announced four photographic exhibitions to be held at 291 during the next season. The first, of British work, was to include David Octavius Hill, Julia Margaret Cameron, and J. Craig Annan, eight of whose images from a trip to Spain in 1913 were reproduced in that issue. Stieglitz wrote of them, "Annan has never done any finer work. His work is always a delight. . . . As an artist he continues to grow."[9] The Britons were to be followed by the Frenchmen Robert Demachy, Charles Puyo, and René Le Bègue, and then by the Austrians Heinrich Kuehn, Hugo Henneberg, and Hans Watzek. An exhibition of American work was to include Annie Brigman, Frank Eugene (whose photographs of the male nude were intercepted by the U.S. Post Office in April), Keiley, Steichen, and Stieglitz.[10]

But Marius de Zayas felt that such a schedule would be a step backward. He convinced Stieglitz that if 291 had only one season left, it should be climactic. Agnes Meyer agreed. De Zayas decided to spend the summer of 1914 in Europe gathering work for a series of exhibitions that would explore the ways in which modern art had been affected by developments in the physical and social sciences. In mid-May he arrived in Paris, where he stayed with the Picabias. Francis, involved with all the latest undertakings, introduced de Zayas to Apollinaire, editor of *Les soirées de Paris*, which increasingly resembled *Camera Work*. A fantastic cross section of Parisian artists and writers showed up at the office of *Les soirées* every day, just as their New York counterparts frequented 291.

Agnes Meyer joined de Zayas in Paris in June. She spent much of her time studying Chinese art in the Louvre and in private collections, but she was excited about meeting Brancusi, whose works she would continue to collect. Over the course of the next two years he would execute in wood a study for a "portrait" of her. Fortuitously, she sailed for New York on July

31, two days before the first declarations of war. When Steichen cabled well-connected Eugene Meyer for his advice, the financier replied, "Suggest immediate orderly retreat." The Steichens soon set out for New York, leaving Voulangis only two days before the arrival of the first patrol of German troops.

After commuting again to Elberon during June and July, Stieglitz was in New York when the war broke out in Europe. Although a pacifist, he speculated at first that a brief conflict might be cathartic, purging Europe of the poisonous materialistic rivalry that had prevailed so long. Because of his deep ties with Germany, he apportioned blame equally. "Colleagues tried to prove to me that Beethoven was no German," he later reminisced, "that all the cruelty in the world came from Germany and that every Frenchman and Englishman was a saint. I was truly sick at heart."[11] He held the United States ultimately responsible for the war because the Americans had "inaugurated an epoch of conspicuous waste."[12]

At 291, Emil Zoler and Abraham Walkowitz naturally took the socialist line that the workers of the world owed their allegiance not to any nation but rather to their class — the international proletariat. Moreover, they should not fight and die to defend the bourgeois nationalism, capitalism, and imperialism that were enslaving them. This position was propounded forcefully in the articles and cartoons in *The Masses*; in its September issue John Reed called the war "a clash of Traders" and wrote, "We must not believe this editorial buncombe about Liberalism going forth to Holy War against Tyranny. This is not Our War."[13] Stieglitz agreed that America should under no circumstances allow itself to be dragged into the fray.

After a month at Lake George with Kitty, while Emmy explored New England with a female friend, Alfred returned to New York in mid-September to greet the newly arrived Steichens, on their way to the Meyers' farm in Mount Kisco, New York. He immediately began to prepare for the early November opening of 291. It turned out that de Zayas had been unable to secure many of the works he wanted for his projected series. But at a time when many people were abandoning their possessions as they fled Europe (Steichen, for instance, had left behind all of his heavy glass-plate negatives, which would be destroyed by humidity and mildew), de Zayas had managed to bring to New York material for three splendid exhibitions.

The first of these was given the unfortunate title "Statuary in Wood by African Savages: The Root of Modern Art." In Paris, through Apollinaire, de Zayas had met Paul Guillaume, a collector and dealer who had connections that enabled him to import very fine work from West Africa. After the outbreak of war, Guillaume was only too glad to lend de Zayas all the sculptures he could put into a trunk. De Zayas had been interested in African art ever since meeting Picasso, and as early as April 1911 he had proposed an exhibition at 291 devoted to it. As a caricaturist, he felt an affinity with the Africans, who, he posited, represented their emotional responses by exaggerating certain aspects of the human face and body. In his preface for the exhibition catalog he wrote that African sculpture was "created by a mentality full of fear," by people "who see the outer world only under its most intensely expressive aspect and not under its natural one." It would be far too painful to quote the passage in its entirety, for it is full of patronizing racist nonsense.[14]

Stieglitz was fascinated by the relationship between African sculpture and the Brancusis he had exhibited in the spring. The carvings would also provide a wonderful context for Picasso and Braque, whose works he was planning to hang next. There had been a small African show at Coady's Washington Square Gallery in the spring of 1914, but Stieglitz touted the 291 exhibition as the first anywhere to present African sculpture "as a medium of art expression" rather than as the object of ethnographic interest.[15] He wrote to Arthur Dove, "It is possibly the most important show we have ever had."[16] The reactions of the critics ranged from that of J. Edgar Chamberlin, who noted that the exhibition proved the people who made the sculptures "are real artists, expressing a definite idea with great skill," to that of Forbes Watson, which was despicably dismissive.[17]

When Steichen appeared at 291 after the exhibition had been open for a few days, he was appalled to see the burlap walls covered with dust, the atmosphere stale and stagnant. Having persuaded Stieglitz to let him reinstall the exhibition, Steichen bought several reams of yellow, orange, and black paper, which he pinned to the walls to create rhythmic patterns, a geometric abstraction of "crude and violent color," as *Camera Work* described it.

De Zayas had been distressed to learn that Picasso's dealer, Daniel-Henry Kahnweiler, had agreed to make Coady the artist's exclusive representative in New York. Picabia then volunteered to lend his own extensive collection of Picasso's work, ranging from the large Blue period etching *The Frugal Repast* (which Stieglitz would buy) to an early Synthetic Cubist still life in which the artist pasted newspaper over a charcoal drawing. Stieglitz would also acquire that collage.

Since there weren't enough Picassos to make an exhibition, Picabia suggested adding Braque, who had been collaborating closely with the Spaniard. Although Braque had made the very first *papier collé*, he was completely overshadowed by Picasso in the public mind. Stieglitz and Steichen agreed that it would be highly instructive to see their often-indistinguishable work exhibited together, especially with the addition of a few pieces of African sculpture and a beautiful wasp's nest that Zoler had found.

The Picasso-Braque show was followed by An Exhibition of Recent Paintings — Never Before Exhibited Anywhere — by Francis Picabia (January 12–26, 1915). De Zayas had written Stieglitz from Paris that "it would make quite an impression" to hang three large abstract paintings at 291, where they would cover "almost the entire three walls from the floor to the ceiling."[18] A New York critic speculated that one of the canvases appeared to be "a picture of the wreckage resulting from the collision of an automobile, an aeroplane and a submarine."[19] The promised exhibition of paintings by Le Douanier Rousseau did not materialize. Nor did a show of de Zayas's recent caricatures or a second group of "Younger American Painters."

Stieglitz received sixty-eight replies to his question, "What Is '291'?" and he printed them all, unedited, in the issue of *Camera Work* published in January 1915.[20] The result is a revealing inventory of his friends. The majority were painters, by no means all of whom had exhibited at 291. Besides Steichen and Haviland, the only photographers of note were the Californians Annie Brigman and her friend Francis Bruguière.

Other contributors included Belle Greene (J. P. Morgan's librarian), Stieglitz's sister Selma, the "illustrator and writer" Djuna Barnes, and the principal backers of 291, including both Agnes and Eugene Meyer. The latter's bromide sums up the tenor of the entire issue:

> An oasis of real freedom —
> A sturdy Islet of enduring independence in the besetting seas of
>   Commercialism and Convention —
> A rest — when wearied
> A stimulant — when dulled
> A Relief —
> A Negation of Preconceptions
> A Forum for Wisdom and for Folly
> A Safety valve for repressed ideas —
> An Eye Opener

A Test —
A Solvent
A Victim and an Avenger.[21]

Among the miscellany of friendly dealers and critics was one implacable skeptic, Arthur Hoeber, who wrote that what he had witnessed at 291 was "a tearing down of the old faith . . . without substituting anything in its place." He regretted that Stieglitz had put aside his camera in order to exhibit modern art, "for in photography you were supreme."

The most forceful reply was from Steichen, who wanted the Photo-Secession to be replaced by a new organization that would include not only visual artists but also writers, poets, musicians, and people in the theater. He believed it necessary to "organize art like armies are organized to meet the demands we make upon it. — Poetry, painting, music — the theatre can no longer stand aloof as exquisite expressions of an individual. — We must have something bigger."[22] He envisioned that as the center of such an organization, 291 could become "a civilizing force in the world."[23]

Praising Stieglitz as the benevolent "despot" who had maintained the gallery's "eager receptivity to the unforeseen," Steichen wrote that his friend had "shown his greatest '291' potentiality" by "transforming . . . or . . . eliminating" the reactionaries who had opposed successive "mutative movements." Steichen did not find it surprising that after the Armory Show, Stieglitz spent a year "marking time." But he could not understand why 291 wasn't roused from its lethargy by the outbreak of the war.

It had failed for once, and on this, an occasion of the greatest necessity, to realize its relationship to the great unforeseen. It failed, as every human institution failed, demoralized by the immensity of the event and blinded by the immediate discussion of it, instead of instantly grasping the significance of the great responsibility that was suddenly ours. It failed to grasp the necessity of making of itself a vast force instead of a local one.[24]

CHAPTER FORTY·SEVEN

HAVING EXHAUSTED THE material that de Zayas brought back from Paris, Stieglitz turned to artists closer to home for the rest of the season. The first of the domestic shows (opening on January 27, 1915) was an exhibition of work by Agnes Meyer's friends Marion H. Beckett and Katharine Nash Rhoades, who, together with Meyer, were known around 291 as the Three Graces. In the Armory Show, Beckett had exhibited two portraits — one of Steichen, with whom she had a brief romance — and Rhoades had shown a French landscape. Their work at 291 was in the same genres. It was probably Paul Haviland who wrote that the public was surprised by the sudden appearance of "paintings of a naturalistic character" in the gallery. "They thought that the sanctuary of the mystery of abstract art was profanated by the work of Miss Beckett and Miss Rhoades."[1] The official 291 line was that the show was intended to stimulate the development of these two artists by exposing them to the public's criticism. But there was more to it than that.

Alfred, married to Emmy for twenty-one years, doubted that he could ever escape. He felt trapped in a situation of living death, as he revealed in the first section of a prose poem entitled "One Hour's Sleep — Three Dreams" that he published in March 1915.[2] These "dreams" clearly were consciously devised parables based on his involvements with three women.

In the first he wrote, "I was to be buried. The whole family stood about. Also hundreds of friends. . . . A door opened and a woman came in. As the woman came in I stood up; my eyes opened." The woman was certainly Katharine Rhoades, an aristocratic and statuesque thirty-year-old who was nearly six feet tall, magnificent, and coolly luminous. She generally radiated the aloof self-confidence of a beautiful and talented young woman of independent means, though in Stieglitz's 1915 portrait of her she looks wistfully at the photographer, while she touches a doorjamb erotically, as if she were giving his body a gentle caress.

Stieglitz was in love with her, but he was also intimidated by her. She was so young, so tall, and so strong that beside her he felt old, small, and weak. Many years later he told photographic historian Nancy Newhall that "if he had been a real man, which, he said, he wasn't — if he had been six feet tall, all sinew and strength, he would have carried Rhoades off to some mountain top, built them a little house, given her children, and let her paint."[3] He didn't say anything about letting her write poetry. Although he published quite a bit of her writing during 1915, he must have realized later that it was dreadful.

In Stieglitz's dream-poem the woman fixed her gaze upon him and asked, three times, "Friend, are you really dead?" Unable to answer her, he lay down again and waited to be buried. He feared that he had missed his last chance for a new life. His sense of loss was so intense that he almost wished he were dead. But soon he vowed that if given another opportunity, he would not falter again. He was finally ready to meet Georgia O'Keeffe.

Rhoades may have been as distraught as Stieglitz was. She burned all her work and, beginning in the fall of 1915, devoted herself to assisting the founder of the Smithsonian Institution's Freer Gallery of Art, to whom Agnes Meyer had introduced her. Rhoades seems to have had one last fling, with Steichen; in 1919 she would be named in his widely publicized divorce battle. The unmarried Rhoades spent the last years of her life engaged in religious pursuits.

Stieglitz's second dream, which has already been described, possibly referred to the mysterious Miss S. R., whom he had evidently met in Europe during the summer of 1904. But the subject of the third dream cannot be even tentatively identified. The woman recounted to Stieglitz the story of her desperate, unfulfillable love for another man. As she spoke, she became deranged and began to tear at her clothes and at Stieglitz's. Then she kissed him passionately and cried: "Why are you not HE? . . . What makes me kiss you —- it is He I want, not you." Spellbound, Stieglitz didn't dare to move. Suddenly the woman screeched: "Tell me you are He — tell me —

you are He. And if you are not He I will kill you. For I kissed you." At that point she took a knife from the folds of her dress and stabbed him in the heart. When she turned around, she saw written on the white wall in blood-red letters, "He killed himself. He understood the kisses." She screamed, and Stieglitz awoke.

During January 1915, Marius de Zayas, Agnes Meyer, and Haviland resolved to get 291 out of its rut and rescue the art world from the effects of the war. Many people had regarded the "What Is '291'?" issue of *Camera Work* as an obituary for both the gallery and the magazine. The April 1914 issue (published in October) had promised that upcoming issues would include "a Number devoted to photography, by younger and older workers who have not, as yet, appeared in the pages of *Camera Work*," and "a Number devoted to Children's Work, in picture and in words."[4] But those promises were never kept, and the next issue would not appear until the fall of 1916.

De Zayas, Haviland, and Meyer wanted to start a folio-size monthly to be called *291*, which would feature modern art, caricatures, and satire of the art world. (The magazine turned out to be more serious than Stieglitz had expected, partly because Agnes Meyer's husband "thought that too much satire, too much truth telling about how the game of art and its business were played, should not appear in *291*."[5]) The impact of the contents and design would, the planners felt, make up for the paucity of pages: usually between four and six per issue. Having decided that it would be a good project for "the youngsters," Stieglitz gave his blessing and agreed to join Haviland and Meyer in underwriting it.

Not at all to Stieglitz's surprise, they soon found that costs greatly exceeded both their estimates and their revenues. Wanting to live up to the example set by *Camera Work*, they printed the magazine on heavy white paper and decided to publish a deluxe edition, limited to one hundred copies, on Japanese vellum. A regular subscription cost one dollar a year, the deluxe edition five times that amount. Little attempt was made to attract subscribers, and the magazine would contain no advertisements, but about one hundred people took the regular edition and eight the deluxe, in addition to which sixty complimentary copies were sent to the modernist enclaves in Paris and Zurich. Some English texts were accompanied by French translations, though, perversely, some texts contributed from France were printed without an English translation. One might have begun to wonder whether the magazine was aimed primarily at an American or a European audience.

The contents of the first issue, dated March 1915, were of very uneven quality. On the cover was an amusing de Zayas caricature of Stieglitz as a Brancusi-like sculpture, but all straight lines and angles rather than curves. On the verso was a tediously self-righteous and overcapitalized article by Agnes Meyer that began, "The best one can say of American art criticism is that its CLEVERNESS OFTEN CONCEALS ITS LACK OF PENETRATION." Beneath a fine Picasso pen drawing on the third page was a section of press clippings and rather adolescent satirical pieces, including a dig at Max Weber's eclecticism. Page 4 was filled with a dialogue written by Paul Haviland. When "a professor" pompously informs 291, "You are about to enter your second period, in which you will arrive at the laws which govern the phenomena you have observed," 291 replies, "But laws are the very things I have been fighting against all my life." Such was the struggle between Stieglitz and his pretentious protégés.

At the top of the fifth page was a charming "idéogramme" by Apollinaire in which the words form pictures of a locomotive, a bird, and a cloud. Below were Stieglitz's three dreams. On the back cover was Steichen's drawing entitled "What Is Rotten in the State of Denmark," an insipid parody of the de Zayas on the front — and a rather ineffective statement of his disapproval of the whole business. Years later he would write, "The Dadaism of Picabia did not interest me. I felt it was not a time for mockery and discouragement."[6]

Having come to consider himself almost as much French as American, Steichen was passionately anti-German and strongly favored American intervention on behalf of the Allies. The tensions between the two photographers nearly reached the breaking point with the sinking of the Cunard liner *Lusitania* on May 7, 1915, in response to which Stieglitz infuriated Steichen by stating, "It served them right. They were warned in advance that the ship would be sunk."[7] Stieglitz feared that the British had deliberately allowed the sinking, which killed 128 Americans, in the hope that the United States would enter the war. Steichen was further outraged when the German ambassador to Washington, Count Johann Heinrich von Bernstorff, visited Oaklawn several times during the summers of 1915 and 1916 as the guest of Alfred's sister Selma. Alfred found him sympathetic and approved of his efforts to keep America out of the war.

Steichen was not the only one of Stieglitz's old friends who disliked the new magazine. Another was Charles Caffin, who, in the *New York American*, wrote of the first issue:

Uncouth in shape, its whole make-up is one of self-assertion and self-assured superiority, while it bristles with antagonism. Affecting a high plane of intellectualism, it is as devoid of mental nutriment as of human feeling. It is sterile. It proves how completely the old spirit of "291" is dead; and to many beside myself must bring the shock of a cruel disillusionment.[8]

The next day he wrote in a letter to Stieglitz, "The old spirit was mutual helpfulness. But during the past winter I have felt, rightly or wrongly, that a new spirit, one of bitterness, was creeping in. . . . The whole thing has saddened me so much, that I have not had the heart to come into lunch. . . . But from *you* I cannot separate myself for long."[9] At the other extreme was Georgia O'Keeffe, who would write to a friend regarding the first issue that she was "crazy about it."[10] Unfortunately, she did not specifically record her reaction to Stieglitz's morbidly erotic dreams.

Subsequent issues were somewhat less annoying and more adventurous. On the May cover was an extremely powerful Walkowitz ink drawing of a face. This wild image, which appears to have been produced in an almost insane frenzy, is fully the equal of the most frightening African masks. In marked contrast was the lyrical, calligraphic, and quite abstract Marin drawing of skyscrapers on the next cover, each copy of which the artist embellished, by hand, with a long, meandering squiggle of blue watercolor.

Earlier that spring Marin had had a show of forty-seven "Water Colors, Oils, Etchings, Drawings, Recent and Old" at 291. In the summer of 1914 he had visited Maine for the first time; along its jagged coast and on its ragged islands, around Casco and Penobscot bays, he found his spiritual home. When Stieglitz gave Marin a check for the $2,000 he had earned from his show, he told the painter that he hoped it would get him through the next twelve months. However, soon after Marin returned to Maine early in the summer of 1915, he used half of the sum to buy a small island in Casco Bay with which he had fallen in love. Stieglitz was aghast at the news, and all the more so when he learned that the island lacked potable water. But soon after Marin returned to New York that fall with a large batch of superb watercolors, Stieglitz sold several of them for more than the island had cost.

Indeed, many people were coming to agree with Henry McBride, who had pronounced in his review of Marin's 1915 exhibition, "Not to like Marin is as inconceivable as not to like Chopin."[11] Somewhat to his surprise, Stieglitz found himself representing an artist whose works sold readily and for considerable sums. This situation, too, Stieglitz was able to construe as a "demonstration" — one, as his friend Paul Rosenfeld was to put it, "conducted for the purpose of proving that an artist in America could remain completely obedient to the promptings of an imperious, uncompromising, revolutionary spirit, and yet maintain himself beneath the statue of Commerce and Industry."[12]

When Haviland and de Zayas proposed an issue of *291* devoted to photography, Stieglitz decided that since he had been deluged with requests for prints of *The Steerage*, he would commission an edition of large photogravures of it to be tipped in. The double number (dated September-October 1915) sold for two dollars, not included in the price of the regular subscription, but it consisted of nothing but the gravure and two texts, short but pretentious, by de Zayas and Haviland, printed both in English and French. Although Stieglitz assumed that many nonsubscribers would buy the issue, not a single one did.[13]

Such as it was, the photography issue of *291* marked Stieglitz's renewed commitment to his own photographic work. In June 1915 he wrote to a friend, "I am in the midst of experimenting along many lines. The first real chance I have had in years to do what I want to do in photography."[14] During that year he continued making portraits of his friends and began a series of sharply focused views of the surrounding buildings from the windows of Lawrence's room, chronicling the effects of the seasons, of construction, and of the constantly changing light throughout the day and into the electrically lighted evening. He wanted to spend an entire night at the gallery to "watch the lights gradually go out one by one — until the buildings stood up as vast silhouettes — & then the vast dawn — the sun rises behind those giants."[15] But he never quite got around to it.

For the rest of his life, Stieglitz's subjects would be limited almost entirely to portraits (in an extraordinarily broad sense of the term), views of New York from the windows of his galleries and apartments, highly expressive photographs of clouds, and studies of trees and grasses at Lake George. He considered all of this work to be interrelated, not only in its intense directness and honesty but also in its exploration of the essence of life and death, and its revelation of profound natural forces that transcend the terms "good" and "evil."

CHAPTER FORTY·EIGHT

FRANCIS PICABIA HAD been drafted into the French army in August 1914, but his father in-law, who had been a colonel in the cavalry, was able to get him a posting as the chauffeur of a cavalry general stationed first in Bordeaux, where the government was in exile, and then back in Paris. In the spring of 1915, however, Picabia was faced with the horrifying prospect of being demoted to the infantry as an ordinary soldier. Once again his family rescued him, this time with an assignment to buy sugar in Cuba for the army. Traveling via New York, the anarchistic and irresponsible young man impulsively decided, upon his arrival in June, that he was out of harm's way and would simply remain in the city. Excited about *291*, he joined in at once, contributing drawings and helping de Zayas with the editing.

Even more momentous was the arrival of Marcel Duchamp on June 15. The previous fall Walter Pach had found Duchamp, who was exempt from military service on account of a mild heart condition, depressed and lonely. The French were suspicious of any young man not in uniform, and his brothers and most of his friends were in the army. So Pach had suggested that Duchamp settle in New York until the end of the war.

Pach met him at the pier and took him straight to Walter and Louise Arensberg's duplex in the studio building at 33 West Sixty-seventh Street. Since the Arensbergs would spend the summer at their house in Connecticut, Duchamp would live in their apartment, which had seventeen-foot-high ceilings and huge windows, for three months. Even after he moved out in the fall, he would spend many evenings there, for the Arensbergs' living room became *the* salon of modern art.

In 1907 the wealthy, Harvard-educated Walter Conrad Arensberg had married the even wealthier Mary Louise Stevens and settled in Cambridge, Massachusetts. Fancying himself a poet and an intellectual, Walter immersed himself in a study of Dante and translated Mallarmé's *L'Après-midi d'un faune* into English. Ineluctably drawn to puzzles, mysteries, paradoxes, and ciphers, he searched Shakespeare's plays for cabalistic clues to prove that they had been written by Francis Bacon, read up on psychoanalysis, and was fascinated by the aesthetic and philosophical aspects of chess.

On a visit to New York in March 1913, Walter went to see the Armory Show on its last day and was overcome with excitement. A year later he and Louise moved to New York to join in the whirl of art and artists. They would assemble a great modernist collection, including the world's largest concentration of works by Duchamp, liberally seasoned with African and pre-Columbian pieces, all of it now in the Philadelphia Museum of Art. But the canvas that Walter most coveted — Duchamp's *Nude Descending a Staircase, No. 2* — eluded him until the late 1920s. As an anodyne, the artist made his friend a replica by embellishing with watercolor and pastel a full-size black-and-white photographic reproduction of the painting.

Eager and earnest Walter was something of a puppy dog, jumping around from one enthusiasm to another. A chain-smoker, with his tie loosened around his unbuttoned collar and a lock of hair falling onto his forehead, he looked like a young professor or a cub reporter, the sort of man who would revel in all-night bull sessions. And that's more or less what he had almost every night from early fall to late spring during the years 1915 to 1921. The Arensberg apartment became an informal and perpetual open house, with lavish spreads of food and drink. There were no preordained topics of discussion, as at Mabel Dodge's. Walter would play chess for hours with Duchamp and Alfred Kreymborg, who had competed professionally. On the piano, Louise would perform pieces ranging from transcriptions of opera arias to compositions by Satie. The impassioned discussions and arguments about art, poetry, and music would last until two or three o'clock in the morning, at which point Walter might invite the few who were left to sleep on the couches or in the extra bedrooms — so that he could wake them up a few hours later to pick up where they had left off.

Duchamp was clearly the main attraction, joined by his Section d'Or friends Picabia and Albert Gleizes. Man Ray and Charles Demuth both formed important friendships with Duchamp at the Arensberg salon. Many evenings Duchamp and Demuth would head off together to listen to jazz in Harlem or to carouse at the Golden Swan saloon, a Greenwich Village dive nicknamed the Hell Hole, where Eugene O'Neill held court.

Among the other habitués of the salon at various times were Pach, Charles Sheeler, Morton Schamberg, Joseph Stella, Marsden Hartley, and Marius de Zayas. Doing her best to steal the show was Baroness Elsa von Freytag-Loringhoven, who might appear with half her head shaved or wearing a coal scuttle on her head. She once told William Carlos Williams, another regular, that only if he had the good sense to contract syphilis from her could he ever become a great poet.

Since Walter Arensberg was the patron of the poetry magazine *Others*, edited by Kreymborg, the salon drew many poets: Wallace Stevens (who had been Walter's classmate at Harvard), Marianne Moore, Amy Lowell, Arthur Cravan, Mina Loy, and Williams. The last of these had attended the medical school of the University of Pennsylvania and, in his student boardinghouse, had met Demuth, attending the Pennsylvania Academy of the Fine Arts. Since Williams was then trying to choose between poetry and painting, they became friends. During the teens, Williams, a general practitioner in Rutherford, New Jersey, would take the ferry to New York whenever he could steal an afternoon from his busy practice to visit Stieglitz, with whom he had many friends and acquaintances in common.

Miscellaneous members of the Arensberg circle ranged from Isadora Duncan to the three Stettheimer sisters and from Carl Van Vechten to Max Eastman. The composer Edgard Varèse, who was very friendly with Stieglitz, became an intimate, as did poet Louise Norton, who divorced her husband (her co-editor of the Arensberg-subsidized poetry magazine *Rogue*) to marry Varèse. Although Stieglitz was friendly with most of the Arensberg artists and poets, his visits were infrequent, since the salon was too rambunctious for his liking.

In staid Zurich, on February 5, 1916, would take place the grand opening of the assertively bizarre Cabaret Voltaire, where the Dada movement would soon be named. Its spirit had, however, been abroad *avant la lettre*: as early as 1913 Stieglitz had published in *Camera Work* articles and poems, by Hartmann, de Casseres, and others, imbued with a proto-Dadaistic spirit, and he had pioneered in exhibiting children's art and African sculpture, both of which would appeal greatly to the European Dadaists. Furthermore, the magazine *291* is universally hailed as one of the most important harbingers of the movement.

Dada was, in effect, a parlor game played during World War I by non-combatants in comfortable parlors in neutral countries. Thoroughly disgusted by the bourgeois rationalism and the traditional values that in their view had caused the war, the Dadaists embraced everything that seemed directly opposed to the conventional notions of art — all that was grotesque, primitive, absurd, insane, random, ridiculous, or shocking. They adored the "gratuitous act," which is to say, any spontaneous and pointless gesture. They attacked logic, sought startling juxtapositions, and proclaimed the beauty of machines. Jean Arp, one of the movement's leaders, wrote that Dada "stood for a wholly eclectic freedom to experiment; it enshrined play as the highest human activity, and its main tool was chance." Much of this aesthetic was obviously related to Stieglitz's own, but Dadaism was ultimately too self-indulgent for his taste. Chez Arensberg, not 291, would become the New York home of Dada.

Stieglitz reacted against the post–Armory Show commercialization of the New York art world by becoming even more stubbornly anticommercial than ever. In response to the horrors of the war, and to the hypocrisy, the censorship, and the prejudices that prevailed, he insisted with increasing vehemence that 291 be an oasis of reason, honest self-expression, integrity, decency, and purity. He felt that he was responsible — sometimes, with characteristic egotism, that he alone was responsible — for keeping the flame alive during a period of madness.

De Zayas, Haviland, and Meyer, joined by Picabia after his arrival, were frustrated and exasperated by Stieglitz's curious mixture of idealism, cynicism, amateurism, pessimism, and high-handedness. They believed that he was doing a great disservice to his artists by not deigning to make a more aggressive effort to sell their work. Many people were so intimidated by Stieglitz, fearing he would snub or otherwise embarrass them, that they didn't dare ask the price of anything on exhibition at 291. Stieglitz's educational demonstrations and "scientific" experiments were all very well, his friends complained, but the times were especially hard for artists, and there was a need for enlightened commercialism. After all, they argued, other New York dealers were reaping considerable profits from the market that Stieglitz had done so much to open up. Why shouldn't 291 and its artists get a share — indeed, the largest share — of that money?

Picabia had arrived bearing tales of how desperately European artists needed an outlet for their work. Things were so bad that Parisian dealers would find it worth the risk to send their inventories across the Atlantic to be sold at bargain prices. If 291 could not be transformed, he suggested, the obvious solution was for de Zayas and Haviland to open a second gallery as its commercial extension, using Stieglitz's name and that of 291 in their advertising.

De Zayas soon arranged a meeting to seek the photographer's blessing for such an enterprise. Stieglitz, who remained in New York for the month of July 1915 while Emmy again traveled in New England with a friend and Kitty went to summer camp, objected that there were too many commercial galleries in New York already — and they weren't doing very well. In any case, he was tired and didn't want to talk, or even think about the venture until August, when de Zayas and Picabia could visit him at Lake George. Perhaps he felt that these two consummate urbanites would be at a psychological disadvantage in a rural setting.

De Zayas and Picabia seem to have decided upon the odd course of embarrassing Stieglitz into either action of his own or acceptance of action on their part. In the July-August issue of 291 appeared a piece that was both an appreciation and a criticism of Stieglitz by de Zayas, who wrote that the photographer had "fought to change *good taste* into *common sense*" and to bring out "the individualistic expression of the spirit of the community." However,

> in pursuing his object, he employed the shield of psychology and metaphysics. He has failed. . . . America has not the slightest conception of the value of the work accomplished by Stieglitz. Success, and success on a large scale, is the only thing that can make an impression on American mentality. Any effort, any tendency, which does not possess the radiation of advertising remains practically ignored.

In contrast, wrote de Zayas, Picabia "does not protect himself with any shield. He has married America like a man who is not afraid of consequences. He has obtained results."

The cover of that issue featured Picabia's mechanomorphic portrait of Stieglitz, printed in black and red. It is obviously based very closely — form for form, and almost line for line — on a mirror image of the de Zayas caricature that had appeared on the cover of the first issue. Picabia has taken de Zayas's drawing, and like the ancients fleshing out the constellations into human and animal forms, he has elaborated it into a carefully rendered drawing of a broken camera that lies on its back, its detached bellows drooping like an impotent penis, unable to penetrate the vaginal lens opening, beyond which hovers, printed in German Gothic type, the word "IDEAL." Added to the camera are the automotive accessories of an engaged parking brake and a gearshift positioned in neutral, together symbolizing

Stieglitz's inertia. To the left of the drawing, above the bold numbers "291," is the inscription "Ici, c'est ici Stieglitz / foi et amour." Picabia acknowledges Stieglitz's qualities of faith and love but obviously implies that they have proven inadequate. It is probable that the artist intended *foi et amour* as a pun on the phrase *froid et au mur*, meaning cold or impotent and on the defensive.

In June, Paul Haviland received a letter from his father summoning him back to Limoges to manage the family business. A few days after a farewell party for him on July 4, he sailed for France, having committed himself to participation in the financial support of the new gallery. Unaware of that development, Stieglitz surely hoped that the departure of his friend, whom he would miss greatly and with whom he would long continue to correspond, would at least have the beneficial effect of hobbling the gallery plan.

When Picabia and de Zayas arrived at Lake George in mid-August, they found Stieglitz relaxed and in a good mood — partly because, away from Emmy's disapproval, he had allowed himself to fulfill his long-entertained fantasy of nocturnal swims, solitary and naked, in the lake. These highly sensuous returns to the womb exhilarated and rejuvenated him. After his frustrated romance with Katharine Rhoades, he was evidently feeling very aroused. That summer he made one of his most intensely erotic photographs — more so than all but a few of his later pictures of O'Keeffe — in which the wet black bathing suit of a woman named Ellen Morton is stretched tightly against her buttocks as she climbs up onto a dock piling to dive into the lake.[1]

During de Zayas and Picabia's stay at Lake George, Stieglitz received a forceful letter from Agnes Meyer, who wrote that she had "a firm conviction that something must be done to keep us all from getting into a deep gulf of inactivity and aimlessness, to keep 291 from dying an involuntary and nasty death." She stressed that the "only future left" for them was to open the new gallery for "the scattering of works of modern artists among the American public."[2] She conspired to withhold from Stieglitz the vital information that Eugene Meyer, Picabia, and Haviland had already agreed to contribute the $6,000 capital needed to launch the venture, with Meyer bearing most of the costs — as he could easily afford to do, having more than recovered from his crisis of 1912–13. (It has been estimated that by 1915 his investments in copper mines, oil, and the automobile industry were worth between $40 million and $60 million.) Moreover, they had already leased space on the eighth floor of 500 Fifth Avenue, directly across Forty-second Street from the public library. De Zayas was to be director of the Modern Gallery, which would open in October, with or without Stieglitz's blessing. Bowing to the pressure from two of his principal backers, Stieglitz gave in.

De Zayas prepared a pretentious announcement whose pompous language signified that the new gallery would blaze a middle course between Stieglitz's rejection of commercialism and "the chicanery of self-seeking" that characterized the other New York dealers who exhibited modern art. The gallery would perform "the legitimate function of commercial intervention — that of paying its own way while bringing the producers and consumers of art into a relation of mutual service" — and would "serve the public by affording it the opportunity of purchasing at unmanipulated prices whatever '291' considers worthy of exhibition."

This announcement was withheld, as Stieglitz later wrote, "because '291' felt it owed no explanations to anyone." In its stead a terse notice appeared in the October 1915 issue of 291, giving simply the name of the new gallery, its address, the nature of the work it would show, and the information that "the work of '291' will be continued at 291 Fifth Avenue in the same spirit and manner as heretofore. The Modern Gallery is but an additional expression of '291.'"[3]

De Zayas hoped to present a series of exhibitions tracing the development of modern art, beginning "with the work of Gauguin who first introduced into European contemporary art the exotic element and with the work of van Gogh who started talking about the psychological meaning of color."[4] He was unable to obtain any of Gauguin's paintings, but a selection of canvases by van Gogh constituted the second exhibition at the new gallery, which would show work by such precursors and early modernists as Constantin Guys, Daumier, Toulouse-Lautrec, Cézanne, Derain, and Maurice de Vlaminck. The suppressed announcement promised that the gallery would "also keep on hand a supply of photographic reproductions of the most representative modern paintings, drawings, and sculptures, in order to give the public an opportunity to see and study modern works of art that are privately owned in Europe and elsewhere."[5]

The announcement in 291 stated that the gallery was opening "FOR THE SALE OF PAINTINGS OF THE MOST ADVANCED CHARACTER OF THE MODERN ART MOVEMENT — NEGRO SCULPTURES — PRE-CONQUEST MEXICAN ART — PHOTOGRAPHY." Of the twenty-nine exhibitions mounted during the gallery's existence, seven were wholly or partially devoted to African sculpture, but only one show included "Pre-Conquest Mexican Art," appropriately paired with paintings by Diego Rivera. Although the opening show included photographs by Stieglitz, and another was devoted to paintings and photographs by Charles Sheeler, a purely photographic exhibition of work by Paul Strand, Morton Schamberg, and Sheeler was unique.

The Modern Gallery opened on October 7, 1915, with paintings and drawings by Picasso, Braque, Picabia, de Zayas, Dove, Marin, Walkowitz, and Frank Burty; sculpture by Adolf Wolff; photographs by Stieglitz; and African sculpture. Installing so much work was not easy; the gallery's wall space was quite limited, since the wall facing south onto Forty-second Street was almost entirely glass, admitting an excess of sunlight and traffic noise. Worse, de Zayas recalled, for a while "there were two bands in front of the Library playing the Marseillaise one right after the other from early morning until night."[6]

De Zayas, claiming that he did not have "the ability, intelligence, and facility of speech that Stieglitz lavished on the public," did not attempt to imitate his mentor's ceaseless monologue.[7] Those who therefore found the new gallery sterile could make a point of going to 500 Fifth Avenue on one of the three days a week on which Stieglitz minded the store during lunch hour.

Stieglitz opened the 1915–16 season at 291 with an exhibition of New Jersey landscapes by Oscar Bluemner, who had graduated from the Technische Hochschule in Berlin in 1892. Born in 1867 in Hanover, where his father and grandfather had both been architectural draftsmen, Oscar had followed them into that profession before immigrating to America at the age of twenty-five. Working in a Park Avenue office, he eventually began dropping by 291 at noon or after work. In 1911 he started to make Fauvist oil sketches and spent most of the following year in France and Germany, where he immersed himself in modern art. He soon resolved to give up architecture for painting, though he would be forced to continue doing some drafting in order to subsist.

One critic would write of Bluemner in 1916 that he "strives to heighten all color forms and lights to such a degree that, in the immensely restricted space of a picture, their intensity will overshadow the sensitive spectator even as he is awed by nature's effects." Bluemner said it would "take him twenty years to achieve his aim."[8]

It must have seemed revealing to Stieglitz that when he had Bluemner sit for a portrait early in the teens, the artist moved, throwing his face slightly out of focus. What we see is a harried man, a bit disheveled, with his derby tipped back on his head and a curved pipe hanging from the corner of his mouth. The idealistic dreamer looks lost, tired, and hopeless, as if he already senses that he will be destroyed by the public's neglect of his work.

On December 8 an exhibition of sculptures and drawings by Elie Nadelman opened at 291. Born in Warsaw in 1882 to a prosperous and cultivated family, Nadelman had lived in Paris from 1904 to 1914, during which period he became friendly with Leo and Gertrude Stein. At the outbreak of the war, his patroness — cosmetics queen Helena Rubinstein, who had bought all fifteen of the marble heads he exhibited in London in 1911 — helped him to immigrate to America with much of his work.

The pièce de résistance in his 291 exhibition was the large plaster *Man in the Open Air*, a body-stockinged, bow-tied, and bowler-hatted standing figure whose tapering legs are elegantly crossed like those of a blasé sophisticate. Nadelman's distinctive sculptural style was highly eclectic, inspired as it was by classical Greek sculpture and vase paintings, Rodin, Seurat, Cycladic figures, cave paintings, dolls, toys, folk art, and — though it was difficult to discern — Michelangelo. Nadelman's technical finesse was consummate, and his playfulness can be delightful, but much of his work is irritatingly precious. Henry McBride, who became one of the sculptor's most loyal advocates, gallantly wrote in the *New York Sun* that his work was "almost as artificial as modern life."[9] One less kindly disposed might say that Nadelman was Brancusi for the genteel. His exhibition at 291 gave him a cachet he did not deserve. The following year he had a large show at the fashionable gallery of Scott and Fowles, from which most of the seventy sculptures and drawings were sold, and he was swamped with commissions for portrait busts of socialites.

Although Stieglitz wrote on the day the Nadelman show opened that 291 had "not been so alive in quite some time," he was in a depressed and bitter mood. In that same letter he said that he did not "care a rap" whether anyone would come to see the show, and he confessed that during the past month he had "simply shrunk from all letter writing — even dictating letters." His relations with Meyer and de Zayas were worsening rapidly, since they disagreed vehemently about drumming up business for the Modern Gallery. "Cold facts stagger and drive away one's 'best friends,'" Stieglitz continued,

> but cold cash, I feel, would soon attract them back again. . . . I have no cash. I am having a sweet time in paying off all the debts I have incurred through 291 and all that includes. And before those debts are

paid off I will not feel free, and without feeling free I am no earthly good to myself or anybody else. . . . It is very quiet at 291 and I have lots of time . . . to get a clear perspective of what has been and what is — and a pretty fair idea of what I think is very likely to be.[10]

The explosion came in January 1916. It was probably then that Agnes Meyer wrote to de Zayas, "My advice to you is have nothing more to do with Stieglitz — never see him, never think of him."[11] Perhaps if Paul Haviland had still been in New York, he might have been able to work the diplomatic miracle needed to reconcile the opponents. As things were, however, Stieglitz acidly commented in the next issue of *Camera Work* that since "Mr. De Zayas, after experimenting for three months on the lines contemplated, found that practical business in New York and '291' were incompatible," it had been suggested that the two galleries sever their connection. "The suggestion automatically constituted a separation," wrote Stieglitz imperiously.[12] The Modern Gallery survived the upheaval, but the magazine *291* did not; the last issue appeared in February.

Angry as it was, the January crisis did not result in a break as absolute as that with Weber. Stieglitz was able to remain on speaking terms with de Zayas and Meyer, though they both grew increasingly distant from him. Meyer had met Charles Lang Freer in 1913, and because of their shared passion for Chinese art they soon became close friends. During 1915 the ailing fifty-nine-year-old Freer, who had made his fortune manufacturing railroad cars, moved from Detroit to a New York hotel to be near his doctor. From then on Meyer saw little of Stieglitz, since she spent as much time as she could with Freer, for whom Katharine Rhoades then began to work. The three of them would sample the treasures of Freer's extraordinary collection or eagerly unpack the almost daily shipments from abroad, never knowing what superb hand scroll or porcelain object might emerge from the beautifully crafted boxes concealed in layers of straw. Meyer's interest in Chinese art was so serious that, having learned classical Chinese, she went on to spend five years studying the influence of Confucianism, Taoism, and Buddhism on painters of the Tang and Sung dynasties. Her monograph on the Sung painter Li Lung-mien would be published in 1923.

When the United States entered the war, in the spring of 1917, Eugene Meyer took a government job as a dollar-a-year man, and the family moved to Washington. Meyer would remain in government service until May 1933, when he retired as governor of the Federal Reserve Board. The following month he bought the *Washington Post*, of which his married daughter Katharine Graham (who had been named for Rhoades) would become editor in chief.

By the fall of 1915, Picabia had worked himself into a manic-depressive state, aggravated by his heavy drinking and addiction to opium. Left to his own devices, he would have stayed in New York for the duration of the war, but finally his wife arrived to conduct him on his dangerously delayed mission to procure sugar in the Caribbean. After he carried out his orders in a perfunctory way, the Picabias still didn't dare return to France. They proceeded instead to Barcelona, where the growing community of artistic exiles and nomads already included Albert and Juliette Gleizes, Marie Laurencin and her German husband, and the outrageous poet and boxer Arthur Cravan. In January 1917 the Picabias and their friends in Barcelona would launch a publication entitled, rather obviously, *391*, which would have a complicated, transatlantic life lasting through nineteen issues, published erratically until 1924.

CHAPTER FORTY·NINE

DURING 1915, WHILE yet another of Stieglitz's circles was falling apart, he was gathering around him a new set of friends and protégés. One was the twenty-eight-year-old critic Willard Huntington Wright, who later became well known under the pseudonym S. S. Van Dine, with which he signed the Philo Vance mystery novels that he began to write in the mid-1920s. A conceited, arrogant, and nasty fellow, Wright cultivated a Mephistophelian Vandyke beard and was addicted to cocaine and opium. Very Germanophile in his tastes and mannerisms, and pro-German in his views about the war, he edited an anthology of Nietzsche's writings, provocatively published in 1915. Wright evidently decided that it would be worth his while to cultivate a friendship with Stieglitz, who seems to have been flattered by the attentions of this fascinating young man.

Raised in Santa Monica, California, where his father prospered as a hotel owner, Wright had landed a job as a book reviewer and reporter for the *Los Angeles Times* at the age of twenty-one and within a few months was made literary editor. Affecting a style of criticism marked by a tone of pained exasperation, he demolished all but Dreiser and the most advanced European authors. Audacity was his stock-in-trade.

In 1912, upon the recommendation of his friend and fellow Nietzschean H. L. Mencken, Wright became editor of the sophisticated New

York magazine *The Smart Set*, but he was fired at the end of 1913 for having published too many expensive and controversial pieces. Although he had treated the Armory Show as something of a joke, Wright proceeded to make his debut as an expert on modern art in the December 1913 issue of *The Forum*. He praised Cézanne, Renoir, and Matisse but attacked Picasso, Cubism, Futurism, and Orphism — and then concluded that a new movement called Synchromism (from the Greek, meaning with color) was clearly "destined to have the most far reaching effects of any art force since Cézanne." Nowhere in the article was the reader given a clue that the painter who went by the name of Stanton Macdonald-Wright, and who constituted half of the Synchromist movement, was Wright's younger brother.

In 1907 the homely, pasty-faced, droop-shouldered Macdonald-Wright (whom Georgia O'Keeffe would describe ten years later as looking "glum diseased — physically and mentally") had settled in Paris with his bride and her wealthy mother.[1] Four years later he met Morgan Russell, an American painter who was studying in Paris on a stipend from Gertrude Vanderbilt Whitney. Drawing upon the innovations of Robert and Sonia Delaunay, and perhaps of Kandinsky and František Kupka as well, these two ambitious upstarts developed their "Synchromist" style and claimed that their increasingly abstract paintings (which looked much like patchwork "crazy" quilts of intense colors) were the first and only ones capable of exalting the spirit as music could do.

Their best publicist was Willard Wright, who arranged a New York show of their paintings at the Carroll Galleries in March 1914, became *The Forum*'s monthly art critic beginning in July 1915, and expanded his first article into a book, *Modern Painting: Its Tendency and Meaning*, published in October 1915. In it he avowed that "Synchromism embraces every aesthetic aspiration from Delacroix to Cézanne and the Cubists." It was the ultimate style, he insisted, beyond which no further advances could be made.

One who dissented was Leo Stein. "I hold that Mr. Leo Stein is one of the ablest and most searching living critics of painting," wrote Wright, "despite the fact that he and I disagree wholeheartedly when we discuss the subject."[2] A frequent sight at 291, beginning in the fall of 1915, was the intellectual wrestling of these two men. Early in 1913 Leo had had an angry, sibling-rivalrous break with his sister and stopped attending the Saturday night soirees. Leo was frustrated because he had much to say but suffered from writer's block, while, in his view, Gertrude had nothing to say but was praised for her logorrhea, which he dismissed, along with the work of his erstwhile hero, Picasso, as "the most Godalmighty rubbish that is to be found."[3]

After a stay in Italy, Leo moved to New York in 1915 and went into psychoanalysis, until he decided that he was his own best analyst. Although he still wasn't able to compose his treatise on aesthetics, he did, between 1916 and 1919, write many perceptive reviews and articles about art for *The New Republic*. Thereafter he became more and more of a crank, and when, in 1927, he published his minor opus, *The ABC of Esthetics*, it was disappointing.

For Stieglitz, the climax of the fall of 1915 certainly came on the day when twenty-five-year-old Paul Strand brought him a portfolio of his recent platinum prints to critique. Strand, born in New York in 1890, was the only child of Jacob and Matilda Strand, second-generation Jewish immigrants from Bohemia who had changed their name from Stransky. Paul entered the Ethical Culture School, on Central Park West, in 1904. One of the outstanding teachers was Lewis W. Hine, who taught biology and geography when not working on his great photographic documentation of immigrants arriving at Ellis Island.

In 1905 Hine, the official photographer of school activities, converted a small top-floor classroom into a darkroom and began teaching an extracurricular course in basic photographic techniques. It wasn't until the fall of 1907 that Strand, who had been given a Kodak Brownie when he was twelve, enrolled, along with four or five others, in Hine's course. The highlight was a class visit to 291 to see the exhibition of members' work. Dazzled, Strand left the gallery with the conviction that photography was his vocation. In his junior year at Ethical Culture, he would take both an art-appreciation course taught by Charles Caffin and "Nature Study and Photography," taught by Hine, who resigned from the school at the end of that year to photograph, for the National Child Labor Committee, the terrible exploitation of children forced to work in factories and mines.

After Strand graduated from Ethical Culture, in 1909, his father and uncle gave him a job as a clerk and salesman in their firm, which imported enamelware from Germany. Paul joined the Camera Club of New York and spent his evenings and weekends diligently experimenting with photographic techniques and materials. He imitated the soft-focus Pictorialist styles of Clarence White and Gertrude Käsebier, both of whom he sought out for advice and criticism.

When the family's importing business was sold, he went into business for himself as a photographer, specializing in portraits, advertising shots, and hand-tinted platinum prints of college campuses and fraternity houses. Occasionally he would get up the courage to take a portfolio of his recent noncommercial images to show Stieglitz, who, Strand later recalled, "would look very attentively and kindly tell me where they succeeded and where they failed." Stieglitz's most persistent advice was to throw away his soft-focus lens.

On a cross-country sweep of college campuses in the spring of 1915, Strand finally began to heed Stieglitz, making relatively sharply focused views of sights including Niagara Falls and the Grand Canyon. After his return to New York, he took the summer off from his commercial work and wandered the streets with his camera. The resulting pictures captured a sinister sense of the city. In the most powerful of them, tiny people walk, as if crushed or terrorized, past the huge, dark, blank rectangular windows of the Morgan bank on Wall Street. In one long-distance shot of new apartment buildings, undeveloped land and rocks in the foreground seem like a gaping wound. A shot of pedestrians and traffic at Fifth Avenue and Forty-second Street could illustrate Stieglitz's comment that New York "is like some giant machine, soulless, and without a trace of heart."[4] These images may be called Dadaist in their bitterness and rage and in their depiction of random, chaotic movement.

Although some of the pictures obviously owed a debt to A. L. Coburn and Karl Struss, some were truly individual. In any case, the resemblance to the work of Coburn and Struss was fitting, for Strand would now assume the mantle they had once worn. And if some of Strand's pictures could almost be mistaken for Stieglitz's, that too was fitting, for in the close personal relationship that would quickly develop between the two men, the gifted but immature and insecure Strand would be the son who constantly tries to supplant his father by imitating and outdoing him.

When Strand took his recent work to 291 in the fall of 1915, Stieglitz told him, "This is your place, too. You belong here. Come in whenever you want." Then he summoned Steichen, who was in another room, and said to him, "Here is a man who has done something in photography that I have not seen done anywhere. I think we should show these things."[5] Stieglitz would do so in the spring of 1916.

Shining only somewhat less brightly than Strand was the thirty-two-year-old painter and photographer Charles Sheeler. Tall and lean, aloof and austere, Sheeler was quite unlike his best friend and fellow artist Morton Livingston Schamberg, who was two years older and given to wearing dandified clothes, marcelled hair, a carefully trimmed and waxed mustache, and a pince-nez. The former classmates at the Pennsylvania Academy of the Fine Arts shared not only a studio in Philadelphia but also an eighteenth-century fieldstone weekend and summer house in Bucks County, Pennsylvania. Furthermore, they shared a succession of styles, so that it is often possible to distinguish their works only by keeping in mind that Sheeler specialized in landscape and still life, Schamberg in portraits and figures. Casting about for personal styles, they would experiment with Fauvism and Synchromism and would react strongly to the examples of Picabia and Duchamp, especially after they became friendly with the latter at the Arensberg salon.

In 1912, by which time it had become apparent that they could not support themselves as painters, both Sheeler and Schamberg had taken up commercial photography to make a living. Consistent with their painterly interests, Schamberg established himself as a portraitist, specializing in children, and Sheeler began by documenting suburban houses for Philadelphia architects but soon turned to photographing works of art for New York dealers and collectors. Impressed by some prints that Sheeler sent him, Stieglitz struck up a correspondence and introduced the young artist to Marius de Zayas, who, in 1916, gave him several commissions to photograph works of art from the Modern Gallery's stock and from his own collection. By the next year, Sheeler was the gallery's staff photographer and would later act as its manager in de Zayas's absence.

When Sheeler paid his first visit to Stieglitz's apartment, the older man showed him "a large and comprehensive collection" of his photographs.[6] In reply to Sheeler's grateful letter and his assurances of friendship, Stieglitz replied, "I cannot tell you how glad I am that you feel as you do about me. . . . And as you know this feeling that you have could not exist if I did not have a similar feeling towards you. And I have always had it. From the first moment that you came into 291."[7]

In January 1915 the kindly teacher and anarchistic socialist Dr. John Weichsel, who had written for *Camera Work* during 1913 and 1914, led a group of Jewish painters and sculptors, most of them involved with the Ferrer Center, in forming the People's Art Guild. Born in Poland in 1870 to prosperous, middle-class Jewish parents, Weichsel had been extraordinarily precocious as a child — but can we really believe the claim that he was awarded his baccalaureate degree in engineering from the Zurich Polytechnik at the age of thirteen? After further studies in engineering, psychology, and aesthetics in Berlin, he immigrated to America in the early

1890s. While working days as a machinist's assistant, he spent his nights completing his doctorate in psychology at New York University. In 1900 he was appointed chairman of the department of mechanics and drafting at the Hebrew Technical Institute in New York, a position he would retain until shortly before his death, in 1946.

The People's Art Guild, which met on Friday evenings at Weichsel's apartment in the Bronx for a Sabbath supper and discussion of art and politics, had two principal purposes. One was to exhibit the work of living Jewish artists, both those dealing with Jewish themes and those who espoused modernism. The other was to enable the Jews living in the tenements of the Lower East Side to see, and even to buy, first-rate contemporary art. Weichsel wrote, "To make art more social and life more artistic — that is the leading idea of the People's Art Guild." He wanted to provide an alternative to the commercial galleries, which catered to the rich and would never show work with Jewish subjects. Indeed, Weichsel hoped that the guild would subvert the entire gallery system, that it would "eventually do away with the commercial gallery-owner as a force, and . . . place him in a position of a small broker."[8] Weichsel planned to establish stores where artists could buy their materials at cost and to open shops where painters could make their own frames or buy inexpensive ones.

Stieglitz was naturally in sympathy with all this. In reply to Weichsel's appeal to enlist his "eternal flame" in support of the guild, Stieglitz wrote in December 1915 that after the first of the year he might join "to prove, if proof is necessary, that I have courage besides sympathy."[9] Although he may not actually have joined the guild, in January 1916 Stieglitz did begin working closely with Weichsel as one of the three principal organizers of the so-called Forum Exhibition of Modern American Painters, which would open on March 13. It would be hung at the Anderson Galleries, on Fortieth Street at Madison Avenue, to which Mitchell Kennerley, the new president of that auction house specializing in books, had moved his publishing operations, which included *The Forum*. The exhibition's professed purpose was to offset all the attention and sales garnered by European modernists in New York galleries since the Armory Show. However, the truth was that many dealers were showing the American avant-garde. In February 1916 Montross had a show entitled Fifty Painters of Independent Spirit, which included some of the artists appearing in the Forum Exhibition, as did the Bourgeois Gallery's April exhibition, Paintings, Drawings and Sculpture Arranged and Selected by a Group of American Artists. In addition to 291 and the Modern Gallery, Charles Daniel also regularly exhibited many of the Forum artists.

The real purpose of the Forum Exhibition, masterminded by Willard Wright, was to promote his brother's work and that of Morgan Russell. Both artists were back in New York, and both were broke, as was Wright himself. The brothers had each inherited exactly one dollar from their father, and Stanton's separation from his wife had put an end to his allowance. As for Russell, eye strain and headaches caused by his "vivid color work" had forced him to return to a more subdued and semirepresentational style in the fall of 1915, leading Mrs. Whitney to withdraw her patronage.

Since the arrogance of the Synchromists and their flack at the time of their first New York show had won them more enemies than friends, they decided to try another strategy. This time they would invite a number of their contemporaries to participate, and they would recruit some of the most influential men in the art world to sponsor the show. Wright had been busy currying their favor. Stieglitz, of course, headed the list, followed by Weichsel and Robert Henri, whom Wright had praised as "one of the most sincere and intelligent products of American art."[10] Christian Brinton was the critic who had most favorably reviewed Wright's book *Modern Painting*. And W. H. de B. Nelson was the American editor of *The International Studio*. Only Wright, Stieglitz, and Weichsel actively worked on the show; the others merely lent the prestige of their names.

Most of the seventeen artists in the Forum Exhibition were championed by Stieglitz. Besides Marin, Dove, Hartley, Walkowitz, and Bluemner, he invited Andrew Dasburg, Alfred Maurer, Henry L. McFee (a Cubist who, in Wright's opinion, rivaled Picasso), George Of ("America's best landscapist," Wright pronounced), Man Ray, and Charles Sheeler. Weichsel nominated Ben Benn (influenced by Rousseau) and the husband-and-wife team of William and Marguerite Zorach. (According to Wright, they made "highly decorative pictures" in which were "woven legends and fairy tales.") In addition to the two Synchromists, Wright proposed the twenty-six-year-old Thomas Hart Benton, who had been a good friend of Macdonald-Wright in Paris and who was vacillating between Synchromism and the Realism championed by his new mentor, Weichsel. Benton began spending time at 291 in the hope (so Stieglitz later claimed) of being given a one-man show.

The many eminent painters who were not included might have been less resentful if Wright could have resisted boasting in print that "next to the Armory show" the Forum Exhibition was "the most complete and comprehensive exposition of the new school's work which this country has ever had."[11] Among the top contenders for inclusion would have been Rockwell Kent, Maurice Sterne, Joseph Stella, and such leading members of the People's Art Guild as Samuel Halpert and John Sloan. Of three other notable absentees — Arthur Davies, Charles Demuth, and Max Weber — Wright sneered in the February issue of *The Forum* that they belonged "to that type of secondary workmen who are, in large part, responsible for the current adverse opinions concerning modern art. Such painters are in greater number than the really significant ones; and from them arises the notion that modern painting is charlatanism."[12] So much for making friends.

Nor were the New York dealers spared. The catalog, an insufferable specimen of hypocritical holier-than-thouism, accused them all of being mercenary and of favoring Europeans. In his shameless article in the April issue of *The Forum*, Wright claimed that the exhibition was "non-commercial, its sole aim being to stimulate interest in our native art and thus benefit serious and deserving painters."[13] And yet he went on to tout the work of Maurer and the Zorachs as "suitable to beautify any interior."[14] Most of the 166 paintings and twenty-seven drawings in the show were for sale, at prices ranging from $10 to more than $1,000. In a catalog note to "the buying public," Wright went so far as to assert that the sagacity of the judges could assure any purchaser that his investment was a blue-chip one. Despite respectable attendance, few works were sold.

Between 1915 and 1918 the guild would mount some sixty exhibitions in settlement houses, though its most important show was that held in May 1917, in the building of the Yiddish daily newspaper *Forverts* (Forward) on East Broadway. Considerably more than half of the eighty-nine artists in the show were Jews, many of them little-known residents of the Lower East Side, but the exhibitors also included Henri, Sloan, and George Bellows, along with most of the participants in the Forum Exhibition. Stieglitz lent two of his own photographs to the exhibition, including a print of *The Steerage*.

Stieglitz hung Strand's photographs at 291 during the Forum Exhibition, just as he had pitted his own work against the Armory Show.[15] The gallery had displayed no photographs during the interim, as he would explain in the October 1916 issue of *Camera Work*, "primarily because '291' knew of no work outside of Paul Strand's which was worthy of '291.'" What thrilled Stieglitz about Strand's work was that it was "pure" and "direct," that it did "not rely upon tricks of process," and that it was "related to life in its fullest aspect."[16] It was photography, not imitative and formulaic "picture making," as Stieglitz — in repudiation of his old term — called work that did not add "to the idea of photography, nor to the idea of expression."[17]

Fine as they were, most of the photographs in Strand's March 1916 exhibition would pale beside the work that he would do that summer and fall (though he often claimed an earlier date for his breakthrough). On vacation in Twin Lakes, Connecticut, he began a series of compositional experiments to see whether he could reconcile the "absolute unqualified objectivity" of photography with the abstraction of modernist painting. Stieglitz had, of course, been making photographs for years that echoed cubistic structure, but Strand's new pictures were much more radical, for they attempted to minimize the recognizability of what was depicted, "without tricks of process or manipulation, through the use of straight photographic methods."[18]

For one of his first successes, Strand turned a round table onto its side so that the bold stripes of shadow cast by a porch railing continue from the floor to the tabletop. To make the resulting picture even more of a visual puzzle, he rotated the finished print 90 degrees for exhibition and publication. In another experiment, Strand nestled together four kitchen bowls, tilted at various angles, and illuminated them to create a complex pattern of highlights and shadows. Photographing them so close up that only part of each bowl is within the frame, he produced an image that is reminiscent of some of Dove's purest abstractions — and yet is still clearly a picture of four bowls. As if it were an exclamation point, this extraordinary image would be published as the last picture in the final issue of *Camera Work*.

In the fall of 1916, Strand turned to a very different challenge. Inspired by, and in competition with, Stieglitz's psychological portraits of artists as victims of New York's materialistic civilization, he set out to make a series of close-up portraits of some of the city's poorest and most hopeless residents as they went about their business, unaware that they were being photographed. To make that possible, Strand deceived his subjects by attaching a conspicuously shiny false lens to one side of his quarter-plate reflex camera and concealing the real lens with his sleeve. Later, he used a right-angle lens.

Although in the 1880s Stieglitz had found the idea of a concealed "detective" camera "distasteful" and had disdained "sneaking up on somebody and photographing them unawares," he found Strand's pictures extremely powerful and would publish six of them in *Camera Work*.[19] One unforgettable image depicts a formidable and, indeed, noble woman clothed in black and wearing a white sign on which is painted the word "BLIND." All are superior to Adolf de Meyer's studio portraits of London street characters, which had been reproduced in *Camera Work*, and they certainly equal not only Stieglitz's portraits but also Julia Margaret Cameron's and even Hill and Adamson's, which, wrote Strand, had "never been surpassed."[20]

For *Camera Work*, Stieglitz had Strand's gravures printed directly onto rag paper, instead of the usual Japan tissue, to emphasize "the spirit of their brutal directness." In the accompanying text he wrote, "The eleven photographs in this number represent the real Strand. The man who has actually done something from within. The photographer who has added something to what has gone before. . . . Devoid of all flim-flam; devoid of trickery and of any 'ism;' . . . These photographs are the direct expression of today."[21]

PART VI

GEORGIA O'KEEFFE

CHAPTER FIFTY

IT WAS AFTER FIVE o'clock on the afternoon of Stieglitz's fifty-second birthday — New Year's Day, 1916 — when a young woman named Anita Pollitzer appeared at 291, where the Nadelman show was still on. She was carrying under her arm a cardboard mailing tube filled with about ten large charcoal drawings by her twenty-eight-year-old friend Georgia O'Keeffe, who was teaching art at Columbia College, just outside Columbia, South Carolina.

Pollitzer had been "astounded and awfully happy" when she opened the package of drawings, from the series rightly entitled "Special." In these abstractions, employing a rich vocabulary of organic forms and resonating with feeling, Pollitzer felt that the artist had at last "gotten past the personal stage into the big sort of emotions that are common to big people [important artists] — but it's your version of it."[1]

Six weeks earlier, in response to a previous batch of drawings, Pollitzer had written to O'Keeffe, whom she called Pat in affectionate reference to her Irish ancestry, "I'd love to ask Mr. Stieglitz, Pat. Of course I never should till you said the word & I don't feel the time's come yet."[2] But now Pollitzer was so certain that she didn't bother to wait for O'Keeffe's permission.

Twilight had fallen, and Stieglitz, "feeling more dead than alive," was standing alone in the gallery.[3] He later said that this period of his life had been "the darkest of the many dark periods he passed through."[4] He could no longer endure his fiasco of a marriage. Although he had lots of new acquaintances, the desertion or departure of so many old friends had left him feeling terribly alone. And he was disgusted and depressed by the war, regarding which he was unable to take sides. He simply wanted to see it end and believed that America could hasten a conclusion by refusing to sell arms to any combatant nation.

He was pleased to see Pollitzer, whose occasional visits he had enjoyed for several years. At their first meeting she had impressed him as "radiant, a hundred per cent alive, intelligent, unafraid of her own emotions."[5] She now asked him whether he would like to see the drawings she had brought. They took the tube into the back room and unrolled its contents under the light of a small lamp. "Examining the first drawing, I realized that I had never seen anything like it," Stieglitz recalled. "All my tiredness vanished."[6] He looked at the drawings silently for a long time before exclaiming, "Finally a Woman on paper!" As Pollitzer was leaving, Stieglitz asked her to tell O'Keeffe that her drawings were "the purest, finest, sincerest things that have entered 291 in a long while." He added, "I wouldn't mind showing them in these rooms one bit — perhaps I shall."[7]

Stieglitz soon wrote O'Keeffe that her drawings had given him "much joy," though he professed, "I do not know what you had in mind while doing them."[8] He was being disingenuous, for the enthusiasm of his first response was in direct proportion to his certainty that he knew exactly what the artist had been thinking about: sex. Or rather sexuality in the fullest sense of the word, encompassing not only specifically sexual desires and acts — there did seem to be transparent, if perhaps not altogether conscious, allusions to genitalia — but also love, passion, death, creation, maternity, intuitiveness, secretiveness. The drawings reverberated with all the qualities that the Germanic Stieglitz, who constantly used initial capitals in his writing and implied them in his speech, associated with *das ewig Weibliche*, Goethe's eternal Feminine — "a Woman on paper."

It was fitting that O'Keeffe called her drawings "Special," as she had always felt herself to be. Since childhood she had been defiantly independent, aloof, unafraid, capable, and proud to the point of arrogance. She enjoyed being different from everyone else, commanded respect, expected deferential treatment as a matter of course, and had no patience for rules that did not impress her as sensible.

The young woman was handsome rather than conventionally pretty, with large and somewhat boyish features. Her long brown hair was usually pulled back from her forehead and done up in a bun. In certain regards she seemed like a frontierswoman, and yet there was something exotic about her undemocratically aristocratic bearing and her dark complexion. One early critic mistakenly spoke of her "Levantine mother," and as O'Keeffe aged she would come to look increasingly like a Native American.

Georgia Totto O'Keeffe was named for her maternal grandfather, Count György (George) Victor Totto, a Hungarian nobleman who had been stripped of most of his property and exiled to America after the revolution against Austria in 1848. In Wisconsin, Totto married Isabella Wyckoff, of Dutch extraction, and prospered as a farmer in the town of Sun Prairie. Their daughter Ida married Francis Calyxtus O'Keeffe, a second-generation Irish-American farmer whose family owned a neighboring property. In November 1887, on her parents' large and bountiful farm, Georgia O'Keeffe was born, the second of seven children and the eldest of five daughters.

After having attended a one-room elementary school in Sun Prairie, thirteen-year-old Georgia was enrolled as a boarding student at a convent school outside the nearby city of Madison. The following year she and her older brother attended high school in Milwaukee, where they lived with an aunt. That winter the O'Keeffes, seeking a warmer climate, which they incorrectly thought would protect them from the family scourge of tuberculosis, moved to the then still unrestored town of Williamsburg, Virginia. Georgia and her brother rejoined the family at the end of the school year, and she would complete high school at the neighboring Chatham Episcopal Institute, a finishing school with a preponderance of ministers' daughters among its students.

In the fall of 1905, O'Keeffe began classes at the Art Institute of Chicago. The following spring a bout of typhoid fever forced her to go home to Virginia to recuperate. Instead of returning to Chicago, she went to New York in September 1907 and enrolled at the Art Students League.

Obliged to earn her living, twenty-one-year-old O'Keeffe headed back to Chicago in the fall of 1908. She worked there as a commercial artist until an attack of measles in 1910 affected her eyesight and forced her to convalesce with her family, which had by this time moved to Charlottesville, Virginia. In 1912 she got a job as art supervisor and teacher in the public schools of Amarillo, Texas, where she would remain for two years.

Her second stay in New York, beginning in the fall of 1914, was devoted to studying with Arthur Wesley Dow at Teachers College, Columbia University. It was there that she met Anita Pollitzer. After a summer as a drawing instructor at the University of Virginia, O'Keeffe began teaching art at Columbia College in the fall of 1915.

Stieglitz had met O'Keeffe several times before Pollitzer's fateful visit, but she had not made a memorable impression on him, and he had not previously seen any of her work. After her visits to 291 during the first few months of 1908, she didn't return until December 1914 or January 1915, when she came to see the Picasso-Braque show. But O'Keeffe, who was accompanied by two friends, was again put off, this time because Stieglitz began asking the three young women embarrassingly personal questions. As before, she retreated to a safe distance. Nevertheless, she would occasionally drop by 291 over the course of the next few months and even, once or twice, risked a conversation with Stieglitz. During the Marin show, she asked him whether the artist could make a living from the sale of works like a small blue abstract crayon drawing that was hanging on the back of a door. She was greatly encouraged when Stieglitz replied affirmatively. The last time she had gone to 291, late in the spring of 1915, "there was nothing on the walls — chairs just knocked around — tracks on the floor and — talk behind the curtain," she wrote to Pollitzer, adding, "I even liked it when there was nothing."[9]

At that time O'Keeffe had not yet done any work she thought worthy of showing to Stieglitz. In October 1915, however, she had written to Pollitzer, "I believe I would rather have Stieglitz like some thing — anything I had done — than anyone else I know of — I have always thought that — If I ever make any thing that satisfies me even ever so little — I am going to show it to him to find out if it's any good."[10]

O'Keeffe recalled that when she saw Stieglitz in 1914, he impressed her as "a rather well-groomed, serious-looking person."[11] A few years later a friend described him as "a short, lean man, dressed like a conservative broker."[12] Edmund Wilson would observe that "there was more in his outward appearance of the expert 'technician' than the artist. Still less did he give the impression of the dedicated spiritual teacher."[13]

Stieglitz usually wore a dark three-piece suit with a bow tie, though in more relaxed moments he might substitute a cardigan and a four-in-hand. Because there was no heat in the gallery's exhibition rooms, he wore his overcoat or his black loden cape indoors, with collar turned up, through much of the winter. Anyone seeing him out of his milieu might well have guessed that he was an inspiring professor or perhaps a progressive journalist, but hardly a great artist — let alone the revolutionary that he considered himself to be.

By the mid-teens, the explosion of dark hair that had taken O'Keeffe aback in 1908 had become "a shock of graying hair whose tangles seemed to fling off tangents of rebellion."[14] O'Keeffe and her friends evidently found that look appealing; Pollitzer reported approvingly in a November 1915 letter to O'Keeffe that on her most recent visit to 291, "Stieglitz was great! He talked a blue streak & his hair was extra bushy."[15] And, related another observer, even his ears were "hair-tufted like a faun's."[16] Or like a terrier's, and there was much about Stieglitz to augment that resemblance, for he was as compact, keen, and relentless as any specimen of that family.

Stieglitz was pleased that O'Keeffe was from a pioneer family and that she had never been to Europe. She was, however, fairly well read, and her abstractions were probably not generated quite as spontaneously as she and Stieglitz would later maintain. It seems likely, for instance, that she had been influenced by the work of Pamela Colman Smith. Since we know that O'Keeffe visited the Rodin show at 291 in January 1908 and the Matisse show in April of that year, it is possible that she saw Smith's work in late February or early March. There certainly are some striking resemblances between O'Keeffe's "Special" drawings and Smith's work, though perhaps they simply had common sources in Dow and Odilon Redon, who had said that his goal was "to transform human emotions into arabesques." Or the link between O'Keeffe and Smith may have been their shared preoccupation with trying to express in visual terms their reactions to music. In the fall of 1915, Pollitzer advised O'Keeffe, who was practicing the violin, "Hear Victrola Records, Read Poetry, Think of people & put your reactions on paper."[17]

Whatever O'Keeffe's conscious or unconscious sources, the immediate catalyst for her drawings was her love for Arthur Macmahon, a handsome twenty-five-year-old professor of political science at Columbia University. Like O'Keeffe, he had taught at the University of Virginia's summer school in 1915. In a letter to Pollitzer early in December of that year, O'Keeffe said of Macmahon (who was quite "straight, prim and proper" and three years younger than she was), "He has the nicest way of saying things — and making you feel that he loves you — all the way round — not just in spots."[18] On January 4, 1916, less than a week after making the drawings that overwhelmed Stieglitz, O'Keeffe confided to Anita that she was "balancing on the edge of loving like I imagine we never love but once."[19]

This romance precipitated more than just O'Keeffe's mature sexual awakening. It heightened all her experiences and intensified her emotions. After Macmahon had visited her in South Carolina over Thanksgiving, O'Keeffe told Pollitzer, "The world looks all new to me."[20] She was so full of confusing, frightening, and exhilarating feelings that she thought she might go mad. Being in love sometimes made her feel stronger than ever before, and sometimes made her feel so weak and giddy that she was unable to work — and she resented that terribly. She was afraid that she was too much in love with Macmahon, afraid that she would lose him, afraid that she would end up being hurt badly. "I want to love as hard as I can and I can't let myself," she complained.[21] She wanted to cast off all restraints and conventions. In her art she was determined to stop imitating her teachers and to jettison her vestigial need to make work that would please them. She felt a desperate need to be completely free, to live full out, to express herself uninhibitedly in her life and in her art without worrying about the consequences.

O'Keeffe's increasing freedom in her work was all the more important to her as she grew to resent her economic limitations. She would have loved to move to New York to be near Macmahon and participate in the cultural life of the city, of which she always took full advantage when she was there, going to art exhibitions, concerts, and the theater. But she was not ready to marry Macmahon — or anyone else. And, having a very practical side, she feared that if she were on her own, her life in the city would be quite unromantic. In September 1915 she had told Anita, "If I went to New York I would be lucky if I could make a living — and doing it would take all my time and energy — there would be nothing left that would be just myself for fun."[22] For the time being she would have to remain at her job, although she told her friend, "Columbia is a nightmare to me — everything out here is deliciously stupid."[23] Nevertheless, even South Carolina had its pleasures. "Some of the fields are green — very very green," she would write Stieglitz in February 1916, with clear under- or overtones of eroticism, "almost unbelievably green against the dark of the pine woods — and it's warm — the air feels warm and soft — and lovely."[24]

It was out of the vortex of these emotions that her "Special" drawings emerged. O'Keeffe wrote to Anita one night late in December 1915, "Did you ever have something to say and feel as if the whole side of the wall wouldn't be big enough to say it on and then sit down on the floor and try to get it on to a sheet of charcoal paper[?] . . . I wonder if I am a raving lunatic for trying to make these things. . . . I hope you love me a little tonight — I seem to want everybody in the world to."[25]

*   *   *

In March 1916, O'Keeffe received an offer that she couldn't bear to turn down. The West Texas State Normal College, in the Panhandle town of Canyon, not far from the New Mexican border, would make her the head of its art department if she would return to New York at once to receive some additional instruction from Dow. So she abandoned South Carolina in midsemester and headed north. We do not know what part a desire to see Stieglitz may have played in her decision. But soon after arriving in the city, she made her way to 291, where a Hartley show was up.

In December 1915 the hardships of wartime Berlin and his own poverty had driven Hartley back to New York. The following April, Stieglitz exhibited his German paintings, the most powerful of which commemorated the death of his adored friend Karl von Freyburg, who had been killed in action. In these memorials, whose bright colors belied Hartley's profound depression, the artist threw together — in a highly original blending of Picasso's Synthetic Cubism, de Zayas's absolute caricatures, and the traditional style of classicizing trophy reliefs — piles of flags, white-feathered helmets of the kaiser's Royal Guards, epaulets, spurs, regimental insignia, the Iron Cross, von Freyburg's initials, and the number 24, representing his age at the time of his death. Although Hartley declared in his catalog statement that the paintings were purely formal abstractions, completely devoid of pro-German sentiment, it was miraculous that the show didn't cause a riot.

O'Keeffe recalled disapprovingly that looking at Hartley's paintings at 291 was like hearing "a brass band in a small closet."[26] She went to the gallery alone and had a chance to talk with Stieglitz; when she expressed her reservations about the exhibition, he took from storage some of Hartley's earlier paintings. She liked one of the 1909 "Dark Landscapes" so much that he let her borrow it.

Steichen, who still paid occasional visits to 291 in the hope of salvaging his friendship with Stieglitz, was at the gallery one day in the spring of 1916 when a batch of new drawings arrived from O'Keeffe. "Dumbfounded" by their "amazing psychological frankness," he said they should be exhibited as soon as possible.[27] By May 23, when Stieglitz — without even bothering to notify O'Keeffe, let alone ask her permission — hung an impromptu show of her work with that of two other young artists, Charles Duncan and René Lafferty, most of the New York critics were already on vacation. Duncan, a twenty-four-year-old New York painter and poet who was a friend of Marin's, earned his living as a sign painter. In Stieglitz's spectral

1919 portrait of him, sitting in an interior space apparently illuminated by an open fire, the tight-lipped artist holds a handkerchief in one hand and a pipe in the other and looks like an old man haunted by his past. Anita Pollitzer would characterize him as "queer — but fine."[28] Hardly anything is known about Lafferty, a Philadelphian, except that he had attended Robert Henri's classes at the Ferrer Center and had been a patient in a mental hospital for two years some time before his show at 291. Stieglitz felt that the work and the "big, fine natures" of the three artists were related.[29]

Stieglitz hung ten of O'Keeffe's large charcoal drawings in the main gallery. In the smaller room were two abstract watercolors and one drawing by Duncan, as well as three oils by Lafferty. Duncan commented that like O'Keeffe, he used "the method of picturing non-visual experience while Lafferty has interpreted the significance to himself of a comet, a dragonfly, and a fountain."[30]

According to *Camera Work*, it was "mainly owing to Miss O'Keeffe's drawings" that the exhibition "attracted many visitors and aroused unusual interest and discussion."[31] Stieglitz wrote that the unframed drawings, which he put up by tacking sheets of glass over them, "besides their other value were of intense interest from a psycho-analytical point of view. '291' had never before seen woman express herself so frankly on paper."[32] One female visitor wrote of "the woman pictures" that she had been "startled at their frankness" and had marveled "how new a field of expression such sex consciousness will open."[33] But Willard Wright scoffed, "All these pictures have to say is 'I want to have a baby.' "[34] One "remarkable girl, who . . . had in her potentially the thing O'Keeffe had painted" (probably Katharine Rhoades) told Stieglitz that the drawings were "too obvious." His response was to take "her gently by the arm and [lead] her out of the room."[35]

O'Keeffe herself didn't learn of the show until a classmate at Teachers College — misremembering the notice posted at the gallery stating that the work was by Georgia O'Keeffe of Virginia — mentioned to her that she had seen an exhibition of drawings by Virginia O'Keeffe at 291. The artist immediately went to the gallery but was told that Stieglitz was on jury duty. She was finally able to confront him a few days later. When she demanded, "Who gave you permission to hang these drawings?" he shot back, "You have no more right to withhold these pictures than to withdraw a child from the world, had you given birth to one."[36] The drawings remained on the gallery walls. "Listen," she later remarked of the incident, "you try arguing with him and see where you get."[37] So completely did he win her trust that she would write him in July, "Nothing you do with my drawings is 'nervy.' I seem to feel that they are as much yours as mine."[38]

O'Keeffe had been angered by Stieglitz's high-handedness in failing to notify her of the exhibition, but she had also been ambivalent about having her drawings shown at all. She had written Pollitzer in the fall of 1915, "I always have a curious sort of feeling about some of my things — I hate to show them . . . I am afraid people won't understand — and I hope they won't — and am afraid they will."[39] On the other hand, she was pleased when Stieglitz wrote to her in January 1916 that he would like to show her drawings "if at all possible . . . but we will see about that. I do not quite know where I am just at present. The future is rather hazy, but the present is very positive and very delightful."[40] O'Keeffe wrote to Pollitzer that same month, "Of course I would rather have something hang in 291 than any place in New York — but wanting things hung is simply wanting your vanity satisfied — of course it sounds good . . . Wouldn't it be a great experiment — I'll just not even imagine such luck."[41]

O'Keeffe left New York in June to teach drawing once again at the University of Virginia's summer school. Her return to Charlottesville was traumatic, for her tubercular mother (who was only two weeks younger than Stieglitz) had recently died there, separated from her husband and in pitiful circumstances, months behind in her rent payments. For O'Keeffe, depression always manifested itself as exhaustion; she was so prostrated upon her arrival in Virginia that she spent several days in bed and griped to Pollitzer, "I get so tired that I almost feel crazy."[42]

O'Keeffe had hardly left New York before Stieglitz sent her five back issues of *Camera Work* and Willard Wright's novel *Man of Promise*, an odd choice, since it is a story of how a creative man is frustrated and thwarted by a series of women. She told Pollitzer that the pictures in *Camera Work* "excited me so that I felt like a human being for a couple of hours."[43] A few weeks later Stieglitz sent her, as she told Pollitzer, "nine wonderful photographs of my exhibition — that he had taken himself. . . . Isn't it funny that I hate my drawings — and am simply crazy about the photographs of them. Really — Anita — he is too good to be true."[44]

In his first letter of the summer Stieglitz wrote O'Keeffe sadly, "Queerer still that during your stay here we never had a chance to compare notes — to be alone to compare."[45] Making up for that loss, they began writing each other at least once a week. In July O'Keeffe exulted to Pollitzer, "I think I never had more wonderful letters than [Stieglitz] has been writing me . . . [T]hey have been like fine cold water when you are terribly thirsty."[46]

Not for Stieglitz the three-ring circus of Provincetown, the Cape Cod resort that was to Greenwich Village what Newport was to Fifth Avenue. Marsden Hartley, Charles Demuth, Eugene O'Neill, Leo Stein, Mabel Dodge, Maurice Sterne, the Zorachs, and Hutchins Hapgood were all in Provincetown in the summer of 1916, along with Max Eastman, John Reed, Louise Bryant, and many others associated with *The Masses*. Demuth shared a room in Polly Holladay's boardinghouse with Stuart Davis; Hartley was staying with John Reed; and everyone was involved, in one way or another, with the productions of the Provincetown Players, which had been organized the previous summer. Under the direction of George Cram Cook, plays by O'Neill and others were acted by amateur casts, which occasionally included Hartley or Demuth, in the improvised Wharf Theater, a refurbished fish house. Beginning that fall, when the Provincetown Players opened their first New York season in a little house next to the Liberal Club on MacDougal Street, in the Village, Stieglitz would regularly attend their performances.

He had asked O'Keeffe to send him more drawings, carefully packed, by Railway Express, collect. In August, shortly before she headed off to Texas to begin her new job, she put a batch of drawings and watercolors in a simple cardboard mailing tube and sent it by ordinary post to Lake George, where Alfred was relaxing while Emmy again toured New England. Delighted by the new work, and aghast at the thought of how easily it could have been lost or damaged, he increased both the frequency and the intensity of his correspondence. "Such wonderful letters," O'Keeffe marveled to Pollitzer. "Sometimes he gets so much of himself into them that I can hardly stand it — it's like . . . too much light — you shut your eyes and put one hand over them — then feel round with the other for something to steady yourself by."[47]

CHAPTER FIFTY·ONE

AFTER OPENING the 1916–17 season on November 22 with a group show that included some drawings and watercolors by his ten-year-old niece Georgia S. Engelhard, Stieglitz hung an exhibition of watercolors by Abraham Walkowitz. Then he showed the blandly attractive Synthetic Cubist abstractions based on nautical motifs that Hartley had made during the summer in Provincetown. Angry because the political climate made it impossible to sell his paintings based on German themes, the artist had turned to neutral subjects and had intentionally suppressed his personality. In the emotionless geometry of his paintings he intended an ironic, Dadaistic spirit, which was appreciated only by the most sophisticated viewers.

Although Stieglitz had announced in *Camera Work* in 1915 that 291 would not exhibit any more work by European modernists, he relented once. In March 1917, after the nearly annual Marin show, from which John Quinn bought four watercolors for $1,200, Stieglitz showed a group of twenty-five paintings, drawings, and pastels by the Italian Futurist Gino Severini. He did so, at de Zayas's request, partly because Futurism had been omitted from the Armory Show. (The anarchistic Italians had promised to send their work but predictably failed to do so.) Since the movement had not been taken up by the New York dealers, it was granted a reprieve from Stieglitz's taboo. Presumably with mixed feelings, Stieglitz allowed the bellwether Quinn to purchase ten works from the exhibition for a total of more than $1,100.

The last two shows of the season, solos by Stanton Macdonald-Wright and Georgia O'Keeffe, were intended to complement each other, for Stieglitz believed that their work represented the masculine and feminine extremes of abstraction.[1] In fact, during the next two years O'Keeffe would make a number of paintings that seem inspired by her male counterpart's Synchromism, which she praised as a "wonderful" blend of "theory plus feeling."[2]

Macdonald-Wright had said that he desperately needed to earn at least $500 from his show. Thanks to the suddenly dependable Quinn and a few other collectors, that goal was surpassed. Soon after returning to California in 1919, the artist, who had toyed with a colored-light machine for years, wrote Stieglitz that painting was dead and would be replaced by the superior art of musiclike projections of pure color.

O'Keeffe's exhibition, which opened on April 3, 1917, included work in oil, watercolor, and charcoal, as well as a small phallic sculpture she had made early in the summer of 1916. "It's like everything else," she had written Stieglitz, "I want to show it to you — but — at the same time — hate to show it to anyone."[3] Among the works in the show, according to critic Henry Tyrrell in the *Christian Science Monitor*, was "a water-color impression of an approaching railway train rushing steaming out of space across the limitless prairie, like a vision-bearing cloud in the skies of heaven." He also mentioned "two oil paintings of lovely but singularly disquieting color tonality, which may be interpretively called 'The Embrace,' and 'Loneliness'." Tyrrell stated that O'Keeffe had "found expression in delicately veiled symbolism for 'what every woman knows,' but what women heretofore have kept to themselves."[4]

Another critic, William Murrell Fisher, wrote for *Camera Work* that "it is only in music that one finds any analogy to the emotional content of these drawings — to the gigantic, swirling rhythms, and the exquisite tendernesses so powerfully and sensitively rendered." He said that the drawings and paintings were "more truly inspired" than any other work he had seen and that "even the least satisfactory of them has the *quality* of completeness — while in at least three instances the effect is of a quite cosmic grandeur."[5]

Just as he had juxtaposed his 1913 show of his own photographs with the Armory Show, and Strand's work with the Forum Exhibition, Stieglitz undoubtedly timed the O'Keeffe exhibition specifically to coincide with the huge first exhibition of the American Society of Independent Artists, which opened in the Grand Central Palace on April 9. Late in 1916 the society, modeled on the French Société des Artistes Indépendants, had been formed, largely through the efforts of Walter Pach, to replace the Association of American Painters and Sculptors. The new organization bridged four major groups: the Stieglitz circle, the Arensberg salon, the Eight, and Robert Henri's students, who included Rockwell Kent and George Bellows. William Glackens was the society's first president, but the board of directors was dominated by Arensbergites, including Walter himself, John Covert (an artist who was Arensberg's cousin), Duchamp, Man Ray, Joseph Stella, Morton Schamberg, and Katherine Dreier (a wealthy artist who would soon become a leading force in the art world). John Marin was the only director from the Stieglitz camp.

The society's rules stipulated that any artist who paid the one-dollar initiation fee and the five dollar annual dues was automatically entitled to exhibit two works. Some twelve hundred artists (including O'Keeffe) submitted more than two thousand entries for the first exhibition. As in the 1910 Independents exhibition, there were no jury or prizes, and all works were hung in alphabetical order. Stieglitz went the society one better by suggesting,

> Wouldn't it be advisable next year during the exhibition, to withhold the names of the makers of all work shown[?] The names, if on the canvases, or on the pieces of sculpture, etc., exhibited could be readily hidden. The catalogue should contain, in place of the names of artists, simply numbers, with titles if desired. On the last day of the Exhibition . . . each number would be publicly identified.[6]

Although Arensberg was the managing director of the 1917 show and Duchamp head of the hanging committee, they cooked up a Dada prank that nearly subverted the entire venture. In 1914 Duchamp had bought, in Paris, a rack for drying several dozen bottles, an object as elaborate as the papal triple tiara, and had declared it a "ready-made" work of art. In the fall of 1915 he bought another ready-made, a snow shovel, which he entitled *In Advance of the Broken Arm*. Now, accompanied by Arensberg and Joseph Stella, Duchamp went to the J. L. Mott Iron Works on lower Fifth Avenue and bought a porcelain urinal, which he rotated so that the side normally attached to a wall lay flat on the top of a wooden pedestal. Having signed it "R. Mutt" (a cross between the name of the iron works and A. Mutt of the comic strip *Mutt and Jeff*) and having secretly paid the six-dollar fee for "Richard Mutt," he smuggled the ready-made, which he called *Fountain*, into the Grand Central Palace two days before the opening of the exhibition.

When the society's other directors saw *Fountain*, they denounced it as an indecent joke that might compromise the show and insisted that it could not be displayed. But Arensberg countered, "A lovely form has been revealed, freed from its functional purpose, therefore a man clearly has made an aesthetic contribution."[7] On April 9, the day of the opening, about ten of the fifteen directors were assembled for a vote. According to the *New York Herald*, "Mr. Mutt's defenders were voted down by a small margin."[8] Duchamp resigned from the society, though he still did not acknowledge his authorship.

A few days later Stieglitz, who was amused by the episode but also felt that an important principle was at stake, gave Duchamp permission to take the rejected work to 291. According to one account, Duchamp and Man Ray carried it through the crowded galleries of the Independents exhibition, while Arensberg waved his checkbook and announced his intention of buying it. Once *Fountain* had arrived at 291, Stieglitz set about photographing it for the little magazine *The Blind Man*, published by Arensberg and Duchamp to print commentaries and criticism about the show. Although the O'Keeffe exhibition was then hanging, Stieglitz placed the ready-made in front of a 1913 Hartley painting of mounted, helmeted, and pennant-bearing Germanic soldiers going off to battle. He chose the Hartley for two reasons: a form at its center coincidentally echoed the shape of the urinal (in his 1919 article "The Beautiful Neglected Arts," Hartley would speak of plumbers as "creators of aesthetic delight") and, like the Duchamp, the Hartley could not then be exhibited in New York. The U.S. Senate had passed a declaration of war on the German Empire on April 4, and the House had passed it on the morning of the sixth. President Woodrow Wilson had signed the declaration that afternoon. Because of the Hartley's apparently pro-German subject matter, to exhibit it would be widely viewed as treasonous.

Stieglitz fully understood the complexity of Duchamp's gesture, which was intended not only as a provocation but also as a sincere aesthetic statement. Echoing Stieglitz's 1908 statement to Agnes Ernst, Duchamp remarked in reference to *Fountain*: "Beauty is around you wherever you choose to discover it."[9] The urinal was indeed, as Arensberg had argued, a beautiful form. Stieglitz shot it close up and took great pains to emphasize its curvaceous beauty. Apparently without knowing the Stieglitz image, Edward Weston would photograph a toilet in Mexico in 1925. "Here was every sensuous curve of the 'human form divine' but minus imperfections," wrote Weston. "It somehow reminded me, in the glory of its chaste convolutions and in its swelling, sweeping, forward movement of finely progressing contours, of the Victory of Samothrace."[10] When Stieglitz's photograph of *Fountain* was published in the second issue of *The Blind Man*, the article by Louise Norton on the opposite page was entitled "Buddha of the Bathroom."

Stieglitz must have appreciated the parallel between Duchamp's readymades and photographs, whose detractors had, of course, argued that they were not made by hand. The unsigned editorial in *The Blind Man* argued, "Whether Mr. Mutt with his own hands made the fountain or not has no importance. He CHOSE it. He took an ordinary article of life, placed it so that its useful significance disappeared under the new title and point of view — created a new thought for the object." *Fountain* represented an important step in Duchamp's growing insistence on the primacy of the eye and the mind over the hand — which would lead him to give up painting altogether in 1918.

The second issue of *The Blind Man* was its last, thanks to Picabia, who on April 4 had once again arrived in New York with his wife. He won the magazine in a chess game and discontinued its publication in favor of *391*, three issues of which would appear before the Picabias left New York that fall, never to return. Although Stieglitz and Francis still remained friends, they saw relatively little of each other during this visit. In July Stieglitz spent an enjoyable evening at the Picabias' apartment in Louise Norton's house with Duchamp, the Arensbergs, and the Gleizeses, who lived upstairs. However, the photographer could certainly no longer view his friend as one of the "cleanest propositions" ever, for he was suffering bouts of delirium tremens, was more addicted than ever to opium and cocaine, and was having a tumultuous affair with Isadora Duncan.

If, in 1917, one had mentioned the name Stieglitz to a scientist, he would probably have assumed that one was referring to Alfred's brother Julius, who was among the leading research chemists in the United States. Author of the standard two-volume text *Qualitative Chemical Analysis*, published in 1911, he had become chairman of the chemistry department at the University of Chicago in 1915 and president of the American Chemical Society in January 1917. The following month he was appointed chairman of the National Research Council's Committee on Synthetic Drugs, charged with developing substitutes for the German-manufactured medicines rendered unavailable by the British blockade.

It was perhaps for the best that Julius lived as far away as Chicago, since

Alfred might have found it uncomfortable to live near a brother whose career was, in certain respects, not much different from what an observer in Berlin during the 1880s would probably have predicted for Alfred himself. Julius was especially concerned with the close relationship between aniline dyes, which had been of such interest to his brother, and the substances that could be manufactured from dye intermediates: explosives, war gases, synthetic drugs, and photographic chemicals. As if he weren't stepping painfully enough on Alfred's toes in his professional life, Julius was also a dedicated amateur photographer who refused to grant that his pictures were in any way inferior to his brother's.

Through his connections in Washington, Julius heard that the War Department was thinking of asking Alfred to form a group to develop techniques of high-speed photography. Alfred was interested in the possibility "not because he believed in the war but for the experience," as a friend later reported. However, his participation was vetoed by an officer who warned that Stieglitz was "a hell-raiser."[11]

Edward Steichen, wanting to be the Mathew Brady of the Great War, volunteered for the U.S. Army Signal Corps as a photographic reporter and was commissioned a first lieutenant. Learning of the importance of aerial reconnaissance photography — and relishing the challenge of making sharply focused, legible pictures from a fast, shaky plane at a high altitude — he decided to specialize. Despite their strained friendship, Steichen suggested to the Signal Corps that Stieglitz be placed in charge of expediting shipments of photographic supplies to France, but the suggestion was disregarded — leading Stieglitz to claim later that supplies had not reached the front until after the armistice.

Before boarding his ship for France (where he would arrive just in time to attend Rodin's funeral), the thirty-eight-year-old Steichen paid Stieglitz a visit in his handsomely tailored uniform, cutting a dashing figure. "Pity I'm not young enough," lamented Stieglitz, almost fifty-four, to Marie Rapp soon afterward. "I'm sure I would have made a pretty good looking officer when I was 35 — Gosh! — Now I have to be on the outside of Everything — Just OLD."[12]

A few weeks after the United States entered the war, Congress began debates on a food-control bill, to which temperance forces tried to add an amendment prohibiting the manufacture of all alcoholic beverages. Such a measure would obviously impoverish Emmy. A wealthy Emmy was bad enough from Alfred's standpoint; a poor one was out of the question. And so it came to pass that Alfred finally began to think seriously of leaving her.

He evidently felt that because Kitty would enter Smith College that fall, and would thus be away at school most of the year, he could at last do so in good conscience. As a first step, he stopped sharing a bedroom with his wife and began sleeping in his study.

As it turned out, the compromise reached in Congress ended the production of distilled spirits as of September 1917 but left beer and wine to be dealt with by the president at his discretion. In December 1917, Wilson cut by 30 percent the amount of grain allowed to the beer industry and drastically reduced the legal strength of beer. Worse seemed sure to follow.

In the June 1917 issue of *Camera Work*, which went to the printer early in May, Stieglitz announced that the next issue would feature O'Keeffe's work and that three shows scheduled for the season just ended had been "unavoidably held over": a ten-year retrospective of his own portraits and views from the back window of 291, a second exhibition of Strand's photographs, and a show of Alfred Maurer's recent work, which, Stieglitz had told Arthur Dove, was "undoubtedly a development."[13]

Although Stieglitz had agreed in February 1917 to renew his lease for the gallery space, he suddenly decided in mid-May, when it looked as though the prohibition amendment would be passed, that he couldn't possibly keep 291 open for another season and that he would have to discontinue *Camera Work*, at least temporarily. Only thirty-seven subscribers remained, and with America's entry into the war, the services of Bruckmann Verlag would obviously be unavailable.

On May 16, two days after the closing of the O'Keeffe show ended the season, Stieglitz wrote to Aline Meyer Liebman, who had become a dependable supporter, "I have finally decided that it would be sheer madness to continue 291. . . . I will have to change practically everything in my life. At least the outside of it."[14] He was then considering the possibility of turning the running of the gallery over to someone else, perhaps Marius de Zayas.

He wrote at that time to Mitchell Kennerley, "My family and I have been badly hit. So badly, that I am compelled to give up 291 and *Camera Work*."[15] He even told Emmy they would have to move to a smaller apartment, but she raised such a howl of protest that he shelved that idea for the moment. Stieglitz's decision to close his gallery, however, was based on more than the cost of its yearly upkeep, approximately $1,000. In the spring of 1916 he had thundered that "never since the tower of Babel has there been such general chaos of utterance and confusion of understanding as prevails in the art world today."[16] During 1917 there would be more than sixty one-person or group exhibitions of modern art in New York, and Stieglitz was disgusted by the commercialism and competitiveness that had infected artists and dealers alike. One friend would relate, "It was not because of the public's attitude that the gallery closed. It was because of the smallness of the artists that it had to be destroyed. . . . The American artists with the soul-shrivelry characteristic of the new-worlder were knifing one another, or seeking to capture the laboratory for a formula, socialism, anarchism, patriotism, intellectualism, estheticism."[17]

When he vacated his gallery, Stieglitz would have to sell, give away, or destroy many of the thousands of copies of *Camera Work* and *291* stored there. He had Marie Rapp send out a flood of letters to possible buyers, and he himself wrote to such patrons as Aline Liebman, of whom he inquired, "Perhaps you still know a few people who might be interested in wanting some of the numbers. They can be had at almost any price. To the poor people I am virtually giving them away. As I have always done."[18]

Burdened with some eight thousand unsold copies of *291* and filled with a mixture of anger, bitter amusement, and a sense of vindication, Stieglitz sold all the copies of the regular edition to a ragpicker for $5.80 and gave the money to Marie Rapp, telling her to buy herself a pair or two of gloves. Because he couldn't manage to sell — for a dollar apiece — a single copy of the deluxe edition of the special photography issue, containing the magnificent photogravure of *The Steerage*, he eventually destroyed most of them as well.

By this time Stieglitz and O'Keeffe were writing to each other almost every day. No doubt having received a letter from him about his decision to abandon 291, O'Keeffe boarded a train for New York late in May. "Stieglitz — Well — it was him I went to see," she wrote her best friend. "Just had to go Anita — There wasn't any way out of it — and I'm so glad I went."[19]

They spent Decoration Day, May 30, with Alfred's friend Henry J. Gaisman, who had invented the "Autographic" camera back. (By opening a little door in it, a photographer could use a stylus to record names, the date, and so on in the margin of a negative. George Eastman had paid Gaisman $300,000 for his patent in 1914 and adapted the autographic process to a wide range of Kodak cameras.) Gaisman drove Stieglitz and O'Keeffe, along with Paul Strand, to the exclusive, enclosed community of Sea Gate, on Coney Island, and to the nearby amusement area. Dreamland had been destroyed by fire in 1911, but Steeplechase and Luna parks — the latter a miniature city of more than a thousand towers, spires, and minarets — were thriving. O'Keeffe, who liked both Gaisman and Strand, reported to Pollitzer that despite the cold, windy weather, it had been "a great party and a great day."[20]

During the next week, Stieglitz rehung O'Keeffe's show as a brief command performance amid the clutter of his preparations to abandon 291. There, on June 4, he made his first photographs of her. Perhaps it was at his request that she wore that day a prim black dress with a white collar, the combination that had so enchanted him since childhood. Of the images that survive from that session, three used as background a watercolor suggestive both of a womb and of swirling clouds. In one of the photographs we see only O'Keeffe's hands touching the work. The two others are portraits in which the young provincial schoolteacher looks directly into the camera. Cracking a smile in one, revealing her dimples and her modest amusement at her situation, she is pensive in the other. With her close-fitting helmet of hair, she looks like an American Joan of Arc who has just heard her call.

O'Keeffe's ardor for Arthur Macmahon had cooled. She told Anita Pollitzer that he was "really pretty fine" but admitted, "I sort of feel that I have gone on past [him.] I dont know." It was Paul Strand who suddenly interested her. She confessed to Pollitzer that she "fell for him."[21]

One day he showed her "lots and lots" of his photographs. "I almost lost my mind over them," she told Anita, "photographs that are as queer in shapes as Picasso drawings."[22] She was so excited by Strand's work that while looking at it she loved him "both armsful."[23] She wrote him on the train back to Texas, "I believe I've been looking at things and seeing them as I thought you might photograph them — Isn't that funny — making Strand photographs for myself in my head."[24]

Strand fell even more in love with O'Keeffe than she did with him. In her letters that summer and fall she stressed that while she was very fond of him and loved his work, she did not, despite her initial response, want a romance. "If you knew more of me you would probably be disappointed," she claimed in July. "I seem to like many people enough to make them miserable — no one enough to make them happy."[25] In October she asked, "Isn't our little mutual admiration tendency amusing[?]"[26] Mentioning how much she liked a student from Canyon who was going off to war, she told Strand that she felt true reciprocity of feeling with that man, while "you pull me in spite of myself."[27]

Although O'Keeffe was delighted by Stieglitz's attentions, she still did not think of him romantically. He was a father figure, wise and sensitive. "[Men] never understand me — unless maybe Stieglitz does — don't know that I understand myself," she told Strand in July.[28] But Stieglitz was obviously in love with O'Keeffe. Herbert Seligmann recalled that one night he accompanied him on a long walk that ended at 1111 Madison Avenue, "where he lived, isolated from his family, in a single room, every available inch of wall space crowded with pictures. There he drew out the drawings of Georgia O'Keeffe and with passion pointed out the new language in which the course of a woman's life was being unfolded."[29] This sacred and intimate ritual was repeated for so many friends that Marsden Hartley called it "Stieglitz's celestial solitaire."

The day after their expedition to Coney Island, Stieglitz sent a note to O'Keeffe informing her, "I have decided to rip 291 to pieces after all — I can't bear to think that its walls which held your drawings & the children's should be in charge of any one else but myself."[30] He would arrange for Charles Daniel, N. E. Montross, and other dealers to represent his artists. The space his gallery had occupied was to be taken over by a commercial picture library. He had planned to keep the little side room as his office, but he ended up renting a cubicle on the second floor, where he could spend his days and receive his friends. It was unthinkable for him to be at home with Emmy.

With the help of Marie Rapp, Emil Zoler, and various young volunteers, Stieglitz spent the month of June emptying out the gallery. They moved his photographs, the works of art that he was keeping, and the remaining copies of *Camera Work* to his room downstairs. In his cathartic zeal, he threw away many vital records of the business that he had never acknowledged to be one. On June 24 he wrote O'Keeffe, "This afternoon I set Zoler ripping down more shelving in the old little room — & ripping down the remaining burlap — . . . . The place looks as if it had been raped by the terrible Germans!"[31]

CHAPTER FIFTY·TWO

IN THE FALL of 1917, after his return from a restful and unproductive summer at Lake George, Stieglitz began spending his days at the little office that he called the Vault or the Tomb. To Annie Brigman he wrote,

> I'm still daily at 291 — but am free. Have another tiny room now on the second floor — lots of light — & the fellows, Strand, Wright, Marin, Hartley, Walkowitz, Zoler, Marie (she's one of the fellows), Dove, Bluemner, etc. gather there in all the tininess — The spirit has not changed an iota — my spirit — There are no exhibitions — but all the new work is brought to me — & much of it is magnificent.[1]

Although there was only one chair, as many as eight of the fellows at a time might sit wherever they could find a spot on the desk or shelves.

Among the less frequent visitors was Charles Sheeler, who would drop in during his visits from Philadelphia. Late in March 1917 de Zayas had opened a show of photographs by Sheeler, Schamberg, and Strand at the Modern Gallery, and in December he would give Sheeler a one-man show of his paintings and photographs. Under the heading "Cubism Justified," Henry McBride wrote that in his photographs of the staircase, doors, windows, and woodstove of the Doylestown house he shared with Schamberg, Sheeler's camera had "registered certain effects and qualities hitherto seen only in the works of Pablo Picasso and his ablest followers."[2] Stieglitz traded prints with Sheeler (four of the younger man's for one of the elder's) and had planned to devote an issue of *Camera Work* to him.

In March 1918 Stieglitz headed a jury whose four other members were Philadelphia painters, including Arthur Carles, to judge the thirteenth photographic salon sponsored by the John Wanamaker department store in that city. They awarded the first prize, of $100, to Sheeler and the second to Strand. Serving on the juries of the Wanamaker salons, as he had done every year since 1912, went against many of Stieglitz's avowed principles: everything submitted was hung, the jurors were mostly undistinguished painters, and prizes were awarded. Stieglitz's participation was, however, an investment in the future. "The pictures come from all sections of the country, from Maine to California," he wrote in his foreword for the catalog of the 1916 show. "We know of no other Annual Exhibition of Pictorial Photographs that brings together the work of so many sincere workers in this field. It might almost be called the 'Photographic Salon of America,' and the time may come when it may be considered sufficient honor merely to have one's pictures accepted for this exhibition." In 1917 Stieglitz and Steichen had judged the Wanamaker salon very harshly, designating only fifty-five of the eleven hundred entries as truly worthy of being hung. The first prize had gone to Strand for his photograph *Wall Street*.

After Morton Schamberg's death, of pneumonia, in October 1918, the bereft Sheeler could not bear to remain in Philadelphia. He soon moved to New York, where he continued to see Stieglitz frequently. He also took on a commission to make an extensive photographic documentation of Agnes and Eugene Meyer's new mansion and estate in Mount Kisco. During 1920, Sheeler would collaborate with Paul Strand on a short film — essentially a series of extended stills — of buildings and streets, entitled *New York the Magnificent*. (A few years later the title was changed to *Manhatta*.) In August 1919 Strand had declined an invitation to exhibit with the Pictorial Photographers of America by saying, "Photography . . . is either an expression of a cosmic vision, an embodiment of a life movement or it is nothing — to me. This quality I find only in the work of . . . Charles Sheeler and Alfred Stieglitz."[3]

Sheeler's close association with de Zayas would continue long after lack of sales forced the Modern Gallery to close in April 1918. (The only dependable buyers had been Agnes Meyer, Arthur Davies, John Quinn, and, toward the end, the Arensbergs.) The Mexican dealt privately until the fall of 1919, when, with the backing of several friends, he opened the de Zayas Gallery at 549 Fifth Avenue, where Sheeler worked as the assistant manager. During its two seasons, it showed African sculpture, Chinese paintings, and Post-Impressionism, but no living artists except Sheeler and (for reasons that could hardly have been disinterested) Davies, Walt Kuhn, and John Covert.

Davies and Kuhn were also involved with the Whitney Studio Club, established in February 1918 by Gertrude Vanderbilt Whitney (whom Stieglitz had despised ever since she failed to buy Matisse's *Serf*) and her lieutenant, Juliana Force. Among the other early members of the club, located on West Fourth Street off Washington Square, were Ernest Lawson, Maurice Prendergast, Rockwell Kent, Samuel Halpert, Bryson Burroughs, Kenneth Hayes Miller, and William and Marguerite Zorach. Especially popular were the life classes on the skylighted top floor of the club's building. With exhibition galleries, a library, sitting rooms, and a billiard room, the clubhouse was soon attracting a broad spectrum of New York artists. Since Stieglitz strongly disapproved of the enterprise, only peripheral members of his circle were lured by its comforts and its congeniality, in striking contrast to the cramped austerity of the little room at 291–293 Fifth Avenue.

Among the new regulars were several associated with a short-lived but influential magazine, *The Seven Arts*, the first issue of which was published in November 1916. Conveniently, the *Seven Arts* office was at Madison Avenue and Thirty-first Street, just two blocks from 291.

The principal founder and editor in chief was the Minnesota-born, Columbia-educated poet and novelist James Oppenheim, whose experiences as a social worker on the Lower East Side had filled him with reforming zeal. The magazine's angel was Mrs. A. K. Rankine, who was said to have sold her collection of Whistlers to underwrite it.

The thesis of *The Seven Arts* — which published articles by Theodore Dreiser, Leo Stein, Willard Wright, Marsden Hartley, and Paul Strand — was that the war was bringing about America's cultural and spiritual emancipation from Europe. The magazine's manifesto proclaimed, "It is our faith, and the faith of many, that we are living in the first days of a renascent period, a time which means for America the coming of that national self-consciousness which is the beginning of greatness. In all such epochs the arts cease to be private matters; they become not only the expression of the national life but a means to its enhancement."[4] Stieglitz had, of course, held such ideas for years.

Oppenheim and his colleagues fervently believed that America was beginning to fulfill the destiny promised by Walt Whitman, whom they revered as the greatest artist the nation had produced. Whitman was the evangelist of the new America, in which (so the young writers hoped) a robust spiritual embrace of truth would triumph over materialism, puritanism, and hypocrisy.

The brightest star on the staff of *The Seven Arts* was Randolph Bourne, a hunchbacked dwarf whom Paul Rosenfeld would praise as "perhaps the strongest mind of the entire younger generation in America."[5] While they were undergraduates at Columbia University, Bourne (whose poverty had delayed his matriculation until the age of twenty-three) was the roommate of Arthur Macmahon, O'Keeffe's beau.

Bourne, a cosmopolitan internationalist who wrote on subjects ranging from literature to politics, believed (as did Stieglitz) that Americans "should turn our eyes upon our own art for a time, shut ourselves in with our genius, and cultivate with an intense and partial pride what we have already achieved against the obstacles of our cultural humility."[6]

For both moral and pragmatic reasons, Bourne passionately opposed America's entry into the European cataclysm. Van Wyck Brooks wrote that Bourne argued that "between the War and American promise one had to choose, for the effect of the war would be to impoverish American promise, and one should turn one's energies to promoting what was truly best in the country's life."[7] Once the nation was embroiled, Bourne fearlessly told readers of *The Seven Arts* that America had suffered a great reverse, for even if it emerged on the winning side, it was already poisoned by the militarism and chauvinism that were destroying Europe. So adamant was Bourne in his pacifism, and so loyal to him were the magazine's other editors, that Mrs. Rankine, an orthodox Republican, withdrew her subsidy. Bourne's astounding career would be cut short by a fatal bout of influenza in December 1918.

At the age of twenty-seven, Waldo David Frank became the associate editor of *The Seven Arts*. Named for Ralph Waldo Emerson and Henry David Thoreau, Frank was born in 1889 to an upper-middle-class New York Jewish family. After graduating from DeWitt Clinton High School, the intense young man, who played the cello and wrote fiction, spent a year at a prep school in Switzerland before entering Yale in 1907. Something of a wunderkind, he graduated Phi Beta Kappa in 1911 with both a bachelor's and a master's degree.

Frank — who had thick, unruly black hair, penetrating eyes, and a toothbrush mustache — looked like a gentle anarchist. A nexus of contradictions, he passionately espoused democracy but felt that he was one of the elect. He longed for a mystical union with God but became an egotistical careerist. Restlessly searching for his own identity, he was eager to preach to his compatriots on the subject of America's destiny.

Frank was obsessed with the Americanness of American culture. Confused about what it meant to be a Jew in America, he turned to Stieglitz as a role model. "Alfred Stieglitz is a Jew," wrote Frank. "He is the prophet. And his ways are near to the old ways of his people. He has been the true Apostle of self-liberation in a destructive land. . . . Stieglitz is primarily the Jewish mystic. Suffering is his daily bread: sacrifice is his creed: failure is his beloved. . . . He is a man who has seen God and who has dared to speak."[8]

Frank's interest in all of the arts and his search for father figures had led him to Stieglitz, whom he revered as "perhaps to-day the one major American in art."[9] Often beginning his letters to the photographer "Cher Maître," he admired not only the older man's own work as an artist but also his efforts on behalf of others. To translate Stieglitz's dual rôle into the world of letters, Frank set out to be both a novelist and a critic. As the first, he was determined to prove himself a great artist. As a critic, he would be judge and prophet. In his book *Our America*, published in 1919, he declared himself the spokesman for a new generation revolting against the crassness of American industrialism — the successes of which naturally underwrote the revolt. "Ours," he wrote, "is the first generation of Americans consciously engaged in spiritual pioneering."[10]

It was Waldo Frank who introduced Paul Rosenfeld, one year behind him at Yale, both to Stieglitz and to *The Seven Arts*, in the first issue of which appeared an article about 291 written by Rosenfeld under the pseudonym Peter Minuit. Born in 1890 to prosperous German-Jewish parents who loved literature and music, Rosenfeld was unhappily packed off to military academy at thirteen, three years after his mother had died. Following his graduation from Yale, where he was an editor of the "Lit," he entered the first class at Columbia's School of Journalism and received a bachelor of literature degree in 1913. Having a comfortable independent income, which Frank always envied, Rosenfeld traveled extensively in Europe and devoted himself to writing criticism of music, literature, and the visual arts.

Attractively plump, turning quite stout during the twenties, Rosenfeld had a pink complexion, innocent and expressive brown eyes, auburn hair, and a trim mustache. William Carlos Williams called him "a baroque cherub."[11] He looked the part of a country squire in his brown tweed

Brooks Brothers suits, and it was perhaps a fear of being thought provincial that led him to such excessive affectations as coining the word *eclaircised* when he meant enlightened and using *genial* to mean marked by genius.

Lewis Mumford observed that of the men associated with *The Seven Arts*, Rosenfeld "was the most generous and outgoing to all the new manifestations in the arts: the readiest to search the sand and grit, laboriously, for the sake of the grain or two of gold he might bring to light, the most ready to submerge his identity in that of other creative talents."[12] If he erred in a judgment, he would always prefer to do so on the side of generosity. Rosenfeld would write that he believed "the best attack on the bad is the loving understanding and exposition of the good."[13]

The critic would remain one of Stieglitz's closest friends for the rest of their lives. (They would die a week apart). Edmund Wilson wrote of the eligible bachelor that "his strongest tie was with Stieglitz, toward whom he stood in something like a filial relation; and the group around Stieglitz became for him both family and church." Rosenfeld, said Wilson, revered Stieglitz as a prophet:

> It was difficult, if not impossible, to persuade him to pay attention to any contemporary American painter who was not a protégé of Stieglitz', and if Stieglitz had excommunicated a refractory or competitive disciple, Paul, following the official directive, would condemn him, not merely as an artist but as a reprobate who had somehow committed an unpardonable moral treason.[14]

Frank and Rosenfeld hailed a middle-aged Ohio writer, Sherwood Anderson, as an avatar of the new America. Frank wrote that Anderson's stories were informed by "a consciousness of life and love which must create for us the America of our to-morrow."[15] Rosenfeld called Anderson a "phallic Chekov" and described him as looking "like a racing tout and a divine poet, like a movie-actor and a young priest, like a bartender, a business-man, a hayseed, a mama's boy, a satyr, and an old sit-by-the-stove."[16] He was a true heir of Walt Whitman, representing the essence of America and embracing life in all its complexity.

Not only Anderson's powerful fiction but also the story of his own life was taken as an epic of the America that seemed to be dawning. Born in Ohio in 1876, Anderson had settled in Chicago after serving in the U.S. Army at the end of the Spanish-American War. Working for an advertising firm, he had become known, according to Rosenfeld, as "one of the best mail-order copy-writers in America," writing paeans to manure spreaders and patent medicines.[17] In the early teens he began the haunting stories that he would publish, in 1919, in his book *Winesburg, Ohio*. Three appeared in *The Masses* during 1916, the year in which his first novel, *Windy McPherson's Son*, came out. Early in 1917 Anderson made a brief trip to New York to meet the *Seven Arts* editors, who were impressed by his novel and published several of his stories. During the summer of 1918 he took a leave of absence from his advertising firm to live in New York for a few months. Listing the most important events of that stay, Anderson wrote Frank, "I saw the O'Keeffe things and the Stieglitz things."[18] Anderson and Stieglitz liked each other immediately. For several years they would see little of each other and correspond only rarely, though by the summer of 1920 the writer had sent Stieglitz a group of watercolors he had painted.[19]

In 1919 Anderson told Frank, "One thing I have found out. I cannot continue to live the life I have lived as a businessman. In a sense I have been like one living in a damp, dark cellar since I went back into business after my few months of freedom in New York last year."[20] Soon he would revolt, and his rejection of the world of business in favor of the world of art would be celebrated, at least by Stieglitz and his friends, as nothing less than a messianic rebirth.

CHAPTER FIFTY·THREE

IN THE SPRING of 1918 Leopold Stieglitz's daughter Elizabeth, perceiving that her uncle was in love, wrote O'Keeffe a series of long letters
trying to persuade her to leave Texas and settle in New York. But O'Keeffe
had no such intention. "Just because I want to talk to him, I may go East
this Spring — I don't know — I can't tell," she told Elizabeth. "He is probably more necessary to me than anyone I know, but I do not feel that I have
to be near him. In fact I think we are probably better apart." As for Elizabeth's attempts to pressure her into reciprocating Stieglitz's love, the artist
reprimanded her, "Nobody can make me feel something I just don't feel."[1]

Nor could the war hysteria that prevailed in Canyon convert O'Keeffe
to a Germanophobia that disgusted her. In December she had outraged
her neighbors when she complained that it was un-Christian for a local
store to sell viciously anti-German Christmas cards. Already suspected because of her unconventional behavior and her against-the-rules romance
with a student, she was widely slandered by the town's busybodies. So depressed about the war that she was unable to paint, O'Keeffe suffered a
nervous breakdown in February, accompanied by a persistent sore throat
and cough — symptoms disturbingly suggestive of the tuberculosis that
ran in her family. She was granted a leave of absence from her job and considered going to New York but went instead to her friend Leah Harris's
isolated farm in Waring, not far from San Antonio. Well cared for by the

capable Harris, who seems to have fallen in love with her, O'Keeffe wrote to Stieglitz in April, "It's a wonderful place — I wonder why everyone doesn't live here."[2] But her physical ailments persisted.

Using his very real concern about her health as a pretext, Stieglitz dispatched Paul Strand to Texas early in May both to report on her condition and to encourage her to seek better medical care in New York. Strand was an odd choice for the rôle of John Alden, since Stieglitz knew of his epistolary courtship. Perhaps Alfred felt that Paul would be the most attractive bait to lure Georgia to New York, after which she would have to choose between her two suitors. Despite her obvious affection and respect for the older man, she had given him little reason to expect more.

Strand remained with O'Keeffe in Texas for nearly a month, during which time Stieglitz went through agonies of anxiety and hope. In response to tantalizing reports about her health and her wavering in regard to New York, Alfred wrote his emissary reams in which he revealed the intensity of his concern. "I want her to live — I never wanted anything as much as that — She is the spirit of 291 — Not — I," he avowed, but he stopped short of professing that he was desperately in love with her. Instead, he instructed Strand not to put any pressure on O'Keeffe. "The coming or not coming is entirely in her hands," he insisted. "There must be no suggestion of interference one way or another."[3]

In spite of his resolution, Alfred did offer inducements. He recognized a major factor in O'Keeffe's decision as her "lack of funds not stated but existing." What she obviously needed and wanted was quiet, "which means the need of some funds." Those he promised to provide. "Rest — a simple home — peace of mind — whoever can give her that will give her what she needs above all things," he wrote to Strand on May 27. "If she wants to come — really wants to — feels the necessity — and feels that she can stand the trip physically — all else would arrange itself."[4]

Specifically, Elizabeth had told her uncle Al that O'Keeffe could live in her studio on East Fifty-ninth Street; Lee had said that he would continue to pay the rent if his brother would compensate him with prints. Having studied painting in Munich with Sime Herrmann, twenty-one-year-old Elizabeth was now enrolled at the Art Students League, but she and several friends would spend the next few months farming on the grounds of her father's country house in Westchester County, New York.

Toward the end of May, O'Keeffe finally decided to go to New York for a week or two to visit Stieglitz, whom she had not seen for a year. She wanted to explain to him in person that the city didn't suit her as a place to live. Traveling by train via New Orleans, O'Keeffe and Strand arrived early on the morning of Sunday, June 9, at New York's Pennsylvania Station, where Alfred met them. Besides being exhausted from the trip, O'Keeffe was still coughing and had a fever. The two men took her straight to Elizabeth's studio, on the top floor of the brownstone house at 114 East Fifty-ninth Street, between Park and Lexington avenues. To make the skylighted studio as bright as possible, Elizabeth and Donald had painted the walls pale yellow and the floors yellowish-orange. Preferring the studio to the small, dark bedroom, O'Keeffe moved her bed to a spot directly under the skylight.

Once O'Keeffe was in New York, Strand was pushed aside. Having provided her with a place to stay, Alfred took charge of her and arranged for his brother to examine her. When Lee prescribed bed rest, Alfred, who called himself a "strict nurse," stopped by at least once a day but warned Strand that she was too weak to have any other visitors. For her sake, Alfred even learned how to cook eggs. When Dove brought some from his farm to build up O'Keeffe's strength, Herbert Seligmann taught him how to coddle them.

On June 18 Alfred told Dove, "These last 10 days have been very full ones — possibly the fullest I have had in my life." He went on to glory about O'Keeffe, "She is much more extraordinary than even I had believed. — In fact I don't believe there ever has been anything like her. Mind & feeling very clear — spontaneous — & uncannily beautiful — absolutely living every pulse-beat."[5]

Alfred stayed out as late as possible every night to avoid Emmy. Once, for instance, he walked with Strand from 11 P.M. to 1:30 A.M., no doubt spending much of that time tormenting the young man with praises of, and plans for, O'Keeffe. As a conscientious objector, Strand received an agricultural deferment with Stieglitz's help. After first working briefly on Arthur Dove's farm, he did an equally brief stint in Westchester, where he proceeded to fall in love with Elizabeth. She, however, loved forty-year-old Donald Davidson, a wiry Scot who had been employed as the gardener at Oaklawn before joining her project. A scion of a family that had lost its fortune in the panic of 1893, the congenial and sensitive Davidson would become one of Alfred's closest friends. When Elizabeth and Davidson decided to get married in the spring of 1919, Alfred successfully pleaded their case to an initially opposed Lee. Late in the summer of 1918 Strand would be assigned to a medical unit in Minnesota. He wrote in September that he didn't mind, since he had "nothing else to look forward to particularly."[6]

*   *   *

It was presumably only because Alfred said nothing to Emmy or to Kitty, who got home from Smith on June 13, that he could inform Dove, "Everything is running without friction. — I seem to have the situation in hand for the present."[7]

About ten days after O'Keeffe's arrival in New York, Lee declared her healthy, and she began to paint. Alfred visited her daily, sometimes bringing along a friend or two to meet her. On July 8, he conducted her to 1111 Madison to photograph her in his study while Emmy was out on what was supposed to be an extended shopping trip. When she returned early and found them, Alfred claimed that it was all perfectly innocent. "There was no more between me and O'Keeffe than there is between us here," he later told Seligmann.[8] Alfred and Georgia fled, and he stayed out even later than usual that night. Emmy waited up and gave him an ultimatum: Stop seeing that girl or get out! Alfred, whose self-serving martyr complex was one of the least attractive aspects of his psychology, wrote to Dove, "I was virtually 'kicked' out of home — like I was 'kicked' out of the Camera Club 10 years ago."[9] To Seligmann he whined, "It was the unfairest thing that ever happened to any man."[10] Now if anyone criticized him for deserting his wife, he could retort that she had positively forced him into O'Keeffe's arms.

Having secured O'Keeffe's permission for him to share the studio with her, Alfred began moving his personal possessions and photographic equipment there early the next morning. Mitchell Kennerley let him store his books in the subcellar of the Anderson Galleries' new building, a four-story palace at the southeast corner of Park Avenue and Fifty-ninth Street, half a block from the studio. Within forty-eight hours Alfred had vacated 1111 Madison, though he would later claim that he had gotten his "thousands of pictures and books" out of the apartment by five o'clock on the day of the interrupted photographic session.[11]

In the studio, Alfred and Georgia strung up a clothesline, over which they draped a blanket to separate their beds — for they had not yet become lovers. It shouldn't surprise us that a man who protested so vehemently against puritanism had a streak of conventional propriety. Today it seems rather quaint for Alfred to have written to Joe Obermeyer, "Emmy charged me with something which was absolutely untrue. She slandered an innocent woman — girl. It seems you can't understand any fine or decent relationship between man and woman."[12] Although it was hypocritical for Alfred not to acknowledge that he was in love with O'Keeffe, he was certainly telling the truth about their chastity. It was apparently not until late July that they finally had sexual intercourse. Informing Dove of that momentous step, Alfred wrote him in a letter dated August 15, "O'Keeffe & I are One in a real sense."[13]

As soon as Emmy "kicked" him out, Stieglitz had his brother-in-law George Herbert Engelhard, a lawyer, begin preparing divorce papers. Because of determined opposition from Emmy and her brothers, the proceedings would take six years. Indeed, three days after Alfred moved out, Emmy implored him to return. "Home already 'regrets,'" he told Dove.[14] During the next several months Alfred would be engaged in extricating himself from his marriage. He was fighting to save his life. His desperation, self-righteousness, and guilt sometimes led him to remarks and strategies whose cruelty he seems not to have recognized. For instance, the first time he saw Emmy after leaving her, he suggested that he, she, and O'Keeffe have dinner together. He believed that the two women should become friends. Revealingly, he wrote to Dove late in July, "It's about the maddest time of my life these days. — Tragedy & comedy — all the same it seems. . . . I sometimes wonder . . . whether I have any real feeling of any kind for anyone or anything. — Whether I'm not like nature itself — just a force relentless. — Isn't that what everyone really is."[15]

About August 1, Alfred and Georgia went to Lake George. Hedwig was thrilled to see her beloved son so happy — and welcomed O'Keeffe as the cause. Because Emmy had so obviously made him miserable, Hedwig had never liked her. Around 1910, Alfred's mother had hinted that he should divorce Emmy and marry the newly widowed Maggie Foord.

"The family like [O'Keeffe] hugely," Stieglitz told Dove. "Everyone laughs at us."[16] They did so because Alfred and Georgia were like two teenagers in love. Several times a day they would run up the stairs to their bedroom, so eager to make love that they would start taking their clothes off as they ran. Georgia wrote to Elizabeth Stieglitz, "I was never so happy in my life," but Alfred felt a bit guilty about being so happy while the war still raged in Europe.[17]

Not everything was perfect at Lake George. O'Keeffe, who had assumed that Alfred could be at home only in Spartan surroundings, was shocked by the Victorian clutter of Oaklawn. She was even more shocked, indeed repelled, by Alfred's self-indulgently temperamental sister Selma, an obnoxious prima donna; by Selma's alcoholic husband, Lou Schubart; and by her pampered and vicious Boston terrier, nicknamed Rippy with good reason. Georgia felt rather overwhelmed by the noisily contentious family gathered around the dinner table, where she asserted her independence and self-sufficiency by concocting her own fresh and lightly dressed salads while everyone else ate dull, heavy fare. Whenever the conversation became unbearably heated, she would carry her plate out to the porch to finish in peace.

Alfred and Georgia spent their days working, hiking up Prospect Mountain, swimming, and making love. After dinner almost every evening they would row out on the lake to watch the sunset and the falling of darkness. There, in silence, they enjoyed some of their happiest moments. "The Lake is our great Companion," Stieglitz wrote Dove. "It is virtually neglected this year — the War. — So we have it nearly to ourselves."[18]

About a week after their arrival at the lake, the tranquillity was broken by a desperate telegram from Kitty, asking Alfred to come immediately to her summer camp on Lake Winnipesaukee. She was so confused about her parents' situation that she didn't know whom to believe. Emmy, staying nearby, was exhausting her with daily bouts of hysteria in which she voiced her pathetic determination to change everything about herself that had displeased Alfred and so win him back. He, on the other hand, was insisting that his daughter spend several weeks in September with him and O'Keeffe at Lake George. Kitty felt that to do so would constitute a betrayal of her mother.

Leaving O'Keeffe at Oaklawn, Alfred went to New Hampshire at once. The first afternoon he met with Kitty alone. During five "terrible" hours, he poured out all his grievances against her mother to make it clear that he would never return. He also did his best to convince her that Emmy would ultimately be much better off without him. He hated to subject his daughter to such "cruel" and "selfish" talk, but it was absolutely necessary for her to understand why her parents were separating. His revelations had the intended effect, and the next morning he was relieved to see Kitty "calm & ready" for a meeting with both her parents in a lakeside cottage, their "first true meeting," as Alfred called it. At the end of a long discussion of their future arrangements, he promised Kitty that O'Keeffe would not be at the lake in September. A few days after this session he wrote, "I have been living as I never lived before. — I have gone through a great deal — some very painful hours — but all intensely real. . . . Every moment is a happy eternity — sometimes — rarely — the moment is of intensest pain — but even that turns into a great glory."[19]

Certain that Kitty would be won over to complete acceptance if only she could meet O'Keeffe and spend some time with her, Alfred broke his promise. When Kitty arrived at Oaklawn and found O'Keeffe still there, she threw such tantrums that Alfred and Georgia hastily retreated to New

York. In response to a letter from Kitty, melodramatically delivered late one night by her uncle George Engelhard, Alfred traveled to Oaklawn, alone, by the first train the next morning. Still at an impasse at the end of two days of tears and anger, he left the lake and returned to New York alone. From then on, father and daughter saw little of each other. They maintained a perfunctory correspondence, in which the rage on both sides was cloaked with routine assurances of love, but Kitty could not forgive Alfred for his desertion, and he could not forgive her for wishing that his happiness with O'Keeffe would come to an end.

CHAPTER FIFTY·FOUR

ON AUGUST 7, 1918, a month after he had moved in with O'Keeffe, Stieglitz wrote that he had "done a great deal of photography[,] some of the best I ever did."[1] He was shooting portraits of O'Keeffe "with a kind of heat and excitement," as she put it, recalling elsewhere, "We'd make love. Afterwards he would take photographs of me."[2] For Stieglitz, the latter was a continuation of the former, since he remarked in general about his entire photographic career, "When I make a picture, I make love."

O'Keeffe recounted that Stieglitz always kept his tripod-mounted view camera set up in her studio so that he could expose a few plates whenever inspiration struck. He insisted that they arrange their schedules to be in the studio when the light was at its best. Even then, as O'Keeffe later remembered, the combination of slow emulsions and tiny aperture settings required him to use exposure times as excruciatingly long as three or four minutes. If she blinked or otherwise moved, "a great deal of fuss was made about it."[3]

Stieglitz photographed O'Keeffe obsessively between 1918 and 1925, a period that was by far the most prolific in his life. The resulting cumulative portrait, on which he continued to work sporadically until the mid-1930s, eventually comprised about 350 mounted prints. It was effectively the resumption of his interrupted aggregate portrait of Kitty. But Stieglitz did not regard O'Keeffe as a daughter, despite the fact that he was fifty-four and she was thirty, only nine years older than Kitty. It is true that he called O'Keeffe "The Great Child" and a "Woman-Child" and that he spoke of her "childlike pure loveliness."[4] But he considered himself a "child" as well, insofar as he approached the world freshly and honestly. He wrote in August 1918 that they were "both either intensely sane or mad children."[5]

Stieglitz believed that in O'Keeffe he had finally found the twin he had always sought. They soon discovered uncanny coincidences that allowed them to feel that they were secret sharers. In the spring of 1908, a still life by O'Keeffe had won her a stay of several weeks that summer at Amitola, an artists' retreat on Lake George. The house was the former Crosbyside Hotel, where Alfred had stayed with his family in the summer of 1880. As Stieglitz and O'Keeffe compared memories, they realized — or chose to convince themselves — that they stayed in the same room. It also turned out that when Alfred had helped his father to judge a painting competition at Amitola late in the summer of 1908, they had awarded the first prize to Eugene Speicher's portrait of O'Keeffe.

Nothing in the world could have made Stieglitz happier than to be able to say, as he did in a July 1918 letter to Arthur Dove, "O'Keeffe is truly magnificent. . . . We are at least 90% alike — she a purer form of myself."[6] O'Keeffe accentuated their kinship externally with a black cape like Stieglitz's and a hat somewhat similar to his porkpie. In 1919 he would write, "O'Keeffe and I are really a queer team — more like a couple of pal tramps in spirit — and in fact too perhaps — than anything else."[7]

The fact that Stieglitz's "twin" was possibly a bisexual woman (the evidence is inconclusive) introduced an undercurrent of homosexuality and hermaphroditism both into their relationship and into his photographs of her. His lover could appear either masculine or feminine, by conventional standards, and his camera aped the functions of the female reproductive system. Although much has been made of the phallic quality of a camera, it is actually more like a womb. In this paradigm, it is the subject — O'Keeffe — who takes on the masculine role of impregnation in photographic intercourse. O'Keeffe is said to have told a male homosexual friend late in her life that Stieglitz had had some erotic interest in men — though he seems to have concealed it well except, ironically, in his relationship with her.[8] Of course, the erotic component of narcissism — the self-proclaimed motive for all of his photography — is by definition homosexual.

Stieglitz subsumed his entire artistic and photographic history into his series of portraits of O'Keeffe, in which images range from the maudlin Symbolism of Franz von Stuck or the *retardataire* Pictorialism of Clarence White to the radical abstraction of Picasso and its photographic equivalent pioneered by Paul Strand. Some of Stieglitz's most erotic photographs were probably inspired by Rodin's drawings, while one of O'Keeffe in bed, her head on a pillow, clearly echoes not only his similar picture of the Berlin prostitute Paula but also his Brancusi bronze, *Sleeping Muse I.*

The series also encompasses Stieglitz's personal history, for he photographed O'Keeffe as all the women he had ever loved: the black-and-white-clad teenage girl in Central Park, Paula, Duse, the net mender, Miss S. R., and Katharine Rhoades. He photographed her in many moods and states — happy, anguished, seductive, annoyed, haughty, exhausted. He also made images of her engaged in such activities as working, sewing, and sitting at the wheel of her car.

In the splendid book of fifty-one images from the series that O'Keeffe edited in 1978, it seems almost as though we are watching a striptease as the prim schoolteacher removes her rather masculine clothes to reveal a voluptuous female body, with a lithe form, full breasts, and gracefully swelling hips. Stieglitz shot many close-up studies of parts of her body — especially of her hands, often making exaggeratedly emotional gestures. As Paul Rosenfeld wrote, he

> based pictures not alone on faces and hands and backs of heads, on feet naked and feet stockinged and shod, on breasts and torsos, thighs and buttocks. He has based them on the navel, the mons veneris, the armpits, the bones underneath the skin of the neck and collar. He has brought the lens close to the epidermis in order to photograph, and shown us the life of the pores, of the hairs along the shin-bone, of the veining of the pulse and the liquid moisture on the upper lip.[9]

The portrait was an homage not only to O'Keeffe but also to Walt Whitman (whose poems had been criticized, shortly after their first publication, as excessively photographic, with one reviewer unperspicaciously complaining that "according to Whitman's theory, the greatest poet is he who performs the office of camera to the world, merely reflecting what he sees"[10]). Stieglitz surely conceived of his project as the visual equivalent of Whitman's great omnicelebratory poetic inventories of remembered pleasures, such as that in "I Sing the Body Electric" savoring

> womanhood, and all that is a woman
> . . . .
> The womb, the teats, nipples, breast-milk, tears, laughter, weeping,
>   love-looks, love-perturbations and risings,

The voice, articulation, language, whispering, shouting aloud,
Food, drink, pulse, digestion, sweat, sleep, walking, swimming,
Poise on the hips, leaping, reclining, embracing, arm-curving
   and tightening,
. . . .
The curious sympathy one feels when feeling with the hand the
naked meat of the body.[11]

The photographer's friend Lewis Mumford observed that "it was Stieglitz's endeavor . . . to translate the unseen world of tactile values as they develop between lovers not merely in the sexual act but in the entire relation of two personalities — to translate this world of blind touch into sight . . . Stieglitz achieved the exact visual equivalent of the report of the hand or the face as it travels over the body of the beloved."[12] But even that did not fully satisfy his desire to make a photographic exploration of sexuality. Mumford related that "Stieglitz conceived, though he never carried out, a series of photographs of the heads of stallions and mares, of bulls and cows, in the act of mating, hoping to catch in the brute an essential quality that would symbolize the probably unattainable photograph of a passionate human mating."[13] He also talked about working on other series: studies of the faces and bodies of pregnant women and of women in love, as well as detailed photographic explorations of various women's bodies to reveal the differences among individuals. The principal corollary on which Stieglitz actually began working in 1918 was a new series of portraits of his friends.

   Stieglitz's photographs of O'Keeffe constitute an intricate psychological pas de deux. As O'Keeffe self-consciously presented herself to the camera, whose persona was recorded on the film? Her own? Hers as she wanted to be seen by Stieglitz? Hers as she thought Stieglitz would like to see her? Hers as Stieglitz perceived her? Hers as Stieglitz shaped her? Indeed, the portrait series may well be the ultimate expression of Stieglitz's Pygmalion complex. It is as though every time he photographed O'Keeffe, he was striking another blow of his sculptor's chisel. If so, was he imposing his vision on her? Or did he feel that he was doing what many sculptors have claimed to be doing, liberating the form implicit in the block of stone they are carving? Stieglitz said that O'Keeffe enjoyed studying the proofs of his photographs of her, as if she would discover by looking at them who she was — as he himself had perhaps done with Erdmann Encke's portraits in Berlin.

*   *   *

When Stieglitz began printing his images of O'Keeffe in the fall of 1918, platinum paper had recently become unavailable, for the Russian Revolution had disrupted the supply of platinum from the Urals, at that time the principal source. Manufacturers soon substituted palladium, which is next to platinum on the periodic table. Less expensive than its cousin and available from Canada, palladium produced a paper that yielded a rich reddish-brown tone when developed. In December 1918 Stieglitz complained, "Palladium is all right but I yearn for Platinum. It has so much *inner* quality & black lives at all times — deep brown does not."[14] During the next six years he would make most of his prints on palladium paper, though he gradually switched over to the gelatin-silver paper that he would use exclusively after 1924.

In January 1919 Stieglitz wrote to Paul Strand, "Visitors galore all coming to see our work. . . . All say our work is unlike anything they have ever seen. — And it is — Both very direct — very powerful — very beautiful."[15] Among those visitors were Edward Steichen, Charles Sheeler, Marius de Zayas, Leo Stein, Arthur Davies, Frank Crowninshield, and Walter Arensberg. Stieglitz claimed that when Steichen saw O'Keeffe's paintings, he was so moved by them that he grew pale; when he saw Stieglitz's photographs, "tears rolled down his cheeks."[16] Stieglitz felt friendly enough toward Steichen to invite him to Lake George in the summer of 1921, but the younger photographer declined on the grounds that he realized "how small the place was and how much family there was to occupy and permeate it."[17]

Stieglitz was so excited about his photographs of O'Keeffe that he wrote he was "mad enough to occasionally dream of more numbers of *Camera Work*." In spite of "*No Cash*," he would try to get in touch with Bruckmann Verlag after the end of the war, in November 1918.[18] But nothing would come of his overtures.

Stieglitz's portraits of O'Keeffe were first seen by the public in a small exhibition of work by 291ers at Aline Meyer Liebman's pet institution, the Young Women's Hebrew Association on 110th Street, in March 1919. That spring Alfred and Georgia threw themselves into their individual and collaborative work, though he had to spend much time clearing out his room at 291–293 Fifth Avenue, for the brownstones were to be torn down, along with the others on the block, to make way for a huge office building, which still stands.[19] Alfred added to the books already stored in the subcellar of the Anderson Galleries, and many of the works of art from the Tomb were moved to the studio on Fifty-ninth Street.

Alfred and Georgia finally went to Lake George in July for what would be the family's last summer at Oaklawn, since they could no longer afford to maintain the old mansion. When it was sold that fall they retained not only the farmhouse and its property (called the Hill) but also the rights to a stretch of lakefront for swimming and boating.

Surely Alfred amazed even himself when, during an August storm that had come up suddenly, he managed to save a twelve-year-old boy whose canoe had capsized. Alas, there was nothing he could do to help the boy's older companion.

From mid-August until mid-September the weather was, as Alfred grumbled, "more than trying," with ceaseless "gray — rain — penetrating dampness."[20] When the sky finally cleared and he got to work in earnest, photographing and printing, Paul Strand arrived for a visit on his way back to New York after having been discharged from his military service in Minnesota. Although O'Keeffe seems to have been somewhat apprehensive about seeing her rejected suitor, Strand was able to reestablish his friendship with the couple quite easily.

Stieglitz and O'Keeffe were working so well at the lake that they postponed their return to New York until around November 1. We can only wonder about the cause of the distress to which Stieglitz (always keenly responsive to the weather) was referring when he described to Waldo Frank a storm that they experienced shortly before their departure. "The lake was whipped into a Bacchanalian Fury — Southeaster blew a hot gale," he wrote. "And all reflected on the waters of the Lake below us. Passion to the Last Degree. — Nature seemed to be tearing itself to pieces. . . . I was particularly miserable just before the storm. — The storm brought some peace to me."[21]

CHAPTER FIFTY·FIVE

ALTHOUGH STIEGLITZ HAD been deeply gratified by visitors' responses to his and O'Keeffe's work, Georgia had been less so. She was, in fact, so upset by the consistently sexual interpretations of her paintings, whether representational or abstract, that she had the first of the many debilitating crises she would suffer while she lived with Stieglitz. During the first half of 1920, she felt she had reached a dead end and found herself unable to face a canvas. Stieglitz worried whether she would "paint at all this summer. — Or even soon thereafter. — Or ever perhaps."[1]

Late in the spring, O'Keeffe resorted to what would become her most dependable remedy for such crises: to get away from Stieglitz for a while. She accepted a long-standing invitation from Marjorie ("Marnie") and Bennet Schauffler to visit them at their summer place in York Beach, Maine. There she enjoyed not only the Spartan comfort of the house, which she later described as "a large, very plain, almost empty place with a few good old Indian rugs kicked about in rather disorderly fashion over the otherwise bare floors," but also the pleasures of good food and a beautiful, nearly deserted beach.[2]

Despite O'Keeffe's paralysis, the winter and spring were quite productive for Stieglitz. In addition to helping with the organization of a ten-year retrospective of Marin's watercolors that opened at Charles Daniel's gallery in March, he was busy making portraits of his family and friends.

During the course of 1919 and 1920 he photographed, among others, his sister Agnes's husband, George Engelhard; their daughter Georgia; Donald Davidson; Marin; J. Nilsen Laurvik; and O'Keeffe's friend Dorothy True, of whom he accidentally made a double exposure, superimposing her face onto a shot of her calf (he was delighted when he saw the result). Most he simply asked to sit for him, but he would occasionally — and reluctantly — agree to photograph a patron for $1,000 or $1,500, some or all of which would go into the fund he maintained to aid artists.

During 1920 Stieglitz also added a few negatives to his portrait of O'Keeffe. One, of her hands sewing, is among the masterpieces of the entire series. The disembodied hands, the right with a thimble on its middle finger, the left holding a needle, stand out against an expanse of dark fabric with folds like those in the dress of a Flemish Renaissance Madonna. The hands are outlined beautifully with dark lines; Stieglitz claimed that this was "the first use of solarization as an integral part of a picture." Although the image was obviously shot as a horizontal, with O'Keeffe's left hand lower than the bethimbled right, Stieglitz (disregarding anatomical possibility) wrote on the back of one print, "The photograph can be hung in 4 ways — each a 'different' picture."[3] Today the image is usually exhibited and published as a vertical.

In 1921 Stieglitz sent Aline Meyer Liebman, whom he wanted "to have something AA + 1," a magnificent reddish-brown palladium print of the image, a print whose emulsion he had deliberately scratched through to highlight the needle.[4] Liebman, who had studied photography with Clarence White and had a darkroom in her house on East Eighty-seventh Street, wanted to choose another image. In February 1924 Alfred wrote her, "Don't think I have forgotten about that print of the hands you want exchanged for another print."[5] Her heirs have reason to be glad that the exchange was never made; on October 8, 1993, Christie's auctioned it off for them to the tune of $398,500, setting a new world record for a single photographic print.[6]

In April 1920 the brownstone at 114 East Fifty-ninth Street, in which Stieglitz and O'Keeffe had been living, was put up for sale. In mid-June the new owners announced that they were going to quintuple the rents. Any tenants not willing to sign a lease on those terms would have to vacate by July 15. Unable to afford an apartment of their own, Alfred and Georgia fortunately did not have to worry about where they would live when they returned to the city in the fall. Lee and Lizzie told them that space could be made for them in their house.

Now Stieglitz became obsessed by the chore of packing and storing, in the Lincoln Warehouse, all of his and O'Keeffe's work, as well as his collection of works by others and the possessions they had accumulated at the studio. He also sorted through his books in the subcellar of the Anderson Galleries and threw many away. "With the future for us an enigma," he wrote to Arthur Dove, "why keep anything not really of real need or real pleasure-giving?"[7]

Stieglitz mused that perhaps the Bolsheviks would take over America and seize their stored possessions, for the success of the Russian Revolution had encouraged many socialists throughout the world to convert to communism. In January 1920 Attorney General A. Mitchell Palmer ordered the arrest of thousands of alleged "reds" — most of them completely innocent — and warned that the "Red Menace" was planning to begin a revolution on May 1. When nothing happened on the dreaded day, Palmer became widely discredited, but fears were revived later that month when the Socialist party held its national convention in New York and gave its presidential nomination to Eugene Debs, who was then serving a ten-year prison sentence for violations of the Espionage Act. That same month, two Italian-American anarchists, Nicola Sacco and Bartolomeo Vanzetti, were arrested and charged with having murdered the paymaster and the guard of a Massachusetts shoe factory during a holdup. Many people expected a financial panic (it didn't occur until 1921), which some believed might create conditions for a revolution. In August 1920 Stieglitz would write to Dove, "With the quiet of this morning it is hard to believe that there is greater Hell in the world than during the War — & that sooner or later something must 'happen' dramatically and positively over here."[8]

Alfred and Georgia were in no hurry to get to Lake George in the summer of 1920, since the farmhouse on the Hill was undergoing major renovations to make it habitable for at least six months of the year. A new furnace was being installed, some large rooms were being divided for more efficient use of the available space, and most of the former servants' rooms were being transformed into guest rooms. During the next year or so the house would be wired for electricity and O'Keeffe would have many of the rooms repainted to lighten the interior.

Before their departure for the lake on July 15, Stieglitz made so many trips up and down the four flights of stairs, carrying boxes and parcels from the studio, that (so he boasted) the labor "finally became positively enjoyable & healthgiving."[9] Nevertheless, having worked frantically right up to the last possible day, he would be exhausted for a month. On top of that, it was "so cold and autumn-like" during their first two weeks at Lake George that they had trouble keeping warm.[10]

With the coming of hot weather, they swam in the lake, went out rowing, and took long walks up Prospect Mountain. Alfred felt "a joy of being — & an amusement at many things I took very seriously in former days."[11] Georgia, too, began to feel better and decided that to get herself painting again she needed a proper studio. For some time she had had her eye on one of the outbuildings that were scattered about the Hill's forty acres. In a meadow not far from the farmhouse was a dilapidated shanty that had been built for the Saturday night dances of farmhands and hired help. Georgia felt that if it could be repaired, she would be able to work there in peace and privacy. The local contractor's estimate of $500 was prohibitively high, but when the Davidsons arrived around August 1, Donald enthusiastically suggested that they undertake the project themselves. Waldo Frank and his wife, Margaret Naumburg, a Montessori-trained educator who had founded the Walden School in New York, were staying at a nearby inn for a few weeks. Since Margy was getting bored while Waldo spent every day writing, the others recruited her to help. The Davidsons and O'Keeffe, the latter wearing "bloomers & as little else on above her waistline as possible — for the sun was hot," clambered up a rickety improvised scaffold, pried the rotten shingles off the roof, and laid down tar paper.[12] When he wasn't photographing the proceedings, Stieglitz helped to lay a new floor and oil the rafters.

"Finally Georgia & I have our own shanty," Alfred excitedly told Dove.[13] But she soon put him straight: the shanty was to be hers alone. (Whenever the weather was hot, she would take off all her clothes and work there naked.) As soon as the repairs were completed, O'Keeffe began retiring to her new refuge and finally took up her brushes. It was as though she were starting all over at the Art Students League. Returning to the most basic subject matter, she began painting careful still lifes of fruit — a bunch of grapes on a white plate and, when the apple trees became exceptionally prolific that fall, so many paintings of them that Alfred exclaimed she had "the apple fever."[14] Still later, she would make her first canvases of autumn leaves, a theme to which she would return every year during the 1920s. Surely, she must have resolved, no one could possibly impose sexual interpretations on such paintings.

Apples may have appealed to O'Keeffe for their matter-of-factness, but they were also an important symbol for Stieglitz, who frequently told his listeners that an artist was like an apple tree, "taking up sap from the ground and bearing apples."[15] Furthermore, the apple was a symbol of America. For Stieglitz, the true American artist was like a hardy apple tree, his or her roots reaching deep into the native soil, naturally producing art true to his or her environment. Deploring the number of American artists who imitated French modernism, Alfred would say that if American apple trees heard people praising plums, they would try to bear plums.[16]

During the summer of 1920, Stieglitz was stimulated by the prospect of a large show of his photographs at the Anderson Galleries early the following year. He felt that "photography does need a real awakening & perhaps I can help bring that about with what I have done."[17] He exposed many new negatives and worked hard to make good prints for his show, spending seven or eight hours some days bent over a bathtub in the farmhouse to develop and wash his prints, which he dried on lines strung above the kitchen stove.

That summer he tried the experiment of making some humorous photographs, including *The Way Art Moves*, in which we see Moses Ezekiel's bust of Judith, and two other pieces of sculpture, being transported in a cart from Oaklawn to the Hill. He also photographed Waldo Frank, sitting on the porch of the farmhouse with a manuscript on his lap, holding three partially eaten apples. The cores of two more are at his feet. Like his portrait of Dove as J. P. Morgan, this picture of Frank is something of a private joke deriving from Stieglitz's long-standing interest in caricature. Dressed as an urban schmo, Frank is depicted gorging on apples in an attempt to get in touch with the essence of rural America. In a similar spirit, Stieglitz photographed his niece Elizabeth — who, practicing Hinduism, abstained from alcohol and tobacco — holding a pipe, a cigarette, and a bottle of beer.

In the fall Stieglitz made some rather silly related photographs of O'Keeffe to emphasize her Americanness: in one she holds a branch laden with apples, and in another her head rests uncomfortably on the rim of a basket of apples. A much more powerful image from that period depicts an especially mannish O'Keeffe stoically resisting the temptation posed by an unmistakably testicular and phallic arrangement of two apples and one long leaf hanging from a branch and protruding into the left side of the picture. Here we see O'Keeffe as the new Eve, a woman who does not fall victim to the serpent offering forbidden fruit. No other Stieglitz photograph of O'Keeffe so hauntingly suggests the subtle but complex currents of homosexuality that ran beneath the surface of their relationship.

*   *   *

Late in September, Georgia came upon Alfred's mother in the throes of a stroke. As soon as Hedwig was well enough to be moved, Lee had her taken to New York by ambulance. The rest of the family followed by train, but Alfred and Georgia, having been assured that the immediate danger was past, remained at the lake. They simply couldn't bear to return yet to the city. Stieglitz had recently called New York "the City of Terribleness" and had written to Dove, "New York does an ugly thing to me. — I feel less & less a part of it."[18] To Aline Meyer Liebman he confided, "I like New York less & less — possibly having loved it too much & having given it a little too much of myself."[19]

After thoroughly enjoying a weeklong visit from Paul Rosenfeld and Charles Duncan early in October, Stieglitz and O'Keeffe stayed on at Lake George for another six weeks, though Alfred found it "queer" to be there while his "Ma" lay ill in New York. They both put in long, satisfying days of work, followed by evenings during which Stieglitz read *Madame Bovary* aloud to O'Keeffe or listened to Victrola records, ending with nights of lovemaking. Alfred wrote that never before had he experienced "such feeling of being actually alive." He felt that he had "worked much out of [his] system" and was finally "nearing freedom."[20]

Beneath his outward tranquillity, however, Alfred was deeply upset about his mother. He later told Herbert Seligmann that after a rainfall, on one of the many exceptionally still days that fall, he "had gone out seeking to put his feeling into a form" and when, by the barn, he saw a little apple tree covered with raindrops, he photographed it. "Perhaps the raindrops are tears," he explained. "And perhaps that dark entrance that seems to you mysterious is the womb, the place whence we came and where we desire when we are tired and unhappy to return, the womb of our mother, where we are quiet and without responsibility and protected."[21]

Early in December Alfred and Georgia finally left for New York and moved into two rooms on the top two floors of Lee and Lizzie's brownstone house at 60 East Sixty-fifth Street, between Madison and Park avenues. In deference to Lizzie's ninety-year-old mother, whose room was on the front of the fourth floor, Alfred and Georgia would be assigned separate quarters. They were given the red-carpeted front room on the fifth floor to use as their living room. (The two maids shared the rear bedroom on that floor.) It had an alcove that Alfred could use as a rudimentary darkroom and a couch on which he could sleep. Georgia's studio-cum-bedroom, with a southern exposure providing lots of sunlight, was on the floor below, at the rear of the house. It had been occupied during the past five school years by Steichen's elder daughter, Mary, who graduated from her New York private school in June.

Franklin Delano Roosevelt lived across the street, at number 47. In the fall of 1920 the former assistant secretary of the navy was the vice-presidential candidate on the Democratic ticket that lost to Warren Harding and Calvin Coolidge, who campaigned on the slogan "Back to Normalcy" and won by a landslide. The following summer Roosevelt was stricken with polio while vacationing at the family's summer place on Campobello Island, New Brunswick. During the four years they lived in Lee and Lizzie's house, Stieglitz and O'Keeffe must often have seen the young man, paralyzed from the waist down, being taken for an outing in his wheelchair or being helped in and out of his car.

Alfred and Georgia made their own breakfast every day and dined out every evening. Each Wednesday night they would have dinner with Hedwig, and one night a week with the Engelhards. Other evenings they would eat at a modest restaurant in the neighborhood and often receive two or three guests at home afterward in Alfred's cluttered room, all around which O'Keeffe's paintings were stacked. Some evenings they would go to a concert, perhaps with Paul Rosenfeld, the new music critic for *The Dial*, which Scofield Thayer was beginning to transform into the most important American literary and artistic magazine. Or they might go to see the Provincetown Players, whose production of Eugene O'Neill's play *The Emperor Jones* opened in November 1920.

On Saturdays, Stieglitz and O'Keeffe would usually go with a few friends, or as many as a dozen, to the Far East China Garden, a moderately priced restaurant with marble-topped tables at Columbus Circle. After dinner twenty people might sit around the room on East Sixty-fifth Street and talk until after midnight. Besides Stieglitz's closest artistic and literary friends, one might encounter there Walter Lippmann, composer Ernst Bloch, orchestra conductor Leopold Stokowski, Carl Sandburg on a visit from Chicago, or Frank Harris from London. One notable absence was Abraham Walkowitz, who was banished after an unspecified "betrayal" in 1920.

Beginning late in 1922, Alfred and Georgia were also regulars at the salon of the three eccentric Stettheimer sisters — Florine, Ettie, and Carrie — who lived with their widowed mother in an opulent house on West Seventy-sixth Street. O'Keeffe became especially friendly with outspoken Ettie, the possessor of a doctorate in philosophy from the University of Freiburg. She also liked shy Florine, who wrote poetry and painted in a studio decorated with flounced cellophane curtains, glass-topped tables, and clear vases holding crystal flowers. Florine became widely known for faux naïf, white-background portraits of her friends (including one of Stieglitz, in 1928) and for depictions of the sisters' picnics and soirees.

Among the Stettheimers' "personas gratas," as Henry McBride called them, were such expatriate European artists as Marcel Duchamp, Elie Nadelman, Gaston Lachaise, and Pavel Tchelitchew; Americans Jo Davidson, Charles Demuth, and Marsden Hartley; and writer Carl Van Vechten and his wife, the dancer Fania Marinoff. Other photographers among the habitués included Steichen, Arnold Genthe, and the Baron de Meyer and his wife, who, in 1916, acting on the advice of an astrologer, had changed their names from Adolf and Olga to Gayne and Mhahra.

CHAPTER FIFTY·SIX

STIEGLITZ HUNG THE first exhibition of his own photographs since 1913 on the red plush-covered walls of two large rooms on the skylighted top floor of the Anderson Galleries' building. The show previewed on Sunday, February 6, 1921; opened to the public the next day; and ran for two weeks. Ranging in date from 1887 to 1920, the 146 prints, "effectively centered in their mats of white," were, in the words of Paul Rosenfeld, "majestic little harmonies of gorgeous shadows and burning lights . . . their colors lying within strangely pungent tonalities of black and white, gray, silver, bronze, fawn, and pearl."[1] Stieglitz wrote that the exhibition represented the "quintessence" of his photographic development during four decades.

Only seventeen of the images had been exhibited before, and more than half of the total had been made since O'Keeffe's arrival in New York in June 1918. Twenty-one of the photographs dated from 1887 to 1910, including *A Good Joke*, *The Terminal*, *Winter — Fifth Avenue*, *The Hand of Man*, *The Steerage*, and *The City of Ambition*. These were followed by nine views from the back window of 291 and three installation shots of exhibitions at that gallery. Of the four photographs in a section entitled "Water," three were studies of Ellen Morton in her bathing suit.

More than two thirds of the show was devoted to portraits, for Stieglitz defined the term to include studies not only of faces but also of parts of the body. The final section, "A Demonstration of Portraiture," featured forty-six photographs of O'Keeffe — whose name did not appear in the catalog and whose face was excluded from the nudes, but whose identity was an open secret — grouped into sections entitled "A Woman," "Hands," "Feet," "Hands and Breasts," "Torsos," and "Interpretations." The last of those categories probably included an image in which O'Keeffe's phallic sculpture was erotically placed in front of her vaginal abstraction *Music — Pink and Blue I* (1919). Stieglitz tantalizingly stated in the catalog, "Some important prints of this period are not being shown, as I feel that the general public is not quite ready to receive them." He was referring to the fact that his family, and perhaps O'Keeffe as well, had dissuaded him from exhibiting his close-ups of her pubic region and buttocks.

The exhibition "made a stir," Henry McBride recalled many years later. "Mona Lisa got but one portrait of herself worth talking about. O'Keeffe got a hundred. It put her at once on the map. Everybody knew the name. She became what is known as a newspaper personality."[2] She was embarrassed, but Alfred soon sold several of her paintings, and her next exhibition would be a succès de scandale.

"Never was there such a hubbub about a one-man show," wrote John Tennant in the *Photo-Miniature*.[3] "People did stop you on the street to tell you that you ought to see [Stieglitz's photographs] and people did dispute about them," reported McBride in *The Dial*.[4] Marsden Hartley exclaimed that even for people like himself, who "had found a place for good unadulterated photography in the scheme of our appreciation of the art production of this time," the exhibition had been "a huge revelation."[5] "And then, all at once," continued McBride, "someone ran down Fifth Avenue crying that Alfred Stieglitz had put a price of $5,000 on one of the photographs, a nude, one that was a unique impression with the plate destroyed. . . . And then everyone had to go see the exhibition over again, the crowd about the nude being particularly dense."[6]

In his *New York Herald* review, McBride stated that everyone was excited to see the photographs "about which there had been so much private conjecture, but greater than the photographs was Alfred, and greater than Alfred was his talk — as copious, continuous and revolutionary as ever."[7] Much of the old crowd from 291 turned up on the first two afternoons and began to feel as though nothing had changed. At the Anderson, just as in the heyday of the old place, observed Rosenfeld, "a slender, medium-sized man in a business suit, with a shock of iron-gray hair and intensely bright eyes glowing through iron-rimmed spectacles, [stood] in a corner of the gallery, talking humorously, passionately, debonairly to the people, battling for the Ideas."[8]

It was in the catalog of this exhibition that Stieglitz made his famous declarations "I was born in Hoboken. I am an American. Photography is my passion. The search for Truth my obsession." Sounding very much like P. H. Emerson on his hobbyhorse, Alfred appended the following:

> PLEASE NOTE: in the above STATEMENT the following, fast becoming "obsolete", terms do not appear: ART, SCIENCE, BEAUTY, RELIGION, every ISM, ABSTRACTION, FORM, PLASTICITY, OBJECTIVITY, SUBJECTIVITY, OLD MASTERS, MODERN ART, PSYCHOANALYSIS, AESTHETICS, PICTORIAL PHOTOGRAPHY, DEMOCRACY, CEZANNE, "291", PROHIBITION. The term TRUTH did creep in but may be kicked out by any one.

Most of the banished terms would nevertheless surface in the many reverent and even illuminating reviews written by Stieglitz's disciples and friends. Rosenfeld, for instance, claimed that in the photographs "there has been made an expression ideal as is music; an order as pure, as complete, as that of Cézanne or of any of the great masters of the aesthetic pictural organization."[9]

Rosenfeld's long article in *The Dial* began, "Alfred Stieglitz is of the company of the great affirmers of life." For him, the critic astutely noted, "there seems to be scarcely anything, any object, in all the world without high import, scarcely anything that is not in some fashion related to himself. The humblest objects appear to be, for him, instinct with marvellous life." Rosenfeld went on to utter the resounding judgment that "save for Whitman, there has been amongst us no native-born artist equal to this photographer."[10]

Much of the praise naturally focused on Stieglitz's portraits. Hartley wrote, "I am willing to assert now that there are no [other] portraits in existence, not in all the history of portrait realization either by the camera or in painting, which so definitely present, and in many instances with an almost haunting clairvoyance, the actualities existing in the sitter's mind and body and soul."[11]

The acolytes obediently stressed the plainness, the objectivity, and the absolute straightforwardness of Stieglitz's photographs, which is to say their complete dissimilarity to the painterly efforts of the Pictorialists. McBride, however, dissented. "In spite of Alfred's care not to rob the product of a machine of any of its machinelike attributes," he wrote, "a number of the photographs have painterlike aspects. One or two of the large heads look like things by Rossetti or Courbet; and one — save the mark — bears a suggestion of the lamented Bouguereau."[12]

In the exhibition catalog, Stieglitz claimed that his ideal was "to achieve the ability to produce numberless prints from each negative, prints all significantly alive, yet indistinguishably alike, and to be able to circulate them at a price not higher than that of a popular magazine, or even a daily paper." McBride feared that Stieglitz would never realize his ideal. "His photography is essentially aristocratic and expensive. He spends an immense amount of time making love to the subject before taking it. His impressions are printed luxuriously upon the rarest papers to secure a richness of effect that must always lie beyond the appreciation of the multitude."[13] Alfred was certainly not pleased.

All spring Stieglitz was far too busy to do any photography. He helped to mount an exhibition of Marin's etchings at Weyhe's bookstore in March. He worked closely with Arthur Carles on the preparations for the April 16 opening of an Exhibition of Paintings Showing the Later Tendencies in Art at the Pennsylvania Academy of the Fine Arts. And he organized an auction of Hartley's paintings in May. "So you see," he wrote, "what my withdrawal has done for me!"[14]

The Pennsylvania Academy, at which Carles was a teacher, had offered the painter the use of its galleries for a major survey of American modernism — the first to be held in any museum — but it declined to sponsor the show officially. Stieglitz helped with the selection process until the misogynistic Carles said that he didn't want "any goddam women in the show." Stieglitz then replied that he would have nothing more to do with the exhibition unless O'Keeffe was included. "Take it or leave it," he announced. Carles relented, and O'Keeffe, represented by three paintings, was one of three women among the twenty-seven artists in the show.[15]

Stieglitz certainly felt that advanced American art needed the prestige of the Pennsylvania Academy that season, when both the Metropolitan and the Brooklyn museums opened their doors to French modernism for the first time. Under pressure from a group that included John Quinn, Lillie Bliss, Agnes Meyer, and Gertrude Vanderbilt Whitney, the Met reluctantly hung, beginning May 2 and running through the summer, a Loan Exhibition of Impressionist and Post-Impressionist Paintings from New York collections. Some militant reactionaries, outraged to see canvases by the likes of Matisse and Picasso in such a bastion of civilization, formed an anonymous committee that distributed a foaming-at-the-mouth condemnation of modernist art as "a symptom of a general movement throughout the world having for its object . . . the Revolutionary destruction of our entire social system."[16] Upon receiving a copy of the four-page circular, Stieglitz wrote, "It is . . . not so many years ago that some of those loaning pictures to the [current] Exhibition at the Museum 'had no use' whatever for Cézanne, Matisse, Picasso & Co. — Now they are proud owners . . . and pioneers!" He went on to exclaim, "Ye Gods. — So why this surprise and indignation that a cowardly Anonymity should re-echo what the 'Wise' of To-Day themselves labelled 'Modern Art' not so long ago at 291! — Degenerates, Paranoiacs, Fakirs, Anarchists (Bolshevism was still unknown) and what not."[17]

Late that spring Stieglitz, O'Keeffe, and a friend took the subway out to Brooklyn to see the exhibition Paintings by Modern French Masters Representing the Post-Impressionists and Their Predecessors. Although Stieglitz was opposed to the attention given to French modernism at the expense of American, he found himself delighted by the show, which included canvases by Courbet, Manet, Degas, Renoir, Gauguin, Cézanne, Toulouse-Lautrec, Derain, Picasso, and Matisse. Comparing the bold French paintings with insipid works by Sargent, Winslow Homer, and Arthur Davies elsewhere in the museum, he wondered, "What ailed us — us the supposedly freest of all peoples. Why the repression? That half-light? Why the soft pedal? The half-whisper? The fear of full color? Are we afraid? If so, of what? Ourselves?"[18]

Stieglitz's biggest problem in the spring of 1921 was what to do about Hartley, who had very little money and was becoming terribly discouraged about his prospects. The previous summer the artist had written to Stieglitz, "You understand too well all things that make up the insult called life in one like myself." He added that "after the years of hope and faith and love," he had "dropped the two former and love has turned to a kind of devilish tenacity to keep from letting the whole thing die on one's hands like a sick lizard."[19] Two months later he implied that because his existence had become "one long drawn out tension of pain," he was toying with the idea of suicide.[20]

Having dabbled with Dadaism since 1915, Hartley finally embraced the movement in 1920 — just as it was about to expire. This tragically frustrated, hypersensitive, and lonely misfit claimed, "I have achieved great mastery to my own thinking in that I have brought up the inevitable smile of satire on to my cheek."[21] He relished Dadaism's "exhilarating quality of nihilism" and hailed the movement because it offered "the first joyous dogma . . . which has been invented for the release and true freedom of art."[22] Hartley even announced that since Stieglitz was a "modern artist expressing present day notions of actual things," he was "an artistic idol of the Dadaists."[23]

Hartley's commitment to Dadaism cemented his friendships with Marcel Duchamp and Man Ray, who by this time had begun collaborating on works of art. Duchamp had returned to New York in January 1920, after a stay in Paris during which he spent much time with the leading Dadaists and made his notorious mustachioed and goateed Mona Lisa, entitled *L.H.O.O.Q.* (pronounced "*elle a chaud au cul*," meaning She's got a hot ass). Man Ray soon photographed Duchamp in drag as Rrose Sélavy ("*Eros, c'est la vie*"), the Frenchman's alter ego.

In the fall of 1920 Hartley was appointed the secretary and chairman of publicity for the Société Anonyme (French for corporation), an organization founded by Katherine Dreier, Duchamp, and Ray in April of that year to exhibit modern art and to sponsor lectures and publications. (Stieglitz declined Dreier's invitation to become a trustee.) In November, Hartley was included in a group show with Man Ray, Joseph Stella, Kurt Schwitters, Kandinsky, and others in the society's cramped, walkup headquarters on East Forty-seventh Street; Dreier called the place a "Museum of Modern Art." Mostly with her money, the Société Anonyme would assemble a great collection: 135 oils and nearly four hundred works in other media, by a total of 141 American and European artists. In 1941 Dreier would give the entire collection to Yale University.

One evening at the Far East China Garden, Hartley put a penny in the palm of his right hand and thrust it dramatically under Stieglitz's nose, announcing, "This is all that stands between me and starvation. I know it isn't fair to do this to you, but I am desperate." In a Dadaist spirit, he said that if he could somehow raise $1,200, he would go to Florence, where he would write a book in which he would vent his rage about the way Americans treated artists. After sending copies to one hundred Americans whom he respected or hated, he would commit suicide.

In any case, he was earnest about needing $1,200 for a European sojourn, since he couldn't stand New York any longer. So Stieglitz made a radical suggestion. There were more than a hundred of Hartley's paintings in storage. Surely either Charles Daniel (who had given the artist a one-man show in January 1920) or N. E. Montross (who had included five Hartleys in a group show that fall) would be willing to buy the entire lot for an average of about $10 per painting. The artist accepted the proposal, but both Daniel and Montross refused the offer. Stieglitz then went to Mitchell Kennerley, who had just agreed to auction seventy-five paintings by the wealthy lawyer and amateur painter James Rosenberg on the evening of May 17. Kennerley said that Hartley's pictures could be included in that session.

Stieglitz and O'Keeffe hung Hartley's 117 paintings at the Anderson Galleries, where they went on view a week before the sale, and Stieglitz wrote a foreword for the catalog. The upcoming auction, which was both a curiosity and a human drama, received lots of publicity, and hundreds showed up for the event. People who couldn't ordinarily afford to buy paintings leapt at the opportunity to acquire a Hartley for a few dollars. Hartley's friends filled the room, along with dealers, critics, and collectors. Many others couldn't even get in. The irascible Dr. Albert Barnes, there with his friend and adviser William Glackens, bought three canvases. Charles Daniel bought a few others for Ferdinand Howald. William Carlos Williams paid $105 for a New Mexican pastel. Stieglitz, who had planted friends in the audience to keep the bidding lively, bought some things for himself and, with checks for more than $3,000 in his pocket, acted as agent for a number of collectors who could not be present.

The auction was a huge success. The *New York Herald* reported that Hartley grossed $4,913. Kennerley waived the Anderson Galleries' usual commission, but Stieglitz evidently took $1,000 for his artists' fund, from which he had so often helped Hartley. Even so, the painter ended up with three times the amount for which he had been willing to settle. The money he received would assure him of "three or four years of perfect freedom" in Europe.[24] Stieglitz exulted, "Hartley from absolute poverty & despair — has suddenly become a Capitalist & free to really work. — A miracle really happened. — My faith remains unshaken — & bears fruit."[25]

The painter arrived in Paris in July 1921. He didn't stay long. In November he returned to inflation-ravaged Berlin, where he could live very inexpensively. Enjoying the city's atmosphere of decadence, he would remain there for more than two years, after which he finally went to Florence. His initial choice of destination was probably influenced by Duchamp, who had returned to the French capital in June. Man Ray also arrived in July, having, on Stieglitz's advice, successfully petitioned Ferdinand Howald for a $500 advance. That fall the Arensbergs moved to California. Perhaps they realized that the New York Dada movement was dead, or perhaps they had simply become bored by the nightly circus in their apartment.

Hartley — who had contributed essays about a wide variety of artists and poets to such magazines as *The New Republic, The Seven Arts, The Dial,* and *The Little Review* — didn't write his "book of hate," but a collection of his essays, entitled *Adventures in the Arts: Informal Chapters on Painters, Vaudeville, and Poets,* was published in New York in the fall of 1921. Stieglitz, to whom it was dedicated, took a great interest in the book and recruited Herbert Seligmann to correct the galleys at Lake George during the summer. In September, Stieglitz would write letters to friends announcing the publication of "the first book of the kind written by an American" and stressing that it was "important that the book find a wide circulation."[26] He was even taking orders for it, recommending it as a gift, asking for lists of potential buyers to contact, and encouraging his friends to review it favorably. O'Keeffe was less than happy about all this, for in the section about her, Hartley purple-prosed that she had "had her feet scorched in the laval effusiveness of terrible experience" and that her works were "probably as living and shameless private documents as exist, in painting certainly, and probably in any other art." When she first read the manuscript, she nearly wept and thought about "losing" it before it could be set in type.[27]

"I came up here virtually all in," Stieglitz wrote to Arthur Dove from Lake George in July. "There are but few cheery faces this year up here. — And still all is outwardly peaceful — & my mother is doing very well."[28] Or, at least, well under the circumstances. Hedwig was partially paralyzed, and she was not in good spirits. That summer she would nag about little annoyances and complain a great deal about the running of the household. Furious at his mother for not being her old self, Alfred sulked like a spoiled child, ignored her, avoided her as much as he could, and replied testily to her questions and requests. Devastated by the prospect of her death, he was so depressed that he even developed a psychosomatic heart flutter that sometimes woke him during the night. "A decided grayness pervades both of us," he wrote concerning the shared depression that had kept O'Keeffe from "feeling brilliant colors" that summer. "Red seems to hurt."[29]

Georgia, too, had physical problems. For weeks after they arrived at the lake, trouble with her eyes prevented her from working. She was miserable, and Alfred was terribly worried about her. Finally, in mid-August, they went to New York for a week to see an ophthalmologist, who was able to help her greatly. Georgia then began to spend a lot of time in her shanty and would complete twenty-five paintings, including a rather sinister landscape entitled *Lake George with Crows,* by the time they returned to New York in late October.

At the end of August, Stieglitz told Dove that he had not made a single negative all summer. "A few prints. — Several good ones. But my 'heart' has not been in anything much, I don't seem to have any ideas. And still I have not been entirely stale. — Something will come out of the indulgence. . . . I have gotten away with several novels. — Proof of my own lack of creative desire."[30]

Toward the end of the summer, Alfred finally began to emerge from his funk. Even Hedwig responded by perking up. During a final month at the lake alone with O'Keeffe, Alfred threw himself into a spurt of printing. He was in such a good mood that he could even joke about his frustrations. "I never saw anyone make as many blunders as I did," he wrote to Seligmann in October. The shutter of his camera malfunctioned, he botched the fixing of some negatives, and then he dropped the "few flawless films on the floor." He ended up with the "worst lot of might-have-been masterpieces in my whole career. Thus you see I am *no* Master of Photography as yet."[31]

CHAPTER FIFTY·SEVEN

IN JANUARY 1922 Stieglitz organized a large show of Marin's water-colors, oils, and etchings at N. E. Montross's gallery. The following month, inspired by the success of the Hartley auction, he persuaded Mitchell Kennerley to sponsor an auction of nearly two hundred paintings, by more than forty American artists, to take place at the Anderson Galleries on February 23. Although he had hoped that what he variously called the "Painters'" or the "Artists' Derby" would prove to be "a great sporting event in the art world," it turned out to be a disappointment for almost everyone involved.[1] Both Stieglitz and O'Keeffe, however, were pleased that her painting of the Lake George barn, a tiny canvas only seven inches square, went for $400, the highest price paid for anything in the sale.

Alfred had a new inspiration for a round of portraits of family and friends. In his article entitled "Is Photography a Failure?" published in the *New York Sun* in March, he wrote, "The early painter [Hans] Memling, in his wonderful portraits, was in reality the first photographer. His idea of depicting his subject was photographic as I understand the term."[2] Memling's meticulous and sympathetic portrait of Tommaso Portinari, in which the subject's thoughtful face and palm-to-palm hands emerge from a dark background, had been bequeathed to the Metropolitan Museum by Benjamin Altman in 1913 along with a portrait of Portinari's wife.

In his new portraits Stieglitz concentrated more than ever on physiognomy. In the fall he would tell Edward Weston, "I have put my lens a foot from the sitter's face because I thought when talking intimately one doesn't stand ten feet away; and knowing that it takes time to get deep into the innermost nature of matter, I have given exposures of [three to four] minutes [with the lens aperture stopped all the way down to $f/45$ or even smaller]."[3] It was, he continued, heartbreakingly difficult to get his sitters to forget about the headrest he used to keep them still during such long exposures.

"The ear is given as much consideration as the nose," he declared, so that the eye would find "satisfaction in every portion" of the image.[4] One appreciator of Stieglitz's photographs wrote, "Inasmuch as the lens does not in the same way as the pencil lend itself to the elimination of elements, the problem is so to render every element that it becomes essential."[5]

In the spring of 1922 Stieglitz accepted an invitation to lecture at the Clarence White School of Photography — despite the fact that he dismissed the pupils as "women — half-baked dilettantes — not a single real talent."[6] Ralph Steiner, who would graduate from White's school in June and go on to become a distinguished photographer and filmmaker, recalled that most of the students "had absolutely no idea what Stieglitz was talking about with his insistence that a photograph had to be an 'affirmation.'" Steiner went up to ask about that term after the lecture, but when the young photographer asked whether he could pay him a visit, the elder replied cruelly, "I am not interested in helping individuals."[7] Or at least not the sort of individuals he deemed likely to attend White's school.

Stieglitz's ceasefire with his former protégé and friend came none too soon, for in July 1925 the fifty-four-year-old White would die of a heart attack in Mexico City, where he had taken a group of students. A few weeks after that event Stieglitz would write harshly that when White moved to New York, "his photography went to the devil. . . . He listened to flattery and was jealous of Steichen — That was the beginning of his decline as a friend and human being and artist."[8] Some reconciliation.

When they arrived at Lake George in June, Stieglitz was so "numb with fatigue" that his head felt like "a sucked-out egg," and O'Keeffe had lost so much weight during the winter that her immediate goal was to gain back ten pounds.[9] It seems that she and Alfred had been arguing because she wanted to have a baby. Elizabeth Davidson, who gave birth to a second daughter during 1922, had even promised to help with raising the child. But Alfred was increasingly worried about money. His brothers were able to give him less than in the past since they were paying for nurses to care for Hedwig twenty-four hours a day. Moreover, he argued, he was too old and O'Keeffe too delicate; the death of his sister Flora had left him terrified of childbirth. Then he reminded O'Keeffe that he had been a failure as a father to Kitty. Finally, Alfred, who often spoke of O'Keeffe's paintings as their children, worried that if she had a baby she might no longer need to express her feelings in her work. Their debate would continue for a year.

"My mother of course is a most pathetic sight," Stieglitz wrote Arthur Dove in July.[10] Hedwig would spend the entire summer at the farmhouse, attended by two German nurses. Alfred photographed her sitting in a rocking chair on the porch, bundled up in lap robes and a heavy knitted shawl. Pensive, but with a trace of a smile, she seems to be looking at her death with equanimity.

Alfred, however, was oppressed by a sense of death all around him. "My mother was dying," he wrote of that summer. "Our estate was going to pieces. The old horse of 37 was being kept alive by the 70-year-old coachman. . . . All about me disintegration — slow but sure: dying chestnut trees — the pines doomed too — diseased . . . the world in a great mess."[11]

Although he was depressed about his mother's clearly imminent death, Alfred was able to maintain a show of reasonably good spirits. He soon got down to work. By mid-July he had converted a white-painted potting shed, recently wired for electricity, into a primitive darkroom. His own weathervane-topped "shanty," in front of which there was a tall flagpole, would thereafter be called the Little House and would soon become the subject of several delightful O'Keeffe paintings. It had only cold running water, but at least Alfred wouldn't have to spend hours on his knees bending over the bathtub anymore, though he still dried his negatives in the farmhouse kitchen. Late in July he wrote to Paul Strand, "The splendid cook remarked yesterday seeing me chase in & out — drying negatives over her stove, etc., etc. — 'Why, Mr. Alfred, you are working and looking so hard, as if you were trying to draw the last ounce out of the place!' Not bad for a cook! I guess when I go at something, *all* of me is in the centre of that thing digging into that centre's centre."[12]

Georgia said that if it weren't for work from other years she wanted to finish at Lake George, she would have preferred to spend the summer in Maine, where she had gone for another "really wonderful" visit with the Schaufflers in May. "But there are friends here too and it works out this way."[13] O'Keeffe had extra incentive to paint that summer, since Alfred was arranging for her to have a one-person show at the Anderson Galleries during the coming season. He had already started the publicity machine; Paul Rosenfeld was writing a lengthy article about O'Keeffe to appear in the October issue of *Vanity Fair*.[14] The artist would be embarrassed by the piece, in which Rosenfeld called her "one of those who seem the forerunners of a more biologically evolved humanity," but she understood that "as most people buy pictures more through their ears than their eyes — one must be written about and talked about or the people who buy through their ears think your work is no good and won't buy and one must sell to live."[15]

Stieglitz spent much of July and August trying to focus his inner eye, and to make his camera more than ever a direct extension of himself. He was amused (but also surely half tempted) by a mock challenge posed by a friend in a July letter. "I'll try portraits of eggs," he wrote her humorously, "& see whether I can differentiate between a rotten egg & a fresh one — so that as you look at the pictures you'll get the psychology of that particular (or not particular) egg. — That will be a test of my powers."[16] But apples, not eggs, held his attention for much of that summer, as they were also the subjects of many paintings that O'Keeffe did before she turned to landscapes and autumn leaves late in October.

Stieglitz wrote to Dove early in August that he had accidentally smashed his 8 x 10-inch Eastman view camera one night and so had to rely upon his 4 x 5 Graflex.[17] He missed his big camera while he was working on a "a series of impossible experiments — nothing to do with art — just technical photography." One was an attempt to photograph the front of the barn in bright sunlight and, in the same exposure, to capture detail within the dark interior that could be seen through the doorway — very much the sort of challenge that had preoccupied him as a student in Berlin. Indeed, the upcoming fortieth anniversary of his beginning to study with Vogel (if he remembered the date accurately) was very much on his mind, and he even made a masterful photograph of Ezekiel's bust of Judith to demonstrate the virtuosity he had achieved in the years since his obsessive efforts with the Apollo Belvedere. Describing yet another of that summer's experiments to Dove, he wrote,

> I was trying to hypnotize some apples in the rain — & on the tree — in[to] keeping still for 50 seconds. — The apples seemed very human-like — they would move in spite of that intent gaze of mine, intensity keyed up to 999 degrees of Will. — The Sun was peeping in

& out of slowly moving cloudlets — flirting with my particular apples — that's why that 1° turned achievement into total failure. And so it goes these days with nearly everything — that *one* degree.[18]

One such effort that was not a failure yielded the photograph called *Apples and Gable*, in which four apples on a branch are seen against the background of a top-floor window and the peaked roofline of the farmhouse. Like that in the portrait of O'Keeffe as the new Eve, the configuration of apples is obviously phallic, the two at the top representing testicles. And, remembering what Stieglitz had said about his 1920 image of the apple tree by the barn, we must assume that he intended the dark window directly behind the lowest apple as a vagina being penetrated.

Alfred would have liked to photograph O'Keeffe nude against the weathered wood of her shanty, but he convinced himself that she was not strong enough to pose unclothed outdoors.[19] Instead, he enlisted sixteen-year-old Georgia Engelhard, nicknamed Georgia Minor or the Kid, to pose for one of the corniest photographs he ever made. (He confessed to Dove that he was "doing all kinds of foolish bits."[20]) In the picture we see Alfred's well-developed niece, nude and fully exposed, sitting on the sill of an open window of the shanty (inside which O'Keeffe, the chaperone, was presumably working). The girl is clutching several apples to her abdomen and leaning her head against the window frame for stability during the long exposure. Posing for her uncle, the young model later complained, had required "endless fortitude." Assuming what was "at best a difficult pose to hold even for a few minutes," she wrote, she had to hold it "for more than an hour with no respite. . . . When I became cramped and tried to shift my position, or when I wriggled because a fly was slowly parading down my face, he would roar at me until I was ready to weep with rage and discomfort."[21]

During 1921 Stieglitz had encouraged Paul Rosenfeld and Herbert Seligmann to start a new magazine, *Manuscripts*, which would publish fiction, poetry, essays, and satire. Nothing that was accepted for publication would be cut or edited, and the writers represented in each issue would share at least some of the costs of that issue. The satirical advertisement for the magazine asked readers to send "ten cents a copy if you like it, or Subscribe One Dollar for Ten Numbers to be issued in Ten Days–Ten Weeks–Ten Months–or Ten Years. The risk is yours. Act at once if you want to be One of the First 100,000 Subscribers."

Early in 1922 Paul Strand had accepted the task of editing a special issue of the magazine, to be published in December, devoted to the question
"Can a photograph have the significance of art?" During that entire summer Stieglitz was preoccupied with the progress of the issue, correspond-
ing with Strand, suggesting possible contributors, and tallying up and
weighing the answers submitted. O'Keeffe struggled with hers all summer
and designed the issue's cover. In addition to the usual roster of Stieglitz
friends, contributors included Charlie Chaplin, Walter Lippmann, Carl
Sandburg, and composers Ernst Bloch and Leo Ornstein — but no photographers! Most of the replies were evasive or equivocal, though ten asserted that Stieglitz's photographs, at least, had the significance of art.
Joseph Pennell, however, called photography "the refuge of the inca-
pables" and added, "I have seen, but not attempted to read *Manuscripts*; it is
more inane, artless and vulgar in its appearance than I could have imag-
ined."

One morning late in August, Stieglitz received Waldo Frank's submission, in which the writer stated that in his portraits "the work of Stieglitz is
more than half upon his subject. . . . By talk, atmosphere, suggestion and
the momentum of a personal relationship, Stieglitz lifts the features and
body of his subject into a unitary design that his plate records."[22] Alfred was
outraged at what he perversely took to be an accusation that "the secret
power in my photography was due to the power of hypnotism I had over
my sitters." As he had been thinking of doing for years, he then began a series of cloud photographs to "show that my photographs were not due to
subject matter — not to special trees, or faces, or interiors, to special privileges, clouds were there for everyone." In such a series, he told O'Keeffe,
he would sum up what he had learned in forty years of photographing and
convey his "philosophy of life."[23]

Stieglitz had been fascinated by clouds, and by the special problems of
photographing them, ever since the summer of 1887, when he had used
Vogel's orthochromatic plates to record the approach of storm clouds over
Lake Como. In February 1895, while he was editor of *The American Amateur Photographer*, the magazine carried the editorial comment "Cloud photography is a subject that many amateurs delight in."[24] And four months
later it reprinted an article entitled "Cloud Photography" from *Scientific
American*.[25] On his honeymoon at Lake George in 1903, Edward Steichen
made a magnificent photograph of a cumulus cloud, billowing above silhouetted black hills and reflected on the dark, gently rippled water. Clouds
figured importantly in the photographs that Stieglitz himself made during

1910. Two years later, A. L. Coburn illustrated a limited edition of Shelley's poem "The Cloud." By 1922 the subject was something of a cliché, but Stieglitz was determined to photograph clouds as no one had done before.

He threw himself into his project with great excitement, but he was at first disappointed by his negatives. Even when he made one worth printing, there was "the treachery of the papers nowadays." Because he never knew what to expect from a new batch of the Eastman gelatin-silver paper he was using, he was delighted to discover a cache of old palladium paper. One day he swore when he "lost a wonderful sky picture — & because of my own laxity. — Had a whole day of mishaps — bad emulsions, leaking darkroom — gritty water — electric light turned off without warning — & other trifles like that."[26]

By late August, and throughout most of September, the farmhouse was full. In addition to Alfred, Georgia, Hedwig, and the Engelhards, Julius and Selma were in residence — but Alfred assured Dove in mid-September, "Peace in the house continues."[27] When Paul Strand's vivacious young wife, Rebecca ("Beck"), arrived at the lake on September 7 for what was planned as a three-week stay, she had to be put up at the Pines, a nearby boarding-house. Paul himself was in Maryland, carrying out one of the commercial assignments that Alfred, with uncharacteristic practicality, advised him to accept.

Beck, who had married Paul early in the year, was the daughter of Nate Salsbury, the producer, manager, part owner, and self-described creator of Buffalo Bill's Wild West Show. A certain resemblance to O'Keeffe seems to have been a factor in Paul's eagerness to marry her, and Beck was having some trouble coming to terms with her husband's ambition that he and she be as much like Stieglitz and O'Keeffe as possible. For one thing, she was uncomfortable with the pressure that not only Paul but also Alfred and Georgia put on her to develop her modest artistic talents. Trained in short-hand and typing, she was working part-time as a secretary for two neurologists.

The first summer of the Strands' marriage was difficult, for Paul was working so hard, and traveling so much, that Beck was bored, lonely, and depressed. When she and Paul were together, they were "unaccountably happy" and were growing "closer daily," as Beck had written to Alfred only a few weeks before she arrived at Lake George. But a Strand portrait dating from that year tells a different story. With her chestnut hair cut as short as a man's, Beck is looking fixedly and directly at the camera. Her strong features betray a tremendous sadness, and tears seem to be welling up in her big eyes. She looks as though she might be wondering how she could have married Paul. What a contrast to a photograph Strand took at Lake George in September. Alfred, wearing a sleeveless bathing costume, is emerging from the lake and grinning as he cradles the head of Beck, who is lying on the dock and beaming up at him. One might well take it to be a picture of radiantly happy lovers.

Indeed, Alfred flirted extravagantly with Beck, of whom he enthused, "She's a lively girl & nice to have about. She knows how to laugh."[28] Innocently, Beck wrote to her husband, "A lovely relationship has developed between us and we have lots of fun gamboling about."[29] The presence of such an attractive woman had certainly brought Alfred's eyes down from the clouds. He spent many hours photographing her, making "snapshots" with his Graflex as well as more serious studies with his 8 x 10 camera, which had been repaired. After he and Georgia introduced Beck to the pleasures of nude swimming, Alfred made "a quintillion" photographs of her magnificent body immersed in shallow water at the edge of the lake, her breasts and buttocks covered with gooseflesh.[30]

Deeply impressed by Stieglitz's photographs of O'Keeffe, Strand had been photographing Beck similarly — too similarly for the elder's liking. Alfred later told Nancy Newhall that in posing Beck in the icy water of the lake he was trying "to prove to Paul that in Becky . . . he had a much more pliant and vital model than the then rather fragile O'Keeffe, [who] could not at that time have endured such a trial."[31] More to the point, Alfred was demonstrating his photographic and amatory superiority over the model's husband. We can only wonder what O'Keeffe thought about all this. After all, she often used to relate how, when they saw his photographs of her in his 1921 exhibition, some men had wanted Alfred to photograph their wives or girlfriends. "If they had known what a close relationship he would have needed to have to photograph [them] the way he photographed me — I think they wouldn't have been interested," commented O'Keeffe.[32]

To complicate matters further, a neighbor had observed one of Alfred's sessions with Beck and had notified the police; as a result a plainclothesman kept an eye on the shore for several days. When Paul arrived at the end of September, Alfred encouraged him to savor with Beck the pleasures of swimming au naturel, of which she had written her husband such enthusiastic reports. They were promptly arrested and taken to the local courthouse, where they were fined $10 each. Alfred insisted upon paying the fines himself.

After the departure of Alfred's family on October 1, Paul and Beck moved into the farmhouse. "While Strand was here," Stieglitz wrote to

Paul Rosenfeld, "I virtually did no photography. He photo-ed [*sic*] like one possessed — shooting right and left — forward & backward — upward & downward & in directions not yet named."[33] Alfred was disgusted by such behavior, which, he felt, demonstrated no correlation between the mind's eye and the camera. By way of a reprimand, as if the triumph of his own prints of Beck were not sufficient, he had O'Keeffe read aloud her contribution to *Manuscripts*, in which her praise of Strand's work was quite faint compared with what she wrote about Sheeler's. She called Paul's friend and rival "one of America's most distinguished young modern painters," whose photographs she esteemed as "of equal importance" to his paintings and drawings.[34] Strand was hurt and angry, as Stieglitz had intended. With renewed determination to produce work that would win his mentor's approbation, Paul would soon begin making wonderful close-up studies of the gears of the Double Akeley movie camera that Beck had bought him just before she left for Lake George. He did well to shift his attention to subject matter far away from Alfred's aesthetic and erotic interests.

Although Alfred and Georgia had been looking forward all summer to being alone in October, they invited Beck to stay on for a few more weeks after Paul left on the fourth. But she was no longer there as Alfred's model, for soon he was "frantically photographing skies and landscapes."[35] He and O'Keeffe both usually gained momentum in their work as the summer progressed and were at their peak by fall. Beck wrote to Paul that it was "a very strenuous time with these two people a-going like mad."[36]

Stieglitz was intoxicated with the music of the skies. "I never felt life more extraordinary — more beautiful than now," he wrote to Rosenfeld in October. "Beethoven would go mad . . . were he here today. Music beyond music!"[37] In June, just before leaving New York for Lake George, he had shown some of his photographs to Ernst Bloch, who had responded enthusiastically and perceptively. Now Stieglitz felt certain that in his cloud pictures Bloch would be able to see the visual equivalent of violins, flutes, oboes, and brass instruments. Out of the dozens of images he shot that fall, he would entitle his final selection *Music: A Sequence of Ten Cloud Photographs*.

His work was interrupted in mid-October by a four-day whirlwind trip to New York, during which he got a total of thirteen hours' sleep. "I was under fullest pressure all the time," he told Dove. "Couldn't squeeze in another thing." While in the city he joined his brothers and sisters to celebrate their mother's seventy-eighth birthday, retrieved some prints for an article in *The Ladies' Home Journal*, called on friends and various editors, collected more statements for *Manuscripts*, and had an "extraordinary" meeting with R. Child Bayley, visiting from London, where he was the editor of *The Amateur Photographer & Photography*. Alfred, who had not seen Bayley for fifteen years, showed him some of his new cloud photographs and was gratified by the enthusiastic response. After their encounter he wrote to Dove, "Real men are scarce in the U.S. Bayley is a Man."[38]

Alfred and Georgia were getting ready to leave for New York when, on November 16, they learned that Hedwig had had another stroke, this one massive and likely to prove fatal. They hurriedly finished their packing and rushed to town. Almost as soon as they arrived in New York, Alfred received a call from a thirty-six-year-old photographer named Edward Weston, who was in the city on a visit from California. Stieglitz later told him, "I knew from your letters that you were sincere — and I felt I had something to offer."[39] Weston wrote in his diary that Stieglitz promised to see him "as soon as his mother died. She was sinking rapidly."[40] Her death occurred on the twenty-first. As he had done after he lost his father, Alfred attempted to bury his grief in work.

Weston, a short, intense man, was born in Highland Park, Illinois, in 1886. At the age of twenty he went to visit his older sister in Tropico (now Glendale), California, and decided to remain. Having become a skilled amateur photographer, he began to earn his living as a door-to-door portraitist. In 1911, by which time he was married and had two sons, he opened a commercial studio in Tropico and became a successful portraitist working in a soft-focus style. He fell in love about a year later with an enchanting bohemian photographer named Margrethe Mather, who joined him as a partner in his studio and posed for many of his early Pictorialist nudes.

In 1921 Weston, who had begun to turn away from Pictorialism, was greatly impressed by the reviews of Stieglitz's exhibition written by Paul Rosenfeld, Herbert Seligmann, and John Tennant. During a visit to his sister and her family in Middletown, Ohio, in the fall of 1922, he photographed the towering smokestacks and snaking pipes of the American Rolling Mill Company (Armco); he would later consider those pictures his first mature works. When he mentioned how much he would like to show them to Stieglitz, his sister and her husband gave him money to go on to New York.

Stieglitz began the visit, which took place at his East Sixty-fifth Street studio, by stressing the importance of "a maximum of detail with a maximum of simplification." "With these words as a basis for his attitude toward photography," wrote Weston (who was accompanied by a young woman named Jo), "Alfred Stieglitz talked with Jo and me four hours, or rather he talked to us, for we had no chance, nor desire, to say much. He spoke brilliantly, convincingly with the idealism of a visionary, enforcing his statements by an ever repeated, 'You see, you see.'"[41]

As Weston showed his prints, Stieglitz would pounce "quick as a flash" on an "irrelevant detail" here, an "unrelated background" or area of "bad texture" there, saying over and over, "Nothing must be unconsidered. There must be a complete release." But Stieglitz also offered praise. "I like the way you attack each picture as a fresh problem," he commented. "You are not formulated." He told Weston that if he were still publishing *Camera Work*, he would reproduce several of his nudes as well as the Armco smokestacks.[42]

At the end of July 1923 Weston would go to Mexico City and open a portrait studio there with sultry Tina Modotti, with whom he had fallen in love in California. Whether or not Stieglitz had shown Weston any of his recent clouds, the first photographs "other than matter-of-fact records" that Weston made in Mexico were, as he wrote, of "a marvellous cloud form . . . a sunlit cloud which rose from the bay to become a towering white column."[43] In September, Weston would comment that the clouds were "sufficient to work with for many months and never tire."[44] His interest in clouds, however, was primarily sculptural. He was attracted to the extraordinary shapes floating and metamorphosing in the piercingly blue sky over pre-pollution Mexico City. They are the forerunners of the studies of contorted nudes, peppers, shells, and trees that he would begin to make after his return to California in 1927.

Stieglitz and Weston corresponded for several years, but the young photographer never became one of the elder's "sons." In May 1924, when he dreamt that someone said to him "Alfred Stieglitz is dead," Weston realized that he was on the verge of casting off the particular ideal for which the New Yorker stood.

CHAPTER FIFTY·EIGHT

એજી

ON JANUARY 29, 1923, almost six years after her first one-person show, at 291, O'Keeffe's second solo exhibition opened, on the top floor of the Anderson Galleries, for a two-week run. The brochure, which listed the dates of the included works but no titles, proclaimed:

ALFRED STIEGLITZ PRESENTS
ONE HUNDRED PICTURES
OILS, WATERCOLORS
PASTELS, DRAWINGS
BY
GEORGIA O'KEEFFE
AMERICAN

When Stieglitz billed O'Keeffe emphatically as an American, he meant, as he explained later in the year to Paul Rosenfeld, that her work represented "America without that damned French flavor!" He continued, "No one respects France [more] than I do. But when the world is to be France I strenuously hate the idea quite as much as if the world were to be made 'American' or 'Prussian.'"[1]

Sherwood Anderson recalled that O'Keeffe always felt ill at the very thought of having "greasy, vulgar people" come into contact with her "intimate and beautiful" works, which were to her "like beautiful children."[2]

However, in the exhibition brochure — which, at Stieglitz's insistence, reprinted Hartley's mortifying text from *Adventures in the Arts* — O'Keeffe admitted that she wanted her paintings to be shown, so that she could compare them with others she had seen. She even acknowledged that she was interested in what people had to say. Nevertheless, the strain of all the work — "frames and hanging and publicity" — proved too much for her.[3] A week after the opening she came down with the "grippe" and was confined to bed for six days.

The reviews were excellent. Henry McBride pleased O'Keeffe "immensely" when his piece for the *New York Herald* stated that in the show "there is a great deal of clear, precise, unworried painting," which Stieglitz was calling "color music."[4] The *Sun*'s critic, Alan Burroughs, marveled that in the concurrent exhibition of still lifes and flower pieces by the likes of Cézanne, Manet, Monet, and Renoir at Durand-Ruel, "one sees no canvases with the intensity of Miss O'Keeffe's."[5]

Intense, expressive color was certainly the hallmark of the exhibition. "Flowers and fruit burn in [O'Keeffe's] conception of them with deep, luminous colors," wrote Burroughs.[6] Her paintings of flowers, apples, plums, eggplants, and grapes, as well as abstractions, "line the brave walls of the Anderson rooms with pinks and purples and greens," observed another critic.[7] Some of the walls seemed to glow with flaming canna lilies, like fiery eruptions of red, orange, yellow, and violet.

As many as five hundred people a day thronged the galleries. Although many went out of curiosity aroused by Stieglitz's photographs of the artist, once there they mostly liked what they saw. O'Keeffe's work was sensuous, easily understandable, greatly appealing, often decorative, and much of it seemed quite overtly sexual in a fashionably liberated way. Some twenty paintings were sold, for a total of about $3,000, to such buyers as Lee Stieglitz, O'Keeffe's sister Anita (married to budding financier and railroad magnate Robert Young), Beck Strand, George Engelhard, Katharine Rhoades, and Paul Rosenfeld. Arthur Dove — who had left his wife to live with painter Helen Torr (nicknamed Reds) on a houseboat without electricity moored in the Harlem River — even managed to scrape up enough to buy a tiny painting, which, he reported, held up well under lantern light.

Sherwood Anderson was "a good deal disconcerted" to see how Stieglitz "so patiently worked with the stupid people who came in" to see the exhibition.[8] The photographer exerted himself so greatly that Anderson sometimes feared the effort might kill him.[9] "There is one person I shall always remember," he wrote to O'Keeffe, "just the figure of heavy, pompous stupidity standing on his two heavy legs like a bull, and before him the small, tired, intense figure of Stieglitz trying to tell that man something of his own delicately fine feeling about the artist's work. . . . There was something in it of the whole story of the artist and his life."[10] Not everyone was so impressed. Photographer Dorothea Lange's husband, western artist Maynard Dixon, who was then visiting New York, wrote in his diary, "Listening to Stieglitz expatiate. Impression of cleverness and futility; hot-house atmosphere. . . . Stale-air existence. Glad to get away."[11]

Stieglitz and O'Keeffe had become very friendly with Anderson since his arrival in New York in August 1922. "The few times you came to us were . . . like fine days in the mountains . . . clear sparkling and lots of air," O'Keeffe would write him.[12] During the summer of 1921 Rosenfeld had taken the writer, who had never been to Europe, on a tour of the Continent as his guest. The trip permanently cemented their friendship. A year later Anderson resigned from his advertising firm and moved to New York. It was only then that he and Stieglitz became really close. "As for myself, I freely admit that I have often been stupid about you," Anderson wrote the photographer in June 1923,

> and it was only last year that I came to know and really value you. One day I was going to the country, and as I sat in the train, I suddenly began to weep bitterly and had to turn my face away from the people in the car for shame of my apparent[ly] causeless grief. However, I was not unhappy. It was just that I had at last realized fully what your life had come to mean to me.[13]

With the casual anti-Semitism of the Protestant Midwest that even an artist of Anderson's caliber was slow to shake off, he wrote that Rosenfeld and Stieglitz were "sweet and sound Jews . . . intense men, not sour, very fine," in contrast to men like Waldo Frank, who were unable to rid themselves of "something of the Jewish prophet spirit" and were therefore "preachers really, and by just that much corrupt."[14] With Rosenfeld, who was fourteen years younger than Anderson, he enjoyed an easy kinship. In regard to Stieglitz, Anderson wrote, "I feel him above me, in a quieter place."[15]

Writing about Stieglitz in the October 1922 issue of the *New Republic*, Anderson contrasted the photographer with Henry Ford, who represented the mechanical suppression of the human spirit. Stieglitz, on the other hand, was fighting "to make machinery the tool and not the master of man."[16] Alfred admitted that he was "amused (& tickled) to be the other pole to Henry Ford" and thought the article "unusually fine."[17]

In the fall of 1922 Anderson fell in love with a young woman named Elizabeth Prall; a few months later he left for Reno, Nevada, to get a divorce from his second wife, Tennessee Mitchell. When Anderson, who ended up spending a year in Reno, asked for a photograph or two to hang in his room, Stieglitz sent not only three portraits of the writer standing in front of O'Keeffe's paintings at her exhibition but also two cloud studies. The subject felt that one of the portraits showed him at his best. "The two others are in a way terrible but wonderful to have about," he wrote Stieglitz. "They are to me the man disintegrated, gone to pieces, fallen down before the ugliness in himself and others. I'll look at them on certain days, when I dare perhaps."[18]

Toward the end of 1922 Mitchell Kennerley told Stieglitz that the Anderson Galleries could no longer spare the room in which he had been storing his prints, books, and hundreds of issues of *Camera Work*. In February 1923 the photographer proceeded to destroy many copies of his magazine and, in one day, tore up more than four hundred prints. When he told his friend Carl Zigrosser of his plan to have all his books carted away as rubbish, Zigrosser immediately called the librarian at the Metropolitan Museum, who dispatched a truck to pick them all up.

After another Marin exhibition at Montross, which elicited from Henry McBride a review calling the watercolorist "the most considerable artist in these States at present," Stieglitz opened the second exhibition of his photographs at the Anderson Galleries, on April 2.[19] In the catalog he defiantly stated,

ART OR NOT ART   THAT IS IMMATERIAL
THERE IS PHOTOGRAPHY

The show of 116 photographs, most of them made since 1921 and only one of them previously exhibited, was dominated by portraits. More than half of the total were of twelve women, including O'Keeffe, Rebecca Strand, Claudia O'Keeffe, and Selma Stieglitz Schubart. Among the men represented were John Marin, Charles Demuth, Sherwood Anderson, Donald Davidson, and Marcel Duchamp, who had been back in New York for a year beginning in early February 1922. Stieglitz included many nudes of O'Keeffe, though not yet his most daring studies, for, he wrote in the catalog, "New York is still not ready for some of the most significant photographs I have made." The remainder of the show was composed of *Music: A Sequence of Ten Cloud Photographs* and images of Lake George trees, apples, and barns.

One evening at the beginning of March 1923, Stieglitz had given a preview of his exhibition to Ananda K. Coomaraswamy, the curator of Indian and Islamic art at the Boston Museum of Fine Arts and himself a dedicated amateur photographer. Coomaraswamy would later say that Stieglitz was "the one artist in America whose work truly matters," because "his photographs are 'absolute' art, in the sense that Bach's music is 'absolute' art."[20] The Bostonian, who championed the idea of beginning a photography collection within his museum's print department, asked Stieglitz that first evening whether he might be willing to donate ten or twelve prints to form its nucleus — since the trustees would certainly not agree to *buy* photographs. Although such a gift violated his principles, Stieglitz felt it would be a great victory to have the prestigious museum accession photographs as works of art and exhibit them together with etchings and woodcuts by the old masters. He stipulated that the museum would have to exhibit his prints at least once every five years and that they must always remain exactly as he mounted and framed them. On April 25, Coomaraswamy wrote Stieglitz to say the trustees would be willing to accept a gift on such conditions.

Stieglitz and Edward Steichen were still on only guardedly cordial terms. Nonetheless, Steichen, who had just returned from France to begin working for Condé Nast Publications as chief photographer, must certainly have paid a visit to his old friend's exhibition. The preceding year he had become disillusioned with his painting and proceeded to burn all the canvases in his studio. Thenceforth he would devote himself exclusively to photography. Stieglitz claimed full credit for getting Frank Crowninshield to hire Steichen for Condé Nast, but Crowninshield had, in *Vanity Fair*, recently proclaimed Steichen "the greatest living portrait photographer" and would probably have engaged him even without Stieglitz's blessing. For the next fifteen years Steichen's sophisticated, theatrical portraits of celebrities would appear regularly in *Vanity Fair* and his fashion photographs in *Vogue*. Although his salary at Condé Nast made him the highest-paid photographer in the world, he soon began moonlighting for the advertising firm of J. Walter Thompson. His success dealt his friendship with Stieglitz the coup de grâce. From then on, Stieglitz would sneer at Steichen as an artist whose ambition and greed had led him to prostitute himself.

The visitor to his exhibition who made the greatest impression on Stieglitz was the twenty-three-year-old poet Hart Crane, recently arrived in New York from Ohio. Although he had not previously met the photographer, they had already exchanged a few letters. One year earlier Crane — who had heard much about Stieglitz from Gorham Munson, a writer and editor who was a close friend of Waldo Frank's — had tried unsuccessfully to interest Stieglitz in exhibiting work by Cleveland painter William Sommer.

Looking at the exhibition with Stieglitz, Crane exclaimed when they came to *Apples and Gable*, "That is it. You've captured life."[21] Stieglitz would write him that "there was never truer seeing."[22] When, at the exhibition, Crane proceeded to offer a "short verbal definition" of Stieglitz's work and aims, the photographer was completely won over. The next day, in a letter that began "Dear great and good man, Alfred Stieglitz," the poet recounted, "You so thoroughly confirmed my conjectures as being the only absolutely correct statement that you had thus far heard concerning your photographs. That moment was a tremendous one in my life because I was able to share all the truth toward which I am working in my own medium, poetry, with another man who had manifestly taken many steps in that same direction in *his* work."[23]

Crane decided at once to write "a fairly comprehensive essay" about Stieglitz and enclosed the "kernel" of it in his letter. In his hands, wrote Crane, the camera was an instrument not merely of "personal perception" but of "something more specially vital — apprehension." Stieglitz's photographs permit "nature and all life to mirror itself [*sic*] so intimately and unexpectedly that we are thrown into ultimate harmonies by looking at these stationary, yet strangely moving pictures." Because of Stieglitz's "clairvoyance . . . the essences of things . . . are suspended on the invisible dimension whose vibrance has been denied the human eye at all times save in the intuition of ecstasy."[24]

The photographer was very pleased. In August, Crane would write him,

Every once in a while I [get] a statement or so noted down in regard to my interpretation of you and your photographs. There are still many things in the lucid explanation of them that simply baffle me. To use a modern simile that occurred to me in that connection — it's like trying to locate "the wires of the Acropolis"; indeed, I may call my essay by that name before I get through.[25]

While Crane continued to refer to his hopes of writing his essay, he never managed to realize the project. We can sense the magnitude of our loss from a single extraordinarily beautiful sentence that he wrote Stieglitz in response to one of his cloud photographs: "I never saw the Venus in her sphere before — looking on the world with the wind from Delphos in her hair!"[26]

*   *   *

Amazingly, the largely epistolary friendship that blossomed between Stieglitz and Crane was little affected by the battles then raging among Stieglitz's other literary friends. The photographer's most valued relationship in the world of letters was the triangle formed by himself, Paul Rosenfeld, and Sherwood Anderson. These three men thought the world of each other, but Rosenfeld and Anderson had misgivings about Waldo Frank.

A feud had developed because Frank fancied himself a great novelist, and Rosenfeld repeatedly stated in print that Frank's gifts were analytical and critical, not imaginative. In 1920 Rosenfeld had published a harsh review of his erstwhile friend's first novel, *Dark Mother*, and he didn't see much sign of progress in subsequent efforts. Anderson fully agreed.

Early in 1923, Rosenfeld attacked Gorham Munson's recently published book, *Waldo Frank: A Study*, in which a Stieglitz close-up of Frank's face — the subject called it "the Christ likeness" — appeared as the frontispiece. The vindictive Munson was soon plotting a satire to be called "Rhapsodic Criticism with 39 Metaphors and no ideas, by Paulina Roseyfield."[27]

Forced to choose between Rosenfeld and Frank, Stieglitz unhesitatingly sided with the former. Naturally hurt and angry, Frank rationalized that he had outgrown his friendship with the photographer and, in July, accused him of being able to remain friends only with people "in a state of adolescence." Since "most artists in America" were "spiritually, intellectually, aesthetically, socially, economically" adolescent, taunted Frank, Stieglitz got along with them well. They became his disciples, and that relationship "served to arrest their own growth." But if one of those disciples happened to mature into true adulthood, Stieglitz would drop him. "You are incapable of a relationship of equality with anyone," fumed Frank. "You demand that, in some way, the 'other person' accept your ascendancy before you function in serving him, in understanding him, enlightening him, in helping him."[28] The rupture between Frank and Stieglitz would prove to be brief, and in May 1927 *McCall's* would publish an article by Frank entitled "Alfred Stieglitz: The World's Greatest Photographer."

In 1920 Frank had befriended a twenty-five-year-old writer named Jean Toomer, who said of himself, "Racially, I seem to have (who knows for sure), seven blood mixtures: French, Dutch, Welsh, Negro, German, Jewish, and Indian." With light honey-colored skin, the breathtakingly handsome Toomer was generally classified as "Negro" and wrote much about the African-American experience in America, though he had lived in a black neighborhood for only two months of his life. Toomer had grown up in the luxurious Washington, D.C., house of his grandfather, who, in post–Civil War Louisiana, had become the only African American ever to have served, albeit very briefly, as the governor of any state. In the summer of 1922 — when Toomer was working on his masterpiece, *Cane*, and Frank was writing a novel about a lynching, called *Holiday* — the two men developed a deep bond of friendship during a week they spent together in a black section of Spartanburg, South Carolina.

By the spring of 1923, Frank, Toomer, Munson, and Crane formed a closely knit group. Sharing a longing for spiritual enlightenment, the four friends were drawn to the teachings of the Armenian "prophet" George Ivanovitch Gurdjieff and to those of his disciples P. D. Ouspensky (whose book *Tertium Organum* Crane devoured) and A. R. Orage, an Englishman who edited the magazine *New Age*. Gurdjieff claimed that through study and the practice of "sacred" gymnastics and dervishlike dances one could integrate the three centers of the self — instinct, emotions, and intellect — and thus awaken from the sleep of ordinary life into "cosmic" consciousness. With Orage's arrival in New York, late in 1923, to drum up recruits and donations for the master's new center outside Paris, Gurdjieff's doctrines and exercises became the rage among a large segment of New York's literati.

During the summer of 1923, Toomer went for the first time to Frank's house in Connecticut and met Frank's wife, Margaret Naumburg. Both Jean and Margaret experienced a *coup de foudre*. That fall she would leave Waldo and move to New York in order to see more of Jean. Toomer then shifted his allegiance to Rosenfeld, who introduced him to Stieglitz and O'Keeffe, both of whom were enchanted by the young man. Toomer and Stieglitz were soon exchanging long, heartfelt letters.

Further fragmentation soon occurred. In the spring of 1922, while he was living in Vienna, Gorham Munson had founded the avant-garde literary magazine *Secession*, for which he enlisted critic Kenneth Burke and Dadaist *littérateur* Matthew Josephson as fellow editors. Josephson — who had just become the American editor of Harold Loeb's peripatetic magazine *Broom*, published in various European cities — declared war early in the fall of 1923 by denouncing what he viewed as the mushy spirituality of Munson and Frank, as well as the overly adjectival floridity of Rosenfeld. William Carlos Williams sided with Josephson, straining the poet's friendship with Stieglitz. The conflict became something of a public spectacle, climaxing the following spring with the publication, in *The New Republic*, of Edmund Wilson's notorious "Imaginary Conversation" between Josephson and Rosenfeld in which the author's sympathies clearly lay with the latter. Josephson's rearguard attempt to conquer America in the name of Dada was doomed, as were *Broom* and *Secession*, both of which would fold in 1924. All this factional fighting greatly distressed Stieglitz, who (alluding to Goethe's last words, "More light!") wrote to Crane in August 1923, "We're all after Light — ever more Light. So why not seek it together — as individuals in sympathy in a strong unsentimental spirit — as men — not as politicians."[29]

In the spring of 1923, while these teapot tempests were raging, Stieglitz became engaged very directly in a bitter quarrel with Charles Sheeler. The title page of the April 1923 issue of *The Arts* announced that the following month Sheeler would "discuss the art of Stieglitz with the sympathy of a friend and with the knowledge of a skilled photographer of the first order." When the review duly appeared, prominently featured, Sheeler had high praise for Stieglitz's photographs, but echoing McBride's 1921 review, he criticized his palladium prints for a "material preciousness" reminiscent of that of gold leaf in Italian painting. Sheeler favored "prints growing out of a less aristocratic element, such as silver." Again following McBride's lead, Sheeler also commented that Stieglitz's cloud photographs reminded him of "the landscapes of Mantegna" and observed that "now and again there reappears a trace of the Munich tradition of painting," as in a 1922 photograph entitled *The Hay Wagon*. That was tantamount to accusing Stieglitz of the terrible sin of Pictorialism.

"Sheeler has something wrong about me in his make-up and has had for some time," wrote Stieglitz, calling Sheeler's attitude "small and ugly."[30] The older photographer's anger may well have been increased by the context of the review in an issue that also featured an encomium of Sheeler by Forbes Watson. *The Arts* had been founded in 1920 by Hamilton Easter Field, whose death in April 1922 moved Stieglitz to compose a eulogy to his old friend. Gertrude Vanderbilt Whitney soon bought the rights to the magazine from Field's heir, the sculptor Robert Laurent, a member of the Whitney Studio Club. Whitney and her assistant, Juliana Force, proceeded to install Force's lover, Forbes Watson, as the new editor in chief.

Stieglitz and Watson had taken an intense dislike to each other during the teens. A graduate of Harvard and Columbia Law School, the patrician Bostonian never bothered to practice law. Afraid of no one, outspoken, knowledgeable, and witty, the dashing Watson, who was then the art critic for the *New York Post*, found Stieglitz pushy, manipulative, and — evidently anti-Semitism again — not quite a gentleman. Since Watson didn't like being told what he should write, he would never go up to 291 unless Hodge

Kirnon, the elevator operator, confirmed that the resident monologist was out to lunch.

Stieglitz was surely sorry to see Sheeler, along with Marius de Zayas, drawn into the Whitney orbit. De Zayas's financial troubles had forced him to put his fine collection of modern French paintings, old-master drawings, and African and pre-Columbian art up for auction at the Anderson Galleries in March 1923. Since the results of the sale were disappointing, de Zayas then accepted Juliana Force's invitation to take charge of organizing exhibitions at the Whitney Studio. He had already begun writing for *The Arts*, though that didn't stop him from contributing an appreciation of Stieglitz's cloud photographs to the *New York World* in April.

De Zayas had introduced Sheeler to Force, who also had a house in Doylestown, Pennsylvania, and who shared with Sheeler an interest in American antiques. She greatly admired his paintings — which looked increasingly like colored photographs — and, in August 1923, would invite him and his wife to live in the apartment above the Whitney Studio Club's new galleries on West Eighth Street, in return for which he acted as gallery manager. Sheeler would have a one-man show at the club in March 1924.

His review ended his friendships with both Stieglitz and Strand, who wrote a letter to the *New York Sun* complaining of the "irrelevance of the ever present comparison of photography to a totally different medium" and of "Mr. Sheeler's errors and omissions" regarding Stieglitz's use of platinum paper.[31] Sheeler had already written diplomatically to Strand, "Any exception that Stieglitz may have taken, through you . . . is quite alright."[32] But neither Stieglitz nor Strand could be appeased.

As Stieglitz heard bits of news about Sheeler over the next few years, he must have felt that his former protégé was going from bad to worse. Early in 1926 Sheeler would accept an invitation from Steichen to join him on the staff of Condé Nast. That same year he was given a one-man show by the Pictorial Photographers of America. And in 1927 he went to Detroit to photograph the new Ford Motor Company plant at River Rouge for the advertising firm of N. W. Ayer. The paintings he based on his dramatic photographs would earn him the title "the Raphael of the Fords."

CHAPTER FIFTY·NINE

BY THE END of Stieglitz's winter and spring of discontent, as O'Keeffe wrote during the summer of 1923, his "nerves seemed tied up so tight that they wouldn't unwind."[1] He himself conceded that his "vitality had been so much sapped" that he "was at the breaking point for a long time."[2] It was then that the greatest tragedy of his life occurred.

For the past two years Kitty had been doing very well. Having majored in chemistry, she graduated from Smith with honors in 1921. During her senior year, her letters to her father indicated increasing maturity and forgiveness. However, since it would be disastrous to have both Alfred and Emmy present at her commencement exercises, she gently asked her father not to attend.

The following year, in a Unitarian service to which no members of either family were invited, Kitty married Milton Sprague Stearns, a Bostonian whom she had first met at summer camp. A graduate of Phillips Exeter Academy and Harvard, Milton worked in sales for a firm that imported hides. The newlyweds initially lived in a middle-class suburb of Boston. In the fall Kitty announced that she was pregnant, and soon she and Milton moved to White Plains, New York. Her letters to her father became more frequent and more affectionate.

Early in June 1923, after giving birth to a son, Kitty began sinking into a deep postpartum depression. The day before leaving for Lake George,

Alfred went up to White Plains to visit her in the hospital. Although "far from satisfied with her state of mind," he didn't feel there was much cause for alarm.[3] But her condition grew steadily worse. Soon she was alternating between expressions of love and hate for her father. Some of the terrible, unexpressed rage that Kitty had long felt toward Alfred, for his neglect and subsequent desertion, percolated to the surface in angry outbursts, and some turned ever more deeply inward in the form of debilitating depression.

Alfred was devastated by his worries about Kitty and by guilt for his past treatment of her. "I certainly failed in so many ways in spite of all my endeavour to protect and help her prepare herself for life," he wrote in the fall. "I realize with every new day what a child I have been & still am — Absurdly so. It sometimes disgusts me with myself."[4] "Poor, poor girl," he moaned. "Completely innocent."[5]

Both Alfred's worry and his guilt were assuaged somewhat by the knowledge that after Emmy's birth her mother had developed postpartum depression and had recovered. Alfred consoled himself with the certainty that the condition was both hereditary and temporary. Lee, who was in frequent contact with the doctors in White Plains, told Alfred that Kitty should be back to normal within three or four months. His optimism would prove to be completely unjustified.

Because there had been talk of selling the Hill after Hedwig's death, everyone in the family except Alfred and Georgia had made plans to spend the summer of 1923 elsewhere. When they arrived at Lake George, Alfred was so "dazed" for weeks that he felt "more dead than alive." "If I had a mind to lose," he wrote to Arthur Dove, "I guess it would have gone for good."[6] O'Keeffe said that he "was just a little heap of misery — sleepless — with eyes — ears — nose — arm — feet — ankles — intestines — all taking their turn at deviling him — one after the other."[7] For more than a month one arm hurt so badly that he could barely raise it. Then his feet "gave way" so that he was "forced to sit & finally look after them."[8] And since his eyes were "raising hell," he had trouble reading.[9] "In his misery he was very sad," O'Keeffe told Sherwood Anderson in midsummer, "and I guess I had grown pretty sad and forlorn feeling too."[10] Caught in a vicious circle of depression, Alfred became all the more upset when he realized how adversely his state of mind affected Georgia, even though he knew "it would be unnatural were it different."[11]

A visit from Beck Strand late in June cheered them up a bit, but not much. Then, in mid-July, Alfred was delighted by the arrival of George and

Marie Rapp Boursault with their two-year-old daughter, Yvonne, whom their host called "the livest proposition imaginable."[12] Acknowledging that the little girl sometimes sounded like "21-cats-on-the-fence," he nevertheless was charmed by her games and made innumerable snapshots of her. After George returned to the city to look for work, leaving his again-pregnant wife and Yvonne at the lake for another two months, O'Keeffe would come to loathe the little "brat," the sound of whose voice, whether talking or crying, penetrated every room in the house and nearly drove her to a nervous breakdown. If Kitty's plight confirmed once and for all Alfred's conviction that O'Keeffe must not have a baby, Yvonne convinced the artist herself that she was not cut out to be a mother.

During July, "still too tired to feel," Alfred did no work. "I have done nothing so far but tried to put myself physically & psychically in halfway decent working shape," he wrote. Despite continuing trouble with his eyes, he read and reread the autobiography of John Stuart Mill, which he found "full of meat — solid stuff. Marvellously clear thinking & writing. Much fitting into my own condition. — Digging into roots without sentimental twaddle spoken or unspoken."[13]

With no mention of Kitty, saying only that he had received staggering news, Alfred wrote many long letters to such friends as Dove, Sherwood Anderson, and Hart Crane and derived much comfort from their replies. On June 30, for instance, Anderson wrote from Reno, "You do so make the world a living place for so many people. . . . Whatever blows the actuality of life may deal you, I think you may well know that no other man of our day is so deeply loved. You have kept the old faith that gets so lost and faint, but that always has some man like yourself to make it real again to the younger ones."[14]

On July 4 Crane apologized for not having responded sooner to Stieglitz's "testament of pain and accident," explaining that his copywriting job at J. Walter Thompson and his work on his poem *The Bridge* filled almost every waking moment of every day. Crane — who, later that summer, signed one letter "I am your brother always" — assured his new friend,

I am always seeing your life and experience very solidly as a part of my own because I feel our identities so much alike in a spiritual direction. . . . [W]e center in common devotions, in a kind of timeless vision. In the above sense I feel you as entering very strongly into certain developments in *The Bridge*. May I say it, and not seem absurd, that you are the first, or rather the purest living indice of a new order of consciousness that I have met?

He then encouraged Stieglitz to "go on with your photographic synthesis of life this summer and fall, gathering together those dangerous interests outside of yourself into that purer projection of yourself."[15]

At the beginning of August, O'Keeffe, who had "almost given up hope," gratefully reported that during the past few days Alfred had begun "to be himself again."[16] Heartened by good news about Kitty's progress, he had finally roused himself to work, spending up to ten hours some days trying to coax the most beautiful prints possible from old negatives for the Boston Museum of Fine Arts. Early in February 1924 he would send not the ten or twelve prints he had originally promised but a "comprehensive collection" of twenty-seven, including five *Songs of the Sky*, after spending $300 to have George Of frame them to his specifications.

During August he made dozens of shots of clouds with his 4 x 5 Graflex, more than in any other year. The sun itself appears in many of these biblical struggles of light and dark, full of intense emotion. Stieglitz would write to Marsden Hartley in the fall, "I have gone through a great deal even this summer. That's why 'Clouds' (really the Sun) and I became fast friends."[17] It was, he said, when light was "in the ascendancy" that he felt moved to photograph.[18]

Some of his images include treetops or hilltops, but most float completely free of the ground. He called a few small series "portraits" — of O'Keeffe and others — and he sometimes even claimed to see female forms in the shapes of the clouds. O'Keeffe, however, said that she could "never find the woman."[19] In general, the cloud "portraits" are purely symbolic, though Stieglitz obviously made some in the O'Keeffe group that summer because the formations bore an uncanny resemblance to her abstractions. As with his Picasso drawing, he felt that the similarity vindicated both his photographs and her paintings.

Stieglitz was thrilled that his perfectly sharp, absolutely straightforward photographs of clouds seemed to him more purely abstract than did most "so called" abstract canvases.[20] In the sky he had found the solution to a problem that had been central to his work for more than a decade. "In looking at the photographs of clouds, people seem to feel freed to think more about the actual relationships in the pictures and less about the subject-matter," he said. "True meaning . . . comes through directly, without any extraneous or distracting pictorial or representational factors coming between the person and the picture."[21] He believed his cloud photographs were "different from anything the eye has seen in any medium."[22]

When he exhibited his cloud photographs from 1923, he wrote, "'Songs of the Sky — Secrets of the Skies as revealed by my Camera' are tiny photographs, direct revelations of a man's world in the sky — documents of eternal relationship — perhaps even a philosophy."[23] When Stieglitz looked up into the sky and saw configurations that seemed to embody his feelings at that moment, he felt in harmony with the divine order of the universe. It was as though he and God were experiencing the same feelings at the same moment, and God's emotions were manifested so potently in the clouds that anyone looking at one of the photographs would not only recognize, but actually experience, the particular state of mind it represented. In December 1923, after having shown his summer's work to a few friends, he wrote to Crane, "Several people feel I have photographed God. May be."[24]

Stieglitz made contact silver prints of his new negatives on Eastman Kodak postcard stock. Stung by the criticisms of Henry McBride and Charles Sheeler regarding his expensive materials, he was now determined to turn "poor innocent postal card paper" into "a living thing of beauty."[25] He would labor for hours, or even for days, to produce a perfect print on paper so cheaply made that he feared it wouldn't last more than thirty years. According to Herbert Seligmann, "Stieglitz often said that what he was aiming for was a small photographic print which would contain a maximum of detail together with a maximum of simplicity, his ultimate goal being a print the size of a postage stamp which would express everything he had experienced in life."[26]

Hart Crane wrote late in August, "It's good to hear that you have been 'at the camera' again and that you are recovering with physical and nervous rest, that extremity of delicate equilibrium that goes into your best activities."[27] By the time Stieglitz received that letter, his recovery had been set back by a report from Milton Stearns that Kitty was worse than ever. In addition to her emotional outbursts, she was now suffering hallucinations and held tenaciously to the delusion that her father was dead. Her doctors were forced to admit that she was suffering from something more serious than depression. She was a victim of dementia praecox, as schizophrenia was then called. The prognosis was not encouraging.

At times of emotional crisis, Alfred needed desperately to be surrounded by family and friends. Late in August his need was satisfied by the return of Beck Strand and soon thereafter by the arrival of the Engelhards, the Davidsons, and Katharine Rhoades. Alfred proceeded to make a series of six tree-and-sky photographs that constituted a "portrait" of Rhoades; a critic would write that "a tree that dances and sparkles in the first plates be-com[es] in the last print a thing of dignity and completeness." Stieglitz had "let his imagination work out two future possibilities — a happy and an unhappy ending, as it were."[28]

If Alfred no longer had any romantic interest in Rhoades, that was at least partly because he was infatuated with Beck, to whom he had been writing erotic letters all summer. He told her on August 6, for instance, that he had been touching up with ink some dust spots on prints of his nude photographs of her. "For an hour or more I have been tickling up your rear into most perfect condition of delight," he teased provocatively.[29]

O'Keeffe, worn down by a summer of Alfred's misery and Yvonne's yowling, was not happy to see the Hill fill up. She needed peace and quiet to work, and she felt like a visitor in her own house. Further exasperated by Stieglitz's flirting with Beck, and confident that he would be well taken care of by the Engelhards and the Davidsons, she abruptly left for York Beach on September 8.

Before Georgia's departure, Beck had written Paul that Stieglitz — sleepless, "like a haunted man pursued by his daemon" — would come into her room in the middle of the night to talk. "I wish I could take him to my broad bosom and comfort him," she confided to her husband.[30] But even after the Engelhards and the Davidsons left, and Alfred and Beck found themselves alone, she seems to have resisted the temptation to go to bed with him. Terribly disappointed, Alfred complained to his most dependable confidante, Elizabeth Davidson, that Beck had "seemed millions of miles removed from me — She's all right — but there is a messiness somewhere which will ever remain messy — I'm sorry."[31]

Beck's "messiness" made Alfred appreciate Georgia all the more, and the tranquillity of Maine enabled her to regain her strength. The mail had "brought a very beautiful letter from Georgia," Alfred reported to Elizabeth on September 24. "Rather sad. But very beautiful. There is no doubt that if any woman should be close to me it's Georgia — For she is truly beautiful at the root."[32]

Paul Rosenfeld arrived at the lake on September 18, and during the early part of his "very complete" stay, he and Alfred spent many hours going over the essays in his forthcoming book *Port of New York*. On the twenty-seventh, however, Alfred passed from depression to a manic phase. Frantic with guilt and self-pity, he overwhelmed Beck and Rosenfeld with an obsessive monologue that went on relentlessly for hours. He said that he was stricken with guilt about Kitty, that his life was a tragedy, that he was universally misunderstood, and that he seemed to destroy everyone around him. Furthermore, he said he could never give up the house at Lake George, however miserable O'Keeffe might be there.

"Stieglitz wants his own way of living," Beck wrote her husband the next day, "and his passion for trying to make other people see it in the face of their own inherent qualities really gets things into such a state of pressure that you sometimes feel as though you were suffocating."[33] Rosenfeld wept and told Beck that he had never experienced such hell.

On the morning of the twenty-eighth, after receiving a telegram from O'Keeffe saying that she would be returning later that day, Stieglitz went into further paroxysms of despair. He had not wanted her to come back until he had regained his equilibrium. Fortunately, his frenzy had spent itself by the time she arrived. He was pleased to see her "in much improved condition."[34] The next day he told Dove that he himself was "in 'fighting' shape once more" and eager to tackle the work that was to be done.[35] Over the course of the succeeding days Alfred and Georgia had "some real Talks," he informed Elizabeth. "They showed her some things in a new light. She listened and heard. And I was much clearer. The days of adolescence are over & the relationship reestablished finely free. . . . It is all working out."[36]

Since Kitty showed no improvement, she was admitted in mid-October to Craig House, a private sanatorium overlooking the Hudson River in Beacon, New York, about two hours north of Manhattan. With a minimum rate of nearly $8,000 a year (which would be divided among the Obermeyers and the entire Stieglitz family), Craig House was a luxurious establishment for the wealthy. On the 350 acres of the estate's landscaped grounds was a private cottage for each patient, attended around the clock by a nurse. Every effort was made to give the place the feeling of a perpetual house party, with bridge and Ping-Pong tournaments. The facilities included tennis courts, an indoor and an outdoor swimming pool, and a nine-hole golf course. Because they were under constant supervision, patients were never locked up. As for treatment, Craig House's owner, Dr. Jonathan Slocum, believed in daily chats and dispensed liberal doses of paternalistic "advice and encouragement."[37]

Alfred had apparently suffered so much all summer that he was now beyond pain. "I'm not worrying. There is too much to do — too much to enjoy," he wrote to Dove early in November. "Every day is a life in itself — as a matter of fact every hour has become that — moments each possessing their eternity."[38]

A few days earlier, however, he had become extremely upset when he received from Marsden Hartley, who was then in Germany, some autobiographical notes for the appendix of Rosenfeld's book. Stieglitz wrote an irate letter to the artist on October 26, and then the next day wrote him two more.

> Not a mention of 291. . . . Not a mention of the real generous spirit of the place. . . . And if I didn't have a keen sense of humor and one of values and a very good memory because of these, what you wrote would make me commit suicide. . . . And I certainly want no credit for it. But when I think of your record of fourteen years in connection with me — and that is 291 — when I have the catalogues, *Camera Work*, your letters — and know how it is that you have been able to go about as I have not been able to do — nor wish to do — why the picture you have given of me in connection with you and 291 in the notes becomes a grimace.[39]

Hartley promptly revised his notes.

Stieglitz's spirits were certainly buoyed at the end of October by the arrival of Ida O'Keeffe, a strong, radiant, and good-humored woman who had given up her career as an art teacher to become a nurse. Georgia wrote during the week Ida was at the lake, "My sister . . . is like nothing else that ever grew — She keeps the house very gay with wild flowers — and amuses Stieglitz much — You have never seen anything funnier."[40]

During early November's "perfect days of perfect quiet sunshine," Georgia told Sherwood Anderson, "Stieglitz is in great form — working like a beaver — taking great strides ahead as usual — and in quite a happy frame of mind."[41] Alfred confirmed to the same correspondent that he was "crazily mad with work — fun."[42] He assured another friend that his passion for photography was "greater than ever."[43] And to Hart Crane he wrote of the summer's tribulations, "My work finally saved me."[44]

After Lee Stieglitz had a mild heart attack on September 1, he prescribed for himself an apartment without stairs. Although the house on East Sixty-fifth Street was sold in late October, the occupants would not have to move out until June 1, 1924. Despite the fact that the family was still talking about selling the Hill, Stieglitz and O'Keeffe now considered the possibility of living there year-round. It was not the place itself that she hated, only the conditions that sometimes prevailed there. She confessed to Anderson in November that the house and its setting seemed so perfect that she sometimes wanted "to tear it all to pieces" but conceded, "It is really lovely — And when the household is in good running order — and I feel free to work it is very nice."[45]

They had hired Hedwig's former maid, Catherine Colton, whose company O'Keeffe enjoyed, to work as housekeeper. Reveling in her freedom to paint, O'Keeffe wrote Anderson, "We all spend most of our time alone — each tending to his own particular job — and get on wonderfully — it is a very amusing household."[46]

"It's too glorious here, and the Silence is perfect," Stieglitz told Crane. One day, when he and O'Keeffe had hiked up to the top of Prospect Mountain, the excitement was overwhelming. "In fifty years I have been up there at least fifty times," he said, "and I have seen some marvelous pictures from there — but on this occasion nature actually vied with art and I feel that all the pictures I ever saw put together could not hold a candle to what lay there at my feet — as I turned around 360 degrees! — An unforgettable hour."[47]

On the last Sunday in November they woke up to find the ground covered with a foot of snow. "White–White–White–& soft & clean," exclaimed Stieglitz. Having always dreamt of such conditions but having never before remained at the lake sufficiently late in the year, he stayed outdoors until dark, "photographing like [one] possessed." O'Keeffe, "as happy and beautiful as the day," spent hours "wandering about in the woods — & rushing down to the Lake." That evening, he wrote to Anderson, "the moon came out clear — & I stood watching the barns & trees — & ground — & hills — the sky — an unbelievable dignity. . . . I'll never forget the barns that I saw in the moonlight. Talk about the Sphinx & pyramids — there was that barn — nothing could be grander."[48]

CHAPTER SIXTY

ON JANUARY 1, 1924, Stieglitz celebrated his sixtieth birthday. It was no coincidence that one week later the Royal Photographic Society of Great Britain conferred its highest honor, the Progress Medal, upon him for "services rendered in founding and fostering Pictorial Photography in America, and particularly for your initiation and publication of 'Camera Work,' the most artistic record of Photography ever attempted."

Paul Rosenfeld's book *Port of New York*, published early in 1924, was also something of a sixtieth-birthday present. Hart Crane wrote that the chapter on Stieglitz, a reworking of Rosenfeld's 1921 *Dial* article, was "very fine indeed." Susan Sontag would call it "the finest essay ever written in praise of photography."[1] Among the subjects of the book's thirteen other essays on "American moderns" were O'Keeffe, Marin, Dove, Hartley, Sherwood Anderson, William Carlos Williams, Carl Sandburg, Randolph Bourne, Van Wyck Brooks, and Albert Ryder. Spitefully, Rosenfeld omitted Waldo Frank but included Margaret Naumburg.

The RPS award prompted P. H. Emerson to initiate a correspondence in which he would hound Stieglitz for "a dozen or 20" recent prints to evaluate for possible inclusion in the "true history of the development of artistic photography" he was writing.[2] Emerson promised that if the work was *really* fine, he would send Stieglitz a medal, silver or bronze in accordance with the degree of merit. That, of course, was precisely the sort of request most likely to antagonize Stieglitz, but, while adamant in his refusal to send prints, he was determined to enlighten his former mentor with long letters and with articles by Seligmann and Strand, as well as with Rosenfeld's book. Emerson was not impressed. "Somehow I think you are wandering far from the track in your thoughts," he wrote Stieglitz. "Why be so sensitive about not having any 'ism' and objecting to Pictorial Photography[?]"[3] As for Strand, Emerson dismissed him as "an ignorant and pretentious duffer — he can neither write nor take a fine photograph judging from his portrait of you which is all wrong and proves he does not know the elements." Rosenfeld, he complained, "does not understand at all and his style makes my head ache."[4] Such missives continued to cross the Atlantic for a year, to no avail.

In February 1924, when N. E. Montross was taken ill on the eve of the opening of his by then annual Marin show, he asked Stieglitz to man the gallery. "Once more 291 on deck," exclaimed Alfred with relish.[5] Montross was highly skeptical when his colleague insisted that some of the watercolors be priced at an exorbitant $1,500, which was $300 more than any Marin had ever sold for. But the architect Philip Goodwin, who had previously bought a Marin from Stieglitz for $1,200 (and whose collection would eventually be housed in the building he designed in 1939 for the Museum of Modern Art), gladly paid the specified top price for a particularly beautiful watercolor of a sailboat. Stieglitz rejoiced in such a vindication of his "idealism" over Montross's "so-called practicality."[6]

Stieglitz had already decided, late in 1923, that Marin should not have to depend on dealers like Montross and Charles Daniel for his living. So he had come up with the idea of raising a Marin fund, every contributor to which would be guaranteed a 250 percent return on his or her investment in watercolors at the current valuation. Rosenfeld, Paul Strand and his father, and Katherine Dreier were among the contributors who, for the next three years, would relieve Marin of the need to worry about money.

O'Keeffe had been looking forward to a small exhibition of her "objective" work "to confirm what started last year."[7] Stieglitz had not intended to exhibit his own work again, since he had come to feel that for himself "exhibitioning is out-of-date, offensive." However, he wrote in the third person, "his modesty tells him that his most recent photographs are not only an addition to his past achievements but that they are something not before accomplished in any medium as expression — as scientific fact."[8]

They decided to have simultaneous shows, opening March 3, in the usual space at the Anderson Galleries. One large gallery was filled with fifty-one oils, watercolors, pastels, and drawings by O'Keeffe. In two smaller rooms Stieglitz installed sixty-one of his own photographs. At the entrance to his show was a small print of a close-up side view of the hindquarters of the old horse at Lake George in harness, an image that he called *Spiritual America*. Most viewers were mystified by this beautifully composed, and quite abstract, picture — but the point was that the horse was a gelded stallion, a perfect symbol of America's condition. In contrast, Alfred had noted with surprise and pleasure on his trips to Paris, many carriages there were drawn by intact stallions.

The rest of Stieglitz's exhibition consisted of forty-five *Songs of the Sky*, six early works, and several shots of the barn and other outbuildings on the Hill after the November blizzard. "Then with proper humor, and a relief to intensities," wrote one critic, "the exhibition ends with a scolding old shrew of the sky, berating all humanity."[9]

Alfred spent every day on his feet at the exhibitions and was especially voluble, for, as Henry McBride mischievously commented, "the effort that used to be spent by Mr. Stieglitz during an entire year now must be compressed into a fortnight."[10]

McBride praised the cloud photographs as being "about as far in finish and subtlety and richness as the camera can go, or need go."[11] Another critic proclaimed that Stieglitz was inventing "the hieroglyphics of a new speech."[12] Alfred was even pleased with the review that appeared in *The Arts*. There, Virgil Barker wrote that the "wordless sky-songs" had come to him "as a revelation — a call to adventure, an enlargement of experience, a spiritual release. A perceiving soul has trapped sublimity in a machine and on sheets of paper a hand's breadth wide has fixed immensity."[13] The photographer was, however, outraged by the critique in *The Nation*, where Thomas Craven chided, "Alfred Stieglitz, probably the most accomplished photographer in the world, . . . asks us to believe that the reduplication of natural phenomena carries an emotional freightage identical with that of creative art."[14]

O'Keeffe had hoped that Anderson, who was still in Reno and in a state of "horrible depression," would write a foreword for her catalog, but he declined, saying that because he had the flu, anything he wrote would be dull.[15] Instead O'Keeffe reprinted a mixed bag of reviews of her previous show and ended her own brief statement with two defiantly un-Stieglitzian admissions: "Incidentally I hope someone will buy something. I have kept my pictures small because space in New York necessitated that."

Most of the critics praised her technical skill and noted both a more purely decorative quality and a wider range of color than in the past. In addition to her signature red cannas were cool white-and-yellow calla lilies, purple-green avocados (which were then called alligator pears), and leaves of all colors, ranging (as O'Keeffe wrote) from "summer green" to "dark somber blackish purplish red."[16] The reviewers surmised, correctly, that her straightforward realism was meant to minimize psychological and sexual interpretations — though nearly pornographic calla lilies seemed perhaps not the best choice of subject matter for such a purpose. One writer offered a key to the emotional tension in the paintings by describing the artist herself as

> an ascetic, almost saintly appearing, woman with a dead-white skin, fine delicate features and black hair severely drawn back from her forehead. Saintly, yes, but not nun-like, for O'Keeffe gives one the feeling that beneath her calm poise there is something that is intensely, burningly alive, and that she is not only possessed of the most delicate sensibilities but is also capable of great and violent emotions.[17]

The spring of 1924 was very trying. During April, Stieglitz was racked with pain caused by kidney stones; once he recovered, all of their possessions in Lee and Lizzie's house had to be packed and put into storage by June 1. The actual task would have been demanding enough, but, as Georgia told Anderson, with a mixture of impatience and fondness, Alfred turned moving into an existential dilemma:

> It seems we have been moving all winter — Stieglitz has to do everything in his mind so many times before he does it in reality. . . . It really isn't the moving with him. It is many things within himself that he focuses on the idea of moving . . . trying to understand what it is that he is and why — in relation to the world — and what the world is and where is it all going to and what it is all about — and the poor little thing is looking for a place in it — and doesn't see any place where he thinks he fits.[18]

When they arrived at Lake George early in June, Stieglitz predictably declared himself "so down & out" that he felt barely human.[19] But O'Keeffe judged him "certainly in much better condition than he was when we came up last year" and thought that once his materials arrived he would "get to work earlier this year than usual."[20] A major factor was good news about Kitty, who was discharged from Craig House in June to spend the summer with Milton and their baby in a rented house at Sagamore Beach,

Massachusetts. Nevertheless, wrote O'Keeffe of Alfred, "he is a forlorn little soul — I do what I can — but I have to keep some of myself or I wouldn't have anything left to give."[21]

"It is the first time I have come here that I have really liked it," O'Keeffe confided to Anderson. The difference was that they were completely alone and were "really masters of the house," since the old coachman and general handyman, Fred Varnum, had died during the winter.[22] "Georgia is in her element," Stieglitz reported to Dove three weeks after their arrival. "She is boss. And she is happy. And paints diligently. And cooks sufficiently to keep us from starving."[23] He tried to help her, but he wasn't much use. O'Keeffe mused to Anderson, "I almost think that left to himself he would absent mindedly throw away the dishes because they are dirty."[24] She was so content that she was looking forward to spending the next five or six months at the lake, as much of that time as possible alone with Stieglitz. Acknowledging that he missed having other people around, she nevertheless claimed, "Being alone is good for Stieglitz too — He doesn't get excited — he reads a little — writes letters — and pokes around, a funny little soft grey creature."[25]

While Alfred read James Joyce's *Ulysses*, a biography of Voltaire in German, and books by Bertrand Russell and J.B.S. Haldane about the future of science, Georgia gave the house a thorough cleaning and, with the help of a local man, got the garden plowed and planted — to grow food for the table, flowers for delight, and subjects for her paintings. During those first weeks, she made a great breakthrough in her work when she painted her first bee's-eye view of a flower, a petunia. Although Alfred called it "silly but lovely," Georgia was not deterred.[26] That summer she would paint close-ups not only of flowers but also of corn, whose leaves would fill her narrow, vertical canvases. Edmund Wilson later observed that "the dark green stalks of one of her 'Corn' pictures have become so charged by her personal current and fused by her personal heat that they have the aspect of some sort of dynamo of feeling constructed not to represent but to generate, down the centre of which the fierce white line strikes like an electric spark."[27] At the end of the summer O'Keeffe would write to Anderson, "I am much excited over my work this year . . . [I]t has given me a great time and some of it I enjoy very much — and I really don't often enjoy my own things."[28]

After the first few happy weeks at the lake, trouble arose in paradise. Early in June, Alfred had at last received an interlocutory divorce from Emmy, to become final after ninety days. Soon he raised the question of marriage to

Georgia, who didn't like the idea one bit. The issue would rankle them all summer.

On top of that, guests began to arrive. Collector-patrons financier Arthur Schwab and his wife, writer Edna Bryner, came for a week and were joined by Paul and Beck Strand for the Fourth of July weekend. Forced to relinquish both her cherished solitude and her creative momentum, and exasperated by having to cook and care for four demanding guests, Georgia became so depressed by the time they left that she had no appetite, lost almost ten pounds within a short time, and wanted to stay in bed all day. "I don't know why people disturb me so much," she had written to Anderson in June. "They make me feel like a hobbled horse."[29]

Greatly alarmed, Alfred, who felt "so damned useless," got Catherine Colton to take over again as cook.[30] He also pressed the Davidsons to come earlier than originally planned — though without two-year-old Sue, who would be more than Georgia's shattered nerves could stand, and with a young Swiss woman to take care of five-year-old Peggy, whom Alfred declared "a wonder."[31] Until nearly the middle of July, Georgia would continue to feel "very miserable," but the warm, capable, and independent Davidsons would gradually succeed in getting her back on her feet.[32]

Paul Strand made the mistake of returning for a brief visit before she was fully mended, and she proceeded to launch into him — probably over his effusive but patronizingly sexist article about her that was to appear in the next issue of the magazine *Playboy: A Portfolio of Art and Satire*, along with an article by Egmont Arens on Stieglitz's cloud photographs. Furious at what he perceived as Georgia's ingratitude, Strand left unappeased by Alfred.

O'Keeffe had had it with the Strands. She was disgusted by what she viewed as Paul's obsequiousness and obtuseness, and she blamed his wife for encouraging Alfred's flirting. Beck was due to arrive at the end of July, but Georgia put her foot down — she didn't want her in the house. She could stay at the Pines and take her meals there. Terrified lest anything impede Georgia's recovery, Alfred obediently wrote Beck with a concocted excuse for the change of plans.

When Beck arrived, she was full of righteous indignation at Georgia's treatment of Paul and at her own banishment from the Hill. After a heated argument, the two women avoided each other for days. While Georgia sulked indoors, Alfred photographed Beck and assured her, as he would reiterate in a letter that fall, "Beckalina, mia carissima . . . You really had nothing to do with the, let's call it unrest — inner — of G. — as I see it."[33] Alfred finally talked to Georgia and reached something of an understanding. "It has been a very difficult week," he wrote to Elizabeth Davidson on August 3. "But there has been some clearing up . . . I & my women folk seem to be on a working basis."[34]

One day, down by the lake, Georgia opened her heart to Beck. "Weeping uncontrollably," Beck reported to Paul, Georgia lamented that she didn't know how she could go on living with Stieglitz.[35] He was gregarious, and she craved solitude. He wanted to get married, and she already felt too cramped by their present relationship. She loved him, but what was she to do?

By the end of the first week of August, O'Keeffe had resumed painting, and Stieglitz was printing both old and new negatives. He was also mounting prints, slaving to find the precise size and shade of mount that would best suit each, as well as its proper orientation and placement. "A trying ordeal for the eyes," he wrote to Sherwood Anderson. "It's sometimes the toughest part of the picture making. I've been months sometimes solving such a problem. . . . I wish you could see the difference between right & not right. In the *feel*. The release of spirit when everything is organically functioning as one."[36]

Stieglitz had been hoping to make a thousand prints of his "sky songs" that summer. But, to his dismay, he discovered early in August that Eastman had suddenly lowered the quality of its postcard paper. Instead of the "rich black" and "sparkling white" of the old stock, the new yielded gray and "dirty white." "It is enough to kill a sensitive human," he wailed to Anderson. "And no redress. — God knows murder comes into one's blood." As precious work days slipped away, Stieglitz was

> slaving once more, trying to "adapt" myself — knowing only too well by the time I've evolved some way of turning their really impoverished product into something living by instilling it with my own life blood these monsters will be ready to sink their own standard a little lower for the good of the people–& for the bonuses of their workmen! it's all horrible.

And that despite his claim, earlier in the same letter, "Perhaps I've meant the most to the 'common' people I meet casually–& have met since I was a kid."[37]

With the family still talking about selling the Hill, Alfred deemed it prudent to invite Lee and Lizzie to spend a few weeks there during late August and early September. The stratagem worked too well. They enjoyed themselves so much that at the end of their stay they announced they would spend every summer from then on at the lake. Softening the blow to O'Keeffe only somewhat was their decision not to live in the farmhouse but to build a cottage for themselves on the property.

"September was a marvelous month for us," Stieglitz wrote to Arthur Dove. "Ida O'Keeffe, Catherine . . . , & we in the house. Each one really a free soul & all in harmony — natural cooperation — no words or theories — no tension — much work each in his own way — much laughter. — Ida is a gem — so is Catherine."[38]

Ida told Georgia that when Alfred met her train in Albany, he "jumped around like a little dog wanting to play." He continued to flirt with her ribaldly, but she handled the situation beautifully by refusing to take him the least bit seriously. If he wanted to be bawdy, to slap and pinch her rear, to tease her and steal an occasional kiss, fine — she would tease and slap him right back.

He borrowed his nickname for her from the Ida Red variety of apple and called himself Old Crow Feather. Summing up his sexual fantasies, he stuck a crow's feather deep into an apple and photographed the symbolic construction for Ida's benefit. Late one night he even tiptoed out onto the sleeping porch to gaze longingly at her while she slept. But when he wanted to photograph her nude back, she put her foot down.

Late in September, Paul Rosenfeld — who had just returned from Europe and who had, in Stieglitz's estimation, "matured greatly" — spent five days on the Hill.[39] During his visit, Alfred's jealousy was aroused when he realized that Paul was falling in love with Ida and that she was encouraging his attentions. With Rosenfeld, as with Strand, Alfred felt an intense sexual rivalry. It was as though he could assuage his fears about losing Georgia, who would turn thirty-seven in November, only if he could defeat his "sons" on the field of love. That winter Rosenfeld would see much of Ida in New York and would ask her to marry him. To Alfred's relief, she refused.

When Alfred went into the town of Lake George to pick up the mail on the afternoon of October 10, he found the drugstore full of people listening to the World Series on the radio. "My heart nearly stood still when I was informed that it was the last half of the 11th inning — tie," he related to Anderson. "I've been rooting for Washington for years. . . . and here was Johnston in the box in the final tie after having lost two games for the team and all the U.S.A. rooting for him. . . . Gosh! talk about breathless moments — Washington wins!"[40] Stieglitz cared far less about the upcoming presidential election. "If Coolidge is elected the Winter ought to be 'good' in business — should [Robert] LaFollette upset 'calculations' business is in for merry hell," he wrote to Dove. "But we go right ahead either way."[41]

In October, Stieglitz received an advance copy of Anderson's autobiographical book *A Story Teller's Story*, which he read with "intense joy" and lauded as "a splendid performance — full of humor & fineness — a great simplicity & loveableness — broad — a living thing. And of today. No 'artiness.' "[42] His pleasure was enhanced no small amount by the page that read:

To

ALFRED STIEGLITZ

who has been more than father to so many
puzzled, wistful children of the arts in
this big, noisy, growing and groping
America, this book is gratefully
dedicated.

When Stieglitz and O'Keeffe returned to New York in mid-November, their first chore was to find a place to live. They had thought about moving into a moderately priced hotel near the Anderson Galleries, and various friends had offered them temporary quarters. But O'Keeffe wanted a place of their own at last, with a room she could use as her studio. Flush with Lee's promise to give Alfred $1,000 a year for as long as he could afford to do so, and confident that Georgia's paintings would continue to sell well, they soon rented the top floor of the four-story brownstone at 38 East Fifty-eighth Street, on the south side of the block between Madison and Park avenues.

It was bad news about Kitty that finally brought about their marriage. In October, Milton had written them that after a pleasant summer Kitty had suffered a severe relapse and returned to Craig House. Her doctors suggested that if Stieglitz and O'Keeffe would now marry, Kitty might become able to understand her father's situation. Very reluctantly, Georgia yielded to Alfred's entreaties.

Since Alfred's divorce decree forbade him to remarry in the state of New York, they went to New Jersey on December 8 to get their marriage license. On that cold, wet Monday, John Marin picked them up at the Weehawken ferry, in his brand-new Chandler touring car, and they set off for Cliffside (now Cliffside Park), where he had bought a house. In high spirits, Marin turned his head to share a joke with O'Keeffe, who was sitting in the backseat. As he did so, he sideswiped a grocery wagon, then skidded out of control and smashed into a lamppost. Fortunately, he had not been driving quite as fast as usual. The car was rather badly damaged, but its occupants, though bruised and shaken, emerged without serious in-jury. "There were crowds, altercations, exchangings of license numbers," O'Keeffe later told an interviewer.[43] They walked the rest of the way, in the rain, to the hardware store whose owner was both the mayor of Cliffside and the justice of the peace. Having obtained their license, they would have to return three days later for the civil ceremony.

On the afternoon of Thursday, the eleventh, accompanied by Marin and George Engelhard, their witnesses, they were married without further in-cident — though the J.P.'s eyebrows were surely raised when O'Keeffe in-sisted that he omit from her vows the promise to honor and obey her husband. The couple did not exchange rings, and they didn't bother to cel-ebrate with a dinner or even a toast. No formal announcement was made; indeed, only a few close friends were told. In the future, whenever anyone asked whether he and Miss O'Keeffe were really married, Stieglitz would snap, "What do you think?"

Their marriage had no discernible effect on Kitty, who had regressed to the mentality of a young child and was subject to occasional fits of self-destructive rage. She would remain institutionalized for the rest of her life, eventually being transferred from Craig House to the almost equally luxu-rious Westchester Division of New York Hospital, in White Plains, where she died in 1971. Alfred sent occasional gifts of fruit or candy but was never allowed to see her, and he could hardly bear to mention her. On the other hand, until her death in 1953 Emmy visited Kitty nearly every week. Mil-ton Stearns would raise their son, Milton, Jr., sending him to Exeter and Harvard. Alfred had little contact with his son-in-law and grandson be-yond brief meetings whenever they visited New York.

PART VII

THE INTIMATE GALLERY

CHAPTER SIXTY·ONE

STIEGLITZ HAD WRITTEN to Arthur Dove in the summer of 1924, "I don't feel that Marin, Georgia or I should show this year. Even if we should have 'extraordinarily' (!) good work ready."[1] He had a change of heart, however, when he realized that 1925 would be the twentieth anniversary of the opening of 291. The result was an exhibition with the Barnumesque title Alfred Stieglitz Presents Seven Americans: 159 Paintings, Photographs & Things, Recent & Never Before Publicly Shown, by Arthur G. Dove, Marsden Hartley, John Marin, Charles Demuth, Paul Strand, Georgia O'Keeffe, Alfred Stieglitz. The show occupied the top floor of the Anderson Galleries for about three weeks during March 1925.

In the catalog, which ended with an account of the rôle that 291 had played in introducing modern art to America, Sherwood Anderson proclaimed, "Here are seven artists bringing to you city dwellers their moments of life . . . when life, pumped through their bodies, crept down into their fingers. When they were alive and conscious of all — everything." On the evening of Monday, March 9, as Henry McBride reported, "the seven live ones . . . and their half alive friends assembled in the Anderson Galleries and something as near to a French vernissage as we can manage took place. There was an immense buzz of talk of people who were as much interested in each other as in the new pictures, for the Stieglitz premieres do bring out all the chic types in town."[2]

Among the strays who turned up during the course of the show to greet a pleased and conciliatory Stieglitz were Waldo Frank and Max Weber. Stieglitz wrote that he was "certainly delighted" to see Weber, who would, during the next several years, drop by exhibitions to chat and would even, on at least one occasion, accept an invitation to dinner. "As I had been fascinated by him twenty years ago I again was fascinated," wrote Stieglitz.[3] In 1930, however, the renewed friendship would be permanently ended when Stieglitz felt that he and 291 had been completely misrepresented in the monograph by Holger Cahill that accompanied Weber's Museum of Modern Art retrospective.

At the entrance to the Seven Americans exhibition were several symbolic "poster portraits" of 291ers by Charles Demuth, executed in a signboard-like style with poster paints on panels. The one representing O'Keeffe consists of a potted sansevieria plant (popularly known as a snake plant), beside which the letters of her surname are arranged in the form of a Christian cross; scattered around the base of the pot are three gourds and an apple. It is puzzling that no writer, then or since, seems to have understood the work's fairly obvious meaning. Even more explicitly than Stieglitz's photograph of O'Keeffe resisting the evil apples, Demuth's poster portrait declares her the new Eve, as Christ was the new Adam. In the Demuth, rays emanating from O'Keeffe's name have scorched the tip of one of the snake plant's leaves; the translation is that the artist's holy radiance has killed the tempting serpent and forced it to drop the offending apple, which lies next to a particularly phallic gourd. O'Keeffe, in Demuth's eyes, had done nothing less than to free women from the guilt of original sin.

As one would infer from this poster portrait, Demuth and O'Keeffe had become very close friends. Although she had greater admiration for Dove's work than for Demuth's, she would recall shortly before her death, "Demuth was a better friend with me than any of the other artists."[4] She liked his wit and charm and his not taking himself too seriously. At one point they even talked about collaborating on a canvas full of flowers. "I was going to do the tall things up high," she said, "and he was going to do the little things below."[5] In his will Demuth would leave O'Keeffe all of his unsold oil paintings.

He had begun working with oils in 1921, responding to continued accusations that his work was insufficiently American in character. In his crisp new style (known as Precisionism), simplified representation of subjects limited mostly to Lancaster's commercial and industrial buildings was combined with Cubist-derived linear faceting — which the artist often wittily forced to do double duty as crisscrossing electric power lines. Stieglitz favored Demuth's oils, since they could not possibly be mistaken for the work of O'Keeffe or Marin, and farmed out to other galleries his concurrently painted watercolor flower studies and still lifes of fruits and vegetables, in many of which the juxtapositions are slyly genital.

While in Paris in 1921, Demuth became very ill and was diagnosed with diabetes, a usually fatal illness in those days before insulin. In November of that year he returned to Lancaster and soon went on a drastic diet that reduced him to emaciation. William Carlos Williams later wrote that in his entire medical career he had never seen a thinner person who was still able to walk. The regimen kept Demuth alive until the advent of insulin, which he began taking in March 1923. Shortly thereafter, when he received the portraits that Stieglitz had made of him when he was at his thinnest, Demuth wrote the photographer, "You have me in a fix: shall I remain ill, retaining that look, die, considering 'that moment' the climax of my 'looks,' or, live and change[?] I think the head is one of the most beautiful things that I have ever known in the world of art."[6]

In *The New Republic*, Edmund Wilson trumpeted that O'Keeffe, showing "enormous yellow lilies and wide-open purple petunias, ... outblaze[d] the other painters in the [Seven Americans] exhibition." He went on to gush sexistly, "In Miss Georgia O'Keeffe America seems definitely to have produced a woman painter comparable to her best woman poets and novelists." He felt that during the past year she had made a great leap forward and that her new paintings were "astonishing even to those who were astonished by her first exhibition two years ago." Since her last show she had allowed her art to expand in "decorative gorgeousness" but had "lost nothing in intensity." Her recent work, he believed, showed a new "insistence on dissonance . . . bringing together things which cannot possibly live in the same picture — not only vagueness and sharpness, but mutually repellent colors."[7] He would have been even more astonished had Stieglitz allowed O'Keeffe to hang her recently completed first painting of New York buildings.

Henry McBride opined,

It is Mr. Dove and Miss O'Keeffe and Mr. Stieglitz who emerge in this exhibition above the heads of the other members of the group. . . . Mr. Dove, due to his years of seclusion, becomes the chief curiosity of the show and rewards it well. It is too much to pretend that his canvases are profound, but they are undoubtedly charming.

They are also genuine. . . . Mr. Dove's color is tender, imaginative and lyrical.[8]

Dove had been unusually prolific during 1924 and early 1925. Among the twenty-four works he showed were not only some very fine semi-abstract landscapes but also a number of whimsical assemblages, including a symbolic portrait of Stieglitz composed of a mirror, a lens, a clock spring, and some steel wool. After the exhibition, when Dove said he would go crazy unless he could take a year off from illustrating to paint full-time, Stieglitz gave him the necessary $500.[9]

Disastrously, McBride — or perhaps an editor cutting his review — confused Stieglitz and Strand, whose eighteen photographs included close-ups of machine parts, studies of leaves, and views of New York. Instead of discussing Stieglitz's twenty-eight *Equivalents* (as the photographer would call his images of clouds from then on), McBride wrote, "Mr. Stieglitz concentrates all of his soul upon some amazing photographs of machines. . . . What used to be expended upon madonnas is here lavished upon pistons and revolving steel wheels."[10] It's no wonder that Stieglitz accused McBride of becoming senile.

That summer Stieglitz would complain in a letter to Dove, "Hartley wants admiration — & Cash!"[11] He had been tempted not to include Hartley in the exhibition, both because the artist never seemed adequately grateful when the coveted cash was forthcoming and because his recent work left much to be desired. Having exhausted the proceeds of his auction, Hartley had spent much of 1924 in America, negotiating with four businessmen, including William Bullitt, who was married to John Reed's widow, Louise Bryant. The consortium agreed to pay the artist $3,000 a year for four years, in return for which he would remit ten paintings per year. As soon as the deal was settled, Hartley left for another extended period abroad. Respecting him as a genuine artist and as an individual, Stieglitz included twenty-five of his recent European landscapes and still lifes in the Seven Americans show. McBride yawned that the paintings were "old world, old souled, and awfully fatigued."[12]

There was certainly no consensus among the critics. Each of the seven artists received a share both of high praise and of sneering dismissal. Even Marin's watercolors of Maine and New York were berated by a couple of reviewers. Stieglitz blamed himself, for he believed that if he had not been kept in bed by kidney stones so many days during the show, he could have favorably influenced more of the reviewers. "Still," he assured Dove, "I feel the Show was by no means a failure."[13]

*   *   *

Stieglitz had been looking forward to the summer to recover from "a tough Winter & Spring."[14] But as soon as he and O'Keeffe arrived at Lake George on June 4, 1925, he took to his bed with "kidney colic." After finally passing a kidney stone, Alfred would go so far as to claim in July, "I believe I'm much better — that is not so totally lacking in all energy as I seemed to be for so long."[15]

O'Keeffe also took to her bed. She had been vaccinated for smallpox a few days before they left New York and developed such a severe reaction in the glands around her hip that it would be the end of July before she was able to walk without pain. Depressed and lethargic as well as immobilized, she couldn't tend the garden or do the cooking. A comedy of errors ensued. The first woman they hired to cook for them soon sprained her ankle. Then Paul Rosenfeld, who arrived in June to spend most of the summer, tried his hand at cooking until he also sprained his ankle. "So Stieglitz had to stew the peaches and bake the potatoes for a day or two," reported O'Keeffe with amusement. The woman they hired next "put onions in the salad and no Stieglitz could risk that."[16] At last they found a cook who satisfied them — and then kept her busy with family and guests for the rest of the summer.

Because Donald and Elizabeth Davidson were renovating a farmhouse in Rockland County, New York, they sent their two daughters to Lake George late in June with their grandparents Lee and Lizzie to stay in their newly completed bungalow, nicknamed Red Top. Peggy and Sue Davidson (the latter not quite three) had been instructed by their grandmother to call O'Keeffe "Aunt Georgia." For her obedience, Sue was rewarded with a swift slap on the face and Georgia's barked order never, ever to call her an aunt.

Since Red Top had no kitchen or dining room, they all ate lunch and dinner at the farmhouse. "We had two yowling brats here for six weeks who carefully kept anyone from tasting their food or having anything resembling peace or conversation at table," O'Keeffe griped. "Except for breakfast — Stieglitz, Rosenfeld and I ate that alone with great pleasure and appreciation."[17] One can only wonder just how much pleasure and appreciation Alfred could have derived from his Spartan fare of "Zwieback & Hot Water called Tea by me."[18]

Upon his arrival, Lee had bound O'Keeffe's legs and ordered her to remain in bed. The treatment helped; by July 7 Alfred, who had been very worried, was delighted that she was "finally rounding to be herself again," though she would not be fully back on her feet until the end of the month.[19] Soon, the very practical O'Keeffe was able to oversee the dozens of chores and repairs that had to be done around the house: cleaning the closets, the attic, and the wood room; installing a new hot-water heater; seeing that the part-time hired man kept the icebox filled with heavy blocks of ice; putting up a "much needed shelf" in the back bathroom; painting all the benches. By early August she was even strong enough to withstand the noisy battles that broke out around the dinner table with Selma's arrival. She found that Selma's histrionics actually bothered her less than did Lizzie's mousy, self-effacing deference to Lee, Alfred, and every other man around. Nevertheless, O'Keeffe thanked her lucky stars that Selma ate breakfast in bed. She was also pleased that the Strands would not be visiting that summer and that Alfred's flirtation with Beck was finally over.

At first, Paul Rosenfeld's presence did little to cheer Alfred up, for the visitor was spending eight or ten hours a day writing. In the evenings they were joined by Alfred Kreymborg and his wife, who stayed at the Pines until mid-July, when they moved into the farmhouse. Kreymborg was "a wreck — at the end of his tether" because of the indifference that had greeted his autobiographical book *Troubador*, published by Horace Liveright in the spring. For that reason there wasn't "much theorizing going on — not even much talking."[20] Neither Rosenfeld nor Kreymborg was in the mood for their usual imitation of the vaudevillians Weber and Fields.

Rosenfeld would perhaps have been even glummer if he had been aware that Stieglitz was deliberately thwarting any possible renewal of his romance with Ida O'Keeffe, who had come to regret her hastiness in rejecting his proposal of marriage. Alfred had decided that Paul needed "to get clarity about himself — & he can get that only in working & keeping away from petticoats & all they signify." Therefore, when Ida inquired where Paul was spending the summer, Alfred refused to tell her, forbade Georgia to tell her either, vetoed inviting Ida to the lake, didn't let Paul read her letters, and wouldn't even tell him that she was asking about him.[21] By September, when Alfred admitted what he had done, Paul's and Ida's feelings had cooled beyond revival.

During the months they spent in New York each year, Alfred and Georgia looked forward to Rosenfeld's weekly soirees, which brought together poets, novelists, composers, painters, and a variety of cultural commentators. In November 1924, for instance, Hart Crane related that besides Stieglitz and O'Keeffe the guests one evening included Aaron Copland, Jean Toomer, Paul and Beck Strand, Alfred Kreymborg, Marianne Moore, Van Wyck Brooks, Edmund Wilson, Lewis Mumford, Herbert Seligmann, and a French visitor, Jean Vatel. After Copland played some of his compositions, there were readings by Moore, Crane, and Kreymborg of their own work and by Vatel of a long poem of Paul Valéry's, in the original French.

Among those present that evening, one who became a close friend of Stieglitz's was twenty-nine-year-old Mumford, author of *The Story of Utopias* (1922) and of the more recently published *Sticks and Stones: A Study of American Architecture and Civilization*. As the cofounder of the Regional Planning Association of America, he was already helping to design the enlightened housing development of Sunnyside Gardens in Queens. Mumford would go on to write more than thirty books, as well as hundreds of art reviews and articles about architecture, urban planning, philosophy, and the history of science and technology for such magazines as *The New Yorker* and *The New Republic*.

As the summer of 1925 wore on, Kreymborg, Rosenfeld, and Stieglitz began having nightly sessions about the state of American literature and art. Rosenfeld, as Kreymborg later recalled, "was dismal concerning the absence of a purely esthetic magazine," while Stieglitz lamented "the strewn hopes of American art as a whole" and demanded at each nightly session "that something drastic be undertaken against conditions hounding all dreamers alike."[22]

Kreymborg suggested that he and Rosenfeld start a literary yearbook. It happened that Samuel Ornitz — whose Lower East Side saga *Haunch, Paunch and Jowl* had also been published by Liveright, who encouraged friendships among his authors — was at Lake George that summer to be near his new friend Kreymborg. Ornitz liked the idea of a yearbook and proposed that the Macaulay Company, of which he was the literary editor, publish it, though the firm was known for its "devotion to pot-boiling novels, lurid biographies, and mystery thrillers."[23] Rosenfeld and Kreymborg then invited Van Wyck Brooks and Lewis Mumford to join them as editors of the yearbook, which they called *The American Caravan*. The first volume, dedicated to Stieglitz, would appear in 1927, meeting with both critical acclaim and, as a selection of the Literary Guild, financial success. Four more volumes would be published at lengthening intervals until 1936.

Stieglitz's eyes had been "acutely bothering" him again for months. "But I can stand a lot of pain," he boasted, "[and had] hoped they'd gradually let up."[24] Since he was "looking rotten & feeling worse" at the beginning of August, Lee insisted that he go into New York to see an ophthalmologist and have his lungs X-rayed.[25] For two weeks after his return from the city,

Alfred's eyes were worse than ever. He was in such "agony day & night" that he couldn't read, make prints, or even write letters.[26]

By the end of August, his eyes were at last no longer torturing him, and he told Dove he was "working at a great intensity — am enjoying it."[27] From then on, both he and O'Keeffe gained momentum, though neither would have as much to show for the summer as in previous years. In October they thoroughly enjoyed a visit by Jean Toomer and a return visit by Rosenfeld. Toomer, then writing an autobiographical narrative, was spending more and more of his time working for Gurdjieff and at Christmastime would go to Taos to visit Mabel Dodge Luhan, who fell madly in love with him and urged him to set up a Gurdjieffian institute there.

In November, Alfred wrote to Dove, "We are working our heads off not wasting a moment. I've been going great guns & finally feel fit to enjoy activity — lots of it. — And so I'm putting in 18 hours daily — destroying hundreds of prints after making them — keeping few. Eastman is a fiend — & I'm not always Master."[28] About that same time he wrote to Elizabeth Davidson, bragging of his sexual as well as photographic prowess, "Both G. and I are going at a great pace. . . . It's really great to be able to put in 18 hours a day and feel the energy still left of 17 stallions."[29]

Because O'Keeffe had felt burdened with too much housekeeping in their apartment on East Fifty-eighth Street, and because it seemed silly to pay a full year's rent for a place they occupied fewer than seven months annually, she and Alfred resolved that when they returned to the city in mid-November 1925 they would move into the Shelton Hotel, at Lexington Avenue and Forty-ninth Street. The thirty-four-story Shelton, with twelve hundred rooms, was the tallest hotel in the world. From its hybrid Romanesque and Venetian-Gothic two-story entrance loggia, the brick building — one of the first skyscrapers to make aesthetic use of the setbacks required by the 1916 zoning laws — soared far above its neighbors "in three great leaps of rhythmic height."[30] One contemporary writer hailed it as being like "some titanic result of the force of nature rather than a building by the hand of man" and proclaimed that "the mass seen at dusk is as impressive as Gibraltar."[31] Others called it a wonder of the world and compared it to the Pharos of Alexandria.

The Shelton had opened in 1924 as a residential club-hotel, providing an alternative to boardinghouses for bachelor office workers. As the YMCA would soon begin to do, the Shelton offered such facilities as a gymnasium, a swimming pool, bowling alleys, and squash courts, as well as lounges, reading rooms, and spectacular covered terraces adjoining the restaurants and cafeteria on the sixteenth floor. In the fall of 1925, a huge number of vacancies would force the hotel to accept mixed-occupancy transients, "semi-transients," and residents.

Right up to the last minute, it was uncertain whether women were really going to be admitted. Finally, the management came through and offered Stieglitz and O'Keeffe the two-room Suite 3003, on the twenty-eighth floor. They took it, even though they couldn't really afford it. In December, Alfred would write to Sherwood Anderson that they were staying in the Shelton "for a while — may be all winter."[32] As it turned out, they would live there during their New York seasons for the next ten years.

Their sunny bedroom, with twin beds, was tiny. About the somewhat more spacious living room, which doubled as O'Keeffe's studio, a visitor wrote in 1928:

> The door opened and I entered a room as bleak as the North Pole. It might have been a cloister or the reception room of an orphanage, so austere was it, with its cold gray walls, and its white covers over dull upholstery. There was no frivolous pillow, no "hangings." The only spot of color was a red flower on an easel. There was not an inch of cretonne or a dab of chintz anywhere. It seemed all windows — windows overlooking housetops, steel framework, chimneys; windows to the east through which the panorama of the river and the bridge came flooding. . . . There are no distractions in the room, it is colorless. All the charm of life is out there beyond the windows.[33]

To Stieglitz it seemed as though they were living on an ocean liner sailing far above the madness of New York. There was no noise except the howling of the wind and the groans of "the trembling shaking hulk of steel."[34] He certainly agreed with Claude Bragdon, an architect and Gurdjieff disciple who lived in the Shelton and who often breakfasted with Stieglitz and O'Keeffe in the cafeteria, that the upper floors of the hotel provided "the most successful escape from the dirt, ugliness, noise, promiscuity of the city."[35] "It's a wonderful place," crowed Alfred.[36]

During the months before the Seven Americans show, Mitchell Kennerley had let Stieglitz use Room 303 at the Anderson Galleries to store works included in the exhibition and to give private showings of them.[37] Afterward, Kennerley told him that for $1,800 a year he could rent the room to use as a gallery. Stieglitz had good reasons to accept: he had loved being "on deck" during exhibitions the past several years, and he wanted to show Montross, Daniel, and all the other dealers what he could do. Too, he commented, he felt obliged to provide an alternative to "the humbug going on at the Art Center," a noncommercial gallery on East Fifty-sixth Street that exhibited much second-rate work and played host to the annual exhibitions of the Pictorial Photographers of America.[38] In July, regretting "more than ever" that there wasn't "another little place like '291,'" Alfred wrote resignedly to Dove, "Room 303 has absolutely nothing to do with any of us. — It isn't even a good storage room. — But I see no way out. — Will have to make it a go."[39] He found it auspicious, at least, that the numbers 3003 and 303 echoed each other, suggesting that, despite his misgivings about both the gallery and the apartment, they were decreed by destiny.

One possibility nearly postponed the opening of the new gallery. John Quinn died at the end of July 1925, leaving a collection of about 2,500 works of modern art (approximately 600 paintings, over 1,700 drawings and prints, and more than 150 sculptures) as well as hundreds of African, Asian, and Polynesian works. His holdings of Matisse, Picasso, Rousseau, Redon, Seurat, and Brancusi were probably the finest in private hands anywhere. Kennerley, who had sold Quinn's equally important and even larger collection of books and manuscripts (12,108 lots) in a series of five auctions at the Anderson Galleries in 1923 and 1924, proposed to the executors of the estate that he sell the artworks in a single auction of several sessions. The five-volume catalog Kennerley had commissioned for the literary sales not only provided meticulous bibliographic information but also contained sensitively written commentaries about the significance of many items. Kennerley argued that a similar illustrated catalog of the visual works would, after the auction, constitute an invaluable record of what had been the world's foremost collection of modern art. Moreover, Kennerley promised that he would mount a monthlong exhibition of the collection — most of which had never been seen, even by visitors to Quinn's apartment, where the collector had kept many of the paintings stacked face to the wall.

Stieglitz offered to devote himself entirely to helping Kennerley until the sale was over.[40] But Quinn's executors felt there was so little demand for modern art that such an auction would be a disaster. Even Kennerley was less than sanguine about the prospects; he guaranteed only $250,000 for the sale, an average of $100 per work.

Responsibility for selling the collection piecemeal in New York and Paris was given to the dealer Joseph Brummer, who organized an exhibition of eighty-four paintings and drawings and eight sculptures at the Art Center during January 1926. The dregs of the collection would be auctioned off, early in February 1927, at the American Art Association, Kennerley's principal rival. Estimates of the total revenues from private sales and the auction range from $400,000 to $750,000, not much more or less than the $500,000 Quinn had spent.

The collector had hoped that his friend Arthur Davies might be able to raise $250,000 to buy, as the nucleus of a museum of modern art, all of his best holdings. Frederick James Gregg and Henry McBride, both of whom wrote for the *Sun*, beat the drum to no avail. Alas, the idea was sprung too suddenly on an unprepared New York. No individual could be found to secure the collection, and there was no organization in existence to coordinate the project. Although the Société Anonyme had, in 1920, subtitled itself Museum of Modern Art, by 1925 it had hardly any active members and was subsidized solely by Katherine Dreier, who managed to buy only a few works from Quinn's estate.

Ultimately, the dispersal of Quinn's great collection had a positive effect. Alarmed by their loss of a golden opportunity and eager to provide a memorial for Davies, who died in 1928, Abby Aldrich Rockefeller, Lillie Bliss, and a few of their friends soon mobilized themselves to found the Museum of Modern Art, into whose collections many of Quinn's treasures would eventually find their way.

Room 303, measuring about twenty feet by twenty-six, was located on the northwest corner of the third floor of the Anderson building, where there were several little shops selling antiques, silver, and jewelry. The room had a very high ceiling, and its huge, arched windows opened onto small balconies that looked out over Park Avenue and Fifty-ninth Street. When Stieglitz began to set up his gallery, in mid-November 1925, the walls, from the dark oak chair rail to the picture molding, were covered with stamped black velour. O'Keeffe proceeded to cover them with unbleached white cheesecloth, thereby making the room seem not only lighter but also much larger.[41] Hating smudges on catalogs or walls almost as much as he hated any speck that spoiled the perfection of one of his prints, Stieglitz would routinely roll a carpet sweeper over the room's black rug until it was perfectly clean.[42]

Since so much of the gallery's wall space was taken up by the windows and the door, only the finest paintings in each show would be hung, the rest placed on the floor and leaned against the baseboard or set on top of bookcases, cabinets, and chairs. Also scattered around were such objects as African masks, Stieglitz's bronze Brancusi head, and a crystal ball, which was usually "rolled into a corner . . . out of sight save for prying eyes or chance discovery."[43] As at 291, Stieglitz refused to lock the door when he left.

He called Room 303 the Intimate Gallery and announced that it was not a business but "a Direct Point of Contact between Public and Artist. It is the Artists' Room. . . . Alfred Stieglitz has volunteered his services and is its directing Spirit." The gallery would be open from ten to six Monday through Saturday and from two to five on Sunday. Its purpose, a broadside asserted, was "the intimate study of Seven Americans: John Marin, Georgia O'Keeffe, Arthur G. Dove, Marsden Hartley, Paul Strand, Alfred Stieglitz, and Number Seven (six + X)." O'Keeffe would probably have liked Demuth to occupy the seventh slot permanently, but Alfred, who would give him one-man shows during the first and last of the gallery's four seasons, wanted some flexibility. In any case, Edmund Wilson recalled that when Stieglitz accompanied him through the Seven Americans show, the photographer had "played Demuth down."[44]

Although he declared that "all but Time-killers" would be welcome, Stieglitz wanted his gallery to be rather exclusive. In July he had written to Dove, "I, for one, know that my own work is for very few who 'know' anything about Art. — And that I really don't care to have it seen by more than a few — if by those. — And I can imagine Georgia beginning to feel that way about her work. And Marin has always felt more or less that way. — And I know your feelings."[45] Stieglitz did not ever exhibit his own work at the Intimate Gallery.

It opened on December 7 with a show of Marin's recent work. Stieglitz told Anderson that Room 303 was "very real and has a sense of space — a reserve power, still all the aliveness and movingness of the streets." In a crescendo he continued, "The Marins are marvellous. The room gives them a chance to be. There is no artiness — just a throbbing pulsating being — Marin is a great person — greater than even I had realized."[46]

CHAPTER SIXTY·TWO

AN EXHIBITION OF recent paintings and assemblages by Arthur Dove — the artist's first one-man show anywhere since 1912 — opened at the Intimate Gallery on January 11, 1926. Henry McBride's three-minute-long visit bore out the accusation explicit in Dove's 1925 collage of a top-hatted and monocled critic whizzing through the galleries on roller skates, pushing a vacuum cleaner.[1] Longer and more important was the visit of Duncan Phillips, who would become the painter's chief patron and who would, between 1926 and 1947, acquire more than sixty of his works. In March 1926 Phillips wrote Dove to express his hope that he would "paint many more cosmic things" like the first two paintings he had recently bought, in which he sensed the artist's "consciousness of the rhythm of the universe."[2]

Tall, thin, and rather pompous, the patrician forty-year-old Phillips, who lived in Washington, was very well meaning and eager to learn. A grandson of one of the founders of Pittsburgh's Jones and Laughlin Steel Company, he graduated from Yale in 1908 and then traveled extensively abroad. In 1912, by which time he was active in the American Federation of Arts, he began writing articles on subjects ranging from Giorgione to Impressionism for various magazines. The following year he attacked the Armory Show as "quite stupefying in its vulgarity" and denounced Cézanne and van Gogh as "unbalanced fanatics."[3]

After the deaths of his father in 1917 and his brother in the influenza epidemic of 1918, Phillips decided to transform several rooms of his mother's large brick mansion in Washington into the Phillips Memorial Gallery. It opened in 1921 with a collection of about 240 paintings, including works by Daumier (who was then Phillips's favorite artist), Monet, Puvis de Chavannes, Henri Fantin-Latour, Whistler, Ryder, Homer, and five members of the Eight. That same year Phillips married a painter named Marjorie Acker. Although her work was a blandly pretty derivative of Impressionism, she succeeded in getting her husband to revise his feelings about modernism.

Stieglitz was cultivating Phillips not only as a collector but also as a patron who might contribute to the fund he maintained both to help Marin, Dove, and Hartley through difficult times and to aid worthy artists whose work he did not show, as well as "literary people, a dancer [probably Angna Enters, who married art critic Louis Kalonyme], and other workers in the arts."[4] In 1928 Stieglitz wrote,

> One very brilliant man received quite a sum of money to be able to spend time in a European sanatorium to see whether his eyes could be saved. This is not charity. The man has done much for artists although he has no money himself. I look upon him as a co-worker, as a force needed in America. Another white soul, tubercular, penniless, proud, needed a year in Europe — six hundred dollars. A writer and painter. I knew of it — the man was given the opportunity.[5]

The tubercular artist-author was Jennings Tofel, who had been born Yehudah Toflevicz in Poland in 1891 and had immigrated to America in 1905. The hunchbacked Tofel had a show of his paintings at the Bourgeois Gallery in 1919, participated in the Société Anonyme, wrote poems and essays for various Yiddish publications, and was one of the founders of the Jewish Art Center, in Greenwich Village. Stieglitz never exhibited Tofel's work but managed to sell a few paintings the artist gave him on consignment. In 1927 he raised the money Tofel needed to go to Europe, where he settled in Paris for a year and a half after marrying a woman from his native village. He returned to New York in 1929, but Stieglitz quickly raised enough money to make possible another year in Paris.

Among the regular contributors to Stieglitz's fund, which also paid the Intimate Gallery's rent and covered the costs of printing catalogs, were Paul Rosenfeld, Paul and Beck Strand, Maurice and Alma Wertheim, Aline Meyer Liebman, her sister Florence Meyer Blumenthal, and Lee Stieglitz,

who not only gave generously but also encouraged those of his wealthy patients with whom he was on friendly terms to do so. All of these donors
were given Stieglitz photographs or other works of art by way of thanks.
Indeed, some of these transactions were difficult to distinguish from sales,
from which Alfred habitually deducted 20 percent for his fund, unless the
artist was in desperate need of money.

Stieglitz resented the fact that Agnes Ernst Meyer and Henry Gaisman,
both of whom stopped by the Intimate Gallery occasionally, did not contribute. Although Meyer had bought a total of seventeen Marins over the
years, Stieglitz fumed that, like most art patrons, she would never consider
making a grand gesture that would guarantee a great artist the freedom to
work without having to exhibit or worry about money, even if only for a
year or two.[6] Indeed, Stieglitz couldn't understand why one of the rich
people who admired the work he showed didn't just hand him enough
money to pay the gallery's rent for several years.[7]

The Dove exhibition, which had netted the artist more than $1,700, was
taken down promptly at 6:00 P.M. on February 6. Then Stieglitz, O'Keeffe,
the Strands, Emil Zoler, and Herbert Seligmann worked until after midnight hanging O'Keeffe's show, which the critics would view before it
opened to the public on the eleventh. The fifty recent paintings, dominated by several large canvases of dark purple-black petunias with blue and
rose highlights, also included images of other flowers, of leaves, and of
trees, as well as abstractions and — to everyone's surprise — O'Keeffe's
first two New York scenes, one of which was bought on opening day.

The show drew large crowds and garnered glowing reviews. In *The New
Yorker* Murdock Pemberton praised O'Keeffe as a "raging, blazing soul
mounting to the skies" and wrote that if one of her paintings were to be
hung in Grand Central Station, it "would even halt the home-going com-
muters."[8] Chicago critic Blanche Matthias proclaimed, "This woman who
lives fearlessly, reasons logically, who is modest, unassertive and spiritually
beautiful and who, because she dares to paint as she feels, has become not
only one of the most magical artists of our time, but one of the most stim-
ulatingly powerful!"[9] To counter such hyperbole Henry McBride understated, in the most anti-Rosenfeldian terms possible, "I like [O'Keeffe's]
stuff quite well. Very well. I like her colour, her imagination, her decorative
sense. Her things wear well with me . . . but I do not feel the occult element in them that all the ladies insist is there."[10] The show, originally
scheduled to close on March 11, was extended nearly three weeks, both because of its popularity and because Hartley, who was living in the southern

French town of Vence, did not have enough paintings ready for his show, slated to open after O'Keeffe's.

Late in February O'Keeffe spent several days in Washington, where she visited the Phillips Memorial Gallery and saw her two recently purchased oils in a small Exhibition of Paintings by Eleven Americans and an Important Work by Odilon Redon. She had gone to the capital to speak at a large banquet during the convention of the National Woman's party, to which she had belonged since 1913 and of which Anita Pollitzer was the executive secretary. Stieglitz had seen her off at Pennsylvania Station and then, as he had not done in years, walked alone through the streets. The next day he said that her departure had made him intensely aware that "no one could ever be for him the white thing O'Keeffe was," in comparison with which he felt gray. As he walked, he was so overwhelmed by his love that the city seemed to disappear.[11]

Pollitzer told Stieglitz that in her speech O'Keeffe "had created an equivalent of her painting" and that "what she said had been clear above all the other speeches."[12] We can infer the content from an article published the following year in *The Nation*, which asserted that if O'Keeffe had "any passion other than her work it is her interest and faith in her own sex. . . . She believes ardently in woman as an individual — an individual not merely with the rights and privileges of man but, what is to her more important, with the same responsibilities. And chief among these is the responsibility of self-realization. O'Keeffe is the epitomization of this faith."[13]

In a marriage between two artists, perhaps more overtly than in any other, the key issue is how to maintain a balance between creative independence and loving involvement. "Any true relationship is tragic," Stieglitz told Seligmann in the fall of 1926. "Marriage, if it is real, must be based on a wish that each person attain his potentiality, be the thing he might be, as a tree bears its fruit — at the same time realizing responsibility to the other party."[14] That was all very well, but he had an exceptionally strong need to dominate and to control everyone around him, especially women. Earlier that year he had spoken to Seligmann of an unidentified "woman, like many others, who had utter faith in him." Stieglitz continued, "Such innocence is ghastly. She is like a somnambulist. Anything I tell her she would do. But a fine relationship is dependent upon such utter confidence. She feels I would not ask her to do anything unless it was the thing to do."[15]

His Pygmalion complex was so powerful an element of his psychological makeup that it extended to men as well as to women. It is with a degree of incredulity and revulsion that one reads Seligmann's summary of remarks the photographer made in the spring of 1927: "Neither Marin's nor O'Keeffe's work would have existed without Stieglitz. Marin would have been making pleasant etchings, nice little water colors. O'Keeffe's work would not have existed at all. So the question was, was not their work also an expression of Stieglitz?"[16] Such appalling egotism could only lead to trouble with O'Keeffe.

A week after he and Georgia went to Lake George, about June 1, 1926, Alfred was doubled over with the pain of a bout of kidney stones so serious that he was forced to return to New York. He was admitted to Mount Sinai Hospital and remained a patient there for two weeks, until he was finally able to pass the stones. "I have had a tough deal," he wrote to Dove late in June. "16 awful days. But I'm up. And we expect to leave for Lake George today midnight. I need much quiet — much peace."[17]

During Alfred's convalescence, Ida O'Keeffe stayed at the farmhouse to help care for him, but there were no other guests. Paul Rosenfeld, who could not have been eager to spend another summer with Stieglitz after the Ida episode in 1925, was in the Southwest, as were the Strands. There was, however, one unfamiliar face on the Hill, that of a young woman from Texas whom O'Keeffe had agreed to take on as a student and who boarded at the Pines for a few weeks. In a 1928 interview O'Keeffe would say of her earlier career, "I liked teaching. I have missed it terribly. I liked the contact with those students who earned the money they spent."[18] But that did not mean she was enthusiastic about Alfred's proposal to make the Hill self-sustaining by turning it into an informal summer school of the arts at which he would teach photography, she painting, and Rosenfeld writing.

Stieglitz would refer to the summer of 1926 as "five rotten months of illness & suffering."[19] Despite the presence of Ida and of the cook whom Lee and Lizzie had considerately sent to the Hill while they were in Europe, O'Keeffe bore the burden of taking care of Alfred, an extremely demanding patient. She was getting plenty of exercise, but she became "terribly nervous" and "run down," began sleeping badly, and lost fifteen pounds.[20] The problem was not only Alfred's condition but also the prospect of his siblings' arrival. Throughout the summer, Selma — who claimed that she had at last suffered a complete nervous breakdown — kept threatening to turn up. And Lee and Lizzie were due late in August, after their return from abroad.

In February, Herbert Seligmann had recorded Stieglitz's comment that

O'Keeffe "wanted to build a house to suit herself, a house in which there would be no wood, and the only furniture she could endure — kitchen furniture."[21] Anita Pollitzer stated that in 1928 O'Keeffe thought about constructing a simple cottage for herself on the Hill, a retreat where she could have a few possessions arranged as she wanted them.[22] And Juan Hamilton, O'Keeffe's companion in her old age, recalls that she told him that in the years before she began going to New Mexico, she considered building a house in Virginia or North Carolina, where she and Stieglitz could have some time to themselves. She went so far as to have blueprints drawn up.[23] But Stieglitz consistently vetoed any such proposal.

As soon as Lee and Lizzie arrived, about August 20, with the two little Davidson girls, O'Keeffe left for York Beach. Lee would see that Alfred was well taken care of, and the children were more than she could bear in her weakened condition. Distraught about O'Keeffe's absence and feeling miserable with fear that her trip might be the prelude to her leaving him for good, Stieglitz took the train to York Beach about September 1. "I *had* to see Georgia for her own and my own sake," he wrote to Seligmann. She reassured him that she simply needed some time away from him and his family, a change of scenery, and a chance to paint without so many distractions. He returned alone to Lake George, where he promptly took to his bed with a "miserable cold." Even so, he told Seligmann, he felt much better than he had before going, for O'Keeffe had once again shown him what an "extraordinary woman" she was.[24]

Although she was scheduled to come home on September 15, she decided to stay in Maine for another two weeks. She had begun a series of six paintings of clamshells, which she would follow with seven canvases juxtaposing one of the shells and a piece of shingle. It is tempting to conclude that O'Keeffe turned to this subject matter to exorcise the pain caused by the thoughtful but lukewarm review of her recent show published in *The Art News*. The anonymous critic had complained that each of O'Keeffe's paintings "beckons the eye with promises, only to shut up like a clam when the gaze becomes too inquisitive."[25]

When O'Keeffe finally returned, she was fully restored to physical and psychological health, strong enough even to deal with Selma, who was hysterical about a hideous boil on her nose. Once Alfred got back from escorting his sister to New York to have it treated, he and Georgia enjoyed a few weeks of peace together before heading to the city on November 1.

Despite "much time to do some very direct thinking," Stieglitz had little more than "a handful of small prints" — some of which he considered "a further development" — to show for the summer.[26] He had been able to work relatively few days and even then had lacked the strength to handle his 8 x 10 camera. O'Keeffe, however, had accomplished quite a lot. In addition to her clamshell paintings, she had completed canvases of the barn and of trees, some rather frilly flowers, and a series of dark irises culminating in the most overtly vulval of all her paintings.

One of the big events of New York's 1926–27 art season was the Société Anonyme's International Exhibition of Modern Art, which borrowed the Armory Show's official name and opened at the Brooklyn Museum on November 19. Katherine Dreier, assisted by Marcel Duchamp, had traveled in Europe for several months selecting the show's more than three hundred works, most of them executed since 1920. The emphasis was on constructivist abstraction, especially by artists associated with the Bauhaus.

Although Stieglitz constantly addressed visitors to his gallery, he hardly ever agreed to speak before a large audience. In the fall of 1926, however, he did so twice, first at the New School for Social Research (at that time located on West Twenty-third Street) and then, two weeks later, on December 4, at the Brooklyn Museum. Much of his talk on the latter occasion was a recitation of his more-than-twice-told tales of the history of 291. He ended by equating "experimental" modern art with pure scientific research and expressed his hope that the museum would dedicate even a small section of its galleries permanently to exhibitions of such work.[27]

Speaking from a platform in the main gallery of the Société Anonyme exhibition, Stieglitz had begun by saying that he considered it a privilege to sit beside Duchamp's *Bride Stripped Bare by Her Bachelors, Even*, generally known as *The Large Glass*, which he called "one of the grandest works in the art of all time." The artist had worked intermittently on this masterpiece, from 1915 to 1923, when he declared it "definitively incomplete"; it was now being exhibited for the first time. Sadly, the glass panels between which mechanical images made of foil and wire were sandwiched would be badly cracked during transport at the end of the show, though the damage wasn't discovered until the crate was opened several years later. In the best Dada spirit, Duchamp then announced that he welcomed the accident as the intervention of chance.

In mid-December Stieglitz would comment that "a motion picture made by Marcel Duchamp . . . was the first thing made by another person which he had ever wished he had done himself."[28] He must have been referring to the almost palindromically entitled *Anémic Cinéma*, which Duchamp had recently shown at the Fifth Avenue Theater. A seven-minute film, made in collaboration with Man Ray and Marc Allégret, it consisted entirely of footage of a sequence of ten rotating disks bearing complex linear spiral designs that seemed to pulsate or undulate, alternating with nine disks on which nonsensical French sentences full of puns were printed spirally. In 1931 Stieglitz would tell Charlie Chaplin that for twenty years he had been wanting to make "a movie of a woman's eyes, their changing expression, the hands, feet, lips, breasts, *mons veneris*, all parts of a woman's body, showing the development of a life, each episode alternated with motion pictures of cloud forms on the same theme."[29]

A Marin show, which Stieglitz trumpeted as the artist's "greatest achievement," opened at the Intimate Gallery in mid-November 1926.[30] Duncan Phillips — who in the spring of that year had bought three Marins from Stieglitz and one from Charles Daniel — went to Room 303 on the morning of December 3 to see the exhibition. He was especially interested in the watercolor entitled *Back of Bear Mountain*, which Henry McBride had singled out as the finest in the show. Phillips called the work "soul-stirring," and when he asked its price, Stieglitz informed him that "even if Marin had to starve" he would not let anyone have it for a penny less than $6,000, three times the usual price.[31] Stieglitz was annoyed that because Marin worked almost exclusively in watercolor, he was widely regarded as not quite of the first rank — and his income was unjustly limited, since it was generally taken for granted that even the finest watercolor was intrinsically worth much less than an oil by the same artist.

In 1930 Stieglitz would write to Demuth, "I seem always to be in the position of money-gouger — most amusing when in all the years of gouging I have yet to receive a penny from the gouging! And none of the artists I have gouged for have become rich like the French artists so lovingly supported by art loving America! Why aren't you & Marin & O'Keeffe & Dove Frenchmen? — & I at least a Man Ray in Paris?"[32] Stieglitz knew that Phillips had paid $150,000 for a Renoir in 1923 and that during 1926 he had acquired paintings by Bonnard and Constable, as well as two canvases by Courbet, all for substantial prices. Whenever Phillips appeared at the gallery, he would complain that he was broke because he had already spent so much on works by artists who were either French or dead, or both, and then he would expect Stieglitz to offer him bargains. The photographer was not willing to play that game.

He wrote that when he stated the price of $6,000, "Mr. Phillips actually gasped and said that of course he could not pay any such ridiculous figure." According to Stieglitz, Phillips returned the next morning with his wife, who told him that if he felt so strongly about the Marin, he should buy it.

But he "frankly confessed that his position with dealers and artists would become very difficult if they heard that he had paid $6,000 for a Marin watercolor." Stieglitz then assured him that he would tell no one except Marin and "a few insiders," whereupon Phillips agreed to pay the record price. "I congratulate you," Stieglitz burst out. "A miracle has happened. An American has become a sportsman before an American picture. For years I've waited for that miracle."[33]

Because Mrs. Phillips had urged her husband to spring for the Marin, Stieglitz offered her, as a gift, *Sunset, Rockland County*, which was priced at $1,800. When Phillips then inquired about *Hudson Opposite Bear Mountain*, valued at $2,000, Stieglitz said that in honor of the occasion, he could have it for half that amount.

Stieglitz told Marin, O'Keeffe, and several other people, one of whom leaked the news to the *New York Times*. Phillips then claimed that Stieglitz was misrepresenting the transaction, and they proceeded to exchange increasingly angry letters over the next several months. Early in April 1927 Phillips claimed, in print, that he had agreed to pay $6,000 for the Marin only because Stieglitz had already promised to give him two others as gifts. The collector had written privately to Forbes Watson in March: "Field Marshal Stieglitz maneuvered negotiations so that I paid his record price for the Marin I liked best, receiving as a compensation two others of the very finest of Marin's 1925 vintage as *gifts*. Thus I secured for $6000 three of the best Marins in existence at an average of $2000 each."[34]

Outraged by Phillips's "moral cowardice," Stieglitz then considered publishing their correspondence in order to set the record straight.[35] Instead, he privately printed a four-page account in which he meticulously, with a tone of pained exasperation, explained "how $6,000 happened to be given" for one of Marin's watercolors.[36]

It was during the Marin show that twenty-one-year-old Dorothy Norman first appeared at the Intimate Gallery. This shy and sensitive woman, with large brown eyes and a pale complexion, was eighteen years younger than O'Keeffe and seven years younger than Kitty. Born in Philadelphia in 1905, Norman was the daughter of a wealthy Jewish clothing manufacturer. After a year at a New England boarding school, she entered Smith in the fall of 1922 but left at the end of her first year. Thereafter she lived at home and took art-appreciation courses at the Barnes Foundation, in the Philadelphia suburb of Merion, while attending classes at the University of Pennsylvania. Soon she met Edward Norman, whose father, a founder of Sears, Roebuck, had changed the family name from Nusbaum. Edward, five years older than Dorothy, had dropped out of Harvard and was involved with the consumers' cooperative movement. They were married in June 1925. On their wedding night her gentle husband — whom she would continue to revere as "the most intelligent, knowledgeable, beautiful young person" she had ever met — turned into a selfish monster who essentially raped her. He had told her before the wedding that he had long had psychological troubles; he would work himself into terrible rages against his parents and sometimes suffered from "vagueness" that blocked his concentration and memory. Dorothy would soon become the principal target of her husband's verbally abusive outbursts of temper.

After the Normans settled in New York, in the fall of 1925, Dorothy began doing volunteer work for the American Civil Liberties Union. On one of her occasional rounds of the galleries, she went to Room 303 for the first time simply because it was on a list she had torn out of an art magazine. She had never heard of Marin but was very excited by his works on the walls of the gallery. Stieglitz, whom she had not met, was deep in conversation. Wanting to ask him about Marin, Norman raised her hand and tried to catch his eye, but he ignored her.

When she went back a few days later, the Marin show was still up. She finally found the courage to ask about her favorite painting, but Stieglitz curtly informed her that it had been "acquired" and resumed talking to another visitor.

Dorothy soon returned, finding the Marins stacked facing the wall and an O'Keeffe show on view. When Stieglitz told a young woman that a work of art could not be explained, Norman was captivated by his words, his voice, and his face. She began going to the gallery frequently, to see the exhibitions but even more to see Stieglitz, to talk with him, and to listen to his conversations with others. She began writing down his pithiest remarks when she got home. He told her about 291 and showed her his photographs and copies of *Camera Work*. But the Normans left early for their summer house on Cape Cod, after which Dorothy entered the final months of pregnancy. It was not a particularly auspicious beginning for one of the greatest love affairs of Stieglitz's life.

CHAPTER SIXTY·THREE

A LETTER FROM Stieglitz published in the March 1927 issue of *The Art Digest* announced that "the Georgia O'Keeffes have attracted 9,000 visitors in forty-two days. Not curiosity seekers, but an audience of rare intelligence, discriminating." To counter charges that he was becoming as extortionate as any dealer, he claimed that he didn't quote any prices whatsoever to people who wanted paintings, asking them instead to make an offer. "In order to become guardian of the 'Shelton-Sunspots' one woman offered to give O'Keeffe an annuity of $1,200 a year for five years," Stieglitz boasted. "And although quite a few of the pictures went at what the world might call 'high' figures, it might be well to add that people of very small means also were considered. Some pictures found homes at as low as $75."[1] It was later reported that the "shingle-and-shell" series was sold to a woman who agreed to pay what she would otherwise have spent on a new Rolls-Royce.[2] Such a triumph of art over materialism was precisely what Stieglitz was striving for, and although the deal fell through, at least the point had been made.

O'Keeffe's show of more than forty new paintings, including flowers, the two shell series, four canvases of the Shelton, and three of the East River as seen from their apartment, was a critical as well as a financial success. Murdock Pemberton stated in *The New Yorker*, "We think she steadily enriches herself from year to year and whatever she touches seems to be magic."[3] Louis Kalonyme (who was probably the L.K. to whom one of the paintings, of a white calla lily and roses, was dedicated) enthused that O'Keeffe's "paintings ripple with the singing colors and the symphonic urge of the earth's dynamic music."[4] In *The New Republic* Lewis Mumford called O'Keeffe "perhaps the most original painter in America today."[5] With his usual reaction against such effusiveness, McBride wrote in the *Sun*, "The work is more frankly decorative than it used to be and the canvases have a tendency to grow very large."[6] O'Keeffe herself said, in a letter to Waldo Frank, that she thought her show was "too beautiful" and hoped that her next would be "so magnificently vulgar that all the people who have liked what I have been doing would stop speaking to me." O'Keeffe, who would turn forty in November, concluded, "I have come to the end of something."[7]

That season Stieglitz gave "the utmost of himself" and got "the utmost out of others."[8] Because some visitors to the Marin show had evidently complained that his monologue interfered with their ability to concentrate on the works of art, he declared on the broadside for the O'Keeffe exhibition that from 10:00 A.M. until noon on Mondays, Wednesdays, and Fridays would be "hours of silence."[9]

The third and final show of the Intimate Gallery's 1926–27 season was of sculpture by Gaston Lachaise. Born in France in 1882, he had settled in America in 1906. Recently, Lachaise had been kept busy by steady commissions for portrait busts and garden sculpture, but he still found time to make innumerable female figures with massive breasts and buttocks, for which his wife, Isabel, was the model.

No artist was featured and praised more often than Lachaise in the pages of *The Dial*, which, between 1920 and 1929, was the most distinguished and widely read of American literary and artistic magazines. But the sculptor was a difficult character. As his mammary obsession implies, he was like a big baby (and even looked a bit like one); he was ravenous, unruly, selfish, petulant, and demanding. No matter what his income, he was always in debt and behind with his rent. Stieglitz would chide him that his dealings with clients were "rather messy" and that as a businessman, he was his "own worst enemy."[10]

Among the twenty works in Lachaise's show were a frigid alabaster portrait bust of O'Keeffe, which reflected the sculptor's dislike of her, and a plaster of an exaggeratedly youthful Stieglitz, to be cast in bronze that summer. It took the photographer a while to accept his portrait, for, as he wrote Lachaise, "it's a devilishly difficult thing for even one as *free* as myself to get away from the stupid 'likeness' habit — it is ever getting in the way — at first."[11] Lachaise evidently made these two busts as thanks for his show, since Stieglitz had written the sculptor in December 1926, "In case of sales we would not accept commissions. It is as our guest that we want you here and a most welcome one you would be."[12]

The show was well received, and quite a few works were sold. Stieglitz himself bought a tiny version of a recumbent woman-as-mountain, a little alabaster torso, and a small chrome-nickel figure of a woman, for a total of $1,200. In addition he arranged for some portraits and other commissions, and he kept a few sculptures at the gallery to sell on consignment.

Despite the success of an exhibition of his work in the spring of 1928 at the prestigious Joseph Brummer Gallery, on Fifty-seventh Street, Lachaise called on Stieglitz the day the latter returned to New York from Lake George that fall and pleaded for a loan of $200, saying that he was "in desperate circumstances" and that his wife was sick in Maine. Stieglitz reluctantly gave him the money. A few days later Lachaise returned "in despair" to ask for an additional $500, which the photographer also gave him. Soon thereafter Stieglitz agreed to cash a $200 check from Lachaise that they both knew would bounce. After apologizing for having "obeyed to an impulse to be nasty" during a telephone conversation, the sculptor asked for yet another $100 and received it — making a total of $1,000 he had borrowed. He then took four small sculptures to the Intimate Gallery to serve as collateral, and in May 1929 he insisted that Stieglitz accept them as payment in full. Later that month the photographer returned the four sculptures and told Lachaise, in insulting terms, that he could keep the $1,000. "I am satisfied to pay for the lesson," he wrote, "and hope you are satisfied with your bonus."[13] When Lachaise protested, Stieglitz replied, "I wish you to know that my admiration for much of your work is as great as ever and that as an individual I esteem you but have come to the realisation that for some reason or other your way and my way of doing things do not seem to come together any more."[14] They would have no further business dealings.

Although Stieglitz had been in good health throughout the entire 1926–27 exhibition season, he was sick for three days after arriving at Lake George early in June. "I thought Hell — all of it — had been let loose," he told Arthur Dove.[15] A few weeks later he complained to the same correspondent, "My ailments hold me back so much. And Georgia is handicapped with her rheumatism in the right hand! So there is always something pulling down — or away."[16]

It wasn't until nearly the end of July that Stieglitz reported, "We are both finally 'working' & feeling better. — If my eyes would behave themselves I'd feel fitter than in some years. But I suppose without some torture to remind me that Life is not & cannot be an unadulterated joy, I'd be apt to do many more foolish things than I do & have done." He had made a few negatives that pleased him, and he had found some old printing paper, marked "Guarantee ceases July 1–1924," that was "golden compared to the fresh lots now made & supposed to be similar to the old."[17]

Some of Stieglitz's improvement may be attributed to the pleasure he and O'Keeffe had derived from a six-day visit in mid-July by Cyril Kay-Scott, their first guest of the summer. After stints as a physician, bacteriologist, entomologist, anthropologist, big-game hunter, world traveler, rancher, miner, and author, he had passionately taken up painting and had just returned to America after studying art in Europe for four years. Stieglitz found him "really an extraordinary person. Mature — measured. Has lived. And is without theory. A very sad person in a way."[18] Kay-Scott praised O'Keeffe's sense of "peace-in-intensity" and the "fine virility" of her work, attributing her "amazing psychic balance" to "a courageous self-acceptance."[19]

In mid-August, when O'Keeffe discovered a lump in one of her breasts, Lee immediately sent her to Mount Sinai Hospital for surgery, which revealed the lump to be benign. Ten days later she returned to the lake and was soon swimming, hiking, and enjoying the company of a solicitous Alfred. After visits from Paul Rosenfeld, Emil Zoler, and the newly widowed Selma, who was mercifully subdued, Stieglitz and O'Keeffe had only a few days — in contrast to their usual two months — alone at the lake before going back to New York about November 1.

Two paintings from that difficult summer suggest that O'Keeffe, depressed about Alfred's unwillingness to share a new retreat or to travel with her, was longing for the Southwest. In one spectacular canvas the colors and contours of a red poppy are strongly reminiscent of a mountainous New Mexican landscape, and in another the artist used the light from a red sun to transform the oppressively green hills surrounding Lake George into wish fulfillment. Her longing would soon become too strong to resist.

Duncan Phillips stayed away from the Marin show that opened the Intimate Gallery's season on November 9, 1927. His boycott and generally poor sales discouraged Stieglitz so badly that many visitors to Room 303 were astonished to see him sulking in silence. To Herbert Seligmann he explained, "I'm not quite mad enough to deliver a magnificent oration in a graveyard."[20]

Dove could not afford to have the feud with Stieglitz deprive him of Phillips's support. Having obtained Stieglitz's blessing, he wrote to the collector offering to meet him alone at the gallery during his show, which opened on December 12. Phillips replied that even such an arrangement would be "out of the question" and went on to elaborate, "Mr. Stieglitz and I had a serious misunderstanding last year and he treated me in a way which I cannot easily forgive. . . . Perhaps in time he will feel like telling me how sorry he is and if that time comes I shall be able to resume my active and wholehearted interest in the work of the artists who exhibit under his patronage."[21]

On Christmas Day, Stieglitz wrote Phillips, "If you will let me know what I have done which is to be forgiven I will certainly ask you your forgiveness."[22] Surprisingly, Phillips replied that he did not wish to revive the "unfortunate controversy" and that he and Mrs. Phillips would visit the Dove show.[23] After they spent two hours at the gallery, Stieglitz told Dove, "I'm glad the Phillips matter has been cleared up. I dislike animosities. — Life is too short."[24]

The collector would have liked to buy four paintings, but because — true to form — he claimed to have "spent all his money so far ahead," he bought only one, *Huntington Harbor*, an assemblage of sand, cloth, and wood on a metal panel. It was an odd choice for Phillips, who proceeded to add insult to injury by advising Dove to make fewer assemblages and to "paint more pictures in the conventional way with brush and pigment for I think you owe it to the world to do so."[25]

CHAPTER SIXTY·FOUR

◊

ON JANUARY 9, 1928, after O'Keeffe had again been hospitalized for surgery to remove what turned out to be a benign cyst, her show of some forty paintings opened at Room 303 to gratifying reviews. Henry McBride wrote that O'Keeffe seemed "to pursue her way in calmness toward the ideal she clearly indicated for herself at the beginning of her career. She comes nearer to it this year than ever before."[1] Murdock Pemberton noted a similar composure, hazarding that O'Keeffe had "come into her heritage of serenity. Her beauty is not so militant and seems to approach you unarmed."[2] It was left to brash *Time* to proclaim that "Miss O'Keeffe's paintings are as full of passion as the verses of Solomon's Song."[3]

For the rest of the season, Stieglitz extended the hospitality of the Room (as he often called the Intimate Gallery) to two old friends — Oscar Bluemner and Francis Picabia — and to one new one, Peggy Bacon, a young caricaturist who specialized in skewering the celebrities of the art world.

Stieglitz admired Bluemner's persistence in a world that could hardly care less about his work, and he called the artist, who was living in Braintree, Massachusetts, "the first painter to introduce red in America, the first who really dared to paint red."[4] Indeed, the dominant color of his paintings was a fiery scarlet that seemed to symbolize the rage that smoldered within him. However well the color may have suited his temperament, there was also a tragicomic aspect to Bluemner's chromatic bias; because he had allowed a friend who owed him money to settle the debt with innumerable cans of red paint, he had become known as the Vermilionaire.[5] In 1938 his characteristic color would take on a ghastly significance when the seventy-year-old painter, ill and penniless, cut his own throat.

In mid-April Stieglitz announced dramatically that he had sold a group of six O'Keeffe calla lily paintings dating from 1923 for the astounding price of $25,000 by a collector who wished to remain anonymous. The two large canvases of the group had brought $20,000, and the four smaller panels raised the price another $5,000. Three weeks earlier a group of thirty-two paintings by John Sloan had gone for $41,000, but the O'Keeffes set the record "for so small a group of modern paintings by a present day American."[6]

Stieglitz subsequently revealed that the buyer was an "American business man" and that the paintings had been "acquired to go to France," where, the collector had promised, they would always be kept hanging in his home. Thrilled by this reversal of the relentless flow of art from France to America, and alluding to the historic flight that had taken place a year earlier, Stieglitz rather crassly crowed of O'Keeffe, "She is the Lindbergh of art. Like Lindbergh, Miss O'Keeffe typifies the alert American spirit of going after what you want and getting it!"[7]

The collector was Mitchell Kennerley, who seems to have bought the paintings as a premature wedding present for himself and Margery Durant Campbell Daniel, the daughter of the onetime president of General Motors, William C. Durant. Mitchell and Margery were planning to marry as soon as they were both able to obtain divorces from their current spouses.

Kennerley had been involved in complicated business negotiations since May 1927, when he had let it be known that he was willing to sell the Anderson Galleries, of which he held most of the stock. His principal rival, Cortlandt Field Bishop, owner of the American Art Association, bought the Anderson in January 1928, though Kennerley stayed on as its president and retained the building's lease in his own name. Bishop and Kennerley agreed that in the near future the latter would buy back the Anderson along with the American Art, for $1.5 million — to be provided by Margery, who had a large independent fortune. The firms were to be merged (Anderson excelled in books, American in art) and moved to the American Art Association's building. All the while, Kennerley was talking about retiring from the auction business and moving back to England to return to publishing.

The one mystery is why Stieglitz said the paintings were "to go to France." Kennerley did in fact spend a vacation there early in the summer of 1928, and perhaps he and Margery talked of living in Paris. Or perhaps he anticipated having to live in France for a while to facilitate his divorce. His wife, Helen, would be awarded a divorce in Paris in 1929. Whatever the case, Kennerley told Stieglitz in August 1928 that some of the paintings were in Reno with divorce-seeking Margery Durant and some at his own apartment in New York's Sherry-Netherland Hotel.

All of Kennerley's plans came to naught, for on May 3, 1929, Margery married a man whom the *New York Daily Mirror* called "younger and handsomer" than the auctioneer-publisher.[8] After the latter went bankrupt in 1930, he asked Stieglitz for permission to postpone payments on the O'Keeffes, all of which were then at his apartment. Margery said she would buy them, but she failed to keep her word. So Kennerley returned them to Stieglitz in 1931.[9]

Although one writer has called the original transaction a fraud concocted to publicize O'Keeffe's work and to raise her prices, the deal appears to have been made in good faith.[10] Stieglitz was, however, undeniably elated by the publicity that the announcement of the sale generated. Typical of the hoopla was an article in the *New York Evening Graphic* entitled "She Painted the Lily and Got $25,000 and Fame for Doing It!" Embarrassed by all the fuss, O'Keeffe fled to Bermuda for a few weeks.

Because he considered photography the technological extension of the traditional graphic media, William Ivins, the curator of prints at the Metropolitan Museum of Art, wanted to extend the collection to include photographs as works of art. Stieglitz, resenting the museum's unwillingness to buy his work, resolutely ignored Ivins's fishing for a gift.

In May 1928 his operating and artist's welfare fund received an unusually generous donation of shares of stock from tobacco tycoon David Schulte, one of Lee's patients. Alfred, who gave his benefactor a group of his photographs, then decided that he would also thank him publicly by giving what he called "seven of my finest prints" to the Met in Schulte's name. He subsequently resolved to donate another fifteen in the names of Rebecca Strand, Alma Wertheim, Paul Rosenfeld, and "an anonymous friend" — probably O'Keeffe, one fifth of whose $25,000 from the sale of the calla paintings was earmarked for Stieglitz's fund.[11] His Byzantine scheme, which would allow him not only to thank his patrons (albeit in an odd manner) but also to get his photographs into the Met without losing face, was to present the twenty-two prints (which the museum valued at

$1,000 apiece) not as his gifts in honor of his patrons, but rather as their gifts in his honor. The ruse worked so well that an article in *Time* magazine seemed to take for granted that the donations had come as a surprise to Stieglitz.[12]

The images were, according to Ivins, "representative of the various aspects of his work during the last several years. Among them are portraits, studies of the nude, landscapes, cloudscapes, and the well-known print of hands sewing, which some sensitive observers regard as one of the most extraordinary prints of modern times."[13] The latter was designated as a gift from Rebecca Strand rather than, as one might have expected, from Schulte. Nothing if not contrary, Stieglitz also gave the collection's two most voluptuous nudes of O'Keeffe in the name of the elderly Alma Wertheim.

On May 11, after a show of Picabia's recent paintings — onto at least one of which the artist, who was feeling overshadowed by the young Surrealists, had pinned butterflies — Stieglitz hung a brief semiprivate exhibition of the $25,000 calla lilies. As soon as it was over, O'Keeffe went to Maine for two weeks, where, at first, she "slept and slept." Then, despite rainy weather, she spent her days outdoors and had "a great time." Toward the end of her visit she wrote to her sister Catherine, "I am quite a normal human being here — it is quiet — wonderful food — busy people who leave me alone — and the ocean."[14]

She desperately needed such conditions to recuperate from a trying winter and spring. If her January exhibition had impressed the critics as serene and assured, the painter herself was neither. Stieglitz had reported to Dove while she was still in the hospital that although she was beginning to regain her strength, it was "a question now of nerves building up."[15] Throughout the winter she would complain of feeling tired and would accomplish little. Unsure of the direction to take in her work, flustered by the fuss over her record-setting callas, and depressed about Stieglitz's refusal to spend summers anywhere but at the Lake George farmhouse, O'Keeffe was probably also upset because she had heard her husband speaking more and more frequently and enthusiastically of Dorothy Norman.

After the birth of her daughter in November 1927, Norman had returned to the Intimate Gallery. On one of her first visits, Stieglitz asked whether her marriage was emotionally and sexually satisfying. When he inquired, "Do you have enough milk for your child?" he electrified her by touching her breast through her coat.

Norman soon found that she wanted to go to the Room daily but forced herself to wait a couple of days between visits. Finally, on April 17, 1928, she wrote Stieglitz, "I would love to help you with what you are doing. I instinctively feel pulled toward doing that. I should like to devote a lot of time to it. . . . I want to incorporate knowing you into my life."[16] In response to Stieglitz's reply that she should come in whenever she felt the need to do so, she offered to "park as a handyman to answer the phone, shut the door — hang the pictures — make order out of chaos among the what-nots — or I might see whether long-hand would be possible as a means of taking the place of short-hand."[17] Although she had never published anything, she decided to write an article about him. He then gave her copies of *Camera Work*, let her go through boxes of his prints, and soon presented her with a cloud photograph whose "thrust," she later wrote, was "reserved, reverent, yet erotic."[18] She eventually realized that she couldn't possibly get all she felt about Stieglitz into a single article. For the next eighteen years, until his death, she would collect material for her book *Alfred Stieglitz: An American Seer*, which would not be published until 1973.

When Norman finally met O'Keeffe, two of whose small paintings she had expressed an interest in buying, the artist peremptorily asked her why she didn't devote her efforts to the National Woman's party and "drop all other 'nonsense.'"[19] But Norman was not to be shaken off. After she donated $100 to Stieglitz's fund, they began to correspond regularly. Soon, she recalled, "a day without receiving a magnificent envelope was a day lost."[20] The letters were, however, not yet intimate. One from Stieglitz, at the end of August, consisted only of a few sentences responding to Norman's question about "Objectivity and Subjectivity" and was signed simply "Greetings."[21] But he was disguising his true feelings. He was falling in love with her and knew perfectly well that she was falling in love with him. Whenever they sat in the gallery to talk, he would ask her to sit at some distance from him — "out of danger," he would tell her.

During the week between O'Keeffe's return from Maine, about June 1, and their departure for Lake George, Stieglitz slipped on a freshly mopped floor at the Shelton and hurt his back. He then proceeded to injure the middle finger of his right hand while he was getting undressed; it would remain in a splint all summer, making it "agony" for him to write letters. And since his eyes were again "on a rampage," he would not be able to read much until mid-July. Although he had looked forward all winter to going to the lake and letting "nothing interfere with getting to work at once," that now seemed "out of the question" except for mounting about a hundred old prints during the course of the summer. He was not able to make any new negatives.[22]

At Lake George, distractedly dating her letter May instead of June, O'Keeffe voiced her depression to Henry McBride:

> I try to remind myself I am here — in the country — that there are things one always does here — but I feel in a sort of daze — I don't seem to remember that I am here — and it is difficult to remember how to wind up the machinery necessary for living here . . . I look around and wonder what one might paint — Nothing but green — mountains — lake — green . . . and Stieglitz sick.[23]

A few weeks later, complaining of "a constant battling with batteries of ailments — old & new — physical & psychic," Stieglitz wrote to Dove, "It is good to be away from the City. Whether it is good to be here or not I don't know. — So far I can see no substitute."[24]

O'Keeffe thought they might both be restored by a trip to Wisconsin to visit her two elderly aunts, whom she had not seen for twelve years. Stieglitz recited a daunting list of real and exaggerated ailments that would prevent his going, and he insisted that he could not possibly manage without O'Keeffe to take care of him, even though they had hired a local woman named Margaret Prosser as full-time housekeeper. At the end of June he wrote to Herbert Seligmann, "I sometimes wish I had a few ailments instead of the many so that I might be able to take a few months off and accompany O'Keeffe to 'her' America. I know that is what she craves for. I wonder can it ever be."[25]

O'Keeffe was so upset by her husband's stubbornness that she couldn't paint. Finally, early in July, Elizabeth Davidson managed to convince Alfred that Georgia should go to Wisconsin for a month. After receiving a report of how happy they had been during the two weeks before O'Keeffe's departure, Elizabeth wrote Uncle Al, "It was so good to hear that there is again understanding — togetherness." Referring no doubt to Dorothy Norman, she continued, "I hope nothing will be infected from the outside — to disturb the new peace. Even in the case of a stupidity — Beck or such — it should not go deep."[26]

While O'Keeffe was away, Stieglitz was alone in the farmhouse for four weeks, but Lee, Lizzie, and the Davidson girls were at Red Top, to which an annex containing a kitchen and dining room had been added. Because Alfred's splinted finger still made it difficult for him to write letters or to work, he had lots of time to think about the upcoming season, which might be the last in Room 303, since Kennerley was trying to sell the lease to the

Anderson building. Stieglitz wrote to Dove that he wanted the season to be "still more intensely effective" than former ones and added, "What after this year heaven knows."[27]

One possibility developed after he read *Lady Chatterley's Lover*, sent to him by D. H. Lawrence, who had just had it printed privately in Florence. The photographer thought that the book was "one of the grandest that had ever been written, a sort of Bible, on a par with Goethe and Shakespeare."[28]

Although the two men had never met, they had corresponded, occasionally but warmly, since the summer of 1923, when Stieglitz found Lawrence's new book of essays, *Studies in Classic American Literature*, a "rare pleasure."[29] He immediately wrote a letter of praise to the author, who replied very gratefully a week later.[30] In recommending that book to friends, Stieglitz characterized Lawrence as "an amazing person."[31]

By mid-August 1928, plans were afoot to exhibit at the Intimate Gallery during November Lawrence's recent high-spirited but rather silly paintings, which Stieglitz had never seen. Lawrence wrote from Switzerland, where he was battling the tuberculosis that would kill him in 1930, "Don't be alarmed about the pictures — they're quite good. Anyhow, they *contain* something — which is more than you can say about most moderns, which are all excellent rind of the fruit, but no fruit."[32] Lawrence, eager to meet Stieglitz and O'Keeffe, was hoping to go to his ranch in Taos late in the fall and would try to be in New York during the show. Stieglitz was so excited about the prospect of the exhibition that he wrote Lawrence a fourteen-page letter.

Having already said that he was "not really keen on exhibiting," Lawrence wrote in mid-September that "it would be useless to send [his paintings] to America now — too much stupid fuss over *Lady C*."[33] (When they were shown in London the following year, thirteen of them were officially condemned as obscene and removed by the police.) Because the U.S. Post Office was intercepting and confiscating copies of *Lady Chatterley's Lover*, pirated editions began to circulate. Appalled by the censorship and the "bootlegging," Stieglitz would say in November, "If I did not have to spare myself, I'd give the entire year in Room 303 to Lawrence. I'd challenge the entire country on the book and what is being done to it."[34]

After O'Keeffe returned to Lake George, around August 15, she and Stieglitz had three blissful weeks together. One morning at the end of the first week of September, Alfred even announced that he had finally regained the full use of his finger. That night his heart "started off on trot, pace & gallop simultaneously — & at a record-breaking speed." He had apparently suffered a heart attack, though it may only have been his first attack of angina pectoris. For more than three weeks he would be confined to bed and "absolute isolation."[35]

Despite the help of a local nurse and her sister Ida, O'Keeffe shouldered much of the responsibility for taking care of Alfred. Two weeks after the attack she wrote to a friend, "Not a thought in my head — unless strained spinach, peas, beans, squash . . . five drops of that — a teaspoon in a third of a glass of water — or is it half a glass — pulse this — heart that — grind the meat four times."[36] By then she felt reassured, however, for Stieglitz had resumed his habitual complaining — a sure sign of recovery. Determined to open his gallery on schedule, he continued to improve steadily. He told Dove that as a result of his attack, "I'll have to spare spending myself too lavishly on Tom, Dick & Jane."[37] During this last season of the Intimate Gallery he would show no outsiders but would mount a one-person show of each of the Seven Americans (including Charles Demuth) except himself.

When Stieglitz and O'Keeffe returned to New York, early in November, they saw a good deal of Mabel Dodge Luhan, now married to her former chauffeur, a member of the Taos Pueblo named Antonio Lujan (whose name she unilaterally anglicized). Tony remained in New Mexico while Mabel spent a few weeks in New York, accompanied by her friend the Honorable Dorothy Brett, a painter who specialized in stylized, primary-color depictions of the ceremonial dances of the Pueblo people. The daughter of the second viscount Escher, she had gone with D. H. Lawrence and his wife, Frieda, to Taos in 1925 and had stayed there after the Lawrences returned to Europe the following year. Brett, who was quite deaf and relied on an ear trumpet nicknamed Toby, lived most of the year in a caretaker's cabin on the Kiowa Ranch (which Mabel had sold to Lawrence in return for the manuscript of *Sons and Lovers*). In the winters she lived at Mabel's house in Taos. Before he canceled his show, Lawrence had encouraged Stieglitz to show Brett's paintings together with his own. Since that had fallen through, Brett had brought a group of her works to New York in the hope of a solo. Stieglitz was not sufficiently impressed to exhibit them himself, but he sent her to the dealer Frank Rehn, who offered her a show.

After first meeting Mabel, in 1925, O'Keeffe wrote her that she had never met "a more feminine person" and suggested, "I thought you could write something about me that the men can't."[38] The essay Luhan produced was nothing short of outrageous. She wrote that in O'Keeffe's art "is made manifest the classical dream of walking naked on Broadway." The artist, she continued, "externalizes the frustration of her true being out onto canvases which, receiving her outpouring of sexual juices, . . . permit her to walk this earth with the cleansed, purgated look of fulfilled life!" Then Luhan turned upon Stieglitz, a "filthy, frustrated showman." She accused him, not unjustly, of being a "watchman standing with a club before the gate of [O'Keeffe's] life, guarding and prolonging so long as you may endure, the unconsciousness within her. Stieglitz, let live. Let live this somnolent woman by your side. But, Camera-man, do you dare, I wonder, face the sun?"[39] Some of this must be discounted as Luhan's attempt to outdo the dramatic analysis and style of Rosenfeld and Hartley's essays about O'Keeffe. Regardless, had it been published, no one would have blamed O'Keeffe and Stieglitz if they had permanently broken off relations with Luhan. Instead, they remained on very friendly terms with her, and she gave them an open invitation to visit her in Taos, which by then was known as Mabeltown.

CHAPTER SIXTY·FIVE

ONE DAY WHEN Stieglitz and Dorothy Norman were alone in Room 303 during the fall of 1928, she worked up her courage to tell him that she loved him. He smiled, extended his hand to her, and said, "We do." He proceeded to kiss her, she wrote, "as I have never dreamed a kiss could be." From then on, Norman recalled, "we [had to] be in touch in person, by letter, by phone at every possible moment. No day [was] complete without communication, contact, repetition of the magic words that join[ed] us."[1] In one of his first letters after that kiss, Stieglitz assured her, "We are one. — Every day proves it *more and more to be true.* Dorothy, do you have any idea how much IWY."[2] Whether he wanted or worshiped her must remain a mystery.

Although Norman wrote of having "a complete erotic experience again and again" with Stieglitz, whose love aroused her "to perfect fulfillment," it seems that for some time to come their amatory activities would be limited to kissing. It would be several years before Norman could even bring herself to call him Alfred.

After the Marin show with which the season began, Hartley's first Intimate Gallery exhibition opened on Stieglitz's sixty-fifth birthday, January 1, 1929. It featured still lifes brushed in Paris and landscapes from the south of France, especially a series of Cézannesque paintings and drawings of

Mont Sainte-Victoire that Hartley had executed when he was living in the revered master's Aix. In March, while in Paris, Hartley heard rumors that during his exhibition Stieglitz had been telling people that his work had "gone down terribly" during the previous four years. The artist wrote to a friend that he didn't believe Stieglitz held any such opinion himself but conceded that "with his heavy and distorted regard for the truth" he could well have repeated what the critics had written.[3]

The reviews that followed the February 4 opening of O'Keeffe's show of thirty-five recent paintings were excellent, but Georgia herself felt that something vital had gone out of her work — and out of her life. "I knew I must get back to some of my own ways or quit," she wrote. "It was mostly all dead for me."[4]

Utterly exhausted when they had returned to New York in November, O'Keeffe had wanted to do nothing but rest. "We do not go out nights and do not have guests so it is much easier than other years," she wrote her sister. "I thrive on it."[5] But the truth was that she was very depressed about the state of her marriage and consequently suffered several bouts of illness. On March 1 Stieglitz reported to Dove that she had been miserable and had "virtually done no painting all this winter so far."[6] Various doctors, relations, and friends proposed a trip to Europe, even though *Time* had stressed a few months earlier that O'Keeffe had "never gone abroad and doesn't want to."[7] Soon she resolved that a sojourn in the Southwest was what she needed. If Stieglitz wouldn't go with her, she would go alone.

He was strongly opposed to both versions of the plan. For one thing, he felt that the strain of the long trip would certainly be too great for him. He didn't dare to be so far away from Lee, who had warned him that the high altitude of Taos would be dangerous for his heart. As Stieglitz had done so often in the past, he tried to bind O'Keeffe to him with cords of hypochondria. He insisted that she was far too weak for such a strenuous journey and that, in any case, he was a very sick man who could not possibly manage without her constant attention. Moreover, he worried about her whenever she was out of his sight. During the past summer he had become very nervous every time she went into the town of Lake George alone. Because of his involvement with Norman, he was certainly afraid that if O'Keeffe went to New Mexico, she might never come back.

Throughout the winter of 1929, Alfred and Georgia argued bitterly about her going away. While he poured out endless monologues of self-pity and self-righteousness, she became withdrawn and silent until she would finally burst into tears. The previous summer Stieglitz had confessed, "I oftentimes — most times — feel like a criminal . . . in being the cause of keeping Georgia from where she really naturally belongs."[8] Never before had he been so thoroughly justified in such feelings of guilt. O'Keeffe would soon confide to Mabel Luhan, "I think I would never have minded Stieglitz being anything he happened to be if he hadn't kept me so persistently off my track."[9] Late in life she averred, "I think I only crossed him when I had to — to survive."[10] This was one of those times.

Stieglitz decided that "in order to bring about a real break after Georgia's show," he would follow it with a Paul Strand exhibition, the first and only time photographs were hung on the walls of the Intimate Gallery. The images were mostly close-ups of machine parts and natural forms. Although some of the latter had been shot in Colorado during the summer of 1926, most of the finest were made during the Strands' 1927 and 1928 visits to the Lachaises' in Maine. Among them were pictures of a toadstool and grasses, of ferns, and of iris leaves that surely reminded many viewers of O'Keeffe's paintings, while almost transcendently beautiful close-ups of eroded seaside rocks and arrangements of driftwood are obvious translations of Stieglitz's clouds. During the exhibition Stieglitz spoke critically, both to the photographer and to visitors, of Strand's tendency to imitate and his excessive emphasis on technical perfection. As always, the elder was convinced that no one could possibly take offense at his expression of what he regarded as the obvious truth. Surprised by his protégé's anger, he wrote, "I'm afraid you have misunderstood many things I have said during your show."[11] The two men were reconciled, but not for long.

One of the visitors to whom Stieglitz spoke deprecatingly of Strand was Berenice Abbott, recently returned to New York after eight years in Paris. Having worked as Man Ray's assistant for three years, she had opened a portrait studio, to which flocked such Parisian luminaries as Marcel Duchamp, Jean Cocteau, André Gide, James Joyce, and Peggy Guggenheim. In 1925 Man Ray showed Abbott some photographs of Paris taken by Eugène Atget, who lived nearby. Gripped by the poetry of these ostensibly documentary images, she sought out Atget and befriended him. After his death, in 1927, she managed to acquire all of the prints and negatives that remained in his studio. She had hoped that Stieglitz might exhibit some of the photographs, but after hearing his criticisms of Strand she was afraid that Atget would be subjected to the same treatment.[12] Stieglitz later told a friend that he would not have shown Atget's work in any case, since he was committed to showing only living artists. But if he had known Atget's images while he was publishing *Camera Work*, he said, he would have reproduced them.[13]

Abbott and Atget were each represented by eleven prints in the important international exhibition *Film und Foto*, which opened in Stuttgart in May 1929. The American section, organized by Edward Steichen and Edward Weston, also included work by Charles Sheeler and Ralph Steiner, as well as six of Steichen's fashion photographs. Stieglitz naturally refused to participate. The gulf between him and his old friend was further widened by the publication that year of Carl Sandburg's book *Steichen the Photographer*, in which the poet celebrated his brother-in-law's belief that commercial work presented the photographic artist with his most worthy challenge. Only a consummate artist, Steichen argued, could meet the technical standards of a firm like Condé Nast and also manage to infuse advertising and fashion photographs with real feeling and drama. Stieglitz's disgust with such an attitude is evident in Strand's protest published in *The New Republic*.[14]

Although Stieglitz wrote Duncan Phillips that Dove "should be given the fullest opportunity to go ahead without wasting his time with illustration" and vowed to see the artist through, "even at my having to dig into my own small capital," the Washington collector bought nothing from his show in April 1929.[15] Between the paintings Stieglitz and O'Keeffe bought from the show and a sum from the aid fund, Dove cleared $1,000.

Among the five paintings in Demuth's show, the last of the season, was *The Figure 5 in Gold*, a dynamic homage to William Carlos Williams, from one of whose poems the title was taken. Despite some misgivings about it, Williams called it "the best American picture of its time."[16] Inexplicably, Demuth didn't include his great 1927 painting *My Egypt*, whose title referred to his exile in Lancaster and suggested a comparison between the depicted grain elevators and the Pyramids. An unsigned pamphlet that Stieglitz issued in 1935 stated that the painting offered "perhaps the finest sense of a modern age that has been expressed."[17]

Eventually Stieglitz and O'Keeffe reached a compromise. They agreed that she would spend the months of May and June in the Southwest and then return east for the remainder of the summer with him at Lake George.[18] Furthermore, Rebecca Strand would accompany her. Stieglitz felt that Beck, his ally, would make sure that O'Keeffe came back to him. And since Beck and Paul had stayed with Mabel in 1926, she would be a useful guide not only to the geography of the region but also to the complexities of social life in Taos.

In retrospect, Stieglitz — who had a genius for convincing himself that things always turned out exactly as he had wanted them to — would claim that he had known all along that the Southwest was "*the* thing" for O'Keeffe.[19] More to the point, he surely realized that only by accepting her absences could he hope to keep her at all.

Stieglitz spent his life fighting against, and denying, his extremely possessive nature. He strove for the selfless love that, he wrote, "tends to make one desire to release the other — even from oneself, to make one try to understand the other, rather than to seek the dedication of the other to oneself."[20] But during the winter and spring of 1929, he desperately wanted O'Keeffe to achieve her self-fulfillment without any lessening of her dedication to him.

Right up until her departure, O'Keeffe had some hesitation about going. "If I can keep up my courage and leave Stieglitz," she told a friend late in April, she would be setting off for New Mexico in a few days. "It is always such a struggle for me to leave him."[21]

After a train trip that Beck told Paul "even little Stieglitz" could have stood, the two women were soon settled very comfortably in Mabel's twenty-room adobe house, called Los Gallos for the ceramic roosters that adorned its roof.[22] Mabel gave O'Keeffe the use of a beautiful studio some distance from the Big House. Through the large window of what O'Keeffe called the finest studio she had ever had, she looked out across "a rich green alfalfa field — then the sage brush and beyond — a most perfect mountain," as she wrote to Henry McBride. "It makes me feel like flying."[23]

Only five days after they had left New York, Beck wrote her husband that O'Keeffe looked "so well already — all the tension gone and a real serenity flowing." She instructed him, "Tell Stieglitz this, and that she has not had a single ache or pain or physical distress since we arrived . . . She is a new woman."[24] O'Keeffe herself soon wrote McBride, "You know I never feel at home in the East like I do out here — and finally feeling in the right place again — I feel like myself." She was enjoying "one perfect day after another" and had "never felt better."[25]

Mabel's house was always full of interesting people, one of the most extraordinary of whom was her husband. Tony Lujan was an imposing and dignified man, over six feet tall, with a barrel chest, long braids that he sometimes sheathed with white ribbons, and a large-featured face full of noble character. A man of few but well-chosen words, he had a reverence for nature and a dry sense of humor, both of which appealed greatly to O'Keeffe. Later in the summer she would write to Mabel, "I want to tell you that next to my Stieglitz I have found nothing finer than your Tony."[26]

And in another letter she said, "Tony just being what he is — seems to pull out of me the best things that are in me."[27] When he and Mabel had visited the Intimate Gallery in February 1926, Stieglitz had spoken of him as "a magnificent specimen physically" and wondered how he could photograph him.[28]

Among the lively and congenial assemblage of guests then at Mabel's house were photographer Ansel Adams and writer Mary Austin, who were collaborating on *Taos Pueblo*, which would turn out to be one of the most beautiful photographic books ever published. Also there was Hutchins Hapgood, with his wife (writer Neith Boyce) and their daughter. Mabel, always ready to add a famous artist to her collection, was thrilled when Georgia and Beck suggested sending John Marin a wire to invite him out. He responded with alacrity and arrived about June 10, leaving his wife at home. He quickly fell in love with the mountains around Taos and would return the following summer.

O'Keeffe reported that everyone seemed "to go like Mad all day."[29] In the evening, after dinner at the Big House, accompanied by lots of wine and "Taos lightning," Tony would occasionally arrange for dancers from the pueblo to perform. Or perhaps Adams, who was still considering a career as a concert pianist, might play Mabel's grand piano. O'Keeffe found everything to be "perfect" or "wonderful" and exulted that her days seemed "to be like the loud ring of a hammer striking something hard."[30] After reading her first glowing letters, Stieglitz nervously teased that she was "being ruined for home."[31]

The festivities were dampened somewhat when Mabel was taken ill at the end of Georgia and Beck's first week in Taos. Then, on May 13, Tony left for Santa Fe, where he had to spend several days taking care of some business. Whenever he went away, Mabel worried about his faithfulness. The night after his departure, O'Keeffe shared her hostess's huge roughly hewn, wooden-framed bed, which had had to be built in place and is still there. Because Mabel's first serious adolescent love affair had been with the sister of a classmate — a relationship she later described as exquisitely sensual but "chaste" — and because O'Keeffe may have been bisexual, some biographers would have us imagine a night of sexual passion. But O'Keeffe was probably in Mabel's bed as a consoler rather than as a lover. "I feel like snuggling up to you and crying about it all," she wrote to Mabel later in the summer, in the midst of a crisis of her own, regarding Stieglitz.[32]

Nor is it likely that Georgia and Beck became lovers, though they certainly acted as though they were in love. Temporarily liberated from their difficult husbands and intoxicated with the joy of being in such a beautiful place, they sunbathed in the nude, gave each other little gifts, and reveled in high jinks. They had such a wonderful time that they talked about going away again the next year and even of "trying to find a little house somewhere near New York" where they could spend time together.[33]

On April 12, 1929, Mitchell Kennerley suddenly left for England, having just resigned from the Anderson Galleries. His resignation and departure were evidently the direct result of his having learned that Margery Durant was not going to marry him. Without her money at his disposal, all of his business schemes evaporated. But he retained the lease of 489 Park Avenue, and in early May Stieglitz was still wondering whether he would have Room 303 for another season or would have to vacate it immediately.[34] It was soon announced that the Anderson Galleries would move into the American Art Association's building on Madison Avenue and that Kennerley would remain in London to set his two sons up in publishing. The fate of 489 Park Avenue would be uncertain for some time — Kennerley even considered turning it into a movie palace. In any case, the Intimate Gallery would have to close.

After the Demuth show ended, on May 18, Stieglitz spent several weeks clearing out the gallery and putting hundreds of works of art into storage. He was so busy he hardly had time to miss O'Keeffe. He complained that she should have been there to help him, but Zoler, Strand, and Seligmann all devoted themselves to the project, and Marin even came in from New Jersey a few days to lend a hand. Closing another chapter of his life, Stieglitz asked himself what good he had really accomplished. He moaned that he had exhausted himself to enable a few artists to live and work, and they weren't even grateful to him. "It makes me sick that I have not carried on my Photography," he told Seligmann. "I have not had the chance to do what I might have done."[35]

Stieglitz didn't arrive at Lake George until June 14, more than six weeks after O'Keeffe's departure for New Mexico and only two weeks before the originally scheduled date of her return. By this time, however, Georgia had already informed him that because she and Beck were enjoying themselves so much they were going to stay on in Taos after July 1 — and perhaps even remain there all summer. He was more or less reconciled to this development by June 11, when he wrote to Dove, "I'll be glad to get away altho the Hill will seem a bit forlorn with Georgia not there. Still I'm glad she is where she is. Lake G. is not for her."[36] A week later he wrote to Seligmann from the lake, "Georgia continues to have a very gorgeous time, and as I see this I realize fully how silly (criminally so) [it would be] were she to come here this summer."[37] He was putting up a brave front. More candidly, he would tell one historian that O'Keeffe's going to the Southwest had "nearly killed him, because he knew something had come to an end."[38] He realized from her letters that she would never again be content to divide her life between New York and Lake George.

Zoler accompanied Stieglitz to the lake and stayed on for four weeks as his live-in companion, helper, and nurse. During the first two weeks, Stieglitz told his niece Elizabeth, "I certainly went through Hell itself."[39] Because Georgia and Beck were on a camping trip with Tony Lujan, Alfred didn't hear a word from Taos and worried terribly. Several nights he and Zoler had great bonfires of "negatives, prints, over 1000 copies of *Camera Work*, including a complete set — nearly a library of books — just to get rid of things. It was a great sight watching all these things disappear into the starlit night."[40] In the fall he told Dove that this had been "just a real cleaning up. — And all without any resentment," though he confessed, "A wonder I didn't burn up cameras & even house."[41] But early in the summer he remarked to other friends that he had cremated the dreams of his youth.

The dramatic storm clouds in the *Equivalents* dating from 1929 are suggestive of angels of death, terrifying forces, an angry God, and the Four Horsemen of the Apocalypse. Of such images Stieglitz said, "My photographs are a picture of the chaos in the world, and of my relationship to that chaos. My prints show the world's constant upsetting of man's equilibrium, and his eternal battle to reestablish it."[42] Indeed, Stieglitz rode a manic-depressive roller-coaster all summer. Afterward, he would describe those months as "a very curious time for me. — Maybe the most trying in my whole experience. With Georgia away — and no Room — the Future — very ???"[43]

One night at the end of June, he took something to help him sleep and awoke eleven hours later feeling reborn. "A miracle had happened," he wrote to Elizabeth Davidson. "I believe I'm finally actually beyond all Hurt."[44] Bolstered by Georgia's assurances of her love and cheered by the arrival of the Davidsons, he had a few good weeks. After he heard that Georgia and Beck had bought a Ford, he got Elizabeth to give him driving lessons — though he never did master the art of driving. During the day he photographed, went for walks, and rowed on the lake. Evenings he stayed up late talking, reading, and listening to Bach, Beethoven, and Brahms on his new Victrola.

Soon he fell again into the slough of despond. The problem this time was a misunderstanding between Georgia and Mabel, who was in her hometown of Buffalo for a hysterectomy. Mabel feared that as soon as she

had left Taos, her husband had returned to his first wife, as he did periodically. Then she received a letter from O'Keeffe about the six-day camping
trip with Beck and Tony from which they had just returned. Although the
letter was filled with assurances of Tony's love for Mabel, what leapt from
the page were the sentences "I feel you have got to let him live and *be* his
way — however much it might hurt you. . . . Even if he does go out and
sleeps with someone else it is a little thing."[45] The almost pathologically
possessive Mabel took that to mean that O'Keeffe had slept with Tony, and
she wrote of her suspicions to Stieglitz, who was thrown into paroxysms of
jealousy.

It was at that point that Paul Strand and his friend Harold Clurman, a
young theatrical director who had known Stieglitz since 1924, stopped at
Lake George one morning on their way to New England. As soon as they
sat down on the porch of the farmhouse, Stieglitz began pouring out his
life story in "a long discourse on life, part lament, part harangue" that
lasted for eighteen straight hours, with "enough detail in his rambling —
which progressed by a process of free association — for a full-scale biography." He talked, without respite, all morning, all through lunch, throughout the afternoon, dinner, and the evening. "As we retired for the night,"
recalled Clurman, "the lights in the house still blazing — Strand said that
in view of Stieglitz's excited state we ought not to leave — Stieglitz came to
our room with us and stood over our beds, continuing his monologue."[46]

Strand and Clurman decided that they had better stay on for a few more
days. While they were there, Stieglitz wrote O'Keeffe several letters a day
and read them to his guests. Then he would think of something so urgent
that he would send her a telegram. As soon as he had done so, he would sit
down to write her another letter explaining what he had meant in his wire.
In a portrait that Strand made that summer, Stieglitz appears to be in a
state of shock.

O'Keeffe sighed to Mabel, "I have been having telegrams from Stieglitz
all day today. . . . I am about decided to go back to Stieglitz next
week. . . . He seems to be in a bad state and I feel I have little choice in the
matter. I can't tell you how it grieves me."[47] But when she wired him that
she would return if necessary, he was so relieved by her offer that he told
her not to come. He wrote elatedly to Elizabeth, "I had a marvellous wire
from Georgia this morning — She feels as I feel — Exactly. It all seems as
if I were in a trance — She will stay in Taos & paint awhile & will come
soon if I promise honestly to take care of myself. . . . She feels a greater &
more wonderful togetherness — the first coming together in purity on a
much higher plane!"[48]

That peak of joy was quickly succeeded by another chasm of despair. When Strand, who was distressed because Beck had made it clear that she did not want him to join her in Taos, returned to Lake George at the end of July for a longer visit, the two men commiserated about their troubled marriages. "Common suffering does bring souls closely together," commented Stieglitz.[49] He informed his niece, "I had the toughest day & night yet, up 40 hours writing — & writing — But sent no letters nor telegraphs — couldn't. Georgia was fortunately out of reach."[50] A day or two later, he received four "wonderful" letters from O'Keeffe, in which she explained that his fanatical devotion to his gallery, which, she complained, always "came first," had done much to separate them during the past four years. "My Vision is Clear once more," exclaimed Alfred, who had "believed G. understood the Room was another form of her."[51]

Shortly before Beck reluctantly left Taos, late in July, to care for her ailing mother in Atlantic City, she encouraged Georgia to remain indefinitely in the Southwest, where she was so happy and healthy. In support of that suggestion, Beck mentioned that in the spring Alfred had told her that he had never loved anyone but himself. In his view of things, of course, by loving O'Keeffe he was loving himself, since he was constantly saying that she was a finer manifestation of his own spirit. But Beck took, or professed to take, his remark at face value. This crisis resolved itself in yet another squall of letters.

After Beck departed and Mabel returned from Buffalo, nursed by Ida O'Keeffe, Georgia felt it would be anticlimactic to remain at Los Gallos. Instead, she spent about a week at the Lawrence ranch with Dorothy Brett, the Hapgoods, and Charles Collier, son of the director of the Bureau of Indian Affairs. While there, she painted her striking canvas of a pine tree soaring into the stars, as she had observed it while lying on a table at its base. After seeing a very fine dance at the Santo Domingo Pueblo, she stayed three or four days at the sprawling H & M Ranch, near Alcalde, owned by documentary filmmaker Henwar Rodakiewicz and his wealthy wife, Marie Tudor Garland, author of such books as *Hindu Mind Training* (1917) and *The Marriage Feast* (1920). From there O'Keeffe drove west out toward Abiquiu, prophetically finding the region "very beautiful."[52]

Then Marie proposed that they take a *real* trip, and on about August 8 she, Henwar, Collier, Spud Johnson (a poet who worked as Mabel's private secretary), and O'Keeffe set off on a glorious, rollicking ten-day journey in two touring cars, a Rolls-Royce and a Packard, with their tops down most of the way. They first proceeded westward across New Mexico to the Navajo country of Arizona, then crossed the Painted Desert to the Grand

Canyon before heading north to Bryce Canyon, Utah, and on nearly to Salt Lake City. From there they drove in a great eastward arc to Aspen and Colorado Springs, then south to Taos, arriving there late on the seventeenth. They encountered broiling heat, torrential rains, even a hailstorm that blanketed the ground with white. "Stieglitz thought me dead on that trip," O'Keeffe told Beck.[53]

"The week has been a terror," Stieglitz wailed to Elizabeth on August 18. "6 days without a word — finally yesterday a telegram saying she'd be back in Taos by last night — who knows? . . . I wrote 12 letters & didn't mail them til after the telegram came."[54] Fortunately, Louis Kalonyme was staying at the Hill for at least the first few days of that terrible week. Kalonyme, who "had just returned from Europe where he was with [Eugene] O'Neill," was, according to his host, "a rare person. — Was a treat to have him."[55] The visitor decided that the thing to take Stieglitz's mind off his troubles was a round at the miniature golf course that had just opened nearby. Alfred, recalling his days of glory as a billiards champion, not only was delighted but also demonstrated exceptional aptitude. He developed a real passion for the game and during the next several years would be a regular at the local course, which survived the rapid passing of the craze that swept the country the following summer.

When the effectiveness of that diversionary anodyne began to pale, the resourceful Kalonyme prescribed stronger medicine: a flight in one of the seaplanes that took sightseers on half hour jaunts over Lake George. The experience was so exhilarating that Stieglitz, who had some business in New York, decided to charter a four-passenger plane to fly down on August 19. Still awaiting a letter from Georgia, he wired her of his intention — surely both to boast of his exploits and to give her a taste of worry. He also asked Elizabeth to keep all of Dorothy Norman's correspondence if anything happened to him. "Under no condition do I want Georgia to have anything to do with it," he stressed.[56]

He later told a friend that he had loved seeing what the Hudson River valley and New York City looked like from the air — and that "when he was flying along he thought what a wonderful way it would be to die if the pilot, not knowing that Stieglitz had a bad heart, went up to a very high altitude."[57] He was so enthralled by the flight that he wrote to Dove, "If I were young enough I'd certainly get a machine."[58] More immediately, he was thinking about flying out to Taos to see what Georgia was really up to.

That would prove to be unnecessary. Driving back to Taos from Colorado, she had concluded that she was as ready as she would ever be to return east. "If it were not for the Stieglitz call I would probably never go —

but that is strong," she wrote.[59] She also wanted to paint the autumn foliage at Lake George. Her decision to leave was reinforced when she found Mabel's household in great disorder. Mabel, Tony, and Ida had gone to Albuquerque, where Mabel — whose syphilis, probably contracted from her first husband, had flared up — was in a sanatorium. She told her friends she was being treated for heart troubles, but Ida, shocked to see that her patient was addicted to painkillers, gave her sister the real scoop. ("The tales Ida told me . . . ," O'Keeffe wrote tantalizingly to Beck.) Mabel had quarreled with almost everyone in sight before she left, and the insulted Neith Boyce had stormed home. Moreover, the turmoil was not only emotional. Construction workers had "the whole place dug up for pipes" and were breaking through walls to make new doorways. "You never saw such wreckage," wrote O'Keeffe.[60]

Elated by his flight to New York, Alfred became nearly delirious with joy to find there Georgia's wire saying that she would arrive in Albany early on the morning of August 25. He felt he had been blessed with a miracle. "My aim will be to keep it perfect," he wrote to Elizabeth. "I'll do more than my share . . . I have learned a lot — & shall apply what I have learned."[61]

Having spent the night at a hotel in Albany, he met Georgia when her train pulled into Union Station at 6:00 A.M. O'Keeffe, who had written a friend the previous day "I feel so alive that I am apt to crack at any moment," was amazed and very pleased to find Stieglitz seeming "better physically than in four or five years."[62] During the coming weeks at the lake, he would even be able and willing to walk up Prospect Mountain. "I just look at him and wonder if I can believe my eyes," O'Keeffe confided to Mabel.[63]

Nor was Alfred's dramatic improvement only physical. Psychologically as well, he seemed like a phoenix risen from the ashes. "I have thrown overboard all my ideas — and all my ideals — and everything else," he told his wife, "till there is nothing left but myself."[64] Painful as it had been at times for both of them, their separation had done them both a world of good. O'Keeffe wrote Mabel in September, "The summer had brought me to a state of mind where I felt as grateful for my largest hurts as I did for my largest happiness — in spite of all my tearing about, many things that had been accumulating inside of me for years were arranging themselves — and rearranging themselves. The same thing had been happening to Stieglitz." Their reunion, she sang, was "the most perfect thing that has ever happened to me." Her "funny little Stieglitz" seemed to her "the grandest thing in the world . . . the most beautiful thing I ever knew," and she wondered how she "ever was able to stay away from him so long."[65] It was as though they were falling in love all over again. Stieglitz told his niece, "Our relationship is sounder than [ever] before."[66]

O'Keeffe was so happy that she didn't "seem to see family about or anything else."[67] In any case, she knew that Lee and Lizzie would leave in the middle of September; she and Stieglitz would then be alone, except for a visit from the Strands, until early November. During the late summer, the sun shone, the air was warm and still, and a haze hung over the lake and the intensely green mountains. O'Keeffe was eager to get back to work. That fall she would paint not only landscapes but also a shutter-flanked composite of a window and the front door of the farmhouse. *Lake George Window* is a tentative affirmation of the artist's return to Alfred's world, tentative because a black horizontal line — part of the window sash or of a screen door — seems to block entry.

That fall Stieglitz took more photographs of O'Keeffe than he had made in years. Some capture her pixieish delight with the summer's dénouement, while others emphasize her strength and independence, particularly as symbolized by her car, which arrived at Lake George in mid-September, driven by Charles Collier. On the eighteenth, Stieglitz, O'Keeffe, and Collier set out for a few days at York Beach, where Rosenfeld was staying with the Schaufflers.

Alfred and Georgia thought about remaining at the lake for all but three or four weeks of the winter. That seemed possible because until the end of October he did not expect to have a gallery that season. "We have no 'Plans.' — I'm 'ready' for anything," he told Dove in September.[68]

PART VIII

AN AMERICAN PLACE

CHAPTER SIXTY·SIX

IN THE SPRING of 1929, Paul Strand and Dorothy Norman had offered to spearhead efforts to raise rent money for a new gallery. Stieglitz was skeptical about the prospects since, as he noted in a letter to Dove late in March, Wall Street was "in a smash."[1] Although the stock market recovered over the summer, by early October the irreversible decline into the Great Depression had begun in earnest. The wealthy, Alfred assumed, would not be inclined to give money for an art gallery.

And yet the talk of the town was the November 8 opening of the Museum of Modern Art, which was to be housed on the twelfth floor of the Heckscher Building, at Fifth Avenue and Fifty-seventh Street. Alfred, who had nothing good to say about the venture, dismissed the museum's three "founding mothers" — Abby Aldrich Rockefeller, Lillie P. Bliss, and Mrs. Cornelius J. Sullivan — as rich women whose interest in art was superficial, dilettantish, and merely fashionable. He told Nancy Newhall that when "the crash came, [he] said to himself that the Rockefellers — their fortunes unshakable — would get the same stranglehold on art that they had gotten on finance, the church, and to some extent, education."[2]

Stieglitz hated the very idea of institutions run by committees and denounced them as "contrary to the spirit of art." He derived little comfort from the appointment of Duncan Phillips and Frank Crowninshield to the new museum's board of trustees. In 1931 Alfred would write to Dove regarding that group, "I know the gang called Trustees. None but the Rich need apply — & of course those who bend the knee to their arrogance are the only welcome servants."[3]

By mid-September 1929, Stieglitz had somewhat reluctantly decided that it was important for him to have a place in which to continue his work, both for its own sake and as a rebuke and example to the new museum. The announcement that the latter — which as yet had only an inconsequential collection of its own — would debut with a loan exhibition of works by Cézanne, Gauguin, van Gogh, and Seurat seemed to confirm his fear that it would favor European modernism over American. Nor was he appeased when he heard that the second show, scheduled to open on December 13, was to be Paintings by Nineteen Living Americans. (Demuth quipped in a letter to Stieglitz that he hadn't realized there were that many.) Evading responsibility, the museum's director, Alfred H. Barr, Jr., had the trustees choose the artists by ballot. O'Keeffe was the only woman invited to show. Marin and Demuth were also selected, along with others ranging from Ernest Lawson and John Sloan to Charles Burchfield, Edward Hopper, Walt Kuhn, and Max Weber. As Barr's catalog foreword put it, "Included are artists who are so 'conservative' that they are out of fashion and so 'advanced' that they are not yet generally accepted." The uneven quality of the works in the exhibition prompted one critic to hit home with the suggestion that it should have been called "Some Pictures We Thought Good and Some That Have Been Bought by the Directors."[4]

Stieglitz would certainly have liked all his artists to boycott the show, just as in the old days he had marshaled the Photo-Secession to snub the salons of which he disapproved. But times were especially hard for artists, and Stieglitz could not afford to alienate Phillips, who was intending to lend two of his Marins, including the $6,000 watercolor. Nonetheless, Stieglitz did not want O'Keeffe to show any of her stunning new works — including her first canvas of the adobe church in Ranchos de Taos and *Black Cross, New Mexico*, one of the great masterpieces of American modernism — before he had had a chance to exhibit them as the main attractions of his new gallery's first season. Therefore, she lent the museum several older paintings, among them her 1927 night view of the American Radiator Building, a mischievous choice, since the name Alfred Stieglitz appears in it, in red lights, substituted by the artist on a sign that had actually read "Scientific American."

Stieglitz stipulated that Norman and Strand raise the necessary money for his new gallery and that the lease be in their names. Moreover, all contributors should understand that they would have no say in the running of the gallery; Stieglitz was not about to change his anticommercial ways in order to repay their investments. If they weren't pleased at the end of the first three years, when the lease expired, they would have no obligation to renew.

Stieglitz agreed to reward patrons with his own photographs, but he found the whole business distasteful and embarrassing. "You have no idea how it goes against my grain to have anyone called upon to give money 'for me' in days like these," he wrote to Beck Strand on October 24 — Black Thursday, the day on which the financial decline turned into a panic.[5] By then the Strands and Norman had collected commitments of $16,500. Norman herself pledged $1,000 a year for three years. Among the other most generous donors were Strand's father (whose investments on Wall Street had yielded rich returns), Alfred's friend Jacob Dewald, Lee Stieglitz and his family, and Aline Meyer Liebman and her husband.[6] When the stock market crashed, Stieglitz insisted that the patrons not be held to their promises, but no one withdrew his or her support.

By mid-October, Norman and the Strands had rented a corner suite on the seventeenth floor of the just-completed twenty-two-story office building at 509 Madison Avenue, at Fifty-third Street. Bubbling over with excitement, Paul and Beck took the floor plans to Lake George, expecting Stieglitz to be not only enthusiastic but also grateful for their efforts in his behalf. Instead, he took the wind out of their sails by grumpily announcing that he would, in effect, do them the favor of directing the gallery only if the "young ones" would make real contributions of their time to help with the ongoing work. The new gallery would have to be a truly cooperative venture, not "Stieglitz's Room." This demand was, of course, prompted by O'Keeffe's recent revelation that she had resented the amount of time Alfred devoted to his gallery.

The Strands were hurt and angry, Stieglitz self-righteously unyielding. Having reached an impasse, Paul and Beck abruptly left for New York, ready to abandon the project entirely. Stieglitz — incapable of writing a straightforward apology, since he never believed that he had done anything wrong — quickly penned a letter that mollified them sufficiently to retain their commitment but not to remove the residue of bad feeling.

"It seems to me that we never went to town in better condition," Georgia wrote Beck just before they left the lake.[7] They arrived in New York on November 7, in time to attend the launching reception at the Museum of Modern Art the next afternoon.

There was much to do to get Suite 1710 ready for its December 7 opening. It consisted of five rooms: a main gallery, approximately thirty feet deep and eighteen feet wide, which one entered directly from the outside corridor. Four doorless floor-to-ceiling openings led from the large room to smaller ones, two of which would be used as exhibition rooms, a third as Alfred's office, and the fourth as a storage area, in which he would set up his first proper darkroom. (In 1933 one of the small galleries would be converted into a storage room for paintings.) Under O'Keeffe's direction, the cement floors throughout the suite were left uncarpeted and painted gray; all the walls and the ten-foot-high ceilings were white. (At the beginning of the second season O'Keeffe would have the walls of the main gallery painted a luminous gray of her own mixing, though the other galleries remained white. Occasionally, she and Stieglitz would have the main room specially repainted, as for Dove's show in March 1937, when they decided that his work would look best against white.) On the suite's many large windows were shades that rolled up from the bottom, to provide maximum light with minimal glare.

The broadsides issued for each exhibition at Stieglitz's previous venue had stated, "The Intimate Gallery is an American Room." Since the new gallery had three exhibition rooms, Alfred decided to call it An American Place. He wanted people to understand that "509," as he sometimes referred to it, was not a gallery in any usual sense but rather simply a place in which he happened to hang works of art.

Although Stieglitz did not make any formal announcement dedicating An American Place to the Seven Americans, their work would overwhelmingly dominate the gallery's exhibitions during its seventeen seasons under his direction. O'Keeffe, Dove, and Marin — his "Big Three" — would each have a one-person show every year, and Marin would four times have both an exhibition of recent work and a small retrospective. Since there was an average of four or five shows per season, and since one of them was often a group show consisting entirely of, or organized around, the Big Three, there were few slots for other artists. Stieglitz gave only one solo to Demuth (1931) and three to Hartley (1930–31, 1936, and 1937). He mounted two exhibitions of his own photographs (1932 and 1934–35) and one of Paul Strand's (1932), the latter together with paintings on glass by Beck Strand. Five other painters — Helen Torr (Dove's wife, Reds), Stanton Macdonald-Wright, George Grosz, Robert C. Walker (a friend of O'Keeffe's from the Southwest), and William Einstein — and two other photographers, Ansel Adams and Eliot Porter, were each given one show, in some cases sharing the Place (Torr with Dove, Einstein with Adams,

Porter with Demuth). Sometime in the early 1930s, Henwar Rodakiewicz's first experimental film, *Portrait of a Young Man*, was shown at the gallery. Stieglitz grew very fond of Rodakiewicz, whom he would call "an extraordinarily rare soul . . . as sensitive and honest as anyone I ever knew."[8]

Year after year, O'Keeffe's exhibitions drew large crowds, enthusiastic reviews, and enough buyers to guarantee her a comfortable, and eventually even an impressive, income throughout the depressed 1930s. She paid the rent at the Shelton and at her and Stieglitz's subsequent apartments. She also covered all their living expenses, contributed to An American Place, and bought the work of her fellow artists. Stieglitz, whose finances were further shaken by the Depression, was financially dependent upon his wife. "My little capital is shrinking fast," he wrote to Dove in 1931. "And I didn't speculate!! As if living today wasn't the worst kind of speculation for the likes of me."[9]

Marin ran a fairly close second to O'Keeffe. During the 1929–30 season, sales of his work totaled $22,000, of which he gave $3,000 to the gallery. But Dove ran a distant third. By mid-December 1930, he had nearly hit rock bottom. Paul Rosenfeld, his own capital largely wiped out by the crash, had found himself unable to pay for the painting he had reserved at Dove's show that spring. And Duncan Phillips, at whose request Stieglitz had sent five paintings to Washington at the close of the show, still had not made a selection or even offered any money as a deposit. On December 19, Dove wrote to Stieglitz, "Can stick it out for another week and then if neither Phillips nor Paul R. can do anything, the food stops."[10] Stieglitz replied immediately, enclosing his own check for $200 as an advance against money from Phillips. A day or two later Stieglitz received a check from Phillips for $1,000 in payment for the two paintings he had decided to keep. Dove believed that Stieglitz had brought this miracle about by "a will through living your life as an idea that makes things happen."[11]

Until Dove's death, in 1946, Phillips would remain his principal — and exasperating — patron. Every year, when the Phillipses appeared at An American Place for his annual show, they would announce that they were broke — despite maintaining three chauffeurs on their staff and keeping bottles of champagne in the refrigerators in every guest room of their new house, on the outskirts of Washington, for whose land and construction they had paid $1 million in 1930.[12]

After not having bought anything by Dove during 1932, Phillips began the following year by agreeing to buy three Doves for a total of $600, to be paid in twelve monthly installments of $50 each. Stieglitz and Dove accepted the arrangement, which Phillips insisted on calling a subsidy. That year, Stieglitz refused to deduct any money from Phillips's payments to Dove, instead taking paintings for himself and for the Place.

The tiny regular income made a huge difference to Dove and Reds, who were finally able to marry in 1932; the following year they moved to Geneva, New York, where they struggled along as the bank foreclosed on more and more of the family real estate. But the arrangement with Phillips — which he renewed every year, though he rarely provided any guarantee that he would do so — also created new problems, for his payments were often late, requiring tactful reminders from Stieglitz or from Dove himself. Nor could Phillips be counted on to stand by any offer he made. With much justification, Stieglitz wrote to Dove, "I find Phillips absolutely irresponsible — full of good ideas & intentions — but somehow he is like virtually all rich people — they cannot see the poor man's problem nor his position."[13] Too, Phillips's delusion that Dove was on his payroll led the collector and his painter-wife to feel they had the right to make at least one grotesquely impertinent suggestion. In May 1933 Phillips wrote Dove, "The best passage of painting you have ever done is contained in the painting entitled 'The Bessie of New York.'"[14] He then proceeded to say that he would buy the painting if Dove would agree to cut off most of the left half of the canvas, thereby supposedly improving the composition. Of course, Dove refused to do any such thing. With considerable difficulty, he swallowed his outrage.

Although some writers have accused Stieglitz of Machiavellian plotting to keep Dove and Phillips from meeting, the artist seems to have been perfectly content with the nature of what Stieglitz called their "ménage à trois."[15] Dove and the Phillipses would meet only once, at An American Place in April 1936, and while the painter found his patrons in person "much less difficult" than he had expected, he expressed no eagerness to repeat the encounter.

CHAPTER SIXTY·SEVEN

THROUGHOUT THE WINTER of 1929–30, O'Keeffe remained undecided about returning to New Mexico for the coming summer. "It is what
I want to do for my work — and I have been so very well after the summer
out there," she wrote Dorothy Brett early in April. But, she went on to explain, "I couldn't decide until Stieglitz decided — it came quietly — naturally — like the flow of all winter has been . . . He feels it is the thing to
do . . . It is almost as tho Stieglitz makes me a present of myself in the way
he feels about it."[1]

Early in May, O'Keeffe went to Lake George to get the farmhouse
ready for the summer and to plant the garden. While she was there, the
profusion of jack-in-the-pulpits growing in the woods reminded her of her
high school days in Madison, when the art teacher had brought a specimen
to class one day to have the students study its extraordinary construction
and range of colors. By the time she left for the Southwest in mid-June,
O'Keeffe had painted a series of six increasingly abstract, and increasingly
erotic, canvases of the plant as a present for Alfred.

After one of his weekend visits, Georgia wrote to Mabel Luhan, "He is
so nice — I really think I am probably very dumb to go away and leave him
again."[2] The remark was certainly at least partly intended as reassurance
that she had no designs on Tony. Against her better judgment, she had accepted Mabel's invitation to return to Los Gallos. Although Georgia would

enjoy the company of John Marin, Ansel Adams, and Paul and Beck Strand, who would all be staying at the house, she declared Taos "so beautiful — and so poisonous — the only way to live in it is to strictly mind your own business."[3]

For many weeks after his arrival at Lake George on June 11, Stieglitz indulged in "much laziness & sunlight." Of the latter there would be a drought-producing superabundance that summer. Toward the end of July, Alfred reported to Arthur Dove, "Here all is very serene. — No tension of any kind in spite of Wall Street & my mean heart which is kicking up some. Nothing serious but annoying."[4] Enjoying visits from Zoler, Rosenfeld, and Kalonyme, Alfred spent much of the latter part of the summer mounting prints but didn't expose many negatives. Nor was he able to do much printing, for the icy water in his darkroom in the Little House hurt his "rheumatic arms."[5]

"When ever I come back to Stieglitz I always marvel to see again how nice he is," O'Keeffe wrote early in September. "There is something about being with Stieglitz that makes up for the landscape."[6] To celebrate her return, he took her flying over Lake George. But if their reunion was joyous, its effects were not as lasting as the previous year's had been. With Dorothy Norman in the final weeks of her second pregnancy, Alfred became so worried that he was plagued by severe abdominal pains. Around October 1 he finally heard that both mother and newborn son were healthy. Two weeks later, when he and O'Keeffe went to New York for a couple of days to oversee the annual painting of the gallery walls, Alfred was miraculously cured by a visit with Dorothy.

After one last week at the lake, Stieglitz and O'Keeffe returned to New York for the winter. O'Keeffe went somewhat reluctantly, since she would have preferred remaining in blissful solitude to paint. Her decision to accompany Alfred was based in part on her aim of winning him back once and for all. She hoped that with two small children, Norman would have less time for Alfred. But Georgia underestimated Dorothy, who left her children at home with a nurse and resumed her daily visits to the Place a few weeks after it opened its second season with a Marin exhibition, followed over the succeeding months by Hartley, O'Keeffe, Dove, and Demuth shows.

During 1930 Stieglitz began photographing Dorothy, who turned twenty-five that year. Although she was actually quite capable and bold, in his close-ups of her face we see a troubled, shy, and pleading child-woman, who in one picture bites the knuckle of her forefinger. She must have made Stieglitz feel stronger and more needed than he had felt in years. She was eager to play Galatea to his Pygmalion, to hang on every word of his monologues, and to replace O'Keeffe as his twin. Harold Clurman wrote to Stieglitz that conversation with Norman was "like talking to a lake or rather like talking to a mirror in which one didn't see oneself but someone else! . . . She presents no problem, no burden of personality to be dealt with. One can be with her and at the same time alone with oneself."[7]

Wanting to share every aspect of Stieglitz's work, Dorothy spent as much time as possible at the gallery, helping with correspondence, bills, and files. But she understood very well that in order to win his deepest love she would have to prove herself an artist. To that end, she asked Stieglitz to instruct her in the rudiments of photographic technique. At first he let her use his 4 x 5 Graflex, but she found it too heavy to handle comfortably. Because she was afraid to ask her husband to buy her a camera in the depths of the Depression, Alfred bought her a 3¼ x 4¼ Graflex and told her that she could pay him back at her convenience. He advised her to use the smallest possible aperture setting and to make the longest possible exposures. Beyond that she would have to learn through experience. Nor was he much more helpful in the darkroom, where he said developing was a matter of trial and error. Stieglitz was so silly with love that when Norman photographed him, he would begin by sticking out his tongue at her and making funny faces. As if she weren't already trespassing sufficiently on O'Keeffe's territory, she would soon begin making close-ups of flowers.

To get away from Stieglitz in his state of infatuation, O'Keeffe set off for New Mexico in her Ford at the end of April 1931. Refusing to go back to Mabel's, she rented a cottage on Marie Garland's H & M Ranch, in Alcalde. Except for two weeks in June on a pack trip with a group of her new friends, O'Keeffe spent her ten weeks in the Southwest in solitary work and exploration. Almost every day she drove out toward Abiquiu to paint the dramatic landscape of red cliffs and arroyos. "I think I never had a better time painting," she wrote, "and never worked more steadily and never loved the country more."[8]

During May, Stieglitz threw himself into photographing Norman before she left New York for her summer house at Woods Hole, Massachusetts. On June 17, after closing the season with a group show of work by the five painters who had had solos, he went to Lake George with Rosenfeld. Unable to bear his separation from Dorothy, Alfred invited her to visit. Since she had to remain with her husband and children, she suggested in turn that he come to Woods Hole. He arrived on July 7. Of an overnight trip to Boston they then made to see his prints in the Museum of Fine Arts, he marveled, "It was a wonderful day. . . . All of nature, above all the sky, seemed to be singing."[9] He would capture that singing in some of his photographs that summer, the last in which he would make a significant number of *Equivalents*.

One day, while shooting close-ups of Dorothy's face in her garden, Stieglitz looked at her and said, with greater intensity than ever before, "I love you." He then gently coaxed her to call him Alfred. As she finally forced herself to whisper such a forbidden intimacy, he captured her wide-eyed look of wonder on his film. Thereafter, he would call that the Day of Transfiguration, the day on which, he wrote her from Lake George, "you heard the Voice — you saw the Light." He felt he had seen "God's light in your Face" and was ravished.[10]

Intoxicated with his love for Dorothy and hers for him, Alfred ceaselessly sang her praises to everyone in sight and poured out his love in daily letters to her. In one beginning "Oh Dorothy Child," he gushed, "Yes you love me. And I love you. And I know it is no crime. Not before God. Not before right thinking Men and Women."[11]

Alfred and Dorothy managed to convince themselves that their love for each other didn't threaten or even interfere with their marriages but actually enriched them. Norman wrote of that time in her present-tense memoirs, "Each of us loves the core of the rest of our lives. I want to hurt or tear apart nothing. Nor does Stieglitz. One day he says to me, surprisingly almost on the verge of tears: 'Never get divorced.'"[12] Only after his death did Dorothy articulate the great paradox: "He was perhaps the most possessive person I have ever known," she wrote. "Yet the greatness of what he expressed was in terms of how people must be non-possessive."[13]

"Can't leave that man alone too long," O'Keeffe wrote to Henry McBride shortly before she headed east in mid-July, worried about Stieglitz's health and under the impression that he missed her.[14] Once she arrived, it didn't take her long to understand what had been going on during her absence. She wished she had stayed in New Mexico. Fortunately, she had sent to Lake George by express freight a collection of animal skulls and bones that she had picked up in the desert. Since the New Mexican landscape itself is like the exposed, eroding skeleton of the earth, those microcosms helped her to sustain her southwestern elation. Too, in their hardness and clarity they surely represented to O'Keeffe the inner strength that she was trying to cultivate to survive her marital ordeals. In her best-known canvas of that year, she set a cow skull against a background of red, white, and blue — as a play on the idea of the Great American Painting. (It and her other renderings of that skull, which would be the sensations of her next show at An American Place, have become such quintessential American icons that one is dumbfounded to come upon a frieze of bas-relief O'Keeffian cow skulls on the façade of Palladio's sixteenth-century Palazzo Chiericati, in Vicenza.)

Happy about her new paintings, O'Keeffe once again captivated Stieglitz and disarmed him by laughing at his infatuation with Norman, for whom she felt contempt. A few weeks after her return, she wrote to Beck Strand, "We walk and I feel like the top of the world. . . . So — all put together — it seems a pretty good life."[15]

On the other hand, O'Keeffe found Stieglitz family life at Lake George that summer "a bit thick."[16] After her husband's death in 1930, Lee's mistress Amanda Liebman Hoff had demanded that Lee ask Lizzie for a divorce. Although by that time Lee was in love with a third woman, he acceded. Lizzie assented, one of her conditions being that she would keep Red Top, where she was spending the summer of 1931, while Lee and Amanda were on a premature "honeymoon" in Europe. Lizzie would go to Reno that winter, and the lovers would be married on July 23, 1932, more than forty years after they had first met.

Feeling "smothered with green" and bedeviled by Lizzie's four little granddaughters — who enraged O'Keeffe by spying on her while she worked naked in her shanty — the artist drove to York Beach in mid-August with Louis Kalonyme "for a smell of the salt air and a week on the beach," which, she told a southwestern friend, "is the only thing aside from the desert."[17] Five days after she returned to the lake, Alfred set off to spend another few days at Woods Hole.

"I feel fine — really very gay," O'Keeffe bravely told Beck in mid-September, acknowledging that the summer had been "a bit fantastic to say the least."[18] She had decided that after driving Stieglitz to the city on October 7 and helping him to hang the Marin show that would open the season at An American Place, she would return to the lake to work in peace, away from Alfred and Dorothy. She would let him get Dorothy out of his system. In O'Keeffe's absence, Alfred began to take Dorothy to the Shelton to photograph her in the nude — and in bed. Georgia, who drove down from the lake occasionally to show her latest paintings to Alfred in preparation for her show, must have known perfectly well what was going on, for he enjoined her never to appear at the Shelton or the Place without giving him advance warning.

*   *   *

That fall twenty-five-year-old Julien Levy, who, with the encouragement of his friend Marcel Duchamp, was about to open a gallery on the fourth floor of a brownstone at 602 Madison Avenue, asked Stieglitz to lend him some prints for his first exhibition. The gallery would become known for its shows of Surrealist art and of photography by such people as Walker Evans, George Platt Lynes, Man Ray, Henri Cartier-Bresson, Manuel Alvarez Bravo, Berenice Abbott, and Eugène Atget. (It was Levy who had put up most of the money with which Abbott had bought Atget's negatives and prints.)

Levy, who came from an old New York Jewish family and whose father had greatly increased his fortune by building apartment houses on land he owned along Park Avenue and Central Park West, graduated from Harvard in 1927 with a B.A. in art history. After his graduation, he married Mina Loy's daughter Joella and worked for a while at Weyhe's bookstore, where Stieglitz's friend Carl Zigrosser was in charge of the art gallery.

Levy's introduction to photography had not been auspicious. In the summer of 1925 he and a friend had accompanied the friend's mother, who was a student at the Clarence White School of Photography, on White's fatal field trip to Mexico City. Offsetting that baleful episode was the influence of a Harvard professor who delighted in Hollywood movies as works of art. Through that medium Levy become interested in the psychology of vision and spent much of his senior year experimenting with photography.

Having decided that the curtain raiser at his new gallery should be a "Retrospective of American Photography" — to include work by Stieglitz, Steichen, White, Gertrude Käsebier, Annie Brigman, Paul Strand, and Charles Sheeler — Levy made an appointment and went to see Stieglitz. "Salesmanship begins at home," the photographer told him and then went on to explain that since Levy's father was very rich, he should donate $1,000 to An American Place, in return for which he would receive a Stieglitz print that he could lend to his son's show. When promptly approached by Dorothy Norman, the elder Levy gave the money but subsequently declined to lend his print. Finally, Stieglitz sold young Levy an issue of *Camera Work* that contained photogravures of his work and authorized him to frame and hang them.[19]

Stieglitz was much more helpful to Edith Gregor Halpert, owner of the Downtown Gallery. The ambitious and dynamic Russian-born artist had first met painter Samuel Halpert at a meeting of the People's Art Guild. They married in 1918, and through her husband she met Stieglitz. In 1926 she opened Our Gallery on West Thirteenth Street, in Greenwich Village, and a year later changed its name to the Downtown Gallery. In rooms furnished comfortably with American antiques and adorned with examples of American folk art, Halpert showed work by such artists as Max Weber, William Zorach, Charles Sheeler, and Stuart Davis.[20]

In the spring of 1931, Stieglitz and O'Keeffe sorted through the hundreds of paintings he had in storage at the Lincoln Warehouse and decided to consign some of the surplus to Halpert. When Charles Daniel closed his gallery the following year, Halpert inherited many of the artists he had represented, and Stieglitz welcomed her as Daniel's successor.[21] He was also relieved when Marsden Hartley, who felt slighted in favor of O'Keeffe and Marin, enlisted Halpert to be his primary dealer. Halpert was certainly in a position to help her artists, for her most devoted customer was Abby Aldrich Rockefeller, who bought hundreds of works for the Museum of Modern Art.

Stieglitz had not shown his own photographs publicly since 1925, but he was so excited about his recent work that he decided during the fall of 1931 to have an exhibition at An American Place that winter. The most important images in that show would be of New York buildings, shot from the windows of the Shelton and An American Place. Many of the pictures (some of which are reminiscent of early Coburns and Sheelers) chronicle the construction boom then under way in midtown Manhattan. During 1930 and 1931, Stieglitz photographed the lightning-bolt-inspired RCA Victor Building (now the General Electric Building) and the classic Art Deco Waldorf-Astoria Hotel rising within two blocks of the Shelton. Farther away, beyond the spires of St. Patrick's Cathedral, work had begun on the immense Rockefeller Center complex. From his gallery's windows Stieglitz could gaze over the roofs of a jumble of brownstones to the towers of the hotels — the boxy Savoy-Plaza (on the site of the hotel in which he and Emmy had lived), the Neuschwanstein-pinnacled Sherry-Netherland, and the mansarded Pierre — that had sprung up along Fifth Avenue in the late twenties. In one photograph of that view, the old houses seem like trampled peasants cowering beside immense robber barons.

Harold Clurman would eloquently and accurately write that the city shown in Stieglitz's prints of the 1930s had been "built up now to a pyramidal splendor, crowded, immutable, and terribly, terribly deathlike. . . . It is a city in which man has almost completely disappeared; despite all its metallic precision, it is like an enormous graven image of some very ancient civilization in which all signs of humanity have withered and everything is wrapped in silence."[22] Stieglitz's photographs depict the nightmare of demonic, soulless capitalism run amok. Their factual documentation of

New York architecture was incidental. When the director of the Museum of the City of New York asked whether the photographer might be willing to donate second-quality prints to its reference collection, he was given a tirade.[23]

Notwithstanding second thoughts and worries about expense on Stieglitz's part, his exhibition of 127 photographs spanning forty years opened on February 15, 1932, and ran through March 5. In the main room were old and new photographs of New York. The second gallery was filled with *Equivalents* and studies of Lake George trees and grasses, all presided over by portraits of Dorothy Norman. (Presumably at O'Keeffe's insistence, Stieglitz did not include any nudes of his lover.) In the third gallery were recent portraits of O'Keeffe and of male friends such as Marin, Demuth, Hartley, Anderson, Seligmann, Frank, and Rosenfeld.

On his handwritten announcement Stieglitz claimed that the exhibition would be "Open Continuously Day & Night." But not even he could be on the bridge twenty-four hours a day. One afternoon he treated himself to a performance of *Tristan und Isolde*, during which O'Keeffe stayed at the Place. She felt that the gallery was "the most beautiful now that it has been at all — the rooms as a whole are more severe — more clear in feeling — and . . . as you walk down the length of each wall and look closely at each print — it is as though a breath is caught . . . I am glad he is showing them but there is something about it all that makes me very sad."[24] Because of his "distaste for showing publicly" and his "knowledge that all but the fewest were still blind to a photograph," Stieglitz "vowed religiously" (as he later wrote) that he would never have another exhibition of his work.[25]

As An American Place approached the end of its third season, and thus also of its original subsidy, Dorothy Norman set about raising a new rent fund. Her strategy, an article in the *Herald Tribune* explained, was to solicit many small donations rather than a few large ones, since it seemed that people of modest means were "more willing than the rich to support a gallery . . . described as being thirty years ahead of its time."[26] Norman's diligence in writing an avalanche of letters and making a flurry of visits to potential donors was a greater success than Alfred had dared to hope. Moreover, she managed to get the landlord to lower the rent considerably.

Stieglitz had given Dorothy permission to mount her campaign on conditions similar to those he had laid down in 1929, though now the lease would be solely in her name. He would continue his complicated, yet fair and generous, system of finances, based primarily on each artist's needs. If the artist was doing well, Stieglitz would usually deduct 20 percent from his or her sales for the "Dorothy Norman Rent Fund," which covered not only rent but all the expenses of maintaining the gallery. He generally took for himself one work from each show. If he subsequently sold a work he owned, he might divide the money received between his own account and that of the rent fund, or he might give a cut to the artist.

If the Strands played no rôle in the second drive to raise money for An American Place, one reason was that Norman didn't like them. Undoubtedly envious of Beck's former intimacy and continuing friendship with Stieglitz, Dorothy despised her as "coarse" and laughed at her imitation of O'Keeffe's mannerisms and style of dress. As for Paul, she felt that his "great weakness lay in his being by nature a follower rather than a leader" and that his "more ridiculous performances were due to his following the letter, not the spirit, of Stieglitz's fight for workmanship and the respect of photography." Norman would tell Nancy Newhall that "the Strands were her best teachers and therefore her best friends: they showed her exactly what *not* to do."[27]

In what he admitted was a "diabolical" attempt to expose their failings, Stieglitz mounted a joint exhibition of Paul's photographs and Beck's paintings on glass at An American Place in April and May 1932.[28] Even he acknowledged that Paul's photographs of the Gaspé Peninsula and of Colorado and New Mexico, where the Strands had spent the past two summers, were magnificent. Indeed, he believed that the Gaspé series was the best work Paul had done since the teens. Nevertheless, he found plenty to criticize. He was angry because Paul had come to feel that in the midst of the Depression, a purely aesthetic approach to photography was socially irresponsible — a case of fiddling while Rome was burning.

The exhibition marked the end of their friendship. When the show closed, Paul went to the Place and silently handed back his key to the gallery.[29] Many years later he would write, "The day I walked into the Photo-Secession in 1907 was a great moment in my life . . . but the day I walked out of An American Place in 1932 was not less good. It was fresh air and personal liberation from something that had become, for me at least, second-rate, corrupt, meaningless."[30]

That year Paul would part ways not only with Stieglitz but also with Beck. At the end of their third consecutive summer in the Southwest, she returned to New York when Paul left for Mexico. They would get a divorce the following year, and in 1937 Beck, who continued painting on glass, would marry a wealthy New Mexican rancher named Bill James.

While staying at Mabel Luhan's, Paul had met the Mexican composer

Carlos Chávez, conductor of the Mexican Symphony Orchestra and director of the National Conservatory of Music. Chávez used his influence to have Strand appointed chief of photography and cinematography for the leftist government's Secretariat of Education. In that capacity, he would spend a year making a social realist film entitled *The Wave*, re-creating and dramatizing a strike by exploited fishermen in a town on the Gulf Coast.[31] Newhall would recount that years later "the mere recollection" of the film "could send Stieglitz off into gales of laughter" as he exclaimed, "Those men in the white hats!"[32]

In 1934 Strand returned to New York, where he became very involved with the Group Theatre, founded by Harold Clurman, Cheryl Crawford, and Lee Strasberg three years earlier. Strand spent two months in Moscow with Clurman and Crawford during the summer of 1935. Later that year, he joined with photographer-cinematographers Leo Hurwitz and Ralph Steiner and film critic Pare Lorentz to make a documentary about the Dust Bowl, *The Plow That Broke the Plains,* for the U.S. Resettlement Administration. Strand, who remarried in 1936, would remain primarily involved with films until 1943. The next year O'Keeffe commented in a letter, "Stieglitz is mad at Strand now so not very fair to him."[33] They would never make up, but after a Museum of Modern Art retrospective in 1945, Strand would resume his glorious career in photography.

CHAPTER SIXTY·EIGHT

∽

IN MAY 1932 the Modern inaugurated its new home, an old five-story house at 11 West Fifty third Street, a block and a half away from An American Place, with the exhibition Murals by American Painters and Photographers, organized by recent Harvard graduate Lincoln Kirstein and his friend Julien Levy. The show — the first at the museum to include photographs — materialized in response to widespread complaints that too many commissions to decorate the walls of new American buildings were going to Mexican muralists, led by Diego Rivera, to whom the Modern had given a one-man show in the fall of the previous year.

Fifty-three painters and twelve photographers (including Berenice Abbott, Charles Sheeler, and Edward Steichen) were invited to enter a small study for "a horizontal composition in three parts," one section of which was "to be carried through to completion" on a larger panel. Since the subject was to be "some aspect of 'The Post-War World,'" it seems odd that the organizers were surprised when several artists followed Rivera's example and submitted entries that were militantly leftist. O'Keeffe was delighted to be one of the two women among the invited painters; she prepared three panels of New York buildings painted in a cubo-futuristic or constructivistic style and embellished with incongruous floating gardenias.

In 1926 a critic had written of O'Keeffe, "What is the matter with our architects and interior decorators that they have not singled her out as THE person to design wall panels and decorations?"[1] Although she had been eager to receive such a commission, no one had taken the hint. Within the context of the Modern show, in which even many of the less politicized murals were depressingly sociological or industrial, her entry was among the most decorative. Partly because of that circumstance, and partly as a result of conversations between Edith Halpert and Radio City Music Hall's interior designer, Donald Deskey, O'Keeffe was offered a $1,500 contract to paint the walls and ceiling of the powder room on the second mezzanine of the theater, scheduled to open at the end of the year. Without saying a word to Stieglitz, she signed the contract.

When he learned what she had done, he was furious. He hated the very idea of Radio City and of Rockefeller Center, which he condemned as a monument to the Rockefellers' greed. How dare they spend millions on such a project, he ranted, when the trustees of the Modern claimed they couldn't afford a few hundred dollars for a Dove painting? He insisted that the Rockefellers were already harming the arts in America through the museum's malign influence, and now they were exploiting artists for pittances.

Furthermore, Stieglitz argued that the contract meant economic suicide for O'Keeffe, whose finest and largest paintings — rarely more than four feet high or wide — were then selling for several thousand dollars. In February, for instance, the Whitney Museum of American Art (which had opened in 1931) bought two of her canvases, one for nearly $2,500 (discounted from $3,500) and the other for nearly $3,500 (reduced from $4,800). Now O'Keeffe had agreed to paint hundreds of square feet, in a room whose floor measured about eighteen by twenty feet, for $1,500. Designing and executing the mural would surely occupy her for most of the summer and fall, the seasons when she usually produced most of her paintings for her annual shows at An American Place. Those shows provided not only the income on which they lived but also underwrote a good part of the gallery's expenses. Finally, Stieglitz took it as a personal betrayal that O'Keeffe had signed the contract without consulting him.

He stormed into Deskey's office, insisted that he was O'Keeffe's exclusive agent, and declared that without his approval the contract was invalid. Deskey retorted that it was perfectly legal and binding. Stieglitz left in a huff, and we must imagine a stormy night in Suite 3003 of the Shelton, for O'Keeffe was absolutely determined to do the mural. When he returned to Deskey's office the next day, Stieglitz blustered that she was "a child and not responsible for her actions."[2] In order to protect her prices, he offered to waive her fee entirely, as long as she was reimbursed for the expenses she would incur, which he estimated at $5,000. Of course, Deskey remained adamant. Stieglitz was flabbergasted at what he saw as the designer's unreasonableness.

Right up until the very last minute before she would have set out from Lake George, where she had settled in around May 15 for a few weeks of solitude, O'Keeffe was uncertain about whether to go to New Mexico for the summer. "I am divided between my man and a life with him — and something of the outdoors . . . that is in my blood," she wrote that spring.[3] She decided to stay, both because she was apprehensive about leaving Stieglitz with Dorothy and because she wanted to be able to drive down from the lake to see her room at Radio City as it approached completion. Her decision may have been clinched by the certainty that neither Lee nor Lizzie would be at the lake that summer.

Soon after Stieglitz arrived at the Hill on June 23, three of his new disciples appeared for extended stays. Of them Cary Ross, whom Stieglitz later characterized as "a fine refined quiet capable young man — very sympathetic," would remain closest and most loyal over the coming years.[4] From a wealthy family in Knoxville, Tennessee, Ross was then in his late twenties. After graduating from Yale in 1925, he had studied medicine for a year or two at Johns Hopkins and had then gone to Paris, where he befriended Ernest Hemingway and Scott and Zelda Fitzgerald. In 1929 Ross began working at the Museum of Modern Art, without pay, as Alfred Barr's assistant. One of his colleagues at the museum recalled, "He was as brilliant a conversationalist as I have ever known. He was a man to do odds and ends in an intelligent way, to fill in, and he had ideas about presentation of exhibits."[5] Ross also had literary aspirations of his own. In 1932 Stieglitz issued some of his writings in pamphlet form and the following year published his translation of excerpts from Rilke's *Letters to a Young Poet*.

Walker Evans's 1932 photograph of Ross's Bauhaus-austere bedroom shows identical reproductions of a Picasso hanging above chrome-framed twin beds. Whether this arrangement was the result of sophisticated wit or of neurosis is unclear; both seem to have figured in Ross's psychology. In Stieglitz's portrait from that same year, Ross, wearing a V-necked sweater and with a neatly barbered flounce of straight brown hair, fixes a troubled gaze directly on the camera. Indeed, he had already made at least one attempt at suicide, and some of his colleagues feared that he might be schizophrenic.

Another of the faithful in attendance that summer was forty-nine-year-old Ralph Flint, a bald and stooping painter who wrote art criticism for the *Christian Science Monitor* and was an editor of *The Art News*. The third member of the triumvirate was Frederick J. Ringel, a swarthy, weasel-faced writer in whose book *America as Americans See It*, published that year, there was a chapter on photography written by Edward Steichen.

These three visitors were assigned two impossible tasks by Alfred — to whom they referred, with reverence that one hopes was at least partly mock, as the Master. The first was to persuade O'Keeffe to give up her Radio City project. The second was to convince her that she should recognize Stieglitz's love for Dorothy Norman as an enrichment of her own life and that she should therefore develop a friendship with her. O'Keeffe simply laughed at the dour trio, whom she called the Happiness Boys. But her laughter was forced, since she had finally come to fear that she was losing Stieglitz to Norman. The rage and fear that she was unable to express turned inward and filled her with depression as she faced the prospect of divorce. Although she did not refer directly to her feelings in letters from this time, after the death of her brother, Alexius, in 1930, she had written to her widowed sister-in-law, "All this happening to you makes me feel how utterly empty all my living would be without my Stieglitz."[6]

Early in August — depressed by her marital woes, exasperated by her tormentors on the Hill, and no doubt inspired by the photographs Strand had exhibited in the spring — O'Keeffe took off for the Gaspé Peninsula with Alfred's niece Georgia Engelhard, herself an aspiring painter. O'Keeffe, who painted many fine canvases of the region's white barns and wooden crosses, wrote Dorothy Brett that she considered the Gaspé "very good country for painting . . . quite perfect if it had New Mexico sun."[7] Unfortunately, it lacked more than warmth. Because the two Georgias had trouble finding good food and comfortable places to sleep, they were soon so hungry and tired that they couldn't paint and decided to return to Lake George.

Meanwhile, Stieglitz was very worried about Dorothy, who had developed a persistent low-grade fever and sore throat and felt generally debilitated. That summer she would have an operation in Boston to remove her adenoids, but she recognized that the causes of her condition were more psychological than physiological. On the one hand, she was deeply in love with Stieglitz; on the other, she was committed to her marriage, despite her husband's severe emotional problems. They would not get a divorce until 1953.

Stieglitz reported to Dove in August that his heart had been "on a rampage the last weeks."[8] Consequently, it was a strain for him to carry his 8 x 10 camera; he was nevertheless lugging it up and down the hillside to photograph grasses and trees. One of his close-ups of a dying poplar tree is animated by an upward-sweeping dynamism reminiscent of the van Gogh landscape with cypresses that he had published in *Camera Work* in 1913.

Late in April, Stieglitz had received the terrible news that Hart Crane had committed suicide by jumping overboard from a ship bound for New York from Mexico, where he had spent most of a year on a Guggenheim Fellowship. During the first week of August word followed that sixty-four-year-old Alfred Maurer had hanged himself. Even though his recent Cubist-inspired still lifes, male heads, and studies of emaciated women were the strongest work of his career, his annual exhibitions at Weyhe's bookstore had been ignored. Stieglitz wanted to mount a memorial show, but since Maurer's family insisted on what he considered unrealistically high prices, he abandoned the project.

Paul Rosenfeld finally managed to persuade Stieglitz to yield, with something approximating grace, to O'Keeffe's desire to paint her mural at Radio City. But when they went to New York late in September to check on the progress of her room, which she was planning to emblazon with white flowers, she herself began to waver. Construction was so far behind schedule that she decided to undertake the project only if the opening date, set for December 27, was postponed a month. "I can't paint a room that isn't built," she wrote to Dorothy Brett, "and if the time between the building and the opening isn't long enough I can't do it either."[9]

O'Keeffe felt that even under the best of circumstances "experimenting so publicly is a bit precarious in every way."[10] The problem was that because she would have to paint not only curving walls punctuated with nine mirrors but also a domed ceiling, she would have to work in situ. Stuart Davis, who had been commissioned to paint a mural for the men's lounge of the theater, had a much easier job. Since his painting was to cover an unbroken flat surface, he was able to complete his eleven-by-seventeen-foot canvas, which he called *Men Without Women*, in the peace and privacy of Provincetown that fall and then send it to New York to be installed. O'Keeffe, however, couldn't begin work until the plaster on the walls and ceiling of the powder room had dried thoroughly.

On a return visit to New York in October, during which she found Radio City "a mad house," O'Keeffe wrote a friend, "I think I'll go back to the country tomorrow and let someone else paint the room on the wet plaster."[11] But the management would not release her from her contract. In any case, O'Keeffe still had her heart set on the project and continued to hope that the opening would be postponed. She made several more trips to the city during October and early November, each time expecting to get to work at last. With each disappointment, her tension mounted. Of course, if she had been happy in her marriage she would probably have been more able to maintain her equilibrium.

Finally, with only six weeks left before the unchanged opening date, O'Keeffe was told the room was ready. On the morning of November 16, the day after her forty-fifth birthday, she went to Radio City to begin work, terribly nervous about not having enough time to do the job properly. Accompanied by Donald Deskey and the assistant who had been assigned to her, she finally saw the walls of her room covered with gessoed canvas. But when she noticed that in one corner it was coming loose, she became quite upset. She simply couldn't begin unless she felt absolutely confident of stable conditions. Deskey promised to have the flap reattached at once and assured her that there would be no further problems. After lunch, however, O'Keeffe saw yet more canvas peeling away from the inadequately dried plaster. She yelled at Deskey, then burst into tears and ran out of the building.

The next day Stieglitz called Deskey and informed him that O'Keeffe was having a nervous breakdown. He threatened that unless the contract was immediately canceled, he would sue the Radio City Commission for criminal negligence. Deskey capitulated and contacted Edith Halpert, who arranged for Yasuo Kuniyoshi, one of the stars of her gallery, to paint the powder room. Kuniyoshi, whose family had immigrated to America from Japan in 1906, when he was thirteen, was best known for his faux naïf genre scenes. Nevertheless, he rose to the occasion and covered the powder room walls with O'Keeffe-like white flowers.

O'Keeffe retreated to Lake George and spent most of her time there reading, wrapped in a blanket on a couch by a window. Disturbing symptoms appeared gradually. She became short of breath, experienced pains in her chest, and had trouble speaking. Severely depressed, she began to suffer terrible headaches, felt tired all the time, and was subject to fits of weeping. She lost her appetite and slept very badly. Noise bothered her so much that she couldn't even bear to listen to music. After she returned to New York around December 10 to be examined by Lee, she found that she couldn't walk anywhere in the city without succumbing to terrible feelings of panic.

Lee diagnosed her condition as shock and prescribed extended bed rest. Four days before Christmas she moved into her sister Anita's Park Avenue apartment, where she could have a room of her own and be pampered around the clock. (Already shaken by Georgia's crisis, the Stieglitzes were further grieved by the death of Julius's wife, Anny, on Christmas Day.) O'Keeffe took no part in hanging her annual show at An American Place, which opened on January 7 and featured her well-received paintings of Gaspé barns and crosses. In mid-January 1933 Stieglitz wrote to Dove, "Georgia is very very sick & I am really worried more than I dare admit."[12]

On February 1 she was admitted to fashionable Doctors Hospital, on East Eighty-fifth Street. Around that time she told a friend that her problem was "an irregular heart that seems to be quieting down a bit now — is pretty good while in bed — by inches and minutes I begin to try to get up."[13] But at the hospital she was diagnosed as suffering from "psychoneurosis." Once a week, Alfred, who attributed her psychological problems primarily to menopause, was allowed to pay her a ten-minute visit.[14]

Since Stieglitz extended O'Keeffe's show until mid-March, she was able to see it shortly before it closed, on one of her first outings from the hospital. As soon as she was discharged, toward the end of the month, she sailed for Bermuda with her friend Marjorie Content and Content's daughter, Sue Loeb, who was on vacation from college. A warm, vibrant, and cultivated woman who had run an avant-garde bookstore and enjoyed making costumes and props for Village theaters, Marjorie had been married during the teens and twenties to Harold Loeb, the editor of *Broom*, and had recently separated from her third husband. She had recently spent several summers photographing at the Taos Pueblo for the Bureau of Indian Affairs; while in New Mexico she met O'Keeffe. They continued their friendship in New York, where Marjorie's stockbroker father had bought her a comfortable house on West Tenth Street.

In the fall of 1932 Dorothy Norman had shown Stieglitz her blank-verse poems about God, religion, art, love, and jealousy. He was so besotted that he claimed he was as excited by his first reading of them as he had been by his first encounters with the work of Marin and O'Keeffe. When he failed to find a publisher for the poems, he decided that they should be issued by An American Place, which had, in 1931, published a volume of Marin's letters, edited by Herbert Seligmann.

Norman's book, entitled *Dualities* and dedicated to "Alfred Stieglitz and the spirit of An American Place," appeared in March 1933. Four hundred numbered copies of the collection of ninety-one poems were printed on fine paper. The first thirty copies included an original print of a Stieglitz portrait of the author.

Norman wisely included a disclaimer: "These expressions were not written down with any desire that they should be regarded as Poetry." One paean, "The Purity of Alfred Stieglitz: White Disc Against Any Color," rhapsodized about their "untouchable" lines converging where truth and ecstasy are to be found. We hardly dare to imagine what Georgia's reaction must have been to "O'Keeffe — Neo-Primitive Iconographer," if she could even bring herself to read it.

The publication of Norman's book effectively marked the end of her romance with Stieglitz. Adept though he was at representing his every action as beneficial to all, he found himself forced to acknowledge that the affair had done much to precipitate O'Keeffe's breakdown. Badly frightened, he backed off. Norman would remain extremely important to him and would continue to see him almost daily, but thereafter they were friends, not lovers.

In the spring of 1933 Stieglitz decided that he could no longer afford to pay for the storage of his large collection of works of art at the Lincoln Warehouse, especially since the smallest of the three exhibition rooms at An American Place could easily be converted to house the collection. Under the direction of Cary Ross and Dorothy Norman, Emil Zoler (who now came in only on Saturdays) installed shelves and painting racks. During the process of sorting and packing the works in the warehouse, Stieglitz resolved to rid himself of many photographs he had collected while editing *Camera Notes* and *Camera Work*. Because he had come to despise Pictorialism, had long since fallen out with many of the photographers, and had sadly abandoned his hopes for a museum of photography in which such a collection could be "of living significance," he thought about destroying most of the prints — which, he estimated, had cost him about $15,000 to assemble and store.

Stieglitz certainly wasn't willing to present the collection to the Metropolitan Museum of Art, for to do so would suggest both that he felt the museum's attitude toward photography made it worthy of such a gift and that he deemed those prints worthy to represent photography in the museum. Instead, he mentioned his cathartic intention to Carl Zigrosser, who once again, as in 1923, contacted the Met. Since William Ivins was then in Europe, his assistant went immediately to An American Place, where Stieglitz said he would allow her to salvage what he was discarding, as long as the prints were in no way regarded as a gift from him. The museum could have the collection "without any restrictions of any kind provided it would be called for within twenty-four hours."[16] The next day a truck arrived to pick up 418 prints by about fifty photographers. Stieglitz kept only a small number of images that still pleased him, by such photographers as J. Craig Annan, Julia Margaret Cameron, F. H. Evans, Hill and Adamson, Steichen, and Strand. He also retained most portraits of himself and of Kitty — but gave away all the portraits of Emmy and pictures in which she appeared.

While O'Keeffe was in Bermuda, Stieglitz received an unannounced visit from a scraggly-bearded, gangly, and disarmingly sweet thirty-one-year-old San Francisco photographer named Ansel Adams, of whom he may or may not have remembered hearing O'Keeffe speak as a fellow guest at Mabel Luhan's in 1929 and 1930. During the second of those summers, Adams met Paul Strand and was so impressed by his work that he decided to give up his hopes of a career in music to devote himself entirely to photography. In 1932 Adams and six fellow Californians, including Edward Weston and Imogen Cunningham, formed Group f.64, whose name referred to a very small aperture setting yielding sharp focus at near and far range simultaneously. The three principal purposes of the group were to exhibit the work of contemporary West Coast photographers (who were generally neglected by eastern editors, curators, and dealers), to combat Pictorialism (an egregious variety of which was represented by the kitschy prints of nude witches and Madonnas by the group's bête noire, Los Angeles photographer William Mortensen), and to promote sharp-focus images printed on glossy silver papers that would reveal every detail that was in a negative.

Although Adams had already made many beautiful images of Yosemite and the Sierra Nevada, much of his work from the early 1930s would not be recognized by the majority of his current admirers. In his portfolio when he set out for New York in 1933 were probably prints of the Golden Gate before the bridge was built, a pine cone among fallen eucalyptus leaves, thistles growing at the base of a wall onto which boards had been nailed every which way, and even a rather cubistic shot of a San Francisco factory building.

As soon as he arrived in New York, on the morning of March 28, Adams made his way to An American Place with his portfolio and a letter of introduction from his friend and patroness Rosalie Stern, one of Eugene Meyer's older sisters. When Adams introduced himself and presented Mrs. Stern's letter, Stieglitz snapped, "All this person's got is money, and if this Depression keeps on much longer she's not going to have that." When the offended Adams said that he would just like to show Stieglitz his prints, the latter curtly told him to come back at two-thirty.

Infuriated by such rudeness, Adams nevertheless returned at the appointed time. Stieglitz sat at his desk and opened the portfolio. Since there was no other chair, Adams sat on the adjacent radiator, which became increasingly uncomfortable as the steam came up. In unbroken silence, Stieglitz looked very carefully at all of Adams's prints, then put them back in the portfolio and tied it up. Suddenly, and still without saying a word, he reopened the portfolio and studied all the prints a second time. When he had finished, he turned to Adams and said, "You are always welcome here." In some of his retellings of the episode, Adams claimed that Stieglitz remarked, "Some of the most beautiful photographs I've ever seen." But in the definitive text of his autobiography he has Stieglitz say simply that the photographs were "what he called 'straight' and seen with 'sensitivity.'"[17]

That falls short of the praise Stieglitz lavished in September on O'Keeffe's friend Carl Van Vechten, who had begun making portrait photographs as an amateur the previous year. "If I wore a hat I would take it off before your photographs," Stieglitz saluted. "They are damn swell. A joy. You are certainly a photographer. There are but few."[18] Over the course of the next thirty years, until his death in 1964, Van Vechten would make portraits of hundreds of luminaries in all the arts, with a special emphasis on African Americans, from Langston Hughes and Bessie Smith to Leontyne Price and Alvin Ailey.

Stieglitz did not offer a show to either Adams or Van Vechten. Instead, Adams's first New York exhibition would open in November at the Delphic Studios, on Fifth Avenue at Fifty-seventh Street. Alma Reed had established that gallery a few years earlier to show the work of her lover, the Mexican painter and muralist José Clemente Orozco, who had left his wife to follow Reed to New York. Having been tremendously impressed by Edward Weston's photographs, Reed exhibited them in New York and opened her gallery to other photographers.

That fall, Adams would tell Paul Strand that he had been "amazed" and inspired by the power of Stieglitz's personality.[19] In fact, Adams was so struck by Stieglitz's dual accomplishments as photographer and impresario that when he got back to San Francisco he rented a studio, in part of which he decided to open a gallery for photography and painting. He wanted to devote the first exhibition entirely to Stieglitz's work, but Alfred declined to send the requested twenty-five prints, explaining that "of the things I'd want the world to see there are rarely 'duplicates.'"[20] He was simply not willing to submit his unique prints and their delicate white metal frames to the ordeal of shipping and handling. Stieglitz and Adams did, however, initiate a voluminous correspondence that they would carry on until Stieglitz's death.

O'Keeffe arrived back in New York from Bermuda on May 19, improved but far from well. The next morning Stieglitz accompanied her to Lake George to get her settled on the Hill. After returning to New York on the evening of the twenty-third, he was distraught to learn that Henri Matisse, together with the philosopher and educator John Dewey, had stopped by An American Place while he was away. Because he had not missed a single day at the gallery all season, Stieglitz was both annoyed and amused to have such "tough luck." Matisse had arrived in America on May 11 and spent most of his two-week stay in Pennsylvania, installing a mural at the Barnes Foundation. Abraham Walkowitz, who had once again rejoined the faithful, was tending the gallery when Matisse appeared. "Funny," Stieglitz wrote to Dove. "But all right if there can be any right in such a situation when I'm not here."[21] At least an articulate artist had been there to play host, not the taciturn Zoler.

After a two-person show of the Doves (he never again exhibited the work of the disappointed Reds, whose hopes were raised by this duet), Stieglitz ended the season with a group of early works by Dove, Marin, and O'Keeffe. About June 20 he joined Georgia at the lake for the summer — the only extended period they spent together between September 1932 and January 1935. A few days after his arrival, Stieglitz lamented to Dove, "Georgia's condition is pathetic. I'm certainly far beyond my depths. . . . I see no light of any kind. I dare not hope nor dare I despair. — At times I feel like a murderer. There is Kitty. Now there is Georgia."[22]

Stieglitz was reconciled to the necessity of a quiet summer, since everyone and everything still seemed to get on O'Keeffe's nerves. Not until late August did they invite Louis Kalonyme and Donald Davidson, whose company Georgia always enjoyed. "I have done nothing all summer but wait for myself to be myself again," she told a friend in October.[23] She spent most of her time reading, sewing, walking, lying in the sun, and driving her new Ford V-8 roadster, against whose gleaming spare-tire cover Stieglitz photographed her hands. Early in the summer she had some thoughts of going out to New Mexico late in July, but she soon realized that she was not yet strong enough for such a trip.

That summer and fall O'Keeffe didn't even try to paint, though she made one drawing that she considered "very good." "Nothing seems worth being put down — I seem to have nothing to say," she admitted in October.[24] About that time Stieglitz confided to Ansel Adams that he feared she might "never paint again."[25] The year was almost equally unproductive for him; he suffered from a hernia during the summer, making it more difficult than ever for him to carry his large camera. In spite of his pain, he continued to make studies of grasses and trees and embarked on a series of views of the farmhouse and the Little House. But he would not photograph at all in New York during that fall, winter, and spring. "It's the first time in 50 years that a winter has passed by without my making a single exposure," he wrote to Adams in June 1934. "And there was no printing either."[26]

Stieglitz returned to the city at the end of September 1933 and opened An American Place with a Marin retrospective, of which he exclaimed to Adams, "This Exhibition is perhaps the apex of my lifework."[27] Throughout the fall, O'Keeffe — "still a very sick woman," according to Alfred — would remain at the farmhouse, where he would spend a few weekends with her. Late in November, feeling much better, she went to New York to see the Marin show and a Brancusi exhibition. "The principal things about it all for me were that I could again walk the street a little without fear of losing my mind — even sat through dinner in a room with music one night," she told Strand.[28] She went to the first half of a concert with Paul Rosenfeld, paid a visit to Florine Stettheimer's studio to see her recent paintings, and enjoyed seeing Duchamp and Demuth.

One of the purposes of her trip was to meet with Jean Toomer, whose wife, writer Margery Latimer, had died giving birth to a daughter in August 1932, after only ten months of marriage. Toomer, who was still involved in the Gurdjieff movement, was in New York during October and November 1933 to collect Latimer's letters for publication. O'Keeffe had been a friend of Margery's and had promised Toomer to give him all the letters she had received from her. When she saw Jean, she invited him to Lake George, where she would return in a few days. He could stay to work for as long as he liked.

Toomer arrived at the end of the first week of December, finding O'Keeffe in bed with a cold. "For the first ten days I was sort of in the house by myself," he wrote Stieglitz.[29] Then O'Keeffe began to emerge, gradually, from her cocoon. Toomer, appropriately writing an essay about the photographer, typed away upstairs all day. But in the evening he and Georgia would sit together in front of the living room fireplace and talk or read. By December 21 he was able to report to Stieglitz that he was astonished by O'Keeffe's dramatic improvement. The fact of the matter was that O'Keeffe was falling in love with Toomer, whom she described in a letter to Strand as "an unusually beautiful — clear person — with a very amusing streak in him — lots of real fun."[30]

Toomer's revivifying magic worked as well for Stieglitz as it did for O'Keeffe. When Alfred arrived on the evening of the twenty-third to spend Christmas at the farmhouse, Georgia thought he "looked bad." But he was pleased to see her so healthy and happy, and he enjoyed the quiet that prevailed within the cozy house as snow fell outside. "It was all sort of still — but so alive," wrote O'Keeffe. By the time Alfred left for the city on the morning of the twenty-sixth, he was "looking like a different person."[31] Six days later he celebrated his seventieth birthday with friends, including Dorothy Norman, in New York.

"You seem to have given me a strangely beautiful feeling of balance," O'Keeffe would acknowledge to Toomer. "I seem to have come to life in such a quiet surprising fashion — as tho I am not sick any more — Everything in me begins to move and I feel like a really positive thing again."[32] Stieglitz apparently didn't mind that Georgia's recovery owed much to the erotic attraction between her and Toomer, as he must have sensed. During the weeks following Jean's departure on December 30, she would dispatch to him a stream of passionate letters, in one of which she declared, "I wish so hotly to feel you hold me very very tight." It seems, however, that although they expressed their affection physically, they did not have intercourse. In one of his letters to O'Keeffe, Toomer sent his greetings to "the bundling-bed," referring to the early New England custom of allowing an engaged couple to keep warm on cold nights while they were courting by lying fully clothed in a bed with a board between them.

In love though she was, O'Keeffe certainly had no intention of marrying Toomer. "I want you — sometimes terribly," she wrote him soon after he had left. "But I like it that I am quite apart from you . . . for now I need it that way." He had given her a miraculous gift, but now she knew that she needed to be alone. "If the past year or two or three has taught me anything," she told him, "it is that my plot of earth must be tended with absurd care — By myself first — and if second by someone else it must be with absolute trust."[33] After what she had gone through as a result of Stieglitz's involvement with Dorothy, O'Keeffe was determined that she would never again find herself in such a vulnerable situation. "[I am] moving it seems — more and more toward a kind of aloneness," she told Toomer in March, "not because I wish it so but because there seems no other way."[34] Stieglitz's unfaithfulness had pierced her heart, and she would never fully recover.

*   *   *

Late in January 1934, O'Keeffe went to New York for nearly two weeks to hang her show at An American Place. Since she had not made any paintings during 1933, the exhibition of forty-four canvases that opened on January 29 and ran until the end of March was a retrospective of work she had done between 1915 and 1929.

One of the several thousand visitors to the exhibition was Zelda Fitzgerald, who had taken up painting as a hobby in 1924 but had since become quite serious about it. *Time* said her work was that of a "brilliant introvert" and called it "vividly painted, intensely rhythmic."[35] On the other hand, Zelda's friend Gerald Murphy later said of one of her paintings that the "monstrous, hideous men" in it were "figures out of a nightmare."[36] Because Zelda longed to support herself by selling her work, she adulated O'Keeffe, whose canvases she found "lonely and magnificent and heartbreaking."[37] It so happened that, beginning on March 29, Zelda was having a show of her own paintings and drawings at the little gallery that Cary Ross had opened on East Eighty-sixth Street. (Her favorite among the paintings in her show was on the O'Keeffian theme of white flowers.) It also so happened that Zelda, who had been in and out of sanatoriums in Europe and America since her breakdown in 1930, had recently entered Craig House, where Kitty was still a patient. Against her doctors' advice, Zelda, accompanied by a nurse, took a trip to New York to hang her show and to see O'Keeffe's. The excitement was too much for her. On the train back to Beacon, she became hysterical and had to be sedated.

At the beginning of March, O'Keeffe had sailed again for Bermuda, this time by herself. Just before going, she had spent a few "very dear" days in the city with Alfred. "It was very difficult to leave him but I knew I could not stay," she wrote Toomer from on board her ship.[38] In Bermuda she received the deeply gratifying news that the Metropolitan Museum had bought a 1929 painting entitled *Black Hollyhock, Blue Larkspur* from her show. Even more momentous was the news that greeted her upon her return early in May: while she was away, Toomer and Marjorie Content had met and promptly fallen in love. Georgia affectionately wrote to Jean, "I like it for both of you because I feel deeply fond of both of you."[39] Despite her unvoiced regrets, she realized that it was for the best.

During her stay in Bermuda, O'Keeffe began "to think of New Mexico with a vague kind of interest."[40] When she informed Alfred, he regretted her need to go away but put up little resistance. He continued to worry about her and wrote to Adams in June, "[O'Keeffe] is still not painting. Looks well enough but has no vitality."[41] He felt reassured when it was decided that she would go to the Southwest with Marjorie. Toomer would join them in July, and Georgia would be a witness at their wedding in Taos on September 1.

Georgia had written Beck Strand that since the social life, intrigues, and squabbles both at Mabel Luhan's and at Marie Garland's exhausted her, she wanted to find a place where she could have a house to herself and not be disturbed. Nevertheless, O'Keeffe and Content rented a cottage at the H & M Ranch until Toomer arrived. O'Keeffe then sought out the vast and remote Ghost Ranch, a dude ranch for millionaires, situated in the spectacular landscape northwest of Abiquiu. There she settled into a small house that she would rent for the next several summers and buy in 1940.

On June 21 Stieglitz, who described himself to Adams as "a tired, very tired person," left for Lake George, where Ralph Flint would spend two months with him.[42] The Hill was quiet but tense, since Lizzie, who had gone to Europe with the four Davidsons, gave Lee and his new wife permission to stay at Red Top. Alfred despised Amanda and refused to have anything to do with her, ostentatiously going out of his way to avoid speaking to her. Lee protested, but no one could outdo Alfred when it came to stubbornness.

The family was all abuzz with the news that Julius was about to marry one of his colleagues at the University of Chicago. Dr. Mary Meda Reising, born in Ainsworth, Nebraska, in 1889, was twenty-two years younger than Julius and two years younger than O'Keeffe. After receiving her degree from Mount Holyoke in 1912, she had done her graduate work in chemistry with Julius, subsequently remaining in Chicago as an associate professor. In 1932 the unmarried Dr. Reising had adopted a baby girl, whom Julius adopted after their civil marriage ceremony, which took place in Chicago on August 30, 1934.[43]

That summer Alfred resumed working on his series of photographs of grasses, trees, and buildings on the Hill, but his excitement about his new negatives was eclipsed by his amazement and delight when he discovered, as he was rummaging through the farmhouse attic, twenty-two of his glass plates dating from between 1884 and 1894. Among them were exposures from Gutach, Katwijk, Bellagio, Venice, and Berlin, including *Sun Rays — Paula*. He was "startled to see how intimately related their spirit is to my latest work."[44] Although many of the plates were "scratched and battered," he immediately began to make prints from them.

All summer Stieglitz was preoccupied with the preparation of a book that was to be published in honor of his seventieth birthday. Entitled *America and Alfred Stieglitz: A Collective Portrait*, it was being edited by Dorothy

Norman, Waldo Frank, Paul Rosenfeld, Lewis Mumford, and Harold Rugg, a professor of education at Teachers College. Neither Stieglitz nor O'Keeffe wrote anything for it, but the twenty-five contributors included, in addition to the editors and the other five of the Seven Americans, William Carlos Williams, Sherwood Anderson, Gertrude Stein, Jean Toomer, Harold Clurman, Dorothy Brett, Edna Bryner, Jennings Tofel, R. Child Bayley, Herbert Seligmann, and Ralph Flint. Lengthy essays by Williams and Mumford described the historical, social, and cultural milieus in which Stieglitz had lived and worked. Rosenfeld wrote about Alfred's youth; Seligmann covered the teens and the twenties; Norman rhapsodized about An American Place; and Clurman contributed a very fine essay, "Alfred Stieglitz and the Group Idea." Although the editorial statement proclaimed "This book is not a collection of tributes," most of the remaining pieces were precisely that, many of them reminiscent of the puffs in the "What Is '291'?" issue of *Camera Work*. The plates at the back included small reproductions of a generous selection of images by Stieglitz and photographers he had championed, as well as works by the painters and sculptors to whom he had given exhibitions.

When the editors turned in the completed manuscript, around Labor Day, the publisher rejected it, claiming that the amount of text and the number of illustrations were greatly in excess of what had been agreed upon originally. Terribly disappointed, Stieglitz went to New York for five days in mid-September "because of various things including the book, which is gradually killing me." At that point he was thinking that he would have to publish it himself and told Dove, "If I live, the Book will appear even if it busts me." The morning after he returned to Lake George, he had an attack of angina (he called it a "heart attack") that he took as "a warning to let up for a day."[45]

Norman soon heard that the Literary Guild was looking for an illustrated art book to be its December selection. Carl Van Doren, the guild's editor in chief, was very impressed by the manuscript and illustrations; he would write that "the book at once clarifies and elevates the whole issue of art in America."[46] He agreed immediately to publish what was in the middle of the Depression a staggering thirty thousand copies in conjunction with Doubleday, Doran and Company, the guild's parent company.

Excited by the discovery of his early negatives, Stieglitz decided to break the vow he had made in 1932 and open the season at An American Place with an exhibition of his own work, old and new. When he heard the news about the Literary Guild, however, he postponed it until December, to co-incide with the publication of the book.

To help him prepare the Marin show with which he then began the season, Stieglitz hired a lanky youth named Andrew Droth. Told that his services would be needed for only six weeks, Andrew (one of the very few people whom Stieglitz called by first name) would work at the gallery until 1950, cutting mats, making frames, taking care of packing and mailing, and handling other chores. Alfred soon came to feel that "loyal & orderly" Andrew — "a first-class workman" who was "devoid of all intellectualities & curiosities," who didn't smoke or drink, and who was "absolutely prompt & reliable" — was his irreplaceable mainstay.[47]

The exhibition of sixty-nine Stieglitz photographs opened at An American Place on December 11. It juxtaposed new prints from his old negatives with recent portraits of O'Keeffe and a few male friends, a small group of New York views, seven *Equivalents*, and studies of the farmhouse and of grass and trees at Lake George. Significantly, the show did not include any photographs of Dorothy Norman. The reviews were generally appreciative, and with all the publicity about the book, attendance was high — fourteen hundred during the first week alone. At the end of the show Alfred renewed his vow never to mount another solo exhibition of his work. This time the vow would remain unbroken.

Although the typography and photographic reproduction in *America and Alfred Stieglitz* fell considerably short of his usual standards, the subject gratefully pronounced the tome "a Wonder."[48] Most of the reviewers disagreed. "The Book seems to be selling steadily in spite of the asininities of professional critics," Stieglitz reported to Dove on Christmas Day.[49] He was undoubtedly referring, in particular, to the review that had appeared in the *New York Times* two days earlier. Generally a friendly critic, Edward Alden Jewell had written that the effect of Stieglitz's leadership upon his disciples had been to foster "a sort of half-idolatrous worship, an atmosphere of incantation and pseudo-mystical brooding upon the thisness and thatness of life and the human soul; a cult — it really seems to amount to that — befogged by clouds of incense and bemused by an endless flow of words."[50] Ironically, Stieglitz had written to Ansel Adams a year earlier, "I am trying to sustain life at its highest — to sustain a *living* standard. To let every moment *actually live* without any ism or any fashion or cult attached to it."[51]

There was worse to come — much worse. Thomas Hart Benton, whose self-portrait appeared on the cover of the December 24 issue of *Time*, was becoming the star of the American Scene movement, depicting rural virtues and urban evils in a self-consciously folksy manner that was the right-wing, apple-pie counterpart of Stalin's contemporaneous Socialist Realism. Benton's principal flack was the despicable Thomas Craven, an outspoken bigot and demagogue. In his book *Modern Art: The Men, the Movements, the Meaning*, a rabid attack on modernism published in the fall of 1934, Craven had sneered at Stieglitz as a "Hoboken Jew without knowledge of, or interest in, the historical American background." He acknowledged that Stieglitz had long dedicated himself to supporting American artists and to pushing Americans to recognize "the value of art as a human activity." But he insisted that the artists shown at An American Place drew their fundamental inspiration from Europe. He also compared Matisse to a rich Jew and denounced his followers as "Negro-maniacs" who worshiped everything "savage and undisciplined."

Claims of being more-American-than-thou were, of course, by no means disinterested. In those bitter years of the Depression, the chief source of patronage was the federal government, which commissioned artists to paint patriotic murals in post offices and other civic buildings. The competition for the plum commissions was tough — and success could mean the difference between eating and starving.

In the January 1935 issue of the magazine suspiciously called *Common Sense*, Benton began his review "America and/or Alfred Stieglitz" by accusing the photographer of "a mania for self-aggrandizement." He went on to boast that because American art had finally come to its senses and had embraced "a socially and environmentally conditioned expression," abandoning the "empty purity" of abstraction, "Stieglitz's influence on art has vanished." Mockingly, he concluded,

> In the conception of himself as "seer" and "prophet" lies Stieglitz's real tie to the ways of our country. America produces more of these than any land in the world. . . . They have not heretofore made the "Literary Guild"; and I think it a little unfair that Stieglitz's contemporaries Father Divine and Aimee McPherson, who have such large followings, should be slighted, while he, with such a small band, should be enthroned.[52]

A rather pitiful exchange of letters ensued, in which each man took nasty little potshots at the other, while both pretended that there were no hard feelings. In one letter Stieglitz disingenuously assured Benton, "I'd love to be able to work myself into a white heat about what you've written . . . but for the life of me I can't be anything but gently amused." It is sad that he would abase himself by whining, "What I can't understand is the animus which prompted you to pour your slops over my head. Just because some people insisted on writing a book about me because I happened to be seventy years old and in service for fifty years without ever having received any remuneration personally in any form for all this service."[53] In a letter to Dove, however, Stieglitz expressed his old fighting spirit. "Gangsterism in every field is in the ascendancy," he wrote. "One can't escape envy — malice — being hit below the belt by bullies & cowards. . . . It is too bad 'Camera Work' no longer exists. — That's the one thing I do miss. A weapon in the form of one's own printing press."[54]

CHAPTER SIXTY·NINE

FROM 1935 UNTIL Stieglitz's death, in 1946, O'Keeffe would spend from three to six months of every year except 1939 in New Mexico. It is less remarkable that she needed time away from Alfred than that she always returned to him, her love renewed. In the early 1940s she would write to Henry McBride, "I see Alfred as an old man that I am very fond of — growing older — so that it sometimes shocks and startles me when he looks particularly pale and tired — Aside from my fondness for him personally I feel that he has been very important to something that has made my world for me — I like it that I can make him feel that I have hold of his hand to steady him as he goes on."[1] Toward the end of her life, the proudly unsentimental O'Keeffe wrote candidly of her husband, "For me he was much more wonderful in his work than as a human being. I believe it was the work that kept me with him — though I loved him as a human being. I could see his strengths and weaknesses. I put up with what seemed to me a good deal of contradictory nonsense because of what seemed clear and bright and wonderful."[2]

During the same period Stieglitz spent at least a month every summer except the last at Lake George with his family and such friends as Cary Ross and Emil Zoler. There he devoted most mornings to reading the day's harvest of letters, writing replies, and, if he felt well enough, walking to the post office to mail them. Afternoons were taken up with reading and napping, evenings talking with family and guests.

Increasingly important to Alfred were his daily tête-à-têtes with a succession of teenage grandnieces staying at the Hill. In sessions even more intense than those he had enjoyed with Elizabeth Davidson and Georgia Engelhard, he would recommend and lend parentally forbidden books to his latest infatuation, tell his well-worn anecdotes, and lecture about art and social values. He also listened sympathetically, gave good advice, and asked his current protégée too many questions about her sexual development. In their late teens the girls would begin to receive what his grandniece Sue Davidson Lowe has called the "not-so-avuncular pinches and pats he reserved for the nubile."[3] Lowe recalled, for instance, that Alfred, with a "satyr's twinkle" in his eye, grasped her knee one day and observed, "Nice firm leg. Don't ever shave."[4] Today, Alfred's "pinches and pats" sound dangerously close to molestation, but Lowe summed up, "The experience . . . was a generally salutary rite of passage. . . . An exhilarating and harmless catharsis was had by all."[5]

The one case in which Alfred lost his balance was with Ann Straus, the elder of the two daughters of Lee and Lizzie's daughter Flora. Ann was not quite fifteen in the summer of 1937, the first in many years during which her family visited Lake George. By the end of three long talks with her, Alfred found himself enchanted and invigorated. When O'Keeffe met her, she understood at once: Ann looked like a teenage version of Dorothy Norman. Alfred's devotion to Ann soon became so ardent that there appeared to be some cause for worry. As his health deteriorated badly during the next year or two, he seemed to reach out toward her more desperately, as if a bond with her youth could restore him. He obsessed about her, corresponded with her, looked forward impatiently to her next visit, and wished that he could photograph her. Not until the summer of 1941, when she brought her fiancé to the lake, did Alfred's passion for her finally cool.

In 1934 one of Stieglitz's young friends, Fairfield Porter, a painter and critic, had him to dinner in his Greenwich Village apartment to meet his older brother. A graduate of Harvard College and Harvard Medical School, Eliot was still at the university, doing advanced research in biochemistry. His love of nature had been reinforced during summers spent on Great Spruce Head, the Maine island owned by their family, whose money came from Chicago real estate. Like P. H. Emerson, Porter was an amateur ornithologist who first used a camera to photograph birds. Although he is now best known for his superb color photographs of nature, during the 1930s his wildlife studies and landscapes shot in Maine and Europe were all in black-and-white. Stieglitz later wrote, "In the very beginning I felt he had a vision of his own. I sensed a potentiality."[6] But he did not then offer to hang his work. Instead, like Ansel Adams before him, Porter had a show at the Delphic Studios, in 1936.

Stieglitz finally exhibited Porter's work in December 1938. The show included pictures of birds and nests; studies of trees, roots, and flowers on Great Spruce Head; Tyrolean landscapes; and an image of his infant son sound asleep. The reviews were nearly unanimous in their praise, and Stieglitz wrote Porter, "Some of your photographs are the first I have ever seen which made me feel 'there is my own spirit' — quite an unbelievable experience for one like myself."[7] Dissatisfied with scientific research, Porter decided to devote himself exclusively to photography from then on.

Ansel Adams returned to New York every year to show Stieglitz his recent work. In January 1936 his batch of prints included one of a white marble nineteenth-century tombstone in a San Francisco cemetery, the image that would remain Stieglitz's favorite among Adams's photographs. The elder photographer immediately announced that he would give the Californian a show during the next season. His offer may not have been entirely disinterested, for he was coming to hope that Adams might be the man to carry on his fight for photography. Stieglitz misjudged him so greatly that for several years he would continue to believe that the devoted outdoorsman could eventually be persuaded to move to New York.

Stieglitz did not expect Adams to take over the job of representing O'Keeffe, Marin, Dove, et al. For that he had pinned his hopes on a twenty-nine-year-old painter named William Einstein, who had returned to New York in 1932 after a lengthy sojourn in Paris. He had first appeared at An American Place in the spring of 1935, and although Alfred was not very impressed by William's canvases, he thoroughly enjoyed the rather chubby young man's perceptive and witty conversation. He was all the more pleased when they discovered that they were distant cousins. William, whose trust fund spared him from having to earn a living, soon began volunteering his services almost daily at the Place, taking on such tasks as labeling the works of art in the storage room to identify those that belonged to Stieglitz.

The two heirs apparent had a joint show at An American Place in November and December 1936, with Adams's prints in the main gallery, Einstein's paintings in the smaller. Adams, who traveled to New York for his show, was pleased with Stieglitz's selection and hanging, which he felt to be in perfect taste. He was also thrilled to feel at last completely accepted as a member of Stieglitz's circle.[8] The most enthusiastic visitor to the show was David McAlpin, a lawyer and investment banker whose mother was a Rockefeller. McAlpin had been wanting to buy an O'Keeffe painting, but Stieglitz wouldn't let him, saying, "You're not ready for it yet." He did, however, allow him to buy eight of Adams's prints. McAlpin would become the young photographer's close friend and loyal patron.

As for Einstein, a few months after the show he gently informed Alfred that he cherished his independence and his career as a painter too much to take on any permanent responsibility for the gallery.

Although most photographers and painters knew that Stieglitz now hardly ever exhibited the work of anyone outside his established group, many still took their portfolios to An American Place in the hope of a critique, and possibly even an accolade, from the legendary figure. "My first impulse is to state that I will not look at work," Stieglitz declared, "but when a person seems woebegone and persists, despite my 'No,' something rises up within me and I can no longer refuse."[9] His hesitation was due to his frustration that there was little he could do to help those sensitive, vulnerable artists whose work he liked and little he could say to help those in whose work he saw no spark of life. Furthermore, he was repelled by what he viewed as the crass materialism of most young artists. "They all want money & fame & what not," he complained to Dove in 1935. "I'm too old to adopt young-sters."[10]

He was profoundly discouraged by most of the photographs he saw. "It's a pathetic situation," he lamented to Edward Weston in 1938. "So little vi-sion. So little true *seeing*. — So little *inness* in any print. — Lots of clever-ness. Lots of imitation of imitation. — In all innocence and ignorance. And ye gods, tricks & 'effects' banal and stupid."[11] It is certainly not to his credit that he included among the latter André Kertész's sublimely playful distorted nudes or that he found Walker Evans's superb Flaubertian vi-gnettes cold and unfeeling. Perhaps his antipathy to Evans was more per-sonal than aesthetic. The young photographer, like his friend Berenice Abbott, had no patience for Stieglitz's paternalism and self-righteousness.

Adams was at An American Place one day when a terrified and obviously impecunious young artist (Adams couldn't remember his name) showed Stieglitz his watercolors. After looking at them in silence, Stieglitz aston-ished the artist first by saying that they were "very fine" and then by an-nouncing that he would like to buy one for $150. He gave the man a check for the full amount as well as a five-dollar bill with which to go out and get a good lunch. He said that although he couldn't exhibit the watercolors, he would certainly be able to sell a few if the artist would leave them at the gallery.[12]

Stieglitz strongly advocated such individual acts, in direct and spontaneous response to specific bodies of work, over what he condemned as the counterproductive Federal Art Project, one of whose administrators was his longtime nemesis Forbes Watson. To anyone who would listen, Alfred insisted at length that no real artist would prostitute his talents to paint post office murals, no matter how badly he needed money. As for making a contribution to society, an artist could do that only by being true to himself. Among others, critic Elizabeth McCausland (who was Berenice Abbott's lover) deplored Stieglitz's attacks on the FAP, which she felt were "uncalled for from a man who lived on an unearned income."[13]

To friends and strangers alike Alfred continued to speak out bravely against American materialism and philistinism. Less admirably, he would rail against all museums, all dealers, most artists, most photographers, and everyone with whom he had ever had a falling-out. At times he seemed as much a crank as P. H. Emerson had been, directing endless harangues and letters against any writer who called his gallery a business or who failed to give him adequate credit for championing photography as an art form or for introducing modernism to America. "The repetitive insistence of his thoughts and opinions could wear the patience of angels," wrote Adams. "There was deep truth in many of his statements, but some merely indicated pique and disappointment over situations he might have handled better."[14] Peggy Bacon described Stieglitz as "tottering but determined, pursuing, crusading, charged with some high explosive which seems about to shake the structure to bits. A gallant fanatic."[15]

Although still profoundly committed to representing only American artists, Stieglitz was not insensitive to the plight of Europeans in the middle and late 1930s. When László Moholy-Nagy, who had fled Germany after the Nazis closed the Bauhaus, wrote him in 1937 to ask for help in getting to America from England, Stieglitz sent him some money. But after Moholy was settled at Chicago's New Bauhaus, they had a disagreement and Stieglitz developed what he called "a personal prejudice" against him.[16]

In March 1935 Stieglitz exhibited the drawings and watercolors of George Grosz, the Dada satirist and caricaturist who had visited America in 1932 and come back in 1933 to settle in New York. When Grosz turned his acerbic eye on Depression-racked America, the grotesque juxtapositions of poverty and wealth he recorded were not very different from those

he had drawn in Weimar Germany. Stieglitz told Dove that he was showing the German because he was "in line with de Zayas" but added, "I fear
this country has already taken the *bite* out of Grosz."[17]

That fall saw the premature deaths of two artists whom Stieglitz
had shown. On October 18, seven months after his triumphal retrospective
at the Museum of Modern Art had closed, fifty-three-year-old Gaston
Lachaise died of leukemia. Stieglitz would miss his difficult old friend and
would always keep a small alabaster female torso by him on the shelf in his
office, hanging near it an O'Keeffe abstraction that echoed its thighs and
groin. A week after Lachaise's death, Charles Demuth died in Lancaster
from the effects of diabetes. Stieglitz would continue to exhibit Demuth's
work until 1939, usually in group shows, though once filling the small
gallery with a group of his oils and watercolors.

When the Modern proposed a Marin retrospective for the fall of 1936,
Stieglitz's first impulse was to refuse. "But I had to think of Marin & [his]
family & not my own feelings about Institutions," he wrote to Adams.[18] Before going to Lake George in July 1936 he finished selecting the 160 watercolors, twenty-one oils, and forty-four etchings to be included. In
October, when he was supervising the hanging of the exhibition, which
filled two floors of the museum, he spoke so eloquently about the pictures
that, according to the *New York Herald Tribune,* the "carpenters and electri-
cians putting the finishing touches on the exhibition stopped their work to
listen to him."[19] The show, part of which traveled to the Phillips Memorial Gallery, greatly broadened Marin's audience.

In December 1935, Marsden Hartley arrived back in New York after a year
in Mexico on a Guggenheim, a year in Bavaria, the summer of 1935 in
Bermuda, and the fall in Nova Scotia. The artist, once again in desperate
need of money, persuaded Stieglitz to give him a show, which opened in
March 1936. That summer, as during the previous one, Hartley — who
would never return to Europe — lived on a small Nova Scotia island,
boarding again with the Masons. He adored the entire family of fishermen
and had fallen in love with one of the sons, Alty, a big bear of a man who
seems to have reciprocated. In September 1936, while Hartley was still
there, Alty and his brother were drowned in a storm. Although the tragedy
would lead Hartley to paint some of his strongest canvases (just as Karl von
Freyburg's death had done in 1914), his heart was broken, and he would
rapidly decline physically.

Even though he was sick and tired of Hartley's demands for money, his
accusations of betrayal, and his failure to return to Maine, Stieglitz gave

him one last exhibition, in the spring of 1937. Elizabeth McCausland, who would write a biography of the painter, later claimed that when she went to see the show, Stieglitz followed her around and kept insisting that Hartley was not an important artist. At that rate, it is hardly surprising that not a single painting was sold. Everyone was relieved when a young dealer named Hudson Walker, who had opened a gallery the previous year, enthusiastically accepted Stieglitz's suggestion that he take over the chore of representing Hartley.

The following year, Stieglitz published — without any mention of Hartley's name — the indignant letters he had written to him in 1923. He probably intended less a rebuke to his prodigal son than an airing of his perennial and increasingly whining complaint that the public did not sufficiently appreciate 291's contribution. Indeed, he had opened the 1937–38 season with an exhibition he called "Beginnings and Landmarks, 291: 1905 to 1917," to mark the twentieth anniversary of the Little Gallery's closing. Saturday afternoons were generally the busiest times at An American Place, but one during the show's run was the first ever on which not a single visitor appeared.

O'Keeffe had a great triumph in the spring of 1936, when Elizabeth Arden commissioned her to paint a six-by-seven-foot mural for one wall of the Gymnasium Moderne of her Fifth Avenue salon. Perhaps to show Georgia what he could have accomplished if she had let him negotiate her Radio City deal for her in 1932, Stieglitz held out until Arden agreed to pay a reputed $10,000. O'Keeffe immediately rented a light and airy three-bedroom duplex penthouse at 405 East Fifty-fourth Street, between First Avenue and Sutton Place, to use as a studio. There she finished her mural of several white jimsonweed flowers, entitled *The Miracle Flower*, before she left for New Mexico.

That fall she and Stieglitz would move from the Shelton into the penthouse, whose previous tenant had been *New Yorker* cartoonist Peter Arno. With white walls, dark floors, and uncurtained windows, the apartment was sparsely but comfortably furnished, its black-and-white austerity relieved only by a few colorful Navajo rugs. Alfred, who was slow to feel at home there, complained that it was too expensive and inconveniently located, since he had to take a taxi to the Place and back every day, as well as to his favorite restaurants, the Café St. Denis and Child's.

He also found the penthouse too cold and drafty. He now wore long underwear year-round and often wore his overcoat or cape even in well-heated places. He was really feeling his age. "I haven't been well," he told

Adams in July 1936. "Heart. Damn it. . . . My memory isn't what it was. It's like the heart. A bit on the blink."[20]

Alfred received a sad and unsettling intimation of his own mortality with the death of his younger brother Julius on January 10, 1937. Alfred worried about Lee, but the identical twin would live until 1956.

On April 22, 1938 (three months after hearing the terrible news of Oscar Bluemner's suicide), seventy-four-year-old Alfred suffered a nearly fatal heart attack. Two weeks later he developed double pneumonia. Not until around the first of June could he get out of bed or resume his correspondence, limited at first to one letter a day. For a month he was forced to use pencil, since he was still too shaky to manage pen and ink.

When he went to Lake George in mid-July, Alfred was without a camera for the first since the 1880s.[21] He would never photograph again — not because he was too weak to hold a camera, but because the excitement of striving for a perfect negative was more than he felt his heart could stand. He would, however, continue to print for another two years. After Eliot Porter's exhibition in December, Alfred would exhibit photographs only once more: his own in a 1941 group show. With that one exception, he devoted his last seven seasons at An American Place exclusively to the work of O'Keeffe, Marin, and Dove.

Determined to get himself back in shape to open An American Place in the fall of 1938, Alfred was feeling well enough by August to be excited by Ann Straus's visit to the Hill. A few weeks later he went to New York for a day to see a skin specialist about the pubic itch that had been tormenting him for three months, apparently an allergic reaction to the sulfa drug with which his pneumonia had been treated. "The Hill is very peaceful & if I hadn't that damned itch I'd think the world a pretty swell affair in spite of big & little messes everywhere," he wrote to Dove. "In spite of itch & torture, I think it anyway."[22]

"[Cary] Ross is here & is taking down stories out of my life," Stieglitz reported in September. "Not an autobiography. Just episodes, anecdotes or whatever the business should be called."[23] Between 1925 and 1928 Herbert Seligmann had recorded in his diary what he heard Stieglitz tell visitors to the Intimate Gallery, and for the past ten years Dorothy Norman had been making notes of Stieglitz's anecdotes, parables, and observations, which, she wrote, "were not taken down literally in most cases, but represent an attempt to put into form in as direct a manner as possible, the essence of certain things that Stieglitz has said and stood for."[24] Although he complained of her occasional inaccuracy and incomprehension, he had given his blessing to the publication of some of her notes in the first issue of her new hardcover magazine, *Twice A Year: A Semi-Annual Journal of Literature, the Arts and Civil Liberties,* due out in November 1938. Many additional Stieglitz reminiscences, transcribed by Ross and by Peggy Davidson, would appear in four subsequent issues over the next eight years.

Originally planned as an unillustrated publication, Norman's magazine reproduced four Stieglitz photographs in its first issue. *Twice a Year* was dedicated to Stieglitz, and the cover of every issue bore the three-word title in his distinctive script. Stieglitz, who did not participate in the actual editing of the magazine, allowed Norman to use An American Place as its headquarters. For the next few years a steady stream of American and European intellectuals, poets, and novelists (including Stieglitz's old friend Theodore Dreiser, whom he had not seen for decades) would meet with Norman at the gallery, to which some would return to visit with its genius loci. Most notable of these new friends was Henry Miller, who would write, "I never knew him in the days of '291'; if I had met him then . . . the whole course of my life would probably have been altered."[25]

Dorothy was spending part of almost every day at An American Place, but her presence was no longer a threat to O'Keeffe. Alfred and Dorothy had settled into a very fond friendship, albeit with some of the expected tensions. He became jealous of her devotion to some of the writers she met through her magazine, and her adoration of him would become tinged with disappointment at his occasional failures to live up to the ideals he continued to espouse so fervently. After Stieglitz's death she would confide to Steichen that Alfred's "possessive instinct and his ego often got the better of him," and she regretted that he had reached "a point where establishing a certain success for things on which he had staked his own life became his almost basic preoccupation even while he was denying it."[26] Nevertheless, she resisted her occasional temptation to break away from him completely.

Throughout the last decade of his life, Stieglitz's relations with the Museum of Modern Art were mercurial, to say the least. Central to those relations was Beaumont Newhall, the brilliant and likeable young Harvard-trained art historian who had been hired in 1935 as the museum's librarian. An amateur photographer who was passionately interested in the history of the medium, Newhall supplemented his modest salary by making installation shots of exhibitions and developing them in the men's room.

In the spring of 1936, while Stieglitz was preparing the Marin retrospective for the Modern, Alfred Barr assigned Newhall to spend a year organizing an exhibition that would survey the entire history of photography. Anticipating by two years the centennial of Daguerre's announcement, it would completely fill the museum's galleries. Thrilled, Newhall rushed over to An American Place to ask Stieglitz to be chairman of his advisory council. Not only did Alfred refuse to participate in the preparation of the show, he also declined to lend any of his own prints. Like Julien Levy in 1931, Newhall would have to content himself with exhibiting photogravures from *Camera Work*. Stieglitz later explained to Ansel Adams, who functioned as Newhall's liaison with West Coast photographers, "I have nothing against the Museum of Modern Art except one thing & that is politics & the social set-up come before all else. . . . In short the Museum has really no standard whatever. No integrity of any kind." Stieglitz said he had told Newhall "that in spite of its good intentions the Museum was doing more harm than good."[27]

A revised edition of the catalog of Newhall's landmark show was published in 1938 as *Photography: A Short Critical History*; a further enlarged edition remains the classic text on the history of photography. While Stieglitz was recovering from his 1938 heart attack he had O'Keeffe summon Newhall and Adams to his bedside, where he granted the curator's request for permission to reproduce one of his photographs as the frontispiece and to dedicate the book to him. He then told the two young men, who were nearly in tears, that he expected them to assume his mantle as the leaders of photography.[28]

Early in 1939 David McAlpin made a contribution to the Modern for the purpose of establishing a photography department, the first in any major art museum in the world. Newhall was to be head of the new department, and he was determined that the inaugural exhibition should be a full-scale Stieglitz retrospective. Although opposed to the idea at first, Alfred gradually relented and began going through his lifework with the young curator to make selections. But everything fell apart that fall, when Alfred Barr wrote in his catalog for the museum's Picasso retrospective that the artist's show at 291 was "probably" his first in America. Stieglitz immediately canceled his exhibition and vowed that he would never again have anything to do with the museum.[29]

Because of the Modern's move into its new International Style building, the photography department was not actually set up until late in 1940. Its first exhibition, entitled "Sixty Photographs," opened on December 31 and included (since he had yielded to the combined entreaties of Newhall, Adams, and McAlpin) Stieglitz's 1920 photograph of O'Keeffe's hands sewing and a later image of poplars at Lake George. Among the thirty-odd photographers represented in this survey of photography from the 1840s to the 1930s, mostly drawn from Newhall's 1937 show, were a few surprises, notably Dorothy Norman and Henwar Rodakiewicz. Stieglitz consented to visit on the morning of the opening day and gave his approval to most of what he saw.

O'Keeffe was at first apprehensive when Alfred became friendly with Newhall's young wife, Nancy, who had begun as a painter and had become interested in photography when she married Beaumont, in 1936. During 1941 and 1942 she conducted extensive interviews with Stieglitz for a biography, but the project was put on a back burner when she took over Beaumont's job at the Modern while he was in the army, and she never picked up where she had left off. She did, however, continue to visit Stieglitz frequently at An American Place, and he became very fond of her — though she had no interest in a romantic involvement. She recalled that "at a crucial moment when [Stieglitz] was at outs with both Georgia and Dorothy, he proposed moving in with me."[30] Newhall wisely concluded that she could neither manage the responsibility of ensuring his comfort nor risk the danger of being caught between the two formidable rivals.

During the late 1930s and early 1940s Stieglitz was also telling the story of his life to his friend Jerome Mellquist, a critic whose book *The Emergence of an American Art* (1942) is very much the gospel according to Alfred. Mellquist devoted entire chapters to O'Keeffe, Marin, Dove, and Hartley, while he gave most artists outside the Stieglitz fold a page or two. The story of Stieglitz's careers as photographer and impresario provided the backbone of the book, the first in which the history of photography was intertwined, and related on equal terms, with the history of painting and sculpture.

At the end of January 1939, O'Keeffe left for Hawaii, where she would spend more than two months at the expense of the Dole Pineapple Company. During her stay she flew to several of the islands and marveled at their variety, from lush tropical regions to "bare lava land more wicked than the desert."[31] She made enough paintings in Hawaii for twenty-one of them to constitute her entire 1940 show. Upon her return to New York in mid-April, she chose two for Dole — one of a heliconia flower and one of a papaya tree — but the company rejected the latter, arguing that it did not market papaya, though its principal competitor did. When Dole airfreighted a pineapple tree to O'Keeffe's studio, she grudgingly tried to paint it. Within three weeks she fell victim to the headaches and insomnia that had followed her Radio City fiasco. In mid-June, Stieglitz somewhat overdramatically announced in a letter to Dove, "Georgia has had a nervous breakdown. — Has been laid up for 4 weeks. — Came back in bad condition. — For the present there is no thought of Lake George or anywhere else for either of us."[32]

This time, however, O'Keeffe recovered in a matter of weeks. On August 17, after finally completing her painting of a pineapple bud for Dole, she drove Alfred to Lake George in the new car she had bought for her upcoming trip to New Mexico. Alfred was so distraught about the news of Germany's invasion of Poland, on September 1, that he suffered a severe attack of angina the next day. Although O'Keeffe referred to it as a "heart attack," she qualified it as "not as bad as last year but bad enough."[33] She was sufficiently worried to cancel her trip.

After their mid-September return to New York, Stieglitz went to the Place mornings and rested at home in the afternoons. When he began to go in for longer stretches, Dorothy Norman volunteered the part-time assistance of her two secretaries and, for Alfred's increasingly frequent naps, set up an army cot, with a mattress and pillows, in a corner of his office.

In the middle of June 1941, Stieglitz was "bowled over" by the "glorious & gloriously generous" article "The Fighting Photo-Secession" in *Vogue*, by Edward Steichen, who had never reciprocated Stieglitz's animosity. "If you were here I'd grasp your hand & stand before you," Stieglitz wrote his old friend. "And words would not be possible from either of us. . . . My love to you."[34] Steichen's article and Stieglitz's response finally opened the way to a reconciliatory meeting, which soon took place.

Despite that one bright spot, Stieglitz was increasingly depressed. A month and a half after Steichen's article appeared, he complained to Dove from Lake George, "I'm managing to scrape through one day after another. Am pretty sick of myself. — Do absolutely nothing but lie about — sit about — eat & sleep. Not a thought in my head or elsewhere — wherever."[35]

He felt himself suspended in a purgatorial state of uncertainty between life and death, plagued by ailments ranging from angina to sinusitis and miserably itchy skin. He was also disturbed about the war and feared that it would bring An American Place to an end, just as World War I had forced the closing of 291. Feeling lonely, he remarked to Nancy Newhall in January 1942, "If I have the misfortune to live a year or two longer, I shall find myself where I was in 1917."[36] A few weeks later he told her that he wished his 1938 heart attack had been fatal.

An American Place was often deserted, and Stieglitz's torrent of oratory abated. "The Place should be called The Sarcophagus wherein I lie entombed with the glory of the Marins, O'Keeffes, Doves, your photographs as well as mine & what else," he wrote to Adams in 1943.[37]

O'Keeffe and Marin continued to prosper, and even Dove was now relatively secure. In the spring of 1938 the last of his family's holdings in Geneva were foreclosed by the bank, but his work was selling well enough to enable him to buy a little former post office in Centerport, on the north shore of Long Island. A week after the move, in April 1938, he developed pneumonia, which laid him up for six months. A burst of creativity followed, and Dove's 1940 show was widely hailed as his best ever. Duncan Phillips's annual payments rose to $2,400 in 1941. The following year Stieglitz was deeply touched when Dove and Reds asked him to accept a check for $200 as payment for an *Equivalent*. Having divided the money between the rent fund and Andrew Droth, he sent them two specially framed *Equivalents*.

Nor did Stieglitz have to worry any longer about Hartley, who was spending summers and autumns in Maine and winters in New York. Staying at a hotel not far from the Place, he would frequently drop in for an hour or two to sit in friendly silence with Stieglitz. Embarrassed to open his mouth, for he was now almost toothless, Hartley was also quite deaf. The Hudson Walker Gallery, where he had three annual one-man exhibitions, closed in 1940, but the following year Walker bought twenty-three paintings from the artist for $5,000. Doing some of the finest work of his career, Hartley had a two-man show with Stuart Davis at the Cincinnati Art Museum in 1941 and a critically if not financially successful New York solo at the Macbeth Gallery in March 1942. His February 1943 show at Paul Rosenberg's prestigious gallery elicited sales as well as praise. After his death, on September 2 of that year, Stieglitz wrote enviously to Dove, "What a lucky man Hartley to have passed out in his zenith."[38]

In 1942 the rationing of gasoline led O'Keeffe to worry that taxis might become so scarce that Alfred would have trouble going to and from An American Place. She also worried that a shortage of heating oil might make the penthouse unbearably cold, since its rooms were too large to keep warm with electric heaters. As soon as she returned from New Mexico, around October 1, she went out hunting for an apartment. It had to be within easy walking distance of the gallery and have a bedroom small enough to heat with electricity, if necessary. She soon found a suitable floor-through in a brownstone at 59 East Fifty-fourth Street, a block from the Place, and they moved in almost immediately. O'Keeffe furnished the living room so simply that the uninitiated, on a first visit, might ask when the furniture was going to arrive. Nothing was hung on the walls, though a framed Dove collage was placed on the mantel. The principal ornament was a large, plain Steuben glass bowl. Only a few sizeable plants relieved the sense of barrenness.

They were hardly settled before O'Keeffe was off to Chicago for a retrospective of her paintings at the Art Institute. This first large survey of her work, organized by Daniel Catton Rich, opened on January 21, 1943. Stieglitz had commented that it was wrong for the masterpieces of the Metropolitan Museum to have been taken away to safety from enemy bombers just when the public needed the inspiration and consolation of great art for its well-being.[39] But O'Keeffe told Nancy Newhall that she was pleased to have her paintings going to Chicago, where she felt they would be in less danger than in blacked-out New York, assumed to be a higher-priority target.[40]

The end of the war brought the safe return not only of Stieglitz's grandson, Milton Stearns, Jr., a navy lieutenant who had served in the Pacific, but also of such friends as Beaumont Newhall and Todd Webb. The latter had been working for the Chrysler Export Corporation in Detroit in the late 1930s when he turned to photography as an avocation. Inspired by a ten-day course with Ansel Adams at the Photographic Guild of Detroit in 1941, he visited An American Place the following year on his way to navy boot camp. Liking both the man and his photographs (including a portrait of a teenage African-American boy that Dorothy Norman would publish in *Twice A Year*), Stieglitz would correspond with Webb while he was stationed in New Guinea. After his discharge, Webb moved to New York and began a photographic documentation of the city's architecture and inhabitants, from Fifth Avenue to Coney Island. At least twice a week, particularly on days when the weather didn't allow him to work outdoors, he would stop by the Place for a few hours to visit with Stieglitz, to listen to his woes and his old stories, and to look at his prints.

Another young photographer who visited Stieglitz after the war was Minor White. In the fall of 1945 he enrolled in Columbia University's extension division and began taking courses in art history and the philosophy of art. After his move to San Francisco in July 1946 to assist Ansel Adams in teaching photography, White wrote to Stieglitz, "The first long talk I had with you . . . was the first contact I had with a man who had faith in anything anymore. That did me more good than you will ever realize. Somewhere in combat faith in anything but evil disappeared and it was slow in returning."[41] White would go on to an influential career as a photographer, teacher, and editor, his philosophy strongly influenced by Zen Buddhism and the teachings of Gurdjieff.

One of the most bizarre encounters in the history of photography was that which took place sometime during 1945 between Stieglitz and Arthur Fellig, whom one of his editors described as a "rather portly, cigar-smoking, irregularly shaven man." He was known as Weegee because people said he must use a Ouija board to predict the crimes and disasters at whose scenes he was usually the first photographer to arrive. The truth was that he listened day and night to a police radio, whether cruising the streets in his old Chevrolet or half-asleep in his room across from police head-quarters. Knowing in his heart that he himself was an artist, Weegee coveted the blessing of "the most famous photographer in the world." He had noticed the old man walking on Madison Avenue many times, but — being, according to the same editor, "as shy and sensitive as if he had spent his life photographing babies and bridesmaids" — he had been afraid to bother him. When he finally got up his nerve, Stieglitz invited him back to An American Place, where "there was a smell of disinfectant like in a sick room." The cot onto which Stieglitz collapsed led Weegee to believe that the office was the old man's home.

For the next several hours Stieglitz poured out, to this very curious stranger, his life story, his opinions, his complaints, and even the details of his finances.

> He told me that he had a private income of eighteen hundred dollars a year [wrote Weegee]. That three hundred and fifty dollars went for income tax. (Not that he had to pay it but he felt that the government needed the money worse than he did), that the rent money and expenses, about four thousand dollars a year for the studio, was contributed by the artists when they sold the paintings which were on exhibit. . . . That few paintings were being sold now . . . that the rent was not going to be ready and he was afraid he was going to be dispossessed.[42]

It is hardly any wonder that Weegee accepted at face value Stieglitz's own judgment of himself as a failure and included a portrait of him, along with his account of their meeting, in the rogue's gallery that he published later that year under the title *Naked City*.

*   *   *

Soon after America had entered World War II, Edward Steichen was commissioned a lieutenant commander in the U.S. Navy with the responsibility of overseeing photographic coverage of naval aviation, and he was eventually placed in charge of all navy combat photography. In the fall of 1945 Thomas J. Maloney, an advertising executive and the publisher of *U.S. Camera* magazine, for whose annual supplement Steichen had selected the photographs since 1935, promised to raise $100,000 a year to support the Modern's photography department if Steichen was appointed its new head. The trustees of the museum — for which Steichen had curated an extremely successful propaganda exhibition entitled "Road to Victory" in 1942 — accepted the offer and invited Beaumont Newhall, who loathed Steichen, to stay on as his curatorial deputy. Newhall resigned in March 1946; two years later he would become director of the International Museum of Photography at the George Eastman House, in Rochester.

Despite a second teary reunion with Steichen, in the spring of 1946, Stieglitz still did not think highly of his former protégé and was thoroughly disgusted by what he viewed as the Modern's latest display of perfidy. He was, therefore, not at all happy that on May 14 of that year a retrospective of seventy-five O'Keeffe paintings was going to open at the museum. When he saw the show, however, he was very pleasantly surprised by how well it had been installed, and he would write to curator James Johnson Sweeney, "I say once more it is a glorious exposition. In a sense a miracle in a time like this."[43]

Three weeks after the opening, O'Keeffe set off for New Mexico, having hired a young woman to cook, clean the apartment, and generally take care of Stieglitz. He was planning to settle in at Lake George a month later, though as the date approached, he decided to postpone his departure. Late in June he told Dorothy Norman, who stopped by with Henri Cartier-Bresson before leaving for Woods Hole, that he really didn't want to go to the lake (where he had been bored since his health had forced him to stop photographing), for he loved having his young friends — Todd Webb, Jerome Mellquist, the Newhalls, Henwar Rodakiewicz — visit him at the Place. So, having taken down Dove's show, the last exhibition he would ever hang, he continued to go every day to the gallery. He almost preferred the walls when they were bare.

On Friday, July 5, Stieglitz was feeling so well that when Webb appeared with Ferdinand Reyher, who was starting to work on a book about Atget, he got out boxes of his old prints and showed them with a running narration. The next morning, however, after someone had come in and bought an O'Keeffe, Stieglitz had a bad spasm of angina. Alone in the gallery, he called the doctor himself and then lay down on his cot, where he remained until the Newhalls stopped by during the afternoon, bringing him his favorite treat — a chocolate ice cream cone. "We wanted him to be quiet," Nancy reported to Ansel Adams, "but he wanted to talk, in pain, and with a racing pulse." He asked them to read him James Thrall Soby's critique of O'Keeffe's show in the new issue of *The Saturday Review* and was pleased with Soby's observations. The Newhalls stayed with him until his housekeeper-nurse stopped by. They wanted her to take him home, but he insisted on staying at the gallery. When Nancy returned late in the afternoon, all the shades had been pulled to shut out as much light as possible, and Stieglitz was still in his office "worriedly dictating letters."[44]

His doctor notified O'Keeffe, but these attacks had become quite routine. She called Donald Davidson, who agreed to stay nights at the apartment. Andrew would take care of him during the day. Stieglitz reassured her the next day: "Nearly all right. Nothing for you to worry about. Lucky that I had decided not to go to the Lake today."[45]

Stieglitz stayed at home in bed for a few days, but by Tuesday, July 9, he felt well enough to write O'Keeffe that he was planning to go to the Place the next day "for a while."[46] That evening Mellquist joined him at the apartment for dinner. On the morning of the tenth, Davidson had to leave the apartment before Andrew arrived to escort Stieglitz to the gallery. Alfred apparently spent the morning writing letters in O'Keeffe's room, where he sat at her desk to read his letters — always, he had assured her only the day before, reading her letter first — and to write his replies. When Andrew arrived about noon, he found Stieglitz lying, unconscious, with his pen beside him, on the floor of the hallway between his room and O'Keeffe's. He had suffered a massive stroke. Taken by ambulance to Doctors Hospital, he would remain in an oxygen tent and never regain consciousness.

It wasn't until the morning of Thursday, the eleventh, when she drove from the Ghost Ranch to the nearby town of Espanola, that O'Keeffe received the telegram informing her of Stieglitz's stroke. Without returning to the ranch, she drove straight on to Albuquerque to get the next plane to New York, where her friend Mary Callery, a sculptor, picked her up at the airport and took her to the hospital.

Dorothy Norman, who had rushed back to New York as soon as she was notified, visited him on Thursday morning. With Callery and Rodakiewicz she spent several hours, in silence, at his bedside. After O'Keeffe's arrival that afternoon Norman did not return to the room.

Stieglitz died about 1:30 A.M. on Saturday, July 13. O'Keeffe spent that morning searching for a plain pine coffin, which she lined with a white sheet. Although the obituary that appeared in the *New York Times* on Sunday stated, "No funeral service is planned by the family," about twenty people, including family members, Norman, and Paul Strand, gathered at Frank Campbell's funeral home, on Madison Avenue at Eighty-first Street, at 11:30 Sunday morning to bid Stieglitz farewell.[47] Emmy apparently was not present. Strand told the Newhalls, who were out of town, that O'Keeffe had been "strained but under control" while Norman was "utterly shattered, weeping." There were no tributes, no music, and few flowers. Steichen arrived late and placed upon the black cloth draped over the closed coffin a bough from a pine on his Connecticut farm that he had always called "Alfred's tree."[48] Stieglitz had been correct when he predicted, after their last meeting, that Steichen would be his "greatest mourner."[49]

O'Keeffe went alone in a limousine following the hearse to the Fresh Pond Crematory, in Maspeth, Queens. Toward the end of July, David McAlpin drove her to Lake George, where she and Elizabeth Davidson mingled Alfred's ashes with the earth at the base of an old tree near the shore.

The day after the funeral, O'Keeffe called Dorothy Norman to demand "absolute control" of An American Place. O'Keeffe, who was going back to New Mexico for a couple of months, wanted Norman to clear all her things out of the gallery by the fall. She then announced that she would take over the rent fund, claiming that Stieglitz had let Dorothy handle it "only because he and all his family liked making things difficult." She ended by saying that she considered Dorothy's endlessly "wrangling" relationship with Stieglitz "absolutely disgusting."[50]

In 1927, with the messy dispersal of John Quinn's collection fresh in his mind, Stieglitz had told Herbert Seligmann, "The dealers were waiting for his death — and an auction. There would be no such auction. Rather, the pictures would be burned."[51] There would not, however, be any such suttee. Instead, O'Keeffe would spend much of the next three years dividing among several museums Stieglitz's collection of paintings, sculpture, and works on paper — about 850 items in all — as well as his own photographs. Although Stieglitz had told Nancy Newhall in 1942 that O'Keeffe would probably destroy his nude photographs of her, she did nothing of the sort.

She chose the finest example of each Stieglitz image for a master set of 1,550 prints, which she gave to the National Gallery of Art. Had Beaumont Newhall still been in charge of the Modern's photography department, she might perhaps have given the master set to that museum. But in 1946 Ansel Adams had written to Nancy Newhall that both he and Stieglitz would rather destroy their prints than let the Modern have them if Steichen remained its curator.[52] Nonetheless, O'Keeffe allowed her friend James Johnson Sweeney, who had recently retired as the Modern's director of painting and sculpture, to organize a double exhibition of Stieglitz's photographs and works from his collection, filling two floors of the museum during the summer of 1947. If the trustees expected a donation of some of the exhibited art, they were disappointed.

In her division of the works that Stieglitz had collected, O'Keeffe strove to achieve a balance between preserving the continuity of each artist's development and enriching institutions throughout America. (Stieglitz had commented, "One does not scatter the works of a Shakespeare over the face of the earth, page by page.")[53] In the end, she gave the lion's share, nearly six hundred items, to the Metropolitan Museum of Art. Thanks to the influence of Carl Van Vechten, another 101 went to African-American Fisk University, in Nashville. The Boston Museum of Fine Arts received forty-two Stieglitz prints to supplement the photographer's 1924 gift. The remaining photographs and other works of art were divided among the Art Institute of Chicago, the Library of Congress, the San Francisco Museum of Modern Art (thanks to Ansel Adams), and the Philadelphia Museum of Art, where native Philadelphian Dorothy Norman would later establish an Alfred Stieglitz center. O'Keeffe gave all of Stieglitz's correspondence and papers to Yale University, which houses them in the Beinecke Rare Book and Manuscript Library. The library now owns some fifty thousand letters from and to Stieglitz.

O'Keeffe spent the summers of 1947 and 1948 in New Mexico, overseeing the renovation of a second home, in Abiquiu, not far from the Ghost Ranch. The rest of each year she was in New York, preparing Stieglitz's collection for distribution. After finishing that task early in 1949, she moved permanently to New Mexico, where she would live at the Ghost Ranch in the summer and autumn and in Abiquiu during the winter and spring.

Although she had had little time to paint since Stieglitz's death, O'Keeffe mounted a show of her work from that period at An American Place, in October and November 1950, after which the gallery closed. Thenceforth, Edith Halpert would represent O'Keeffe as well as Marin and the estates of Dove (who died in November 1946) and Demuth.

Georgia O'Keeffe died in Santa Fe on March 6, 1986, at the age of ninety-eight.

NOTES

Abbreviations Used in the Notes

PERIODICALS

AAP	*American Amateur Photographer*
CN	*Camera Notes*
CW	*Camera Work*
TAY	*Twice A Year*

INSTITUTIONS

AAA	Archives of American Art, Washington, D.C.
ASA/YCAL	Alfred Stieglitz Archive, Yale Collection of American Literature, Beinecke Rare Book and Manuscript Library, Yale University, New Haven, Connecticut
CCP	Center for Creative Photography, University of Arizona, Tucson
CU	Rare Books and Manuscript Library, Columbia University, New York
MoMA	Museum of Modern Art, New York
NL	Newberry Library, Chicago
RPS	Royal Photographic Society, London
UPA	University of Pennsylvania, Philadelphia
YCAL	Yale Collection of American Literature, Beinecke Rare Book and Manuscript Library, Yale University, New Haven, Connecticut

CORRESPONDENTS

AA	Ansel Adams
AD	Arthur Dove
AML	Aline Meyer Liebman
AP	Anita Pollitzer
AS	Alfred Stieglitz
DN	Dorothy Norman

ES   Edward Stieglitz
ESD   Elizabeth Stieglitz Davidson
GOK   Georgia O'Keeffe
HS   Herbert Seligmann
MDL   Mabel Dodge Luhan
MH   Marsden Hartley
PHE   Peter Henry Emerson
PR   Paul Rosenfeld
PS   Paul Strand
RSS   Rebecca Salsbury Strand
SA   Sherwood Anderson
SH   Sadakichi Hartmann

Chapter 1 • *(pages 3–11)*

1. Edward Stieglitz Papers, YCAL.
2. ES to Ida Werner, July 1873, Edward Stieglitz Papers, YCAL.
3. New York State, Adjutant General's Office, *New York in the War of Rebellion, 1861–1865*, Frederick Phisterer, ed., 3d ed. (Albany, N.Y.: J. B. Lyon, 1912), 539ff.
4. *New York Herald*, April 22, 1861.
5. Siegmund Stieglitz to ES, May 3, 1861, Edward Stieglitz Papers, YCAL.
6. Helena Stieglitz to ES, May 16, 1861, Edward Stieglitz Papers, YCAL.
7. ES to Marcus and Sara Stieglitz, June 3, 1861, Edward Stieglitz Papers, YCAL.
8. ES to Marcus Stieglitz and family, July 14, 1861, Edward Stieglitz Papers, YCAL.
9. New York State, Adjutant General's Office, *New York in the War of Rebellion*, 546–547.
10. Maj. Gen. John A. Dix to Col. E. D. Townsend, July 24, 1861, in *The War of the Rebellion: A Compilation of the Official Records of the Union and Confederate Armies* (Washington, D.C.: U.S. War Dept., 1880), series 1, vol. 2, 759–760; reprinted by National Historical Society (Harrisburg, Penn.), 1985.

Chapter 2 • *(pages 12–17)*

1. The address was both 178 Hudson Street and One Sea View Place. The block of Hudson Street between Fifth and Sixth streets was known as Sea View Place.

2. The system of street numbering in Hoboken was changed about 1890. The Stieglitz house is now 219 Garden Street, between Second and Third streets. Edward Stieglitz is named as the owner of the house in *Combined Atlas of the State of New Jersey and the County of Hudson* (Philadelphia: M. Hopkins and Co., 1873).

3. AS, "The Organ-Grinder," *TAY*, no. 5/6, 1941, 160.

4. Dorothy Norman, *Alfred Stieglitz: An American Seer*, 15–16.

5. Lewis Mumford, *The Brown Decades*, 3.

Chapter 3 • *(pages 18–21)*

1. AS, "A Statement," in catalog of Exhibition of Stieglitz Photographs, Anderson Galleries, New York, 1921.

2. James Jackson Jarves, *The Art-Idea*, 137, 149.

3. Quoted in Francis Steegmuller, *The Two Lives of James Jackson Jarves*, 220.

4. *Harper's Weekly*, April 16, 1864, 246.

5. Quoted in Roger B. Stein, *John Ruskin and Aesthetic Thought in America, 1840–1900*, 106.

6. Although the modern scholarly literature nearly always refers to the "Association for the Advancement of Truth in Art," the first issue (May 1863) of the organization's journal, *The New Path*, announced that it was published by the "Society for the Advancement of Truth in Art."

7. Quoted in William H. Gerdts, "Through a Glass Brightly," in Linda S. Ferber and William H. Gerdts, *The New Path* (Brooklyn, N.Y.: Brooklyn Museum, 1985), 40.

8. Quoted in *The Pursuit of Beauty* (New York: Metropolitan Museum of Art, 1986), 388.

Chapter 4 • *(pages 22–27)*

1. John Towles in *Humphrey's Journal*, June 15, 1864; quoted in Martha A. Sandweiss et al., *Photography in Nineteenth-Century America*, 62.

2. Vicki Goldberg, ed., *Photography in Print*, 104.

3. Quoted in Aaron Scharf, *Art and Photography*, 146.

4. Scharf, *Art and Photography*, 149–153.

Chapter 5 • *(pages 28–34)*

1. For a photograph of the area in 1871, see M. Christine Boyer, *Manhattan Manners*, 176. The Stieglitz house was one of the group of three in the background, with white skylights, three blocks north of the church at Madison Avenue and Fifty-seventh Street.
2. "Democratic Vistas," in Walt Whitman, *Poetry and Prose* (New York: Library of America, 1982), 937–939.
3. Quoted in Lewis Mumford, *The Brown Decades*, 6.
4. *National Cyclopedia of American Biography*, vol. 13, 416.
5. Ibid., vol. 3, 309.
6. Solomon Willis Rudy, *The College of the City of New York*, 153–154. Letter from R. R. Bowker published in *New York Evening Post*, August 29, 1919; reprinted in *Campus* (CCNY), September 24, 1919.
7. "Adolph Werner," by Lewis Sayre Burchard (CCNY class of 1877), in *College Mercury* (CCNY), September 1919, 8ff.
8. Dorothy Norman, *Alfred Stieglitz: An American Seer*, 20.

Chapter 6 • *(pages 35–41)*

1. John B. Bachelder, *Popular Resorts and How to Reach Them* (Boston, 1873).
2. Quoted in Allen Dulles, *America Learns to Play*, 182.
3. Dorothy Norman, *Alfred Stieglitz: An American Seer*, 19.
4. Bachelder, *Popular Resorts*, 176.
5. Edward Stieglitz's name does not appear on the surviving membership lists of the American Jockey Club (founded in 1866), of its successor, the Coney Island Jockey Club (founded 1879), or of the Jockey Club (founded 1894).
6. Quoted in Barbara Novak, *The Thyssen-Bornemisza Collection*, 84.
7. Seneca Ray Stoddard, *Lake George* (Albany, N.Y.: Weed, Parsons and Co. Printers: (1873), notes that the name of the post office in Caldwell had just been changed to Lake George (37), but most people continued to refer to the village as Caldwell.
8. William Cullen Bryant, ed., *Picturesque America* (New York: D. Appleton and Co., 1872–74), vol. 2, 256.
9. Ibid.
10. Bachelder, *Popular Resorts*, 177. Georgia O'Keeffe mentioned this tradition in a letter to Ettie Stettheimer dated August 6, 1925 (Jack Cowart et al., eds., *Georgia O'Keeffe: Art and Letters*, 182).
11. Broadside from Catskill Mountain House. On verso: bill from AS to ES, August 7, 1873, Edward Stieglitz Papers, YCAL.
12. Stoddard, *Lake George*, 42.
13. Norman, *AS: An American Seer*, 20–21.

Chapter 7 • *(pages 42–46)*

1. Edward L. Wilson, "Personal Recollections of Dr. H. W. Vogel," *Wilson's Photographic Magazine*, March 1899, 97–100.
2. *National Cyclopedia of American Biography*, vol. 18, 217–218. Thieme, Ulrich, and Felix Becker, *Allgemeines Lexicon der bildenden Künstler* (Leipzig, 1908–50), vol. 11, 145.
3. Dorothy Norman, *Alfred Stieglitz: An American Seer*, 19.

Chapter 8 • *(pages 47–54)*

1. AS, "The Scissors Grinder," *TAY*, no. 10/11, 1943, 256–257.
2. Dorothy Norman, *Alfred Stieglitz: An American Seer*, 16–17.
3. Adolph Werner to AS, January 1, 1913, ASA/YCAL.
4. Norman, *AS: An American Seer*, 16–17.
5. Sue Davidson Lowe, *Stieglitz*, 64.
6. Norman, *AS: An American Seer*, 16–17.
7. AS, "The Scissors Grinder," 260.
8. Ibid.
9. Norman, *AS: An American Seer*, 16–17.
10. AS to ES, December 8, 1877, Edward Stieglitz Papers, YCAL.
11. AS album entitled *Autographs*, vol. 1, ASA/YCAL.
12. In *Mental Photographs: An Album for Confessions*, which AS filled out on December 31, 1876, ASA/YCAL.
13. AS, "Thoroughly Unprepared," *TAY*, no. 10/11, 1943, 252.
14. Paul Rosenfeld in Waldo Frank et al., *America and Alfred Stieglitz*, 64.
15. Alice Miller, *The Drama of the Gifted Child* (New York: Basic Books, 1990), 30–45.
16. Norman, *AS: An American Seer*, 17–18.
17. AS, "Thoroughly Unprepared," 252.

Chapter 9 • *(pages 55–59)*

1. Solomon Willis Rudy, *The College of the City of New York*, 111–112, 161, 165–166, 206.
2. During the spring of 1878, a movement was begun to repeal that rule. The state senate did not approve the repeal until 1882. Ibid., 124–126.
3. AS, "Thoroughly Unprepared," *TAY*, no. 10/11, 1943, 245.
4. Ibid.

5. Ibid.

6. Adolph Werner, "The Later Faculty," in Philip J. Mosenthal and Charles F. Horne, eds., *The City College: Memories of Sixty Years* (New York: G. P. Putnam's Sons, 1907), 151.

7. Lewis Freeman Mott (CCNY class of 1883), "The Eighties," in Mosenthal and Horne, eds., *The City College*, 310.

Chapter 10 • *(pages 60–67)*

1. Solomon Willis Rudy, *The College of the City of New York*, 162.

2. James D. McCabe, Jr., *New York by Gaslight*, 132.

3. Mark Twain, *A Tramp Abroad* (New York: Hippocrene, 1982), 131.

4. AS and Louis H. Schubart, "Two Artists' Haunts," *Photographic Times*, January 1895, 9–12.

5. Nancy Newhall, *From Adams to Stieglitz*, 124. In 1882, however, Leopold inquired in a letter whether Alfred received his "$3,000 a year from Pa" in weekly or monthly instalments or in an annual lump sum (Leopold Stieglitz to AS, September 20, 1882, ASA/YCAL).

6. Dorothy Norman, *Alfred Stieglitz: An American Seer*, 31–32.

7. AS, "Four Happenings," *TAY*, no. 8/9, 1942, 105.

8. Norman, *AS: An American Seer*, 31.

9. AS, "Four Happenings," 105.

10. Norman, *AS: An American Seer*, 31–32.

11. Friedrich Paulsen, *German Education, Past and Present* (New York: Charles Scribner's Sons, 1908), 174–175.

12. Norman, *AS: An American Seer*, 25.

Chapter 11 • *(pages 71–79)*

1. AS, quoted in Thomas Craven, "Stieglitz — Old Master of the Camera," *Saturday Evening Post*, January 8, 1944, 14. See William Innes Homer, *Alfred Stieglitz and the Photo-Secession*, 7.

2. Dorothy Norman, *Alfred Stieglitz: An American Seer*, 25–26.

3. AS in *TAY*, no. 1, 1938, 93–94.

4. Robert Taft, *Photography and the American Scene*, 334.

5. Reproduced in William Welling, *Photography in America*, 233.

6. Unsigned [Agnes Ernst], "The New School of the Camera," *New York Morning Sun*, April 26, 1908.

7. *Photographic Times*, August 1883, 403–404.

8. Taft, *Photography and the American Scene*, 334.

9. Theodore Dreiser, "A Master of Photography," *Success*, June 10, 1899, 471.

10. AS in *TAY*, no. 1, 1938, 93.

11. Hermann Vogel, *Handbook of the Practice and Art of Photography*.

12. AS in *TAY*, no. 1, 1938, 94.

13. Ibid., 93.

14. Vogel, *Handbook*, 294. On p. 327, Vogel illustrates the Apollo Belvedere bust photographed from three angles, creating very different effects.

15. AS in *TAY*, no. 1, 1938, 94.

16. Charles H. Caffin, *Photography as a Fine Art*, 28.

17. Dreiser, "A Remarkable Art, The New Pictorial Photography," *Great Round World*, May 3, 1902, 430–434.

18. Unsigned [Agnes Ernst], "New School of the Camera."

19. Herbert J. Seligmann, *Alfred Stieglitz Talking 1925–1931*, 76.

20. AS in *TAY*, no. 1, 1938, 94–95. Nancy Newhall, *From Adams to Stieglitz*, 124.

21. Eaton S. Lothrop, Jr., *A Century of Cameras*, 26.

22. Norman, *Alfred Stieglitz: Introduction to an American Seer*, 6.

23. AS, "A Word or Two About Amateur Photography in Germany," *Amateur Photographer* (London), February 25, 1887, 96.

24. AS, quoted in Thomas Craven, "Stieglitz," 14. Homer, *Stieglitz and the Photo-Secession*, 7.

25. Homer, *Alfred Stieglitz and the American Avant-Garde*, 13, quoting Norman, *Introduction*, 6.

26. AS, quoted in Welling, *Photography in America*, 291.

27. Norman, *AS: An American Seer*, 29.

28. Newhall, *From Adams to Stieglitz*, 124.

29. Rosenfeld in Waldo Frank et al., eds., *America and Alfred Stieglitz*, 69.

Chapter 12 • *(pages 80–85)*

1. AS, "Photography and Painting," *TAY*, no. 5/6, 145.

2. AS, untitled note accompanying reproduction of his photograph *After the Rain*, in *Sun and Shade*, January 1892, n.p.

3. Quoted in William Welling, *Photography in America*, 291.

4. AS in *TAY*, no. 1, 1938, 94–95.

5. AS, "A Word or Two About Amateur Photography in Germany," *Amateur Photographer* (London), February 25, 1887, 97.

6. *Photographic Times*, August 1883, 403–404.

7. *Der Amateur-Photograph* (Düsseldorf), March 1887, 48.

8. AS, "Amateur Photography in Germany," 97.

9. AS, "Photography and Painting," 144–147.

10. Catalog of International Exhibition of Pictorial Photography, Albright Art Gallery, Buffalo, New York, 1910.

11. Mark Twain, *The Innocents Abroad* (New York: Library of America, 1984), 160.

12. The Pensione du Lac is now known as the Hotel du Lac.

13. AS also gave the girl's name as Marina.

14. The fountain no longer exists. Early in the twentieth century Bellagio's harbor was filled in to create a piazza. The arcade visible in the background of *A Good Joke* is that of the Hotel du Lac.

15. "Our Views," *Amateur Photographer* (London), November 25, 1887, 253–254.

16. PHE to AS, June 20, 1888, ASA/YCAL.

17. Paul Rosenfeld, *Port of New York*, 310.

Chapter 13 • *(pages 86–93)*

1. AS, "Das Chlorsilber-Gelatine-Papier . . . ," *Jahrbuch für Photographie und Reproductionstechnik für das Jahr 1890* (Halle), 111.

2. AS, "The Platinotype Process and the New York Amateur," *AAP*, 1892, 153–154.

3. AS, "Platinum Printing," in *Picture Taking and Picture Making* (Rochester, N.Y.: Eastman Kodak Co., 1898); reprinted in *The Modern Way of Picture Making* (Rochester, N.Y.: Eastman Kodak Co., 1905), 122–128.

4. AS letter, *Amateur Photographer* (London), July 22, 1887.

5. AS, "Sammler und Vorzugsdrucke," *Camerakunst* (Berlin), 1903, 55–56.

6. P. H. Emerson lecture, "Photography: A Pictorial Art," March 1886; quoted in Nancy Newhall, *P. H. Emerson*, 39–40.

7. Quoted in Newhall, *P. H. Emerson*, 34–35.

8. PHE to AS, June 20, 1888, ASA/YCAL.

9. PHE to AS, September 29, 1889, ASA/YCAL.

10. Ibid.

11. PHE to AS, September 18, 1889, ASA/YCAL.

12. AS review of the 1899 American edition of P. H. Emerson's *Naturalistic Photography*, in *CN*, October 1899, 88.

13. Quoted in Newhall, *P. H. Emerson*, 66.

14. Ibid., 81.

15. Newhall, *From Adams to Stieglitz*, 98.

16. "Naturalistic Photography," *Photographic Journal*, March 28, 1893; quoted in Newhall, *P. H. Emerson*, 99.

17. Newhall, *P. H. Emerson*, 3.

18. AS, "The Joint Exhibition at Philadelphia," *AAP*, May 1893, 202.

19. AS review, *CN*, October 1899, 88.

20. AS, "Pictorial Photography," *Scribner's*, November 1899, 528.

Chapter 14 • *(pages 94–100)*

1. AS, "A Day in Chioggia," *Amateur Photographer* (London), June 1889 (Prize Tour Number).
2. The house, greatly altered on the exterior as well as utterly transformed inside, is now the centerpiece of a condominium community called the Quarters at Four Seasons Inn.
3. AS, "Photographic Exhibition, Berlin," *Amateur Photographer*, September 6, 1889, 154.
4. Obermeyer's *Anticipation* is reproduced in *AAP*, October 1893, opposite 468. His *Delight in Disorder* is reproduced in *AAP*, January 1894, 5. In the "Editorial Comment" on p. 22 of that issue AS says of the latter: "It is probably the most interesting piece of work done by him."
5. Nancy Newhall, *From Adams to Stieglitz*, 125.
6. Ibid.
7. AS, "Cortina and Sterzing," *Sun Pictures from Many Lands*, published by *Amateur Photographer* (London), 1892, 60.
8. Ibid.
9. "Our Views," *Amateur Photographer* (London), July 18, 1890.

Chapter 15 • *(pages 101–106)*

1. AS in *TAY*, no. 1, 1938, 95–96.
2. AS, "The Reproduction of Pictorial Photographs by Half-tone Methods," *Practical Process Worker and Photo-Mechanical Printer*, June 1896, 33.
3. AS, "Editorial Comment," *AAP*, January 1894, 22. *The Last Load* is reproduced opposite p. 3.

Chapter 16 • *(pages 107–115)*

1. AS, "A Plea for Art Photography in America," *Photographic Mosaics*, 1892, 135–137.
2. AS, "The Joint Exhibition at New York," *AAP*, April 1894, 153–156.
3. AS, "The Seventh Annual Joint Exhibition," *AAP*, May 1894, 209–219.
4. AS, "Plea for Art Photography," 135–137.
5. AS, "The Joint Exhibition at Philadelphia," *AAP*, June 1893, 251.
6. AS, "Joint Exhibition at New York," 153.
7. AS, quoted by Paul Rosenfeld in Waldo Frank et al., eds., *America and Alfred Stieglitz*, 75.

8. AS, "Joint Exhibition at Philadelphia," 201.

9. Ibid., 207.

10. Alexander Black, "The Amateur Photographer," *Century*, September 1887; reprinted in Beaumont Newhall, *Photography*, 149–153.

11. Frances Benjamin Johnston, "What a Woman Can Do with a Camera," *Ladies' Home Journal*, September 1897.

12. "Editorial Comment," *AAP*, July 1893, 318.

13. AS, "Editorial Comment," *AAP*, November 1893, 518. AS, "Joint Exhibition at Philadelphia," 203.

14. AS, "Joint Exhibition at Philadelphia," 203.

15. Quoted in Margaret Harker, *Henry Peach Robinson*, 79–80.

16. AS, "Modern Pictorial Photography," *Century*, October 1902, 822.

17. AS, "The American Photographic Salon," *American Annual of Photography and Photographic Times Almanac for 1896*, 194–196.

18. AS, "Joint Exhibition at New York," 153–156.

19. AS, "A Plea for a Photographic Art Exhibition," *American Annual of Photography and Photographic Times Almanac for 1895*, 28.

20. AS, "Pictorial Photography in the United States, 1895," *Photograms of the Year 1895*, 81.

Chapter 17 • *(pages 116–122)*

1. AS, "The Joint Exhibition at Philadelphia," *AAP*, June 1893, 251.

2. Brian Coe, *Cameras*, 87. See also Eaton S. Lothrop, Jr., *A Century of Cameras*, 75.

3. AS, "Joint Exhibition at Philadelphia," 251.

4. AS, "The Hand Camera — Its Present Importance," *American Annual of Photography and Photographic Times Almanac for 1897*, 19.

5. "The Men in the Storm," in Hart Crane, *Prose and Poetry* (New York: Library of America, 1984), 577.

6. "Specimen Days," in Walt Whitman, *Poetry and Prose* (New York: Library of America, 1982), 703.

7. AS, "Hand Camera," 19.

8. Sadakichi Hartmann in *The Valiant Knights of Daguerre*, 164.

9. AS, "Hand Camera," 19.

10. Theodore Dreiser, "A Master of Photography," *Success*, June 10, 1899, 471.

11. "Society News," *AAP*, May 1893, 219.

12. AS in *TAY*, no. 1, 1938, 97.

13. AS to Hamilton Easter Field, November 16, 1920, ASA/YCAL.

14. W. E. Woodbury, "Alfred Stieglitz and His Latest Work," *Photographic Times*, April 1896, 161, quoting AS: "Nothing charms me so much as walking among

the lower classes, studying them carefully and making mental notes. They are interesting from every point of view. I dislike the superficial and artificial, and I find less of it among the lower classes. That is the reason they are more sympathetic to me as subjects."

15. Herbert J. Seligmann, *Alfred Stieglitz Talking 1925–1931*, 101; Felix Isman, *Weber and Fields* (New York: Boni and Liveright, 1924), 176, 183.
16. Seligmann, *Stieglitz Talking*, 102.

Chapter 18 • *(pages 123–128)*

1. Nancy Newhall, *From Adams to Stieglitz*, 127.
2. Todd Webb, *Looking Back*, 48.
3. Newhall, *From Adams to Stieglitz*, 127.
4. Quoted in Joan Abse, *John Ruskin*, 129.
5. Paul Rosenfeld in Waldo Frank et al., eds., *America and Alfred Stieglitz*, 78.

Chapter 19 • *(pages 129–134)*

1. Quoted in Sadakichi Hartmann, *The Valiant Knights of Daguerre*, 166.
2. Ibid., 52. Stieglitz may have heard Guilbert only in New York, in 1896.
3. "Editorial Comment," *AAP*, June 1894, 273.
4. AS letter, August 8, 1894, *AAP*, September 1894, 431–432.
5. AS and Louis H. Schubart, "Two Artists' Haunts," *Photographic Times*, January 1895, 9–12.
6. Ibid.
7. Quoted in Hartmann, *Valiant Knights of Daguerre*, 67.
8. AS, "My Favorite Picture," *Photographic Life*, 1899, 11–12.
9. AS, "The Seventh Annual Exhibition," *AAP*, May 1894, 213.
10. George Davison, "Pictorial Photography: The London Photographic Salon, 1894," *AAP*, November 1894, 493.

Chapter 20 • *(pages 137–143)*

1. "To Our Readers," *AAP*, January 1895, 24.
2. "Bolles vs. the Outing Co., Limited," *AAP*, July 1895, 319; Nancy Newhall, *From Adams to Stieglitz*, 105.
3. Newhall, *From Adams to Stieglitz*, 128.

4. *Anthony's Photographic Bulletin*, October 1895, 334, quoted in William Welling, *Photography in America*, 361.

5. "Editorial Comment," *AAP*, September 1894, 418–421.

6. *CN*, July 1902, 33.

7. *AAP*, January 1895, 39.

8. *Amateur Photographer* (London), February 21, 1896, 149.

9. AS, "Four Happenings," *TAY*, no. 8/9, 1942, 114.

10. Theodore Dreiser, "The Camera Club of New York," *Ainslee's*, October 1899, 325.

11. AS, "The Hand Camera — Its Present Importance," *American Annual of Photography and Photographic Times Almanac for 1897*, 19.

12. Dreiser, "A Master of Photography," *Success*, June 10, 1899, 471.

13. Sadakichi Hartmann, "The New York Camera Club," *Photographic Times*, February 1900, 59.

14. Dreiser, "Camera Club of New York," 325.

15. Unsigned [Dreiser], "A Remarkable Art," *Great Round World*, May 3, 1902, 443.

16. Dreiser, "Master of Photography," 471.

17. Ibid.

18. AS, "The Photographic Year in the United States," *Photograms of the Year 1897*, 29.

19. Dreiser, "Camera Club of New York."

20. AS, "Simplicity in Composition," from *The Modern Way of Picture Making* (Rochester, N.Y.: Eastman Kodak Co., 1905), 161–164.

21. Dorothy Norman, *Alfred Stieglitz: An American Seer*, 42–43.

Chapter 21 • *(pages 144–148)*

1. Theodore Dreiser, "The Camera Club of New York," *Ainslee's*, October 1899.

2. AS, "Valedictory," *CN*, July 1902, 3–4. John Francis Strauss, "The Club and Its Official Organ: Special Meeting of the Club," *CN*, January 1901, 154.

3. Letter signed by Publication Committee, *CN*, July 1897, 1.

4. AS, quoted in Jerome Mellquist, *The Emergence of an American Art*, 94–95.

5. AS, "To William M. Murray — An Appreciative Acknowledgement," *CN*, July 1902, 5. Strauss, "Club and Its Official Organ," 155.

6. R. Child Bayley, *CW*, October 1913, 58.

7. SH to AS, n.d., quoted in Sadakichi Hartmann, *The Valiant Knights of Daguerre*, 15.

8. AS note, *CN*, January 1899, 132.

9. *CN*, October 1898, 46–49.

10. Publication Committee, "Free Speech," *CN*, July 1899, 23.

Chapter 22 • (pages 149–152)

1. Preface to catalog of Philadelphia Photographic Salon, Pennsylvania Academy of the Fine Arts, October 24–November 12, 1898, n.p.
2. AS, "Painters on Photographic Juries," *CN*, July 1902, 27–30.
3. AS note in *CN*, January 1899, 132.
4. Jerome Mellquist, *The Emergence of an American Art*, 109.
5. Barbara L. Michaels, *Gertrude Käsebier*, 56–58. Käsebier's first studio was located at 12 East Thirtieth Street. In 1899 she would move her studio around the corner to 273 Fifth Avenue, between Twenty-ninth and Thirtieth streets.
6. Charles H. Caffin, *Photography as a Fine Art*, 55.
7. AS in *CN*, July 1899, 24.
8. Gertrude Käsebier to F. H. Day, December 14, 1899, quoted in William Innes Homer, *Alfred Stieglitz and the Photo-Secession*, 66.
9. Quoted in William Innes Homer, *A Pictorial Heritage*, 26.

Chapter 23 • (pages 153–156)

1. Nancy Newhall, *From Adams to Stieglitz*, 128.
2. Charles H. Caffin, *Photography as a Fine Art*, 48.
3. Newhall, *From Adams to Stieglitz*, 128.
4. Edward Steichen, *A Life in Photography*, n.p.
5. Franz von Stuck, *Sin (Die Sünde)*, 1893, Munich, Bayerische Staatsgemälde-sammlungen.
6. Stuck, *The Kiss of the Sphinx*, c. 1895, Budapest, Museum of Fine Arts.
7. Reproduced in William Innes Homer, *Alfred Stieglitz and the American Avant-Garde*, 25. A similar portrait of AS, by Gertrude Käsebier, is in the Princeton University Art Museum (Barbara L. Michaels, *Gertrude Käsebier*, 74).

Chapter 24 • (pages 157–162)

1. AS, "Notes," *CN*, October 1898, 53.
2. AS, "The Progress of Pictorial Photography in the United States," *American Journal of Photography and Photographic Times Almanac for 1899*, 158.
3. AS, "Notes," *CN*, October 1898, 53–54.
4. AS, "Modern Pictorial Photography," *Century*, October 1902, 825.
5. Unsigned [Theodore Dreiser], "A Remarkable Art," *Great Round World*, May 3, 1902.

6. Joseph Pennell, "Is Photography Among the Fine Arts?" *Contemporary Review*, 1897, 824–836; reprinted in Vicki Goldberg, ed., *Photography in Print*, 210–213.

7. AS's article "Pictorial Photography" in *Scribner's*, November 1899, 528–537, is illustrated with images from his exhibition at the Camera Club. Keiley's article was reprinted as a monograph, with illustrations, published by Tennant and Ward.

8. Charles H. Caffin, *Photography as a Fine Art*, 99–100.

9. Ibid., 39–40.

10. Unsigned [Dreiser], "Remarkable Art."

11. Dreiser, "The Camera Club of New York," *Ainslee's*, October 1899.

12. Caffin, *Photography as a Fine Art*, 46.

13. Paul Martin, "Around London by Gaslight," *Amateur Photographer* (London), October 9 and 16, 1896. In an article he wrote in 1897, AS praised Martin for the unselfishness with which he had explained the details of his procedure, gave him credit for having pioneered the specialty that had been "the novelty of the year," and stated that "Mr. Fraser, of the Camera Club of New York, was the first American to take up the work on similar lines" (AS, "Night Photography with the Introduction of Life," *American Annual of Photography and Photographic Times Almanac for 1898*, 1897). By 1910, however, AS was not prepared to be quite so candid. He then claimed that "simultaneously with Mr. Paul Martin, in London," he himself had been "the first to successfully experiment with night scenes" (catalog of International Exhibition of Pictorial Photography, Albright Art Gallery, Buffalo, New York, 1910).

14. Dorothy Norman, *Alfred Stieglitz: An American Seer*, 44.

15. AS, "Night Photography."

16. AS, "The Pictures in This Number," *CW*, January 1903, 63.

17. Ibid.

18. AS, "Photograph the Flat-Iron Building, 1902–03," *TAY*, no. 14/15, 1946, 188–190.

19. Ibid.

Chapter 25 • *(pages 163–168)*

1. "Mr. Osborne I. Yellott on 'The Issue,'" *CN*, April 1902, 272ff.

2. Reprinted in *CN*, July 1900, 56–64.

3. *CN*, July 1900, 34.

4. AS letter, July 5, 1900, in *Amateur Photographer* (London), July 20, 1900, 44.

5. *CN*, July 1900, 34.

6. SH to AS, September 2, 1904, ASA/YCAL.

7. Sadakichi Hartmann, "A Visit to Steichen's Studio," *CW,* April 1903; reprinted in Hartmann, *The Valiant Knights of Daguerre,* 202.

8. Charles Caffin, "Progress in Photography," *Century,* February 1908, 491.

9. Hartmann [under pseud. Sidney Allan], "Eduard J. Steichen, Painter, Photographer," *CN,* July 1902, 15–16.

10. Nancy Newhall, *From Adams to Stieglitz,* 118–119.

11. Hartmann, "Visit to Steichen's Studio," 209.

12. AS letter, April 10, 1902, "The 'Champs de Mars' Salon and Photography," *CN,* July 1902, 50.

13. *New York Herald,* March 30, 1902.

14. AS letter, April 10, 1902, "'Champs de Mars' Salon," 50.

15. AS, "Postscript. — May 10th," *CN,* July 1902, inserted between pp. 50 and 51.

Chapter 26 • *(pages 169–173)*

1. F. II. Day to AS, n.d. [1898], ASA/YCAL.

2. Quoted in Estelle Jussim, *Slave to Beauty,* 141.

3. Draft of letter reproduced in Jussim, *Slave to Beauty,* 143.

4. AS note in *CN,* July 1901, 33ff.

5. Quoted in A. Horsley Hinton, "Some Further Considerations of the New American School and Its Critics," *Amateur Photographer,* 1900, 383–385; Beaumont Newhall, *The History of Photography,* 160.

6. Note in *Amateur Photographer* (London), September 21, 1900, 222.

7. "The English Exhibitions and the 'American Invasion,'" *CN,* January 1901, 163.

8. Sadakichi Hartmann, "A Decorative Photographer. F. H. Day," *Photographic Times,* March 1900, 102–106.

9. Alvin Langdon Coburn, *Alvin Langdon Coburn: Photographer,* 18.

10. AS to Dudley Johnston, June 25, 1924, RPS Archive. Quoted in Margaret Harker, *The Linked Ring,* 175.

11. Hartmann, *The Valiant Knights of Daguerre,* 259.

Chapter 27 • *(pages 174–181)*

1. AS, "American Pictorial Photography, Series II," *CN,* April 1901, 286.

2. John Francis Strauss, "The Club and Its Official Organ: Special Meeting of the Club," *CN,* January 1901, 153–161.

3. AS review, "The Members' Third Annual Exhibition of Prints" (Camera Club of New York), *CN,* October 1900, 109–111.

4. AS letter in *Amateur Photographer* (London), November 16, 1900, 383.

5. AS, "The Photo-Secession at the National Arts Club, New York," *Photograms of the Year 1902*, 17–20.

6. John Aspinwall to AS, January 16, 1902, ASA/YCAL.

7. *CN*, April 1902, 309.

8. *CN*, July 1902, 80.

9. AS, "Juries and Judges," *CW*, April 1903, 48.

10. AS in *TAY*, no. 8/9, 1942, 116–118.

11. AS, "Pictorial Photography," *Scribner's*, November 1899, 534; reprinted in Beaumont Newhall, *Photography*, 165.

12. *CN*, July 1902, 69.

13. "Valedictory," *CN*, July 1902, 3.

14. Letter, May 26, 1902, *Photo-Era*, 1902, 489.

15. Ibid., 490.

16. Joseph Keiley, "Final Report of Print Committee for 1901–1902," *CN*, July 1902.

17. AS, "Photo-Secession," 17–20.

18. Ibid.

19. AS to F. Dundas Todd, March 17, 1902; published in *British Journal of Photography*, 1902, 459.

Chapter 28 • *(pages 182–188)*

1. *CN*, July 1902, 46.

2. AS, "The Photo-Secession," Bausch and Lomb Lens Souvenir, 1903.

3. Ibid.

4. AS, "The Photo-Secession," *CW*, July 1903.

5. AS, "Four Happenings," *TAY*, no. 8/9, 1942, 117.

6. Of the founders, only Bullock, Fuguet, Redfield, and Strauss were never Links. Mary Devens, who became a Link in September 1902, and Alvin Langdon Coburn, who became one in October 1903, were both made fellows of the Photo-Secession. Only four American Links were never fellows of AS's organization: Day, C. Yarnall Abbott (some of whose photographs would nevertheless be exhibited at AS's gallery in 1907), Margaret Russell Foster, and Rudolf Eickemeyer.

7. AS, "Photo-Secession," *CW*, July 1903.

8. AS, "The Photo-Secession at the National Arts Club, New York," *Photograms of the Year 1902*, 17–20.

9. Edward Steichen, *A Life in Photography*, n.p.

10. "Editorial," *CW*, April 1906, 17.

11. William Post to AS, January 7, 1903, ASA/YCAL.

12. Steichen, *Life in Photography*, n.p.
13. AS letter, November 11, 1902, published in *CW*, January 1903, 60.
14. AS to Frederick C. Beach, November 21, 1902, published in *AAP*, December 1902, 575.
15. AS, "Photo-Secession Notes," *CW*, April 1903, 50.
16. AS letter, December 12, 1903, published in *Photographic Times*, January 1904, 47.
17. Peter Morrin et al., *The Advent of Modernism*, 143.
18. AS, "Photo-Secession," Bausch and Lomb Lens Souvenir, 1903.
19. Georgia O'Keeffe, *Georgia O'Keeffe: A Portrait by Alfred Stieglitz*, introduction, n.p.
20. Ibid.

Chapter 29 • *(pages 189–196)*

1. Temple Scott, "Fifth Avenue and the Boulevard Saint-Michel," *Forum*, December 1910, 670.
2. AS, "*Camera Work* and the New York Public Library," *TAY*, no. 5/6, 1941, 153.
3. *CW*, October 1903.
4. "An Apology," *CW*, January 1903, 15.
5. Ibid.
6. Herbert J. Seligmann, *Alfred Stieglitz Talking 1925–1931*, 85.
7. Edward Steichen to AS, [1901], ASA/YCAL.
8. Nancy Newhall, *From Adams to Stieglitz*, 120–121.
9. PHE to AS, [1904], ASA/YCAL.
10. Seligmann, *Stieglitz Talking*, 79.
11. George Bernard Shaw, "The Exhibitions," *Amateur Photographer* (London), October 11, 1901, 282–284, and October 18, 1901, 303–304; reprinted in Peter C. Bunnell, ed., *A Photographic Vision*, 143.
12. Charles H. Caffin, *Photography as a Fine Art*, 18.
13. Sadakichi Hartmann, "An Art Critic's Estimate of Alfred Stieglitz," *Photographic Times*, June 1898.
14. Hartmann, "A Plea for Straight Photography," *AAP*, March 1904, 101–109.

Chapter 30 • *(pages 197–206)*

1. AS, "The Photo-Secession and the St. Louis Exposition," *Amateur Photographer* (London), April 14, 1904, 287–288.
2. AS letter published in *British Journal of Photography*, August 1904.
3. "Exhibition Notes — The Photo-Secession," *CW*, April 1905, 49.

4. Sadakichi Hartmann [under pseud. The Chiel], "The Salon Club and the First American Photographic Salon at New York," *AAP*, July 1904, 296–305. Reprinted in Hartmann, *The Valiant Knights of Daguerre*, 124.

5. SH to AS, September 2, 1904, ASA/YCAL.

6. Hartman, "Salon Club," 124.

7. AS letter published in *AAP*, August 1904, 358–359.

8. AS, "Some Impressions of Foreign Exhibitions," *CW*, October 1904, 34.

9. Ibid.

10. AS, "One Hour's Sleep — Three Dreams," *291*, March 1915.

11. *Amateur Photographer* (London), July 28, 1904.

12. Roland Rood letter to the editor, *AAP*, October 1904, 421.

13. Quoted in Margaret Harker, *The Linked Ring*, 145.

14. AS in *CW*, October 1904, 36.

15. AS letter published in *Photography*, October 15, 1904.

16. Hartmann [under pseud. Juvenal], "Little Tin Gods on Wheels," *Photo-Beacon*, September 1904, 282–286.

17. Hartmann [under pseud. Caliban], "The Inquisitorial System," *Photo-Beacon*, November 1904, 346–349.

18. Hartman [under pseud. Caliban], "Gessler's Hat," *Camera*, November 1904, 431–434.

19. AS, "The 'First American Salon' at New York" *CW*, January 1905, 50. It came out that Bell had edited the submissions down to eighteen hundred before the judges arrived. See H. C. Rubincam [letter], *Photographer*, February 21, 1905, 267–269, and Sarah Greenough, "The Published Writings of Alfred Stieglitz," 384.

20. Curtis Bell to George Seeley, November 19, 1904; quoted in Weston J. Naef, *The Collection of Alfred Stieglitz*, 430.

21. *AAP*, December 1904, 519–529.

22. AS to Seeley, December 27, 1904, ASA/YCAL.

Chapter 31 • *(pages 209–216)*

1. Joseph Keiley to AS, n.d., quoted in Robert Doty, *Photo-Secession*, 36–37.

2. AS letter published in *Photo-Era*, October 1905, 147.

3. Sadakichi Hartmann, "A Monologue," *CW*, April 1904, 25.

4. AS letter published in *Photo-Era*, October 1905, 147.

5. Ibid.

6. "Photo-Secession Notes," *CW*, April 1906, p. 48.

7. John Kerfoot, "The Game at the Little Galleries," *CW*, January 1911, 45.

8. AS letter published in *Photo-Era*, October 1905, 147.

9. AS, "Editorial," *CW*, April 1906, 17. The catalog of the exhibition gives its dates as November 24, 1905–January 4, 1906.
10. Charles Caffin, "The Recent Exhibitions — Some Impressions," *CW*, October 1906, 33.
11. Charles FitzGerald, *New York Evening Sun*, December 9, 1905; reprinted in *CW*, April 1906, 35.
12. FitzGerald, *New York Evening Sun*, December 2, 1905; reprinted in *CW*, April 1906, 33.
13. Calendar of Exhibitions, *CW*, April 1906, in unpaged advertising section.
14. Roland Rood, "The 'Little Galleries' of the Photo-Secession," *AAP*, December 1905, 567.
15. Caffin, "Recent Exhibitions," 37. On the published price list for the American photographs in the 1905 London salon, Stieglitz's prints were priced from $25 (*Miss S. R.*) to $40 (*Ploughing*) and Steichen's at $50 to $60; Keiley's hand-worked glycerine prints were all $75. The prices of prints by the less distinguished Photo-Secessionists mostly ranged between five dollars and $25.

Chapter 32 • *(pages 217–223)*

1. AS, "Four Happenings," *TAY*, no. 8/9, 1942, 122.
2. AS to Heinrich Kuehn [probably November 17, 1906]; quoted in Robert Doty, *Photo-Secession*, 43.
3. AS, "Four Happenings," 122–123.
4. Joseph Keiley, "The Photo-Secession Exhibition at the Pennsylvania Academy of Fine Arts — Its Place and Significance in the Progress of Pictorial Photography," *CW*, October 1906.
5. F. H. Day to AS, November 30, 1906, ASA/YCAL.
6. Unsigned [Agnes Ernst], "The New School of the Camera," *New York Morning Sun*, April 26, 1908.
7. *New York Evening Sun*, December 11, 1897; quoted in Bennard P. Perlman, *Robert Henri*, 37.
8. AS, "The Editor's Page," *CW*, April 1907, 37.
9. Ibid., 37–38.
10. AS in *TAY*, no. 1, 1938, 82.
11. Charles Caffin, "The De Meyer and Coburn Exhibitions," *CW*, July 1909, 29.
12. AS to Kuehn, August 25, 1925, ASA/YCAL.
13. Clarence White to Day, February 11, 1908; quoted in Estelle Jussim, *Slave to Beauty*, 175.
14. AS to White, May 23, 1912, ASA/YCAL.
15. *CW*, July 1909, 47.

16. Ibid.
17. Gertrude Käsebier to Day, December 28, 1907; quoted in Barbara L. Michaels, *Gertrude Käsebier*, 125.
18. Adolf de Meyer to AS, July 21, 1908, ASA/YCAL.

Chapter 33 • *(pages 224–227)*

1. AS, "Four Happenings," *TAY*, no. 8/9, 1942, 128.
2. AS in *TAY*, no. 1, 1938, 81.
3. AS letter to the editor of *Photography* (London), July 31, 1907; reprinted in AS, "The New Color Photography — A Bit of History," *CW*, October 1907.
4. Ibid.
5. AS letter, n.d., to the editor of *Photography*; reprinted in AS, "New Color Photography."

Chapter 34 • *(pages 228–237)*

1. J. Nilsen Laurvik, *New York Times;* reprinted in *CW*, April 1908.
2. Quoted in "The Rodin Drawings at the Photo-Secession Galleries," *CW*, April 1908, 35.
3. AS letter, December 28, 1916, published in *Bruno's Weekly*, January 1917, 8.
4. Laurvik, *New York Times;* reprinted in *CW*, April 1908.
5. SH to AS, August 22, 1908, ASA/YCAL.
6. "A Woman Waits for Me," in Walt Whitman, *Poetry and Prose* (New York: Library of America, 1982), 259.
7. Jerome Mellquist, *The Emergence of an American Art*, 187.
8. Georgia O'Keeffe, "Stieglitz: His Pictures Collected Him," *New York Times Magazine Section*, December 11, 1949; reprinted in Peninah R. Petruck, ed., *Photography Before World War II*, 42.
9. Georgia O'Keeffe, *Georgia O'Keeffe: A Portrait by Alfred Stieglitz*, introduction, n.p.
10. Ibid.
11. John Hadden to AS, January 4, 1908; reprinted in John Francis Strauss, "Mr. Stieglitz's Expulsion — A Statement," *CW*, April 1908.
12. Strauss, "Mr. Stieglitz's Expulsion."
13. Charles Caffin, "Rumpus in a Hen-House," *CW*, April 1908.
14. Charles I. Berg to unidentified correspondent, March 21, 1908; published in Strauss, "Mr. Stieglitz's Expulsion."
15. *New York Times*, February 14, 1908.

16. "The Camera Workers," *CW,* April 1908, 44. The organization would survive until 1912.
17. Strauss, "Mr. Stieglitz's Expulsion."
18. M. W. Tingley to AS, February 4, 1908; reprinted in Strauss, "Mr. Stieglitz's Expulsion."
19. Dennis Longwell, "Alfred Stieglitz vs. The Camera Club of New York," *Image,* December 1971, 21–23.
20. Strauss, "Mr. Stieglitz's Expulsion."
21. Berg to unidentified correspondent, March 21, 1908; published in Strauss, "Mr. Stieglitz's Expulsion."
22. Addendum to Strauss, "Mr. Stieglitz's Expulsion."
23. Unsigned [Agnes Ernst], "The New School of the Camera," *New York Morning Sun,* April 26, 1908.
24. Ernst to AS, January 5, 1909, ASA/YCAL.
25. Quoted in Bennard P. Perlman, *Robert Henri,* 80.
26. Caffin, *The Story of American Painting,* 378.

Chapter 35 • *(pages 238–244)*

1. Quoted in Alfred H. Barr, Jr., *Matisse,* 113.
2. Quoted in Robert Doty, *Photo-Secession,* 45.
3. AS in *TAY,* no. 1, 1938, 100.
4. *CW,* July 1908, 10.
5. AS to Hamilton Easter Field, September 7, 1921; published in *Arts,* August-September 1921, 61.
6. Unsigned [Agnes Ernst], "The New School of the Camera," *New York Morning Sun,* April 26, 1908.
7. Adolf Wolff, *International;* reprinted in *CW,* October 1913, 43.
8. AS to Walter Zimmermann, August 1, 1910; published in AS, *Photo-Secessionism and Its Opponents.*
9. Quoted in Werner Haftmann, *Painting in the Twentieth Century,* vol. 1, 71.
10. Reprinted in *CW,* July 1908, 10.
11. Ibid.
12. "The Little Galleries of the Photo-Secession," *CW,* July 1908, 13.
13. Jerome Mellquist, *The Emergence of an American Art,* 192.
14. AS, "Four Happenings," *TAY,* no. 8/9, 1942, 125.
15. Unsigned [Ernst], "New School of the Camera."
16. *CW,* April 1909, 36.
17. Mellquist, *Emergence of an American Art,* 185.
18. *CW,* July 1914, 38.
19. AS, "Four Happenings," 127.

Chapter 36 • *(pages 245–252)*

1. Benjamin de Casseres, "Caricature and New York," *CW,* April 1909, 17.
2. Paul Haviland, "The Photo-Secession Gallery," *CW,* April 1909, 36–37.
3. De Casseres, "Caricature and New York," 18.
4. Haviland, "Photo-Secession Gallery," 36–37.
5. Edward Steichen, *A Life in Photography,* n.p.
6. "Photo-Secession Notes," *CW,* July 1909, 27. Smith and Marius de Zayas were first listed as members of the Photo-Secession in that same issue of *CW* (20).
7. Although the name of the old organization is usually given as the "Society of American Painters in Paris," stationery used by Steichen and reproduced in Alfred H. Barr, Jr., *Matisse* (112), has the letterhead "American Art Association of Paris."
8. Steichen to AS, n.d. [early 1909], ASA/YCAL.
9. Gertrude Stein, *The Autobiography of Alice B. Toklas,* 11. AS in *TAY,* no. 1, 1938, 100. Dorothy Norman, *Alfred Stieglitz: An American Seer,* 97.
10. Steichen to AS, n.d. [early 1909], ASA/YCAL.
11. AS, quoted in Norman, *AS: An American Seer,* 97.
12. Reprinted in *CW,* July 1909, 43.
13. Ibid.
14. Ibid., 42.
15. Ibid.
16. Quoted in Townsend Ludington, *Marsden Hartley,* 79.
17. AS to MH, October 26, 1923, ASA/YCAL.
18. AS to MH, October 27, 1923, ASA/YCAL.
19. Marsden Hartley, "Somehow a Past," unpublished ms., YCAL; quoted in Ludington, *Marsden Hartley,* 62.
20. Hartley, "Albert P. Ryder," *Seven Arts,* May 1917, 94, 96.
21. Quoted in Ludington, *Marsden Hartley,* 64.

Chapter 37 • *(pages 253–259)*

1. Joseph Keiley, "Impressions of the Linked Ring Salon of 1908," *CW,* January 1909, 33.
2. AS to George Davison, April 10, 1909, ASA/YCAL.
3. Ibid.
4. AS, "Four Happenings," *TAY,* no. 8/9, 1942, 126.
5. Dorothy Norman, *Alfred Stieglitz: An American Seer,* 111–112.
6. AS, "Four Marin Stories," *TAY,* no. 8/9, 1942, 157.
7. AS to Heinrich Kuehn, March 1, 1909, ASA/YCAL.

8. AS to Edith Halpert, December 20, 1930; published in Percy North, "Turmoil at 291," *Archives of American Art Journal*, 1984, 16.
9. Ibid. AS in *TAY*, no. 1, 1938, 83–84.
10. Temple Scott, "Fifth Avenue and the Boulevard Saint-Michel," *Forum*, December 1910, 668–669.

Chapter 38 · *(pages 260–266)*

1. Waldo Frank, *Our America*, 184.
2. Ibid.
3. Edward Steichen, *A Life in Photography*, n.p.
4. Paul Rosenfeld, *Port of New York*, 261–262.
5. Ibid., 261.
6. Frank, *Our America*, 185.
7. Mabel Dodge Luhan, *Movers and Shakers*, 72.
8. *New York Sun*, March 6, 1912; Sarah Greenough, "The Published Writings of Alfred Stieglitz," 468.
9. Marius de Zayas, "How, When, and Why Modern Art Came to New York," *Arts*, April 1980, 114.
10. Frank, *Our America*, 185. Herbert J. Seligmann, *Alfred Stieglitz Talking 1925–1931*, iv–v, 110.
11. Henry McBride, *The Flow of Art*, 43.
12. Edmund Wilson, *The American Earthquake*, 101.
13. Quoted in de Zayas, "How, When, and Why," 115.
14. Henry Miller, "Stieglitz and Marin," *TAY*, no. 8/9, 1942, 151; reprinted in Miller, *The Air-Conditioned Nightmare*.
15. Georgia O'Keeffe, *Georgia O'Keeffe: A Portrait by Alfred Stieglitz*, introduction, n.p.
16. Thomas Hart Benton, *An American in Art*, 45.
17. De Zayas, "How, When, and Why," 115.
18. Hutchins Hapgood, *A Victorian in the Modern World*, 337–339.
19. Ibid.
20. Seligmann, *Stieglitz Talking*, iv–v.
21. Rosenfeld, *Port of New York*, 257, 259.
22. Edward Weston, *The Daybooks of Edward Weston*, vol. 1 (*Mexico*), 5.
23. AS to SH, December 22, 1911, ASA/YCAL.
24. Ibid.
25. Harold Clurman, *All People Are Famous*, 59.
26. AS, "Is Photography a Failure?" *New York Sun*, March 14, 1922; Sarah Greenough, "The Published Writings of Alfred Stieglitz," 505.
27. De Zayas, "How, When, and Why," 115.
28. Hapgood, *Victorian in the Modern World*, 337–339.

29. AS, "Four Happenings," *TAY*, no. 8/9, 1942, 123.
30. AS in *TAY*, no. 1, 1938, 100.
31. AS letter published in *Art Digest*, March 1927, 20.
32. Marie Rapp, quoted in William Innes Homer, *Alfred Stieglitz and the American Avant-Garde*, 79–80.
33. AS in *TAY*, no. 1, 1938, 86.
34. Quoted in Steven Watson, *Strange Bedfellows*, 184.

Chapter 39 • *(pages 267–273)*

1. Unsigned [Paul Haviland], "Photo-Secession Exhibitions," *CW*, January 1910, 51.
2. B. P. Stephenson, reprinted in *CW*, January 1910, 51.
3. Frank Jewett Mather, Jr., *New York Evening Post*, March 1910; reprinted in *CW*, April 1910, 50–51.
4. "Photo-Secession Notes," *CW*, October 1910, 41.
5. Reprinted in "Photo-Secession Notes," *CW*, April 1910, 47.
6. "Photo-Secession Notes," *CW*, April 1910, 47.
7. Caspar Purdon Clarke interview, *New York Post*, December 30, 1908; reprinted in *CW*, April 1909, 24–26.
8. Alfred H. Barr, Jr., *Matisse*, 115.
9. Israel White in *Newark Evening News;* reprinted in *CW*, July 1910, 45.
10. "Photo-Secession Notes," *CW*, April 1910.
11. James Huneker in *New York Sun*, April 7, 1910; reprinted in *CW*, July 1910, 49.
12. William Innes Homer, *Alfred Stieglitz and the American Avant-Garde*, 109.
13. DN to Edward Steichen, August 13, 1946, Edward Steichen Archive, Museum of Modern Art, New York.
14. "Photo-Secession Notes," *CW*, July 1910, 42.

Chapter 40 • *(pages 277–284)*

1. "Photo-Secession Notes," *CW*, April 1910.
2. AS to George D. Pratt, December 7, 1912, ASA/YCAL.
3. Paul Haviland, "Photo-Secession Notes," *CW*, July 1910, 41.
4. Ibid.
5. AS to A. L. Coburn and Mrs. F. Coburn, [1911], ASA/YCAL.
6. "Photo-Secession Notes," *CW*, October 1910, 41.
7. *Outlook*, February 20, 1924; quoted in Edward Abrahams, "Alfred Stieglitz and the Metropolitan Museum of Art," *Arts*, June 1979, 88.

8. Foreword to catalog of International Exhibition of Pictorial Photography, Albright Art Gallery, Buffalo, New York, 1910.

9. Cornelia B. Sage to AS, November 4, 1909, ASA/YCAL.

10. AS to Walter Zimmermann, June 16, 1910; in AS, *Photo-Secessionism and Its Opponents*, 9.

11. AS, *Photo-Secessionism and Its Opponents*, [3].

12. *American Photography*, August 1910, 476.

13. Max Weber designed the cover of the catalog, on which he placed the mysterious inscription "79–1910–12." Perhaps it should have read "479–1910–124," referring to the numbers of prints in the invitational and open sections, not counting addenda.

14. AS to Coburn, September 1910, ASA/YCAL.

15. F. Austin Library, "Some Impressions of the Buffalo Exhibition," *American Photography*, December 1910, 676.

16. Joseph Keiley, "The Buffalo Exhibition," *CW*, January 1911.

17. AS to F. H. Evans, December 26, 1910, ASA/YCAL.

18. AS to Karl Struss, June 14, 1912, Estate of Karl Struss; quoted in William Innes Homer, *Alfred Stieglitz and the Photo-Secession*, 149–151.

19. Lidbury, "Impressions of the Buffalo Exhibition," 680–681.

20. AS to George Seeley, November 21, 1910, ASA/YCAL.

21. Lidbury, "Impressions of the Buffalo Exhibition," 676.

Chapter 41 • *(pages 285–292)*

1. Quoted in Marius de Zayas, "How, When, and Why Modern Art Came to New York," *Arts*, April 1980, 101.

2. Temple Scott, "Fifth Avenue and the Boulevard Saint-Michel," *Forum*, December 1910, 667.

3. AS to Edith Halpert, December 20, 1930; published in Percy North, "Turmoil at 291," *Archives of American Art Journal*, 1984, 18.

4. Paul Haviland, "Art as a Commodity," *CW*, April-July 1911, 69.

5. AS to Halpert, December 20, 1930; published in North, "Turmoil at 291," 18.

6. Reprinted in "The Exhibitions at '291,'" *CW*, October 1911, 31.

7. F. Austin Lidbury, "Some Impressions of the Buffalo Exhibition," *American Photography*, December 1910, 680.

8. AS to R. Child Bayley, April 29, 1912, ASA/YCAL.

9. AS to Clarence White, May 23, 1912, ASA/YCAL

10. AS to Gertrude Käsebier, December 19, 1910, and her undated reply at the bottom of the same sheet, ASA/YCAL.

11. Joseph Keiley, "The Buffalo Exhibition," *CW*, January 1911, 27.

12. AS to Käsebier, January 4, 1912, ASA/YCAL.

13. Käsebier's "Recollections" (typescript of first-person recollections written or dictated by Käsebier, c. 1929), 184, Gertrude Käsebier Papers, University of Delaware Library, Newark, Delaware; quoted in Barbara L. Michaels, *Gertrude Käsebier*, 128.
14. AS to Ward Muir, January 30, 1913, ASA/YCAL.

Chapter 42 • *(pages 293–298)*

1. AS to SH, December 22, 1911, ASA/YCAL.
2. AS in *TAY*, no. 1, 1938, 83–84.
3. Edward Steichen to AS, undated [summer 1910], ASA/YCAL.
4. Reprinted in *CW*, October 1911, 29.
5. Harold Clurman, *All People Are Famous*, 59.
6. "Art Photographs and Cubist Painting," *New York Sun*, March 3, 1913.
7. AS to Arthur Jerome Eddy, November 10, 1913, ASA/YCAL.
8. AS to Heinrich Kuehn, October 14, 1912, ASA/YCAL.
9. Marius de Zayas, "The New Art in Paris," *Forum*, February 1911, 180; reprinted in *CW*, April-July 1911.
10. AS to SH, December 22, 1911, ASA/YCAL.
11. Ibid.
12. Ibid.
13. Ibid.
14. AS letter to the editor, December 14, 1911, published in *New York Evening Sun*, December 18, 1911.
15. AS to SH, December 22, 1911, ASA/YCAL.
16. Ibid.

Chapter 43 • *(pages 299–308)*

1. AS to Heinrich Kuehn, January 12, 1912, ASA/YCAL.
2. AS to SH, December 22, 1911, ASA/YCAL.
3. AS to Kuehn, October 14, 1912, ASA/YCAL.
4. Benjamin de Casseres, "Modernity and Decadence," *CW*, January 1912, 17–18.
5. AS to MH, October 20, 1913, ASA/YCAL.
6. Edward Steichen, *A Life in Photography*, n.p.
7. Charles Caffin, "Exhibition of Prints by Baron Ad. De Meyer," *CW*, January 1912.
8. AS to SH, December 1911, ASA/YCAL.
9. MH to AS, [July? 1911], ASA/YCAL.

10. AD to Samuel Kootz, written during the 1910s and published in Kootz, *Modern American Painters* (New York: Brewer & Warren, 1930); reprinted in Barbara Haskell, *Arthur Dove*, appendix.

11. Herbert J. Seligmann, *Alfred Stieglitz Talking 1925–1931*, 13.

12. Alfred H. Barr, Jr., *Matisse*, 148–149.

13. Reprinted in "Photo-Secession Notes," *CW*, April 1912.

14. "Some Remarkable Work by Very Young Artists," unsourced newspaper clipping, ASA/YCAL.

15. Quoted in Jerome Mellquist, *The Emergence of an American Art*, 201.

16. "Some Remarkable Work."

17. Quoted in William Innes Homer, *Alfred Stieglitz and the American Avant-Garde*, 140.

18. Reprinted in "Photo-Secession Notes," *CW*, January 1913, 24.

19. "Photo-Secession Notes," *CW*, January 1913, 24.

20. "Some Remarkable Work."

21. "Photo-Secession Notes," *CW*, January 1913, 24.

22. William L. O'Neill, ed., *Echoes of Revolt*, 49.

23. Steichen, *Life in Photography*, n.p.

24. Mellquist, *Emergence of an American Art*, 211n.

25. AS, "Ten Stories," *TAY*, no. 5/6, 1941, 137.

Chapter 44 • *(pages 309–322)*

1. Quoted in Milton W. Brown, *The Story of the Armory Show*, 58.

2. Mabel Dodge Luhan, *Movers and Shakers*, 36.

3. Ibid., 83.

4. Agnes Ernst Meyer, *Out of These Roots*, 102.

5. Luhan, *Movers and Shakers*, 72.

6. Alfred Kreymborg, *Troubadour*, 134. Hutchins Hapgood, *A Victorian in the Modern World*, 274.

7. Hapgood, *Victorian in the Modern World*, 285.

8. Quoted in Jerome Mellquist, *The Emergence of an American Art*, 200.

9. Quoted in Luhan, *Movers and Shakers*, 52.

10. Hapgood in *New York Globe*, February 21, 1913; quoted in Steven Watson, *Strange Bedfellows*, 135.

11. Hapgood, *Victorian in the Modern World*, 283.

12. AS to Heinrich Kuehn, May 22, 1912, ASA/YCAL.

13. Gertrude Stein, "Pablo Picasso," *CW*, special number, August 1912, 29.

14. "Photo-Secession Notes," *CW*, January 1913, 24.

15. "Some Remarkable Work by Very Young Artists," unsourced newspaper clipping, ASA/YCAL.

16. AS to Ward Muir, January 30, 1913, ASA/YCAL.

17. AS to John Cosgrave, January 27 and 29, 1913, ASA/YCAL.

18. AS, "The First Great 'Clinic to Revitalize Art,'" *New York American*, January 26, 1913.

19. AS to Israel White, March 18, 1913. Sarah Greenough and Juan Hamilton, eds., *Alfred Stieglitz*, 196–197.

20. Quoted in Brown, *Story of the Armory Show*, 109.

21. Reprinted in "Notes on '291,'" *CW*, April-July 1913.

22. AS to Muir, January 30, 1913, ASA/YCAL.

23. *CW*, April-July 1913. In the exhibition catalog, AS erroneously assigned a date of 1892 to *The Terminal* and *Winter — Fifth Avenue*.

24. "Notes on '291,'" *CW*, April-July 1913.

25. Ibid.

26. Ibid.

27. Marius de Zayas, "Photography," *CW*, January 1913.

28. AS to George D. Pratt, December 7, 1912, ASA/YCAL.

29. Quoted in Robert Doty, *Photo-Secession*, 63.

30. Quoted in B. L. Reid, *The Man from New York*, 151.

31. Gertrude Stein, *The Autobiography of Alice B. Toklas*, 134.

32. AS to Arthur Carles, April 11, 1913, ASA/YCAL.

33. Marius de Zayas, "Relative and Absolute Caricatures," 291, New York, April 8–May 20, 1913.

34. Paul Haviland, "Marius de Zayas — Material, Relative, and Absolute Caricatures," *CW*, April 1914.

35. Paul Rosenfeld, *Port of New York*, 272–273.

36. Luhan, *Movers and Shakers*, 165.

37. *La Vie Parisienne*, May 3, 1919, 309; quoted in William A. Camfield, *Francis Picabia*, 57.

Chapter 45 • *(pages 323–329)*

1. Hutchins Hapgood, *A Victorian in the Modern World*, 340.

2. AS, "Ten Stories," *TAY*, no. 5/6, 1941, 160–161.

3. Marius de Zayas to AS, September 7, 1913, ASA/YCAL.

4. AS to MH, October 20, 1913, ASA/YCAL.

5. MH to AS, October 1912, ASA/YCAL.

6. AS to MH, October 20, 1913, ASA/YCAL.

7. AS to Edward Steichen, November 26, 1913, ASA/YCAL.

8. Marius de Zayas, "Photography and Artistic-Photography," *CW*, April-July 1913.

9. Walter Pach to Constantin Brancusi, February 6, 1914; quoted in Pontus Hulten et al., *Brancusi*, 94.

10. In the catalog of Brancusi's 291 exhibition, *The First Step* was called *The Prodigal Son*, as Brancusi had specifically requested. Brancusi eventually destroyed *The First Step*, except for the head. The quite different but related sculpture now known as *The Prodigal Son* (Philadelphia Museum of Art, Arensberg Collection) dates from 1915.

11. Reprinted in "Exhibitions at '291,'" *CW*, January 1914 [published June 1914].

12. Ibid.

13. AS to Brancusi, April 14, 1914; quoted in Pontus Hulten et al., *Brancusi*, 96.

14. J. Edgar Chamberlin in *New York Evening Mail*; reprinted in "Exhibitions at '291,'" *CW*, June 1914, 43.

15. "Exhibitions at '291,'" *CW*, January 1914 [published June 1914].

Chapter 46 • *(pages 330–338)*

1. AS, [untitled], *CW*, July 1914 [published January 1915], 3.

2. AS to Charles Caffin, November 17, 1914, ASA/YCAL.

3. Henry McBride in *New York Sun*, February 8, 1914; reprinted in McBride, *The Flow of Art*, 52.

4. AS, "Six Happenings," *TAY*, no. 14/15, 1946–47, 197.

5. "Contributors," *CW*, July 1914 [published January 1915].

6. Alfred Kreymborg, *Troubador*, 210.

7. Peyton Boswell in *New York Herald*, [January 1915]; quoted in Marius de Zayas, "How, When, and Why Modern Art Came to New York," *Arts*, April 1980, 112.

8. Paul Rosenfeld, *Port of New York*, 266.

9. AS, "Our Illustrations," *CW*, January 1914 [published June 1914], 44.

10. Caffin, "Censorship in the Land of the Free," *New York American*, April 20, 1914.

11. Dorothy Norman, *Alfred Stieglitz: An American Seer*, 124.

12. Herbert J. Seligmann, *Alfred Stieglitz Talking 1925–1931*, 116.

13. William L. O'Neill, *Echoes of Revolt*, 269.

14. De Zayas would expand all this claptrap into a small book, *African Negro Art: Its Influence on Modern Art*, published by the Modern Gallery in 1916.

15. Arthur Jerome Eddy, *Cubists and Post-Impressionism*, 2nd ed. (Chicago: A. C. McClung, 1919), 220.

16. AS to AD, November 5, 1914, ASA/YCAL.

17. De Zayas, "How, When, and Why," 110.

18. De Zayas to AS, June 30, 1914, ASA/YCAL.

19. Unsigned review in *New York Herald*, January 19, 1915, 12; quoted in William A. Camfield, *Francis Picabia*, 68.
20. *CW*, July 1914 [published January 1915].
21. Ibid., 40.
22. Quoted in Penelope Niven, *Carl Sandburg*, 272.
23. Edward Steichen, *A Life in Photography*, n.p.
24. *CW*, July 1914 [published January 1915], 66.

Chapter 47 • *(pages 339–344)*

1. [Unsigned], *291*, March 1915, n.p.
2. AS, "One Hour's Sleep — Three Dreams," *291*, March 1915, n.p.
3. Nancy Newhall, *From Adams to Stieglitz*, 124.
4. "Exhibitions at '291,' 1914–1915," *CW*, April 1914 [published October 1914], 52.
5. AS, "Four Happenings," *TAY*, no. 8/9, 1942, 133.
6. Edward Steichen, *A Life in Photography*, n.p.
7. Ibid.
8. Charles Caffin in *New York American*, April 5, 1915; quoted in Sandra Lee Underwood, *Charles H. Caffin*, 121.
9. Caffin to AS, April 6, 1915, ASA/YCAL.
10. GOK to AP, August 25, 1915, ASA/YCAL.
11. Reprinted in Henry McBride, *The Flow of Art*, 81.
12. Paul Rosenfeld, *Port of New York*, 258.
13. AS, "Four Happenings," 134–136.
14. AS to H. C. Reiner, June 11, 1915, ASA/YCAL.
15. AS to GOK, January 22, 1917; quoted in Sarah Greenough and Juan Hamilton, eds., *Alfred Stieglitz*, 201–202.

Chapter 48 • *(pages 345–355)*

1. In the catalog of his 1921 exhibition, Stieglitz dated three photographs of "Ellen" 1916, but his dates are never entirely reliable.
2. Agnes Meyer to AS, August 16, 1915, ASA/YCAL.
3. "'291' and The Modern Gallery," *CW*, October 1916.
4. Marius de Zayas, "How, When, and Why Modern Art Came to New York," *Arts*, April 1980, 117.
5. Ibid., 116–117.
6. Ibid., 118.

7. Ibid., 117.
8. Willard Huntington Wright, "The Forum Exhibition," *Forum*, April 1916, 460.
9. Henry McBride in *New York Sun*; reprinted in *CW*, October 1916.
10. AS to John Weichsel, November 8, 1915, John Weichsel Papers, AAA.
11. Meyer to de Zayas, n.d., Marius de Zayas Papers, CU.
12. "'291' and The Modern Gallery."

Chapter 49 • *(pages 356–365)*

1. GOK to AP, June 20, 1917, ASA/YCAL.
2. Willard Huntington Wright, "The Aesthetic Struggle in America," *Forum*, February 1916, 210.
3. Quoted in James R. Mellow, *Charmed Circle*, 202–203.
4. AS to MH, May 12, 1914, ASA/YCAL.
5. Paul Strand in Paul Hill and Thomas Cooper, *Dialogue with Photography*, 3–4.
6. Charles Sheeler to AS, October 28, 1916, ASA/YCAL.
7. AS to Sheeler, November 1, 1916, ASA/YCAL.
8. Wright, "Aesthetic Struggle in America," 204.
9. AS to John Weichsel, December 8, 1915, John Weichsel Papers, AAA.
10. Wright, *Modern Painting;* quoted in Bennard P. Perlman, *Robert Henri*, 121.
11. Wright, "The Forum Exhibition," *Forum*, April 1916, 457.
12. Wright, "Aesthetic Struggle in America," 217.
13. Wright, "Forum Exhibition," 457.
14. Ibid., 465.
15. Strand photographs: March 13–April 3, 1916. Forum Exhibition: March 13–25, 1916.
16. Unsigned [AS], "Photographs by Paul Strand," *CW*, October 1916, 11.
17. AS to Williamina Parrish, May 8, 1917, ASA/YCAL.
18. Paul Strand, "Photography," *Seven Arts*, August 1917.
19. AS in *TAY*, no. 1, 1938, 95.
20. Strand, "Photography."
21. Unsigned [AS], "Our Illustrations," *CW*, June 1917, 36.

Chapter 50 • *(pages 369–378)*

1. AP to GOK, January 1, 1916, ASA/YCAL.
2. AP to GOK, November 1915, ASA/YCAL.
3. Dorothy Norman, *Alfred Stieglitz: An American Seer*, 130.

4. Herbert J. Seligmann, *Alfred Stieglitz Talking 1925–1931*, 70.

5. Norman, *AS: An American Seer*, 129.

6. Ibid., 130.

7. AP to GOK, January 1, 1916, ASA/YCAL.

8. AS to GOK, [mid-January 1916], ASA/YCAL; published in Anita Pollitzer, *A Woman on Paper*, 124.

9. GOK to AP, [late June 1915], ASA/YCAL.

10. GOK to AP, [October 1915], ASA/YCAL.

11. Georgia O'Keeffe, *Georgia O'Keeffe: A Portrait by Alfred Stieglitz*, introduction, n.p.

12. Waldo Frank, *Our America*, 184.

13. Edmund Wilson, *The American Earthquake*, 102.

14. Frank, *Our America*, 184–185.

15. AP to GOK, [November 1915], ASA/YCAL.

16. Frank, *Our America*, 185.

17. AP to GOK, [November 1915], ASA/YCAL.

18. GOK to AP, December 4, 1915, ASA/YCAL.

19. GOK to AP, January 4, 1916, ASA/YCAL.

20. GOK to AP, [November 1915], ASA/YCAL.

21. GOK to AP, January 14, 1916, ASA/YCAL.

22. GOK to AP, [September 1915], ASA/YCAL.

23. GOK to AP, January 4, 1916, ASA/YCAL.

24. GOK to AS, February 1, 1916, ASA/YCAL; published in Jack Cowart et al., eds., *Georgia O'Keeffe*, 150.

25. GOK to AP, [December 1915], ASA/YCAL.

26. O'Keeffe, *Portrait by Stieglitz*, introduction, n.p.

27. Edward Steichen, *A Life in Photography*, n.p.

28. AP to GOK, [July 1916], ASA/YCAL.

29. "Georgia O'Keeffe — C. Duncan — Réné [*sic*] Lafferty," *CW*, October 1916, 12–13.

30. Ibid.

31. Ibid.

32. Ibid.

33. Evelyn Sayer to AS, published in *CW*, October 1916.

34. Laurie Lisle, *Portrait of an Artist*, 75.

35. Seligmann, *Stieglitz Talking*, 70.

36. Norman, *AS: An American Seer*, 130–131.

37. In Perry Miller Adato's film *Georgia O'Keeffe* (produced by WNET/THIRTEEN, New York, for Women in Art, 1977); quoted in Barbara Buhler Lynes, *O'Keeffe, Stieglitz and the Critics, 1916–1929*, 321.

38. GOK to AS, July 27, 1916, ASA/YCAL; published in Pollitzer, *Woman on Paper*, 140–141.

39. GOK to AP, [October 1915], ASA/YCAL.

40. AS to GOK, [mid-January 1916], ASA/YCAL; published in Pollitzer, *Woman on Paper*, 124.

41. GOK to AP, January 4, 1916, ASA/YCAL.

42. GOK to AP, [June 1916], ASA/YCAL.

43. Ibid.

44. GOK to AP, [August 1916], ASA/YCAL.

45. AS to GOK, [June 1916], ASA/YCAL; published in Pollitzer, *Woman on Paper*, 140.

46. GOK to AP, [July 1916], ASA/YCAL.

47. GOK to AP, [September 1916], ASA/YCAL.

Chapter 51 • *(pages 379–388)*

1. Stanton Macdonald-Wright to AS, March 8, 1920, ASA/YCAL.

2. GOK to AP, June 20, 1917, ASA/YCAL.

3. GOK to AS, July 27, 1916, ASA/YCAL; published in Jack Cowart et al., eds., *Georgia O'Keeffe*, 154.

4. Henry Tyrrell, "Esoteric Art at '291,'" *Christian Science Monitor*, May 4, 1917; reprinted in *CW*, June 1917.

5. William Murrell Fisher, "The Georgia O'Keeffe Drawings and Paintings at '291,'" *CW*, June 1917.

6. AS letter, April 13, 1917; published in *Blind Man*, May 1917, 15.

7. Beatrice Wood, *I Shock Myself*, 29.

8. "His Art Too Crude for Independents," *New York Herald*, April 14, 1917.

9. Quoted in William A. Camfield, *Marcel Duchamp*, 41.

10. Edward Weston, *The Daybooks of Edward Weston*, vol. 1 (Mexico), 132.

11. Herbert J. Seligmann, *Alfred Stieglitz Talking 1925–1931*, 29.

12. AS to Marie Rapp, July 23, 1917, ASA/YCAL.

13. AS to AD, December 28, 1916, ASA/YCAL.

14. AS to AML, May 16, 1917, Aline Meyer Liebman Papers, AAA.

15. AS to Mitchell Kennerley, May 1917, New York Public Library.

16. Tyrrell, "Animadversions on the Tendencies of the Times in Art," *Christian Science Monitor*, June 2, 1916.

17. Paul Rosenfeld, *Port of New York*, 265–266.

18. AS to AML, May 16, 1917, Aline Meyer Liebman Papers, AAA.

19. GOK to AP, June 20, 1917, ASA/YCAL.

20. Ibid.

21. Ibid.

22. Ibid.

23. GOK to PS, October 24, 1917, CCP.

24. GOK to PS, June 3, 1917, CCP.

25. GOK to PS, July 23, 1917, CCP.
26. GOK to PS, October 24, 1917, CCP.
27. GOK to PS, November 15, 1917, CCP.
28. GOK to PS, July 23, 1917, CCP.
29. Seligmann in Waldo Frank et al., eds., *America and Alfred Stieglitz*, 113.
30. AS to GOK, May 31, 1917, ASA/YCAL; excerpted in Sarah Greenough and Juan Hamilton, eds., *Alfred Stieglitz*, 202.
31. AS to GOK, June 24, 1917, ASA/YCAL; excerpted in Greenough and Hamilton, eds., *Alfred Stieglitz*, 202.

Chapter 52 • *(pages 389–395)*

1. AS to Annie W. Brigman, [1917 or early 1918], ASA/YCAL.
2. Henry McBride in *New York Sun*, December 10, 1917; quoted in Marius de Zayas, "How, When, and Why Modern Art Came to New York," *Arts*, April 1980, 104–105.
3. PS to Mrs. Shreve, August 9, 1919, ASA/YCAL.
4. James Oppenheim and Waldo Frank, "Editorial," *Seven Arts*, November 1916, 52.
5. Paul Rosenfeld, *Port of New York*, 235.
6. Quoted in Van Wyck Brooks, "Randolph Bourne," in *Fenollosa and His Circle*, 305.
7. Ibid., 313–314.
8. Frank, *Our America*, 186–187.
9. Ibid., 181.
10. Ibid., 9.
11. William Carlos Williams, *The Autobiography of William Carlos Williams*, 272.
12. Lewis Mumford, "Lyric Wisdom," in Jerome Mellquist and Lucie Wiese, eds., *Paul Rosenfeld*, 48.
13. Alan Tate, "Anomaly in New York," in Mellquist and Wiese, eds., *Paul Rosenfeld*, 141.
14. Edmund Wilson, "Paul Rosenfeld: Three Phases," in Mellquist and Wiese, eds., *Paul Rosenfeld*, 9.
15. Frank, *Our America*, 142.
16. Rosenfeld, "Sherwood Anderson," *Dial*, January 1922, 35.
17. Rosenfeld, *Port of New York*, 307.
18. SA to Frank, [December? 1919]; published in Sherwood Anderson, *The Letters of Sherwood Anderson*, 51.
19. Sherwood's older brother, Karl Anderson, was a painter who had been a charter member of the Association of American Painters and Sculptors.
20. SA to Frank, [December? 1919]; published in Anderson, *Letters*, 50–51.

Chapter 53 • *(pages 396–402)*

1. GOK to ESD, [spring 1918], ASA/YCAL.
2. GOK to AS, April 19, 1918, ASA/YCAL; published in Anita Pollitzer, *A Woman on Paper*, 159.
3. AS to PS, May 28, 1918, CCP.
4. AS to PS, May 27, 1918, CCP.
5. AS to AD, June 18, 1918, ASA/YCAL.
6. PS to AS, September 14, 1918, CCP.
7. AS to AD, June 18, 1918, ASA/YCAL.
8. Herbert J. Seligmann, *Alfred Stieglitz Talking 1925–1931*, 125.
9. AS to AD, [July 1918], ASA/YCAL.
10. Seligmann, *Stieglitz Talking*, 125.
11. Ibid.
12. AS to Joe Obermeyer, October 31, 1918, ASA/YCAL.
13. AS to AD, August 15, 1918, ASA/YCAL.
14. AS to AD, late July 1918, ASA/YCAL.
15. AS to SD, [July 1918], ASA/YCAL.
16. AS to AD, August 15, 1918, ASA/YCAL.
17. GOK to ESD, [August 1918], ASA/YCAL.
18. AS to AD, August 15, 1918, ASA/YCAL.
19. Ibid.

Chapter 54 • *(pages 403–408)*

1. AS to AML, postmarked August 7, 1918, Aline Meyer Liebman Papers, AAA.
2. Georgia O'Keeffe, *Georgia O'Keeffe: A Portrait by Alfred Stieglitz*, introduction, n.p.; Roxana Robinson, *Georgia O'Keeffe*, 212.
3. O'Keeffe, *Portrait by Stieglitz*, introduction, n.p.
4. AS to GOK, March 31, 1918, ASA/YCAL; published in Anita Pollitzer, *A Woman on Paper*, 159. AS to PS, May 27, 1918, CCP.
5. AS to AD, August 15, 1918, ASA/YCAL.
6. AS to AD, [July 1918], ASA/YCAL.
7. AS to PS, February 7, 1919, CCP.
8. Jeffrey Hogrefe, *O'Keeffe*, 27.
9. Paul Rosenfeld, "Stieglitz," *Dial*, April 1921; reprinted in Beaumont Newhall, *Photography*, 209.
10. A critic in *Crayon*, quoted in Roger B. Stein, *John Ruskin and Aesthetic Thought in America, 1840–1900*, 114.
11. "I Sing the Body Electric," in Walt Whitman, *Poetry and Prose* (New York: Library of America, 1982), 258.

12. Lewis Mumford in Waldo Frank et al., eds., *America and Alfred Stieglitz*, 57.
13. Ibid., 53–54.
14. AS to AML, postmarked December 17, 1918; Aline Meyer Liebman Papers, AAA.
15. AS to PS, January 23, 1919, CCP.
16. Nancy Newhall, *From Adams to Stieglitz*, 121.
17. Edward Steichen to AS, October 1921, ASA/YCAL.
18. AS to AD, September 18, 1919, ASA/YCAL.
19. Hamilton Easter Field, in *Arts*, December 4, 1920, 25, noted that "Number '291' is gone, and already a skyscraper filling the entire frontage of the block is taking its place."
20. AS to AD, September 18, 1919, ASA/YCAL.
21. AS to Frank, October 30, 1919, ASA/YCAL.

Chapter 55 • *(pages 409–416)*

1. AS to AD, August 28, 1920, ASA/YCAL.
2. Georgia O'Keeffe, *Georgia O'Keeffe*, n.p.
3. Verso of print of the collection of MoMA, with AS's annotation, reproduced in Beaumont Newhall, *Photography*, 216.
4. AS to AML, postmarked April 4, 1921, Aline Meyer Liebman Papers, AAA.
5. AS to AML, February 18, 1924, Aline Meyer Liebman Papers, AAA.
6. "Stieglitz Photograph Brings Record Prices," *New York Times*, October 9, 1993.
7. AS to AD, August 28, 1920, ASA/YCAL.
8. Ibid.
9. AS to AML, August 28, 1920, Aline Meyer Liebman Papers, AAA.
10. AS to AD, July 29, 1920, ASA/YCAL.
11. AS to AML, August 28, 1920, Aline Meyer Liebman Papers, AAA.
12. AS to AD, August 28, 1920, ASA/YCAL.
13. Ibid.
14. AS to Marie Rapp Boursault, October 6, 1920, ASA/YCAL.
15. Herbert J. Seligmann, *Alfred Stieglitz Talking 1925–1931*, 19.
16. Ibid.
17. AS to AML, August 28, 1920, Aline Meyer Liebman Papers, AAA.
18. AS to PR, August 28, 1920, ASA/YCAL; AS to AD, August 28, 1920, ASA/YCAL.
19. AS to AML, August 28, 1920, Aline Meyer Liebman Papers, AAA.
20. AS to HS, October 20, 1920, ASA/YCAL.
21. Seligmann, *Stieglitz Talking*, 61–62.

Chapter 56 · *(pages 417–425)*

1. Paul Rosenfeld in Waldo Frank et al., eds., *America and Alfred Stieglitz*, 84.
2. Henry McBride, "O'Keeffe at the Museum," *New York Sun*, May 18, 1946.
3. John Tennant in *Photo-Miniature*, quoted in Beaumont Newhall, *The History of Photography, from 1839 to the Present*, 171.
4. McBride, "Modern Art," *Dial*, April 1921.
5. Marsden Hartley, *Adventures in the Arts*, 104.
6. McBride, "Modern Art."
7. McBride, "Steiglitz's [*sic*] Life Work in Photography," *New York Herald*, February 13, 1921.
8. Rosenfeld in Frank et al., eds., *America and Alfred Stieglitz*, 87.
9. Rosenfeld, "Stieglitz," *Dial*, April 1921.
10. Ibid.
11. Hartley, *Adventures in the Arts*, 105.
12. McBride, "Modern Art."
13. Ibid.
14. AS to AML, [March-April 1921], Aline Meyer Liebman Papers, AAA.
15. Laurie Lisle, *Portrait of an Artist*, 110.
16. Quoted in Carol Troyen, "After Stieglitz: Edith Gregor Halpert," in Theodore E. Stebbins, Jr., and Troyen, eds., *The Lane Collection*, 36.
17. AS to Hamilton Easter Field, September 7, 1921, published in *Arts*, August-September 1921.
18. AS, "Regarding the Modern French Masters Exhibition: A Letter," *Brooklyn Museum Quarterly*, July 1921, 112–113.
19. MH to AS, August 2, 1920, ASA/YCAL.
20. MH to AS, October 6, 1920, ASA/YCAL.
21. MH to AS, August 2, 1920, ASA/YCAL.
22. Hartley, *Adventures in the Arts*, 247, 254.
23. Ibid., 111.
24. Rosenfeld, *Port of New York*, 301.
25. AS to AML, n.d., [1921], Aline Meyer Liebman Papers, AAA.
26. AS to AML, September 15, 1921, Aline Meyer Liebman Papers, AAA.
27. GOK to Mitchell Kennerley, [autumn 1922], New York Public Library.
28. AS to AD, [July 1921], ASA/YCAL.
29. AS to Frank, August 25, 1921, ASA/YCAL. AS to AD, August 28, 1921, ASA/YCAL.
30. AS to AD, August 28, 1921, ASA/YCAL.
31. AS to HS, October 2, 1921, ASA/YCAL.

Alfred Stieglitz

Chapter 57 • *(pages 426–436)*

1. AS to Hamilton Easter Field, n.d.; published in *Arts*, January 1922, 254. The auction was officially called the Artists' Derby.
2. AS, "Is Photography a Failure?" *New York Sun*, March 14, 1922, 20.
3. Edward Weston, *The Daybooks of Edward Weston*, vol. 1 *(Mexico)*, 5.
4. Ibid.
5. Ananda K. Coomaraswamy in *Bulletin* of Boston Museum of Fine Arts, 1924; quoted in Roger Lipsey, *Coomaraswamy*, vol. 3, 158.
6. AS to Heinrich Kuehn, August 25, 1925, ASA/YCAL.
7. Ralph Steiner, *A Point of View*, 6.
8. AS to Kuehn, August 25, 1925. Weston J. Naef, *The Collection of Alfred Stieglitz*, 482.
9. AS to AD, July 12, 1922, ASA/YCAL.
10. Ibid.
11. AS, "How I Came to Photograph Clouds," *Amateur Photographer and Photography*, September 19, 1923, 255.
12. AS to PS, July 26, 1922, CCP, ASA/YCAL.
13. GOK to Doris McMurdo, July 1–4, 1922, Chatham Hall School, Chatham, Virginia.
14. Paul Rosenfeld, "The Paintings of Georgia O'Keeffe," *Vanity Fair*, October 1922.
15. GOK to McMurdo, July 1–4, 1922, Chatham Hall School, Chatham, Virginia.
16. AS to RSS, July 15, 1922, ASA/YCAL.
17. AS's large camera was an 8 x 10-inch Eastman view camera with a Packard shutter. His small camera was a 4 x 5 Auto Graflex with two old Goerz lenses.
18. AS to AD, August 7, 1922, ASA/YCAL.
19. Sometime during 1922 Stieglitz made, indoors, a close-up of O'Keeffe's buttocks and thighs — one of the last nude studies of her he would ever shoot. There is a remarkable resemblance between his photograph and certain paintings of petunias that O'Keeffe would soon begin to make.
20. AS to AD, August 30, 1922, ASA/YCAL.
21. Georgia Engelhard, "Alfred Stieglitz, Master Photographer," *American Photography*, April 1945.
22. Waldo Frank in *Manuscripts*, December 1922.
23. AS, "How I Came to Photograph Clouds," 255.
24. "Editorial Comment," *AAP*, February 1895, 118.
25. "Cloud Photography," *AAP*, June 1895, 265–266.
26. AS to AD, August 30, 1922, ASA/YCAL.
27. AS to AD, September 15, 1922, ASA/YCAL.
28. AS to AD, September 21, 1922, ASA/YCAL.
29. RSS to PS, September 30, 1922, CCP.
30. AS to RSS, October 28, 1922, ASA/YCAL.

31. Nancy Newhall, *P. H. Emerson*, 123.
32. Georgia O'Keeffe, *Georgia O'Keeffe: A Portrait by Alfred Stieglitz*, introduction, n.p.
33. AS to PR, October 4, 1922, ASA/YCAL.
34. Georgia O'Keeffe in *Manuscripts*, December 1922, 17–18.
35. RSS to PS, October 15, 1922, CCP.
36. Ibid.
37. AS to PR, October 18, 1922, ASA/YCAL.
38. AS to AD, October 24, 1922, ASA/YCAL.
39. Edward Weston to Johann Hagemeyer; quoted in Naef, *Collection of Alfred Stieglitz*, 232.
40. Weston, *Daybooks*, vol. 1, 4.
41. Ibid.
42. Ibid., 4–6.
43. Ibid., 14.
44. Ibid., 21.

Chapter 58 • *(pages 437–446)*

1. AS to PR, September 5, 1923, ASA/YCAL.
2. SA to AS, July 12, 1924, NL, ASA/YCAL; published in Sherwood Anderson, *Letters of Sherwood Anderson*, 127.
3. GOK to Doris McMurdo, July 1, 1922, Chatham Hall School, Chatham, Virginia.
4. GOK to Henry McBride, [February 1923], ASA/YCAL; Henry McBride, "Art News and Reviews," *New York Herald*, February 4, 1923.
5. Alan Burroughs, "Studio and Gallery," *New York Sun*, February 3, 1923.
6. Ibid.
7. Elizabeth Luther Cary, "Art . . . ," *New York Times*, February 4, 1923.
8. SA to GOK, August 4, 1923, NL, ASA/YCAL; published in Anderson, *Letters*, 104–105.
9. SA to AS, June 30, 1923, NL, ASA/YCAL; published in Anderson, *Letters*, 100.
10. SA to GOK, August 4, 1923, NL, ASA/YCAL; published in Anderson, *Letters*, 104–105.
11. Quoted in Milton Meltzer, *Dorothea Lange*, 58.
12. GOK to SA, [August 1, 1923?], NL.
13. SA to AS, June 30, 1923, NL, ASA/YCAL; published in Anderson, *Letters*, 99–100.
14. SA to Roger Sergel, December 18, 1923, NL; published in Anderson, *Letters*, 117–118.
15. SA to PR, [December 1924?], NL; published in Anderson, *Letters*, 134.

16. Anderson, "Alfred Stieglitz," *New Republic*, October 25, 1922, 217.

17. AS to AD, October 24, 1922, ASA/YCAL.

18. SA to AS, May 18, 1923, NL, ASA/YCAL; published in Anderson, *Letters*, 97.

19. McBride, *New York Herald*, March 11, 1923.

20. Quoted in Roger Lipsey, *Coomaraswamy*, vol. 3, 159.

21. Brom Weber, "Stieglitz: An Emotional Experience," in *Stieglitz Memorial Portfolio*, Dorothy Newman, ed. (New York: Twice A Year Press, 1947), 48.

22. AS to Hart Crane, April 16, 1923, CU, ASA/YCAL.

23. Crane to AS, April 15, 1923, CU, ASA/YCAL; published in Crane, *The Letters of Hart Crane*, 131–132.

24. Ibid.

25. Crane to AS, August 25, 1923, CU, ASA/YCAL; published in Crane, *Letters*, 145.

26. Crane to AS, August 11, 1923, CU, ASA/YCAL; published in Crane, *Letters*, 142.

27. Brom Weber, *Hart Crane: A Biographical and Critical Study* (New York: Bodley Press, 1948), 240.

28. Waldo Frank to AS, July 13, 1923, ASA/YCAL.

29. AS to Crane, August 15, 1923, CU, ASA/YCAL.

30. AS to PS, June 28, 1923, ASA/YCAL.

31. "Photographers Criticized; Support for View That They Do Not Understand Own Art," *New York Sun and The Globe*, June 27, 1923.

32. Charles Sheeler to PS, June 22, 1923, ASA/YCAL.

Chapter 59 • *(pages 447–455)*

1. GOK to SA, [August 1, 1923?], NL.

2. AS to AD, September 29, 1923, ASA/YCAL.

3. AS to ESD, June 26, 1923, ASA/YCAL.

4. AS to ESD, October 11, 1923, ASA/YCAL.

5. AS to RSS, October 16, 1923, ASA/YCAL.

6. AS to AD, July 18, 1923, ASA/YCAL.

7. GOK to SA, [August 1, 1923?], NL.

8. AS to AD, July 18, 1923, ASA/YCAL.

9. Ibid.

10. GOK to SA, [August 1, 1923?], NL.

11. AS to AD, July 18, 1923, ASA/YCAL.

12. Ibid.

13. AS to AD, July 18, 1923, ASA/YCAL.

14. SA to AS, June 30, 1923, NL, ASA/YCAL; published in Sherwood Anderson, *Letters of Sherwood Anderson*, 99–100.

15. Hart Crane to AS, July 4, 1923, CU, ASA/YCAL; published in Crane, *The Letters of Hart Crane*, 137–139.
16. GOK to SA, [August 1, 1923?], NL.
17. AS to MH, October 26–27, 1923, ASA/YCAL.
18. AS, quoted in Dorothy Norman, *Alfred Stieglitz: An American Seer*, 202.
19. Laurie Lisle, *Portrait of an Artist*, 102.
20. AS to Crane, December 10, 1923, CU, ASA/YCAL.
21. AS in *TAY*, no. 1, 1938, 99.
22. AS to Crane, [autumn 1923], CU, ASA/YCAL; quoted in John Unterecker, *Voyager*, 319.
23. Catalog of Third Exhibition of Photography by Alfred Stieglitz, Anderson Galleries, New York, 1924.
24. AS to Crane, December 10, 1923, CU, ASA/YCAL.
25. AS to SA, August 7, 1924, NL, ASA/YCAL.
26. Herbert J. Seligmann, *Alfred Stieglitz Talking 1925–1931*, 81, 116.
27. Crane to AS, August 25, 1923, CU, ASA/YCAL; published in Crane, *Letters*, 145.
28. Elizabeth Luther Cary, "Art: Exhibitions of the Week: 'Spiritual America' Print," *New York Times*, March 9, 1924.
29. AS to RSS, August 6, 1923, ASA/YCAL.
30. RSS to PS, September 4, 1923, CCP.
31. AS to ESD, September 24, 1923, ASA/YCAL.
32. Ibid.
33. RSS to PS, September 28, 1923, CCP.
34. AS to AD, September 29, 1923, ASA/YCAL.
35. Ibid.
36. AS to ESD, October 2, 1923, ASA/YCAL.
37. "The Sanitariums," *Fortune*, April 1935.
38. AS to AD, November 3, 1923, ASA/YCAL.
39. AS to MH, October 26–27, 1923, ASA/YCAL.
40. GOK to SA, [November 1923], ASA/YCAL.
41. Ibid.
42. AS to SA, November 1, 1923, NL, ASA/YCAL.
43. AS to J. Dudley Johnston, October 15, 1923, RPS.
44. AS to Crane, [autumn 1923], CU, ASA/YCAL; published in Unterecker, *Voyager*, 319.
45. GOK to SA, [November 1923], ASA/YCAL.
46. Ibid.
47. AS to Crane, [autumn 1923], CU, ASA/YCAL; published in Unterecker, *Voyager*, 319.
48. AS to SA, November 28, 1923, NL, ASA/YCAL.

1. Susan Sontag, *On Photography*, 118.
2. PHE to AS, February 14, 1924, and June 6, 1924, ASA/YCAL.
3. PHE to AS, March 25, 1924, ASA/YCAL.
4. PHE to AS, April 30, 1924, ASA/YCAL.
5. AS to AD, February 21, 1924, ASA/YCAL.
6. AS to RSS, February 18, 1924, ASA/YCAL.
7. GOK to SA, February 11, 1924, NL.
8. Catalog of Third Exhibition of Photography by Alfred Stieglitz, Anderson Galleries, New York, March 3–16, 1924.
9. Elizabeth Luther Cary, "Art: Exhibitions of the Week: 'Spiritual America' Print," *New York Times*, March 9, 1924.
10. Henry McBride, "Stieglitz, Teacher, Artist; Pamela Bianco's New Work: Stieglitz-O'Keefe [*sic*] Show at Anderson Galleries," *New York Herald*, March 9, 1924.
11. Ibid.
12. Egmont Arens, "Alfred Stieglitz: His Cloud Pictures," *Playboy*, July 1924, 15.
13. *Arts*, April 1924; quoted in AS letter published in *Nation*, May 14, 1924, 561.
14. *Nation*, April 16, 1924.
15. SA to AS and GOK, December 7, 1923, NL, ASA/YCAL; published in Sherwood Anderson, *Letters of Sherwood Anderson*, 113. SA night letter to GOK, February 1924, NL.
16. GOK to SA, February 11, 1924, NL.
17. Helen Appleton Read, "Georgia O'Keeffe — Woman Artist Whose Art Is Sincerely Feminine," *Brooklyn Sunday Eagle Magazine*, April 6, 1924.
18. GOK to SA, June 11, 1924, NL.
19. AS to AD, June 23, 1924, ASA/YCAL.
20. GOK to SA, June 11, 1924, NL.
21. Ibid.
22. Ibid.
23. AS to AD, June 23, 1924, ASA/YCAL.
24. GOK to SA, June 11, 1924, NL.
25. Ibid.
26. AS to RSS, June 18, 1924, ASA/YCAL.
27. Edmund Wilson, "The Stieglitz Exhibition," *New Republic*, March 18, 1925, 97–98.
28. GOK to SA, November [11?] 1924, NL.
29. GOK to SA, June 11, 1924. NL.
30. AS to RSS, July 17, 1924, ASA/YCAL.
31. AS to AD, August 3, 1924, ASA/YCAL.
32. AS to RSS, July 17, 1924, ASA/YCAL.
33. AS to RSS, October 3, 1924, ASA/YCAL.

34. AS to ESD, August 3, 1924, ASA/YCAL.

35. RSS to PS, August 8, 1924, CCP.

36. AS to SA, August 7, 1924, NL, ASA/YCAL.

37. Ibid.

38. AS to AD, October 4, 1924, ASA/YCAL.

39. Ibid.

40. AS to SA, October 11, 1924, NL, ASA/YCAL.

41. AS to AD, October 4, 1924, ASA/YCAL.

42. Ibid.

43. Robert M. Coates, "Profiles: Abstraction — Flowers," *New Yorker*, July 6, 1929.

Chapter 61 • *(pages 469–480)*

1. AS to AD, June 23, 1924, ASA/YCAL.

2. Henry McBride, "The Stieglitz Group at Anderson's," *New York Sun*, March 14, 1925.

3. AS to Edith Halpert, December 20, 1930; published in Percy North, "Turmoil at 291," *Archives of American Art Journal*, 1984, 18.

4. "Demuth Was 'Better Friend,'" *Lancaster New Era*, March 7, 1986; quoted in Barbara Haskell, *Charles Demuth*, 175.

5. Dorothy Seiberling, "Horizons of a Pioneer," *Life*, March 1, 1968, 52.

6. Charles Demuth to AS, May 2, 1923, ASA/YCAL.

7. Edmund Wilson, "The Stieglitz Exhibition," *New Republic*, March 18, 1925, 97–98.

8. McBride, "Stieglitz Group at Anderson's."

9. Herbert J. Seligmann, *Alfred Stieglitz Talking 1925–1931*, 13. AS to AD, June 5, 1925, ASA/YCAL.

10. McBride, "Stieglitz Group at Anderson's."

11. AS to AD, July 7, 1925, ASA/YCAL.

12. McBride, "Stieglitz Group at Anderson's."

13. AS to AD, July 7, 1925, ASA/YCAL.

14. AS to AD, June 5, 1925, ASA/YCAL.

15. AS to AD, July 7, 1925, ASA/YCAL.

16. GOK to Ettie Stettheimer, August 6, 1925, ASA/YCAL.

17. Ibid.

18. AS to AD, July 24, 1927, ASA/YCAL.

19. AS to AD, July 7, 1925, ASA/YCAL.

20. Alfred Kreymborg, *Troubadour*. AS to AD, July 7, 1925, ASA/YCAL.

21. AS to Ida O'Keeffe, September 24, 1925, ASA/YCAL.

22. Kreymborg, "The *Caravan* Venture," in Jerome Mellquist and Lucie Wiese, eds., *Paul Rosenfeld*, 26–27.

23. Ibid., 29.
24. AS to AD, August 27, 1925, ASA/YCAL.
25. GOK to Stettheimer, August 6, 1925, ASA/YCAL.
26. AS to AD, August 27, 1925, ASA/YCAL.
27. Ibid.
28. AS to AD, November 9, 1925, ASA/YCAL.
29. AS to ESD, [summer 1925], ASA/YCAL.
30. Fiske Kimball, quoted in Robert Stern et al., *New York 1930*, 208.
31. George Harold Edgell, quoted in Stern et al., *New York 1930*, 208.
32. AS to SA, December 9, 1925, NL, ASA/YCAL.
33. Lillian Sabine, "Record Price for Living Artist," *Brooklyn Sunday Eagle Magazine*, May 27, 1928.
34. AS to SA, December 9, 1925, NL, ASA/YCAL.
35. Claude Bragdon, quoted in Stern et al., *New York 1930*, 210.
36. AS to SA, December 9, 1925, NL, ASA/YCAL.
37. AS to AD, January 27, 1925, ASA/YCAL. Rönnebeck text in catalog of Seven Americans exhibition.
38. Seligmann, *Stieglitz Talking*, 77.
39. AS to AD, July 7, 1925, ASA/YCAL.
40. Seligmann, *Stieglitz Talking*, 100.
41. GOK to Ida O'Keeffe, [November–December 1925], ASA/YCAL.
42. Seligmann, *Stieglitz Talking*, 5.
43. Edward Alden Jewell, "Georgia O'Keeffe: Mystic," *New York Times*, January 22, 1928. Seligmann, *Stieglitz Talking*, 2, 96.
44. Edmund Wilson, *The American Earthquake*, 101–102.
45. AS to AD, July 7, 1925, ASA/YCAL.
46. AS to SA, December 9, 1925, NL, ASA/YCAL.

Chapter 62 • *(pages 481–490)*

1. Herbert J. Seligmann, *Alfred Stieglitz Talking 1925–1931*, 46.
2. Duncan Phillips to AD, March 13, 1926, Phillips Collection Papers, AAA.
3. Phillips, *The Enchantment of Art as Part of the Enchantment of Experience* (New York and London: John Lane, 1914); quoted in *The Phillips Collection in the Making, 1920–1930*, 19.
4. AS, quoted in Dorothy Norman, *Alfred Stieglitz: An American Seer*, 172.
5. AS to DN, 1928; quoted in Norman, *Encounters*, 65.
6. Seligmann, *Stieglitz Talking*, 90–91.
7. Ibid., 62.
8. Murdock Pemberton, "The Art Galleries: Eight Out of Every Ten Are Born Blind . . . ," *New Yorker*, February 20, 1926.

9. Blanche C. Matthias, "Georgia O'Keeffe and the Intimate Gallery," *Chicago Evening Post Magazine of the Art World*, March 2, 1926.
10. Henry McBride, "Modern Art," *Dial*, May 1926.
11. Seligmann, *Stieglitz Talking*, 63.
12. Ibid., 65.
13. Frances O'Brien, "Americans We Like: Georgia O'Keeffe," *Nation*, October 12, 1927, 362.
14. Seligmann, *Stieglitz Talking*, 84.
15. Ibid., 12.
16. Ibid., 129.
17. AS to AD, June 25, 1926, ASA/YCAL.
18. Lillian Sabine, "Record Price for Living Artist," *Brooklyn Sunday Eagle Magazine*," May 27, 1928.
19. AS to AD, April 6, 1927, ASA/YCAL.
20. AS to HS, August 22, 1926, ASA/YCAL.
21. Seligmann, *Stieglitz Talking*, 60.
22. Anita Pollitzer, *A Woman on Paper*, 198.
23. Author interview with Juan Hamilton, September 29, 1990.
24. AS to HS, September 5, 1926, ASA/YCAL.
25. "Exhibitions in New York: Georgia O'Keeffe, Intimate Gallery," *Art News*, February 13, 1926.
26. AS to AD, October 31, 1926, ASA/YCAL.
27. Seligmann, *Stieglitz Talking*, 110–114.
28. Ibid., 118.
29. Ibid., 138–139.
30. Ibid., 90.
31. Ibid., 117.
32. AS to Charles Demuth, January 28, 1930, ASA/YCAL.
33. AS, untitled pamphlet (New York: Privately printed), April 17, 1927.
34. Phillips to Forbes Watson, March 21, 1927, Phillips Collection Papers, AAA.
35. AS to AD, April 6, 1927, ASA/YCAL. Seligmann, *Stieglitz Talking*, 128.
36. AS, untitled pamphlet (New York: Privately printed), April 17, 1927.

Chapter 63 • *(pages 491–495)*

1. AS letter published in *Art Digest*, March 1927, 20.
2. Robert M. Coates, "Profiles: Abstraction — Flowers," *New Yorker*, July 6, 1929.
3. Murdock Pemberton, "The Art Galleries," *New Yorker*, January 22, 1927, 62–63.
4. Louis Kalonyme, "Scaling the Peak of the Art Season," *Arts and Decoration*, March 1927, 93.

5. Lewis Mumford, "O'Keefe [*sic*] and Matisse," *New Republic*, March 2, 1927.

6. Henry McBride, "Georgia O'Keeffe's Work Shown," *New York Sun*, January 15, 1927.

7. GOK to Waldo Frank, January 10, 1927, UPA.

8. Herbert J. Seligmann, *Alfred Stieglitz Talking 1925–1931*, 132.

9. McBride, "Modern Art," *Dial*, March 1927.

10. AS to Gaston Lachaise, May 16, 1929; quoted in Gerald Nordland, *Gaston Lachaise*, 39–40.

11. AS to Lachaise, May 2, 1927; quoted in Nordland, *Gaston Lachaise*, 36.

12. AS to Lachaise, December 7, 1926; quoted in Nordland, *Gaston Lachaise*, 36.

13. AS to Lachaise, May 16, 1929; quoted in Nordland, *Gaston Lachaise*, 39–40.

14. AS to Lachaise, June 1, 1929; quoted in Nordland, *Gaston Lachaise*, 41.

15. AS to AD, June 26, 1927, ASA/YCAL.

16. AS to AD, July 19, 1927, ASA/YCAL.

17. AS to AD, July 24, 1927, ASA/YCAL.

18. Ibid.

19. C. Kay-Scott to GOK, July 21, 1927; published in catalog of O'Keeffe's 1928 exhibition.

20. Seligmann, *Stieglitz Talking*, 132.

21. Duncan Phillips to AD, December 19, 1927, ASA/YCAL.

22. AS to Phillips, December 25, 1927, Phillips Collection Papers, AAA.

23. Phillips to AS, December 29, 1927, ASA/YCAL.

24. AS to AD, January 7, 1928, ASA/YCAL.

25. Phillips to AD, January 21, 1928, Phillips Collection Papers, AAA.

Chapter 64 • (*pages 496–504*)

1. Henry McBride, "Georgia O'Keeffe's Recent Work," *New York Sun*, January 14, 1928.

2. Murdock Pemberton, "The Art Galleries," *New Yorker*, January 21, 1928.

3. "Art: On View," *Time*, February 20, 1928.

4. Herbert J. Seligmann, *Alfred Stieglitz Talking 1925–1931*, 118.

5. Jerome Mellquist, *The Emergence of an American Art*, 328.

6. Lillian Sabine, "Record Price for Living Artist," *Brooklyn Sunday Eagle Magazine*, May 27, 1928.

7. B. Vladimir Berman, "She Painted the Lily and Got $25,000 and Fame for Doing It!" *New York Evening Graphic*, May 12, 1928.

8. *New York Daily Mirror*, July 16, 1929; quoted in Matthew J. Bruccoli, *The Fortunes of Mitchell Kennerley, Bookman*, 218.

9. Bruccoli, *Fortunes of Mitchell Kennerley*, 199. AS to AD, March 26, 1931, ASA/YCAL.

10. Benita Eisler, *O'Keeffe and Stieglitz*, 371.

11. AS letter, April 16, 1928; published in *Art News*, April 21, 1928, 10.

12. "Stieglitz into Metropolitan," *Time*, February 25, 1929.

13. William M. Ivins, Jr., "Photographs by Alfred Stieglitz," *Bulletin of the Metropolitan Museum of Art*, February 1929, 44.

14. GOK to Catherine O'Keeffe Klenert, May 29, 1928, ASA/YCAL.

15. AS to AD, January 7, 1928, ASA/YCAL.

16. Dorothy Norman, *Encounters*, 57–58.

17. Ibid., 59–60.

18. Ibid., 60.

19. Ibid., 62.

20. Ibid., 66.

21. Ibid.

22. AS to AD, July 4, 1928, ASA/YCAL.

23. GOK to McBride, [dated May 11, 1928, but evidently June 1928], ASA/YCAL.

24. AS to AD, July 4, 1928, ASA/YCAL.

25. AS to HS, June 28, 1928, ASA/YCAL.

26. ESD to AS, July 26, 1928, ASA/YCAL.

27. AS to AD, July 4, 1928, ASA/YCAL.

28. Seligmann, *Stieglitz Talking*, 135.

29. AS to AD, September 29, 1923, ASA/YCAL.

30. D. H. Lawrence to AS, September 17, 1923, ASA/YCAL.

31. AS to AD, September 29, 1923, ASA/YCAL.

32. Lawrence to AS, August 15, 1928, ASA/YCAL.

33. Lawrence to AS, August 15, 1928, and September 12, 1928, ASA/YCAL.

34. Seligmann, *Stieglitz Talking*, 135.

35. AS to AD, October 18, 1928, ASA/YCAL.

36. GOK to Ettie Stettheimer, September 21, 1928, ASA/YCAL.

37. AS to AD, October 28, 1928, ASA/YCAL.

38. GOK to MDL, [1925?], ASA/YCAL.

39. Mabel Dodge Luhan, "The Art of Georgia O'Keeffe," typescript, Mabel Dodge Luhan Archive, YCAL.

Chapter 65 • *(pages 505–517)*

1. Dorothy Norman, *Encounters*, 71.

2. Ibid., 72.

3. MH to Adelaide Kuntz, March 1928; quoted in Barbara Haskell, *Marsden Hartley*, 79.

4. GOK to Ettie Stettheimer, August 24, 1929, ASA/YCAL.

5. GOK to Catherine O'Keeffe Klenert, December 9, 1928, ASA/YCAL.

6. AS to AD, March 1, 1929, ASA/YCAL.

7. "Art: On View," *Time*, February 20, 1928.

8. AS to HS, July 10, 1928, ASA/YCAL.

9. GOK to MDL, summer 1929, ASA/YCAL.

10. Georgia O'Keeffe, *Georgia O'Keeffe: A Portrait by Alfred Stieglitz*, introduction, n.p.

11. AS to PS, March 31, 1929, CCP.

12. Hank O'Neal, *Berenice Abbott, American Photographer*, 14.

13. Todd Webb, *Looking Back*, 28.

14. Paul Strand, "Steichen and Commercial Art," *New Republic*, February 19, 1930.

15. AS to Duncan Phillips, April 26 and May 6, 1929, Phillips Collection Papers, AAA.

16. Haskell, *Charles Demuth*, 191.

17. "It Must Be Said," no. 4 [bis], An American Place, November 1935.

18. GOK to Blanche Matthias, April 1929, ASA/YCAL.

19. AS to RSS, May 17, 1929, ASA/YCAL.

20. AS in *TAY*, no. 1, 1938, 108.

21. GOK to Matthias, April 1929, ASA/YCAL.

22. RSS to PS, April [28?], 1929, CCP.

23. GOK to Henry McBride, [summer 1929], ASA/YCAL.

24. RSS to PS, May 2, 1929, CCP.

25. GOK to McBride, [summer 1929], ASA/YCAL.

26. GOK to MDL, [early July 1929], ASA/YCAL.

27. GOK to MDL, [July 1929], ASA/YCAL.

28. Herbert J. Seligmann, *Alfred Stieglitz Talking 1925–1931*, 39.

29. GOK to PS, [May 1929], CCP.

30. GOK to MDL, [June 1929], ASA/YCAL.

31. GOK to McBride, [summer 1929], ASA/YCAL.

32. GOK to MDL, n.d., ASA/YCAL.

33. RSS to PS, June 19, 1929, CCP.

34. AS to AD, May 2, 1929, ASA/YCAL.

35. Seligmann, *Stieglitz Talking*, 136.

36. AS to AD, June 11, 1929, ASA/YCAL.

37. AS to HS, June 17, 1929, ASA/YCAL.

38. Nancy Newhall, *From Adams to Stieglitz*, 123.

39. AS to ESD, July 2, 1929, ASA/YCAL.

40. AS to SH, November 22, 1930, ASA/YCAL.

41. AS to AD, September 9, 1929, ASA/YCAL.

42. Norman, *Alfred Stieglitz: An American Seer*, 161.

43. AS to AD, September 9, 1929, ASA/YCAL.

44. AS to ESD, July 2, 1929, ASA/YCAL.

45. GOK to MDL, [July 1929], ASA/YCAL.

46. Harold Clurman, *All People Are Famous*, 56–57.

47. GOK to MDL, summer 1929, ASA/YCAL.

48. AS to ESD, July 22, 1929, ASA/YCAL.

49. AS to ESD, July 28–29, 1929, ASA/YCAL.

50. Ibid.

51. Ibid.

52. GOK to RSS, August 24, 1929, ASA/YCAL.

53. Ibid.

54. AS to ESD, August 18, 1929, ASA/YCAL.

55. AS to AD, September 9, 1929, ASA/YCAL.

56. AS to ESD, August 18, 1929, ASA/YCAL.

57. Webb, *Looking Back*, 39.

58. AS to AD, September 9, 1929, ASA/YCAL.

59. GOK to Stettheimer, August 24, 1929, ASA/YCAL.

60. GOK to RSS, August 24, 1929, ASA/YCAL.

61. AS to ESD, August 25, 1929, ASA/YCAL.

62. GOK to Stettheimer, August 24, 1929, ASA/YCAL. GOK to MDL, September 1929, ASA/YCAL.

63. GOK to MDL, [letter 2, September 1929], ASA/YCAL.

64. Ibid.

65. GOK to MDL, [letter 1, September 1929], ASA/YCAL.

66. AS to ESD, September 2, 1929, ASA/YCAL.

67. GOK to MDL, [letter 1, September 1929], ASA/YCAL.

68. AS to AD, September 9, 1929, ASA/YCAL.

Chapter 66 • *(pages 521–526)*

1. AS to AD, March 27, 1929, ASA/YCAL.

2. Nancy Newhall, *From Adams to Stieglitz*, 106.

3. AS to AD, April 2, 1931, ASA/YCAL.

4. Alice Goldfarb Marquis, *Alfred H. Barr, Jr.*, 77.

5. AS to RSS, October 24, 1929, ASA/YCAL.

6. AS to AML, December 25, 1929, Aline Meyer Liebman Papers, AAA.

7. GOK to RSS, November 5, 1929, ASA/YCAL.

8. AS to Eliot Porter, January 21, 1939, Estate of Eliot Porter.

9. AS to AD, May 8, 1931, ASA/YCAL.

10. AD to AS, December 19, 1930, ASA/YCAL.

11. AD to AS, probably December 22 or 23, 1930, ASA/YCAL.

12. AS to AD, probably May 25, 1936, ASA/YCAL. AS to AD, December 13, 1932, ASA/YCAL.

13. AS to AD, March 2, 1934, ASA/YCAL.
14. Duncan Phillips to AD, May 3, 1933, Phillips Collection Papers, AAA.
15. AS to AD, June 8, 1934, ASA/YCAL.

Chapter 67 • (*pages 527–536*)

1. GOK to Dorothy Brett, [early April 1930], ASA/YCAL.
2. GOK to MDL, [spring 1930], ASA/YCAL.
3. GOK to Brett, October [12?], 1930, ASA/YCAL. GOK to MDL, [winter 1933–34], ASA/YCAL.
4. AS to AD, July 25, 1930, ASA/YCAL.
5. AS to AD, September 11, 1930, ASA/YCAL.
6. GOK to RSS, September 4, 1930, ASA/YCAL.
7. Harold Clurman to AS, c. 1931; quoted in Dorothy Norman, *Encounters*, 99.
8. GOK to Russell Vernon Hunter, August 1931, ASA/YCAL.
9. AS, "Ten Stories," *TAY*, no. 5/6, 1940–41, 153.
10. Quoted in Norman, *Encounters*, 104.
11. Ibid., 107.
12. Ibid., 106.
13. Norman to Edward Steichen, August 13, 1946, Edward Steichen Archive, Museum of Modern Art, New York.
14. GOK to Henry McBride, July 1931, ASA/YCAL.
15. GOK to RSS, August 9, 1931, ASA/YCAL.
16. GOK to RSS, September 14, 1931, ASA/YCAL.
17. GOK to Hunter, August 1931, ASA/YCAL.
18. GOK to RSS, September 14, 1931, ASA/YCAL.
19. Julien Levy, *Memoir of an Art Gallery*, 51.
20. Carol Troyen, "After Stieglitz: Edith Gregor Halpert," in Theodore J. Stebbins and Troyen, eds., *The Lane Collection*.
21. Beginning in February 1934, AS would occasionally also lend works to J. B. Neumann's Contemporary New Art Circle, which was located in the same building as An American Place.
22. Clurman in Waldo Frank et al., eds., *America and Alfred Stieglitz*, 272.
23. Nancy Newhall, *From Adams to Stieglitz*, 150.
24. GOK to Brett, [mid-February 1932], ASA/YCAL.
25. Catalog of Alfred Stieglitz: Exhibition of Photographs (1884–1934), An American Place, New York, December 11, 1934–January 17, 1935.
26. *New York Herald Tribune*, April 29, 1932.
27. Newhall, *From Adams to Stieglitz*, 114–115.
28. Ibid., 115.

29. Ibid., 133.
30. PS to RSS, December 13, 1966, CCP.
31. Strand recruited Henwar Rodakiewicz to write the shooting script.
32. Newhall, *From Adams to Stieglitz*, 132.
33. GOK to Carl Zigrosser, April 1944, UPA.

Chapter 68 · *(pages 537–555)*

1. Helen Appleton Read, "Georgia O'Keeffe," *Brooklyn Daily Eagle*, February 21, 1926.
2. Laurie Lisle, *Portrait of an Artist*, 205.
3. GOK to Russell Vernon Hunter, [spring 1932], ASA/YCAL.
4. AS to AD, September 12, 1938, ASA/YCAL.
5. Russell Lynes, *Good Old Modern*, 51.
6. GOK to Betty O'Keeffe, January 24, 1930, ASA/YCAL.
7. GOK to Dorothy Brett, [September?] 1932, ASA/YCAL.
8. AS to AD, August 11, 1932, ASA/YCAL.
9. GOK to Brett, [September?] 1932, ASA/YCAL.
10. Ibid.
11. GOK to Hunter, October 1932, ASA/YCAL.
12. AS to AD, January 19, 1933, ASA/YCAL.
13. GOK to Hunter, early February 1933, ASA/YCAL.
14. "Georgia's condition is psychic & cardiac. The former is the thing to unravel. She is at the age" (AS to AD, June 25, 1933, ASA/YCAL).
15. Dorothy Norman, *Dualities*, 76.
16. AS to Olivia Paine (William Ivins's assistant), May 9, 1933, Archives of the Metropolitan Museum of Art, New York; published in Weston J. Naef, *The Collection of Alfred Stieglitz*, 9–10.
17. Ansel Adams, *Ansel Adams: An Autobiography*, 125.
18. AS to Carl Van Vechten, September 1933; quoted in Van Vechten, *The Letters of Carl Van Vechten*, 133.
19. AA to PS, September 12, 1933, CCP.
20. AS to AA, June 28, 1933, CCP, ASA/YCAL.
21. AS to AD, May 24, 1933, ASA/YCAL.
22. AS to AD, June 25, 1933, ASA/YCAL.
23. GOK to Hunter, October 21, 1933, ASA/YCAL.
24. Ibid.
25. AS to AA, October 20, 1933, CCP, ASA/YCAL.
26. AS to AA, June 9, 1934, CCP, ASA/YCAL.
27. AS to AA, October 20, 1933, CCP, ASA/YCAL.

28. GOK to PS, December 26, 1933, CCP.
29. Jean Toomer to AS, December 21, 1933, ASA/YCAL.
30. GOK to PS, December 26, 1933, CCP.
31. Ibid.
32. GOK to Toomer, January 3, 1934, ASA/YCAL.
33. GOK to Toomer, January 10, 1934, ASA/YCAL.
34. GOK to Toomer, March 5, 1934, ASA/YCAL.
35. Nancy Milford, *Zelda*, 349.
36. Ibid., 347.
37. Ibid., 351.
38. GOK to Toomer, March 5, 1934, ASA/YCAL.
39. GOK to Toomer, May 11, 1934, ASA/YCAL.
40. GOK to RSS, April 26, 1934, ASA/YCAL.
41. AS to AA, June 9, 1934, CCP, ASA/YCAL.
42. Ibid.
43. Herbert N. McCoy, "Julius Stieglitz," *American Chemical Society Journal*, November 1938.
44. Catalog of Alfred Stieglitz: Exhibition of Photographs (1884–1934), An American Place, New York, December 11, 1934–January 17, 1935.
45. AS to AD, September 23, 1934, ASA/YCAL.
46. Catalog of Alfred Stieglitz: Exhibition of Photographs (1884–1934).
47. AS to AD, September 12, 1938, ASA/YCAL. AS to AD, December 3, 1937, ASA/YCAL.
48. AS to AD, December 20, 1934, ASA/YCAL.
49. AS to AD, December 25, 1934, ASA/YCAL.
50. Review of *America and Alfred Stieglitz*, by Edward Alden Jewell, *New York Times*, December 23, 1934.
51. AS to AA, December 7, 1933, CCP, ASA/YCAL.
52. Thomas Hart Benton, "America and/or Alfred Stieglitz," *Common Sense*, January 1935.
53. AS to Benton, January 2, 1935, ASA/YCAL.
54. AS to AD, January 2, 1935, ASA/YCAL.

Chapter 69 · *(pages 556–574)*

1. GOK to Henry McBride, early 1940s, ASA/YCAL.
2. Georgia O'Keeffe, *Georgia O'Keeffe: A Portrait by Alfred Stieglitz*, introduction, n.p.
3. Sue Davidson Lowe, *Stieglitz*, 361.
4. Ibid., 335.
5. Ibid., 230.

6. Catalog of Eliot Porter — Exhibition of Photographs, An American Place, New York, December 29, 1938–January 18, 1939.
7. AS to Eliot Porter, January 21, 1939, Estate of Eliot Porter.
8. AA to Virginia Adams, November 16, 1936, CCP.
9. Dorothy Norman, *Alfred Stieglitz: An American Seer*, 225.
10. AS to AD, February 27, 1935, ASA/YCAL.
11. AS to Edward Weston, September 3, 1938, ASA/YCAL.
12. Ansel Adams, *Ansel Adams: An Autobiography*, 127–128.
13. Elizabeth McCausland papers, AAA; quoted in Sarah Greenough and Juan Hamilton, eds., *Alfred Stieglitz*, 237.
14. Adams, *Autobiography*, 129.
15. Peggy Bacon, *Off with Their Heads*.
16. Beaumont Newhall to Adams, January 1, 1941, CCP.
17. AS to AD, February 27, 1935, ASA/YCAL.
18. AS to AA, July 30, 1936, CCP, ASA/YCAL.
19. Quoted in Anita Pollitzer, *A Woman on Paper*, 117.
20. AS to AA, July 30, 1936, CCP, ASA/YCAL.
21. AS to AD, July 24, 1938, ASA/YCAL.
22. AS to AD, September 12, 1938, ASA/YCAL.
23. Ibid.
24. *TAY*, no. 1, 1938, 77.
25. Henry Miller in *TAY*, no. 8/9, 1942, 153.
26. DN to Edward Steichen, August 13, 1946, Edward Steichen Archives, Museum of Modern Art.
27. AS to AA, April 8, 1938, CCP, ASA/YCAL.
28. Nancy Newhall, *From Adams to Stieglitz*, 154–155.
29. Ibid., 155.
30. Ibid., 129.
31. GOK to Russell Vernon Hunter, October-November 1939, ASA/YCAL.
32. AS to AD, June 16, 1939, ASA/YCAL.
33. GOK to Hunter, October-November 1939, ASA/YCAL.
34. AS to Steichen, June 15, 1941, Edward Steichen Papers, Archive, Museum of Modern Art, New York.
35. AS to AD, July 31, 1941, ASA/YCAL.
36. Newhall, *From Adams to Stieglitz*, 122.
37. AS to AA, August 8, 1943, CCP.
38. AS to AD, September 11, 1943, ASA/YCAL.
39. AS, "Random Thoughts — 1942," *TAY*, no. 10/11, 1943, 264.
40. Newhall, *From Adams to Stieglitz*, 117–118.
41. Minor White to AS, July 7, 1946; quoted in Peter C. Bunnell, *Minor White*, 25.
42. Weegee, *Naked City*, 235. Ellipses in original.
43. AS to James Johnson Sweeney, July 3, 1946; quoted in Pollitzer, *Woman on Paper*, 247.

44. Nancy Newhall to AA, July 15, 1946, CCP.
45. AS to GOK, July 6, 1946, ASA/YCAL; quoted in Pollitzer, *Woman on Paper*, 250–251.
46. AS to GOK, July 9, 1946, ASA/YCAL; quoted in Pollitzer, *Woman on Paper*, 251.
47. "Alfred Stieglitz Dies Here at 82," *New York Times*, July 14, 1946, 38.
48. Pollitzer, *Woman on Paper*, 251.
49. Lowe, *Stieglitz*, 192.
50. Nancy Newhall to AA, July 15, 1946, CCP.
51. Herbert J. Seligmann, *Alfred Stieglitz Talking 1925–1931*, 119.
52. AA to Nancy Newhall, January 7, 1946, CCP.
53. Norman, *AS: An American Seer*, 238.

SELECTED BIBLIOGRAPHY

ABRAHAMS, EDWARD. *The Lyrical Left: Randolph Bourne and Alfred Stieglitz.* Charlottesville: University of Virginia Press, 1986.

ABSE, JOAN. *John Ruskin: The Passionate Moralist.* New York: Alfred A. Knopf, 1981.

ADAMS, ANSEL. *Ansel Adams: An Autobiography.* Boston: New York Graphic Society/Little, Brown, 1985.

————. *Ansel Adams: Letters and Images, 1916–1984.* Boston: New York Graphic Society/Little, Brown, 1988.

ADAMS, HENRY. *Thomas Hart Benton: An American Original.* New York: Alfred A. Knopf, 1989.

ALLEN, FREDERICK LEWIS. *Only Yesterday: An Informal History of the 1920s.* New York: Harper and Bros., 1931.

————. *Since Yesterday: The 1930s in America.* New York: Harper and Bros., 1940.

ANDERSON, SHERWOOD. *Letters of Sherwood Anderson.* Edited by Howard Mumford Jones and Walter B. Rideout. Boston: Little, Brown, 1953.

————. *Selected Letters of Sherwood Anderson.* Edited by Charles E. Modlin. Knoxville: University of Tennessee Press, 1984.

————. *Letters to Bab: Sherwood Anderson to Marietta D. Finley, 1916–1933.* Urbana: University of Illinois Press, 1985.

————. *Sherwood Anderson's Notebook.* New York: Boni and Liveright, 1926.

————. *A Story Teller's Story.* Edited by Ray Lewis White. Cleveland: Press of Case Western Reserve University, 1968.

BACON, PEGGY. *Off with Their Heads.* New York: Robert M. McBride, 1934.

BAIGELL, MATTHEW. *Dictionary of American Art.* London: John Murray, 1980.

————, ed. *A Thomas Hart Benton Miscellany: Selections from His Published Opinions, 1916–1960.* Lawrence: University Press of Kansas, 1971.

BALDWIN, NEIL. *Man Ray: American Artist.* New York: Clarkson N. Potter, 1988.

BARR, ALFRED H., JR. *Matisse: His Art and His Public.* New York: Museum of Modern Art, 1951.

————. *Picasso: Fifty Years of His Art.* New York: Museum of Modern Art, 1946.

BAUR, JOHN I. H. *Revolution and Tradition in Modern American Art.* Cambridge: Harvard University Press, 1951.

BEATON, CECIL, and GAIL BUCKLAND. *The Magic Image: The Genius of Photography from 1839 to the Present Day.* Boston: Little, Brown, 1975.

BENTON, THOMAS HART. *An American in Art: A Professional and Technical Autobiography.* Lawrence: University Press of Kansas, 1969.

———. *An Artist in America.* New York: Robert M. McBride, 1937.

BERGER, MARGARET LIEBMAN. *Aline Meyer Liebman: Pioneer Collector and Artist.* Canandaigua, N.Y.: W. F. Humphrey, 1982.

BERMAN, AVIS. *Rebels on Eighth Street: Juliana Force and the Whitney Museum of American Art.* New York: Atheneum, 1990.

BOYER, M. CHRISTINE. *Manhattan Manners: Architecture and Style, 1850–1900.* New York: Rizzoli, 1985.

BROOKS, VAN WYCK. *America's Coming of Age.* New York: Farrar, Straus and Giroux, 1975.

———. *The Confident Years, 1885–1915.* New York: E. P. Dutton, 1952.

———. *Days of the Phoenix: The 1920s I Remember.* New York: E. P. Dutton, 1957.

———. *Fenellosa and His Circle; With Other Essays in Biography.* New York: E. P. Dutton, 1962.

———. *John Sloan: A Painter's Life.* New York: E. P. Dutton, 1955.

BROWN, MILTON W. *American Painting from the Armory Show to the Depression.* Princeton, N.J.: Princeton University Press, 1955.

———. *The Story of the Armory Show.* 2nd ed. New York: Abbeville Press, 1988.

BRUCCOLI, MATTHEW J. *The Fortunes of Mitchell Kennerley, Bookman.* San Diego: Harcourt Brace Jovanovich, 1986.

BRY, DORIS. *Alfred Stieglitz: Photographer.* Boston: Museum of Fine Arts, 1965.

———. *An Exhibition of Photographs by Alfred Stieglitz.* Washington, D.C.: National Gallery of Art, 1958.

BRY, DORIS, and NICHOLAS CALLAWAY, eds. *Georgia O'Keeffe: The New York Years.* New York: Alfred A. Knopf/Callaway Editions, 1991.

BUNNELL, PETER C. *Minor White: The Eye That Shapes.* Boston: Bulfinch/Little, Brown, 1989.

———, ed. *A Photographic Vision: Pictorial Photography, 1889–1923.* Salt Lake City: Peregrine Smith, 1980.

CAFFIN, CHARLES H. *Photography as a Fine Art.* New York: Doubleday, Page and Co., 1901. Reprint, Hastings-on-Hudson, N.Y.: Morgan and Morgan, 1972.

———. The Story of American Painting. New York: Frederick A. Stokes, 1907. Reprint, Garden City, N.Y.: Garden City Publishing Co., 1937.

CAMFIELD, WILLIAM A. *Francis Picabia: His Life, Art, and Times.* Princeton, N.J.: Princeton University Press, 1979.

———. *Marcel Duchamp: Fountain.* Houston: Menil Collection and Houston Fine Art Press, 1989.

CASTRO, JAN GARDEN. *The Art and Life of Georgia O'Keeffe.* New York: Crown, 1985.

CHAMPA, KERMIT. *Over Here! Modernism: The First Exile, 1914–1919.* Providence, R.I.: Brown University Press, 1989.

CHENEY, SHELDON. *A Primer of Modern Art.* New York: Horace Liveright, 1924.

CLAYTON, BRUCE. *Forgotten Prophet: The Life of Randolph Bourne.* Baton Rouge: Louisiana State University Press, 1984.

CLIFFORD, HENRY, and CARL ZIGROSSER. *History of an American — Alfred Stieglitz: 291 and After.* Philadelphia: Philadelphia Museum of Art, 1944.

CLURMAN, HAROLD. *All People Are Famous.* New York: Harcourt Brace Jovanovich, 1974.

COBURN, ALVIN LANGDON. *Alvin Langdon Coburn: Photographer. An Autobiography.* Edited by Helmut and Alison Gernsheim. New York: Frederick A. Praeger, 1966. Reprint, New York: Dover, 1978.

COE, BRIAN. *Cameras.* New York: Crown, 1978.

CORN, WANDA M. *The Color of Mood: American Tonalism, 1880–1910.* San Francisco: M. H. De Young Memorial Museum and California Legion of Honor, 1972.

COWART, JACK, JUAN HAMILTON, and SARAH GREENOUGH, eds. *Georgia O'Keeffe: Art and Letters.* Boston: Bulfinch/Little, Brown (in association with National Gallery of Art, Washington, D.C.), 1987.

CRANE, HART. *The Letters of Hart Crane.* Edited by Brom Weber. New York: Hermitage House, 1952.

CRAVEN, THOMAS. *Modern Art.* New York: Simon & Schuster, 1934.

CRAWFORD, WILLIAM. *The Keepers of Light.* Dobbs Ferry, N.Y.: Morgan and Morgan, 1979.

DANIEL, PETE, and RAYMOND SMOCK. *A Talent for Detail: The Photographs of Miss Frances Benjamin Johnston, 1889–1910.* New York: Harmony Books, 1974.

DAVIDSON, ABRAHAM A. *Early American Modernist Painting.* New York: Harper and Row, 1981.

DE ZAYAS, MARIUS. *African Negro Art: Its Influence on Modern Art.* New York: Modern Gallery, 1916.

DE ZAYAS, MARIUS, and PAUL HAVILAND. *A Study of the Modern Evolution of Plastic Expression.* New York: "291," 1913.

D'HARNONCOURT, ANNE, and KYNASTON MCSHINE, eds. *Marcel Duchamp.* New York: Museum of Modern Art, 1973.

DIJKSTRA, BRAM. *The Hieroglyphics of a New Speech: Cubism, Stieglitz, and the Early Poetry of William Carlos Williams.* Princeton, N.J.: Princeton University Press, 1969.

———, ed. *A Recognizable Image: William Carlos Williams on Art and Artists.* New York: New Directions, 1978.

DOTY, ROBERT. *Photo-Secession: Stieglitz and the Fine-Art Movement in Photography.* New York: Dover, 1978.

DREISER, THEODORE. *The "Genius."* New York: John Lane, 1915.

DULLES, FOSTER RHEA. *America Learns to Play.* New York: D. Appleton-Century, 1940.

EISLER, BENITA. *O'Keeffe and Stieglitz: An American Romance.* New York: Doubleday, 1991.

EMERSON, PETER HENRY. *Naturalistic Photography.* London: Sampson Low, Marston, Searle and Rivington, 1889. New York: Scovill and Adams Co., 1889.

ENYEART, JAMES. *Bruguière: His Photographs and His Life.* New York: Alfred A. Knopf, 1977.

———, ed. *Decade by Decade:* Twentieth-Century American Photography from the Center for Creative Photography. Boston: Bulfinch/Little, Brown, 1989.

FARNHAM, EMILY. *Charles Demuth: Behind a Laughing Mask.* Norman: University of Oklahoma Press, 1971.

FINE, RUTH E. *John Marin.* Washington, D.C.: National Gallery of Art (with Abbeville Press), 1990.

FORD, COLIN, ed. *An Early Victorian Album: The Photographic Masterpieces (1843–1847) of David Octavius Hill and Robert Adamson.* New York: Alfred A. Knopf, 1976.

FRANK, WALDO. *Memoirs of Waldo Frank.* Edited by Alan Trachtenberg. Amherst: University of Massachusetts Press, 1973.

———. *Our America.* New York: Boni and Liveright, 1919.

———. [Search-Light, pseud.]. *Time Exposures.* New York: Boni and Liveright, 1926.

FRANK, WALDO, LEWIS MUMFORD, DOROTHY NORMAN, PAUL ROSENFELD, and HAROLD RUGG, eds. *America and Alfred Stieglitz: A Collective Portrait.* New York: Literary Guild, 1934.

FRIEDMAN, MARTIN. *The Precisionist View in American Art.* Minneapolis: Walker Art Center, 1960.

GALLUP, DONALD. *Pigeons on the Granite.* New Haven, Conn.: Beinecke Rare Book and Manuscript Library, Yale University, 1988.

———, ed. *The Flowers of Friendship.* New York: Alfred A. Knopf, 1953.

GELDZAHLER, HENRY. *American Painting in the Twentieth Century.* New York: Metropolitan Museum of Art, 1965.

GERNSHEIM, HELMUT and ALISON. *The History of Photography from the Camera Obscura to the Beginnings of the Modern Era, 1685–1914.* New York: McGraw-Hill, 1969.

GIBOIRE, CLIVE, ed. *Lovingly, Georgia: The Complete Correspondence of Georgia O'Keeffe and Anita Pollitzer.* New York: Simon and Schuster, 1990.

GLACKENS, IRA. *William Glackens and the Eight.* New York: Horizon Press, 1957.

GOLDBERG, VICKI, ed. *Photography in Print: Writings from 1816 to the Present.* New York: Simon and Schuster, 1981.

GOLDSCHMIDT, LUCIEN, and WESTON J. NAEF. *The Truthful Lens: A Survey of the Photographically Printed Book, 1844–1914*. New York: Grolier Club, 1980.

GOLDWATER, ROBERT. *Symbolism*. New York: Harper and Row, 1979.

GOODRICH, LLOYD, and DORIS BRY. *Georgia O'Keeffe*. New York: Whitney Museum of American Art, 1970.

GREEN, JONATHAN. *Camera Work: A Critical Anthology*. Millerton, N.Y.: Aperture, 1973.

GREEN, MARTIN. *New York, 1913: The Armory Show and the Paterson Strike Pageant*. New York: Collier/Macmillan, 1988.

GREENFELD, HOWARD. *The Devil and Dr. Barnes: Portrait of an American Art Collector*. New York: Viking Penguin, 1987.

GREENOUGH, SARAH. "Alfred Stieglitz's Photographs of Clouds." Ph.D. diss., University of New Mexico, 1984.

———. *Paul Strand: An American Vision*. Millerton, N.Y.: Aperture (in association with National Gallery of Art, Washington, D.C.), 1990.

———. "The Published Writings of Alfred Stieglitz." Master's thesis, University of New Mexico, 1976. [With an appendix of photocopies of all of Stieglitz's published writings.]

GREENOUGH, SARAH, et al. *On the Art of Fixing a Shadow*. Boston: Bulfinch/Little, Brown (in association with National Gallery of Art, Washington, D.C., and Art Institute of Chicago), 1989.

GREENOUGH, SARAH, and JUAN HAMILTON, eds. *Alfred Stieglitz: Photographs and Writings*. Washington, D.C.: National Gallery of Art/Callaway Editions, 1983.

HAFTMANN, WERNER. *Painting in the Twentieth Century*. 2 vols. New York: Frederick A. Praeger, 1965.

HAPGOOD, HUTCHINS. *A Victorian in the Modern World*. New York: Harcourt, Brace, 1939.

HARKER, MARGARET. *Henry Peach Robinson: Master of Photographic Art, 1830–1901*. Oxford: Basil Blackwell, 1988.

———. *The Linked Ring: The Secession Movement in Photography in Britain, 1892–1910*. London: Heinemann/Royal Photographic Society, 1979.

HARTLEY, MARSDEN. *Adventures in the Arts: Informal Chapters on Painters, Vaudeville, and Poets*. New York: Boni and Liveright, 1921. Reprint, New York: Hacker, 1972.

HARTMANN, SADAKICHI. *The Valiant Knights of Daguerre: Selected Critical Essays on Photography and Profiles of Photographic Pioneers*. Edited by Harry W. Lawton and George Knox. Berkeley: University of California Press, 1978.

HASKELL, BARBARA. *Arthur Dove*. Boston: New York Graphic Society, 1974.

———. *Charles Demuth*. New York: Whitney Museum of American Art, 1987.

———. *Marsden Hartley*. New York: Whitney Museum of American Art, 1980.

HAWORTH-BOOTH, MARK, ed. *The Golden Age of British Photography*. Millerton, N.Y.: Aperture, 1984.

HELM, MACKINLEY. *John Marin.* Boston: Pellegrini and Cudahy in association with Institute of Contemporary Art, 1948.

HENRI, ROBERT. *The Art Spirit.* New York: J. B. Lippincott, 1923. Reprint, New York: Harper and Row, 1984.

HERBERT, ROBERT L., et al. *The Société Anonyme and the Dreier Bequest at Yale University: A Catalogue Raisonné.* New Haven, Conn.: Yale University Press, 1984.

HILL, PAUL, and THOMAS COOPER. *Dialogue with Photography.* New York: Farrar, Straus and Giroux, 1979.

HOGREFE, JEFFREY. *O'Keeffe: The Life of an American Legend.* New York: Bantam, 1992.

HOMER, WILLIAM INNES. *Alfred Stieglitz and the American Avant-Garde.* Boston: New York Graphic Society/Little, Brown, 1977.

———. *Alfred Stieglitz and the Photo-Secession.* Boston: New York Graphic Society/Little, Brown, 1983.

———. *A Pictorial Heritage: The Photographs of Gertrude Käsebier.* Wilmington: Delaware Art Museum, 1979.

———. *Robert Henri and His Circle.* Ithaca, N.Y.: Cornell University Press, 1969.

———, ed. *Avant-Garde Painting and Sculpture in America, 1910–1925.* Wilmington: Delaware Art Museum, 1975.

HUGHES, ROBERT. *The Shock of the New.* New York: Alfred A. Knopf, 1981.

HULTEN, PONTUS, et al. *Brancusi.* New York: Harry N. Abrams, 1987.

HUNTER, SAM, and JOHN JACOBUS. *American Art of the Twentieth Century.* New York: Harry N. Abrams, 1973.

IVINS, WILLIAM M., JR. *Prints and Visual Communication.* Cambridge: MIT Press, 1953.

JARVES, JAMES JACKSON. *The Art-Idea.* Edited by Benjamin Rowland, Jr. Cambridge: Harvard University Press, 1960.

JONES, HAROLD, ed. *Weston to Hagemeyer: New York Notes.* Tucson, Ariz.: Center for Creative Photography, 1977.

JONES, HOWARD MUMFORD. *The Age of Energy: Varieties of American Experience, 1865–1915.* New York: Viking, 1971.

JULLIAN, PHILIPPE. *De Meyer.* New York: Alfred A. Knopf, 1976.

JUSSIM, ESTELLE. *Slave to Beauty: The Eccentric Life and Controversial Career of F. Holland Day.* Boston: David R. Godine, 1981.

KAHMEN, VOLKER. *Art History of Photography.* New York: Viking, 1974.

KANDINSKY, WASSILY. *Concerning the Spiritual in Art.* Translated by M.T.H. Sadler. London: Constable and Co., 1914. Reprint, New York: Dover, 1977.

KELLNER, BRUCE. *Carl Van Vechten and the Irreverent Decades.* Norman: University of Oklahoma Press, 1968.

KERMAN, CYNTHIA EARL, and RICHARD ELDRIDGE. *The Lives of Jean Toomer: A Hunger for Wholeness.* Baton Rouge: Louisiana State University Press, 1987.

KIRSTEIN, LINCOLN. *Elie Nadelman.* New York: Eakins Press, 1973.

KLEEBLATT, NORMAN L., and SUSAN CHEVLOWE, eds. *Painting a Place in America: Jewish Artists in New York, 1900–1945*. New York: Jewish Museum, 1991.

KOUWENHOVEN, JOHN A. *The Columbia Historical Portrait of New York*. New York: Doubleday, 1953.

KREYMBORG, ALFRED. *Troubadour*. New York: Boni and Liveright, 1925.

LASCH, CHRISTOPHER. *The New Radicalism in America, 1889–1963: The Intellectual as a Social Type*. New York: Alfred A. Knopf, 1965.

LAWRENCE, D. H. *The Letters of D. H. Lawrence*. Edited by Aldous Huxley. New York: Viking, 1932.

LERMAN, LEO. *The Museum: One Hundred Years and the Metropolitan Museum of Art*. New York: Viking, 1969.

LEUCHTENBERG, WILLIAM E. *The Perils of Prosperity, 1914–1932*. Chicago: University of Chicago Press, 1958.

LEVIN, GAIL. *Synchromism and American Color Abstraction, 1910–1925*. New York: Whitney Museum of American Art/George Braziller, 1978.

LEVY, JULIEN. *Memoir of an Art Gallery*. New York: G. P. Putnam's Sons, 1977.

LINGEMAN, RICHARD. *At the Gates of the City, 1871–1907*. Vol. 1 of *Theodore Dreiser*. New York: G. P. Putnam's Sons, 1986.

LIPSEY, ROGER. *Coomaraswamy: His Life and Work*. 3 vols. Princeton, N.J.: Princeton University Press, 1977.

LISLE, LAURIE. *Portrait of an Artist: A Biography of Georgia O'Keeffe*. New York: Seaview, 1980.

LONGWELL, DENNIS. *Steichen: The Master Prints, 1895–1914: The Symbolist Period*. New York: Museum of Modern Art, 1978.

LOTHROP, EATON S., JR. *A Century of Cameras*. Dobbs Ferry, N.Y.: Morgan and Morgan, 1982.

LOUGHERY, JOHN. *Alias S. S. Van Dine*. New York: Charles Scribner's Sons, 1992.

LOWE, SUE DAVIDSON. *Stieglitz: A Memoir/Biography*. New York: Farrar, Straus and Giroux, 1983.

LUDINGTON, TOWNSEND. *Marsden Hartley: The Biography of an American Artist*. Boston: Little, Brown, 1992.

LUHAN, MABEL DODGE. *Movers and Shakers*. Vol. 3 of *Intimate Memories*. New York: Harcourt, Brace, 1936.

LYNES, BARBARA BUHLER. *O'Keeffe, Stieglitz and the Critics, 1916–1929*. Ann Arbor, Mich.: UMI Research Press, 1989.

LYNES, RUSSELL. *Good Old Modern: An Intimate Portrait of the Museum of Modern Art*. New York: Atheneum, 1973.

LYONS, NATHAN, ed. *Photographers on Photography: A Critical Anthology*. Englewood Cliffs, N.J.: Prentice Hall, 1966.

MCBRIDE, HENRY. *The Flow of Art: Essays and Criticism of Henry McBride*. Edited by Daniel Catton Rich. New York: Atheneum, 1975.

MCCABE, JAMES D., JR. *New York by Gaslight.* Philadelphia: Hubbard Bros., 1882. Reprint, New York: Greenwich House, 1984.

MAKELA, MARIA. *The Munich Secession: Art and Artists in Turn-of-the-Century Munich.* Princeton: N.J.: Princeton University Press, 1990.

MALCOLM, JANET. *Diana and Nikon.* Boston: David R. Godine, 1980.

MARGOLIS, MARIANNE FULTON, ed. *Camera Work: A Pictorial Guide.* New York: Dover, 1978.

MARIANI, PAUL. *William Carlos Williams: A New World Naked.* New York: W. W. Norton, 1981.

MARIN, JOHN. *Selected Letters of John Marin.* Edited by Herbert J. Seligmann. New York: An American Place, 1931. Reprint, Westport, Conn.: Greenwood Press, 1970.

MARQUIS, ALICE GOLDFARB. *Alfred A. Barr, Jr.: Missionary for the Modern.* Chicago and New York: Contemporary Books, 1989.

MATTHIESSEN, F. O. *Theodore Dreiser.* New York: William Sloane, 1951.

MAY, HENRY F. *The End of American Innocence: A Study of the First Years of Our Own Time, 1912–1917.* New York: Alfred A. Knopf, 1959.

MELLOW, JAMES R. *Charmed Circle: Gertrude Stein and Company.* New York: Frederick A. Praeger, 1974.

MELLQUIST, JEROME. *The Emergence of an American Art.* New York: Charles Scribner's Sons, 1942.

MELLQUIST, JEROME, and LUCIE WIESE, eds. *Paul Rosenfeld: Voyager in the Arts.* New York: Creative Age Press, 1948.

MELTZER, MILTON. *Dorothea Lange: A Photographer's Life.* New York: Farrar, Straus and Giroux, 1978.

MEYER, AGNES ERNST. *Out of These Roots: The Autobiography of an American Woman.* Boston: Little, Brown, 1953.

MICHAELS, BARBARA L. *Gertrude Käsebier: The Photographer and Her Photographs.* New York: Harry N. Abrams, 1992.

MILFORD, NANCY. *Zelda.* New York: Avon, 1971.

MILLER, DONALD L. *Lewis Mumford: A Life.* New York: Weidenfeld and Nicolson, 1989.

MILLER, HENRY. *The Air-Conditioned Nightmare.* New York: New Directions, 1945.

MORGAN, ANN LEE, ed. *Dear Stieglitz, Dear Dove.* Newark: University of Delaware Press, 1988.

MORRIN, PETER, et al. *The Advent of Modernism: Post-Impressionism and North American Art, 1900–1918.* Atlanta: High Museum of Art, 1986.

MUMFORD, LEWIS. *The Brown Decades.* New York: Harcourt, Brace, 1931. Reprint, New York: Dover, 1971.

———. *My Works and Days: A Personal Chronicle.* New York: Harcourt Brace Jovanovich, 1979.

————. *Sketches from Life: The Autobiography of Lewis Mumford.* New York: Dial, 1982.

MUNSON, GORHAM. *Waldo Frank: A Study.* New York: Boni and Liveright, 1923.

NAEF, WESTON J. *The Collection of Alfred Stieglitz: Fifty Pioneers of Modern Photography.* New York: Metropolitan Museum of Art/Viking, 1978.

NEWHALL, BEAUMONT. *Frederick H. Evans.* Rochester, N.Y.: George Eastman House, 1964. Reprint, Millerton, N.Y.: Aperture, 1973.

————. *The History of Photography, from 1839 to the Present.* Rev. ed. New York: Museum of Modern Art/New York Graphic Society/Little, Brown, 1982.

————. *Photography: Essays and Images.* New York: Museum of Modern Art/New York Graphic Society/Little, Brown, 1980.

NEWHALL, NANCY. *From Adams to Stieglitz: Pioneers of Modern Photography.* Millerton, N.Y.: Aperture, 1989.

————. *Paul Strand: Photographs 1915–1945.* New York: Museum of Modern Art, 1945.

————. *P. H. Emerson.* Millerton, N.Y.: Aperture, 1975.

NEWMAN, SASHA M. *Arthur Dove and Duncan Phillips: Artist and Patron.* Washington, D.C.: Phillips Collection/George Braziller, 1981.

NIVEN, PENELOPE. *Carl Sandburg: A Biography.* New York: Charles Scribner's Sons, 1991.

NORDLAND, GERALD. *Gaston Lachaise: The Man and His Work.* New York: George Braziller, 1974.

NORMAN, DOROTHY. *Alfred Stieglitz.* Millerton, N.Y.: Aperture, 1976.

————. *Alfred Stieglitz: An American Seer.* New York: Random House, 1973.

————. *Alfred Stieglitz: Introduction to an American Seer.* New York: Duell, Sloane and Pierce, 1960.

————. *Dualities.* New York: An American Place, 1933.

————. *Encounters: A Memoir.* New York: Harcourt Brace Jovanovich, 1987.

————, ed. *Stieglitz Memorial Portfolio, 1864–1946.* New York: Twice A Year Press, 1947.

NORTH, PERCY. *Max Weber: American Modern.* New York: Jewish Museum, 1982.

NOVAK, BARBARA. *Nature and Culture.* New York: Oxford University Press, 1980.

————. *The Thyssen-Bornemisza Collection: Nineteenth-Century American Painting.* New York: Vendome Press, 1986.

O'KEEFFE, GEORGIA. *Georgia O'Keeffe.* New York: Viking, 1976.

————. *Georgia O'Keeffe: A Portrait by Alfred Stieglitz.* New York: Metropolitan Museum of Art, 1978.

O'NEAL, HANK. *Berenice Abbott, American Photographer.* New York: McGraw-Hill, 1982.

O'NEILL, WILLIAM L., ed. *Echoes of Revolt: The Masses, 1911–1917*. Chicago: Quadrangle Books, 1966.

PARSONS, MELINDA BOYD. *To All Believers: The Art of Pamela Colman Smith*. Wilmington: University of Delaware Press, 1975.

PERLMAN, BENNARD P. *The Immortal Eight: American Painting from Eakins to the Armory Show*. New York: Exposition Press, 1962.

———. *Robert Henri: His Life and Art*. New York: Dover, 1991.

PETERS, SARAH WHITAKER. *Becoming O'Keeffe: The Early Years*. New York: Abbeville Press, 1991.

PETRUCK, PENINAH R., ed. *Photography Before World War II*. Vol. 1 of *The Camera Viewed*. New York: E. P. Dutton, 1979.

The Phillips Collection in the Making, 1920–1930. Washington, D.C.: Phillips Collection and Smithsonian Institution, 1979.

PHILLIPS, SANDRA S., DAVID TRAVIS, and WESTON J. NAEF. *André Kertész: Of Paris and New York*. New York: Thames and Hudson (with Art Institute of Chicago and Metropolitan Museum of Art, New York), 1985.

PISANO, RONALD G. *William Merritt Chase*. New York: Watson-Guptill, 1986.

POLLITZER, ANITA. *A Woman on Paper: Georgia O'Keeffe*. New York: Simon and Schuster, 1988.

PORTER, ELIOT. *Eliot Porter*. Boston: New York Graphic Society/Little, Brown, 1987.

PULTZ, JOHN, AND CATHERINE B. SCALLEN. *Cubism and American Photography*. Williamstown, Mass.: Sterling and Francine Clark Art Institute, 1981.

PUSEY, MERLO J. *Eugene Meyer*. New York: Alfred A. Knopf, 1974.

RATHBONE, BELINDA, et al. *Georgia O'Keeffe and Alfred Stieglitz: Two Lives; A Conversation in Paintings and Photographs*. New York: HarperCollins/Callaway Editions, 1992.

RAY, MAN. *Self-Portrait*. Boston: Little, Brown, 1963.

REICH, SHELDON. *John Marin: A Stylistic Analysis and a Catalogue Raisonné*. Tucson: University of Arizona Press, 1970.

REID, B.L. *The Man from New York: John Quinn and His Friends*. New York: Oxford University Press, 1968.

ROBINSON, ROXANA. *Georgia O'Keeffe: A Life*. New York: Harper and Row, 1989.

ROSE, BARBARA. *American Art Since 1900: A Critical History*. New York: Frederick A. Praeger, 1967.

———. *Readings in American Art Since 1900*. New York: Frederick A. Praeger, 1968.

ROSENBLUM, NAOMI. *A World History of Photography*. New York: Abbeville Press, 1984.

ROSENFELD, PAUL. *Men Seen*. New York: Dial Press, 1925.

———. *Port of New York: Essays on Fourteen Moderns*. New York: Harcourt, Brace, 1924. Reprint, Urbana: University of Illinois Press, 1961.

ROSENSTONE, ROBERT A. *Romantic Revolutionary: A Biography of John Reed.* New York: Alfred A. Knopf, 1975.

RUBIN, WILLIAM S. *Dada, Surrealism, and Their Heritage.* New York: Museum of Modern Art, 1968.

———, ed. *Pablo Picasso: A Retrospective.* New York: Museum of Modern Art/New York Graphic Society/Little, Brown, 1980.

———, ed. *"Primitivism" in Twentieth-Century Art.* New York: Museum of Modern Art, 1984.

RUDNICK, LOIS PALKEN. *Mabel Dodge Luhan: New Woman, New Worlds.* Albuquerque: University of New Mexico Press, 1984.

RUDY, SOLOMON WILLIS. *The College of the City of New York: A History, 1847–1974.* New York: City College Press, 1967.

SAARINEN, ALINE B. *The Proud Possessors.* New York: Random House, 1958.

SANDBURG, CARL. *Steichen the Photographer.* New York: Harcourt, Brace, 1929.

SANDWEISS, MARTHA A., ed. *Photography in Nineteenth-Century America.* New York: Harry N. Abrams (for Amon Carter Museum, Fort Worth, Tex.), 1991.

SCHAPIRO, MEYER. *Modern Art, Nineteenth and Twentieth Centuries: Selected Papers.* New York: George Braziller, 1978.

SCHARF, AARON. *Art and Photography.* Baltimore: Penguin Books, 1969.

———. *Pioneers of Photography.* New York: Harry N. Abrams, 1976.

SCHLEIER, MERRILL. *The Skyscraper in American Art, 1890–1931.* Ann Arbor, Mich.: UMI Research Press, 1986. Reprint, New York: Da Capo, n.d.

SCHWARZ, ARTURO. *New York Dada: Duchamp, Man Ray, Picabia.* New York: Hacker, 1973.

SELIGMANN, HERBERT J. *Alfred Stieglitz Talking 1925–1931.* New Haven, Conn.: Yale University Library, 1966.

SHATTUCK, ROGER, et al. *Henri Rousseau.* New York: Museum of Modern Art, 1985.

SONTAG, SUSAN. *On Photography.* New York: Farrar, Straus and Giroux, 1977.

STEBBINS, THEODORE E., JR., and NORMAN KEYES, JR. *Charles Sheeler: The Photographs.* Boston: New York Graphic Society/Little, Brown, 1987.

STEBBINS, THEODORE E., JR., and CAROL TROYEN. *The Lane Collection: Twentieth-Century Paintings in the American Tradition.* Boston: Museum of Fine Arts, 1983.

STEEGMULLER, FRANCIS. *Apollinaire: Poet Among the Painters.* New York: Farrar, Straus, 1963.

———. *Cocteau: A Biography.* Boston: Atlantic/Little, Brown, 1970.

———. *The Two Lives of James Jackson Jarves.* New Haven, Conn.: Yale University Press, 1951.

STEICHEN, EDWARD. *A Life in Photography.* Garden City, N.Y.: Doubleday, 1963.

STEIN, GERTRUDE. *The Autobiography of Alice B. Toklas.* New York: Modern Library, 1933.

STEIN, ROGER B. *John Ruskin and Aesthetic Thought in America, 1840–1900.* Cambridge: Harvard University Press, 1967.

STEINER, RALPH. *A Point of View.* Middletown, Conn.: Wesleyan University Press, 1978.

STERN, ROBERT, GREGORY GILMARTIN, and THOMAS MELLINS. *New York 1930: Architecture and Urbanism Between the Two World Wars.* New York: Rizzoli, 1987.

STIEGLITZ, ALFRED. *Photo-Secessionism and Its Opponents: Five Letters.* New York: Privately published, August 25, 1910.

STRAND, PAUL. *Paul Strand: A Retrospective Monograph: The Years 1915–1968.* Millerton, N.Y.: Aperture, 1971.

———. *Paul Strand: Sixty Years of Photographs.* Millerton, N.Y.: Aperture, 1976.

SZARKOWSKI, JOHN. *Looking at Photographs.* New York: Museum of Modern Art, 1973.

TAFT, ROBERT. *Photography and the American Scene: A Social History, 1839–1889.* New York: Macmillan, 1938. Reprint, New York: Dover, 1964.

TASHJIAN, DICKRAN. *Skyscraper Primitives: Dada and the American Avant-Garde, 1910–1925.* Middletown, Conn.: Wesleyan University Press, 1975.

———. *William Carlos Williams and the American Scene, 1920–1940.* New York: Whitney Museum of American Art and University of California Press, 1978.

THOMAS, F. RICHARD. *Literary Admirers of Alfred Stieglitz.* Carbondale: Southern Illinois University Press, 1982.

THORNTON, GENE. *Masters of the Camera: Stieglitz, Steichen and Their Successors.* New York: Ridge Press and Holt, Rinehart, Winston, 1976.

TOMKINS, CALVIN. *Merchants and Masterpieces: The Story of the Metropolitan Museum of Art.* New York: E. P. Dutton, 1970.

TOWNSEND, KIM. *Sherwood Anderson.* Boston: Houghton Mifflin, 1987.

TRACHTENBERG, ALAN. *Reading American Photographs: Images as History, Mathew Brady to Walker Evans.* New York: Hill and Wang, 1989.

TRAVIS, DAVID. *Photography Rediscovered: American Photographs, 1900–1930.* New York: Whitney Museum of American Art, 1979.

TROYEN, CAROL, and ERICA E. HIRSHLER. *Charles Sheeler: The Paintings.* Boston: Museum of Fine Arts, 1987.

TUCKER, MARCIA. *American Paintings in the Ferdinand Howald Collection.* Columbus, Ohio: Columbus Gallery of Fine Arts, 1969.

TYLER, PARKER. *Florine Stettheimer: A Life in Art.* New York: Farrar, Straus, 1963.

UDALL, SHARYN ROHLFSEN. *Modernist Painting in New Mexico, 1913–1935.* Albuquerque: University of New Mexico Press, 1984.

UNDERWOOD, SANDRA LEE. *Charles H. Caffin: A Voice for Modernism, 1897–1918.* Ann Arbor, Mich.: UMI Research Press, 1983.

UNTERECKER, JOHN. *Voyager: A Life of Hart Crane.* New York: Farrar, Straus and Giroux, 1969.

VAN VECHTEN, CARL. *The Letters of Carl Van Vechten.* New Haven, Conn.: Yale University Press, 1987.

VOGEL, HERMANN. *Handbook of the Practice and Art of Photography.* 2nd ed. Philadelphia: Benerman and Wilson, 1875.

WATSON, STEVEN. *Strange Bedfellows: The First American Avant-Garde.* New York: Abbeville Press, 1991.

WEAVER, MIKE. *Alvin Langdon Coburn: Symbolist Photographer, 1882–1966.* Millerton, N.Y.: Aperture, 1986.

WEBB, TODD. *Looking Back: Memoirs and Photographs.* Albuquerque: University of New Mexico Press, 1991.

WEEGEE [ARTHUR FELLIG]. *Naked City.* New York: Essential Books, 1945. Reprint, New York: Da Capo, n.d.

WELLING, WILLIAM. *Photography in America: The Formative Years, 1839–1900.* New York: Thomas Y. Crowell, 1978.

WERNER, ALFRED. *Max Weber.* New York: Harry N. Abrams, 1975.

WESTON, EDWARD. *The Daybooks of Edward Weston.* Vol. I: *Mexico.* Rochester, N.Y.: George Eastman House, 1961. Reprint, Millerton, N.Y.: Aperture, 1971.

WIEBE, ROBERT. *The Search for Order: 1877–1920.* New York: Hill and Wang, 1967.

WILKIN, KAREN. *Stuart Davis.* New York: Abbeville Press, 1987.

WILLIAMS, WILLIAM CARLOS. *The Autobiography of William Carlos Williams.* New York: Random House, 1951. Reprint, New York: New Directions, 1967.

WILSON, EDMUND. *The American Earthquake.* Garden City, N.Y.: Doubleday, 1958. Reprint, New York: Farrar, Straus and Giroux, 1979.

WOLF, BEN. *Morton Livingston Schamberg.* Philadelphia: University of Pennsylvania Press, 1963.

WOOD, BEATRICE. *I Shock Myself.* Ojai, Calif.: Dillingham Press, 1985.

WRIGHT, WILLARD HUNTINGTON. *Modern Painting: Its Tendency and Meaning.* New York: John Lane, 1915

Grateful acknowledgment is made to the following for permission to quote from copyrighted and/or unpublished material:

Donald G. Gallup and Patricia Willis for quotations from the Alfred Stieglitz Archive, Yale Collection of American Literature, Beinecke Rare Book and Manuscript Library, Yale University, and for quotations from the book *Alfred Stieglitz Talking 1925–1931* by Herbert J. Seligmann (© 1966).

The Georgia O'Keeffe Foundation for quotations from letters written by Alfred Stieglitz or Georgia O'Keeffe.

Dorothy Norman for quotations from her letters and from her books *Alfred Stieglitz: An American Seer* (© 1973) and *Encounters* (© 1987).

The Metropolitan Museum of Art for quotations from Georgia O'Keeffe's introduction in *Georgia O'Keeffe: A Portrait by Alfred Stieglitz* (copyright © 1978 by the Metropolitan Museum of Art, Introduction copyright © 1978 by Georgia O'Keeffe).

Archives of American Art for quotations from letters in the Aline Meyer Liebman Papers, the John Weichsel Papers, The Phillips Collection Papers, and the Downtown Gallery Papers.

The Phillips Collection, Washington, D.C., for quotations from letters in The Phillips Collection Papers, Archives of American Art.

Rare Book and Manuscript Library, Columbia University, for quotations from letters in the Hart Crane Papers and the Marius de Zayas Papers.

The Newberry Library, Chicago, for quotations from material in the Sherwood Anderson Papers.

Alfred Stieglitz

Professor Charles Modlin and Harold Ober Associates for quotations from letters written by Sherwood Anderson.

Michael E. Hoffman for quotations from letters written by Paul Strand, © Paul Strand Archive, Aperture Foundation, Inc.

John E. Cassel for quotations from letters written by Rebecca Salsbury Strand James.

David Scheinbaum for quotations from letters written by Beaumont Newhall or Nancy Newhall.

INDEX